Component-Based Development with Visual C#™

Component-Based Development with Visual C#™

Ted Faison

Hungry Minds™

Best-Selling Books • Digital Downloads • e-Books • Answer Networks • e-Newsletters • Branded Web Sites • e-Learning

New York, NY✦ Cleveland, OH ✦ Indianapolis, IN

Component-Based Development with Visual C#™

Published by
M&T Books
An imprint of Hungry Minds, Inc.
909 Third Avenue
New York, NY 10022
www.hungryminds.com

Library of Congress Catalog Card No.: 2002100236

ISBN: 0-7645-4914-6

Printed in the United States of America

10 9 8 7 6 5 4 3 2 1

1B/SS/QT/QS/IN

Distributed in the United States by Hungry Minds, Inc.

Distributed by CDG Books Canada Inc. for Canada; by Transworld Publishers Limited in the United Kingdom; by IDG Norge Books for Norway; by IDG Sweden Books for Sweden; by IDG Books Australia Publishing Corporation Pty. Ltd. for Australia and New Zealand; by TransQuest Publishers Pte Ltd. for Singapore, Malaysia, Thailand, Indonesia, and Hong Kong; by Gotop Information Inc. for Taiwan; by ICG Muse, Inc. for Japan; by Intersoft for South Africa; by Eyrolles for France; by International Thomson Publishing for Germany, Austria, and Switzerland; by Distribuidora Cuspide for Argentina; by LR International for Brazil; by Galileo Libros for Chile; by Ediciones ZETA S.C.R. Ltda. for Peru; by WS Computer Publishing Corporation, Inc., for the Philippines; by Contemporanea de Ediciones for Venezuela; by Express Computer Distributors for the Caribbean and West Indies; by Micronesia Media Distributor, Inc. for Micronesia; by Chips Computadoras S.A. de C.V. for Mexico; by Editorial Norma de Panama S.A. for Panama; by American Bookshops for Finland.

For general information on Hungry Minds' products and services please contact our Customer Care department within the U.S. at 800-762-2974, outside the U.S. at 317-572-3993 or fax 317-572-4002.

For sales inquiries and reseller information, including discounts, premium and bulk quantity sales, and foreign-language translations, please contact our Customer Care department at 800-434-3422, fax 317-572-4002 or write to Hungry Minds, Inc., Attn: Customer Care Department, 10475 Crosspoint Boulevard, Indianapolis, IN 46256.

For information on licensing foreign or domestic rights, please contact our Sub-Rights Customer Care department at 212-884-5000.

For information on using Hungry Minds' products and services in the classroom or for ordering examination copies, please contact our Educational Sales department at 800-434-2086 or fax 317-572-4005.

For press review copies, author interviews, or other publicity information, please contact our Public Relations department at 317-572-3168 or fax 317-572-4168.

For authorization to photocopy items for corporate, personal, or educational use, please contact Copyright Clearance Center, 222 Rosewood Drive, Danvers, MA 01923, or fax 978-750-4470.

About the Author

Ted Faison is an independent consultant and researcher who has been in the software field for over twenty years. He has written extensively on object-oriented programming and component-based development issues. Ted has delivered numerous talks at conferences regarding C++, Java, Delphi, XML, and other technologies. Although he presently resides in southern California, he has lived in other countries, such as Italy and Costa Rica. Besides software engineering, Ted's interests also include electronic engineering, philosophy, mathematics, biology, physics, linguistics, and medicine. He holds a B.S. degree in electrical engineering from California State University at Fullerton.

Credits

Acquisitions Editor
Gregory S. Croy

Project Editor
Kathryn Duggan

Technical Editor
Sundar Rajan

Copy Editor
Kathryn Duggan

Editorial Manager
Mary Beth Wakefield

Vice President and Executive Group Publisher
Richard Swadley

Vice President and Executive Publisher
Bob Ipsen

Vice President and Publisher
Joseph B. Wikert

Editorial Director
Mary Bednarek

Project Coordinator
Nancee Reeves

Graphics and Production Specialists
Beth Brooks, Laurie Petrone,
Brent Savage, Erin Zeltner

Quality Control Technicians
John Greenough, Andy Hollandbeck,
Carl Pierce, Dwight Ramsey,
Charles Spencer

Proofreading and Indexing
TECHBOOKS Production Services

Cover Image
© Noma/Images.com

Author Portrait
Linda Faison

To the muse of my life, Marilena

Preface

Half of this game is ninety percent mental.

—Danny Ozark, baseball team manager

The field of software development might be described in a similar way. Developing software is intellectually challenging, but the mental part is only half the game. The other half is discipline and experience. Discipline is important because the quality of software depends to a large extent on the development process. To produce quality software, an organization must ensure that its staff abides by the rules of the adopted development process.

The .NET Framework Is a Huge Undertaking

The .NET Framework is the single most extensive software technology innovation I have ever seen, from any company, in a single release. Windows is a spectacular product, but it matured over the course of many years. The first version supported only crude graphics with a small collection of user interface controls, limited fonts, no help system, no MDI support, no multi-tasking. Not much of anything, compared with what is available now. Still, Windows was a giant leap forward for most people.

In contrast, the .NET Framework was developed from the very start to take on every significant aspect of software development, from the front end to the back end. While the first version of Windows was the product of a handful of people, the .NET Framework was a massive undertaking involving thousands of people at Microsoft, aided by armies of private testers and writers. The Framework, with its associated languages and technologies, took years to develop, starting back in 1997. The Framework covers most of the programming scenarios in use today, from threads to ActiveX interoperability, to asynchronous programming and messaging, to distributed debugging, to multilingual development, and on and on. The Framework's scope is truly daunting.

As the book's title indicates, this is a book about component-based development (CBD) in general, and CBD with Visual C# in particular. Before diving into this book, you might want to have a book on the C# language available, because I won't be describing the syntax of the C# language. However, if you're comfortable with other object-oriented languages, such as C++, Delphi, or Java, or Eiffel, you'll have no problem understanding the code in this book.

The Book's Structure

The book is divided into four sections. Part I is fairly rigorous and academic, describing the component-oriented development process, with references to important research done in the field. This section is pretty much independent of programming languages, giving you information on important topics such as UML and Software Design patterns.

The last three parts are entirely different, written for the developer in the trenches who needs information about specific types of components. The last three parts show you how to accomplish a specific task with Visual C# and Visual Studio .NET (VS .NET). Component-based development is largely a tool-based effort. The idea is to write less code manually and accomplish more tasks using wizards and tools. VS .NET is a phenomenal development environment, with literally hundreds of wizards, so I devote many sections to wizard-based tasks.

The book looks at component-based applications from the *tier* perspective. Many large information systems are distributed across computers into tiers or levels. Part II deals with the first tier: the front end, which is where a program interacts with the end user. The overwhelming majority of programmers deal with user interfaces sooner or later in their careers, so this section will probably be of interest to the greatest number of people.

Part III deals with the middle tier, where business and application logic is often coded. I describe Windows 2000 services, Web Services, and Web Forms in this section.

Part IV deals with the back-end tier, which traditionally is where data is managed and stored. In this part, I deal with issues such as interactions with relational database management systems, stored procedures, and database result sets.

The Index

Most computer books are indexed by a professional indexer, hired by the publisher. Many books have indexes with hundreds of references to things like class names and method names referenced in the text. These items are often of little use to someone trying to find out how to accomplish a programming task. A good index really needs to be created by the author, because only he knows *why* he addresses the various topics, *why* they are important, *how* a reader would look them up in the index, *what* relationship exists between topics, and *what* should be indexed in the first place.

While the table of contents is organized into component-development phases and tiers, the index is designed to let you locate not just the .NET classes and methods referenced through the book but also the programming concepts, technologies, tasks, tips, and code samples described. For example, say you're new to .NET programming and can't remember how to set the mouse cursor to an hourglass. You'll find references in the index under the entries *mouse*, *cursor*, and *hourglass*. Maybe you need to see how to create a textured brush—you'll find index entries under both *brush* and *texture*. Each programming task is generally indexed under multiple cross-references to help you find information.

Bibliographic references

If you have perused this book, you may have noticed that it contains bibliographic references. I took some flak from the publisher about including references, because it makes the book seem scholarly and pedantic to some people. The fact is that many of the ideas and techniques I describe are not my own inventions, and it is only fair to acknowledge the people whose work is referenced.

Bibliographic references appear in square brackets, in the form [Faison 2000]. The good news (if you don't like bibliographic citations) is that the references are largely confined to the first part of the book. To make the references somewhat less intrusive, they are collected in an appendix at the end of the book, rather than appearing as footnotes or notes at the end of each chapter. The appendix lists the references in alphabetical order. If you are interested in the references, you can also look them up using the Index, under the heading *Citations*.

Source Code

The source code for the examples in this book can be found at www.hungryminds.com/extras.

Moving Toward a Component-Centric Process

A lot has been said in the industry about the advantages of moving the software-development process to a component-centric style. The object-oriented programming (OOP) movement of the 1990s is quickly evolving to embrace components, and the expression *component-based development* serves to indicate that components are not simply another name for objects but are at the center of a new development paradigm that is less focused on language issues such as inheritance and polymorphism and more focused on the overall software construction, maintenance, and delivery processes. Before continuing, and to avoid too much confusion, it is essential to address an important issue.

What is a component?

You hear the word *component* thrown around a lot these days, just as the word *object* was in years past. In industry and academia, in the trade press and at conferences, everyone seems to be talking about components, but what exactly does the word *component* mean? Ask a hundred people and you'll probably get a hundred different answers. No book can begin a discussion on components without at least attempting to clarify what is meant by *component*.

The etymology of the word tells us little. The word comes from the Latin verb *componere*, or *to put together*. Anything that can be put together with other parts to yield a larger entity, at compile time, runtime, design-time, whatever, could be considered a software component. C++ objects, DLLs, JavaScript fragments, resource files, and GUI custom controls all qualify as such components. The literal meaning of the word would even let me treat a line of source code as a component, since a program is built by putting lines together. If the etymology is not helpful, let's take a look at some recent definitions of the word, as given by practitioners in the software engineering field:

- ✦ *A component is a physical and replaceable part of a system that conforms to and provides the realization of a set of interfaces.* [Booch 1998]

- ✦ *A runtime software component is a dynamically bindable package of one or more programs managed as a unit and accessed through documented interfaces that can be discovered at runtime.* [Brown 1998]

- ✦ *Software components are binary units of independent production, acquisition, and deployment that interact to form a functioning system.* [Szyperski 1999]

- ✦ *A component is an independently deliverable set of reusable services.* [Brown 1997]

- ✦ *A software component is a program element with the following properties: The element may be used by other program elements (clients). The clients and their authors do not need to be known to the element's authors.* [Meyer 1999]

- ✦ *Software components are reusable building blocks for constructing software systems. . . Components . . . can be modified at design time as binary executables.* [Krieger 1998]

- ✦ *A software component is a static abstraction with plugs.* [Nierstrasz 1995]

There are many other definitions, but you get the picture. Some of them focus on structure, others on function. What is common across all definitions is the notion of *reusability*. Most of the definitions are generic and omit whether components are language-specific, how they are packaged, how they are reused, and how they are deployed. This book deals not only with components in abstract but also with components in the .NET world specifically, so I'll need to define carefully what I mean by *component*. I'll start with a simple definition:

A component is a reusable program, packaged as a binary unit.

This statement seems simple enough, but let's take a closer look at what it entails.

Being a binary entity, a component is not language-specific. It is, however, platform-specific. For example, the machine code that runs on an Intel Pentium will not run on a Motorola chip, an RISC chip, or any other chip that wasn't specifically designed to be binary-compatible with a Pentium. So a component is built for a designated target platform. The platform also identifies which operating system the component is built for. Just because a component executes Pentium machine code doesn't mean it will run on any operating system running on a Pentium machine. (Try taking a component designed to run under Windows and running it under Linux!)

Being *reusable* implies that the functionality contained in the component can be accessed by *others*. Under the heading *others*, I'll include both components and people. In terms of people, there are two groups: developers and end users. While software developers use components at design-time, end users use components at runtime, by running them. Developers use components at design-time, connecting them to build increasingly sophisticated components. The idea is to assemble components incrementally until a complete standalone application or subsystem is built. So a complete program (such as Microsoft Word) can be considered a collection or assemblage of components.

To reduce the development burden of using components, there should be tool-assisted ways to work with and assemble them. The tools should present to the developer information about a component's interface. To do this, the tools must have a means of exploring a component's interface at runtime. So I'll refine my previous definition a bit:

> *A component is a* self-describing, *reusable program, packaged as a binary unit.*

The *self-describing* requirement means there must be a way for a tool to discover, explore, and describe the interface of a component at runtime. The information describing a component could theoretically be anywhere, but the best place is inside the component itself. The self-describing information could not just cover a component's interface, but also include help documents, licensing information, and security certificates that relate to the component.

Does a component have to be contained in a single binary unit? Yes! This is important, because a component defines its own execution environment, including threading and memory control. To guarantee that all portions of a component execute in the same environment, it is important that everything be contained in the same executable binary image. Also, if a component were split across binary units, the component would break if any of the units were missing or unavailable. So I'll refine my definition again:

> *A component is a self-describing, reusable program, packaged as a* single *binary unit.*

What if you have a component that gets so big you want to split it into smaller files? What you'll need to do is partition the code into separate smaller components that are assembled in their own units.

So far I have said nothing about how a component is used, or how its services are accessed. One last refinement will give us the final definition of component, as used in this book:

> ***A component is a self-describing, reusable program, packaged as a single binary unit, accessible through properties, methods, and events.***

This is my final definition. Properties, methods, and events (PME) make up a component's interface. A component need not have all three categories of interface items. For example, a component may expose only properties and methods, or just methods. Among other things, adding the PME requirement means you can use the familiar notation `componentInstance.property` or `componentInstance.method()` to access properties and methods.

Note that my definition of component didn't say anything about where components come from. Most of the time, they come from files containing executable code, but files are not required to create components. A component, with its binary code, could indeed be created entirely *on-the-fly* with your own code, and then used without loading any files at all. Most components are loaded from files, but this is simply a convenience, not a requirement.

What's the difference between a component and an object?

Although components are generally built using objects and object-oriented languages, this is not a strict requirement, according to my definition of *component*. You could use assembly language (good luck) to create components, if you wanted. As long as the finished program was a self-descriptive binary program that exposed its features through properties, methods, and events, you could call it a bona fide component.

A big difference between components and objects is that the former may be made up of any number of the latter. A component may be implemented by one object or by fifty—or by none.

Another difference is that components are language-neutral, while objects are not. Developers reusing a component are not required to use the same programming language or development tools that were used to produce the component. On the other hand, if you instantiate third-party classes in your code, you must use the same language, and often even the same version of compiler, that the vendor used to produce the classes. For example, if you were developing a Delphi class, you couldn't use Visual C++ or Eiffel classes in it. To share classes across language and vendor barriers, you have to use a component technology, like .NET, ActiveX, or CORBA.

Components are evolutionary improvements over objects, because they are designed from the start to simplify software development by supporting a tool-based composition model. To use an object, you have to obtain documentation somewhere that tells you what interface elements are available. With a component, you can use a component-aware development environment (like VS .NET) to extract what properties, methods, and events are available. Because components are self-describing, tools can do this for you, which makes component-based development a much more productive and enjoyable experience than ordinary object-oriented programming.

How is CBD different from OOP?

One of the most important abbreviations for component developers is CBD, for *component-based development*. The expression is synonymous with CBSE, or *component-based software engineering*. A lot of people believe that components are equivalent to objects, making CBD roughly the same thing as OOP. Wrong. Remember that components are binary entities. Developing components is more than just creating and instantiating classes. Components share all the methodologies of OOP, but CBD also addresses packaging, deployment, and licensing issues. OOP is about designing and writing code. CBD goes beyond this to consider how components are assembled, how the packaged code will get into the customer's hands, and how it will be installed and licensed. OOP development is traditionally based on the following development phases: *analysis*, *design*, *implementation*, and *testing*. Once code is debugged, there may be an additional *integration* stage to make it work with other code. In the OOP world, packaging, creating deployment and installation programs, delivery, and licensing are after-the-fact steps that you don't address with classes, objects, or class diagrams. On the other hand, a CBD programmer's job isn't finished until the code is deployed.

You might say that OOP takes code to the point where it runs on the developer's machine. CBD takes it to the point where it runs on the end-user's machine. Big difference.

Is CBD a silver bullet?

Every once in a while, a new tool, technology, or methodology appears on the horizon that promises to revolutionize the software development world, if not the whole world. In the past thirty years, the software world has been swept by a number of tsunamis, including the advent of structured programming in the 1970s [Yourdon 1979] the artificial intelligence craze in the mid-1980s [everyone-and-their-grandmother], the object-oriented programming revolution of the late 1980s [Booch 1994], and the Java gambit in the late 1990s [Arnold 2000]. Now we're in the midst of the component-based development wave. Is CBD just a fad, or will it revolutionize the software industry? Will it *blow away* everything else? Probably not, at least in the foreseeable future.

Frederick P. Brooks Jr. made the following provocative and highly controversial statement in 1986 in his now classic paper entitled "No Silver Bullet — Essence and Accident in Software Engineering" [Brooks 1986]:

> *There is no single development, in either technology or management technique, which by itself promises even one order-of-magnitude improvement within a decade in productivity, in reliability, in simplicity.*

Although more than a decade has passed since Brooks made this statement, it is fair to ask "Is CBD the fabled silver bullet?" It depends. If Brooks's silver bullet slays the software-development monster, then CBD is not one. If a silver bullet is something that *helps a lot in overcoming the beast*, then CDB definitely qualifies. Whether or not CBD provides an order-of-magnitude boost is not essential and would likely depend on the metrics used to analyze the various facets of the software-development process, such as reliability, quality, cost, testability, manageability, and a whole slew of others. But one thing is sure: CBD is a huge step in the right direction.

The .NET Framework Changes Everything

The .NET Framework makes CBD a particularly rewarding experience, not because it is a fresh wave of new technology but because it *dramatically* simplifies the development process. Projects that used to take months can now be developed in weeks or even days.

Before developing the .NET Framework, Microsoft stepped back to look at the big picture of component technologies and decided that ActiveX technology was too complicated to develop, reuse, and deploy with most types of projects. Rather than add a layer on top of COM and ActiveX, to hide the rough edges under some .NET component veneer, Microsoft decided to develop an entirely new technology, to provide rich support for tool-assisted development and simplify development. Microsoft's flagship development environment, VS .NET, has been redesigned from the ground up. VS .NET has wizards that help you every step of the way to build components and applications. New features like Dynamic Help, the Server Explorer, and support for HTML page editing make VS .NET a spectacular development environment. But the .NET Framework is more than a bunch of embellishments and fancy tools — it is a new computing platform. Here is my short list of favorite features of the Framework:

✦ The .NET Framework simplifies the software-development process in a number of ways, by supporting automatic garbage collection, a simple uniform component model, support for common classes like strings or dates, and the seamless integration with standard technologies like WSDL, XML, SOAP, and HTTP.

✦ Applications are more robust. The old "DLL Hell" problem, caused by shared DLLs, is pretty much gone: Installing new programs or uninstalling old ones should no longer break other .NET applications.

✦ The Framework completely eliminates the need for COM, DCOM, and ActiveX components, although it supports them for legacy projects.

✦ The Framework no longer makes massive demands on the Windows Registry or the win\system32 directory. While COM components store all kinds of information in the Registry, resulting in huge Registry files, most .NET components have zero impact on the Registry. The .NET Framework restores the Windows Registry to its original role: that of a central lightweight repository of application data, such as user settings and preferences. The win\system32 directory is no longer used as a catch-all folder for DLLs on your machine. This heavily abused directory is also returned to its intended role, as a repository for those DLLs used by the operating system and its extensions.

✦ Cross-language compatibility. Now you can develop components in different languages, mixing and matching languages based on the skill of your development team. Code reuse is much improved, because you can use classes developed in one language with any other .NET language.

✦ Installation programs are simpler. Because .NET components are packaged as self-describing assemblies requiring no system registration, you can often install a complete application with the equivalent of a simple XCOPY command.

Even with all the exciting new features of the .NET Framework, the subject of software engineering and computer programming is pretty dry. If you interrupted a conversation at a dinner party and even mentioned the subject, you could be banished permanently from the premises. In this book, I've tried to make the subject a bit more entertaining by adding tips, heuristics, aphorisms, some science fiction, stories from the trenches, and personal anecdotes.

Software engineering is a fairly new discipline, in terms of human developments. As such, it borrows ideas, concepts, and approaches from other disciplines. Throughout the first part of the book, I'll connect some of the discussion with passing references to topics of history, philosophy, and biology. I made these connections easy to skip over if they bore you, but I hope they will serve to illustrate how many of the problems we face in software today were discovered and sometimes solved a long time ago in other disciplines.

As I said earlier, the .NET Framework is an ambitious and wide-range technology that I believe will serve to reduce both the development time and the cost of software. With this book, my hope is to be able to convey the enthusiasm I feel for this new exciting technology, and to help you get your job done as a software developer.

Acknowledgments

Creating a book like this was a long and arduous undertaking, extending over a period of fifteen months. During this time, I was fortunate enough to receive support from a number of friends whose feedback helped me eliminate errors or inaccuracies. I'd like to extend my gratitude to the folks at Microsoft, including Anders Hejlsberg, Eric Gunnerson, and Scott Wiltamuth, for their interest and feedback. My appreciation and thanks also go to the publisher, especially Greg Croy, whose unwavering support gave me a large degree of freedom in book layout and structure. Thanks also to Kathi Duggan, whose heroic editing efforts made it possible to get this book into production in record time, considering its size.

Contents at a Glance

Contents

Part II: Front-End Components   191

Chapter 7: Windows Form Components 193

Part III: Middle-Tier Components   573

Chapter 13: Web Forms 575

Chapter 14: Web Controls 627

General Topics

The Development Process

I think it would be a good idea.

> —Mahatma Gandhi, when asked what
> he thought of Western civilization

Using a sound software-development process is also a good idea. Creating software is a nontrivial undertaking, and requires expertise in more domains than just software development. Most projects require team efforts, making it necessary to have layers of people working at different levels of responsibility. In this chapter, you'll find me discussing not just software issues, but also a number of project-management issues, such as estimation, scheduling, and costing.

Component Development

The component-development process defines the steps you follow to manufacture and deploy software components. For the most part, the issues I'll discuss will be applicable to any type of software—not just components. Everyone uses a process to produce software, whether they realize it or not. For example, if you receive a phone call from a customer asking for changes, and then jump straight to code to implement those changes, you have followed a process. Not a bulletproof process, but nevertheless, a process.

Some processes are better than others at producing high-quality results. Good processes divide the tasks between conception and deployment into many smaller tasks, with written documentation describing not just the work to be done, but the purpose of the work, performance requirements, software structure, and other items.

The most important thing about development processes is to find one that works for you, and stick to it. Process is first and foremost about *discipline*, both individually and collectively. If your organization decides on a certain way to do things, but no one abides by those rules, there is no process. There's anarchy. And don't laugh: this type of situation is the order of the day for more organizations than you can imagine. Where there's disorganization, there is invariably confusion, frustration, and inefficiency. At a pathological extreme, software projects sometimes become so-called *Death Marches* [Yourdon 1999]: projects that are doomed to fail from the very beginning. Don't let this happen to you. Learning how projects fail can be useful for identifying problems in your organization, so studying failures can be enlighteningvery useful. Failed projects tend to have things in common, sometimes called *AntiPatterns* [Brown 2000]. If Design Patterns are a distillation of good design ideas and techniques, AntiPatterns are bad things to look out for and avoid.

Every time your organization has to fix something in a software product, there is a cost involved. Whether you pass this cost on to your customers or absorb it yourself, someone is paying for mistakes or oversights. If your competitors have a better process than you, then their costs will tend to be lower than yours in the long run. At some point, you may lose your customers, and then you'll try to figure out what went wrong. By then it's obviously too late.

Even if you don't lose customers due to a bad software-development process, a better process will make your job easier, more predictable, more enjoyable, and probably even more profitable.

Common mistakes

I can't count the number of papers, articles, and books that have been written about software-development processes. We all have our own ideas about what process is best, and what benefits they bring. Let's take a look at some statistics that were compiled by industry experts from the field. Very informative are statistics that focus on software defects, their origin, their cost, and how to avoid them. Some statistics I found interesting were summarized in an article by Barry Boehm titled "Software Defect Reduction Top 10 List" [Boehm 2001]. It listed the top ten areas to concentrate on to reduce software defects The list, reprinted with permission from IEEE, is as follows:

1. Finding and fixing a problem after delivery is often 100 times more expensive than fixing it before code is written.

2. Current software projects spend roughly 40–50 percent of their effort on avoidable rework.

3. About 80 percent of avoidable rework comes from 20 percent of the defects.

4. About 80 percent of the defects come from 20 percent of the modules. About half of the modules are defect free.

5. About 90 percent of the downtime comes from, at most, 10 percent of the defects.

6. Peer reviews catch 60 percent of the defects.

7. Perspective-based reviews catch 35 percent more defects than nondirected reviews.

8. Disciplined personal practices can reduce defect introduction rates by up to 75 percent.

9. All other things being equal, it costs 50 percent more per line of code to develop high-dependability software than low-dependability software. However the investment is more than worth it if the project has significant operations and maintenance costs.

10. Nearly 50 percent of user programs contain nontrivial defects. A user program, in this context, is something the end user works with (such as a spreadsheet or a word processing program), using commercial software.

To summarize the summary, remember three key things:

+ Follow your process. This takes discipline.

+ Communication skills are extremely important. People need to talk.

+ The sooner you identify a problem, the easier it is to fix. Do your homework.

Project-management risks

Software is as much a team effort as any other nontrivial engineering undertaking. Because groups of people are required to work together, to implement requirements that are often of a fluid nature, there are several factors that can cause a project to be late or even die. The chart in Figure 1-1 shows the most important risk factors identified by a panel of project managers from around the world [Keil 1998].

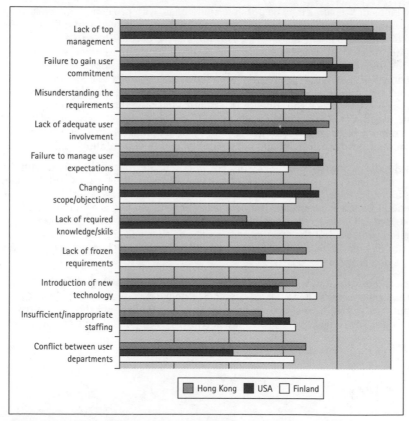

Figure 1-1: The greatest project risk factors, according to one study (Reprinted with permission from ACM)

Perhaps surprisingly, most of the risks are related to people problems, rather than technology. Almost half the risks are dependent on issues with the end-user organization. Also interesting is how the relevance of perceived risks is related to local culture. For example the seventh item, *Lack of required knowledge/skills*, was found to represent a very high risk in Finland, but only a moderate risk in the U.S. Given all the risks in creating software systems, managing their development, and the time constraints teams must work under, it's almost amazing how working systems are produced at all.

Development Phases

From time to time, you hear stories that circulate in the industry about programmers who developed some incredible piece of software *"in a week"* or even *"during their lunch break."* The stories often describe the code as being written with no design at all: straight from idea to working code.

While these kinds of scenarios may be possible sometimes, with projects that have a very limited scope and programmers temporarily exalted by dreams of overnight millions, most software is fortunately not written this way. I say *fortunately,* because there are a number of problems with the straight-to-code development approach. First, there is no documentation describing the intentions of the project, the programmer, or the developed software. The code itself is the only documentation produced. Second, the project tends to be a hash of quick-and-dirty solutions that contain duplications, hard-to-read fragments, and hard-to-maintain code. Third, no one else dares touch the code for fear of breaking something, because it is usually hard to understand. Changes are often made by adding more spaghetti code on top of old code. Imagine being hired years later into a company to maintain this kind of project, with the original developer nowhere in sight, and not a shred of real documentation.

Companies that have one quick-and-dirty project will often approach all projects with the same attitude. The excuse is that they don't have time to write all the specs and documentation. That's like a Formula 1 racer saying he doesn't have time to make a pit stop to refuel. He may be ahead of the pack for a while, but he'll probably run out of gas eventually and lose the race. Also keep this in mind: going directly to code may allow you to hit the market quicker, in some limited projects, but the maintenance costs and time will kill you later. As the saying goes, *"You can pay me now, or pay me later."* And remember, paying later will cost you a lot more than paying now.

OK. So we're all convinced now that straight-to-code and quick-and-dirty are bad processes. So, what is a good process? Elementary, Watson: decide what you're going to do, *before you do it.* And put it in writing. Translated, this means stop and think about the project before writing any code. The basic phases in a sound software development cycle are the following:

- ✦ Analysis
- ✦ Design
- ✦ Implementation
- ✦ Deployment

You may notice the conspicuous absence of a testing phase. Don't infer from this that I don't advocate testing. Quite the contrary: testing is so important that it's an integral part of the overall process. You should test your code incrementally, as it is developed, not all at the end of the coding process. Not too long ago (and even today), companies managed projects by splitting the testing phase out of the development phase. The idea was to write all the code, get it to compile, finish all coding requirements, and then start testing. I hold this approach to be completely wrong. It's like building a complete airplane by bolting everything together, installing the engines, the avionics, and the radars; hooking up all the hundreds or thousands of miles of wires; and adding the in-flight entertainment systems, the carpeting, and passenger seats. After everything is in place, you turn the key to see if it all works, and if not, fix whatever is wrong. Good luck. You'd spend the rest of your life getting everything to work with this approach. When airplanes are assembled, items are tested continuously, both before and after being installed. Many items may even be tested repeatedly *during* the installation phase.

Software requires the same type of testing-intensive approach. Just because a piece of code compiles doesn't mean it works correctly. The moral of the story is that testing is so important that it permeates the entire software-development cycle. The best developers even keep testing in mind during the design phase: they design components to make them easy to test and maintain. They *design systems for easy testability*. The hardware people have been doing this for years: many chips have built-in diagnostics sections that make chip testing easier. Printed circuit board designers often add connectors to allow special diagnostic equipment to be plugged in to check everything out. These days, even cars are designed for automated diagnostics. Most cars have a special connector in the engine compartment that mechanics can plug test and diagnostic equipment into.

The Waterfall process

In the old days (until the 1980s), the prevailing development process was based on a philosophy that was *reductionistic*. I borrow the term from the philosophical current of the same name that swept the biological sciences field during the middle of the 20th century. Reductionists believed that the key to understanding complex systems, such as living organisms, was to reduce them to the smallest components and study these simple parts [Mayr 1997] [Bossomaier 1998]. As was later realized, understanding how low-level cellular processes work, such as the Kreb cycle, is important on one level. Unfortunately the chemical details tell you nothing about what it is to be alive, what consciousness is, what dreams are, or how emotions are possible. The whole is much more than the sum of the parts.

As complex as we may think our software systems and development processes are, they are ludicrously simplistic when compared to even the simplest of life forms. Nevertheless, the early software process model was reductionistic, because it was based on the preface that splitting everything down into a series of neat little independent steps was the key. The tasks in the first box needed to be accomplished before you could go to the next box. There was no overlap between the boxes. Each box was its own little universe. The idea was that even the most complicated project could be handled, if you only followed the box order, finishing one box before proceeding to the next. The scheme was known as the *Waterfall* model, and looked like Figure 1-2.

The Waterfall model [Royce 1970] was the basis of several standard development processes, such as the U.S. Department of Defense's DOD-STD-2167A [DOD 1988]. Apart from its failure to recognize the incremental and iterative nature of the software process, one big problem with the Waterfall model was project-completion monitoring. Until the Integration box was complete, there was basically no working software to be seen. It wasn't uncommon for the final integration phase to stumble upon major show-stoppers, such as discrepancies between subsystem interfaces or subsystems that interpreted the requirements in different and incompatible ways.

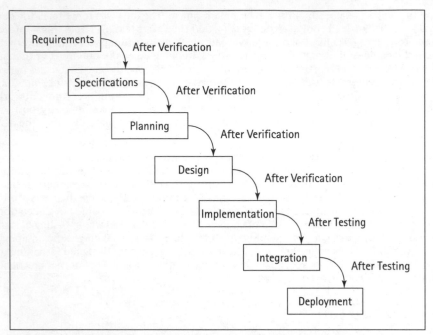

Figure 1-2: The obsolete Waterfall model of software development

Problems with the initial requirements

The Waterfall model was predicated on starting out with absolutely firm requirements. The customer would often produce a User Requirements document that was attached to the project contract. It was fairly common for a User Guide or User Manual to also be produced before the contract was signed. These documents went into details of screen layouts, workflow, database transactions, operating conditions, error messages, and so on.

The problem with this approach is the premise of firm requirements. Don't expect the initial requirements to be exact, complete, or even correct. Regarding initial requirements, the following statement was made over a decade ago [Humphrey 1989]:

> *"The firmer specifications are, the more likely they are to be wrong."*

The problem is that the detailed requirements of most systems are too complex to be fully understood *a priori*. Attempting to nail down every aspect of a system up-front generally leads to mistakes, omissions, and conflicts. If you look back at the third item in Figure 1-1, you'll notice the relevance of misunderstanding the user requirements when it comes to project management risks. We appear to have an unsolvable problem: Misunderstanding the requirements is a key risk in software projects, but user requirements are generally studded with errors. How do you build something, if customers can't tell you exactly what they want? The following statement is a corollary to this dilemma: Customers can always tell you what they *don't* want, but not always what they *do* want.

The solution is to use a development process that starts with a fluid-requirements document and refines the document by successive iterations through design and implementation stages. The customer needs to be part of the refinement process, so there is mutual agreement on all changes and refinements made.

The Continual Refinement process

By considering the initial requirements only as a basis for discussion, subject to potentially substantial changes during the life of the project, the structure of the development process is completely different from the simple Waterfall process. The process entails continuing refinements of the requirements, the design, and the implementation, in ways that don't fit a simple diagram. The various phases and steps of the software development process are not independent from each other, and refining one aspect may require you to go back and refine other aspects.

The development process needs to be broken into two parts: a preliminary one and a refinement one. In the former, the requirements are verified and reviewed with close interaction with the customer. Significant changes are often made to the requirements during this phase. Prototypes may be developed to demonstrate proposed designs and obtain a better understanding of the risks associated with the project.

Due to the iterative and continual way in which changes are made to the requirements, the design and the implementation, I'll refer to this development process model as the *Continual Refinement* (CR) process. Figure 1-3 depicts the preliminary phase.

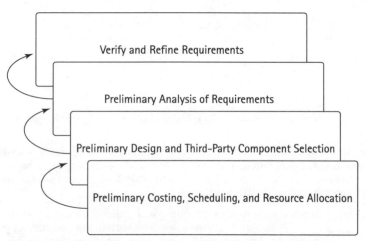

Verify and Refine Requirements

Preliminary Analysis of Requirements

Preliminary Design and Third-Party Component Selection

Preliminary Costing, Scheduling, and Resource Allocation

Figure 1-3: The preliminary phase of the Continual Refinement development process

By adding to the development cycle an initial preliminary phase, you can flush out problem areas and refine the requirements with the customer at a very early stage. The customer doesn't know the exact requirements of the system, and neither does anyone else, but by working with the customer, you should be able to have the requirements converge toward something you can start with. The preliminary phase is complete when the requirements details are deemed to be sufficiently trusted and stable for large-scale development.

Expect requirements to change even after the preliminary cycle. During the preliminary phase, and indeed for the duration of the project, it is essential to have access to domain experts from the customer organization, to ensure that poorly specified areas are implemented correctly.

An important goal of the preliminary process is to reduce the risks and unknowns of a project, in order to come up with good estimates of cost, feasibility, and schedule. Once the preliminary phase is complete and the customer has agreed to the predicted cost and schedule, the next phase starts, in which the preliminary activities are enhanced and refined incrementally until the project is completed. Figure 1-4 depicts the refinement phase.

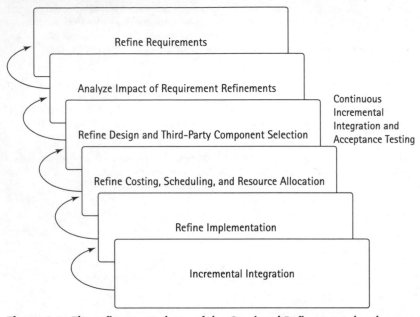

Refine Requirements

Analyze Impact of Requirement Refinements

Refine Design and Third-Party Component Selection

Continuous Incremental Integration and Acceptance Testing

Refine Costing, Scheduling, and Resource Allocation

Refine Implementation

Incremental Integration

Figure 1-4: The refinement phase of the Continual Refinement development process

The CR model is similar to the Spiral model described by Boehm several years ago [Boehm 1988]. For some interesting heuristics that apply to the CR model, see Sotirovski's paper titled "Heuristics for Iterative Software Development" [Sotirovski 2001]. There are two important differences between the CR and the Waterfall models:

✦ The CR model recognizes the fluidity of user requirements, allowing them to be changed at any stage of the project. The greatest changes are dealt with in the preliminary phase, where first-order estimates of schedules, staffing, and costs are determined.

✦ There is continual iteration between the design, implementation, and integration phases, with incremental testing occurring every step of the way. Iteration is necessary when refinements become necessary to address cost, risk, or technology issues that weren't initially contemplated.

Component selection

An important part of the CR model is the decision process that determines whether to make or buy components. The process is often driven by concerns for cost, reliability, technical-support availability, and vendor longevity. Including third-party components in a project may also affect the architecture of the system, because the vendor may have designed them for use in a different scenario or architecture from the one you plan to adopt. Figure 1-5 shows the details of the component-selection process.

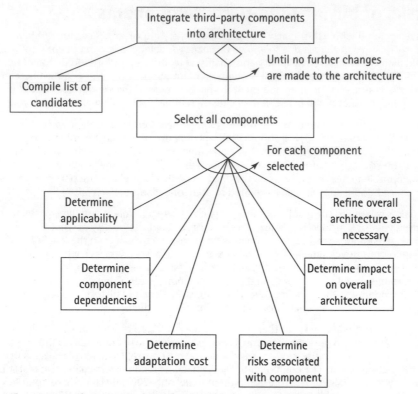

Figure 1-5: The process for selecting third-party components

The process is by successive approximations. You start with an ideal architecture that is created without regard for the existence of third-party components, or using third-party components that you have used in the past and are thoroughly familiar with. Then you create a list of additional candidate components to consider for inclusion in the project. Finally, you go through this list, analyzing each component and making a decision to include it or not. As you select a component for inclusion, you may need to modify or refine the original architecture, which may require changes to components already selected. The selection process ends when all components have been selected and the final architecture has been established. As you can see, selecting a third-party component is not just about opening a sales catalog and picking something that looks really cool. The selection process is coupled with architectural issues and risk analysis.

The order in which you go through the list of candidates is important, and will reflect the priorities your project is governed by. You may choose to analyze components in order of cost, risk, familiarity, vendor reliability, performance, applicability, and so on.

When analyzing a component's applicability, you look at how well it fits your needs. If you have the choice between a component that is overqualified and one that is underqualified, the overqualified one is often best, because it doesn't require you to add new code. Any time you add code, you also increase the probability of adding defects. But don't go overboard on overqualifications, because by selecting a component that is greatly overqualified, you may be introducing unnecessary dependencies on other components that you'll never need.

The risks of buying third-party components

The risks associated with a third-party component are very important. Risks are not just technical in nature. Besides problems due to known or unknown defects in a component's software, you should also consider the availability and quality of technical support and documentation for the component. Adopting a third-party component into your software system will create a dependency between your product and the third-party vendor. If the vendor goes out of business while your product is still in use, it may cause a technical-support nightmare for you.

A similar problem occurs when the vendor develops newer versions of the component you have adopted, eventually dropping support for your version. You may be able to upgrade your software to use the newer version, but there may be situations in which you can't. Purchasing the source code for third-party components will sometimes reduce some of these risks to acceptable levels, but then you may need to dedicate one or more persons from your organization to handle support issues related to someone else's software.

Another risk is related to the quality of third-party components. Unless you have previous experience with a vendor's products, you may know nothing about the quality of what you are buying. An extensive in-house testing program may be necessary to ascertain the level of quality risk, adding to your development costs. The risk is similar to what you face when you buy a car. There may be a particular manufacturer you have had good experience with. Maybe you have heard good things about the company in the news or from friends. Component manufacturers should be considered in the same manner. The more statistical and historical information you have about a particular component from a particular vendor, the better.

Performance unpredictability is another risk. You may decide to buy a component that is advertised with a certain performance, but your system may pose demands on the component that overload it. As an example, say you need a fancy tree control to display the items in a user-interface component. The component is advertised as high-performance. You test it by populating it with 500 nodes. The tree component takes only 200 milliseconds to complete the task, which is acceptable for your system, so you adopt the component. What you didn't discover was the nonlinear relationship between node population and load time. Had you tried the component with 2000 nodes, you would have discovered the unadvertised load time of 5 minutes, which is totally unacceptable. When testing a component's performance, be sure to take into account the conditions under which you will use it.

Risks and problems like these are not limited to software systems using third-party components. Many complex manufactured products use parts or subsystems developed by different organizations, divisions, or factories. Designing a system based on a special part may create a very tight dependency between companies. Consider designing an electronic circuit based on the XYZ chip manufactured by company ABC. If no one else makes a compatible chip, you're at the mercy of ABC. It's what engineers call the *single source problem*. If the company decides to drastically increase the chip's price, or drop it from production, your product may be doomed. If the company goes out of business, you may have a serious problem on your hands.

The Microsoft development process

It may be interesting to know that Microsoft uses an iterative process somewhat similar to the CR model shown previously, but scaled to accommodate multiple teams working in parallel [Cusumano 1997]. The orchestration of the parallel teams is based on a style informally known as *sync-and-stabilize*. At preestablished times (often daily), the various team members are required to perform code check-ins. Complete product builds are performed on a daily basis, generating multiple versions of the product (such as U.S. and major international versions). Microsoft places a great deal of importance on the iterative nature of the development process, recognizing the fluidity of initial product specifications. Reviews of large numbers of Microsoft projects suggest that the feature set laid out in the original specifications may change by as much as 30% by the time the project is finished. An essential part of the Microsoft development philosophy is to *continuously test the product as you build it.* Automatic regression testing occurs on changes as they are checked in. Product development is usually split into three major milestones. One-third of the specified feature set is added at each milestone. A milestone isn't complete until most, if not all, the defects found have been fixed. The third milestone ends with the release to manufacturing.

The Analysis Phase

Before you can begin to design a software system, you obviously need to know what the system is required to do. You need to determine the overall requirements of the system, understand them, and break them down into manageable units. Then you need to study these requirements, estimate how much effort will be required to satisfy them, and determine staffing, individual responsibilities, milestones, overall costs, product delivery times and more. A whole slew of tasks, none of which are very inviting to most of us. Welcome to what I'll refer to in this book as the *Analysis phase*.

The Analysis phase is essentially where you discover or determine the following things:

- ✦ What needs to be done
- ✦ How the system is going to be used
- ✦ What performance is required
- ✦ How difficult the project is
- ✦ How long it's going to take you to do it
- ✦ Who's going to do it
- ✦ What it will cost you
- ✦ Whether you really want to do it

You'll notice that I put the item "*What performance is required*" near the top of the list. The performance requirements of a system affect the architecture and complexity of the software substantially. For example, if you're developing a Web application, it makes a big difference if it needs to serve 20,000 users simultaneously instead of 1 or 2. The former case would probably require more than one server, the latter one would not.

The Analysis phase requires some serious estimation skills, along with a certain amount of preliminary software design work. Whether this preliminary design work can be accomplished in 10 seconds or in 10 weeks depends on the complexity and novelty of the project. Probably the most important single result of the Analysis phase is the decision on whether your organization should consider developing the project or not. If the analysis shows the project as being too costly, taking too much time, or requiring expertise your organization doesn't have, you may want to pass.

When analyzing a project, you'll need to come up with some preliminary estimates of both development time and cost. Will the project take 3 months or 3 years? Will it require 3 people or 30? These estimates are difficult to make with limited information, and sometimes you may need to do some preliminary design work and build one or more rapid prototypes to get a better grasp on the work ahead.

The art of estimating

We've all had our boss ask us in a development meeting, "How long is this going to take?" Most developers hate this question. They just want to hit the keyboard and bang out code, but how long a task will take is important to know. Some people are better than others at estimating effort and completion times. In my experience, we developers tend to be eternal optimists when it comes to schedules. We don't factor in the interruptions that constantly drag us off to other crises. Or the uncertainties that we invariably discover in the requirements (assuming we have written requirements in the first place). Or the learning curve of the new business rules of our customer. Or the time required to learn new tools. Or the overhead of all the meetings. And so on and so forth. (See Ropponen's paper titled "Components of Software Development Risk: How to Address Them? A Project Manager Survey" [Ropponen 2000] for a description of the risks of the estimation and software-development processes, based on a survey of seasoned professionals.)

Estimating software projects is difficult mostly for one simple reason: uncertainties. An aphorism applies to software projects as well as life:

> *Estimating a task is easy, if you've already done it before.*

To which an important corollary applies:

> *The second time you do something, you'll do it better and quicker.*

Unfortunately, software projects always seem to have new, untried tasks to accomplish or technologies to deal with. No two projects are alike. This isn't an accident. Financial incentives and rewards tend to be greatest for projects that solve problems that haven't already been solved.

But not all hope is lost. For those of you with no estimation skills at all, there is an interesting empirical estimation formula that works almost like magic. My boss many years ago taught it to me when I was working at Beckman Instruments, after I told him there was no way I could estimate a job without thinking about it first. He simply replied, "How long do you think it will take to come up with a good estimate?" *The old second-order logic trick.* I replied, "About a week." My boss then returned, "It if takes you 1 week to give a good estimate, then I'll estimate it will take you 10 weeks to do the job." It turned out that he was *very* close. After that, I started testing his estimation formula with other projects. Most of the time, the estimate produced was excellent. To sum up these words of wisdom:

> *To estimate the time required to complete a task, determine how much time you would need to produce the estimate, and then add a zero.*

Try it out. However, I wouldn't recommend telling your boss about how you suddenly improved your estimation skills. For more serious estimation, there are a number of models and techniques in use. One of the best known is COCOMO, an acronym for *Constructive Cost Model*, developed by Barry Boehm in 1981. The original model was based on software practices and technologies common in the 1970s. The model has since been updated to account for changes in the software engineering field, and the current version is COCOMO II [Boehm 2000]. This model is supported by a number of commercial tools, and is highly recommended to people in charge of medium or large projects. Even if you don't use COCOMO II, a book you should consider reading regarding software development cost and effort estimation is Boehm's now classic book *Software Engineering Economics* [Boehm 1981]. The world has changed quite a bit since 1981, but the book is nevertheless invaluable for managers.

The wrong way

Often you'll find companies handling the analysis phase like this: a customer comes in with a request for something. The request is sent to the sales group or the support department. At some point in time, the company decides to support the request. A product manager talks with the sales or support people, and possibly with the customer, to determine the specific needs. Then he or she calls one or more developers (or perhaps just a team leader) and describes what needs to be done. Someone comes up with a cost estimate, a delivery date is set, and the project begins. Handling the Analysis phase like this may work for simple tasks, but in general, it is too weak for most projects.

The first problem is that the developers are hearing a second- or third-hand interpretation of the requirements from the product manager or sales and support person. With complicated tasks, it is better for developers to have direct access to the customers to clear up any doubts or confusion.

The second problem is the lack of documentation. It is always a good idea to write things down, to make sure everyone is on the same page—literally. The Analysis phase should always produce a written document or set of documents describing what the business requirements are, so everybody knows what the goals and assumptions are. In fact, this document should be shown to or discussed with the customer before any design or development work starts.

Third, no one can estimate the amount of time a project will take, or the level of effort necessary, better than people in the development department. Frequently developers work towards unrealistic deadlines that were decided by another department. These projects are guaranteed to run into problems of cost or time—or both.

Fourth, by keeping the development guys out of the loop during the Analysis phase, you preclude them from feeling ownership of the goals, and taking responsibility for the deadlines that were established. You can't just come up with an analysis plan and then *throw it over the wall* into the development department.

A huge mistake made by many organizations is to estimate projects by the number of people it will take, with the assumption that a software engineer is just a warm body capable of delivering a certain amount of work per day—one person, one quantum of work everyday. No! No! No! The U.S. Constitution may say that all men are created equal, but I will tell you that no two programmers are equal. Not even close. Check out the classic book *The Mythical Man-Month* [Brooks 1995] for a detailed account from a highly regarded professional. In his book, Brooks describes the problems caused by considering programmers as interchangeable bodies. Many regard the book as one of the most useful references ever written on real software management. Although the first edition was written over 25 years ago, it deals with problems that can be attributed more to human nature rather than technological shortcomings. This book should be required reading for all software managers. If your department manager hasn't read it, buy him or her a copy.

Often I see companies address the Analysis phase like a business planning session, where a bunch of sales and marketing people and upper-management executives huddle together and come up with a plan, without any input from the development folks. While it's true that this phase is where you decode the business requirements and understand the underlying business rules, many of the requirements for staffing, costs, and delivery times require people with a strong technical background and an understanding of the business requirements and the capabilities of the software organization. An organization should always include at least one developer or developer manager in any project analysis meeting where nontrivial software projects are being discussed.

The right way

Paradoxically, perhaps, there is no single right way. What works well for a multinational corporation working on an Air Traffic Control system is probably too expensive and complicated for a small company with four programmers developing a medical imaging system. What you should remember is that the importance of analysis grows with the size and complexity of a project.

A big project needs more analysis effort than a small one. That's obvious, but what exactly is a big project? A friend of mine had this interesting description:

> *A big project is any project requiring more than one person.*

I agree with him. The idea is that there is a quantum leap in project management and development complexity between one-person and two-person projects. Any time there is more than one person, issues such as documentation, interpersonal relationships, work habits, meetings, working hours, and communication become important. Just because you have a bunch of smart developers doesn't mean you're going to have a good team. As the project size increases, cooperation and communication skills get more important, while individual eccentricities become more problematic.

Projects can be complex for many reasons. There might be a large number of business rules to understand. The relationship between these rules may be complicated. There may be a large number of subsystems to deal with. The relationship between the subsystems may be complex. There may be timing issues that are important to understand. The projects may have multiple modes of operation, based on who is using the system, how many people are using it at the same time, or other aspects.

Moreover, a thorough analysis may require some preliminary design work, or even the construction of a rapid prototype. Many books on software process will tell you that in the analysis phase you should decide the *whats,* but not the *hows.* I disagree, slightly. While understanding what a system is required to do is obviously important, the paramount decision of whether you can afford to develop the system or have the time and capability to do so may depend on design considerations—the *hows.* This is not to say you need to completely design and spec out the whole system while analyzing it, but there may be design issues that you need to know about up front.

One important outcome from the Analysis phase is written documentation. It is important both as a blueprint for the development process, and as feedback to the customer. Make sure the customer signs off on the relevant conclusions reached during the Analysis phase, such as the performance goals, the preliminary delivery schedule, and the features you plan to support (not to mention the cost of the project). The customer can also help you identify incorrect or misleading assumptions regarding the business process. I'll summarize the importance of detail in the Analysis phase with a rule-of-thumb, which may seem obvious:

> *The more precise (and correct) your analysis is, the cheaper your software will be to produce and maintain.*

But don't take the Analysis phase to pathological extremes. You could analyze something to death, finding yourself in *analysis paralysis.* How thorough you need to be will depend on many things, such as the project complexity, the cost of fixing a defect later, whether the software is life-critical, and other factors.

Use cases

A user-centric and effective way of modeling the requirements and determining what a software system needs to do is based on *use cases* [Jacobsen 1994]. Use cases show the interaction between the user (or users) and the system while a required operation is carried out. Consider a system that is required to handle Web orders. One use case may depict what happens when an order is received, and might look something like Figure 1-6.

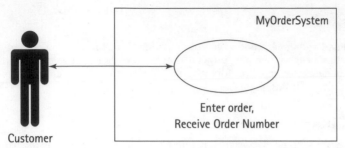

Figure 1-6: A use case depicting an interaction between a typical user and the system

Complex use cases like this one should be broken down into simpler ones, until the operation is described to the level of detail required. Use cases are now considered to be an integral part of the Unified Modeling Language. Use cases are supported by numerous design tools, such as Rational Rose and Microsoft Visio 2000.

Interaction diagrams

Use cases show the flow of events in operations that involve end users. Another way to show this flow is with UML interaction diagrams. The nice thing about these kinds of diagrams is the way they clearly denote the order of a sequence. Each participant in an interaction is represented by a vertical line. Time increases in the downward direction. The interaction diagram shown in Figure 1-7 describes the requirements of a simple order entry system.

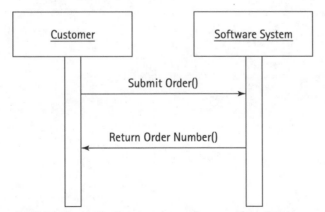

Figure 1-7: A simple interaction diagram describing an order entry system

The diagram shows the customer entering an order and receiving an order number. Interaction diagrams are also useful for documenting design details, because they can show sequences of calls between components. Interaction diagrams are described further in Chapter 3.

For more information on the Analysis phase, a good source is *Developing Software with UML* [Oestereich 1999]. If you want a thorough or rigorous account, check out the books *Mastering the Requirements Process* [Robertson 2000] or *A Discipline for Software Engineering* [Humphrey 1995].

The Design Phase

Once you have determined and understood what your customer's needs are, you're ready to design the system. As stated earlier, complex projects may require you to do some preliminary design work and build one or more rapid prototypes to test high-risk ideas or approaches even before getting to the formal Design phase.

Know the end user

When you design a software system, always keep in mind usability factors. How is the user going to use the software? Too often, software is designed from the inside out: the user or component interfaces expose details that are meaningful to developers, but not to users of the software. Usability means keeping in mind how the software will be used from the perspective of the user. To make software highly usable, you must know something about the class of users that will use the software. The following are important classes of users to consider:

- ✦ Corporate settings
  - Executive management
  - Middle management
  - Office workers
  - Technical users
- ✦ Commercial settings
  - Factory workers
  - Shop clerks
- ✦ Educational settings
  - Universities
  - Primary schools
- ✦ Private homes
  - Young children
  - Teenagers
  - Computer-challenged people
- ✦ Public places
  - Shoppers
  - Travelers

Once you have established the class of user to target, design the software to expose concepts and language that will be familiar to those users. For example, if you're designing software to be used by company executives, you'll want to design the software so the user deals with such items as spreadsheets and financial reports.

If the users are factory workers, you'll want to keep in mind that safety is critical. Operations that cause machinery to move are often dangerous, so you'll probably want to design the system to make it easy for users to stop moving parts if an emergency occurs.

Travelers are often in a hurry, so you'll want to design the software to be easy to understand and fast. Whatever the type of user, keep this in mind:

> *Don't alienate the end users by exposing technical jargon that means nothing to them.*

Software systems that have a user interface should always attempt to use language and concepts that are familiar to the user. For example, if you have a database application that is geared towards nontechnical audiences, you may want to encapsulate database operations as file operations. Most people using computers today are familiar with the concept of a file. Instead of logging into a database, updating records, and committing them, users would think in terms of file operations: opening a file, editing it, and saving it. Database rollbacks might be presented as "Undo" operations.

Know the performance requirements

It's surprising to see how many systems are designed without thinking up-front about performance. People get all caught up in the details of the *what*, and tend to forget or take for granted the *how fast*. It can happen, but don't let it happen to you.

An interesting story about failure to account for performance is the early history of Ada, a programming language commissioned by the U.S. Department of Defense (DOD) in the early 1980s as the answer to the spiraling costs of software. By the end of the 1970s, the DOD owned software systems in every computing language known to man. Each branch of the military had its own pet languages, most of which were unknown to commercial programmers. For example, the Air Force liked to use something called *Jovial*. To make a long story short, the DOD decided to end the Tower of Babel of programming languages, and decided to create a language that could be used for all DOD projects. A few years (and billions of dollars) later, Ada was born — the answer to our prayers. From then on, all new DOD projects had to use Ada. But the marriage between DOD and Ada was not to be a happy one for long. One of the first real deployments of Ada was an avionics package for a fighter jet. Since there was only one Ada compiler certified by DOD at the time, it had to be used. Everything seemed to be going OK, until the software was put on the fighter and somebody turned the key. The software didn't work correctly. While this happens sometimes, it doesn't help when the whole world is watching you, especially when you're a superpower that just spent billions developing the new system. There was nothing wrong with the code or the Ada language itself. The problem was the compiler. Not that it produced incorrect binaries, but the code it produced wasn't fast enough to handle the job with the available hardware. *The old final-integration problem*. The fix was to use a noncertified compiler for the avionics software. The compiler had to cut a few corners in terms of the original Ada specs, but got the job done and produced the necessary performance. The moral of the story is this:

> *Don't forget about performance.*

Where to start

Before starting to design a software system, make sure you have a good understanding of what the system needs to do, and make sure everything significant is documented. How to document the requirements is up to you. You can use word descriptions, flow charts, work flow diagrams, UML diagrams, or whatever. I find that business processes and requirements are often captured well with annotated UML interaction diagrams.

What to accomplish

The outcome of the Design phase should always be some form of documentation that describes the architecture and detailed structure of the software. How the parts of the system interact is also very important, and should be documented using interaction diagrams or other types of drawings. When an interaction starts with a command entered by the user, the diagram essentially depicts a use case. The use cases documented in the Design phase should obviously map to use cases identified in the Analysis phase. Table 1-1 lists the important types of documentation you should generate in the Design phase.

Table 1-1: Important Types of Documentation to Prepare in the Design Phase

Design Documentation	Description
Class diagrams	These diagrams describe the class hierarchies of, and relationships between, classes used in the software system.
Object diagrams	When classes are instantiated in different situations, describe each instance and how it relates to other instances and the system. For example, a class Person might be used to represent a customer, a sales person, and a technical support representative. The object diagram will show these three persons separately.
Interaction diagrams	Also known as *sequence diagrams*, these diagrams describe sequences of interactions between objects or classes. They can also describe use cases.
Text documents	Complex systems often require some type of textual documentation, providing a justification of the architectural choices made, alternatives considered, goals to be achieved, and so on.
Project-management data	This type of documentation shows detailed resource allocations, schedules, costs, milestones, deliverables, and so on.

Don't think of documentation as a necessary evil. Documentation is not only created to aid others, it is also helpful to you. Not only does it force you to think problems through, but it can also help you later on. If your boss five years from now asks you to make some changes to the system, and in the meantime you've worked on ten other projects, wouldn't it be nice to have some documentation to read to refresh your mind?

A potential problem with documentation is staleness. Documentation that is out of sync with the software can sometimes be worse than no documentation, depending on how out of date it is. We all know that documentation should be maintained along with the software. The problem is that changes are often made under time constraints, so we postpone updating the documentation *until we have time*. Some companies never seem to have time, so the documentation doesn't get updated.

Design for testability

Testability is not something that just pops out of a box. It's the result of a deliberate and long-term effort that should start in the Design phase. How do you design software that is easy to test? There are a small number of guidelines that can be applied to any component-based project:

✦ Keep component interfaces simple.

✦ Keep components simple.

✦ Design test fixtures along with the components.

The following sections justify each guideline.

Keep component interfaces simple

Don't have a thousand methods or properties in the interface. No one wants to spend the time understanding the differences and nuances of each method or property. I don't like to use absolute figures, but interfaces with less than 10 methods and 10 properties should be a goal. The fewer items, the better, but don't go pathological on me and build 10 interfaces with one method or property each.

Keep components simple

Just because a component's interface is simple doesn't mean the component is simple. At a limit, you could build an entire application into one component. The interface would only have the application's main entry point, so it would be extremely simple, but the component would probably be ghastly in complexity.

Don't try to accomplish too much in a component. *Divide et impera*. Try to break a component down into subcomponents. Use functional decomposition, top-down design, and whatever method you want. The goal is to have each subcomponent handle one task, or a small group of closely related tasks. Components that have fewer responsibilities are easier to test separately, and easier to reuse. If a small group of components needs tight coupling, for performance or other reasons, at least try to make the group as independent as possible, so you can test them separately as a group.

Simpler components will also have simpler design documentation and be easier to understand. Recall item number 4 in the "Common Mistakes" list, that about half the modules in a project are free from defects. Translated into component language, it means that half the components are free from defects. Components with the greatest probability of being free from defects are those that are simplest in structure and easiest to test.

Design test fixtures along with the components

Many texts on software testing approach the subject of testing as an after-the-fact task: the software guys have finished coding and unit testing, and have *thrown the code over the wall* into the testing department. While having a separate testing department to do final testing is very important, most of the testing should have occurred well beforehand, before the software ever left the development department. The sooner problems are found, the cheaper and easier they are to fix.

The easiest way to discover problems in components is to build a simple test program to exercise the methods and properties exposed by the component. As you implement features in the component under development, add code to the test fixture to test the features immediately. If you wait until all the code is written, you may have already forgotten important boundary conditions or constraints that you coded for.

If your component is tightly coupled with one or more others, developed by other people, you probably can't test it by itself. In these cases, try to coordinate the test fixture with the other team members. Say you are working on component A, which depends on B and C. Create the test fixture skeleton and add test code for A. Then have the other team members add support for B and C. If you plan to test the components like this in advance, each team member may be able to create stubs for the other components to work with, to support incremental testing almost from the very beginning.

Most components I'll develop in later chapters are accompanied by test fixtures. Don't think a test fixture adds a whole new set of headaches to your already busy schedule. Development environments today typically have wizards that automate the task of creating skeleton projects, creating the basis for your test fixture in seconds. Once you get the hang of it, you'll find yourself cutting and pasting code from older test fixtures to create new ones. From my personal experience, test fixtures can often be built in less than a day—some in less than an hour. Most of the ones shown in this book took only minutes to create. It really depends on how complex the interface is of the component to test.

The Implementation Phase

Here's the part you've all been waiting for. If you're like me, you can't wait to jump in and get your hands dirty. Let's face it: documentation is boring and coding is fun. Still, to build quality software, you don't want to jump the gun and forget the other parts of the development process. Fun or not, software development is your job, and your goal should be to produce a high-quality product.

Be sure to track changes

Source code is a living thing. You don't suddenly produce it one day and put it into production. Source code gets developed over a period of time, often with the contribution of more than one person. Most source code files are edited numerous times before the code is ready to be released. If you talk to anyone who knows anything about software configuration management, they'll tell you to use a source code control system. Don't leave home without one. Changes are not always for the better. Sometimes a change breaks the code. When this happens, you may want to recover an earlier version of the software, or find out who made the changes.

Source code control systems (SCCSs), like Visual Source Safe or PVCS, manage your files over time, and save the complete history of edits. SCCSs have tools to compare different versions of a file, so you can easily determine what changes were made, when, and by whom. They also allow multiple people to work on a file at the same time, merging the changes together when the file is checked back in. An SCCS should not just be used with the source code files. You should use it for any file associated with the project, including resources and documentation.

Coding guidelines

There are a number of simple guidelines that can help make code easier to follow. Everyone is different and has his or her own preferences when it comes to coding styles, but the guidelines I recommend in the following sections should be applicable to any coding style.

Keep the code simple

When you pick up someone else's code, it would be nice to be able to read through it and get a sense of what it does immediately. Keeping code simple, by keeping it short and using descriptive names for identifiers, makes the code more readable and easier to manage. Making code readable not only helps others understand your work better, but it also helps you. Consider the code fragment in Listing 1-1.

Listing 1-1: **Unreadable Code**

```
void InitEng()
{
  int i = GetStatus(13);
  i |= 0x02;
  SetStatus(i);
  t = 0;
  while (true)
  {
    i = GetStatus(14);
    if ( (i & 0x04) == 0x04) break;
    t++;
    if (t == 1000) break;
  }
  i = GetStatus(14);
  if ( (i & 0x04) != 0x04) return;
  SetStatus(15);
}
```

What is this code supposed to do? The intentions of the developer are completely opaque. Breaking the code up into smaller methods, and using better names, the method might look like Listing 1-2.

Listing 1-2: **Readable Code**

```
void StartEngine()
{
  TurnOnIgnition();
  WaitForEngineToStart();
  if (EngineIsRunning)
    SwitchIgnitionToRunPosition();
}
```

The code reads like a book and is very short. The reader doesn't run the risk of getting caught up in details or losing track of what was going on. You should always try to break code down into methods of manageable size. Use long names where necessary with methods, variables, and properties.

Some people like the so-called "Hungarian notation," a coding convention whereby variable names are prefixed with a code to indicate the type. The following are some examples:

```
iLength              an integer
cFirst               a character
sName                a string
```

The longer a method is, and the more variables it manipulates, the more useful Hungarian notation is. I personally don't use it. If you break methods down sufficiently in size, they usually wind up dealing with a very small set of variables. I find that long, descriptive variable names, coupled with methods that are short enough to fit on a page, produce code that is easier to read and understand without the extra type prefixes. But that's just my personal choice.

Another justification for keeping code simple and short is that documentation tends to become stale over time. After years of maintenance work and changes to a software system, old documentation may turn out to be outright wrong. When there is a discrepancy between the code and the documentation of code that has been in production for a while, the code is what counts — especially if it works. The code is the ultimate source of documentation, so you want it to be as readable as possible.

Be consistent with indentation

Indentation is purely for the benefit of people. Compilers for most languages ignore white space in source code files. Even though indentation is just to make the code look nicer, we depend on it to a great extent in following the logic of a program. Incorrect or inconsistent indentation in source code can lead to silly mistakes. Take the following code:

```
if (SystemSpeedIsLow() )
   IncreaseSystemSpeed();
   TurnFanOn();
```

The casual reader is led to believe that the fan is turned on only if the system speed is low, while in reality, the fan is always turned on. Code with consistent and correct indentation looks like this:

```
if (SystemSpeedIsLow() )
   IncreaseSystemSpeed();
TurnFanOn();
```

This code makes it easier to follow the logic. Whether you prefer to indent with tab characters instead of spaces, or use eight spaces instead of two, is not the point. Use indentation consistently to emphasize the code logic and help readers.

Use blank lines

Don't jam all the code together. Look at how text is laid out in text documents, like this book. Groups of related sentences are kept together. Some blank space is used to separate paragraphs. Use blank space not only to separate methods, but also inside methods to separate blocks of code. Readers of your code will be grateful.

Don't duplicate code

A particularly pernicious habit some of us have is to duplicate code. Duplicated code wastes time and space, but the main problem is that it potentially spreads defects. If the duplicated code is found to be defective, each copy needs to be fixed. Often it is difficult to find all the copies, so after fixing a few instances of the defective code, we discover the defect was not really fixed completely. Consider this code:

```
if ( Field[5] && Field[6] )
  DoSomething();

// ...
// ...

if ( Field[5] && Field[6] )
  DoSomethingElse();
```

The conditional test is duplicated, not to mention difficult to read. A better approach would be to move the conditional test into a method and use a descriptive name for it, like this:

```
if (IsTimeToDoSomething() )
  DoSomething();

// ...
// ...

if (IsTimeToDoSomething() )
  DoSomethingElse();
```

Code duplication can creep in surreptitiously. Embedding literals in your code is a form of duplication. In the previous code, the method IsTimeToDoSomething () might be implemented like this:

```
bool IsTimeToDoSomething()
{
  return (Field[5] && Field[6]);
}
```

Perhaps when you write this kind of code, you're sure you'll never change your mind about what Field[5] and Field[6] are used for, so the code will never need to be changed. Even if that were true, you shouldn't count on it. Besides, the code is still difficult to read. How does the reader know what Field[5] and Field[6] are used for? A better approach is to eliminate the embedded literals, possibly like this:

```
public class MyClass
{
  private readonly int DiskReady = 5;
  private readonly int DoorClosed = 6;

  protected bool IsDiskReady() { return Field [DiskReady]; }
  protected bool IsDoorClosed() { return Field [DoorClosed]; }

  protected bool IsTimeToDoSomething()
  {
    return IsDiskReady() && IsDoorClosed();
  }
}
```

This way, there is no duplicated code, the purpose of the code is clear, and readers can follow the logic easily.

What about comments?

Conspicuously missing from my list of recommendations are comments. Should you comment your code? Of course. How much commenting should you use? As little or as much as is necessary to describe what your intentions or purposes are. The important thing is that the use of short methods and long identifier names should make the code self-descriptive and self-commenting to a good extent. Don't use comments to state the obvious, like this:

```
// IsTimeToDoSomehing
protected bool IsTimeToDoSomething()
    {
    return IsDiskReady() && IsDoorClosed();
    } // End of IsTimeToDoSomehing
```

Don't laugh: I've seen lots of people do this. (Not you, of course . . .) Comments should not duplicate something that is obvious in the code. I find comments particularly useful when they point out why something was done in a special, perhaps unexpected, way. Consider the code in Listing 1-3.

Listing 1-3: Using Comments in GetMessage() to Point Out Something that Isn't Obvious

```
public class MyClass
    {
    string header, trailer;

    string GetHeader()
        {
        // recompute both the header and trailer
        header = "New header";
        trailer = header + ".";
        return header;
        }

    string GetMessage()
        {
        // use GetHeader() instead of header, to refresh the trailer
        return GetHeader() + "Hello" + trailer;
        }
    }
```

Without the comment, someone might think they could optimize the code in GetMessage() by replacing the GetHeader() call with the variable header. In reality, the call to GetHeader() is not a mistake or an oversight, and the comment makes this clear.

Don't declare things private without a good reason

I can't count the number of times I've come across code that I wanted to reuse, but couldn't because the original developer declared an important field or method private. Just because you can't think of way a field, property, or method could be used in a derived class is not always a good reason to declare it private. People sometimes find unexpected or even amazing ways to reuse code. Don't try to second-guess every possible way to use or extend your classes. Your goal should be to make code as reusable as possible, not as *unreusable* (I think I just invented a new word) as possible.

In the past, C++ programmers were often compelled to declare a data member private, to prevent other classes from changing it. The typical reason for protecting against changes was side effects. If changing a member's value required making other changes to the object's state, or to other objects, it became imperative to prevent direct write-access to the member.

With .NET languages, this type of problem is no longer an issue, because you can control read and write access separately, using properties. By declaring a field private and supplying a protected getter method, you can let derived classes read a private field but not change it. Actually, by allowing changes to be made only via a setter method, you could also make the setter protected. Any derived classes that changed the field would have to do so through your setter method, which would handle any side effects that were necessary.

On the other hand, you may not want descendent classes to read or write a field at all. By barring access, you would have complete freedom in future versions to change the way a field is used, or even to remove it from the class. Is this a good reason to declare a field (and its setter and getter methods, if any) private? Sometimes yes, but let's take a look at this situation more carefully. The reasoning is based on the notion that base class developers should be free to change anything that is private without affecting descendants. Protected and public members would need to be changed carefully, to avoid breaking existing descendent classes.

In the .NET world, versioning problems are avoided by using assemblies with strong names, so existing derived classes would continue to work regardless of the changes made to a base class. Let's say you develop a class called `MyDerivedClass` that is derived from a class called `BaseClass` from a vendor named ACME. In the .NET world, just saying that one class derives from another is not a complete statement. What you need to also specify is which versions of classes you're talking about, because different versions of classes live in different assemblies. For all practical purposes, each assembly is a separate universe. So let's say that version one of `DerivedClass` is derived from version one of ACME's `BaseClass`. At some point, ACME releases version two of the class, with changes that are incompatible with version one. Will this new version break version one of your `DerivedClass`? Not at all. The new version of ACME's class is in a different assembly from version one, and `DerivedClass` has no knowledge of the new assembly. If you decided to create a version two of `DerivedClass`, based on ACME's new version, you would have to create a new `DerivedClass` that referenced ACME's new assembly, at which time you would have to deal with whatever incompatible changes were made to the base class.

The moral of the story is this: Since .NET classes are versioned using assemblies, there is no chance that changes between versions of a base class will break existing code derived from it. If you do make changes that will predictably cause problems for users of your classes, document the changes and offer workarounds. If you think a field or method is likely to change in some future version of a class, let users know this by adding appropriate comments to your code.

Summarizing this discussion, there are few reasons to prevent read access to a field by derived classes. By using property getters and setters, you can allow only read access or both read and write access, with full support for side effects. When talking about methods, there may be reasons to declare one private, if it deals with obscure, delicate, or perhaps proprietary algorithms or code.

Use properties generously

Properties are really wrappers around fields. If you have a field that can be read and written without side effects, you may decide that the overhead of creating property getters and setters is excessive. Consider the property in Listing 1-4.

Listing 1-4: **A Property that Can Be Read and Written without Side Effects**

```
public class MyClass
{
  Color backgroundColor;

  Color BackgroundColor
  {
    get {return backgroundColor;}
    set {backgroundColor = value;}
  }
}
```

There seems to be no justification for the BackgroundColor property. In reality, having a property can be very useful for debugging, because it forces all changes to the BackgroundColor to go through the setter method. If you need to catch changes in the BackgroundColor, you only need to set a breakpoint in one place. Without using a setter method, to catch changes to BackgroundColor you would need to do one of two things:

✦ Track down all the places where the variable is changed.

✦ Set up a debugger to monitor the value of backgroundColor, and trigger a break when the value changed or assumed a certain value.

The first method is time-consuming and may not even be possible if the variable is changed by someone else's code that you don't have access to.

The second method has its own problems. To monitor a variable this way, the debugger would be forced to single step through the code, checking the variable's value continuously. The code would obviously run much slower than normal, perhaps hundreds of times slower. Running code at a different speed than normal may by itself obscure other problems in the code, such as concurrency issues.

Apart from debugging, consider the possibility that side effects, although not contemplated now, may be necessary in the future to support a new feature. Maybe you'll discover later that when the background color is changed, you have to invalidate the component's UI to force it to repaint itself. If you already set up BackgroundColor as a property, adding code later to produce the required side effect is much easier. You only have to change the property's setter, instead of running around and looking for all the places in the code where the BackgroundColor is changed. Think of properties as a way to reduce duplication in your code.

Test fixtures

Components are generally not standalone applications, so you can't test them by just compiling, linking, and running them. You need some sort of application that hosts the component and invokes it, in order to test it. Enter the *test fixture*. Unless you opened this book and jumped straight to this section, you should know by now that test fixtures are crucial for the development and debugging of components.

As you develop a component, test the code incrementally with a test fixture. Don't wait to finish coding to start testing. Sometimes a flaw uncovered by early testing will spur you to change the design or the way you implement something else. The sooner you make these changes, the simpler and cheaper it will be. If you are working on a component that requires other components, you may think it is better to get all the required components finished before you start testing. Not a good idea. The sooner you start testing each component, the better. Create stubs for the components that don't exist yet. Stubs for ancillary components may be useful even if those components *do* exist, because they don't introduce unnecessary complexity into the test arena and they let you focus on one component at a time.

Regarding the order in which components should be developed and tested, people often ask, *"Should I develop components from the top-down, or is bottom-up better? Should I start at the user interface and work down, or start at the data layer and work up?"* Both approaches have pros and cons, and then we all have our own preferences. It's like asking an artist what order you should follow to paint the various parts of a painting. Some programmers prefer to address the high-risk areas first, others prefer to nail down the user interface, and others prefer to set up the database schemas or file layouts. Everyone is different and each project is different.

Testing

The Continual Refinement (CR) development process emphasizes testing throughout most of the development cycle, as opposed to other models that tend to move most testing toward the end. As components are developed, they are incrementally tested using dedicated test fixtures. Once the components have been tested and deemed stable according to some satisfaction criterion, they can be tested with other components. The test fixtures used during testing are important legacies of development, and should be checked into a version control system and treated with the same care as the components tested.

Volumes have been written about how much testing is good, how to conduct tests, and when to stop testing. No matter how much testing you do, there is always the possibility of bugs getting by, so you have to be realistic in determining when to stop testing. Dijkstra made the following statement over 30 years ago [Dijkstra 1970]:

> *"Program testing can be used to show the presence of bugs, but never their absence!"*

There are several types of tests that you can subject a component to. The most important ones are the following:

✦ Unit testing

✦ Integration testing

✦ Acceptance testing

✦ Regression testing

Unit testing

This is the first and most basic type of test. Its purpose is to isolate one component as much as possible from others and test it separately with a dedicated test fixture. Most components are designed to work with others, so unit testing generally requires you to simulate the other components with stubs. A *stub* is a trivial component that has the same interface as another component, but handles only a fixed or limited set of input and output values. The purpose of a stub is only to satisfy the interfacing requirements of the component under test, not to simulate algorithms in the missing components.

Once you develop a unit test fixture, make sure to save it in your version control system, along with any stubs you may have built. Later, during maintenance, you may need to run tests on a specific component to determine if it is the cause of a discovered defect.

Integration testing

Once you have a number of interdependent components built and unit-tested, you'll need to test them all together. Integration testing is generally quite a bit more complicated than unit testing, but should still be approached the same way: create stubs for components that are missing or not part of the test and develop a dedicated test fixture for each step of integration testing. Make sure you save all the test fixtures in your version control system for later.

Integration testing is used to test basically everything from two-component subsystems all the way up to a complete software system. By starting with small numbers of components and scaling slowly upwards, a great deal of problems and defects can usually be found before the code gets to the acceptance-testing phase.

Acceptance testing

Once you have done integration testing on the full software system, you need to verify that it fully satisfies the customer's requirements. Large customer organizations will sometimes provide you with a test script to use for acceptance testing, or even send their own QA people to your site to help or witness testing. Before getting your customer involved, you'll want to do your own deployment testing, and possibly some stress testing.

Deployment testing is required to verify that the deployment process sets up the new software system on the customer's machine or machines correctly. Deployment testing is important, to make sure you didn't forget to copy something to the customer's machine, and that the software will function correctly when delivered.

Stress testing is done to ascertain the performance of a system as a function of load or operating conditions. Often, stress testing entails running software with limited memory, with limited network bandwidth, or with large numbers of concurrent users. Stress testing generally results in two types of performance characteristics: gradual loss and sudden loss. Figure 1-8 shows typical performance graphs.

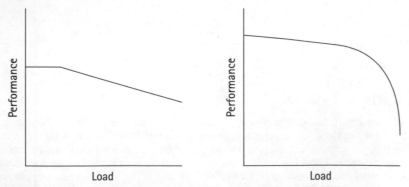

Figure 1-8: Gradual Performance Degradation (left) and Sudden Performance Degradation (right)

Gradual performance degradation is commonly associated with systems that are governed by a bottleneck constraint, such as the bandwidth of the hard disk, the speed of the network connection, or the number of database connection handles in a pool. Before the bottleneck is saturated, performance is essentially constant. As congestion increases at the bottleneck, tasks need to be put on hold for longer and longer periods. Under these conditions, performance declines gradually and predictably. A simple example of gradual degradation is when you download a Web page with a browser. The browser spawns a separate HTTP connection to the server for each separate graphics item contained on the page. All the connections attempt to use the network connection simultaneously. As the number of items to download increases, the time to download increases proportionally.

Sudden performance degradation is characteristic of systems that share a limited resource, whose management represents a significant overhead. Systems sharing memory and processor time fall into this category. As the load increases, the management of the resource becomes important. At a certain point, the system is spending more time managing or allocating the resource than anything else, and the system goes into a state of thrashing.

Regression testing

When you make a change to a software system, it may affect other aspects of the system in unpredictable ways. To verify how the rest of the system was affected, you need to run regression tests. Regression testing is particularly important during the maintenance phase, when defects are fixed or new features are added. But regression testing may also be necessary during development time, during system integration. As you increase the number of components tested during system integration, you may have to regressively test features that were tested previously with unit testing.

The nature and depth of regression testing generally depends on the number of interdependencies between components, and on the cost or consequences of defects in the released software.

Deciding when to release – DDRs and FFRs

How do you decide your software is ready to rock-and-roll? Most project schedules are set up to end with a period of final integration and testing. If you allocated four weeks of final integration and testing, are you going to ship at the end of those four weeks, *regardless of what happens in those four weeks?* Hopefully not. You should base the decision of when to release on when the software is ready, not because *it's Tuesday and somebody promised a customer it would be ready on that day.* How you measure *readiness* is not universal, but many organizations use the *Defect Discovery Rate (DDR)* in the testing department as the meter, counting the number of defects found per day. Let's see how the process works.

It's Monday and final integration and testing begins. You have allocated four weeks to complete everything and ship. The testers start and discover 100 defects the first day, so your DDR is 100. Say 80% of them are minor, but the others are high-priority. You need to establish a system to log and track defects. The system will help you prioritize the defects to be fixed, and make sure that all known defects are accounted for. Even if you decide not to fix each defect, at least you'll know what problems the software will be shipped with. You could include a document in the deployment package, describing the known problems and workarounds that may exist.

Getting back to the 100 defects, let's say you decide to fix all the high-priority ones (20) and half the others (40). That gives you 60 defects to fix on the first day. So you have 40 defects left to fix, right? Wrong. There is that annoying little thing called the *Fault Feedback Ratio (FFR)*. When you fix a defect, you may create other problems. The FFR indicates the number of defects introduced in relation to the number of defects fixed. If you introduce a new defect for every defect fixed, the FFR is 100% and you'll never finish fixing the code. If for every 10 defects fixed you introduce 4 new ones, the FFR is 40%. The value of the FFR of a project is obtained empirically, or is based on the results of previous projects of a similar nature in your organization. For example, during the testing of version 2 of a product, you might use the FFR obtained during version 1 testing.

Assume you have an FFR of 40%. After fixing the defects discovered on the first day, there remain 40 unfixed defects, plus 24 (40% of 60) newly introduced defects, for a total of 64 defects. The second day, the testers find 80 defects. Like before, you find that 80% are minor and the rest are high-priority. You prioritize this new list of defects and fix most of them. As defects get fixed, new defects tend to be discovered with decreasing frequency. A quality-based release policy should be associated with a measurement of the number of known defects the software has, and on the rate at which new ones are discovered (the DDR). Ideally, you would release a product only after *all* defects were fixed and no new ones are discovered. In reality this occurs rarely — if ever. Often, minor defects are based on differences of opinion or preference, and don't compromise the use or dependability of a system.

Software organizations often base their release criterion on the DDR. For example, if all the high-priority defects have been fixed, and only low-priority problems exist, you might decide to release the software when the DDR falls to 5 (five new defects discovered per day). The value your organization chooses will depend on items such as:

✦ **The nature of the known defects.** You may not want to release a product until all the high or medium priority defects have been fixed.

✦ **The cost of fixing defects later.** If the software will be deployed in a remote location, or in large numbers of locations, it may be prohibitively expensive to fix defects later.

✦ **The potential effects of defects.** If combinations of existing defects can create hazards to people, property, or the environment, you may need to choose a low DDR value.

✦ **Marketing pressure.** If you have notified critical customers about the ship date, or committed to a high-profile release date, you may be forced to ship with a larger-than-normal DDR value.

Often, the release of a product occurs in three stages: the *Alpha release,* intended solely for internal testing; the *Beta release,* intended for internal testing and limited external testing by selected customers or organizations; and *product shipment,* which occurs when the Beta release has been fixed and is stable (according to the rate of new-defect discovery).

The Deployment Phase

Deployment is the process of transferring software to your customers' machines and getting it ready to be used. The two most popular deployment models today are *disc-based* and *Internet-based.* The former requires all the software to be put on one or more CDs or DVDs. The disc contains a Setup program that prompts the user for installation options, and then it copies a series of files to his or her machine, installing DLLs, running database scripts, registering components, and doing everything else necessary for the software to run.

The Internet-based model is adequate for smaller and/or simpler software systems. The software is downloaded and installed over the Internet, requiring little or no operator intervention. Internet-based deployment is often used for small components, such as GUI widgets. For components that are sold for-profit, users are typically required to submit a credit card number that is billed. In response, they get a password that unlocks the downloaded software.

Life after Deployment: Maintenance

Most software engineers would agree that the fun part of their job is design and development, when they get to produce large amounts of code, play with their favorite development tools, and work with a fairly structured work plan. Unfortunately, a software project doesn't end when the software is shipped. Someone has to maintain the system after it is deployed, to fix defects and add or change features according to customer requests. Maintaining software is quite different from developing it, both from a software-engineering and a management perspective. Software engineers must understand the notion of *minimum impact solutions,* considering alternative solutions until the one is found that promises to have the smallest impact on the rest of the system. The project-management process required to run a successful maintenance team must deal with constant interruptions, new requests, changing priorities, and very tight schedules.

A large number of organizations have inadequate processes for managing maintenance projects. To an alarming extent, maintenance teams are in a perpetual state of crisis-management: a problem is addressed only if it represents a crisis that threatens the loss of revenue, the relations with an important customer, or the future of the company. The organization is basically fighting fires all the time. The priorities are constantly changing, and resources are spread out to the point that no one has enough time to address issues and fix them according to a plan.

You don't have to be an expert in software process or management consulting to realize that acting in a state of ongoing crisis is a poor way to handle ordinary business. If you plan to maintain a product, your organization should allocate resources to it and establish a plan for dealing with change. When a customer comes to you with a newly discovered bug or a request for a new feature, you should have a procedure in place for managing changes. A good procedure should establish a common way to approve changes, prioritize them, assign them to people, track them over time, verify that they were implemented, and ensure that nothing was broken as a result of the changes.

A large percentage of the cost of software is related to maintenance. Changes are often made without carefully considering alternatives, and without adequately thinking ahead about the repercussions of changes on the future of the product. Often a change made hastily causes a barrage of problems or additional change requests. To properly maintain software, it is extremely important to design changes for minimum system impact. It may take a lot of thinking to come up with minimum impact solutions, and often time is of the essence, but don't let lack-of-time be an excuse. Remember:

> *If you don't have time to correctly fix a problem today, you might need ten times more time to fix it tomorrow.*

How well an organization handles maintenance determines profitability in the medium term, and may determine whether the organization survives in the long term. Don't address maintenance as a necessary evil — plan for it.

Summary

In this chapter, I introduced a generic iterative development model. Whatever specific model you adopt, make sure everyone in your organization understands the purpose and importance of following your development process steps. Everyone needs to abide by the process rules. In the CR model I described, a preliminary phase is useful to gauge the size, complexity, and cost of a project, before getting knee-deep in resource and customer commitments. I also tried to convey the importance of an integrated test policy in the development process. Don't approach testing as an after-the-fact activity.

✦   ✦   ✦

Component Structure

It's déjà vu all over again.

— Yogi Berra, baseball player

If you are familiar with object-oriented programming concepts (and you should be if you're reading this), many of the issues that I'll cover in this chapter will be *déjà vu*. Many design patterns that apply to objects often apply to components. The ways objects and components interact, through interfaces and event handlers, are also similar. However, there are also structural differences between components and objects. For example, objects use language-based inheritance as the basis of reuse. Components, being language neutral, can't use inheritance, relying instead on other techniques.

This chapter will attempt to describe the most common types of structural issues that occur in components today. To some, it may appear that these issues belong in a section dealing with design patterns. Possibly, but while patterns are elegant solutions to specific types of recurring problems, the structural issues I discuss in this chapter are even more generic than patterns, as you will see.

Conway's Law

Over the last forty years or so, the structure of software systems has changed considerably. Many of the changes are related to the declining costs in hardware and the commodity status of computers. Before the advent of objects and components, large systems tended to be designed as a collection of modules. For example a payroll system might have had modules for Screen Handling (no GUIs back then), Report Generation, Data Entry, Database Management, and so on. Each module was designed specifically for the larger system, and therefore could not be used without substantial modifications of other payroll-related projects. A statement made during the 1960s [Conway 1968], known now as *Conway's Law,* described the structure of these large systems:

> *"The structure of a system mirrors the structure of the organization that invented it."*

This statement held true mainly because the Work Breakdown Structure for a project was designed to create software modules that could be assigned on a department or subdepartment basis. However, one could argue that Conway only described half of the equation, with the structure of the organization also being a result of the structure of the systems it designs. Why? Because a large organization doesn't suddenly appear out of nowhere. It starts out as a small group of people charged with accomplishing a business task. As the task grows in complexity, the organization grows and evolves accordingly, in a manner that maximizes efficiency. Inefficient organizations tend to disappear or get taken over by more efficient ones. Efficiency is predicated on the reduction of waste and duplicated effort. To minimize duplicated effort, it makes sense to organize the work force as a function of the work to be carried out. One could refine Conway's Law by saying:

> *An organization tends to initially assume the structure of the systems it designs, and subsequently to design systems that reflect that structure.*

Conway's Law is really just a different incarnation of the eternal philosophical question:

> *Does form follow function, or vice versa?*

I'll let you decide. Regardless of the answer, how does Conway's Law apply in the new world order of CBD? With component-based-development, the top-level architecture of a system tends to be more a function of available technology and cost than organizational structure. Important parts of systems are implemented using off-the-shelf components. Custom components are added to give systems their final shape. To see how program structure has changed over the last few decades, consider the example of a multi-user system designed to provide company payroll reports.

Thirty years ago, the system might have been designed with an IBM 360 mainframe serving several thousand remote users using 3270 terminals. The software would have been designed around an IBM hierarchical database (no relational databases back then), with custom software for presenting information on character terminals (no color or graphics), data entry, database (DB) interaction, and report generation and printing. The whole system was something we would today call a *stovepipe system,* because none of its parts worked alone or could be reused in other software systems without extensive changes.

Today, such a system would be approached much differently. It needs to support thousands of users? That sounds like a Web project. We'll use a Web server to coordinate the user requests. Users will interact with the system using ordinary Web browsers. For the database, we'll use whatever RDBMS the organization is comfortable with, but insulate the application from DB dependencies using OLEDB and ADO. For the user interface, we'll use *WebForms* and *WebControls.* For the reports, we'll use Crystal Reports components, and design the report layouts graphically with third-party tools. We already have a pretty interesting system, and we haven't even had to develop any components yet. Obviously we'll need a number of custom components to handle the interaction between parts of the system, encode business rules, and handle other functions. The point is that the architecture and design of component-based systems tends to rely more on *what cost-effective components are already available* than *what the organization structure looks like.*

Supercomponents and Subcomponents

Probably the most important type of structure used in component-based development is based on the parent-child relationship. Windows programmers have dealt with this relationship for years: The hierarchy of windows displayed on the desktop is an example of it. The desktop is the parent window of one or more child windows that represent applications. When applying the relationship to components, I'll call the parent the *supercomponent* and the child components the *subcomponents.* Supercomponents control the lifecycle of their subcomponents, and encapsulate the interfaces of their subcomponents in various ways, described later. The parent-child relationship for components can be recursive: A subcomponent may in turn be a supercomponent, with its own subcomponents.

A supercomponent is responsible for creating instances of each of its subcomponents. Subcomponents are used to split up and simplify the work of the supercomponent. By convention, subcomponents are drawn inside their supercomponent. Figure 2-1 shows a supercomponent with two subcomponents.

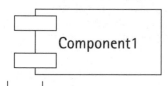

Figure 2-1: A component with two subcomponents

If you are familiar with UML, you know that there is a UML symbol to designate components, shown in Figure 2-2.

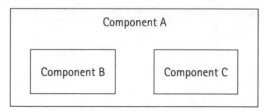

Figure 2-2: The UML notation
for a component

I'll use this symbol only sparingly, because the UML symbol was established in the context of packaging and deployment. For most of the figures in this book, I'll use the UML class symbol to denote components. Apart from packaging and language issues, components and classes are conceptually similar.

Component-based developers consider components first-class design entities, alongside classes, objects, and interfaces. In figures showing components with interfaces, the notation I adopt in this book is similar to the one used with COM: components are labeled boxes, containing zero or more subcomponents. The main difference between components in this book and COM components is that the former can have only one interface, while the latter could have any number. Since all components in this book have exactly one interface, it isn't always useful to show the interface of every component drawn. I'll only show interfaces when their presence makes it easier to understand things that pertain expressly to interfaces. When drawing interfaces, I will use the UML and COM convention that depicts them with a small circle at the end of a line. Figure 2-3 shows the previous example with interfaces.

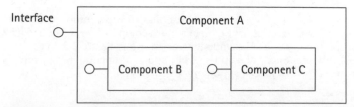

Figure 2-3: Showing the interfaces of components

There is no limit to the number of subcomponents a component may have, although my notation makes it difficult to show subcomponents of subcomponents. A fairly curious arrangement occurs when a component has subcomponents of the same type as the supercomponent, yielding the diagram in Figure 2-4.

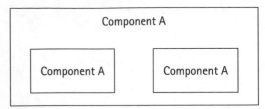

Figure 2-4: A component containing instances of itself as subcomponents

It turns out that this sort of arrangement is not only powerful, but also fairly common. The arrangement has a *self-referential* structure. If component A represented a window on the screen, the arrangement could be used to represent the windows on the desktop, with each window recursively containing others, to any depth. But I'm getting a little ahead of myself here. Discussing this sort of variation is more a subject of patterns, which are addressed in the next chapter.

Component Levels

Components can contain subcomponents nested inside subcomponents, to any depth. Sometimes, when dealing with subcomponents, it is useful to indicate whether they are children, grandchildren, great-grandchildren, or other descendents of a given component. Rather than using terminology from family trees, and to avoid confusing you with expressions like *great-great-great*-something or other, I'll used *levels* to indicate the subcomponent relationship. A level-1 subcomponent is a direct subcomponent, as shown in Figure 2-5.

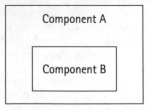

Figure 2-5: A component with a level-1 subcomponent

B is a level-1 subcomponent of A. The level system also applies to supercomponents. In the previous figure, A is a level-1 supercomponent of B. In a more complex hierarchy, a level-2 subcomponent is a subcomponent of a subcomponent, as shown in Figure 2-6. In this figure, component C is a level-2 subcomponent of A and a level-1 subcomponent of B. Conversely, A is a level-1 supercomponent of B and a level-2 supercomponent of C.

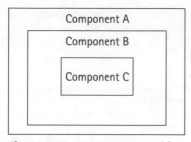

Figure 2-6: A component with a level-1 and level-2 subcomponent

A few big pieces or lots of smaller ones?

A recurring question people have when learning about component-based development is, "How big should a component be?" I'm glad you asked that question. I'll use Mark Twain's answer:

> *"I was gratified to be able to answer promptly. I said, 'I don't know.'"*

Actually, it's not that I don't know. It's more like there is no single answer. There are obviously not absolute limits to how big a component should be, but there are some guidelines that will help you.

Size versus complexity

When dealing with issues of component size and complexity, the first question is this: How do you measure size and complexity? It depends. If your goal is to estimate how long it would take someone to download the component from a Web site, the binary image size is what you need to know. Should you include the size of subcomponents in your calculations? Probably, if the user has to download those, too.

What if you're trying to gauge the complexity of the component? In that case, you could use the binary image size, ignoring the size of subcomponents. Or you could count the number of classes, lines of code, function points [Jones 1997], use cases [Oestereich 1997], or other methods [Szyperski 1999].

What if you're trying to determine how complicated a component will be to reuse? In this case, the internal size and the intrinsic complexity of the component are immaterial. What counts is the number of independent separate business or domain processes the component supports. This number is reflected in the component's interface. How many items are exposed? For example, say you had a component that knew how to do only one thing: *to determine the answer to life, the universe, and everything.* (OK, that's actually three things . . .) Of course, if you read *The Hitchhiker's Guide to the Galaxy* [Adams 1997], you would already know that the answer is *42,* so you wouldn't need your component to figure it out in the first place. But assuming the Adams book didn't exist, your component would have to be fairly complicated to get the answer. From the interface perspective, however, the component would have only one method. Other developers reusing your component would consider it quite simple to use: they would only need to call the `GetAnswerToEverything()` method, and then get the response back as an integer.

Counting the number of methods and properties exposed by a component is a simple way to get an *order-of-magnitude* estimate of the learning curve developers will be faced with when using a component.

Big is bad

In the component world, big is *not* beautiful, big is bad. In the past, we've had monster APIs like Win32 and OLE. Or class libraries like MFC. I can't remember ever coming across anyone that enjoyed learning those APIs. Apart from the difficulty developers may have in getting up to speed, we live on Internet time, when things happen in hours and days, not weeks and months. We don't have time to go off for a few months to learn thousands of pages of details. Even if we did, today's software world is often measured in kilobits per second. Software is more and more frequently deployed by downloading it from somewhere, so the download time can be a crucial parameter.

Large components are likely to contain lower-level functionality that is duplicated elsewhere in the system, increasing unnecessarily the overall complexity. Large components also tend to have narrow focuses, and be difficult or impossible to reuse. They are also much more difficult to maintain over time, because they are difficult to master. If big is bad initially, things gets worse over time as each wave of developers is faced with the daunting task of fixing the code or adding a new feature to it, without fully understanding how the old code worked.

Medium is good

How small is good? Here's one heuristic:

Components should be as small as possible, but big enough to justify a test fixture.

Is there an appropriate or general size that you should aim for? If you exclude from the count the constructors, all private items, and all inherited items, a good heuristic might be to shoot for components with the following number of items in their interface:

✦ <= 10 properties

✦ <= 10 methods

✦ <= 10 events

I'll call this the *10-10-10 guideline*. The idea is that smaller components are more reusable and simpler to use. If you can't list the interface items of a component on a single sheet of paper, then the component may not be simple, or may not be as simple as it could be. Of course not all components *are* simple, so this guideline is only a general goal — not a golden rule of nature.

Simple is best

One of my tenets of software development — *the only one*, in fact — is to strive to make things simple. Einstein may not be known for the good choices he made regarding his personal life [Pais 1983], but he did have some interesting ideas in other areas. One of the lesser-known ones was this:

"Everything should be as simple as possible, but no simpler."

Although Einstein was referring to nature and science, the statement can apply to any field. When applied to technology, it could be followed with the corollary:

All else being equal, simplicity may be the single most desirable goal of a system.

Einstein was not the first person to advocate simplicity. William of Occam (ca. 1285–1349) is famous for his statement known as *Occam's razor*:

"Entities should not be multiplied unnecessarily." (Which translated into current language, would be "Keep it simple, man!")

Paradoxically, simplicity is difficult to achieve, sometimes very difficult. Experience helps. If you have read Chapter 1, you may remember the statement:

"The second time you do something, you'll do it better and quicker."

You'd also make it simpler, if you were building something. To achieve simplicity, sometimes you have to throw away something you already finished and build it over again. Simplicity often goes hand in hand with quality.

Speaking of quality, let me make a small digression. In the U.S., we have the adage, *"If it ain't broke, don't fix it!"* Rubbish! The phrase might have applied back in the past, but certainly not now, with global competition closing in on you from every direction. The adage for these days is:

If it ain't broke, improve *it!*

If you don't, somebody will—if the product has a market. There can be only one leader, but many followers, and those who play *catch-up* typically end up as followers or succumb altogether.

Size also affects quality

It is intuitive that the more code you write, the larger the probability of potential errors. Organizations that have a stable and repeatable development process produce software with a fairly predictable relationship between component size and defects. Accumulated experience indicates that the relationship is approximately linear for small components, as shown in Figure 2-7.

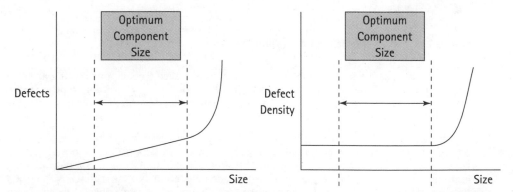

Figure 2-7: Defects versus component size (left) and defect density versus component size (right)

At a certain characteristic size, which varies from organization to organization and from team to team, the number of defects starts growing nonlinearly. This essential flexion-point on the graph is a good indicator of the maximum size or complexity an organization can handle in a time- and cost-effective way. The value is related to the quality of the software development process, the experience of the software engineers involved, and their ability to work together synergistically.

In summary, there are a number of guidelines for determining the appropriate size and complexity of components you should plan for. The following are key considerations:

✦ **Ease of use.** From a reuse perspective, the 10-10-10 guideline is important.

✦ **Ease of development.** Minimize the number of dependencies on other components. Make components as small as possible, while justifying the development of a test fixture.

✦ **Ease of testing.** Keeping the size within the flexion point on the defect graph for your organization will keep the number of defects to predictable and manageable levels. By keeping components in the optimum zone, you can better control the cost associated with defect-removal.

✦ **Ease of deployment.** Keep the number of components and their overall size as small as possible.

Delegation

Delegation is a component composition technique, requiring at least two components. The idea of delegation is very simple. It sounds more complicated than it is. If component A has a subcomponent B that supports a certain feature, then A can expose that feature, too. If you ask component A to deliver this feature, A can internally reroute or *delegate* the request to B, without having to support the feature itself. With delegation, component B is generally a subcomponent of A, and is inaccessible outside A. Figure 2-8 will help.

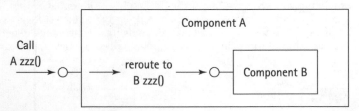

Figure 2-8: Using the delegation model

It's perfectly possible for component A to delegate calls even to components that aren't subcomponents of A. When A is accepting calls that are subsequently rerouted to other external components, the arrangement is really a Façade pattern, as described in the next chapter, "Component Design."

Looking at Figure 2-8, and from the outside of component A, delegation makes it look like the A has features of the subcomponent B: the supercomponent supports the method zzz(), which is a method of the subcomponent. The situation is reminiscent of object-oriented programming inheritance. The big difference between delegation and inheritance is that the latter is essentially free: If class A is *derived* from B, it *automatically* inherits all the capabilities of B. You don't have to add any extra code. The compiler takes care of the details. Not so with delegation: In the previous figure, the method zzz() exposed by the interface of the supercomponent A requires you to write your own code to manually delegate the call to the subcomponent B. Listing 2-1 shows how.

Listing 2-1: A Simple Example Showing How Delegation Works

```
public class A
{
  B b = new B();
  public void zzz() {b.zzz(); }
}

public class B
{
  public void zzz() { }
}
```

Clients of supercomponent A calling the method zzz() have no way of knowing that the call was internally delegated to another component. They may not even know (or care) that subcomponents exist inside the supercomponent. Encapsulation is an OOP technique of wrapping a class around *something* and exposing properties and methods to access that *something*. Delegation is a form of encapsulation, because supercomponent A *envelopes* the subcomponents it delegates calls to.

Specializing a Feature with Delegation

A supercomponent that uses delegation to support a feature has the ability to specialize the feature, because it can run its own code before and/or after calling the subcomponent. By trapping the call, the supercomponent can expand or restrict the subcomponent feature. Feature expansion and restriction should be familiar to you, if you have OOP experience. A couple of examples will help.

Say you have a component B that has a SetColor() method. In supercomponent A, you want to expose SetColor(), but you want to restrict the colors to Black and White. The code in Listing 2-2 could be used.

Listing 2-2: Feature Restriction with Delegation

```
public class A
{
  B b;
  public void SetColor(Color theColor)
  {
    if ( (theColor == Color.Black) || (theColor == Color.White) )
      b.SetColor(theColor);
  }
}

public class B
{
  Color color;
  public void SetColor(Color theColor) {color = theColor; }
}
```

Supercomponent A doesn't delegate the `SetColor()` call to B unless the color is `Black` or `White`.

You can also add code to the supercomponent to expand a feature. Say you want to repaint the supercomponent on the screen when the color is changed. The code might look like Listing 2-3.

Listing 2-3: Feature Expansion with Delegation

```
public class A
{
  B b;
  public void SetColor(Color theColor)
  {
    b.SetColor(theColor);
    Invalidate();  // implemented elsewhere
  }
}

public class B
{
  Color color;
  public void SetColor(Color theColor) {color = theColor; }
}
```

After setting the color, supercomponent A calls `Invalidate()` to refresh the screen.

As stated earlier, delegation is a way for components to simulate OOP inheritance, but this doesn't automatically mean you should resort to it every time a design requires the equivalent of inheritance. Delegation is a good choice in these situations:

✦ The number of subcomponent features to expose is small.

✦ You want to make the services of a subcomponent available, but with restrictions.

✦ You want to modify the behavior of a subcomponent.

Delegation is probably not a good choice in the following situations:

✦ You want to expose the entire interface of a subcomponent. In this case, you should consider aggregation, described in the next section.

✦ The execution overhead of delegation is excessive. For example if one component delegates to another, which then delegates to another, and so on, the execution overhead may become intolerable. Also, if the subcomponents are running in a different process space, the overhead required for parameter marshalling may be a problem.

There are many other reasons for not using delegation, but most are related to special circumstances. For example, if a subcomponent can raise exceptions that interfere with the operation of the supercomponent, delegation may be more of a problem than a solution.

Aggregation

Like delegation, aggregation is also a component composition technique, requiring at least two components. Other than that, delegation and aggregation have little else in common.

Aggregation means different things to different people. The etymology of the word tells us little: it comes from the Latin verb *adgrego*, or *I add to a group*. In the everyday meaning, an aggregation is a bunch of things added or mixed together. When discussing component structure in this chapter, I will use aggregation in a way similar to that of COM/OLE.

The concept of aggregation is easy to understand: If you have a supercomponent A that has a subcomponent B, then B is an aggregate of A if A exposes B. Differently stated, an aggregate is a component that is exposed by its supercomponent. Figure 2-9 may help.

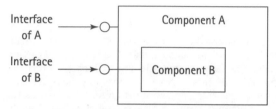

Figure 2-9: Using the aggregation model

From this definition, a necessary condition for a component to be an aggregate is to be a subcomponent of another component. A mathematician would say the condition is necessary, but not sufficient. But who cares, we're programmers. If the parent does not expose the subcomponent's interface, the situation does not represent aggregation, but simple containment.

Aggregation can be an effective way to expose features from a component, because it doesn't have the coding overhead of delegation. Listing 2-4 shows how a component B might be aggregated inside a supercomponent A.

Listing 2-4: A Simple Aggregation Example

```
public class A
{
   public B b = new B();
}

public class B
{
   Color color;
   public void SetColor(Color theColor) {color = theColor; }
}
```

Figure 2-10 shows the situation graphically.

Users of component A have direct access to subcomponent B, so they can call any public item in B's interface, such as `SetColor()`. A user might use the following code:

```
B b = a.b;
b.SetColor(Black);
```

Other than the one line of code fetching a reference to B, there is no runtime performance penalty for users to access the aggregate component B, or for A to expose the interface of B.

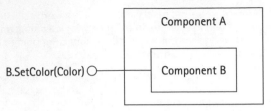

Figure 2-10: Using aggregation to expose the
SetColor() method of subcomponent B

Although implementing aggregation is quite simple in most languages, this doesn't mean you
should use it everywhere in your code. When a component A uses the services of one or
more subcomponents, it may not be desirable for code outside A to bypass A's interface and
call directly into a subcomponent. Consider this simple case: a supercomponent A that acts
as a container for two subcomponents, B and C, that each support an Activate() method.
The requirements dictate that only one subcomponent can be selected at a time. Say you
used aggregation as shown in Figure 2-11.

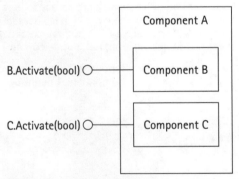

Figure 2-11: Exposing too much information
using aggregation

Clients calling the two Activate() methods could easily create the situation in which both B
and C were active at the same time. To prevent this, you would probably want to use delegation: You might expose two methods from A, called ActivateB() and ActivateC(). These
methods would internally delegate to B and C, coordinating the process to ensure that C was
deactivated before B was activated, and vice versa.

Deep Aggregation

I have only discussed the use of aggregation with level-1 subcomponents. What about level-2
subcomponents and beyond? Can a component expose the interface of a subcomponent of a
subcomponent? Absolutely. Consider the component diagram in Figure 2-12.

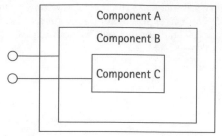

Figure 2-12: Exposing level-1 and level-2 subcomponents

The component A exposes both the level-1 subcomponent B and the level-2 subcomponent C. Listing 2-5 shows a simple implementation.

Listing 2-5: Implementing Deep Aggregation

```
public class A
{
  public B b = new B();
  public C c
  {
    get { return b.c; }
  }
}

public class B
{
  public C c = new C();
  public void MethodForB() {}
}

public class C
{
  public void MethodForC() {}
}
```

You could access components A, B, and C using code like the snippet shown in Listing 2-6.

Listing 2-6: Accessing the Components Implemented in Listing 2-5

```
A a = new A();
B b = a.b;
C c = a.c;
```

The use of a simple property makes it straightforward to access the level-2 subcomponent C from A. Using the technique shown in Listing 2-5, you can expose a subcomponent of an arbitrary level. What if you wanted to expose only a level-2 subcomponent, without exposing the intermediate level-1 subcomponent, as shown in Figure 2-13?

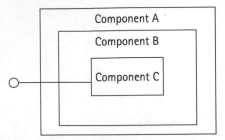

Figure 2-13: Exposing a level-2 subcomponent, without the level-1 subcomponent

No problem. To accomplish this type of structure, all you need to do is make b a private field in A, as shown in bold in Listing 2-7.

Listing 2-7: **Exposing a Level-2 Subcomponent, without the Level-1 Subcomponent**

```
public class A
{
  private B b = new B();
  public C c
  {
    get { return b.c; }
  }
}

public class B
{
  public C c = new C();
  public void MethodForB() {}
}

public class C
{
  public void MethodForC() {}
}
```

There is a fundamental limitation of deep aggregation: For A to expose the interface of a level-2 subcomponent C, the level-1 subcomponent B must also expose C. Applied to subcomponents of arbitrary level *n*, we can say:

To aggregate an arbitrary subcomponent X of level n, all the intermediate subcomponents at levels (1..n-1) must also aggregate X.

For example, in the code shown in Listing 2-7, if B hides subcomponent C by making it `private`, there is no way for A to get to C, so A cannot aggregate C.

Threads

Two heads are better than one. Actually, that would depend on whose heads we're talking about. Threads are not heads, but they do provide a way to structure components to let them do more than one thing at a time. For example, when writing high-performance components, you often need to deal with high volumes of requests from client components.

One solution, which would probably get you fired, is to process one request at a time. A better approach is to handle each client request in parallel, with a dedicated thread. This way, a simple request that arrived after a complex one would not have to wait for the long operation to complete, and would run immediately. Another situation where threads are useful is when complex or lengthy operations need to be carried out, and you don't want your code to seem *dead* while the operation completes. Running the long operation on its own threads allows the rest of the system to continue normally.

Although threads can be considered a component structural issue, they are so important that I dedicated an entire chapter to them. See Chapter 20, titled "Multithreaded Components," for further details.

Summary

In this chapter, I introduced the most common types of component structures. By using aggregation and delegation to put components together, you can achieve a functional equivalence to object-oriented programming inheritance and polymorphism. A key goal in component structure is to keep each component as simple as possible. Where possible, complex features should be supported by using multiple subcomponents, as opposed to a single monolithic component.

✦　　✦　　✦

Component Design

A verbal contract isn't worth the paper it's written on.

—Samuel Goldwyn, movie producer

Mr. Goldwyn was not the first person to recognize the importance of written documents. The ancient Romans had the saying *verba volant, scripta manent*, which loosely translates to *words fly away, writings stay behind*. If design is important, then documenting the design in writing is imperative. Older design techniques, like flow charts and Nassi-Shneiderman charts, are useful for showing the flow of a program's logic. What they don't illustrate well is the structure of a program and the relationship between its parts. Structured charts represented an improvement, but they were most effective with software organized as modules and functions. Object-oriented and component-based systems need a different notation, which recognizes the importance of classes and objects. A number of competing methodologies cropped up to address this new need, of which UML is the best known and most used.

UML

The *Unified Modeling Language* (UML) emerged during the 1990s as a standard way to describe object-oriented software. UML became a formal standard and is currently administered by the Object Management Group. Contrary to its name, UML is not a language, in the ordinary sense, but more of a methodology and notation. Actually, UML encompasses multiple methodologies and notations. I won't attempt to describe UML in detail here. There are excellent books devoted to this subject, such as *The Unified Modeling Language User Guide* [Booch 1998] and *UML Components: A Simple Process for Specifying Component-Based Software* [Cheesman 2000]. What I will concentrate on is the very small subset of UML notations that I use throughout the book, to save those readers that are new to UML from having to go off and buy another book.

Class diagrams

The easiest way to describe the elements of a class diagram is to show you one. In UML, classes are denoted with a rectangular box, showing the class name, properties, and methods, as illustrated in Figure 3-1.

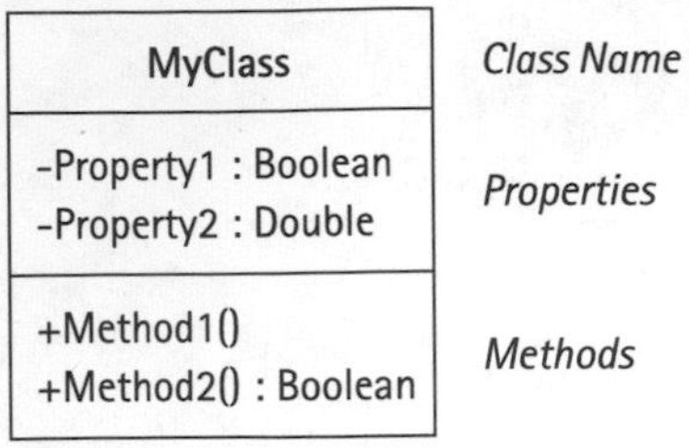

MyClass	*Class Name*
-Property1 : Boolean -Property2 : Double	*Properties*
+Method1() +Method2() : Boolean	*Methods*

Figure 3-1: The elements of the
UML class symbol

Properties can be annotated with their type. Methods can be annotated with their return type. Throughout this book, I use the terms *properties* and *methods* a lot. UML doesn't actually use these terms. The UML notation uses the more generic terms *attributes* and *operations*. Figure 3-2 shows a diagram with five classes and one interface.

A few words will help you understand the figure:

✦ Class1 is a class that doesn't have a base class or super class.

✦ Class2 is derived from Class1 via single inheritance. Interface1 is an interface, in other words a class with no implementation. The purpose of interfaces is to use them as base classes for other interfaces or classes. The small triangle right under a class box denotes derivation through inheritance.

✦ Class3 is derived through multiple inheritance from Class2 and Interface1. Class3 is the only class in the diagram to have properties and methods. A class can have any number (including 0) of properties. Class3 is associated with Class4. Simple links or associations are represented with a line. You can label each end of the association to clarify its meaning. Since associations are references to objects, the labels are often the names of the reference variables used. In the example, Class3 has a variable called MyClass4 that references Class4. Class4 has a reference variable called MyClass3 that references Class3. Associations can also have multiplicities, indicating the number of instances at each end of it. If no numbers are shown (which is the case for the link between Class3 and Class4), the implied value is 1.

✦ Class4 is a composite class. It aggregates multiple instances of another class (Class5, in the example). The small diamond symbol under Class4 denotes the composition relationship. This type of relationship, like associations, can also have multiplicities. In the example, the asterisk next to Class5 indicates there can be any number of them. Each Class5 item belongs to just one Class4 element. Each end of the composition can be labeled. In the example, Class4 has a collection named MyElements that manages the Class5 elements. Each Class5 element has a reference named MyContainer that references Class4.

UML aggregates have nothing to do with the aggregation model described in Chapter 2, "Component Structure." A UML aggregate is just a class used one or more times in another class that acts like a container. Aggregation, as a component model, indicates that the interfaces of subcomponents are visible to users of the supercomponent.

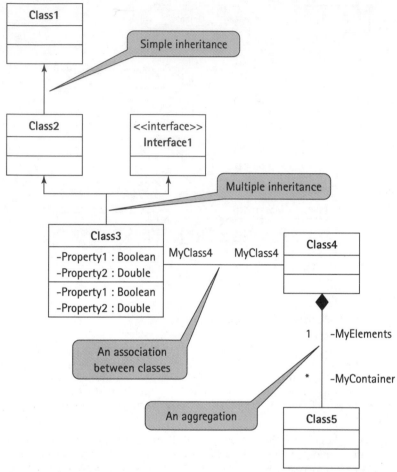

Figure 3-2: A simple UML class diagram, with a number of commonly recurring symbols and notations

Interaction diagrams

The most common name for this type of diagram in the UML literature is *sequence diagram.* I prefer the name *interaction diagram,* because these diagrams generally show how objects or components interact with each other (by showing sequences of messages). The basic elements in an interaction diagram are actors and messages. Actors interact with each other by exchanging messages, as shown in Figure 3-3.

The diagram in Figure 3-3 shows two objects communicating with each other. Actors are defined by a vertical dashed line. At the top is a rectangular box containing the name of the actor. In the interaction diagrams shown in this book, the actors are objects. When there is only one object of a given type in the diagram, I normally use the class name (such as MyClass) rather than an object name (such as MyObject). A thick bar is drawn on top of the vertical dashed line to denote when the object is active. Messages exchanged between actors are denoted by horizontal arrows. Time progresses in the downward direction. Notes and constraints can be added to the diagram, as shown in the figure.

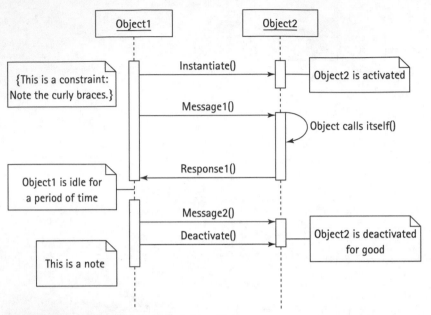

Figure 3-3: A simple UML interaction diagram

In Figure 3-3, Object1 starts the interaction by creating an instance of Object2. Then it sends Message1 to Object2. Object2 reacts by sending a message to itself, and then returning a response to Object1. Object1 then sends Message2 to Object2 and then deactivates Object2. The term *message* is used generically in UML. It represents the transfer of information and/or control flow from one object to another. Most languages use methods or events for this purpose.

Many languages, like C++, give control over an object's lifetime to the programmer. In C++, you need to explicitly deallocate objects by calling the delete keyword. Many newer languages, like C# and Java, manage object lifecycle automatically using a garbage collector. With these languages, you have no way of forcing the destruction of an object at a particular moment in time. Once you stop referencing an object, the garbage collector will deallocate the memory used by the object. The garbage collection process occurs in the background, and is not generally controlled by your code.

There is one drawback in interaction diagrams: Conditional sequences are awkward to represent. Say you have a sequence that, based on a condition being true or not, follows different paths. Such a sequence would be modeled as shown in Figure 3-4.

The diagram has a single conditional statement, and is fairly confusing. Imagine modeling a condition with 5, 6, or more possible values. The diagram would be entirely unreadable. I recommend using a separate interaction diagram for each condition, and documenting only those sequences that are significant. For example, if Object2 has different paths based on whether the Color is red, green, or blue, you may only want to model each path if the differences are important to understand, or perhaps have different side effects. If the Color condition simply made you call SetRed() instead of SetGreen() or SetBlue(), there is no conceptual difference in what happens, so you might just document the sequence with a generic SetColor() message, adding a note to the diagram that setColor() is a placeholder for setRed(), setGreen(), and setBlue().

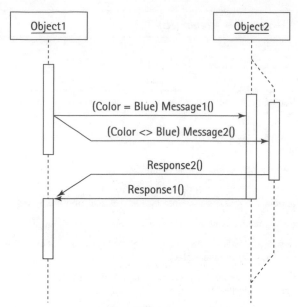

Figure 3-4: Modeling conditional sequences

Design Patterns

Two of the most important events that occurred during the 1990s in the software engineering discipline were the widespread adoption of object-oriented programming and the rise of the design patterns movement. Design patterns are elegant solutions to recurring problems. There are too many patterns in the literature for me to describe in the limited space available here, but Table 3-1 lists some of the significant patterns that are in widespread use today. In subsequent sections, I'll describe them in some detail. For more information, check the sources referenced in the Appendix.

Table 3-1: Some Commonly Used Software Design Patterns

Creational Patterns Overview

Pattern Name	Description
Builder	Helps abstract component instantiation, supporting a homogeneous way to create different types of objects.
Product Trader	Specifies a way to use a common interface to create different types of objects.
Prototype	Specifies a cloning method for creating new objects out of existing ones.
Singleton	Defines a way to implement classes that must only be instantiated once.

Continued

Table 3-1 *(continued)*

Structural Patterns Overview

Pattern Name	Description
Composite	Used when one component is made up of many others that all share a basic interface.
Decorator	Supports a means to extend the features of an object without using inheritance.
Extension Object	Provides a method for adding new features to a class without changing its interface.
Façade	Uses one object to represent the interface into a collection of others.
Manager	Abstracts the management of collections of objects.
Master-Slave	Defines a structure with a master object that carries out operations using a collection of identical worker objects.
Mediator	Serves as glue between objects, allowing objects to interact without having knowledge of each other's structure.
Proxy	Defines one object as a surrogate for another.

Behavioral Patterns Overview

Pattern Name	Description
Asynchronous Completion Token	Supports a way for asynchronous calls to be synchronized using a token.
Chain Of Responsibility	Specifies a way to have multiple receivers process a message.
Command	Provides a way to encapsulate requests for action.
Interpreter	Defines a way to describe grammars and parsers.
Observer	Allows multiple objects that depend on a common object to remain updated when the object is modified.
Reactor	Defines a mechanism to add event handlers to an object.
State	Provides a way to support state-based behavior.
Template	Allows an operation to be specified generically by one class, with derived classes providing refinements.
Visitor	Encapsulates the navigation logic to traverse the items in a graph and apply an operation to each item visited.

There are many other patterns in existence, with new ones being identified all the time, but those in the table have been found by many people to be extremely useful for all sorts of situations.

Creational patterns

Creational patterns are those that have to do with object instantiation, or constraints imposed on instantiation. Some of these patterns provide features similar to virtual constructors. The following sections describe the most popular creational patterns in some detail.

Builder

When you need to transform a complex object into a series of other objects, and there could be several ways to perform the transformation, you can use a common `Builder` interface [Gamma 1995] to represent the generic transformation process. The `Builder` interface embodies the abstract notion of the transformation process. Derived classes can implement the transformation in different ways. A generic class, called `Director`, can use the `Builder` interface to transform each part of the original complex object, step by step. Figures 3-5 and 3-6 show the basic class and interaction diagrams for the pattern.

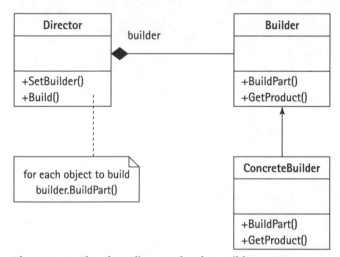

Figure 3-5: The class diagram for the Builder pattern

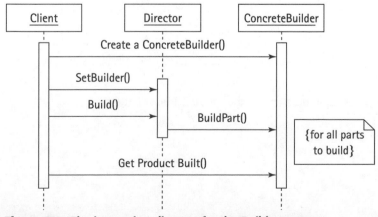

Figure 3-6: The interaction diagram for the Builder pattern

Product Trader

This pattern's name is a bit misleading. The pattern actually defines a way to build objects whose type isn't known until runtime, much like a virtual constructor. With the Product Trader pattern [Bäumer 1998], you need two special items for each class to be instantiated: a class ID and a class factory. The former is passed to the Product Trader to indicate which type of object to build. The class ID is used by the Trader to locate the class factory and to instantiate the class. Figures 3-7 and 3-8 show the basic class and interaction diagrams for the pattern.

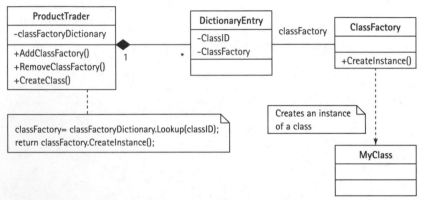

Figure 3-7: The class diagram for the Product Trader pattern

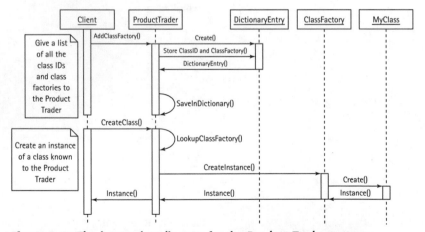

Figure 3-8: The interaction diagram for the Product Trader pattern

Prototype

The Prototype pattern [Gamma 1995] describes the situation in which you need to create copies of an object (which we'll call the *prototype*), whose type is unknown at design time. Rather than writing a huge switch statement for each possible object type, a solution is to have some sort of cloning process that creates copies of the prototype. Figures 3-9 and 3-10 show the basic class and interaction diagrams for the pattern.

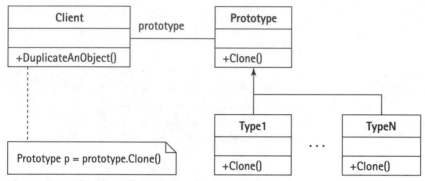

Figure 3-9: The class diagram for the Prototype pattern

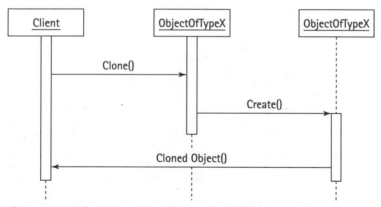

Figure 3-10: The interaction diagram for the Prototype pattern

Singleton

There are many situations in which a system can only allow the existence of one instance of certain types. For example, consider using a SecurityManager to validate operations. Most likely you'll want only one instance of the object to exist at any given time. If multiple client components make use of the SecurityManager, it may be impractical or bug-prone to make the clients responsible for ensuring that only one instance of SecurityManager is instantiated. The solution provided by the Singleton pattern [Gamma 1995] is to hide the class constructor, and force clients to instantiate Singleton by calling a static method, which I'll call `GetUniqueInstance()`. This method checks to see whether an instance of Singleton already exists. If so, it returns that instance. If not, a new instance is created and returned. Figures 3-11 and 3-12 show the basic class and interaction diagrams for the pattern.

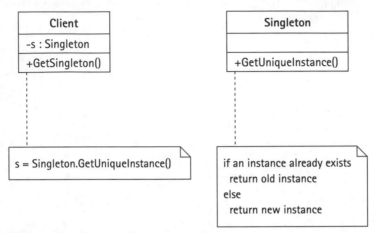

Figure 3-11: The class diagram for the Singleton pattern

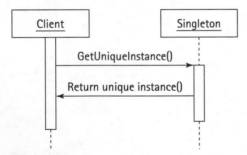

Figure 3-12: The interaction diagram for the Singleton pattern

Structural patterns

Structural patterns can be used to solve certain types of problems that rely on graphs of classes, rather than a single class.

Composite

The Composite pattern [Gamma 1995] is an extremely useful pattern that describes hierarchical relationships. If you have an object that can act as a container to other objects, which can themselves be containers, the Composite pattern represents an elegant solution. An example where the pattern might be used is to represent the windows in a user interface: each window can contain various types of items, including other windows. Figures 3-13 and 3-14 show the basic class and interaction diagrams for the pattern.

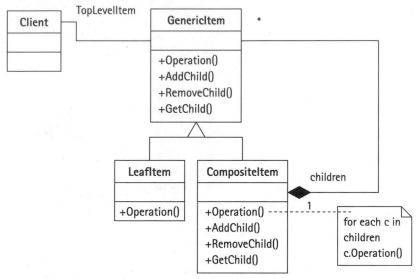

Figure 3-13: The class diagram for the Composite pattern

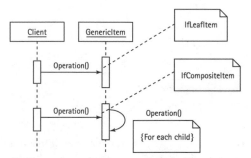

Figure 3-14: The interaction diagram for the Composite pattern

Decorator

When you deal with groups of classes that share basic functionality, it may become necessary to later add features to some of the objects. The Decorator pattern [Gamma 1995] is a way to add features without having to modify the interface of a class, and without disturbing other instances of the same type. Figures 3-15 and 3-16 show the basic class and interaction diagrams for the pattern.

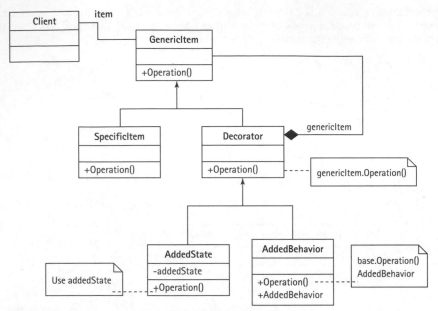

Figure 3-15: The class diagram for the Decorator pattern

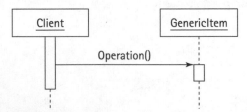

Figure 3-16: The interaction diagram for the Decorator pattern

Extension Object

The Extension Object pattern [Gamma 1998] provides a way to add new capabilities to an object. The extensions are added through add-on objects, so the original object requires no structural or interface changes. Use this pattern with complicated or flexible objects, to which users may need to add features that you can't anticipate at design time. Figures 3-17 and 3-18 show the basic class and interaction diagrams for the pattern.

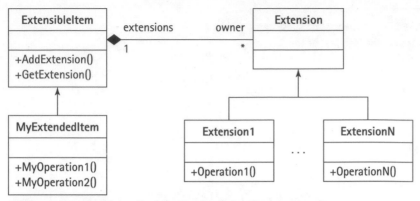

Figure 3-17: The class diagram for the Extension pattern

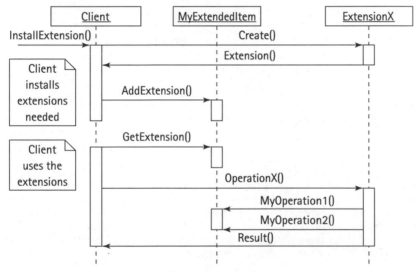

Figure 3-18: The interaction diagram for the Extension pattern

Façade

The Façade pattern [Gamma 1995] uses a single interface to control access to a group of objects forming a subsystem. Components containing subcomponents demonstrate this pattern: the supercomponent's interface hides the subcomponents from direct access. Figure 3-19 shows the basic class diagram for the pattern. You'll notice the absence of an interaction diagram for the Façade pattern. I omitted the diagram because the importance of the pattern lies in the relationship between the Façade class and the classes it hides access to. The interactions that occur between external client components and the Façade class are irrelevant in terms of understanding the Façade design pattern.

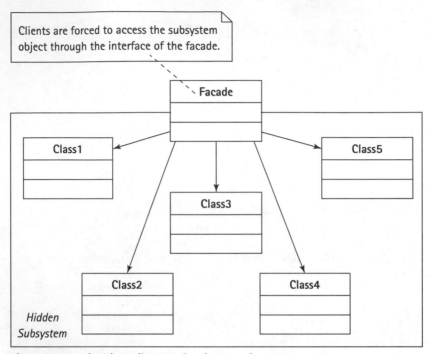

Figure 3-19: The class diagram for the Façade pattern

Manager

A very common programming situation is to have collections of objects that are stored somewhere. Client objects want to be able to retrieve an object from the collection, work with it, and then return it. Picture a public library: you check a book out, read it, and then return it. A more software-oriented example could be a pool of threads. When you need to run a task, you request a thread, run the task on it, and then return the thread to the pool. The Manager pattern [Sommerlad 1998] separates the management functions from the items being managed. Figures 3-20 and 3-21 show the basic class and interaction diagrams for the pattern.

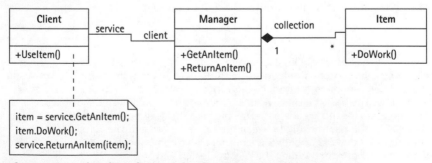

Figure 3-20: The class diagram for the Manager pattern

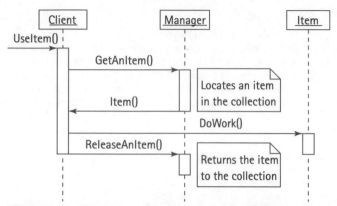

Figure 3-21: The interaction diagram for the Manager pattern

Master-Slave

The Master-Slave pattern [Buschmann 1995] is often used when you want to implement a service using a set of identical worker objects *(slaves)*. Clients using the service deal with a *master* object, which manages the slaves, schedules slaves to handle requests, and hides the slaves from clients. The master may require multiple slaves to work on a request at the same time. The master coordinates the slave activities transparently from the client. From the client's point of view, the only object available is the master. The Master-Slave pattern can be used to support services that require concurrent processing. Slaves can be envisioned as belonging to a pool, from which the master selects available slaves and assigns them to a task. Figures 3-22 and 3-23 show the basic class and interaction diagrams for the pattern.

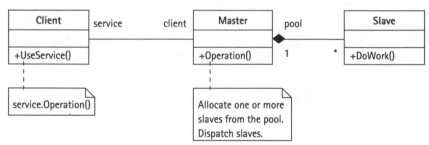

Figure 3-22: The class diagram for the Master-Slave pattern

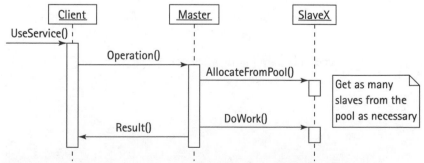

Figure 3-23: The interaction diagram for the Master-Slave pattern

Mediator

The Mediator pattern [Gamma 1995] defines certain objects as glue, to manage synchronization and messaging between other objects, creating a central place for coordination logic to be. It isn't too unusual for mediator objects to also contain business-rule logic. As an example, say you have a dialog box with two controls: a listbox and a label. You want the label to display the string selected in the listbox. By using a mediator, you could have the `OnSelectedItemChanged` event of the listbox call a method in the mediator, which would react by calling the `SetText()` method on the label control. Figures 3-24 and 3-25 show the basic class and interaction diagrams for the pattern.

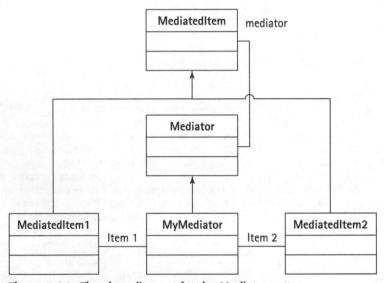

Figure 3-24: The class diagram for the Mediator pattern

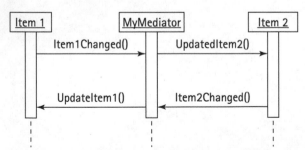

Figure 3-25: The interaction diagram for the Mediator pattern

Proxy

When a client object needs to access another object that may be at a location that is variable, remote, complicated to determine, or even unknown until runtime, one solution is to use the Proxy pattern [Gamma 1995] to set up an intermediate *proxy* object to hide the access details. The client can then talk to the proxy, which forwards requests to the intended object and routes responses back to the client. Figures 3-26 and 3-27 show the basic class and interaction diagrams for the pattern.

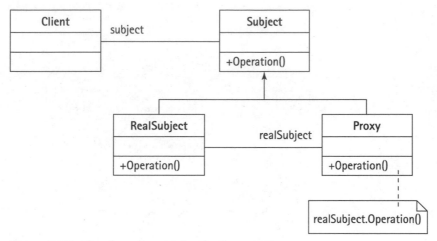

Figure 3-26: The class diagram for the Proxy pattern

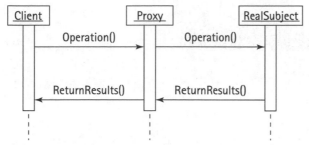

Figure 3-27: The interaction diagram for the Proxy pattern

Behavioral patterns

Patterns in this category are relevant not as much for the way objects are structured, but for the way they act as a whole, how they interact, how one object reacts when another is changed, or how a group of objects handles changes of various types.

Asynchronous Completion Token

When one object (the *client*) makes an asynchronous call to another (the *service*), an important issue is how the client detects when the service has finished carrying out its task. Nonblocking calls return immediately, so a completion notification mechanism needs to be established for the client and service to use. The Asynchronous Completion Token (ACT) pattern [Pyarali 1998] uses a token, which is passed from the client to the service. When the service completes the task, it sends the token back to the client using a callback method. The token can carry arbitrarily complex information, to indicate completion information or errors that may have occurred. Figures 3-28 and 3-29 show the basic class and interaction diagrams for the pattern.

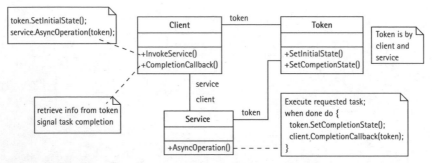

Figure 3-28: The class diagram for the Asynchronous Completion Token pattern

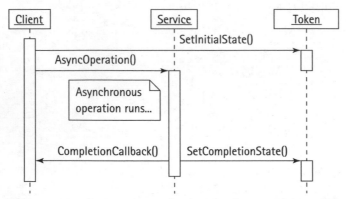

Figure 3-29: The interaction diagram for the Asynchronous Completion Token pattern

Chain of Responsibility

This pattern [Gamma 1995] describes a simple way to handle events that are propagated through an object graph. Consider a SetFocus event that is sent to a control in a dialog box. If the control can accept focus, it consumes the event; otherwise, the control may send the event to the parent window. The event travels up the parent chain until it is consumed or it reaches the top of the hierarchy. Figures 3-30 and 3-31 show the basic class and interaction diagrams for the pattern.

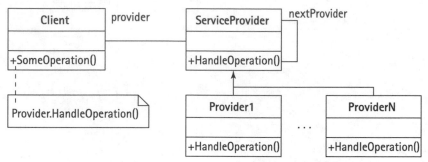

Figure 3-30: The class diagram for the Chain of Responsibility pattern

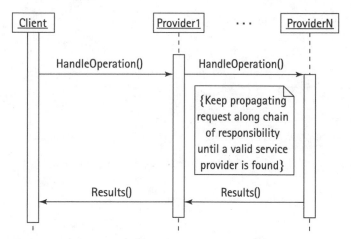

Figure 3-31: The interaction diagram for the Chain of Responsibility pattern

Command

The most direct way of issuing a command to an object is to call one of its methods. If you need to have an object send commands, but won't know who the receiver is until runtime, one approach is to use the Command pattern [Gamma 1995]. This pattern decouples from each other the sender, the receiver, and the command being exchanged. An initializer object creates commands at runtime and establishes the binding between the command sender and receiver. Figures 3-32 and 3-33 show the basic class and interaction diagrams for the pattern.

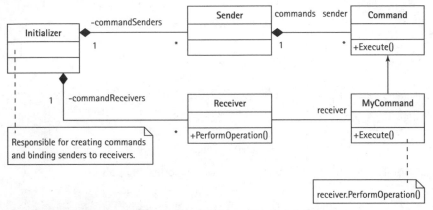

Figure 3-32: The class diagram for the Command pattern

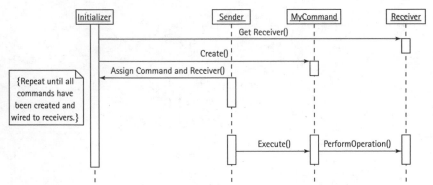

Figure 3-33: The interaction diagram for the Command pattern

Interpreter

When you have a sequence of symbols that need to be parsed, the Interpreter pattern [Gamma 1995] can be useful. Sequences of symbols are common in software projects. A sequence may represent a code fragment written in a programming language, or a regular expression, or a set of commands that are project-specific and use your own private grammar. Consider a simple grammar defined with the following BNF (Backus-Naur Form, a common notation used to describe context-free grammar) code:

```
expression          ::= simple_expression
                        [ ( "=" | "<>" | "<" | "<=" | ">" | ">=" )
                        simple_expression ]

simple_expression ::= [ "+" | "-" ] term { ( "+" | "-") term }
term                ::= number { ( "*" | "/") number }
```

An arbitrary statement that followed this grammar, such as "10+5*2/8" could be parsed using a class diagram that used the Interpreter pattern. Figures 3-34 and 3-35 show the basic class and interaction diagrams for the pattern.

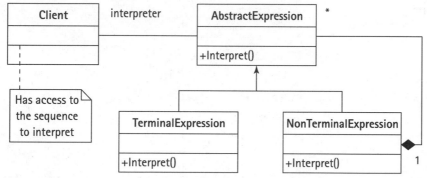

Figure 3-34: The class diagram for the Interpreter pattern

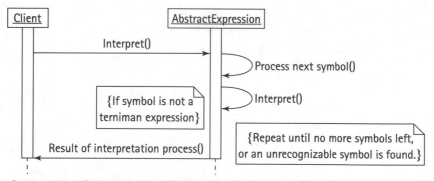

Figure 3-35: The interaction diagram for the Interpreter pattern

Observer

When one object is dependent on the state of another, the former needs to be notified when the latter is changed. The Observer pattern [Gamma 1995] can be useful in this situation. The idea is for the subject (the object being observed) to maintain a list of observer objects. When the subject changes, it sends update messages to all the observers, to give them a chance to refresh themselves and take other appropriate actions. Figures 3-36 and 3-37 show the basic class and interaction diagrams for the pattern.

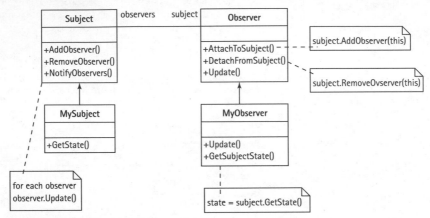

Figure 3-36: The class diagram for the Observer pattern

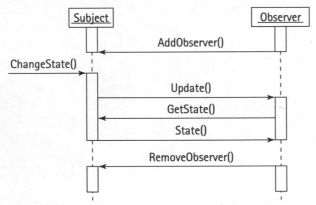

Figure 3-37: The interaction diagram for the Observer pattern

Reactor

This pattern [Schmidt 1995] is the basis of many event-driven architectures. Although its class diagram is reminiscent of the Observer pattern, its operation and motivation are quite different. The purpose of a Reactor is to provide a simple means for a system to process and dispatch events to other objects, without requiring multithreading or complicated queuing mechanisms. The pattern defines a main loop that receives events and dispatches them to one or more event handlers. All the events are processed on this single *event pump* thread, so event handlers are not allowed to block while processing events. Before an event handler can be dispatched events, it must register itself with the event dispatcher, indicating which events it is interested in processing. Figures 3-38 and 3-39 show the basic class and interaction diagrams for the pattern.

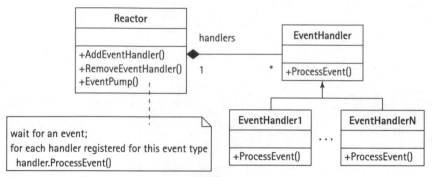

Figure 3-38: The class diagram for the Reactor pattern

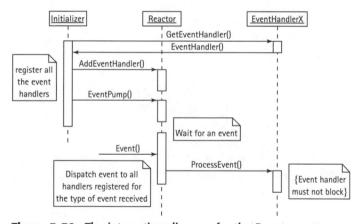

Figure 3-39: The interaction diagram for the Reactor pattern

State

Many systems are associated with states. Such systems behave in a way that depends on the *state* they are in, and are often modeled using state transition diagrams. If the various states share common functions, but must implement them differently, the State pattern [Gamma 1995] can be a solution. Using this pattern, you model the states as classes derived from a common base class. When the system wishes to enter a given state, it instantiates an object of the correct type and invokes it. Figures 3-40 and 3-41 show the basic class and interaction diagrams for the pattern.

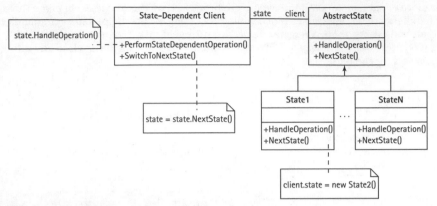

Figure 3-40: The class diagram for the State pattern

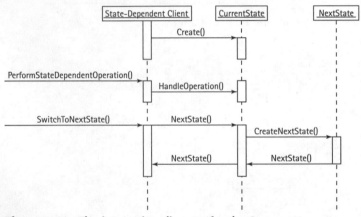

Figure 3-41: The interaction diagram for the State pattern

Template

This pattern [Gamma 1995] is useful when a system uses a service that supports a general algorithm, consisting of many suboperations. The suboperations are defined abstractly, and could have different implementations, but you don't want the client to have dependencies on the specific server implementation. The Template pattern uses a base class to model the general service interface, delegating specialized suboperations to a derived class. Figures 3-42 and 3-43 show the basic class and interaction diagrams for the pattern.

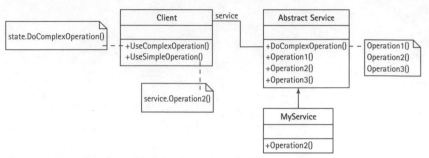

Figure 3-42: The class diagram for the Template pattern

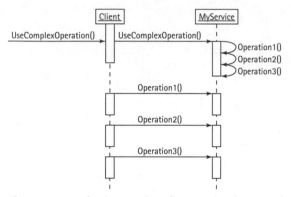

Figure 3-43: The interaction diagram for the Template pattern

Visitor

This pattern [Gamma 1995] is useful when you need to traverse a graph of objects and apply an operation to some, or all, of the visited objects. The pattern allows you to change the operation, without impacting the structure of the objects in the graph. You determine which operation is applied to an element by passing it a given visitor object. Figures 3-44 and 3-45 show the basic class and interaction diagrams for the pattern.

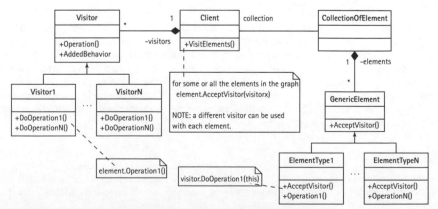

Figure 3-44: The class diagram for the Visitor pattern

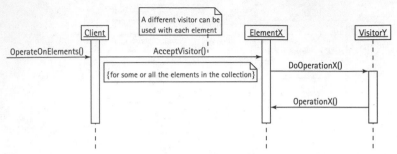

Figure 3-45: The interaction diagram for the Visitor pattern

Don't Forget the *-ilities*

Developing designs that are elegant, fast, and simple is good, but there are a number of non-functional requirements to be kept in mind during the design phase. These are second-order features that are desirable, but often missing from the official requirements. They include such difficult-to-measure things as testability, flexibility, and reliability. Collectively these issues are sometimes called the *–ilities*. The following is a list of some of the important ones:

✦ Manageability

✦ Testability

✦ Usability

✦ Deployability

✦ Maintainability

✦ Reliability

✦ Flexibility

✦ Portability

Many of the *–ilities* are interrelated. Each is discussed briefly in the next sections.

Manageability

Don't design your software system such that none of it can be demonstrated or tested until all the parts are finished. If there is a problem somewhere in the team or the design, you want to know as soon as possible. You should design components to be as independent from each other as possible, so they can be built and verified independently and incrementally. A project that produces no demonstrable parts until the very end is a management nightmare (how would you verify progress or completion percentage?), and runs a high risk of missing production deadlines. Design for incremental milestones in which small but complete parts of the system can be shown to work early on.

Testability

Always try to design components so they can be tested by themselves, or with a small set of ancillary components. Design a test fixture as you design each component. Making good use of design patterns should help produce designs with low coupling between components. The lower the degree of coupling, the easier the components will be to test independently. Once you design and build your test fixtures, save them along with your components. In the future, the test fixtures may turn out to be invaluable if a defect is discovered in the software and you're not sure which component is defective. The test fixtures will allow you to test each of your components separately and help quickly pinpoint the guilty one.

Usability

How easy is it for other programmers to use your designs? If your component has 200 methods and 100 properties, I guarantee it won't be very easy to use—for you or anyone else. Keep the number of items in the interface as small as possible. Remember the *10-10-10* guideline: Try to keep the number of properties, methods, and events to less than 10 each. Also, use *long* names with items in the interface, to make sure they are as self-explanatory as possible. For example, a fictitious method called `bind()` may be easier to use if it were changed to `ConnectToServerAndSetupEventProcessingQueue()`. Don't try to save time typing. If you don't like typing, you picked the wrong profession. Creating software is all about typing. Developing software using visual methods or through spoken commands is not quite there yet, so typing is mandatory now and for the near-term future. Keep in mind that those long names you type may help *you* too, when five years down the road, and three projects later, your boss asks you to pick up some old code and make some changes to it.

Deployability

When it comes to deploying software, there are two important issues, from the customer's point of view: how long it takes, and how complicated the process is. A software system using components in 50 different files, with 25 third-party DLLs each requiring a separate install process is not going to be a simple system to deploy. If your software makes use of third-party components, try to install those transparently. Launching a second or third install program after the main install is finished is not only frustrating for end-users, but sloppy-looking.

While you design the software, keep in mind the manner in which you will distribute it. If you are planning a Web distribution, you may want to plan a deployment based on small, incremental parts. Large, monolithic downloads may not be acceptable for many users. If a new version of a component is released down the road, it would be nice if your customers only had to download that one component. Also, if the software will be deployed over the Web to developing countries, remember that not everyone has a T1, DSL, or cable modem connection. In some countries, just getting a dial tone is itself an accomplishment.

If you are planning to distribute the software on a CD or a DVD, size is probably not as crucial. Still, the number of separate files that need to be installed on the customer's machine should be kept as small as possible. An application's *footprint* is not just a description of physical size, but also an indication of intrusiveness. The bigger the footprint, the greater the potential impact on the end user's machine.

When the user runs the Install program, try not to present too many installation options. Ideally, the user wants to run the program and not have to do anything. If you do need to support different options, hide them on an Advanced or Custom form, and let most users work with reasonable defaults.

Maintainability

The quality of your software's design affects its maintainability. Good design implicitly means low component coupling, low interface complexity at the component level, and good usability.

If you were handed a piece of software to make changes to, what would you want it to look like? You would want the original test fixture to be available. Some documentation would be nice. You would also want the component to be small and independent of other components. You would also want the individual properties, methods, and events of the component to be as independent of each other as possible. If one part of the code affected another part in obscure or undocumented ways, the code would be more difficult to maintain and modify than otherwise.

Another feature that makes a system more maintainable is a clear relationship between causes and effects. If you have a component with a property called `BackgroundColor`, people will expect to use it for setting the background color of the component. If the property's setter does something different, or does other things as well, the code will be more difficult to maintain.

Besides the obvious time and cost advantages of software that is easy to maintain, consider developing maintainable software as a favor to yourself, because *you* may be the person that is called upon to maintain it. And don't think you'll always remember every little detail. Besides, when the time comes to hand the work over to someone else, the next person's job will be easier.

Reliability

Regarding reliability, a cardinal rule with any system is this:

> *The more risk a system is subject to, the less reliable it will be.*

Risk equates to uncertainty, and there are generally several sources of uncertainty in a system. One is related to complexity. Complexity may be required to satisfy the system requirements, but complexity itself injects potential problems into a system. Never introduce complex solutions unless you have explored all the alternatives first. Another source of uncertainty is change. Anytime you add new features to a system, especially features you have never implemented before on other systems, you introduce uncertainty. Look at how Toyota manufactures cars. One of the many reasons Toyota achieves the consistent high marks for reliability in its cars depends on the way the company controls changes [Ohno 1988]. From one year to the next, the highest importance is placed on fixing problems discovered in the previous model. Changes and new features are added sparingly, and not just for the sake of making the next model different.

Reliability is also related to how a system operates, or whether it survives, in unusual or extreme situations. For example, middle-tier or back-end components may be hit by traffic peaks during certain times of the day, month, or year. Consider what would happen if your company advertised on television commercials during the finals of the World Soccer Cup. Your servers might get a sudden surge in simultaneous requests on that one single day. Will the whole system grind to a halt, or will performance degrade gracefully? Software that deals with real-time events has similar problems. What if multiple events occur at the same time? Are you prepared to handle the events concurrently? In multithreaded code, have you been careful about avoiding deadlocks and race conditions?

Software that deals with end users through a user interface is faced with another task: dealing with operator error. You can't always assume people will press the right key or click the right button. Designing reliable software isn't easy, and the more variations in input, traffic, and events you need to plan for, the more difficult it gets. Difficult, but not impossible.

Reliability is not just dependent on how well something is designed, but also on how well it is tested. Junior programmers (and some not-so-junior ones) will often go to their team leader and say they are finished developing a certain piece of code, when in reality the software is known to work correctly only when all the correct values are entered, or when the expected events are triggered in the right order. Design your test fixtures to stress-test your code, to test boundary conditions, and to simulate foreseeable operator errors.

Regarding reliability, I remember a story from the early days of the Space Shuttle program. Within seconds of lift-off, the countdown sequence was aborted for a failure in the onboard computers. The mission was postponed while the software engineers poured over the software systems to figure out what had happened. The problem turned out to be an initialization sequence timing problem: System A was supposed to start first, then System B, then System C, and so on. Apparently, the sequence didn't go this way on that fateful day, so the overall system failed to initialize correctly. No harm, no foul, but lots of time, money, and effort wasted. As it turns out, the engineers familiar with the systems had seen this problem before and knew how to fix it: just hit the reset buttons until the system booted correctly (I'm simplifying here somewhat, but you get the picture). Reliability can be a very important issue. When those computers fire up, they had better fire up! Even if no one is killed or injured, you may lose your credibility if they don't.

Measuring reliability

How do you measure reliability? It can't really be measured, only estimated. Engineers have been estimating the reliability of mechanical and electronic systems for decades. How do they do it? In more ways than one, but always using statistical methods. Perhaps the most common way is to estimate how much time a system will operate until it fails. This estimate is called the *Mean Time To Failure* (MTTF), and is measured generally in *hours.* If a system is estimated to fail after 1000 hours, it has an MTTF of 1000. MTTF estimates don't usually account for the probability of accidents. For example, the MTTF for a hard drive may be 200,000. This value doesn't include the probability of the hard drive dropping off the back of a truck during shipment.

But physical and software systems are very different. The MTTFs of physical systems are usually obtained by operating large numbers of identical systems under artificial conditions to stress them, causing accelerated aging and subsequent failure. There are two problems with this method, when applied to software systems. First, software systems don't age with use. Second, using multiple copies of software in the stress test is pointless, because each copy will operate identically to the master copy.

To measure reliability with software, you need to run the software under all foreseeable conditions and find when or how often it fails. Automatic testing is a very common way of finding faults: A test fixture rapidly exercises all the functions of the system, simulating valid and invalid inputs, while monitoring the outputs. Although automatic testing is extremely effective, in terms of costs and results, it is not a replacement for human testers. Programs that have complex user interactions and graphical user interfaces often require extensive human testing to guarantee that data displayed is correct at all times.

When a system first enters the final test phase, defects will be discovered at a certain rate. As failures are fixed, defects will tend to be discovered less frequently, so the MTTF will increase. As defects get more rare, they tend to require more and more effort to discover and fix. The graph in Figure 3-46 shows how effort-per-unit MTTF is related to the number of defects fixed, according to one study [Littlewood 1993].

As the cost of fixing defects increases, and as the defects become scarcer, there invariably comes a point at which the cost of fixing a defect outweighs the benefits of fixing it. The point at which that occurs will depend on the resources available to the organization building the system; the nature of the remaining defects; the potential danger of defects for people, property, or the environment; and so on.

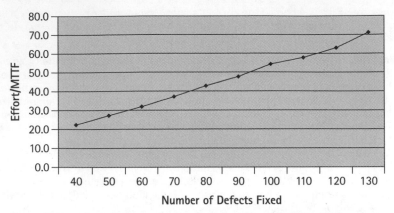

Figure 3-46: The effort required to increase the reliability of a system

As stated earlier, the MTTF is a somewhat simplistic measurement of reliability. It tells you the time between failures, but not the gravity of those failures. Consider two software systems with the same MTTF: the first system occasionally has small, cosmetic problems in the user interface; the second system occasionally hangs and loses all your data. Is one system more reliable than the other? Intuitively, yes: the first system has small problems you can probably live with; the second has severe problems that you may not tolerate. What is common between the two systems is the frequency with which the respective problems manifest themselves. To better specify reliability, there are methods that include the gravity of failures, as well as their frequency, but these methods are beyond the scope of this book.

Flexibility

How difficult would it be to make changes to your design? What impact would a change have on the implementation? How long would it take to make it? The answers obviously depend on what the changes are, so it is impossible to design a system that is *arbitrarily* flexible. Still, systems built with small components that are loosely coupled and easy to understand are probably more flexible than others. Flexibility is also heavily dependent on other *–ilities*.

To design a system that can accommodate evolution in a certain direction, it helps if you know what the direction will be when you design the system. The initial specifications and requirements may have listed items that were removed from the first version, but will need to be supported later. If so, it wouldn't be absurd to consider those items as possible features necessary in the next version, and to design the system with those changes in mind.

Portability

If your software needs to run on multiple platforms, or under different configurations, portability may be an issue. Try to encapsulate the platform dependencies in components, to insulate the rest of the system. Ideally, all the nonportable code should be in one place, or in a small number of places. Portability usually needs to be considered from the design phase, but careful implementation may also be necessary. Will the software be used with 32- and 64-bit operating systems? If so, method arguments and variable types could become critical.

Relax — There's No Such Thing as Perfect Design

I have never seen a software design I would call perfect, and I probably never will. You'll always be able to find software that has a worse design than yours, but then again you'll always be able to find better designs. Perfection is an abstract concept, something we should strive for, even if we never achieve it. The problem is that the amount of time and effort we can devote to design and development is highly constrained, and there are so many different issues to deal with. What is the answer? As for most things in life, the answer is *experience*. Don't be embarrassed to learn.

Hallmarks of Good Design

I think we all agree by now that design is important, but how do you measure the quality of a system's design? What is a good design, in a nutshell? Different types of projects have different priorities, with different design goals. For example, an avionics package may consider redundancy and real-time responsiveness essential. For a business accounting package, the top priority may be guarding against loss of data. A software system controlling intensive-care medical instrumentation may place the highest priority on reliability. Looking beyond the immediate priorities of a project, which vary from sector to sector, there are a number of features that stand out in all good designs:

✦ Components are loosely coupled.

✦ Class diagrams are simple.

✦ Interaction diagrams are simple.

✦ Many of the *–ilities* are satisfied.

It may sound strange at first, but here's an aphorism for you:

The best way to design good software is to use someone else's design.

I'm not talking about plagiarism here: Use patterns! Patterns have been used successfully in large numbers of projects, and represent the distillation of some serious thought by many people. Patterns represent simple, elegant, and often, flexible solutions to many of the scenarios you encounter in everyday projects. But don't get into a pattern binge, shoehorning every pattern in existence into your projects.

Summary

To conclude this chapter, design your systems in detail *before* implementing them. Design documentation is not just something to let others understand what you did: It's also supposed to help you create better software. Use UML, or other equivalent notation, to document your designs. Use patterns as much as possible, and always design test fixtures while designing your components.

✦　　✦　　✦

Component Classifications

*I have orders to be awakened at any time in the case of a
national emergency, even if I'm in a cabinet meeting.*

—Ronald Reagan, former U.S. President

Hopefully, no one will need to awake you while you're reading
this chapter. Classification can be a fairly dry subject, especially
in fields like botany or zoology that deal with thousands or even
millions of different types of plants and animals. The field of software
components is too new to have levels of differentiation even remotely
comparable to those found in the natural sciences. Lucky you—
otherwise, this chapter might have been a whole new book, if not an
entire series.

There are thousands of third-party software components in existence
today, with the number expected to rise exponentially. When dealing
with large numbers of items, it is very important to establish one or
more criteria for cataloging them. Without such criteria, it would be
difficult and time-consuming to locate and retrieve an item. Some
things are easier to catalog and organize than others. For example,
words are organized alphabetically in dictionaries. Encyclopedias are
organized by alphabetical subject. But software components are
much more difficult to classify than simple words. Sure, you could
create a dictionary of components sorted by name or vendor, but
with large numbers of components, it would be almost useless.
Component names are arbitrary, and vendor names may have no
relationship to the features of the components they sell. What type of
classification should be used to make it easy to retrieve a component
with given features?

Software engineering is certainly not the first field to deal with large
numbers of complex items in human history, so it may help to step
back for a minute and look at how other disciplines have dealt with
the problem. Take the field of biology. Since the days of Aristotle, and
probably even before, attempts were made to create classifications of
all living things. In the seventeenth and eighteenth centuries, following an explosion in the number of known plant and animal types, the
whole field seemed to be in chaos. Specialists from different countries
had no common way to refer to plants or animals. Other than the fact
they were alive, there didn't seem to be any relationship between
zebras and mollusks, or between fungi and roses.

As an indication of how disorganized the field was as recently as the eighteenth century, it may be of interest to know that the term *biology* didn't even exist until the early 1800s. Recognition of biology as a separate branch of science didn't occur until the middle of that century. Prior to then, biology was studied by a combination of physicians, naturalists, and philosophers.

A breakthrough occurred when the Swedish naturalist Carolus Linnaeus (1707-1778) published the works *Species Plantarum* and *Systema Naturae*, in which he identified and classified over 8000 plants and 4000 animals, creating a binomial classification system and nomenclature that is the basis for all biological classifications used today. The system uses Latin words and syntax. Linnaeus chose Latin because it was the official language for scientific papers at the time. Expressions like *homo sapiens* or *escherichia coli* are examples of the Linnaeus nomenclature. The creation and acceptance of a universal classification system for living things was a breakthrough that enormously facilitated the sharing of information across cultural divides, and provided the spark for a new renaissance in the study of living things.

Today, we're still in the infancy of component-based development (CBD), much like the field of biology in the late seventeenth century. We don't even have a name for software engineers doing CBD. Who knows, may be in the future we'll call them *componentologists!* Whatever name prevails in coming years, the field of "componentology" will be populated by component developers, assemblers, integrators, brokers, and vendors. If components become the basis of development, repositories will be needed to store them and provide access to them. Once component repositories start growing in size, it will be a challenge to find components for a specific task, unless a suitable and uniform method is established to describe and classify components.

How Do You Classify Components?

Many attempts have been made to classify software components, as in biology before Linnaeus, but no one has yet come up with a system that is simple and general enough to achieve widespread support. If classifying components were easy, we would all have agreed on a single system a long time ago and would be using it today. The problem is that there seems to be no single *right* way to classify components, because any classification is an attempt to create structure and organization by focusing on a certain subset of characteristics. Of the many classification systems that have been proposed, the major ones are based on content, syntax, or semantics. The first category includes systems based on natural language [Girardi 1993]. The second includes systems based on keywords [NHSE 1998] and facets [Prieto-Diaz 1991]. The third includes systems that use formal methods to describe component interfaces and behaviors [Hoare 1985] [Rittri 1990] [Penix 1995] [Zaremski 1997].

The problem with formal methods

The use of formal methods to describe components is very attractive, because it could support advanced search engines based on logic and deductive reasoning. These engines would be able to locate components based on similarities, natural language descriptions, relationships, prerequisites, and other characteristics. Formal methods use the mathematical language of set and group theory to express concepts, attributes, and behaviors. As attractive as they may seem in theoretical terms, a major impediment of formal methods is their intractability. For example, consider the following formal expression for defining the Pipe-Filter architecture style [Allen 1997]:

$\#Components = \#Connectors+1$

$\wedge\forall c:Components\bullet\exists p: Ports\ (c); cn:Connectors; r:Roles(cn)\bullet$

$((c,p),(cn,r))\in Attachments$

$\wedge\exists s: seq\ Components\mid ran\ s = Components\wedge\#s = \#Components$

$\bullet\forall cn:Connectors; i,j:N; p_1:Ports(s(i)); p_2:Ports(s(j))\mid$

$\{(((s(i),p_1),(cn,Sink)),((s(j),p_2),(cn,Source)))\}\subseteq Attachments$

$\bullet i = j - 1$

Almost as easy to understand as machine code! To underscore the difficulty of dealing with math equations to describe things, consider the fact that papers and books describing formal methods frequently have lengthy erratas, to correct the errors that escaped the heroic attention of the authors and reviewers. Formal methods may solve one problem (describing things), but they create another (using an extremely arcane language). Formal logic also has trouble dealing with the notion of time, to express timing constraints, durations, or intervals.

There are also weaknesses in formal logic itself. *Russell's Paradox,* discovered in 1902 by Bertrand Russell [Enderton 1977] is a perfect example. Consider the set defined like this:

$\{x\mid x\notin x\}$

The equation defines a set that includes all the objects that are not members of themselves. If a set A satisfied $A\notin A$, then its elements would qualify as set members. But qualifying elements as members would violate the initial condition $A\notin A$. On the other hand, if we started with a set A, such that $A\notin A$, then A would fail to satisfy the entrance condition in the set, producing the consequence that $A\notin A$.

Solving Russell's paradox required a narrowing of the definition of set, and the introduction of the notion of class. Everything was straightened out. But what if someone were to come up with another paradox? There is no reason to believe this is impossible. The solution would likely require other refinements in definitions, implying that today's set theory is flawed. By applying induction (itself an important, but somewhat controversial logic tool), one could conclude that because paradoxes in the theory have been found before, there is and always will be the possibility of a new paradox, hence undermining the validity of formal logic entirely. This may in fact be the ultimate paradox: *that using induction on the theory of logic proves that logic is itself flawed.*

Logic is a curious animal. People have used it in the past to prove all sorts of interesting claims, such as the existence of God (like Thomas Aquinas in the thirteenth century and Putnam in the twentieth century) and the existence of ourselves (Descartes: *I think, therefore I am*). Over the years, philosophers have used logic to both prove and disprove the same thing, which should raise some red flags over their arguments *a priori*. Regarding what can and can't be proven with logic, a stimulating aphorism is this:

Absence of proof is not proof of absence.

Just because you can't prove something is true, doesn't prove it is false. For example, not being able to prove that a system has defects doesn't mean it doesn't have defects. But to live by this rule is also to die by it. You could use it to back up claims of microscopic extraterrestrials living under your kitchen sink or the existence of a parallel universe where time runs backwards.

It is illuminating to study the results of formal methodology when applied to large projects. For example, one group of practitioners using formal methods on a large Air Traffic Control information system in the U.K concluded, *". . . we found no compelling quantitative evidence that formal design techniques alone produced code of higher quality than informal design techniques"* [Pfleeger1997].

This whole discussion is not meant to say that all logic is bad, wrong, or useless. Formal methods and logic should be used with a certain amount of caution and common sense. Saying that all logic is flawed would be like saying that because the laws of physics have been revised over time, a mathematical treatment of nature is but a pipe dream. Logic is, and should be, the foundation for any rational enterprise, with the recognition that it may have pitfalls that we need to be aware of. Formal logic has its place in software engineering, but where that place is exactly has yet to be established conclusively. Formal methods can be a wonderful tool, but only if applied judiciously, narrowly, and with the help of software tools that hide the opaque math symbology as much as possible.

Classification systems

Having said that a universal software component classification system doesn't exist, let's take a look at some of the current popular *de facto* classifications used by vendors in leading development tools, or by the way components are organized in marketing catalogs.

The Role classification system

One way to classify components is by considering the role they play, or the architectural layer they are on, with respect to a fixed reference, such as the user interface (the top role or layer) or the operating system (the bottom role or layer). Figure 4-1 shows some of the important first-order roles.

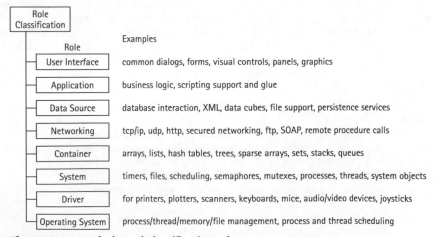

Figure 4-1: A role-based classification of components

Each node is the root of a much more detailed hierarchy of subroles. For example, the Data Source node includes all components that read or write data from files, databases, network connections, and so on. The role of a Data Source component is to retrieve data from a source, format it into an easily consumable shape, and make it available to a data consumer, such as another Data Source, a UI component, or other component. Figure 4-2 shows a possible role-based organization of Data Source components.

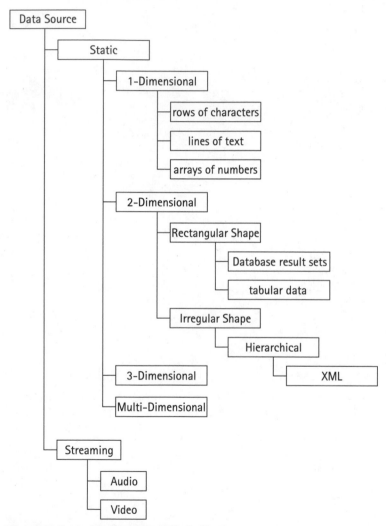

Figure 4-2: A classification of Data Sources

Figure 4-3 shows a possible role-based organization of user-interface components.

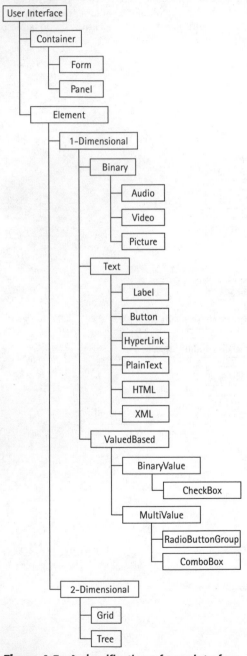

Figure 4-3: A classification of user-interface elements

The Functional classification system

Looking at the function of a component entails focusing on behavior, purpose, and intent, as opposed to size, relationships, or structure. Figure 4-4 shows some of the important functional categories of a Functional classification system.

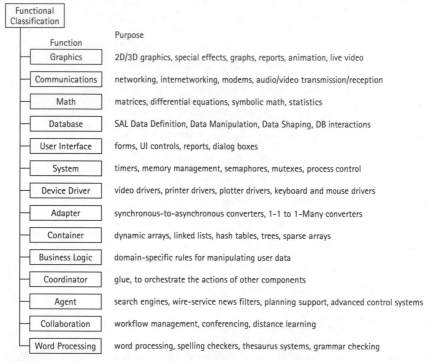

Figure 4-4: Some of the important categories in a Functional classification

Functional classifications focus on specific areas of software development expertise, such as graphics or math. Because the skills required to develop components for one area are often unique, component vendors tend to specialize in only one functional area. If you peruse the brochures of current component distributors, you'll find that they often are organized using a function classification. Each section has a small number of competing vendors specializing in one area, such as device drivers or user interface widgets.

The Domain classification system

Stepping back from the bits and bytes, and looking at the larger picture, components can also be organized based on the type of industry or field they are developed for. Components that are classified by domain tend to be very high-level, including complete applications, or large subsystems of applications, as shown in Figure 4-5.

The components that appear in a Domain classification system will invariably use lower level components, like those shown in role or functional classifications.

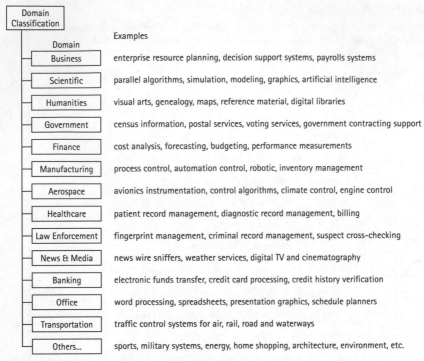

Figure 4-5: Components classified by domain

The Tier classification system

Distributed applications today are often characterized as *tier-based systems*. Each tier is a process, generally running on a different computer system. Because of the popularity and importance of these types of distributed systems, especially those involving the Internet and the Web, in this book I'll use a tier-based classification, following the generic multitier software model shown in Figure 4-6.

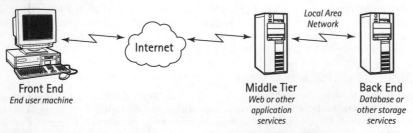

Figure 4-6: The tier-structure of a many distributed systems

Figure 4-7 depicts the Tier classification as a diagram.

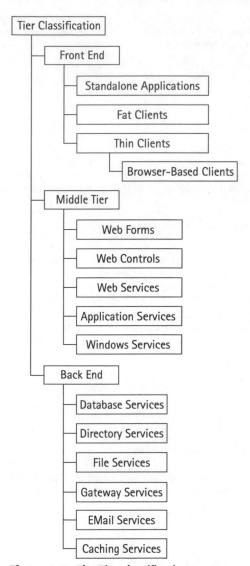

Figure 4-7: The Tier classification system

Like many of the other classification systems, the tier approach is a *macro-classification*, because the components in each tier can be further broken down into smaller components that in general are tier-independent. The tier-based components I'll describe in later sections can be applied in many cases to projects that have a different architecture. For example, back-end components that support database services in a three-tier architecture can often be used in one- or two-tier architectures. Front-end components can be used not just in a multitier system, but also in monolithic, standalone systems. Tier organizations tend to mirror the way many software development groups are set up in enterprises. Each tier requires a different set of skill sets, so programmers and development groups tend to specialize in one tier. For example, programmers that do user-interface development generally are not experts in database admin-istration or distributed computing. Programmers that do back-end database components are generally not user interface or Web page technology experts.

The following sections describe some of the important components identified in the previous figure. Examples of many of these components will be shown in detail in later chapters.

Front-End Components

The *front end* is where the user interface of a program is managed and displayed. Not all pro-grams have front ends. Operating system services and device drivers usually don't, but the development of applications with front ends is the area in which an overwhelming number of developers work. In the following sections, I'll deal with some of the most important types of front-end components and architectures.

Standalone applications

All programmers are familiar at least to some extent with the concept of a standalone applica-tion. The first complete *HelloWorld* program you wrote when you first learned programming was a complete, if not earth-shattering, standalone application. Most professionally developed programs are somewhat more complicated, especially since the advent of GUI environments like Windows. Back in the old days, MS DOS programmers developed standalone applications almost exclusively. There were few other options. Apart from DOS device drivers, some of you may remember *Terminate and Stay Resident* (TSR) programs. Those were programs that were somewhat similar to what we call a *service* today.

Standalone architectures are usually the best choice for programs or utilities that are designed for a single user and that don't make use of networks (except for accessing network resources such as files, printers, or modems) or complicated databases. Good candidates for a standalone architecture are word processing programs, graphics programs, operating sys-tem tools and utilities, single-player games, and software development environments.

If the database requirements are simple, and can be solved with a file-based database system such as Microsoft Access or Borland Paradox, the monolithic approach is still a good one. Lots of programs fall into this database category, such as personal scheduling programs, con-tact management systems, small business accounting programs, small business computer-aided design systems, and others. These programs are designed to be easy to install and use, and are targeted at end-users that don't necessarily work in a networked environment, such as small business employees, students, and home users.

Distributed applications

Not all applications are designed for single users. Ticketing systems; enterprise-level systems; collaboration systems; and military command, communication, and control systems are all programs designed specifically to support large numbers of concurrent users. The users are generally not in the same place, and could be in different countries or continents. By nature, distributed systems allow groups of people to interact with a single base of information — typically a database.

Fat clients

Distributed systems can be designed in different ways. Before the advent of the Web, most systems were designed with two tiers, using the popular client-server architecture shown in Figure 4-8.

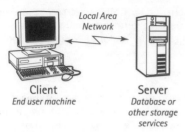

Local Area
Network

Client
End user machine

Server
*Database or
other storage
services*

Figure 4-8: The traditional
client-server two-tier architecture

A large number of these systems are still around and being developed today. They allow large numbers of clients to access a common database over a local area network, but have several drawbacks, from the client and administration perspective.

The first drawback is size. Each RDBMS vendor has its own software for accessing the database over a network connection. On Windows machines, this software takes the form of a series of DLLs to manage everything from network packets to result sets to scrollable cursors. The client applications tend to have large footprints because they contain not just the front-end code, but also all the business logic required to manage the remote database, plus all the DLLs required to communicate with the RDBMS over the network.

The second drawback is that client-server systems are difficult to develop, deploy, and maintain. Client-server systems are notorious for their costs in development and technical support. They are difficult to develop, because programmers must now wear multiple hats: they need to be well versed in user interfaces and domain knowledge, as in the standalone architecture. In addition, they need to have knowledge of SQL and database interaction software like ADO or ODBC, and understand the database vendor's networking software well enough to get it to work correctly. Figure 4-9 shows the software layers of a fat client in a typical client-server architecture.

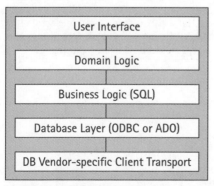

> User Interface
>
> Domain Logic
>
> Business Logic (SQL)
>
> Database Layer (ODBC or ADO)
>
> DB Vendor–specific Client Transport

Figure 4-9: The salient layers in a typical
fat-client system

The vendor-specific code is responsible for setting up and managing scrollable cursors containing result sets of data received from the server over the network. Experience shows that getting the database layer and the vendor-specific client transport software working is a major cost item, both during development and after deployment. The problems are sometimes difficult to diagnose, because developers are not always experts in vendor-specific database issues, or don't have access to complete documentation for the vendor-specific code and error conditions.

Thin clients

A current trend in distributed application architecture is to do away with the database and DB vendor-specific layers from the client side entirely, pushing the creation and management of the result set cursors back to the server side. The result is a lighter client side that is much easier to install, configure, and maintain. Thin clients typically transfer database records back and forth from the server using XML packets. Figure 4-10 shows the general structure of a thin client, in terms of database connectivity.

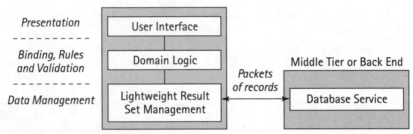

Figure 4-10: The structure of a thin client, from the database perspective

Notice the absence of the Business Layer containing SQL code on the client side. Rather than dealing with SQL code directly, thin clients rely on the server making available a service that can be called to produce the required result set. The client only needs to know the same of the service and method to call to get a result set.

In terms of .NET technology, the interesting part is where result sets are managed on the client side. The .NET framework introduces the `Dataset` class to emulate a local in-memory database. The class fetches records of the result set from the server and fills a local structure. The client accesses database records as local data, through a `DataView`, while `Dataset` invisibly handles the transfer of modified data back to the server. Figure 4-11 shows the .NET components involved in a thin client displaying a grid populated from a database.

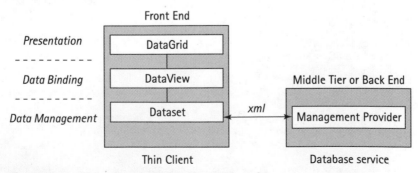

Figure 4-11: Thin client layers in the .NET world

A very important feature of Dataset is the ability to work with subsets of a full result set. If a result set contains 10,000 items, you may not want to send the whole set of records over the wire to the client side. For example, if the client side is only capable of displaying 20 rows at a time in a grid, it may be a good idea to only fetch 20 records from the server. If the user later scrolls down a page in the grid, the client could then fetch the next block of records. By fetching only the minimum amount of records needed to satisfy the user interface, performance is maximized. The Dataset class supports this type of scrollable windowing on the result set. As the client makes requests for rows to Dataset, the component gets this information from the server and caches it locally. If the client subsequently needs to scroll backwards, the Dataset will already have the rows locally and will return them to the client, avoiding a round trip to the server. Dataset is a fairly lightweight component that makes accesses to result sets and RDBMSs look like local in-memory operations, producing very thin and nimble clients.

An added bonus of many thin clients in general, and the .NET implementation in particular, is support for disconnected result sets. This type of result set remains usable after the database connection used to populate the client Dataset is closed. Disconnected result sets are convenient in two situations:

✦ When the number of concurrent users that need a database connection is high.

✦ When users need to be able to work with data after disconnecting from the database.

A disconnected result set is populated using a database connection, and then the connection is released, allowing the server to reuse it. The user may then change the local data, editing, inserting, and deleting records. During this time, the user's machine does not need to have network connectivity with the database server. Later, the changes are posted back to the database using another connection briefly. Database connections, which are generally very valuable and limited resources, are never assigned permanently to users. They are assigned only for short bursts, for the time necessary to read or write data, resulting in very efficient use of the both the database and the network.

Browser-based applications

Front-end systems can be arbitrarily rich and complex, containing widgets like menus, pop-up menus, modeless windows, multiple windows, and other items. Not all applications need all this UI power. Many applications only need to present a single window to the user, where data is read and possibly modified only occasionally. In these situations, it can be advantageous to create the complete user interface using HTML pages, allowing the user to interact with an application's front end through a standard Web browser. This type of application would have the structure shown in Figure 4-12.

The ASP.NET code generates HTML pages based on the URL and the parameters entered by the end user. Because this type of application is implemented entirely by the ASP.NET code running on the Web server, it is often called a *Web application*.

There are both advantages and disadvantages to the Web application architecture. The primary advantage is deployability: If the ASP.NET code is located on a machine other than the end user's, all the client needs is network connectivity (and access privileges) to that machine. The user simply enters the URL of the page in his or her browser. No installation process is necessary, no database components are required, and no files need to be copied to the user's machine (assuming the pages don't contain ActiveX components or Java applets). The application is *click-and-go*.

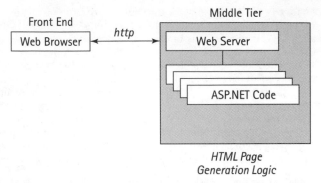

Figure 4-12: The structure of a browser-based application

The disadvantages are limited flexibility in the user interface, poor performance, and restricted access to important user machine resources, such as the file system. Because the application is really just a Web page in a browser, it doesn't have complete control over the user interface of the client's machine. Creating window adornments like toolbars, modeless pop-up windows, and other features may be difficult or impossible, without resorting to technology such as ActiveX components. The problem with ActiveX components is that users may elect to disable them from being downloaded, for security reasons. Not to mention the fact that not all browsers support them.

A couple other disadvantages of browser-based front ends are complexity and sluggishness. Complexity is based on the need for a Web service to run on the server side. If the application uses a database, the Web service is an additional system that may not have been needed if the client was a stand-alone application. The other problem, sluggishness, is due to the fact that every time the user does something that requires updating the screen, a new HTML page needs to be generated on the server and sent back to the client. The use of DHTML on the HTML pages can reduce the number of round trips to the server, but only for simple operations. Even with fast network connections, browser-based front ends are nowhere near as responsive as front-end systems running as applications.

The Middle Tier

Multitier systems typically use a middle tier to handle business logic. Middle-tier components are often used to control workflow, handle data formatting for presentation, share database connection handles, and generally interact with large numbers of concurrent users. Large distributed systems may have more than one middle tier to increase performance. Dealing with large numbers of end users often puts a big load on the middle tier, exceeding the capabilities of a single computer. When one computer isn't enough, the obvious answer is to use more computers. The problem is this: How do you configure software on multiple computers and coordinate all the computers to act as one, from the user's perspective? You want to have a middle tier that splits its work across multiple systems, while giving end users the illusion that there is only one computer there. The next two sections discuss the two most common techniques.

Clustered servers

With clustering, the business components are usually duplicated across an array of similar computers. I'll just call these computers *servers*. The servers are controlled by a higher level computer called the *cluster server,* which receives user requests and redirects them to one of the servers in the cluster. The cluster server is responsible for *load balancing.* When a server is taken off line, the cluster server distributes user requests to the remaining servers in the cluster. The cluster server itself can be set up as two redundant systems, to prevent a single failure in the cluster server from bringing the whole system down. Figure 4-13 shows the basic layout for a clustered middle tier.

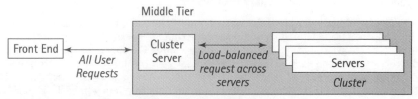

Figure 4-13: Using clustering in the middle tier

A full discussion of clusters and cluster servers is beyond the scope of this book. For a relatively brief description based on Microsoft technology, see the article titled "Application Center 2000 Offers World-Class Scalability" [Kougiouris 2001].

Server farms

With farming, one of the servers (which I'll refer to as the *main Web routing server*) is configured to receive all initial user requests. The information it returns to the user contains links to one of the servers in the farm, so subsequent requests from the user are processed by a farmed server.

For a Web farm, the routing server returns an HTML page with hyperlinks to one of the farmed servers, in order to balance out the overall load. With Web sites, farming is more popular than clustering, because it is much cheaper and simpler to set up. The downside is reliability. If the main Web server that farms the work out goes down, the whole system becomes unavailable. Figure 4-14 shows the basic layout for a farmed middle tier using Web servers.

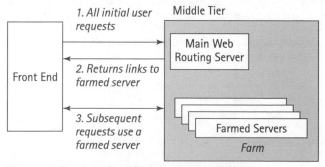

Figure 4-14: Using farming in the middle tier

Although the figure depicts the main Web routing server separated from the farmed servers, it may be part of the farm itself. As an example of farming, assume your Web site is set up with a three-server farm. Server 1 is the routing server and also a farmed server, while Servers 2 and 3 are just farmed servers. The home page of the Web site is www.mywebsite.com/home.htm, which references Server 1. The home page contains link to other pages. Let's say it has a link called *Company Info*. When Server 1 returns the home page to the user, it determines which of the servers in the farm has the lightest load, and uses its address in the *Company Info* link. If Server 3 had the lightest load, the *Company Info* link would be set to something like `www.myserver3.com/companyinfo.htm`. If the user clicked this link, the request would no longer go to Web site's main server, but directly to Server 3. As you can see, the process is very straightforward. Once the user is directed to Server 3, all future Web pages returned to the user from that server will contain links to Server 3.

The servers in a farm don't all have to be able to handle the same requests. Let's say you study your Web site's traffic statistics and determine that 80% of the hits request the `StockQuotes.htm` page. The other 20% of the hits are spread evenly over the Web site. If you allocated two servers in the farm to handle the general Web traffic, you would probably want to allocate a bunch of servers to handle the `StockQuotes.htm` page alone. The idea is that as the traffic patterns of a Web site change, a Web farm architecture lets you easily add more machines to handle specific areas of traffic. For additional information on Web farms, see the article titled "Advanced Basics — Working on a Web Farm" [Pattison 1999].

Tracking user state

Middle-tier components are typically shared among large numbers of users. Most of the time, the components need to keep track of the user's past actions, to provide continuity from one page to the next. For example, if your main page has a login screen prompting the user for a username and password, the next pages should be able to tell if the user is already logged in. Both clustering and farming present challenges in managing user state information, because the user may hit different servers each time he or she logs in. The .NET framework introduces a number of solutions to track user state, which are described in detail in the section titled "Managing State," in Chapter 13.

Database connection pooling

In traditional client-server systems, when a client started his or her application, a database connection was opened and assigned to the user until the application was shut down. Establishing a database connection is an extremely expensive operation, in computational terms. Middle-tier components can eliminate the overhead required to establish database connections by maintaining a pool of connection handles and granting them to users for brief periods of time. Each time a user requires access to the database, to get a result set or to make changes to database records, a connection handle is fetched from the pool, used, and returned to the pool. The interaction diagram in Figure 4-15 shows the basic concept.

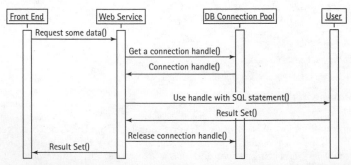

Figure 4-15: The use of a database connection pool at the middle-tier level

Fetching a connection handle from the pool is an in-memory operation that is essentially instantaneous, as far as the user is concerned. Keep in mind that a high performance RDBMS like Oracle or SQL Server, running on single-processor machines, will start having serious performance problems when dealing with more than about 300 simultaneous connections. Connection pooling is a standard technique used to handle large numbers (thousands or more) of concurrent or near-concurrent users without overloading the database-management system with connection requests.

The Back End

Back-end systems often run programs with no user interface. The purpose of these programs is to move data in and out of a repository, ship it over the network to another process, and do all of this as fast as possible and without interruptions of service. The most popular types of back-end systems are e-mail servers and RDBMSs, such as SQL Server or Oracle database systems. Back-end computers often deal with sensitive or mission-critical data and are located in secured areas. Because their performance is so important, they are usually attended by a group of dedicated support engineers that constantly monitor the throughput and make occasional tuning tweaks. Don't assume a back-end computer is a Windows or Unix machine. There are lots of mainframe back-end systems out there, handling things like credit card processing, airline reservations, and transaction processing.

To underscore the significance of performance for back-end systems, one of the most important metrics used to describe them is *TPS,* or the number of transactions per second they can handle. High-end systems can handle over 1000 TPS, sometimes by using terabytes of RAM. These systems often keep an entire database in memory, to avoid the latencies of reading and writing to disk. Memory operations are thousands or even millions of times faster than disk operations. Disk operations often require tens of milliseconds, as opposed to the tens of nanoseconds required to read and write RAM.

The good news is that the back-end system's computing platform is irrelevant to other tiers. All that counts is how to get data in and out of it over the network, and how fast data is moved. The most used back-end systems are the following:

✦ **Database-management systems.** Typical systems are SQL Server, Oracle, or DB2.

✦ **Asynchronous messaging services.** These services use queues to manage and deliver messages asynchronously. When the destination system acknowledges receipt of the message, the sender is given the option of being notified. Messaging services enable one computer to send a message to another without worrying about the details of assuring that the message is received.

✦ **Digital library services**. These services are used to support the retrieval of documents, such as articles, research papers, books, and newspapers. Current copyright laws prohibit public libraries from letting you download the full content of current books, but many organizations support research libraries whose works are fully accessible to qualified members. For software libraries, check out the ACM digital library at http://www.acm.org/dl and the IEEE digital library at http://www.computer.org/publications/dlib.

✦ **E-mail services**. These services support electronic post-office services to manage the delivery of e-mail.

✦ **Directory services.** Typical services are based on LDAP and Active Directory. These services maintain repositories of directories describing, for example, the users of a network, the printers in a company, the back-end servers available, and so on.

✦ **File services**. A file service can be something as simple as a dedicated Windows machine, connected to the network. It can also be quite a bit more sophisticated, supporting caching of commonly requested files, concurrent reading of the same file by multiple users, and so on. File servers are a lot more common than most people think, because they are used to augment RDBMSs. The problem is that some RDBMSs have very poor performance when dealing with tables containing binary fields. Even those that offer good performance have limitations on how big a binary field can be. Unfortunately for RDBMSs, pictures are commonly embedded in Web pages, and they are binary in nature. A common way to deal with pictures is to store them on a file server, instead of a database.

✦ **Multimedia services**. These services support streaming audio and video. While it's possible to store audio and video clips as binary files on a file server, treating them as a file would force users to download the entire file before they could play it. Streaming services allow clips to be played while they are downloaded.

✦ **Mapping services.** These services take the geographical coordinates of a city or location and return a map or satellite image of the area. Some services support thematic data overlays, characterizing statistics such as population density or annual rainfall. Check out the mapping service on the Web at `http://www.terraserver.com/main.htm`. Microsoft also maintains an interesting mapping service that can be accessed as a Web service. Check it out at `http://terraserver.microsoft.net/default.aspx`.

✦ **Gateway services.** These services provide a single entry point to services supported either locally or by remote service providers. A Web site offering stock quotes is an example. The stock quotes are not maintained by the Web site, but rather are obtained by accessing a stock quotes service provider, such as NASDAQ.

✦ **Financial transaction services.** These services support credit card transaction processing, automated clearinghouse operations, merchant services, currency exchange, and others. These services typically are accessible only to financial institutions or government agencies.

✦ **Weather reporting services.** These services provide local, national, and international forecasts, satellite images, radar images, road conditions, snow reports, severe storm alerts, and other weather-related information.

✦ **Time services.** These services provide the current time, based on UTC (Universal Time Coordinated). The times broadcast are generally accurate to about 1 or 2 seconds, due to network transmission latency. Check out the services at `http://www.atomictime.net`, `http://132.163.135.130:14`, and `http://www.worldtimeserver.com`.

✦ **Caching services.** These services are used to speed up access to commonly used resources. Services that cache Web pages are fairly common and help to reduce traffic on congested Internet backbones. Web caching services sometimes run on Web proxy servers.

Conspicuously missing from the list are Web services. In this book, I consider Web services to be on the middle tier. Although it is perfectly possible to run a Web service on a back-end system, in practice this is not done too often, and for at least two good reasons:

✦ That back end is where most organizations store business data. Running a Web service like IIS on a back-end system may be a security risk, allowing intruders to affect the system's performance (for example, via denial of service attacks), or even gain unauthorized access to the system's confidential data. Even for systems connected only to an intranet, the risk may be too great to put IIS on the same machine as the RDBMS. Consider an intranet user running a PC Anywhere server, so he or she can work from home. If this server is not correctly configured, an outside attacker could hack into the user's system by cracking PC Anywhere and from there, gain access to the entire intranet.

✦ Back-end software, such as RDBMSs are expected to be highly available. Running other services, such as a Web service may affect the system's performance and its availability. Most database administrators have a policy that nothing can be installed on back-end systems except for the intended data service and the associated administration tools.

Some components are equally suited for the middle-tier and the back-end systems. Consider a service built with the .NET Remoting framework: such a service might be useful on middle-tier systems that don't use a Web server. The service could be configured to listen for client connections using TCP/IP sockets and require no Web service to run. This kind of component could also run on a back-end system, to accomplish tasks such as remote management or testing.

Summary

In this chapter, I have described some of the major component classification systems in use, focusing in particular on the tier-based system. There is nothing inherently right or wrong about any of the classification systems. The Tier system is merely the classification system *du jour*. In coming years, other systems may well rise up and take center stage as technology evolves.

✦ ✦ ✦

Debugging

If we don't succeed, we run the risk of failure.

—Former U.S. Vice-President Dan Quayle

Although not succeeding is certainly one way to risk failure, there are other ways you could fail as well. One is by not adequately debugging code before shipping it. Debugging is the process of defect removal. Before you can remove a defect, you have to find it, so debugging is typically an effort that takes place in concert with testing. In the past, debugging was fairly straightforward, because most or all of the code of a system was written in a common programming language and the code was run on a single machine. Today, with the advent of components, programming languages are no longer a given and you may need a debugger that is multilingual and supports distributed or remote debugging.

In this chapter, I'll explore some of the best features of the VS .NET debugging environment and give a number of tips on debugging components in different scenarios, such as single-machine, multimachine and multilingual conditions. If you have experience debugging remote applications or ASP components, you'll really appreciate the improvements Microsoft made to the VS .NET integrated debugger. A really cool new feature is the ability to attach a debugger to a running process (this was possible even before the .NET Framework), and then also detach from it. Before the advent of the .NET Framework, you couldn't detach once you were attached. Now you can attach to a service or any other running code, set breakpoints in it, and single-step through the code. Once done, you don't have to kill the process and reload it: the code continues to run normally after you have detached. I'll show you how to attach and detach to a process in one of the later sections.

A Couple of Debugging Stories

Every developer has his or her own debugging war stories. Some describe problems bordering on science fiction, but they usually have a happy ending. It's not only entertaining, but also instructive to read about other people's bugs and how the bugs were fixed. What would you do if your program only worked correctly because it was Wednesday? How would you go about finding a bug that caused a program to crash after 45,000 iterations? Before launching into the thick of debugging, here are a couple of real stories you may enjoy that were compiled by one researcher [Eisenstadt 1997].

" . . . I once had a program that worked only on Wednesdays... The documentation claimed the day of the week was returned in a doubleword, 8 bytes. In fact, Wednesday is 9 characters long, and the system routine actually expected 12 bytes of space to put the day of the week. Since I was supplying only 8 bytes, it was writing 4 bytes on top of the storage area intended for another purpose. As it turned out, that space was where a 'y' was supposed to be stored for comparison with the user's answer. Six days a week the system would wipe out the 'y' with blanks, but on Wednesdays, a 'y' would be stored in its correct places . . . "

" . . . The program crashed after running about 45,000 iterations of the main simulation loop . . . Somewhere, somehow, someone was walking over memory . . . The bug turned out to be a case of an array of shorts (maximum value 32K) with certain elements incremented every time they were 'used'—the fastest use being about every 1.5 iterations of the simulator. So, an element of an array would be incremented past 32K . . . This value was then used as an array index . . . It took 3 hours for the program to crash, so creating test cases took forever . . . "

One of the greatest problems in debugging is the delay between the cause and effect of a bug. For example, if a variable is set to an incorrect value at one point, it may be thousands of lines of code later that the problem manifests itself.

Debugging code running on embedded systems presents a whole new series of challenges. The task is particularly hard when there are real time interrupts that periodically and pseudo-randomly interrupt execution of the main program, overwriting memory.

Common Bugs

Needless to say, development tools keep getting better and better. With the first generation of high-level programming languages, decades ago, compilers didn't have the sophistication we take for granted today. Many problems were actually dependent on programming language issues, which prevented the compiler from detecting problems in advance. For example, early FORTRAN compilers would not warn you if you used a variable that had never been initialized. Some compilers wouldn't tell you if you were passing the wrong number or type of parameters to a procedure contained in a different module. Most modern compilers provide much better warning and error reporting. The current .NET compilers are generally smart enough to catch a good number of potential bugs, such as the following:

✦ Failure to initialize a variable before using it

✦ Assignments to a variable that are never used

✦ Passing incorrect parameters in a method call

✦ The presence of unreachable code

✦ Using integers where an enumeration was expected

Still, there are many types of problems that the compiler can't detect, especially those related to memory. The absence of pointers and pointer-based access to memory in .NET-managed code should help dramatically reduce the number of memory-related bugs, but I'm sure people will find innovative ways to cause new manifestations of memory-dependent defects.

The Different Types of Debuggers

The .NET Framework and VS .NET ship with a set of new debuggers, because previous debuggers for unmanaged code aren't CLR (Common Language Runtime) aware. Moreover, the integrated debugger that shipped with Visual Studio 6 (the last version before the .NET Framework appeared) was weak in a number of areas. For example, debugging ASP pages required you to use Visual InterDev. Debugging ActiveX components called by ASP code was complicated, and sometimes required IIS to be stopped to unload ActiveX components. At times you even had to restart the IIS machine, when things really got stuck. Debugging other middle-tier and back-end components was also challenging.

Microsoft addressed these and other issues with the new .NET debuggers, making debugging a much more enjoyable experience. The following sections describe the debuggers in more detail.

Visual Studio .NET integrated debugger

This is Microsoft's full-blown, no-holds-barred, new GUI debugger. It is entirely integrated into the VS framework, like its predecessor, but has a number of outstanding features that will make your debugging work much easier. The following is a list of some of the best features:

✦ It supports multiple source code languages. Stack traces now show which language each method was coded in. Breakpoints can be set across multiple languages. You can single-step across language barriers.

✦ It simplifies debugging of ASP components. Now you can easily attach the debugger to ASP.NET components, set breakpoints, step through code, and examine variables. With the VS 6 debugger, debugging ASP code required a number of nontrivial settings. It was common to have to shut IIS down completely during or after a debugging session. Sometimes a component would be stuck in memory and force you to restart the machine entirely. The new debugger makes all these kinds of problems a thing of the past.

✦ It supports seamless Web service debugging. If your code calls a remote method contained in a Web service, you can use the debugger to step across machine boundaries and step into the Web service code, then back to your local code.

DbgClr

This is a standalone debugger that has a GUI interface that looks a lot like the VS .NET environment. It has a host of features similar to the VS .NET integrated debugger, allowing you to set breakpoints, step through code and get stack traces. By default, DbgClr is placed in the folder:

```
C:\Program Files\Microsoft.NET\FrameworkSDK\GuiDebug
```

DbgClr doesn't have a built-in compiler, and only a primitive editor, so you'll only want to use it when VS .NET can't be used, or for JIT debugging. Figure 5-1 shows what DbgClr looks like during a typical debug session.

You can set and clear breakpoints by clicking in the gray margin on the left of the Code window. Breakpoints are denoted by a dark red circle. When the breakpoint is hit, the program is stopped there and the source code line is highlighted in yellow. You can single-step through the code, examine variables, and even attach to a running process. To view the stack frame, click the combo box at the top of the Code window labeled Stack Frame.

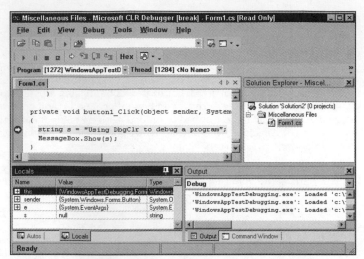

Figure 5-1: The UI of DbgClr while debugging a program

CORDBG

This is a bare-bones debugger that is useful to tool vendors who require debugging at the CLR level. Its name stands for *Command-line Runtime Debugger*. As the name indicates, this debugger runs from the command line and doesn't have a graphical user interface, so you probably won't want to use it unless you absolutely have to. Microsoft created CORDBG for two main purposes: to test the CLR debugging APIs built into the .NET Framework, and to provide an example to tool vendors of how to build a debugger for the .NET Framework.

The full source code for CORDBG is available with the .NET Framework. With the Beta distribution, the code was installed in the folder:

```
C:\Program Files\Microsoft.NET\FrameworkSDK\Tool Developers Guide\
Samples\debugger
```

The code is a combination of C and C++. To build it, you'll need to have the Win32 SDK or Visual Studio 6 installed on your system.

General Debugging Techniques

There are a number of debugging techniques that apply to all types of projects and architectures, so I'll describe them once and for all in this section. I'll refer you back to this section when discussing different types of debugging scenarios, such as local, remote, and mixed debugging.

Breakpoints

A breakpoint is a place where you want the code to stop. There are few things you can debug in a program while it is running, so setting breakpoints in the code is one of the first actions you take to debug code. There are two types of breakpoints you can set: unconditional and conditional.

Unconditional breakpoints

This is by far the most common type of breakpoint. Any time your program attempts to execute a line containing an unconditional breakpoint, it will stop on that line. The two most common ways of setting these breakpoints are by clicking in the gray margin on the left side of the Code window, or by clicking the Hand button on the Toolbar. Once a breakpoint has been set on a line, a dark red circle will appear in the left margin for that line, as shown in Figure 5-2.

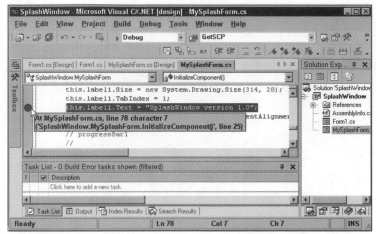

Figure 5-2: The symbol denoting a breakpoint in the Code window

If you move your mouse over the breakpoint circle, a tooltip window will show up, describing the position of the breakpoint in the file and class. Once an unconditional breakpoint has been set, you need to trigger it. In other words, you need to make your program execute the code containing the breakpoint. When the breakpoint is triggered, the Code window will show a small arrow over the breakpoint symbol, as shown in Figure 5-3.

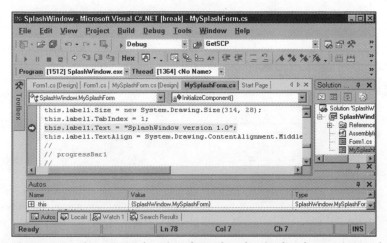

Figure 5-3: The arrow, showing that a breakpoint has been triggered

Once a breakpoint has been triggered, you can use a number of debugging tools to analyze the program, such as viewing the Call Stack window, the Watch window, the Autos window, the Locals window, the This window, the Registers window, and others.

The Call Stack window is described later in the section titled "Stack traces"; the other windows are described in the section called "Examining data," later in this chapter.

Conditional breakpoints

You may want a breakpoint to get triggered only under certain conditions. Say you find a bug that only shows up when the variable i is equal to 10. All you need to do is set a breakpoint on the line you want to stop on, and then right-click on that line and choose Breakpoint Properties from the pop-up menu. You'll see the dialog box shown in Figure 5-4.

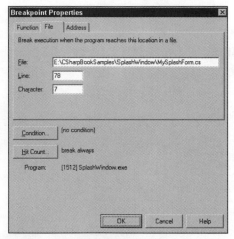

Figure 5-4: The Breakpoint Properties dialog box, which enables you to set the conditions under which a breakpoint will trigger

Clicking the Condition button produces the dialog box shown in Figure 5-5.

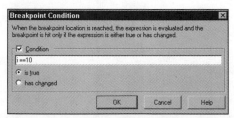

Figure 5-5: Setting breakpoint conditions

I entered the condition i == 10, as shown in the dialog box. After setting the conditional breakpoint, the code will only stop there if the condition is true. You can use any valid Boolean expression you like, such as the following:

```
i < 5
i == k + 2
(i == 10) && (j < z - 3) || (s == 0)
```

The expressions must be valid when the code reaches the breakpoint. If you enter a condition that the debugger can't evaluate or that contains symbols that are undefined or not valid in the context of the breakpoint, a question mark symbol will be placed on the breakpoint, as shown in Figure 5-6.

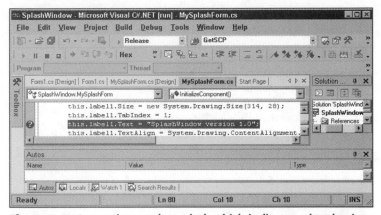

Figure 5-6: A question mark symbol, which indicates a breakpoint condition is incorrect

The question mark indicates that the breakpoint is not triggerable. There may be reasons a breakpoint is not triggerable. Probably the two most common ones are lack of debugging information in the code, and breakpoints in code that is not part of the program being debugged.

Looking back at Figure 5-5, you'll notice the presence of a radio button labeled "has changed." Click this if you want the breakpoint to trigger any time a designated variable changes on subsequent passes over the breakpoint. For example, to stop when the variable i changes, set the breakpoint condition as shown in Figure 5-7.

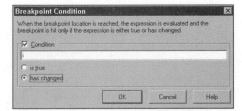

Figure 5-7: Setting the breakpoint condition to monitor changes in a variable

The first time the code sets the value of i, the breakpoint will not trigger. The debugger merely determines the initial value of the variable to monitor. In my example, the initial value of i is 0. The breakpoint will trigger as soon the breakpoint is reached while the variable i has a value other than 0.

You can also set the condition of a breakpoint to cause it to trigger when the code with the breakpoint has executed a certain number of times. Perhaps you have a bug that shows up every fifth pass through a piece of code, or on the 113th pass only. In the dialog box shown previously in Figure 5-4, click the Hit Count button. You'll then see the dialog box shown in Figure 5-8.

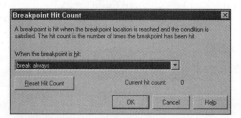

Figure 5-8: The dialog box in which you can set the hit count for a breakpoint condition

The drop-down list lets you choose the following hit count conditions:

- ✦ break always
- ✦ break when the hit count is equal to
- ✦ break when the hit count is a multiple of
- ✦ break when the hit count is greater than or equal to

The settings are self-explanatory. To make the code stop on the seventh pass over a breakpoint, choose the second option and enter a hit count of **7**, as shown in Figure 5-9.

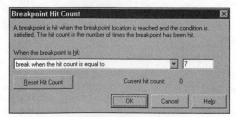

Figure 5-9: Setting a breakpoint for the seventh pass

You can also use Conditions and Hit Counts together in a breakpoint. The breakpoint will trigger when either the Condition is true or the Hit Count is satisfied.

Breaking on exceptions

If your program throws an exception and your code doesn't catch it, the debugger is set up by default to handle it. Say your problem has a function that throws exception. It will look something like this:

```
void abc()
{
```

```
//...
throw new SystemException("Exception from SplashWindow");
}
```

When the code is executed with the debugger, you'll get a message box that tells you about the exception as shown in Figure 5-10.

Figure 5-10: The message displayed when an exception isn't handled in your program

If you click the Break button, the debugger will stop the program on the exception's `throw` statement and display it in the Code window as shown in Figure 5-11.

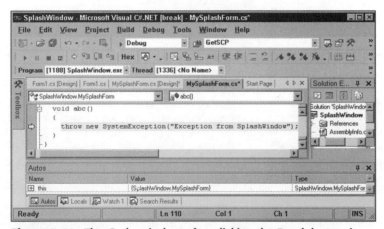

Figure 5-11: The Code window after clicking the Break button in the previous figure

The default settings for exceptions are usually acceptable, but may need to be changed if your code *does* handle an exception. If you have a series of low-level methods that can throw exceptions that are all caught by the same handler, the default behavior of the debugger will be to let your handler deal with the exception. If you put a breakpoint on the `catch` statement, you won't know which of the low level methods threw the exception.

What you need is for the debugger to stop on `throw` statements, even if they are handled later in your code. To set the debugger up this way, use the Debug ⇨ Exceptions command on the main menu. The command displays the Exceptions dialog box, with exceptions organized into groups. By default, all groups have the same settings, telling the debugger to stop the program only for unhandled exceptions. Let's change the default behavior for the `SystemException` thrown in my previous example. I'll change the settings on the Exceptions dialog box, as shown in Figure 5-12.

Figure 5-12: Configuring the debugger to stop on specific types of exceptions, even if the code handles them

I changed the setting in the "When the exception is thrown" group. The default was Continue. I set it to "Break into the debugger." You can also change the debugger's behavior for an entire exception group. Just click one of the parent nodes displayed in bold in the Exceptions tree in the upper part of the window.

Before running my program again with the new setting, I'll wrap the call to `abc()` in a `try` block and add an exception handler. The code now looks like Listing 5-1.

Listing 5-1: Setting an Exception Handler for Exceptions Thrown in abc()

```
void SomeFunction()
{
  // ...
  try
  {
    abc();
  }
  catch (Exception e)
  {
    Console.WriteLine(e.Message);
  }
}
```

Running the program this time produces the error message shown in Figure 5-13.

Figure 5-13: The error message shown when an exception was thrown for which a handler is available

If you click the Break button, the debugger will put you right on the `throw` statement inside `abc()`, as before. If you click the Continue button, the code will wind up in the `catch` statement in the method `SomeFunction()`.

Changing code on-the-fly

When a breakpoint is triggered and you're in hot pursuit of a problem, it would be nice to make changes to the source code, right there on the spot, and be able to continue execution. After all, it might have taken a lot of effort (or luck) to get to a certain point in the code. If you had to stop the program to make changes, and then recompile, link, and start the program all over again, it might be difficult to catch the bug again and get back to where you are.

VS .NET allows on-the-fly changes with the option called Edit and Continue. To check the Edit and Continue settings on your machine, select the Tools ➪ Options command from the main menu. On the Options dialog box that appears, select the Edit and Continue node under Debugging from the list on the left. The options will appear as shown in Figure 5-14.

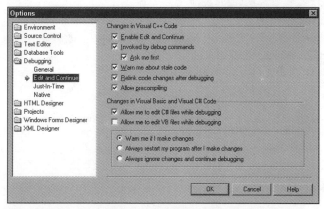

Figure 5-14: The Edit and Continue debugging options

Now for the bad news: If you look carefully at Figure 5-14, you'll notice the caption at the top of the right pane that says "Changes in Visual C++ Code". The caption tells you that the Edit and Continue feature doesn't work with Visual C# or Visual Basic .NET. It only works with native code written with Visual C++. That's too bad, because Edit and Continue is a pretty cool feature.

Changing values on-the-fly

Once your code hits a breakpoint, you can inspect variables, look at the stack, and poke around to spot suspicious code. If you need to change the value of a variable or field, right-click on it and select the QuickWatch command from the pop-up menu. Say you set a breakpoint on some code, as shown in Figure 5-15.

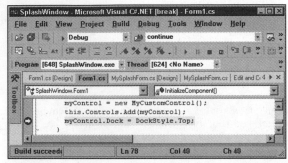

Figure 5-15: A triggered breakpoint in a sample program

If you right-click on the variable myControl, the QuickWatch dialog box will display the values of all the fields of myControl, as shown in Figure 5-16.

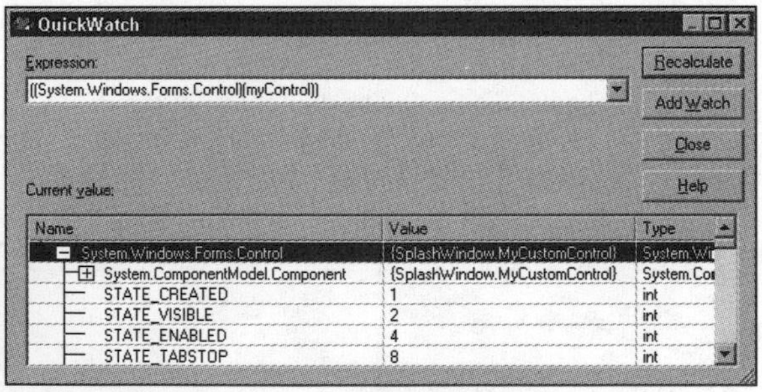

Figure 5-16: The QuickWatch dialog box, showing the values of all the fields of myControl

The dialog box not only shows all the fields, but also lets you change their values, by entering a new expression in the edit box at the top. For example, to change the endingColor field, you could enter the following expression:

```
myControl.endingColor.value = 0x303030
```

Or you could use a predefined color with the following expression:

```
myControl.endingColor = System.Drawing.Color.Blue
```

The Expression text box understands C# syntax, so you can enter C# expressions containing constants, variables, objects, and object properties. Just be sure that all items in the expression are in scope. You can also drill down to see the fields of an object by clicking the + sign next to a field name in the QuickWatch window.

Stepping through code

The debugger enables you to execute code one step at a time, so you can watch variables and other items to verify that your program is behaving correctly. By default, a *step* is one line of executable source code. Comments are always ignored in all stepping modes. You can also configure steps to be measured in statements or instructions, using the Debug ⇨ Step By command on the main menu. Statements are a smaller unit than lines, because a line of source code can contain multiple statements. For example, a `for` statement is commonly written like this:

```
for (int i = 0; i < 20; i++)
```

It contains three statements. To show you which statement the debugger is about to execute, the statement is highlighted on the line. For example, if you step into the previous `for` loop, the Code window will appear as shown in Figure 5-17.

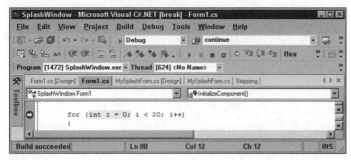

Figure 5-17: The highlights used by the debugger when stepping by statement

Each time you issue a new Step Into or Step Over command, the highlight moves to the next instruction. This may involve moving to another part of the same line or moving to another line.

Step Into

This command steps into a method call, if the next statement to execute is a method call. For statements that are not method calls, the Step Into command is equivalent to the Step Over command.

Step Over

This command always steps over the current statement and stops at the next step (statement, line, or instruction). If the statement is a method call, the method is called and the debugger stops again when the method returns.

Step Out Of

This command executes until a return instruction is found, or the current stack frame is exited. The debugger basically looks at the stack trace and puts an invisible breakpoint on the line after the call to the current method.

Run To Cursor

This command runs the program at full speed (disabling stepping temporarily) until the line containing the cursor is reached.

Stepping into machine code

Each statement in a high-level language corresponds to one or more statements in machine language. The CPU knows nothing about C#, Visual Basic, or any other language. It only understands binary code. Assembly language is the readable form of machine code. It shows the low-level memory and register operations that high-level statements correspond to. If you need to step through code at the machine code level, open the Disassembly window using the Debug ➪ Windows ➪ Disassembly command on the main menu. The Disassembly window is shown in Figure 5-18.

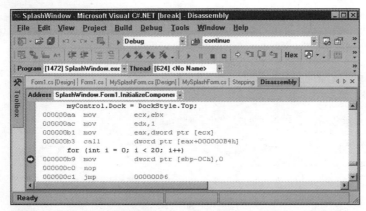

Figure 5-18: Stepping through code at the machine code level

The high-level language statements appear in bold. The assembly language statements are in gray. The 8-digit hexadecimal number on the left of each line of assembly language is the address of each instruction relative to the beginning of the code module.

Symbol table loading issues

In order for you to set breakpoints on high-level language statements, or see method and variables names, the debugger must have access to the symbol table for the code to debug. When you set the Configuration Setting of a project to Debug, the compiler and linker generate symbolic information that ultimately winds up in the program's symbol table. This table is contained in a file with the same name as your project, but with a .pdb suffix (for *Program Database*). You can still use the debugger on code that doesn't have a symbol table, but you'll only be able to see things at the machine code level.

Examining data

Once your program has hit a breakpoint, you typically want to see the value of one or more variables. The VS .NET integrated debugger has the following Debugging windows for variable inspection:

✦ **Autos**. This shows variables that are used in the vicinity of the breakpoint the program has stopped on.

✦ **Locals**. This shows the value of the fields, organized by class. The current class is listed with the keyword `this`. Other objects used in the method that contains the breakpoint will appear, allowing you to inspect their fields as well.

✦ **This**. This window shows all the fields of the current object.

✦ **Watch**. This window enables you to keep an eye on variables that are particularly interesting to you. The window is initially empty. To add a variable to it, the easiest way is to select it in the Code window and drag it into the Watch window.

✦ **Registers**. When you step through code at the machine-code level, you can use this window to track the values stored in each of the CPU registers.

✦ **Modules**. This window shows the various executable files loaded, and can be useful when you're not sure of the order in which modules are loaded, or the paths of the modules loaded. Figure 5-19 shows a typical Modules window.

Modules							☒
Name	Address	Path	Order	Version	Program	Timestamp	Inform
mscorlib.dll	61940000-61B1E000	c:\winnt\microsoft.net\framework\v...	1	1.0.2914.16	[1472] S...	2001-06-07	No sy
SplashWindo...	00400000-00408000	E:\CSharpBookSamples\SplashWi...	2	1.0.677.405...	[1472] S...	2001-08-19 ...	Symbo
system.windo...	5F060000-5F246000	c:\winnt\assembly\gac\system.win...	3	1.0.2914.16	[1472] S...	2001-11-08 ...	No sy
system.dll	5E4B0000-5E61A000	c:\winnt\assembly\gac\system\1.0...	4	1.0.2914.16	[1472] S...	2001-11-08 ...	No sy
system.drawin...	5EC00000-5EC70000	c:\winnt\assembly\gac\system.dra...	5	1.0.2914.16	[1472] S...	2001-11-08 ...	No sy

Figure 5-19: The Modules window, showing the loading order and other details about each module loaded

The window also shows the name of the executable that owns the loaded modules, the version of each module, and the fully qualified path used to load the modules.

Stack traces

When a breakpoint is triggered and you find your program stopped on a line of code, sometimes it is informative to see how the program got there. Often there will be multiple paths a program can follow to get there and you need to see which path got you there. The Call Stack window gives you this information, as shown in Figure 5-20.

Call Stack		☒
Name	Language	
SplashWindow.exe!SplashWindow.Form1.InitializeComponent() Line 80	C#	
SplashWindow.exe!SplashWindow.Form1.Form1() Line 28	C#	
SplashWindow.exe!SplashWindow.Form1.Main() Line 93 + 0x14 bytes	C#	

Figure 5-20: The Call Stack window, showing the execution path followed to reach a breakpoint

The top line in the window is where the breakpoint was triggered. The following lines show the stack trace, down to the bottom of the stack. Each line indicates a call from code in the line below it. The bottom item is the entry point into the application.

Notice the Language column on the right side of the window. It's there because your program may have executed code written in any number of languages before reaching the breakpoint. See "Debugging multilingual code" for more information.

Seeing how a program reached a breakpoint is interesting in itself, but there's more. The debugger also keeps track of local variables for each stack frame. If you open an Autos, a Locals, or a "this" window, it will show you values effective when the breakpoint occurred, as shown in Figure 5-21.

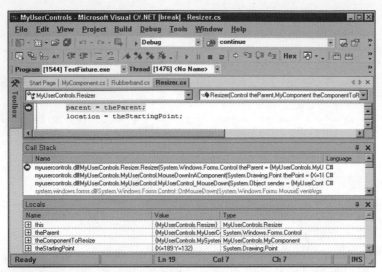

Figure 5-21: Local variables of the method where a breakpoint was triggered

In this example, a breakpoint was set and triggered in the constructor for a class named `Resizer`. To see the values of variables of one of the methods that called your code, double-click on its stack frame in the Call Stack window. For example, Figure 5-22 shows the local variables for a method two calls down on the stack.

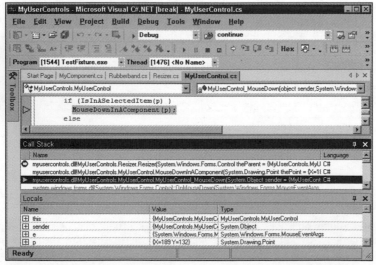

Figure 5-22: The local variables for a method two levels down in the stack trace

Using the Call Stack window to jump around on the stack allows you to examine variables that were set up before your method was called, and often gives you important clues about why your code behaved the way it did.

Debugging multilingual code

Each component you create in VS .NET can only use one language, but you can mix and match .NET languages in a project by calling components developed in different languages. To demonstrate this, I wrote a simple C# program called `DebuggingMultiLanguages`. The main form has a button that calls C# code and a button that calls Visual Basic code. The main project was written in C# and references a DLL written in VB. I put the VB code in a component called `VBComponent`. Figure 5-23 shows the Solution Explorer window of the project.

Figure 5-23: The Solution Explorer for my simple multilanguage project

Putting a breakpoint in `VBComponent` and stopping inside the VB code enables you to use the Call Stack debugger window to see the chain of function calls that led to the breakpoint. The Call Stack window has a column that indicates the language that each method was written in, as shown in Figure 5-24.

Figure 5-24: The Call Stack, showing the Language column

The Call Stack window doesn't show the language of methods contained in the .NET framework, only of methods in your own code.

You can cross language boundaries in the VS .NET debugger, provided the components you debug have debugging information available. In the main form of my example, the C# code shown in Listing 5-2 calls VB code.

Listing 5-2: C# Code that Calls VB Code

```
protected void buttonUseVB_Click (object sender, System.EventArgs e)
{
    label1.Text = Class1.UseVB(this.Text);
}
```

If I put a breakpoint on the C# code in my example that calls VB code and stops on that statement, the Code window looks like Figure 5-25.

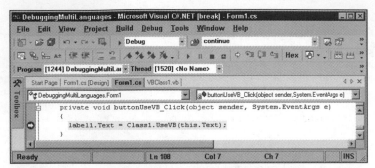

Figure 5-25: The Code window before stepping over a language boundary

Clicking the Step Into button, the Code window seamlessly switches to the VB code, which now looks like Figure 5-26.

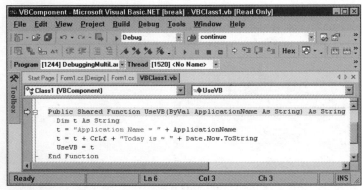

Figure 5-26: Stepping into VB code

The process of stepping across .NET language boundaries is completely automatic. Besides the syntax of the code displayed in the Code window, there are two other clues that tell you what language the code was written in: the file suffix (.vb in this case) and the Call Stack window. The former is only visible during debugging, when the code has stopped on a breakpoint.

Instrumenting Your Code

The process of embedding debug support code in a program is known as *instrumentation*. An instrumented Visual C# program typically uses embedded code, calling Debug and Trace objects to produce messages that describe important conditions in the code at runtime.

The Debug class writes to VS .NET's Output window, and only if the project is built with the debug configuration setting. Calling Debug methods in the code enables you to monitor a running program without using breakpoints. Stopping a program with a breakpoint sometimes makes bugs disappear, especially those related to timing issues. Debug statements are useful to check the operating conditions of your program while the program is running at full speed inside the debugger.

The Trace class is designed to work both with debug and release builds. In debug mode, it sends messages to the VS .NET Output window. For release builds, Trace statements work differently. By default they do nothing, so their impact on performance is minimal. Using a series of switches, you can make Trace statements go to a console window, a file, or elsewhere.

Using the Debug class

The Debug class makes it easy to write debugging information to the Output window at debug time. The class has four important methods that you can use: Write(), WriteLine(), WriteIf(), and WriteLineIf(). The last two methods write only if a condition evaluated at runtime is true. Listing 5-3 shows how you would call the Debug methods.

Listing 5-3: Calling Methods of the Debug Class

```csharp
using System.Diagnostics;

public class MyClass
{
  void MyMethod()
  {
    bool expression = true; // any boolean expression can be used

    Debug.Write("Debug.Write called");
    Debug.WriteLine("Debug.WriteLine called");
    Debug.WriteIf(expression, "Debug.WriteIf called");
    Debug.WriteLineIf(expression, "Debug.WriteLineIf called");
  }
}
```

Make sure your code imports the System.Diagnostics namespace. The Debug class only generates output if the DEBUG symbol is defined at compile time. By default, this symbol is defined for debug builds, but not for release builds. If DEBUG is not defined, your code will still have the overhead of calling into the Debug class methods, but the methods will return immediately. If you want to completely eliminate the overhead of calling Debug methods, you can use conditional compilation, described later.

Using the Trace class

The Trace class is very similar to the Debug class, but it is designed more for release builds than debug builds. Its purpose is to let you embed debugging messages in release builds that can be controlled through external switches. Using the default project configuration settings,

Trace information is compiled into both debug and release builds, and is controlled by the existence of the TRACE symbol at compile time. Like the Debug class, the Trace class has four important methods: Write(), WriteLine(), WriteIf(), and WriteLineIf(). The last two are usually used with TraceSwitches, which can be controlled through settings in the component's configuration file. Listing 5-4 shows how to use WriteLineIf() with a trace switch.

Listing 5-4: **Using Conditional Trace Methods**

```
using System.Diagnostics;

public class MyClass
{
  void MyMethod()
  {
    TraceSwitch mySwitch = new TraceSwitch("MySwitch", "MySwitch
Description");

    Trace.WriteLineIf(mySwitch.TraceError, "Error!");
    Trace.WriteLineIf(mySwitch.TraceWarning, "Warning!");
    Trace.WriteLineIf(mySwitch.TraceInfo, "For your information: ...");
    Trace.WriteLineIf(mySwitch.TraceVerbose, "Lengthy description of
error");
  }
}
```

To increase performance, you should instantiate the TraceSwitch object when the program starts, instead of on the fly, so the object is constructed only once.

Class TraceSwitch has a level property that you can use to control the amount of detail you want in the trace output messages. The level can be set to Off, Error, Warning, Info, or Verbose. The levels form a hierarchy, as shown in Figure 5-27.

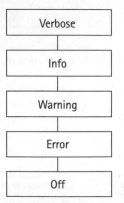

Figure 5-27: The hierarchy of tracing levels

Each level includes the levels below it. For example, setting the level to Info will enable Info, Warning, and Error messages. There are two ways to set the TraceSwitch level: programmatically and by editing the component's configuration file.

To set or clear the level programmatically, use one of the following statements:

```
mySwitch.Level = TraceLevel.Verbose;

mySwitch.Level = TraceLevel.Info;

mySwitch.Level = TraceLevel.Warning;

mySwitch.Level = TraceLevel.Error;

mySwitch.Level = TraceLevel.Off;
```

You can change the trace level as many times as you want, although most programs set it to one level and leave it there. A disadvantage of setting the trace level programmatically is flexibility. By baking the level into the code, you can change it without recompiling. On the other hand, by setting the trace level in the configuration file, you can adjust the trace level after the code is built, which can be extremely useful after the code is deployed if a problem shows up. You could instruct the customer to edit the configuration file, or send him or her a file that you edited, to set tracing to a given level, which might help pinpoint the cause of a problem.

To set the trace level using the configuration file, let's say your code runs in an application called MyApp.exe. In the folder containing the .exe, there would need to be a configuration file named MyApp.exe.config. In this file, you would need to add the XML code shown in Listing 5-5.

Listing 5-5: Configuration File Code Necessary to Set the Trace Level

```xml
<configuration>
  <system.diagnostics>
    <switches>
      <add name="mySwitch" value="1" />
    </switches>
  </system.diagnostics>
</configuration>
```

This code sets the trace level to Error. The value setting for switches is numeric, accepting the levels 0 through 4. The value 0 sets the level to Off; the level 4 sets it to Verbose.

Making assertions

C and C++ programmers have used assertions in their code for many years to detect incorrect conditions found at runtime. The idea behind an assertion is to verify the truth of an expression, notify the user if the expression is false, and allow the program to be stopped if invalid conditions are detected. With C#, assertions are even more powerful, allowing your code to display not just an error message, but also a stack trace that will show the execution path that led to the error. The code in Listing 5-6 makes two assertions.

Listing 5-6: **Making Two Assertions**

```
void UseAssertions(Object theParameter)
{
  // show error message if parameter is invalid
  Trace.Assert(theParameter != null, "Invalid Parameter");

  // show a stack track
  Trace.Assert(theParameter != null);

  // otherwise use the parameter...
}
```

If the parameter passed to the method is null, the assertions are triggered. The first assertion specifies an error message, and will produce a message box with the error message and stack trace that looks like Figure 5-28.

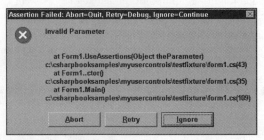

Figure 5-28: Showing an error message for an assertion

The second assertion has no error message and causes a just a stack trace to be displayed, as shown in Figure 5-29.

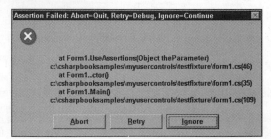

Figure 5-29: The stack trace error message

Clicking the Abort button causes the program to stop. The Retry button will stop execution of the code on the statement following the assertion and put you in the debugger. If the program is running on an end user's machine that doesn't have a debugger, Retry will abort the program. If a JIT debugger is configured, it will be launched to let you debug the code. If symbolic information is not available, you'll have to debug at the assembly language level, which is usually not a good idea. The Ignore button will allow the program to continue after the assertion.

The presence of the Ignore button is extremely important. Because the end user is allowed the option to continue execution, you should only use assertions when your program can make reasonable assumptions and continue processing after the failed assertion.

Using the Fail() method

Assertions force you to test a condition before generating an error message. Sometimes, the mere fact that a piece of code executed at all is an indication of a problem the user may need to know about. You could use a message box, but then all users would see this message if that nasty piece of code ever ran. To restrict who sees these types of messages, you could use a Trace.Assert() method, using the value false for the first parameter. A simpler way is to use the Fail() method, which acts pretty much the same as Assert(), without requiring a condition to be tested. Listing 5-7 shows an example.

Listing 5-7: Using Trace.Fail() to Display an Error Message

```
void UseFail(Object theParameter)
{
  try
  {
     String s = theParameter.ToString();
  }
  catch (Exception)
  {
    Trace.Fail("The parameter is null!");
  }
}
```

This code produces an error message box like the one previously shown in Figure 5-28.

Redirecting debug and trace messages

Debug and Trace classes are called to generate messages. These classes use defaults to determine where to send the messages. If the defaults don't suit you, you can change them, by creating a custom object known as a *listener*. Both classes always use the same listener, which by default sends output to the VS .NET Output window, if available, or to any window registered to receive OutputDebugString messages. Figure 5-30 shows a trace message in the VS .NET Output window.

If the code is running standalone as a Windows application, there will be no Output window, so you may want to send the messages elsewhere. The most common places are console windows and files, but any output stream can be used.

To redirect output to a console window, you just have to replace the default listener with a different one. Listing 5-8 shows how.

Figure 5-30: The VS.NET Output window, showing trace messages redirected to System.Console.Out

Listing 5-8: **Sending Trace Output to the System Console**

```
using System.Diagnostics;

public class MyClass
{
  void MyMethod()
  {

    Trace.Listeners.Clear();
    TextWriterTraceListener console =
      new TextWriterTraceListener(System.Console.Out);
    Trace.Listeners.Add(console);

    Trace.WriteLine("My Message");
  }
}
```

Adding a listener configured with `System.Console.Out` will allow trace messages to appear in a standard output console. To direct the trace messages to a file, use code like what's shown in Listing 5-9.

Listing 5-9: **Sending Trace Output to a Text File**

```
using System.Diagnostics;
using System.IO;

public class MyClass
{
  void MyMethod()
  {
    Trace.Listeners.Clear();
    Stream myFile = File.Create(@"c:\MyTraceLog.txt");
    TextWriterTraceListener li = new TextWriterTraceListener(myFile);
    Trace.Listeners.Add(li);

    Trace.WriteLine("My Message");
```

```
        myFile.Flush();
        myFile.Close();
    }
}
```

You can direct output to any number of listeners, by adding the listeners you need to the Trace or Debug object. You can also redirect output to a Windows Event Log, using the listener class `EventLogTraceListener`.

Conditional compilation

There are many situations in which you might need code to compile conditionally. Say you have two versions of a product, the standard version and the professional version. Both versions share the same code base, but you want the professional version to have slightly different code somewhere. Conditional compilation is one way to solve this type of problem. It is based on the conditional directives #if, #else, #elif, and #endif. Here's how you might use them:

```
#if PRO_VERSION
    MessageBox.Show("This is the professional version");
#else
    MessageBox.Show("This is the standard version");
#endif
```

The existence of the compiler symbol PRO_VERSION controls whether the #if directive evaluates to true or false. The VS .NET editor is smart enough to check for the existence of the symbol at edit time, graying out the conditions that are false. In the previous code, if PRO_VERSION had been defined, the statement in the #else condition would have been grayed out. Where does a compiler symbol like PRO_VERSION come from? There are two ways to define a compiler symbol: You can use a #define directive at the very beginning of a file like this:

```
#define PRO_VERSION
```

Another way is to add the compiler symbol to the list of Conditional Compilation Constants in the Project Properties window, as shown in Figure 5-31.

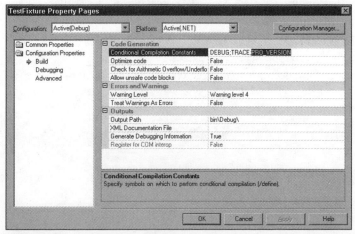

Figure 5-31: Defining a conditional compilation symbol using the Project Properties window

You can use the ! operator in a #if directive to test for the absence of a symbol, like this:

```
#if !PRO_VERSION
  MessageBox.Show("This is the standard version");
#endif
```

You can also use the #elif directive to test for multiple symbols, like this:

```
#if PRO_VERSION
  MessageBox.Show("This is the professional version");
#elif HOME_VERSION
  MessageBox.Show("This is the home version");
#else
  MessageBox.Show("This is the standard version");
#endif
```

Once a symbol has been defined, it can also be deleted from the set of conditional compilation constants with a #undef directive, like this:

```
#undef PRO_VERSION
```

This directive must appear at the beginning of a file. VS .NET by default defines two important compiler symbols: TRACE and DEBUG. You can use them to add debugging code to a file as shown in Listing 5-10.

Listing 5-10: Using the Built-In Compiler Symbol DEBUG to Add Conditional Debugging Code

```
#if DEBUG
  MessageBox.Show("This code is part of a debug build");
#endif
```

I caution against abusing conditional compilation directives, because they can make the code difficult to read. If you have lots of code that needs to compile conditionally, you might want to consider the use of the conditional attribute, as described in the next section.

Using the conditional attribute

With C#, you can mark a method with the special conditional attribute, so it will be included in the compiled code only if a specified symbol is defined during compilation. Listing 5-11 shows how to conditionally include a method called DebuggingMethod().

Listing 5-11: Adding a Conditional Debug Method to the Code

```
class MyClass
{
  void SomeMethod()
```

```
  {
    DebuggingMethod();
  }

[Conditional("DEBUG")]
 void DebuggingMethod ()
  {
    Console.WriteLine("Debug Code");
  }
}
```

The method `DebuggingMethod()` will only be called if the `DEBUG` symbol is defined at compile time. If it isn't, all calls to the method are removed from the code. As mentioned earlier, by default, the `DEBUG` and `TRACE` symbols are defined for debug builds. For release builds, only the `TRACE` symbol is defined.

You can use any compiler symbol you want in a conditional attribute, so you could create a compiler symbol in the Project Options page, as previously shown in Figure 5-31, and use it like this:

```
[Conditional("PRO_VERSION")]
void MyProfessionalVersionCode() {...}
```

The beauty of using conditional attributes on methods is that they completely eliminate conditional directive clutter in your code. You can liberally sprinkle calls to conditional methods throughout your code, knowing that they will be removed from the compiled code if the symbol specified is undefined.

Types of Debugging Scenarios

If you have ever debugged a program — and you should have if you're reading this book — you're probably familiar with the Visual Studio debugging process. You open the solution containing the project to debug, set the configuration for a debug build, build the project, and then run it under the debugger. You set breakpoints, run the program, and away you go. Fairly straightforward.

These days, software systems are often more complicated. With the emphasis towards components, a system may be a collection of components running on any number of computers. Debuggers for the .NET Framework must be able to step into code that runs in a different process or on a different machine. They must support multiple languages, understand distributed procedure calls used for Web services, support debugging of stored procedures, and support debugging of ASP.NET pages. They must do all this and more, and do it seamlessly from a single machine. From a debugging perspective, there are three scenarios you'll be dealing with:

✦ Local components

✦ Remote components

✦ Mixed components

Local components run on the same machine as the debugger, and tend to be the easiest to debug. Remote and mixed systems can be a bit tricky, because remote components are often run as services. One problem with services is that they can hang or crash for no apparent reason. Because they run with no UI, they can't display error messages or exception boxes to tell you what went wrong. Another problem is their privilege level. If they attempt to perform an operation without having sufficient privileges, a runtime exception will occur and they will hang.

The chapters that follow describe the development of front-end, middle-tier, and back-end components, and provide debugging tips that apply to specific types of components.

The following sections will describe some of the important issues that apply to many types of components.

A Few General Tips

Every program has its own bugs, but here are a few useful tips that apply to a pretty much any software system:

✦ **Track bugs carefully.** Just because a bug was found doesn't guarantee that someone will fix it. Make sure you have a system for recording defects and tracking them. This way, you'll know how many problems there are to fix and be able to measure the DDR (Defect Discovery Rate). As stated earlier, apart from telling you how much repair work you have, the DDR may be a criterion for deciding when to release code to production. Forgetting about a defect, or losing track of it in the heat of the battle will not earn you any points with your customers or your supervisors.

✦ **Fix all compiler and linker warnings before you start debugging.** By default, debug builds have the Warning Level set the highest level (Level 4). This is good, because the compiler and linker will give you the most information about possible problems. Let the tools work for you, before launching off into a debugging expedition that may be unnecessary. I've seen projects that produced hundreds of warnings, which the developers completely ignored. While some warnings may be harmless, you can't make that assumption about all of them. Use a defensive debugging tactic, and assume that *all* warnings are potential defects. Clean up the code to eliminate them.

✦ **When you find a bug, don't jump straight into a coding spree to fix it.** Take the time to understand why the problem occurred and how the code is structured. Always try for the *minimum impact correction*. Fixing something with minimum impact requires you to have an understanding of the context in which the code is called, the assumptions made, the data structures affected, and other issues. If you read Chapter 1, you may remember FFRs (Fault Feedback Ratios). Fixing something incurs the risk of breaking something else. The less you understand the system, the higher the probability of breaking it. High values of FFR may be an indication that the system was poorly designed, but may also be an indication that the people debugging the code don't have a good understanding of it.

✦ **Use the VS .NET Call Stack window.** If you find a piece of code that is producing incorrect results, check the stack. Sometimes, the code you are about to debug is not the problem — it was only called at the wrong time by one of the methods listed in the Call Stack window.

Standalone Applications

A standalone application is just a .EXE program. Whether the program calls other components or DLLs or not is immaterial, if all you want to do is debug the source code for the main application.

To debug an application, you need to ensure that it is built with debugging information available. To do so, set the project's configuration setting to Debug, as shown for a project called SplashWindow in Figure 5-32.

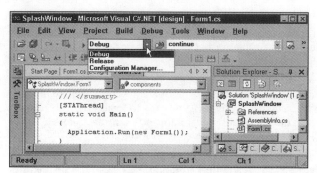

Figure 5-32: Setting the Debug configuration for a project

The next time you build the project, it will contain debugging information. A standalone application doesn't require a test fixture, so after you build it you can immediately set breakpoints in the code and run the program. You're on your way. Using the general debugging techniques described earlier, you should have all the information to get debugging underway. Now you're on your own.

DLLs

Most components you develop are not standalone programs. They are designed to be reused by other components. These components are really just DLLs, and you can't debug a DLL by itself. There needs to be an application that loads it and calls it. Although it is possible to debug a DLL by running the application it is used with, you should generally debug DLLs with a separate test fixture. The idea is reduce the number of variables to a minimum, so you want to eliminate the application code from the arena and concentrate all your effort on a single component, or group of components.

If you took my advice from Chapter 1 and created test fixtures for all components, you're in good shape. Many developers think they will save time by skipping the creation of a test fixture. Big mistake.

Debugging a DLL is actually quite easy, at least in terms of getting the code to run inside the debugger so you can add breakpoints and examine variables. It's not much different from debugging a standalone application, but you'll need a test fixture. There are lots of examples in this book on how to do this. For example, Chapter 9 describes a test fixture for a custom control DLL.

Here is a quick rundown on how to set up a test fixture project to debug a DLL. Open the solution containing the DLL project to debug. Create a Windows Application using the VS .NET project wizard, and add it to the solution. Select the test fixture project in the Solutions Explorer. Right-click on the project and select the Add Reference command to add a reference to the DLL to the project. In the test fixture code, make use of the properties, methods, and events of the DLL component to debug.

Now switch back to the DLL project and specify your test fixture as the Debug Application. Once this is done, you click the VS .NET Run button for the DLL component. VS .NET will load the test fixture, which should load your DLL and get the debugging process started. From this point on, debugging the DLL is pretty much the same as a standalone application.

Common problems

As somebody said once, *"Anything is easy, if you already know how to do it."* Debugging a DLL is easy, unless it isn't. There are a few problems that can stump beginners, which are described briefly in this section.

When you start the debugger on a DLL, you can't set breakpoints. There are two common causes for this. First, make sure your test fixture references the DLL you want to debug. If all your test fixtures have the same name, such as *TestFixture*, it's easy to inadvertently choose the wrong one. For example, say you have a solution containing a DLL project named *MyCustomControls* and a test fixture named *TestFixture,* as shown in Figure 5-33.

Figure 5-33: A solution containing a DLL and a test fixture

To see if the DLL is using the correct test fixture, right-click the project node for MyCustomControls in the Solutions Explorer and choose the Properties command. The Property Pages dialog box will appear for MyCustomControls. In the left tree, expand the Configuration Properties node and select the Debugging node under it. Figure 5-34 shows what the dialog box should look like.

Double-check the test fixture's path. If the path is correct, another possibility is that the DLL project is set for release builds. A glance at the screen will tell if it's right. In the Property Pages dialog box, check the Configuration combo box at the top left, as shown in the previous figure. Make sure it is set to debug, as shown.

Before the .NET Framework came around, DLL debugging problems were sometimes caused by having multiple copies of a DLL on your machine. Say you had a copy in the two folders A and B. The output directory of the DLL project in Visual Studio was set to folder B. Say there was a copy of the DLL in folder A. If the test fixture was in a different directory from the DLL, Windows would load the DLL by following the search path. If folder A was first in the path, the DLL in folder A was loaded, preventing the DLL in folder B from being debugged. The two solutions were to change to output path of the DLL project to folder A, or to delete the extra copy of the DLL in folder A.

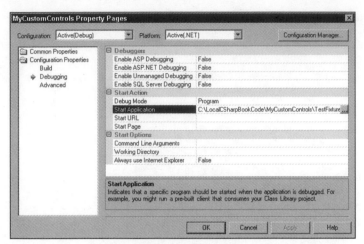

Figure 5-34: The Property Pages for the DLL project, showing the exact path to the test fixture

With the .NET Framework, this scenario should not occur. The manifest information in the test fixture's assembly should unequivocally point to the components it references, including all path information, making the test fixture load the right DLLs from the right paths.

Attaching to a process

If you have a component that is designed to be loaded and called from another process, you may need to attach the debugger to that process to debug your code. This scenario is common when the process that loads and calls your component is a service. To provide a simple example, say you have a custom controls DLL that you want to debug. There is a program called *TestFixture* that loads the DLL. Since TestFixture is a standalone application, the easiest way to start debugging the DLL is to set TestFixture as the debug application for the DLL.

Since I'm discussing how to attach the debugger to a process, I'll use the hard way and show how to attach the debugger to TestFixture. For this short example, I'll assume the DLL is named *MyCustomControls.dll*. With VS NET, load the DLL project. If you have a solution with multiple projects, set MyCustomControls as the startup project, by right-clicking on MyCustomControls in the Solution Explorer and choosing Set as Startup Project from the pop-up menu.

Make sure the process you want to attach to is running. I manually started TestFixture by double-clicking TestFixture.exe in the Windows Explorer. Once the application to attach to is running, go back to VS .NET. On the Debug menu, choose the Processes command. You'll get the dialog box shown in Figure 5-35.

Notice the Machine combo box. You can specify a different machine in your network, if the process is running somewhere else. In the Available Processes section, locate the target process, which is *TestFixture* in this case. If you want to attach to a service, such as IIS, click the "Show system processes" checkbox. By default, the Available Processes list shows only ordinary application programs. Once you have located the process you want to attach to, click the Attach button, and you'll get the dialog box shown in Figure 5-36.

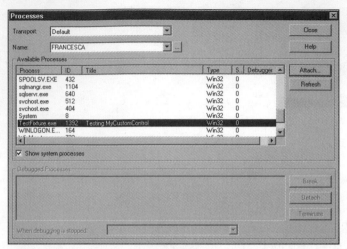

Figure 5-35: The Processes dialog box that enables you to select a running process to attach the debugger to

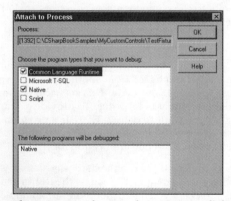

Figure 5-36: The Attach to Process dialog box

This is really just a confirmation window. Click the OK button and you're back to the previous dialog box, which now should look like Figure 5-37.

At the bottom of the window is a drop-down box labeled "When debugging is stopped". The choices available are "Terminate this process" and "Detach from this process." If you're attaching to a service, the best choice is normally to detach from the process.

Note   To select the "Detach from this process" option, there are a couple of additional things that need to be taken care of. See the "Detaching from a process" section later in this chapter for details.

You generally don't want services to stop unless you're using them only as debugging test fixtures or you are debugging them along with your code.

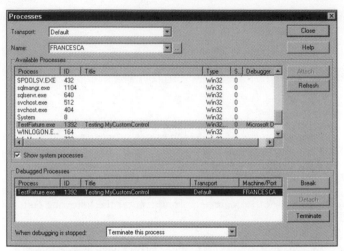

Figure 5-37: The Processes dialog box that enables you to choose
what to do to the attached process when you stop the debugger

Click the Close button. Now you can set breakpoints in the DLL code and debug it as you would
a simple .exe. When you click the Stop Debugging button in the VS .NET IDE, the process you
attached to is stopped if you chose that option. Otherwise, the debugger detaches from the
process and stops the debugging process.

Attaching just in time

Another way of attaching the debugger to a process is with the Just In Time (JIT) method. The
debugger is then launched automatically if an unhandled exception occurs in the process.
To enable JIT attaching and debugging, choose Tools ➪ Options from the main menu. Select
the node labeled General, under the Debugging ➪ Just-In-Time node in the list on the left. The
dialog box shown in Figure 5-38 will appear.

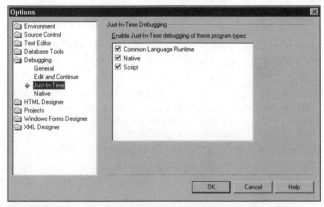

Figure 5-38: The Debugging options that enable you
to configure JIT debugging

Make sure the checkboxes are set for the type of process you want to set up JIT debugging for. By default, all the checkboxes are checked.

The next time the designated type of application throws an unhandled exception, such as a memory access violation, a dialog box will appear offering you the option of starting up the VS .NET debugger, or other registered JIT debuggers you may have, to debug the code.

Detaching from a process

In order for the VS .NET debugger to successfully detach from a process without killing it, you need to have the Visual Studio Debugger Proxy service running on the same machine as the process. If you have never used the Proxy service before, the first step is to install it. Open a command prompt window and navigate to the directory `C:\Program Files\Microsoft Visual Studio.NET\Common7\Packages\Debugger`. Adjust the path based on where you installed VS .NET on your machine. At the command prompt, enter the following command:

```
dbgproxy.exe -install
```

This installs the service. Now you have to start it. On the Control Panel, select the Administrative Tools applet. On the window that appears, double-click on the Services program. The Services snap-in application starts. Scroll down to the Visual Studio Debugger Proxy node, select it, and then click the Start Service button at the top, as shown in Figure 5-39.

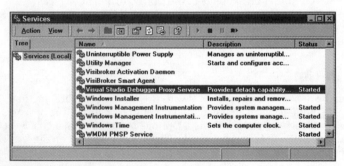

Figure 5-39: Starting the Debugging Proxy service, to allow the debugger to detach from a running process without stopping it

Windows will start the Proxy service. If you chose "Detach from this process" in the drop-down list at the bottom of the dialog box previously shown in Figure 5-39, the debugger automatically detaches when you stop it.

To manually detach from a process, the easiest way is to use the Detach All command on the Debug menu. If you attached the debugger to multiple processes, and only want to detach from some of them, use the Debug ➪ Processes command from the main menu to display the Processes dialog box previously shown in Figure 5-37. In the Debugged Processes list at the bottom, select the processes to detach from, and then click the Detach button.

Later in this book, in the sections dealing with front-end, middle-tier, and back-end components, you'll find more information describing debugging techniques that apply to specific types of components.

Summary

Debugging is as much an art as a skill, but knowing how to use the debugging features of VS .NET is very important. In this chapter, I've shown numerous tools, windows, and commands built into VS .NET to help the debugging process. Developing distributed applications is easier than ever before, due to the seamless way you can step across process and machine boundaries with the debugger.

✦　　✦　　✦

Deployment

"Behind every successful man is a woman; behind her is his wife."

—Groucho Marx

L et me point out first that, contrary to what some may surmise, Groucho was not related to Karl. If you don't have a clue which Karl I'm talking about, don't worry about it: It's not important. More to the point, while successful men have a woman behind them, behind every successful component deployment is a well-engineered setup program. *Deployment* refers to the process of getting software you wrote and debugged in one computing environment to run in the end user's computing environment. The *computing environment* may be one machine, for simple standalone applications. It may also be two, three, or more computers networked together, for multitier applications.

The Old Way

Before the advent of the .NET Framework, deployment entailed users running a setup program to perform the following typical steps:

1. Put application-specific components in the application folder.

2. Put shared components in the \Windows\System32 folder.

3. Register the software's COM components on the user's computer.

4. Update the registry to reflect program settings.

The process was conceptually straightforward, but had a number of potentially serious drawbacks:

✦ Shared components were put in \Windows\System32 folder. Files in this folder are typically shared by more than one application. Installing new versions of a DLL in this folder had the potential of breaking existing applications.

✦ DLLs copied to the application's folder could break older versions of the application.

✦ When registering COM components, large numbers of entries were added to the Windows Registry, causing it to grow considerably. Moreover, the registry entries were fairly arcane and could cause obscure system problems.

✦ The user often had to restart the computer, because the installation program needed to replace DLLs that were already loaded by the system.

✦ Uninstalling applications could break existing applications, by removing shared DLLs or other files.

✦ Installation was often just too complicated, requiring substantial changes to the user's system. The user really had no idea of what changes the installation procedure made on his system, how the registry was modified, what files were added, and so on.

✦ It was impossible to move an installed application to a different folder. The program had to been completely uninstalled and reinstalled.

✦ Development environments like Visual Studio typically didn't include tools to create the setup programs necessary to deploy programs or components. As a result, creating deployment programs was largely based on third-party tools like InstallShield and Wise Installer.

✦ If the installation process encountered an error, it would terminate, sometimes after having partially installed a product. The product was completely unusable. Even worst, the product could sometimes not be uninstalled, because the install process terminated before adding information for the uninstaller.

The New Way

The .NET Framework and VS .NET solve all of the problems listed in the previous section, integrating the creation of setup programs into the VS .NET environment. With .NET components, you may not even need to create a setup program at all. There are basically four ways to deploy .NET components:

✦ Using Xcopy

✦ Using a setup program

✦ Using Merge modules

✦ Using CAB packages

Which method is best for deployment depends on the type of components you are deploying (applications, shared components, Web services, Web applications, and so on), the types of configuration changes required on the client machine (creating new folders, adding registry entries, registering ActiveX components, and so on), and other considerations.

The Xcopy method takes its name from the old DOS program by the same name. XCOPY (for *Extended Copy*) enabled you to copy a folder will all its files and subfolders recursively to any depth. With Xcopy deployments, you copy the folder containing the necessary assemblies, and all its subfolders, to the target machine. When all the files to deploy are arranged hierarchically under a single folder, and no other resources (such as the Windows Registry) need to be updated, Xcopy installs are a great and simple way to deploy software.

I'll discuss the other deployment methods in later sections, but first I need to digress into the territory of .NET assemblies, because they are central to any discussion of deployment.

Assemblies

The deployment of all .NET components is now completely based on the notion of *assemblies*. Not only do assemblies help define what items make up a product, they also define where those items are expected to be, what version they must have, and a lot of other information.

What is an assembly?

A lot of people are a little hazy on exactly what an assembly is. Is it a file? Is it the group of files in a single folder? Is it the group of all the files in an application? Is it a component? To be sure, an assembly is *not* a file, so don't go looking for a file called Assembly.cs, or something like that. Actually, there is a file called AssemblyInfo.cs, but like Groucho and Karl, assemblies and AssemblyInfo files are not related.

A good way to picture an assembly is with an analogy. When you go to the store and buy a computer, it comes in a box. The box contains the product's *assembly* — in other words, all the parts you need to set up the computer and get in running. The box has the computer itself and other smaller boxes, or subassemblies, containing the keyboard, the cables, and the documentation. A .NET Assembly is similar: it is a logical grouping of all the things — in this case files — needed to get software components set up and running on the user's computer. You, the developer, define what the components are, and what files it needs. The files referenced by an assembly don't need to be in the same directory: they can be anywhere you want — including on a different machine or somewhere on the Internet. Some files in an assembly will be executable, others may not be. It's all up to you.

An application might have a single assembly. Or maybe the application makes use of the services of other components that are of a general purpose nature that you want to make available to others. In this case, the application would have multiple assemblies: one for the basic core of the application and one or more assemblies for the other shared parts.

So an assembly contains a group of files, and the files can be of any type, based only on the requirements of your software. They could be .sql scripts, .reg files, .html files, text files, .dll files, .exe files, or any other type of file. Assemblies are entirely self-describing: they don't rely on the system registry at all to describe the files they reference.

The assembly structure

Assemblies are conceptual packages. One assembly can contain any number of other assemblies, which I'll call *subassemblies*. The .NET Framework literature sometimes calls subassemblies *satellite assemblies*. Figure 6-1 shows a logical way to think of assemblies.

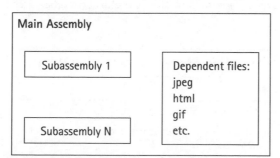

Figure 6-1: A logical view of an assembly containing other assemblies

Before looking at the physical structure of an assembly, let's look at the physical structure of a simple .NET component. Say you have a component called MyComponent that is packaged as the file MyComponent.dll. This component also uses two external shared components in the files ComponentA.dll and ComponentB.dll. From a file perspective, MyComponent uses three files, as shown in Figure 6-2.

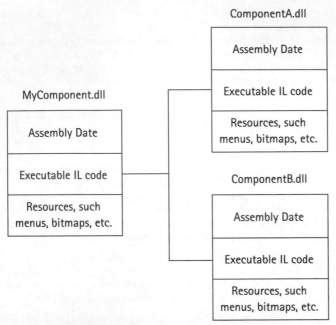

Figure 6-2: The file structure of a .NET component with two subcomponents

The Assembly Data contains a list of all the dependent resource files used by each assembly, along with references to all the subcomponents used. Each shared component has its own Assembly Data, so assemblies conceptually form a dependency tree.

Examining the Assembly Data

The Assembly Data includes various types of information that is useful at runtime, as shown in Table 6-1.

Table 6-1: Types of Information Stored in Assembly Data

Type	Description
Manifest	A list of all the dependent files and subassemblies used.
Type Metadata	A description of the classes, methods, and properties defined in each component in the assembly.
Locale Info	Indicates which locale (for example, US English or Swiss French) the assembly was built for, plus a list of locales the assembly supports.
Versioning Info	Contains version information about the assembly, including the version number, the manufacturer name, and the build number.

There are tools available that allow you to look at the Assembly Data. One is ILDASM.EXE, which displays the contents of an assembly as a hierarchical view. As an example, I created a plain Windows application called *WindowsApplication1*, containing a single empty form. When I opened the application's .exe file (the program's main assembly) with ILDASM *(Intermediate Language Disassembler)*, the Assembly Data shown in Figure 6-3 was displayed.

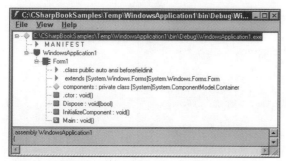

Figure 6-3: Examining the assembly of a simple Windows application with ILDASM

ILDASM shows hierarchy of the components in the assembly (only one component in this case), plus a list of classes, methods, and events. If you double-click any of these nodes, ILDASM will show its contents; if the node is a method, ILDASM will show the disassembled code. The node we're most interested in at right now is the one called *MANIFEST.* Double-clicking it causes a new window to appear, showing the contents of the assembly's manifest, as shown in Figure 6-4.

```
MANIFEST                                                    _ □ ×
  .publickeytoken = (B7 7A 5C 56 19 34 E0 89 )          // ·
  .ver 1:0:2411:0
}
.assembly extern System.Drawing
{
  .publickeytoken = (B0 3F 5F 7F 11 D5 0A 3A )          // ·
  .ver 1:0:2411:0
}
.assembly WindowsApplication1
{
  .custom instance void [mscorlib]System.Reflection.AssemblyCopyrightAttribu
  .custom instance void [mscorlib]System.Reflection.AssemblyKeyNameAttribut
  .custom instance void [mscorlib]System.Reflection.AssemblyKeyFileAttribut
  .custom instance void [mscorlib]System.Reflection.AssemblyDelaySignAttrib
  .custom instance void [mscorlib]System.Reflection.AssemblyTrademarkAttrib
  .custom instance void [mscorlib]System.Reflection.AssemblyConfigurationAt
  // --- The following custom attribute is added automatically, do not unco
```

Figure 6-4: The contents of the assembly manifest of a simple Windows application

The manifest shows the subassemblies used by WindowsApplication1.exe, which version of the subassemblies it uses, and the subassembly hash values. These values are used to verify that the subassemblies loaded at runtime have the same signature as the ones required by the assembly.

Another utility for looking at relationships between assemblies is *DEPENDS.EXE.* This tool uses import information in the Portable Executable (PE) metadata of a file and recursively lists the .dlls it depends on. Figure 6-5 shows how WindowsApplication1.exe looks with DEPENDS.

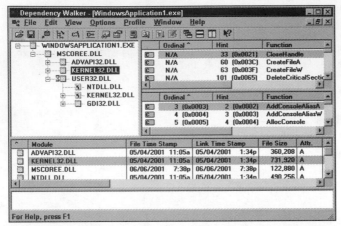

Figure 6-5: Examining a simple Windows application with the DEPENDS utility

The dependencies of an assembly are also shown in the VS .NET Solution Explorer, as shown in Figure 6-6.

Figure 6-6: The list of subassemblies shown in the VS .NET Solution Explorer

The key thing to remember about assemblies is that they are a packaging technology created to aid deployment. When an end user deploys your components on his machine, your assemblies are copied to his machine. You can set up two kinds of assemblies, based on how you expect your components to be used.

Private assemblies

Private assemblies are those designed to be used by a single application, and typically are deployed at the same time as the application. Say you create a package of components designed to be used exclusively by your application called *XYZ.exe*. The components don't need to be visible to other applications, so they are best packaged as a private assembly and installed along with XYZ.exe.

Shared assemblies

Shared assemblies are those designed to be used by more than one component or application. Third-party developers creating custom controls use shared assemblies to distribute their components. Shared assemblies are all installed in the same place on the end user's computer: the Global Assembly Cache (GAC). Side-by-side implementations of multiple versions of components are supported by the GAC.

Viewing the Global Assembly Cache

In case you're interested in finding what shared assemblies are installed on your computer, there are a couple of utilities for viewing the contents of the GAC. The first one is a command-line tool called *GACUTIL.EXE*. By running it with the -l (lowercase L) option, you can get a list of the shared assemblies in the GAC. The output will look something like Figure 6-7.

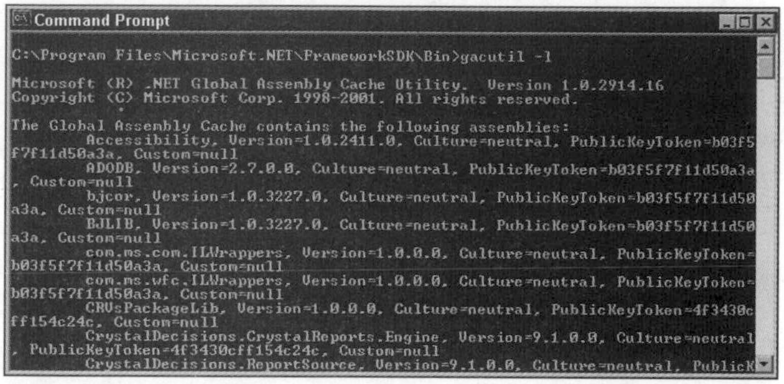

Figure 6-7: Listing the shared assemblies in the GAC using the GACUTIL command-line utility

A much more intuitive interface to the GAC is offered by the *shfusion.dll* Windows Shell Extension, which allows you to display the GAC as a folder in Windows Explorer under the folder c:\WinNT\Assembly. Figure 6-8 shows how the GAC appears in Windows Explorer.

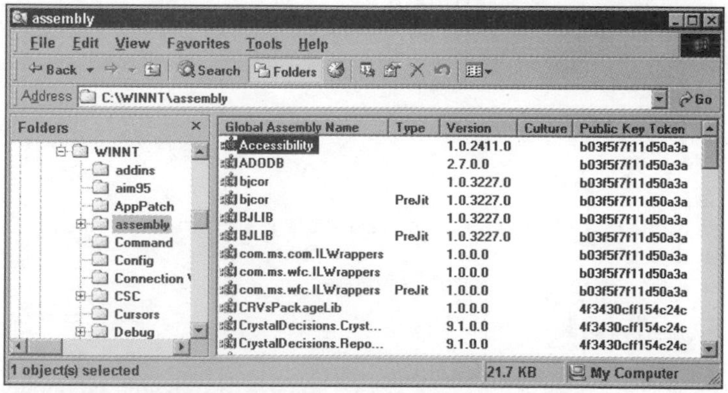

Figure 6-8: Viewing the GAC with Windows Explorer

You can add and delete shared assemblies as you would files. To delete an existing assembly, select it and press Delete. To add a new assembly, drag a file containing Assembly Data to the WinNT\Assembly folder and drop it there. Table 6-2 describes the columns shown in the right pane in the Windows Explorer.

Table 6-2: GAC Information Displayed by the Windows Explorer

Column Name	Description
Global Assembly Name	The name of the shared assembly.
Type	The type of the assembly. Precompiled assemblies have the Type `Prejit`.
Version	The version of the assembly. You can install multiple versions of the same assembly without causing conflicts.
Culture	The locale the assembly supports (for example, `US English`).
Public Key Token	A 128-bit code that represents the strong name of the assembly.

You may not have noticed, but the GAC Viewer shown back in Figure 6-8 has a special button on the toolbar that pertains specifically to the GAC: It's the fifth button from the right and is labeled Configure Cache Settings. Clicking the button opens the Cache Properties dialog box, shown in Figure 6-9.

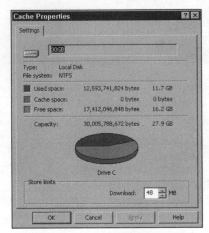

Figure 6-9: The Global Assembly Cache Properties dialog box

The Cache Properties dialog box shows you the total size of the GAC and how full it is. The Download spin box at the bottom lets you adjust the size of the GAC.

Deployment Methods

In this book, *packaging* doesn't refer to the boxes or CDs you use to ship your components. It refers to the way the software is built for delivery to the customer. VS .NET supports four packaging choices:

✦ Windows application setup program

✦ Web application setup program

✦ Shared components

✦ Cabinet files

How you package your software for deployment depends on the type of component you want to ship, the complexity of the software, and the distribution method. The first two choices are very similar, so I'll skip Web applications and describe the other three choices in the remainder of this chapter.

Using the Setup Wizard

The easiest way to create a setup project is with the Setup Wizard, as shown in Figure 6-10.

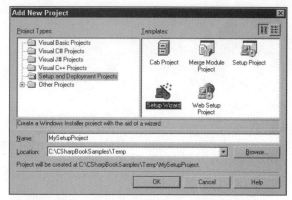

Figure 6-10: Using the Setup Wizard to create a simple setup project

The wizard walks you through some questions about the type of setup project you want to create, as shown in Figure 6-11.

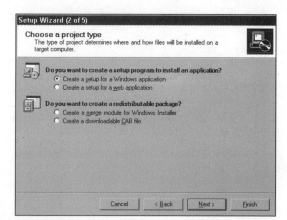

Figure 6-11: Selecting the type of setup project to create

By default, the wizard will create a .msi file for projects in the same solution. The wizard also allows you to include nonexecutable files in the .msi file, as shown in Figure 6-12.

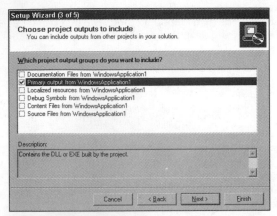

Figure 6-12: Selecting the types of files to include in the setup project

I selected only the "PrimaryOutput from WindowsApplication1" option, which tells the setup program to include the .exe or .dll produced by WindowsApplication1. When the wizard finished, it created a new project in the Solution Explorer, as shown in Figure 6-13.

Figure 6-13: The Windows Installer Package created by the wizard

When you build MySetupProject, a .msi file is created. When you double-click this file, the Windows Installer Service runs it and displays the screens shown in Figure 6-14.

When the installer ends, it displays a final Completion screen. (The screen just tells you you're done, so I won't show it here.)

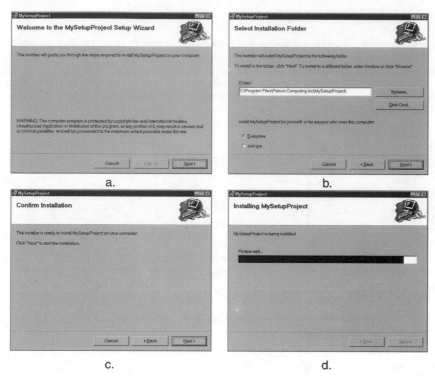

Figure 6-14: The screens displayed by the setup program created by the Setup Wizard

Creating Basic Setup Programs

The Setup Wizard doesn't provide that many options, so I tend not to use it very often. To demonstrate the normal process of creating setup programs, I used the Add New Project Wizard twice: first to create a simple Windows application and then again to create a setup project. Figure 6-15 shows the template used to create the setup project.

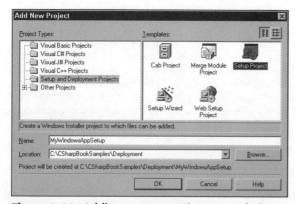

Figure 6-15: Adding a setup project to a solution

The name of the setup project determines the name of the .msi file generated. Most of the time, you'll want the project name to be the product name or something derived from it, because the name will appear on all the installation screens. The setup project can even have the same name as the project it is designed to install. There shouldn't be any name collisions, because setup programs have the file extension .msi *(Microsoft Installer)*. Besides, the setup project lives in its own folder. To avoid confusion in this chapter, I named the setup program differently from the project it installs. After creating the setup project, the Solution Explorer looks like Figure 6-16.

Figure 6-16: The Solution Explorer showing the newly created setup project

The setup project is initially empty, so building it at this stage would be useless. You need to add items to the project, specifying what to include in the installer program. To do this, right-click on the Setup project in the Solution Explorer, choose Add from the pop-up menu, and then select one of the options, as shown in Figure 6-17.

Figure 6-17: Adding items to the setup program

As you can see, there are four kinds of items you can add. I'll describe the Project Output selection separately in the next section. As far as the other items, they just let you specify nonexecutable files, merge modules with shared components, and assemblies to include in the setup program. For example, you would use the Files menu command to include images, .pdf, or Microsoft Access .mdb files with the project. You can reference any file type you want, in any number. You would use the Merge Module menu command to include shared components that your project uses. The Assembly command can be used to include other assemblies not included with the Merge Module command.

Adding a Project Output Group

The Project Output Group indicates what project the setup program is to install. The Project Output can reference either a .exe or a .dll project. For the given project, you can select what files to include in the setup program. Figure 6-18 shows the Add Project Output Group dialog box, after selecting three file types.

Figure 6-18: The Add Project Output Group dialog box

In the Project combo box at the top of the dialog box, you can choose any project you want that is part of the same solution. The Configuration combo box lets you specify whether to use the Release or Debug version. The setting (Active) specifies the configuration that is currently selected. Most of the time, you'll want to select the Release configuration, because you don't normally deploy Debug versions of code. When you close the dialog box with the OK button, a number of items are added to the Solution Explorer, as shown in Figure 6-19.

Figure 6-19: The Solution Explorer showing the newly added file groups

Editing the setup project properties

The next step is to edit the setup project's properties to indicate the name, version, and other attributes of the program to install. It is important that you do so, because many of the items, such as the product and manufacturer name, show up in the Windows Control Panel's Add/Remove Programs applet, or in the Properties dialog box of files. Figure 6-20 shows the properties I entered for my setup project example.

To display the Properties for a project, just select the setup project in the Solution Explorer. The properties shown in the figure are fairly self-explanatory, except for a few that warrant a short discussion.

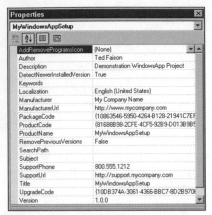

Figure 6-20: Editing the properties
of the setup project

The AddRemoveProgramsIcon property lets you specify an icon that will be used in the Control Panel's Add/Remove Programs applet. A default icon is used if you don't specify one.

The PackageCode and ProductCodes are unique identifiers that tag each version of the setup program and the product it installs. These identifiers are generated automatically when you first create a setup program, or when you change the Version property.

The Keywords property lets you add any number of words. Keywords show up in the Windows Explorer when you right-click on a .msi file, choose the Properties command from the pop-up menu, and then go to the Summary page. Microsoft recommends setting the Keywords property to an expression of the form `<product name>.<version>`. In practice, most companies leave the Keywords property blank.

The UpgradeCode is a value that identifies the product being installed, regardless of version. The UpgradeCode allows the installer to detect whether pre-existing versions of the product to install are already present on the end user's machine. The properties DetectNewerInstalledVersion and RemovePreviousVersions depend on the UpgradeCode. The UpgradeCode is established when you first create a setup program, and should never be changed.

Some of the properties appear in Support Information dialog box for the installed product. To display this dialog box, select the product in the Control Panel's Add/Remove Programs applet, as shown in Figure 6-21.

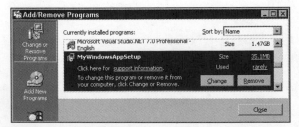

Figure 6-21: The Add/Remove Programs applet

Click the `support information` link to see the Support Info dialog box, shown in Figure 6-22.

Figure 6-22: The Support Info
dialog box

Common issues

In this section, I'll discuss some of the recurring issues that apply to setup programs. In later sections, I'll show you how to use advanced features to customize the way a setup program runs.

Adding a shortcut to the Start menu

It is very common for installed programs to be accessible through a shortcut in the Programs folder of the Start menu. To add such a shortcut, right-click on the Setup project in the Solution Explorer and choose View ➪ File System from the pop-up menu, as shown in Figure 6-23.

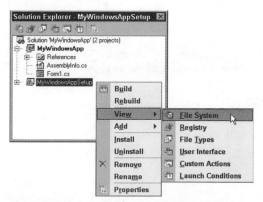

Figure 6-23: Opening the File System Editor
to install a shortcut to your application in
the Start menu

As you can see, besides the File System Editor, there are others editors for the Registry, the user interface, and other resources or tasks. I'll discuss the other editors a bit later. Each editor has its own tab in the Forms Designer area. Figure 6-24 shows the File System Editor.

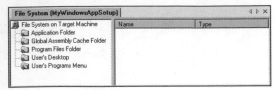

Figure 6-24: The File System Editor

The items on the left side represent some of the *special* folders on the end user's machine. Special folders are those that have special meaning to Windows, such as the Program Files folder, the Windows folder, and so on. You can use the File System Editor to add files to any folder you want.

When adding a shortcut to the Start menu, there are two common choices: to put the shortcut in the Programs folder, or to put the shortcut in its own folder under the Programs folder. The latter option is convenient when you want to add a number of items in a folder that has a company name or product name.

To add a shortcut directly to the Programs folder of the Start menu, select the item labeled *User's Program Menu.* In the right pane, right-click and choose Create New Shortcut from the pop-up menu, as shown in Figure 6-25.

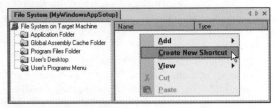

Figure 6-25: Adding a shortcut to the Programs folder of the Start Menu

In the Select Item in Project dialog box that appears, select Application Folder in the top drop-down list, and then choose Primary Output from MyWindowsApp, as shown in Figure 6-26.

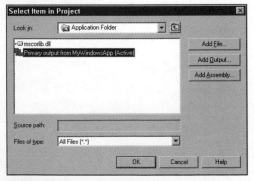

Figure 6-26: Choosing the file to create a shortcut to

Click the OK button. In the right pane of the File System Editor, change the shortcut name to the name of your application, as shown in Figure 6-27.

Figure 6-27: Renaming the shortcut that will appear in the Start menu

To create a shortcut in a folder under the Start menu's Programs folder, select the User's Programs Menu item on the left. Right-click and choose Add ➪ Folder from the pop-up menu, and then add the shortcut to the newly added folder. Figure 6-28 shows how the File System Editor appears after I added a shortcut to a folder named *My Company*.

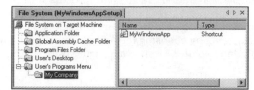

Figure 6-28: A shortcut added to a subfolder of the Programs folder

Adding a shortcut to the desktop

The process is similar to the one described in the previous section. The only difference is which special folder you select in the File System Editor left pane: Just select the User's Desktop item. Figure 6-29 shows the File System Editor after a desktop shortcut has been added.

Figure 6-29: Adding a shortcut to the user's desktop

Adding items to the registry

If you need to add items to the registry, you can do so easily with Registry Editor, shown in Figure 6-30.

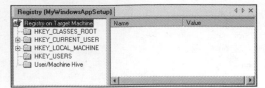

Figure 6-30: The Registry Editor

To display the Registry Editor, select the command View ⇨ Registry from the pop-up menu shown previously in Figure 6-24. You don't have to add entries pertaining to any ActiveX components that you use in the Setup project. These components can be set up to register themselves or to be registered automatically, as described in the next section.

ActiveX components

A setup program can include essentially any type of file. Some file types are special, such as ActiveX components, so you need to handle them with a bit more care than other types. What makes ActiveX components special is the fact that they must be registered before they are used for the first time. Because component registration is a standard process for every ActiveX component, all you need to do is set a property to tell the installer how the ActiveX component needs to be installed. For example, say you want to add the ActiveX component MsHtml.dll to the Setup project. You would begin by choosing the Add ⇨ File command from the Setup project's pop-up menu in the Solution Explorer, as shown in Figure 6-31.

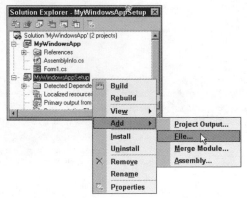

Figure 6-31: Adding an ActiveX component to a Setup project

Navigate to the folder c:\winnt\system32 and add the file MsHtml.dll. The file will be added to the Setup project and appear in the Solution Explorer. Select the file in the Solution Explorer. In the Properties Window, check the Register property. With most ActiveX components, you'll find the property already set to the value vsdrfCOM, as shown in Figure 6-32.

All files (not just ActiveX components) have the Register property. With ordinary files, the property is set to vsdrpDoNotRegister. When the property is set to vsdfrCOM, vsdfrCOMRelativePath, or vsdfrCOMSelfRegister, the ActiveX component will be registered automatically, so you won't have to manually add any entries to the registry.

Figure 6-32: Setting up an ActiveX component to be registered when installed

Built-in dialog boxes

During the install process, a setup program displays a number of dialog boxes, allowing the user to select folders, specify options, read help documents, and so on. In the following sections, I'll show you how to customize a setup program using these built-in windows.

To start working with the built-in dialog boxes, open the User Interface Editor. To do so, right-click on the Setup project in the Solution Explorer and choose View ➪ User Interface from the pop-up menu, as previously shown in Figure 6-23. The User Interface Editor will appear on a new tab in the Forms Designer area, as shown in Figure 6-33.

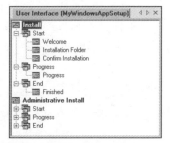

Figure 6-33: The User Interface Editor

As you can see, there are two main sections: Install and Administrative Install. Each can be set up independently, if you want Administrators to have setup features that are different from ordinary users. The dialog boxes will appear at setup time in the same order they appear in the User Interface Editor. To change their order, use the mouse to drag them around.

By default, every Setup project starts off with a small list of default dialog boxes. You can delete them if you don't want them to appear. You can also add others, from a fairly long list of built-in dialog boxes. The following is a list of the built-in dialog boxes:

   ✦ Splash dialog box

   ✦ Welcome dialog box

   ✦ End User License Agreement dialog box

✦ Customer Information dialog box

✦ RadioButton dialog boxes with two, three, or four buttons

✦ CheckBox dialog boxes in various styles

✦ TextBox dialog boxes in various styles

✦ Readme dialog box

✦ Register User dialog box

To add a new dialog box to the Setup project, right-click on one of the sections (Start, Progress, or End) shown in the User Interface Editor and select the Add Dialog command from the pop-up menu, as shown in Figure 6-34.

Figure 6-34: Adding a new built-in dialog box to a setup program

The Add Dialog Wizard will appear, allowing you to choose the type of dialog box to add, as shown in Figure 6-35.

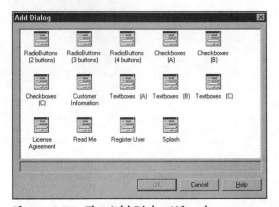

Figure 6-35: The Add Dialog Wizard

The following sections discuss each type of dialog box. But first, I want to show you how to add a custom logo to a dialog box. Except for the Splash dialog box, all the dialog boxes support custom logos, which appear in the upper section of each window. You can decide which dialog boxes to use logos on. If you don't specify a logo, a default logo is shown on all the dialog boxes (except for the Splash dialog box).

Logos

Most companies opt to display a logo on the various windows in a setup program. The built-in dialog boxes reserve a space that is 500 x 70 pixels in size, so this is the optimal size of any logo images you create. If the image is larger or smaller, it will be shrunk or stretched to make it fill the available space. For the image, you'll want to use light colors to produce a faint image, because the image will be used as a watermark, appearing behind black text. If the image contains dark or bold colors, the text will be hard to read. I created an image and saved it in the file My Logo.bmp in the Setup project's folder. The image is shown in Figure 6-36.

Figure 6-36: A 500 x 70 pixel custom logo

Once you have an image file, you need to add it to the Setup project. Right-click on the project in the Solution Explorer and select the command Add ➪ Files from the pop-up menu. In the Add Files dialog box, locate the image file and click the Open button. Once the file is added to the project, you can add it to one of the built-in dialog boxes. For example, to add it to the Welcome dialog box, select that dialog in the User Interface Editor. In the Properties window, select the BannerBitmap property. From the property's drop-down list, choose Browse. In the Select Item In Project window, select the image file, as shown in Figure 6-37.

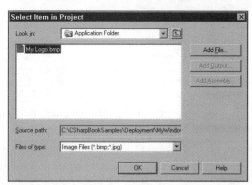

Figure 6-37: Adding a custom logo to a built-in dialog box

After adding the image file, its filename will appear in the Properties window for the selected built-in dialog box, as shown in Figure 6-38.

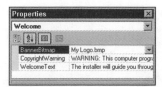

Figure 6-38: The Properties window showing the custom logo filename

Figure 6-39 shows what the Welcome dialog box looks like with my custom logo image.

Like I said, you'll want to use very light colors to minimize interference with the black text displayed on top of the logo.

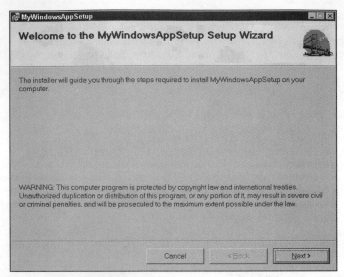

Figure 6-39: A Welcome dialog box with a custom logo

Splash dialog box

This is the generally the first window users see when the setup program is launched. It displays an image inside a window, as shown in Figure 6-40.

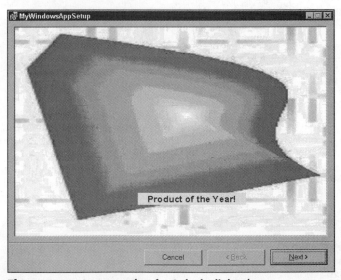

Figure 6-40: An example of a Splash dialog box

The optimal size of the splash image is 600 x 400 pixels. If you specify an image of a different size, the image will be shrunk or stretched to fit it in the allocated space. If the image includes text on it, the text may look really bad if the image is resized.

To create the Splash dialog box shown in the figure, I created a file called My Splash.jpg and added it to the Setup project, as described in the previous section, "LOGOS." I added a Splash dialog to the project using the User Interface Editor, and then set the dialog box's SplashBitmap property to reference My Splash.jpg.

Welcome dialog box

An example of a Welcome dialog box was previously shown back in Figure 6-39. There are a couple of other properties you can customize for this dialog box. The first is called WelcomeText and contains the text to display in the upper part of the dialog box. As you can see from the empty space in the center portion of the dialog box, there is plenty of space to handle long WelcomeText messages.

The other property is called CopyrightWarning, which shows the text in the lower part of the dialog box. Here again, there is ample space for fairly long messages.

User License dialog box

This dialog box displays the End User License Agreement (EULA). The text must be placed in a file, and the dialog box poses no restrictions on how long the EULA text is. The text is contained in a .rtf file, so it can contain richly formatted text, as shown in Figure 6-41.

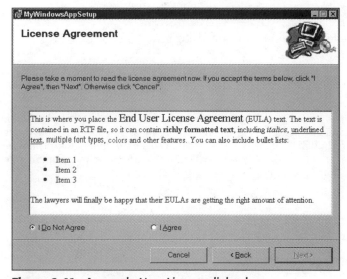

Figure 6-41: A sample User License dialog box

Customer Information dialog box

This dialog box prompts the user for his or her name and organization, as shown in Figure 6-42.

The dialog box can be customized with several properties. The ShowOrganization property can be set to False to hide the Organization edit box. You can also make the dialog box prompt the user for a serial number, using the properties named SerialNumberTemplate and ShowSerialNumber. Using SerialNumberTemplate, you can specify an edit mask for the serial number, using characters like #, ?, and %. The first specifies a digit, the second an alphanumeric character. The third also specifies an alphanumeric character, but uses the character in a simple validation algorithm.

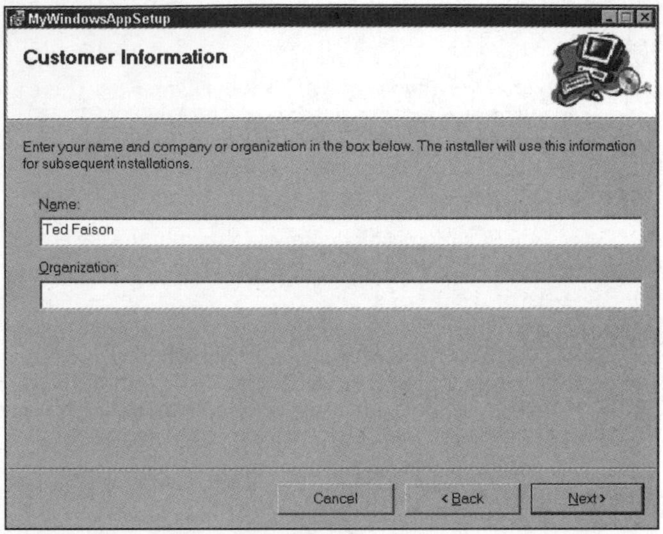

Figure 6-42: The default Customer Information dialog box

For example, the mask ### indicates 3 digits. The mask ?? indicates a string of length 2 made up of numbers or alphabetic characters. The mask %%% indicates a string with 3 alphanumeric characters.

All the characters specified by % are included in a simple validation check: The characters are added together, and the sum is divided by 7. The remainder must be 0 for the serial number to be considered valid. Although it might at first seem that this hard-coded algorithm forces you to create serial numbers in a specific way, it really doesn't. Say your serial number generator came up with the following string:

```
123 AB 876-234
```

You could use the following edit mask:

```
%%% ?? %%% - %%%%
```

The spaces were added to improve legibility. Looking more closely at the edit mask, it defines 3 digits, followed by 2 characters (excluded from the validation check) and then a group of 4 more digits. You'll notice the last group has one more digit than the original serial number. A mistake? No. The last digit in the edit mask is a check digit: It's only there to adjust the sum of the first 9 digits to be divisible by 7, to satisfy the validation algorithm. If the user enters the valid serial number 123 AB 876-234, the sum of the 9 digits is

```
1+2+3 +8+7+6 +2+3+4 = 36
```

To make the value divisible by 7, the check digit needs to be 6, making the sum 42. As far as the user is concerned, the serial number is

123 AB 876-2346

Note that the check digit can be used at any character position, not just the last one. You can place a check digit (or even multiple check digits) anywhere in the serial number.

Any edit mask characters that aren't part of the reserved characters are considered literals and displayed verbatim in the Serial Number edit box.

The Customer Information dialog box uses the edit mask string to display one or more edit boxes for entering the serial number. For each different mask character found, an edit box is created. For example, the mask #|#%%??#|# would produce four edit boxes, because there are four groups of characters. Figure 6-43 shows an example of a Customer Information dialog box that uses the edit mask string #|#|#-%%%%%%%.

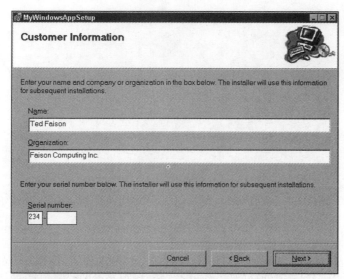

Figure 6-43: A Customer Information dialog box with a Serial Number field

If the serial number entered fails the dialog box's validation algorithm, the user will get the error message shown in Figure 6-44, and will be prevented from continuing the installation process.

Figure 6-44: The error message shown if an invalid serial number is entered

Once a valid serial number is entered, the user can proceed to the next Setup screen.

RadioButton dialog boxes

The RadioButton dialog boxes can contain two, three, and four buttons. These dialog boxes can be used to enable users to specify choices that affect the install process. Figure 6-45 shows a two-button dialog box.

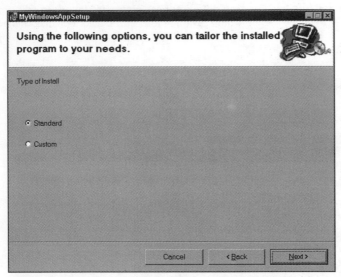

Figure 6-45: A two-button RadioButton dialog box

On this dialog box, you can configure the banner bitmap, the banner text, the body text, and the radio button captions. The dialog box shown was configured with the properties seen in Figure 6-46. You can control which radio button is initially selected by using the dialog's DefaultValue property.

Figure 6-46: The properties used to configure the RadioButton dialog box in the previous figure

The ButtonProperty field is very important. It is the name of the property that returns the selection made on the dialog box. You normally don't read this value in your own code, because there is no code of your own in a typical Setup project. Rather, you reference the ButtonProperty field in the Condition properties of other Setup items. I'll show you how to used RadioButton selections in "Using conditions," later in this chapter.

CheckBox dialog boxes

There are three identical CheckBox dialog boxes you can use. They are referenced using the letters A, B, and C. Why three identical dialog boxes? The reason is that you can only use one instance of each type of User Interface dialog box. The folks at Microsoft decided that one CheckBox dialog box wasn't sufficient for many setup situations, so they threw in two more. Each of the dialog boxes has up to four checkboxes. By using the Visible property, you can control which of the checkboxes are shown on the screen. Figure 6-47 shows a CheckBox dialog box with three visible checkboxes.

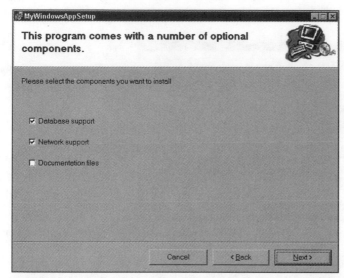

Figure 6-47: A CheckBox dialog box with three visible checkboxes

To make a checkbox show up initially as checked, set its CheckBoxValue property to Checked. Figure 6-48 shows the properties used to configure the dialog box shown in the previous figure.

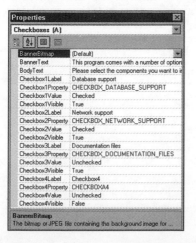

Figure 6-48: The properties used to configure the CheckBoxes dialog box in the previous figure

Notice how two of the checkboxes are initialized as `Checked`. Also, checkbox 4 is hidden. To read back the state of the checkboxes, you need to reference the `CheckBoxNProperty` in the `Condition` property of other Setup items. I'll show you how to use checkbox information in "Using conditions" later in this chapter.

TextBox dialog boxes

You can use TextBox dialog boxes to prompt the user for additional information you may need in your setup program. There are three identical TextBox dialog boxes that you can use. They all have four edit boxes, but you can control how many of them are visible. Figure 6-49 shows a sample TextBox dialog box.

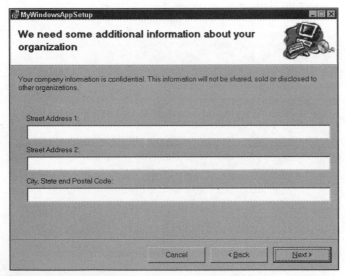

Figure 6-49: A TextBox dialog box showing three edit boxes

On a TextBox dialog box, you can control the banner text, the body text, the captions, and the initial values of each edit box. If you don't need all four edit boxes, hide the unused ones by setting their `Visible` property to `false`. To retrieve the data entered by the user, you'll need to reference the various EditNProperty values in conditions attached to other items. For more information, see the "Using conditions" later in this chapter.

Figure 6-50 shows the properties used to configure the TextBoxes dialog box shown in Figure 6-49.

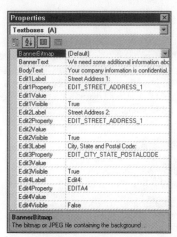

Figure 6-50: The properties used to configure the TextBoxes dialog box shown in the previous figure

Installation Folder dialog boxes

This is a simple dialog box that prompts the user for the main installation folder. If your Setup project needs to prompt for multiple installation folders, use a TextBoxes dialog box. Figure 6-51 shows an example of an Installation Folder dialog box.

The button labeled *Disk Cost* enables the user to see the amount of available space on his or her hard drive. Except for the banner image, all the fields of the Installation Folder dialog box are fixed.

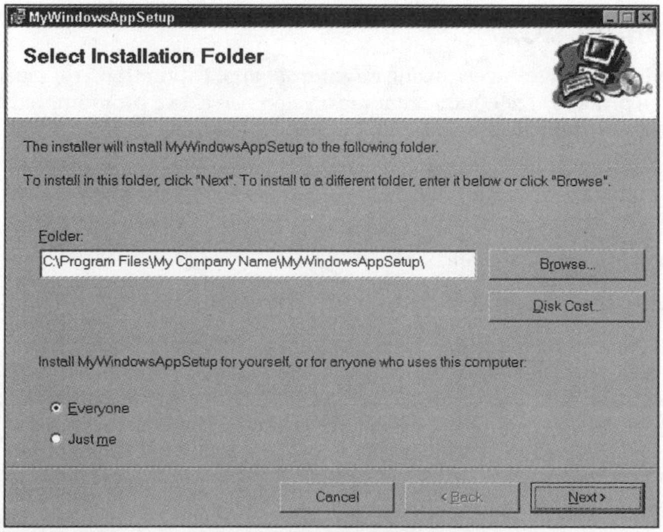

Figure 6-51: An Installation Folder dialog box

Readme dialog box

This dialog box is equivalent to the User License dialog box. It displays the contents of a .rtf file, which can contain an arbitrarily long amount of richly formatted text. To set up a Readme dialog box, create the .rtf file with an editor like Microsoft Word, put the file in the same folder as the other Setup project files, and then add the file to the project. After adding a Readme dialog box to the project, set the dialog box's `ReadmeFile` property to reference the .rtf file containing the text you want to display. Figure 6-52 shows an example.

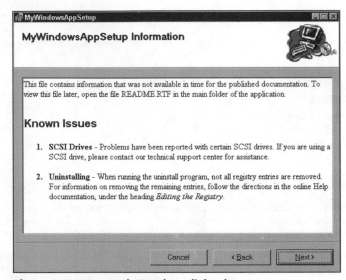

Figure 6-52: A sample Readme dialog box

Register User dialog box

This dialog box enables you to register users, using an external application that you must supply. The dialog box has the property Executable that must reference a .exe program that will carry out the steps you need to get a user registered. Common ways to register users include

✦ Printing out a form to be mailed or faxed

✦ Signing up on a Web site

✦ Submitting user information via e-mail

Figure 6-53 shows a Register User dialog box.

Figure 6-54 shows a simple example of a registration program that submits user information via e-mail. The program is a separate executable that you need to add to the Setup project, using the Add ➪ File context menu of the Setup project in the Solution Explorer. After adding the file, set the Register User dialog box's Executable property to reference the .exe file.

If you don't specify an Executable file for the dialog box, the Register Now button will be grayed out. Note that the setup program doesn't expect a return value or any other kind of result from the registration process. In fact, the user can continue the setup process without clicking the Register Now button.

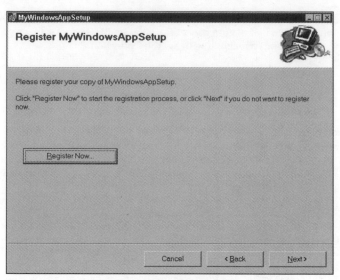

Figure 6-53: An example of a Register User dialog box

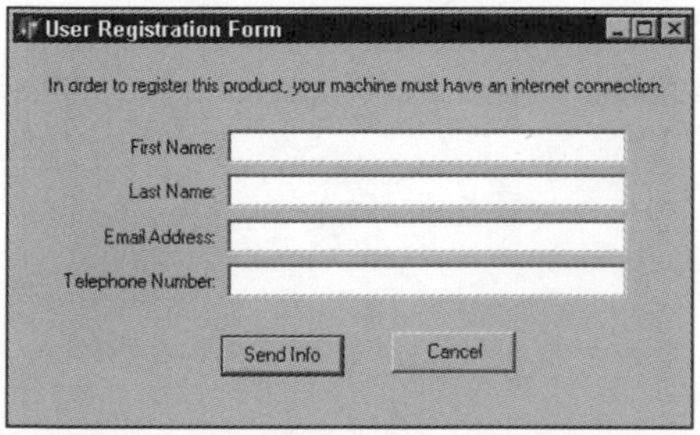

Figure 6-54: A simple user registration program

Using conditions

Many setup programs support different installation options. For example, you may have an application that can be installed only as an upgrade, meaning the user must have an earlier version of the product already installed. Or you may have options that control how much information is copied to the user's hard disk. An option called *typical* might just install the basic files, while the *complete* option might copy all the files from the Setup CD. Options give a lot of flexibility to a setup program, so I'll discuss ways to support some of the most common ones in the following sections.

Blocking the installation process if a resource isn't present

This type of condition is known as a Search Condition. You can add as many Search Conditions to your Setup project as you want. The conditions are evaluated before any User dialog boxes are displayed. The first condition that is found to be false will display an error message and prevent the user from continuing the installation process, rolling back all actions taken (if any) up to that point. The resources can be associated with Search Conditions:

✦ Files

✦ Registry entries

✦ Windows Installer components

To add a Search Condition to a Setup project, right-click the project node in the Solution Explorer and choose View ➪ Launch Conditions from the pop-up menu. The Launch Conditions Editor will appear on a new tab in the Forms Designer space. Right-click the node *Requirements on Target Machine* and select the type of resource you want to verify the presence of (on the machine the user will be running the setup program on), as shown in Figure 6-55.

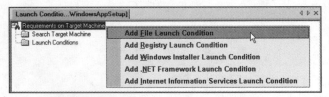

Figure 6-55: Selecting a resource to search for at install time

Figure 6-56 shows the Launch Conditions Editor after adding the first three types of Search Conditions listed in the menu in the previous figure.

Figure 6-56: Adding three different types of Search Conditions

The names of the items can be changed to make them more meaningful, so you could use names like *Search for Version 4 executable*, or *Search for User License file*. Spaces are allowed in names. The *Search for File* and *Search for RegistryEntry* conditions are self-explanatory. The *Search for Component* condition is not. This last type of Search Condition can be used to see if a Windows Installer component, having a specific GUID, is present on the user's machine. Figures 6-57, 6-58, and 6-59 show the properties for each type of search condition.

For all the search items, the Property field is the name of the property that can be accessed by Launch Condition items. For file searches, you specify the filename and the folder to search. All subfolders of the folder will also be searched.

The Launch Conditions items need to be set up with two properties: a condition to test and the error message to display if the condition tested is false. Figure 6-60 shows the properties of the *File1Exists* condition.

Figure 6-57: The properties of the *Search for Component1* item

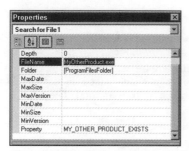

Figure 6-58: The properties of the *Search for File1* item

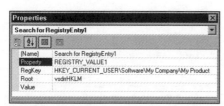

Figure 6-59: The properties of the *Search for RegistryEntry1* item

Figure 6-60: The properties of the *File1Exists* condition

All the Search Conditions are evaluated in the order they appear in the Launch Conditions Editor. The Search Conditions are verified before any other User Interface dialog boxes are shown to the user. When a condition is found to be false, the text from its Message property is shown in a message box, such as the one shown in Figure 6-61 for the condition *File1Exists*.

When the message box is closed, the setup program terminates. Because no actions were taken yet, the program doesn't need to roll any changes back.

Figure 6-61: The error message shown if the file specified in *Search for File1* is not found

Blocking the installation process if a condition isn't met

This type of condition is known generically as a *Launch Condition*. You can add as many Launch Conditions as you want. A condition you specify will be evaluated during the installation process. If the condition is found to be false, an error message will be displayed and the setup program will terminate, rolling back all actions taken up to that point. The kinds of conditions you can check for are:

✦ Operating system type and version

✦ Amount of RAM available

✦ Type of CPU

✦ Conditions from User Interface dialog boxes

The built-in identifiers

There are a number of identifiers that you can reference in your Launch Condition and elsewhere in a Setup project. Table 6-3 shows the main built-in identifiers.

Table 6-3: Most Commonly Used Built-In Conditions

Identifier	Values	Description
Version9X	Version of Windows 95, 98, or ME.	If Windows 95, 98, or ME is installed on the user's machine, this condition will return the major and minor versions.
VersionNT	Version of Windows NT, 2000, or XP	Operating system major and minor versions. For example, use "Version >=500" to test for Windows 2000 or later.
ServicePackLevel	1, 2, 3...	Version of the latest operating system service pack installed. For example, use "ServicePackLevel >=1" to test for Service Pack 1 or later.
WindowsBuild	An integer value (for example, 2195)	The build number of the operating system.
SystemLanguageID	An integer value	Indicates the default language of the user's machine.

Identifier	Values	Description
MsiNetAssemblySupport the user's machine.	A dot-separated series of numbers (for example, 1.0.2914.16)	This is essentially the version of the .NET Framework installed on.
ComputerName	A string (for example, "MyComputer")	The name of the user's computer.
LogonUser	A string (for example, "Chris")	The user name of the user who is currently logged in.
AdminUser	True or False	Indicates whether the user has administrative privileges.
PhysicalMemory	An integer	The number of MB of RAM installed.
Intel	An integer	The version of the CPU, if it's an Intel processor like a Pentium chip.
COMPANYNAME	A string (for example, "My Company")	The name of the user's organization, as entered in the setup program's Customer Information dialog box.
USERNAME	A string (for example, "Ted Faison")	The name of the user, as entered in the setup program's Customer Information dialog box.

User Interface dialog box properties as conditions

Some of the User Interface dialog boxes have controls with values you can use as conditions. The following dialog boxes have conditions: RadioButtons, CheckBoxes, and TextBoxes.

For each dialog box, there are properties that you can name and then use as conditions with Launch Conditions, or to control whether a file is installed or not. With RadioButtons dialog boxes, the property that tells you what radio button is selected is called `ButtonProperty`. For CheckBoxes dialog boxes, each checkbox has a property called `CheckboxNProperty`, where N stands for the number (1–4) of the control. For TextBoxes dialog boxes, each edit box has a property called `EditNProperty`. The value of this property is the name of the condition that you can refer to in conditional statements.

As an example, say you have a RadioButtons dialog box with two radio buttons, configured with the properties shown in Figure 6-62.

Figure 6-62: The configuration settings for a sample RadioButtons dialog box

If you want to install a file only if a radio button is selected, use the following condition:

```
INSTALLATION_MODE = 2
```

Where would you use this condition? Since you want to use it to control whether a file is installed or not, attach it to a file as follows. Open the File System Viewer and select the file to be conditionally installed. Right-click on the filename. In the Properties window, add the condition to the Condition property, as shown in Figure 6-63. (In this example, the file to be conditionally installed is called *EULA.rtf*.)

Figure 6-63: Using a RadioButton selection to control whether a file is installed or not

You can also reference INSTALLATION_MODE from a Launch Condition, using a similar process. Doing so would let you terminate the installation process if a condition (or even a set of conditions) was true.

Custom Actions

Another way to customize a Setup project is with *Custom Actions*. Custom Actions are just executable programs that you can make the setup program call at four specific points in time:

✦ At the end of the install process

✦ After a successful commit has been performed

✦ After a rollback has been performed

✦ At the end of an uninstall process

In many cases, actions performed during installation need to be reversed during uninstallation. For example, if you use a Custom Action to set up a database and populate its tables with records at the end of the install process, you may want to remove the database and its records if the program is uninstalled.

Creating a Custom Action program is straightforward. Actions are executable programs that can be either .exe or .dll files. As an example, I created a program called *MyCustomAction.dll* that writes a message to the Windows Event Log. First, I created a project with the New Project Wizard, specifying **Class Library** as the template. By default, a class called Class1 is created in the project. I deleted this class from the project and used the Add New Item Wizard to add an InstallerClass to the project, as shown in Figure 6-64.

I added some code to the InstallerClass to write a message to the Windows Event Log, as shown in the bolded lines in Listing 6-1.

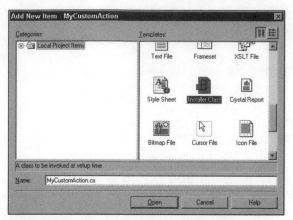

Figure 6-64: Adding an InstallerClass to a custom
action project

**Listing 6-1: Using a Custom Action .dll to Write Information to
the Windows Event Log**

```
using System;
using System.Collections;
using System.ComponentModel;
using System.Configuration.Install;

namespace MyCustomAction
{
  [RunInstaller(true)]
  public class MyCustomActionInstaller :
            System.Configuration.Install.Installer
  {
    private System.ComponentModel.Container components = null;

    public MyCustomActionInstaller()
    {
      // This call is required by the Designer.
      InitializeComponent();

      System.Diagnostics.EventLog eventLog1;
      eventLog1 = new System.Diagnostics.EventLog();
      eventLog1.Log = "Application";
      eventLog1.Source = "Setup Program";
      eventLog1.WriteEntry("MyWindowsApp installed on " +
                      DateTime.Now.ToString() );
    }
```

Continued

Listing 6-1 *(continued)*

```
    public override void Dispose()
    {  // standard wizard-generated code }

    private void InitializeComponent() {  }
  }
}
```

That's it. The Custom Action is complete. To use it in a Setup project, right-click on the Setup project in the Solution Explorer and use the Add ⇨ Files command from the pop-up menu to added the .dll to the Setup project. Figure 6-65 shows MyCustomAction.dll after it has been added it to the Setup project.

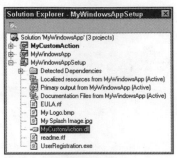

Figure 6-65: A Custom Action program added to the Setup project

After adding the action to the Setup project, open the Custom Actions Editor. To do so, right-click on the Setup project in the Solution Explorer and choose View ⇨ Custom Actions in the pop-up menu. In the Custom Actions Editor, I right-clicked on the Install folder and selected the Add Custom Action command from the pop-up menu, as shown in Figure 6-66.

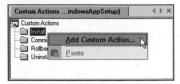

Figure 6-66: Adding a Custom Action to the end of the installation process

I added the file MyCustomAction.dll. All of the Custom Actions you add will appear under the folders they were added to. Figure 6-67 shows how MyCustomAction.dll appeared in the Custom Action Editor.

Figure 6-67: How the newly added MyCustomAction file appears in the Custom Actions Editor

The Custom Actions will be run in the order they appear in the editor. You can arrange the order using the mouse. When you specify a .dll for a Custom Action, and that program doesn't use an `InstallerClass`, you also need to tell the Setup project which method to call in that .dll. You do this using the `EntryPoint` property in the Properties window. You can also pass data to the entry point method, by entering the parameters in the `CustomActionData` property, as shown in Figure 6-68.

Figure 6-68: Setting the properties of the custom action program

If you create a Custom Action program that doesn't have an `InstallerClass`, be sure to set the `InstallerClass` property to `False`; otherwise, the setup program will ignore the `EntryPoint` property and try to call the `InstallerClass` entry point in the .dll. If the Custom Action is a .exe, the entry point will be the program's `Main()` method.

Precompiling Code

The code that makes up your application is in the form of Microsoft Intermediate Language (MSIL) code generated by the C# compiler. When a C# program is run, the CLR normally performs Just-In-Time (JIT) compilation on the methods to execute. The JIT compilation produces native binary code that can be run directly by the CPU. Once the code is compiled into binary, the resulting executable code is cached until the program terminates, so any given method is only JIT-compiled once in the life of a running process.

There are situations in which your program may need to call a large number of methods when it starts up. In these cases, the JIT compiler would be called heavily to compile a large amount of code while the user is sitting there waiting for the program to appear. A simple way to increase the startup speed of a program is to precompile it after installing it. Using this approach, the entire program is compiled down to native binary code at once and caches it away for later use. When the user runs the program, the native code will be used, and the program will start up much faster than before.

The benefits of precompilation are mostly realized at startup time, because that is when the JIT compiler is usually called to do the greatest amount of work at once. After the program has started up, most users will not experience noticeable differences in speed between JIT-compiled and precompiled code.

This last statement may seem like heresy, but the reality is this: The JIT compiler is extremely fast, and .NET code loading and translation is *very* different from Java, in which each class is loaded from a separate file, causing hundreds or thousands of file operations to be performed just to get a program loaded and started. With .NET code, executable code is loaded by module, not by method. A module is either a .exe or a .dll file. When the loader loads a module, all the classes and methods in it are loaded into memory at the same time. Keep in mind that file operations are measured in tens of milliseconds, while in-memory operations are measured in microseconds — a *huge* difference, and it shows: The JIT compiler is faster than most people with Java experience would ever expect. The performance is more due to the fact that the code is loaded in one fell swoop, as opposed to supernatural virtues of the JIT compiler.

To precompile code, there is a command-line tool in the .NET Framework called NGEN.EXE (for Native image GENerator). The program is located in the following folder:

```
C:\WINNT\Microsoft.NET\Framework\v1.0.2914
```

The version number at the end of the path string depends on which version of the .NET Framework you have.

To run NGEN.EXE on a program, use the following notation:

```
ngen <assembly name>
```

For example, to precompile the application developed earlier in the chapter called MyWindowsApp, you would go to the folder containing MyWindowsApp.exe and use the following command:

```
ngen MyWindowsApp.exe
```

Figure 6-69 shows a Command Prompt screen after precompiling MyWindowsApp.exe.

Figure 6-69: Running the precompiler on a program

Once NGEN is run on an assembly, the precompiled code is saved permanently in a cache. Any time the assembly is run in the future, its precompiled version will be used, if available. If a new version of the assembly is installed at some later time, it will need to be precompiled again. Both the old and new precompiled versions of the assembly can remain on the system and can even be used simultaneously by different programs. If you don't precompile the new version, the runtime will JIT-compile it while running it.

You can use NGEN to get a list of the precompiled assemblies on your machine, using the command ngen /show, as shown in Figure 6-70.

Figure 6-70: Using NGEN.EXE to list the precompiled assemblies

The screen is hard to read, because the information for each assembly wraps over multiple lines. By truncating some of the text from each line and aligning the fields, you can read the list much easier, as you can see in Listing 6-2.

Listing 6-2: Using NGEN.EXE to List the Precompiled Assemblies

```
C:\CSharpBookSamples\Deployment\MyWindowsApp\bin\Release>ngen /show

NGen - CLR Native Image Generator - Version 1.0.2914.16
Copyright (C) Microsoft Corp. 2001. All rights reserved.

bjcor,                   Version=1.0.3227.0,     Culture=neutral...
BJLIB,                   Version=1.0.3227.0,     Culture=neutral...
JSharpCodeProvider,      Version=7.0.0.0,        Culture=neutral...
Microsoft.VisualStudio,  Version=1.0.2411.0,     Culture=neutral...
mscorlib,                Version=1.0.2411.0,     Culture=neutral...
MyWindowsApp,            Version=1.0.686.16721,  Culture=neutral...
System,                  Version=1.0.2411.0,     Culture=neutral...
System.Design,           Version=1.0.2411.0,     Culture=neutral...
System.Drawing,          Version=1.0.2411.0,     Culture=neutral...
System.Windows.Forms,    Version=1.0.2411.0,     Culture=neutral...
WFC,                     Version=1.0.3227.0,     Culture=neutral...
```

Much better. You can also limit the list to a specific assembly, using the following command:

```
ngen /show assemblyname
```

To see all the precompiled versions of MyWindowsApp, I could use the following command:

```
ngen /show MyWindowsApp
```

An even easier way to get a list of the precompiled assemblies is to use Windows Explorer, as shown in Figure 6-71.

Windows Explorer uses a Shell Extension (shfusion.dll) to display the contents of the GAC. To see the precompiled assemblies, click on the Type column header to sort by type, and then scroll down to the items with the type *Prejit*. These are precompiled assemblies.

You can delete assemblies from the cache using the DEL key. You can also use NGEN.EXE to delete precompiled assemblies. The command doesn't remove the original assembly file (the .exe or .dll), just the cached data. To delete a precompiled assembly, use the following command:

```
ngen /delete MyWindowsAssembly
```

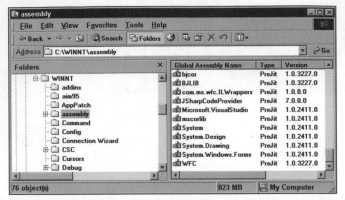

Figure 6-71: Using Windows Explorer to view the precompiled assemblies in the GAC

There are several other uses of NGEN.EXE. Consult the VS .NET documentation for details.

In order to precompile code at installation time, you need to create a Custom Action that calls NGEN.EXE. Unfortunately, there is no checkbox you can click somewhere to enable pre-compilation the easy way. On the other hand, creating a Custom Action that does it is not too terribly difficult.

When to precompile

There are two basic situations in which you'll want to precompile code:

✦ When your program needs to run a large amount of code just to start up

✦ When your code is a shared library that will be used over and over again by many programs

The first situation is really a no-brainer. Stated differently, it says, "*Precompile your code if the JIT compiled code is too slow.*" Gee, thanks. At least you know that if JIT-compiled code is too slow you have an alternative (and an excellent one at that). Java developers would kill to have that kind of option.

The second situation is not a rare one, because shared components are fairly common. For example, the .NET Framework code is all precompiled. Since the Framework code is used with every .NET program you run, it would be absurd to JIT-compile it each and every time a managed code program was run. If you have components that are expected to be heavily used, consider precompiling them.

When *not* to precompile

There is really only one situation in which JIT-compilation is better than precompilation: when the startup time is secondary, but program-cruising speed (the steady speed attained after startup) is primary. To understand why a JIT-compiled program cruises faster than a precompiled program, you need to take into consideration what the JIT compiler does: It doesn't just translate bytes into bytes, it also performs a number of important runtime opti-mizations that make your code run faster. At least with the current release of the .NET Framework, precompiled code is not as efficient as JIT-compiled code.

Deploying Software over the Internet or an Intranet

The Internet and intranets are compelling methods for deploying software. Instead of distributing new CDs to all your customers each time a software update is released, you can have customers download the new components from a URL. There are two ways to support this approach: manually and automatically. I'll describe each method in the next two sections.

Using a Web page

The manual approach uses a Web page that is accessible over the Internet or an intranet. The page contains one or more hyperlinks that users can click to download updates. Figure 6-72 shows a sample page.

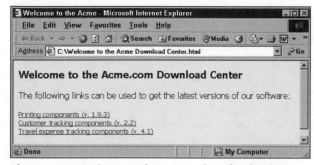

Figure 6-72: Using a Web page to download software

In addition to downloading ordinary files using Web page links, there are two types of compressed packages you can use to deploy software this way: .cab (for *cabinet,* or *CAB* for short) files and .msi (for *Microsoft Installer*) files.

CAB files

CAB files are like Zip files, in that they contain one or more compressed files. CAB files were originally developed by Microsoft as a way to reduce the number of diskettes required to distribute software. Today, CAB files are used primarily in two scenarios, both of which are related to software distribution:

✦ To package ActiveX controls for download and use on Web pages browsed with Internet Explorer

✦ To package groups of compressed files for download using http or ftp and manual installation

Compared to the newer .NET deployment options, CAB files are somewhat simplistic and limited, so I won't spend too much time on them. However CAB files can be useful in tasks other than deployment. For example, you could create a CAB file to compress a group of files you want send to someone using email. To create a CAB package for deployment, use the Add New Project Wizard, as shown in Figure 6-73.

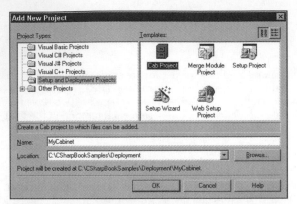

Figure 6-73: Creating a CAB deployment package using the Add New Project Wizard

Internet Explorer has built-in functionality that enables it to download and silently install ActiveX controls contained on Web pages. To add an ActiveX control to a project, right-click the CAB project in the Solution Explorer and choose Add ⇨ File from the pop-up menu. In the Add Files dialog box, navigate to the folder with the *.ocx* file containing with the ActiveX component and add it to the CAB Setup project. Create a *.inf* file that contains instructions on how to use the files contained in the CAB file. The details for creating .inf files are beyond the scope of this book.

To embed an ActiveX component on a Web page, you need to use the <OBJECT> tag. If you added the control MyControl.ocx to MyCabinet.cab and the control had the GUID 1F863546-3950-4264-BC28-21941C7EFAEA, then you would need to add the tag shown in Listing 6-3 to an HTML page that embedded the control.

Listing 6-3: **Embedding an ActiveX Component in a Web Page**

```
<OBJECT CODEBASE="http://MyCompany.com/MyCabinet.cab#version=1,0,0,0"
        CLASSID="clsid: 1F863546-3950-4264-BC28-21941C7EFAEA">
```

When Internet Explorer (IE) loads the page, it will see the <OBJECT> tag, download the CAB file, read the .inf file, extract MyControl.ocx, install it, and run it. If the CAB file is signed using Authenticode, the browser will ask you if you trust the company that signed the file. If you do, the rest of the process (downloading, extracting, installing, and registering) occurs silently. If the CAB file is not signed, IE will block its download if the user has set his or her security settings to disallow downloading of unsigned files.

If you use CAB files just to package compressed files for quicker downloads, then you'll need to use HTTP or FTP to download the file manually, and then use a tool like WinZip to extract the files on the client machine.

Smart clients

You've probably heard about fat clients and thin clients. Now we have *smart clients* too, which are essentially Windows applications that use components downloaded on-the-fly over the

Internet. What makes the clients smart is the fact that every time the user runs the program, the system will go out and check to see if newer versions of its components exist. If so, they are downloaded. If not, the previously downloaded components are run from the Global Assembly Cache (GAC).

The main idea behind smart clients is to load assemblies from a URL rather than a file, using the method `Assembly.LoadFrom(string theUrl)`. Before blindly downloading a new copy of the assembly from the remote server, the runtime checks the GAC to see if the local copy is older than the one on the server. If so, the assembly is downloaded. The client can use the code shown in Listing 6-4 to download assemblies and instantiate classes contained in them:

Listing 6-4: Using Remote Assemblies to Dynamically Get the Latest Version Available on a Web Server

```
// assume the file MyComponent.dll is an assembly containing
//  a component of type Form

Assembly myAssembly =
        Assembly.LoadFrom("http://MyCompany.com/MyComponent.dll");
Type myFormType = myAssembly.GetType("MyForm");
Form myForm = (Form) Activator.CreateInstance(myFormType);
myForm.Show();
```

The beauty of this approach is that software publishers don't need to send copies of each software update to all their clients. When an update is published, the next time a user runs the client software it will automatically check your Web server for updates.

The *smart* part of smart clients entails more than just using remotely loaded assemblies. With the approach described here, the client can only update assemblies it knows about. What if you release a new assembly that wasn't in the original release the customer has? The solution is to have the client query a Web service that returns a list of the assemblies that are needed. The list may be different for various types of users, so you might publish assemblies A, B, and C for typical users and additional assemblies D, E, and F for power users. Because the list of assemblies is not baked into the client's software, you can support just about any kind of software update this way.

Even better is the fact that updates are only downloaded if they contain components the user needs. So if Joe Programmer just needs components from assembly A, he won't need to download assemblies B and C, and won't even know about the existence of D, E, and F that apply to power users.

Deploying Shared Components

When you distribute components that are designed to be used by more than a single program, you need to deploy them using something called a *Merge Module*. (Where the folks at Microsoft come up with these names is beyond me. Technology is complicated enough even without using arcane names for things.) Merge Modules are just a packaging option to support shared components. To create a Merge Module, use the trusted Add New Project Wizard as shown in Figure 6-74.

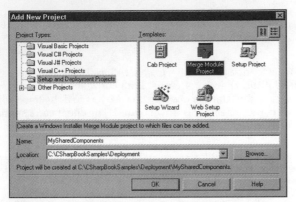

Figure 6-74: Creating a Merge Module to deploy shared components

You develop Merge Module programs using basically the same techniques as those used for Setup projects, with two important differences:

✦ Merge Modules can't be run by themselves. While Setup projects can be run directly by the Microsoft Installer Service, Merge Modules can't. Think of Merge Modules as DLLs. They contain code that can be called only from a running program. To be distributed, Merge Modules must be attached to Setup projects.

✦ Merge Modules are placed in a common folder, for other components to access. For components expected to be of general interest, such as custom controls that any program may want to use, the recommended folder is `C:\Program Files\Common Files\Merge Modules`. If you create a Merge Module that will only be used with your own products, use a more private location. For example, for a company named *MyCompany,* a good place might be the folder `C:\Program Files\My Company\Merge Modules`.

Note   Because Merge Modules are shared with other applications, it is imperative that you not make changes to them, unless you update the version number. Every time you make a change to components deployed in a Merge Module, *always* be sure to update the assembly's version number.

Once you have a Merge Module, you can add it to a Setup project very easily. First add the Merge Module to the solution containing the Setup project. Then right-click the Setup project and select Add ➪ Merge Module from the pop-up menu. For information on other details of Merge Modules, see the earlier sections describing Setup projects.

Licensing

Most of us are in the software business to make a profit. Without a licensing infrastructure, anyone who gets a copy of your components could use them without your permission. The idea of licensing in the .NET Framework is to support an unobtrusive, yet powerful and flexible way to control usage of your components. The .NET licensing model is based on an architecture in which there are four key players, as shown in Figure 6-75.

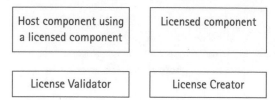

Figure 6-75: The four key players in the .NET Framework licensing model

I'll discuss the role of the players in this and later sections. With the default licensing classes, the licensing model supports only simple, perpetual licenses: If a customer has a valid license, they'll be able to use the licensed components indefinitely. By customizing the license components, you can support different licensing models, such as the following:

✦ Licenses valid only within a given start and end date

✦ Licenses valid for a certain number of runs

✦ Licenses that expire after a given number of days

✦ Licenses that support a maximum number of concurrent users

✦ Licenses based on the number of CPUs installed

Like I said earlier, the .NET licensing architecture is flexible, so it isn't too hard to add custom licensing features. When you create a licensed component, you are responsible for all the parties except the host components, which belong to people using your licensed component. From the very beginning, the designers of the license model worked with the goal of creating a model that didn't change the way customers use licensed components — the way to instantiate a component is the same for both unlicensed and licensed ones, using the familiar new operator. For example, if you develop a licensed component called MyLicensedComponent, a host component would instantiate it using the code shown in Listing 6-5.

Listing 6-5: Instantiating a Licensed Component, Using the Standard New Operator

```
MyLicensedComponent myComponent = new MyLicensedComponent();
```

If the host doesn't have a valid license, a LicenseException will be thrown inside the constructor. Licensed components internally use a LicenseManager component to verify whether the host component is authorized to use the component. The LicenseManager uses a pluggable (customizable) license validator class to verify the license. The NET Framework contains a simple built-in license validator that looks for license keys in files. A licensed component requires very little extra code to handle licensing. Figure 6-76 shows the class diagram for a basic licensed component.

The code for MyLicensedComponent would look something like Listing 6-6.

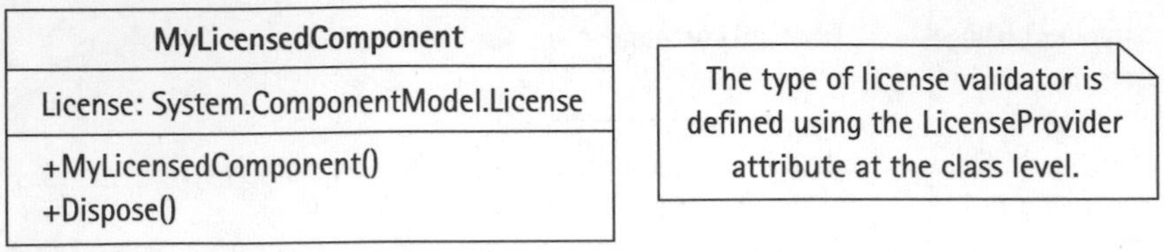

MyLicensedComponent
License: System.ComponentModel.License
+MyLicensedComponent()   +Dispose()

The type of license validator is defined using the LicenseProvider attribute at the class level.

Figure 6-76: The class diagram for a simple licensed component

Listing 6-6: **The Code for a Simple Licensed Component**

```
[LicenseProviderAttribute(typeof(LicFileLicenseProvider))]
public class MyLicensedComponent
{
  private License license = null;

  public MyLicensedComponent ()
  {
    license = LicenseManager.Validate(typeof(MyLicensedComponent),
                                this);
  }
}
```

Notice the attribute attached to the class. To specify what type of `LicenseProvider` to use, you need to use attributes. The presence of this attribute denotes a class as licensed. If your class has a `Dispose()` method, it is recommended (but not mandatory) that you add code to it to dispose of the license as shown in Listing 6-7.

Listing 6-7: **Releasing the License in Classes with a Dispose() Method**

```
protected override void Dispose(bool disposing)
{
  if (license != null)
  {
    license.Dispose();
    license = null;
  }
  base.Dispose();
}
```

The reason for calling `license.Dispose()` like this is to remove licenses from the runtime as soon as possible. Otherwise they will survive until your program terminates, because the `LicenseManager` is holding onto them.

When it comes to using a licensed component, there are two scenarios: design time and runtime. *Design time* is when you're using a tool such as VS .NET to drop licensed components from the toolbar on forms or other components. *Runtime* is when the code containing the licensed components is actually executed.

Design-time licenses

Design-time licenses require the presence of a special license file that contains a license key. To understand how this file and the various licensing components fit in the licensing process at design time, look at the interaction diagram in Figure 6-77.

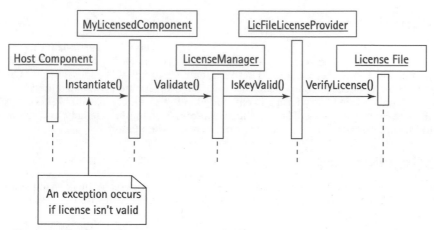

Figure 6-77: The interaction diagram describing the design-time licensing mechanism

A singleton `LicenseManager` manages all the `LicenseProvider`s used by components in the assembly. There is only one type of `LicenseProvider` that is built into the .NET Framework: `LicFileLicenseProvider`. This provider looks for license keys in files.

At design time, the built-in class `LicFileLicenseProvider` searches for a license file in the same folder containing the assembly's executable code. The license file must be a text file with the extension *.lic*. The standard provider `LicFileLicenseProvider` uses extremely simple license keys that consist of a string in clear text in the following format:

```
<assembly name>.<class name> is a licensed component.
```

So to create a license file for `MyLicensedComponent`, you need to create a text file called perhaps *MyAssembly.lic* and save it in a folder with a path that looks something like this:

```
C:\MyProjects\MyLicensedComponent\bin\debug
```

The filename of the license text file is not important, as long as the extension is *.lic*. It is customary to use the assembly name for the filename. In my example license file, I would need the following line of text:

```
MyAssembly.MyLicensedComponent is a licensed component.
```

The text represents the license key. Obviously with such a simple key, it wouldn't be too difficult for unlicensed users to create license files on their own. The purpose of `LicFileLicenseProvider` is not to create an unbreakable license scheme, but to give you a base class to easily customize. By overriding the `GetLicense()` and `IsKeyValid()` methods, you can create your own `LicenseProvider` that perhaps uses encrypted or hashed values in the license file. Or your provider could query a remote Web service to see if the user is an authorized one. Or you could add data to support time-constrained licenses.

In the `GetLicense()` method, a customized provider can return a custom `License` object that is derived from `System.ComponentModel.License`, supporting properties and methods for specific situations. For example, you could create a `MyCustomLicense` class that has the properties `IsRegistered`, `IsSubscriber`, and `IsEndUser` that might be accessed in the `MyLicensedComponent` code. The license properties could be used to constrain features for different types of licensed users.

Runtime licenses

While at design-time, `LicenseProvider`s like `LicFileLicenseProvider` look for licenses in .lic text files, at runtime they can also look for licenses elsewhere. If a .lic file isn't found, they look for a binary license key embedded in the assembly's executable code. When you build a project containing licensed components, all the license information contained in a project's .lic file is compiled into binary form and embedded in the assembly executable code. At runtime, the `LicenseProvider` will find the license information in the assembly, and enable the code to instantiate licensed components whose licenses were found.

Creating licenses

Licenses are always initially created as design-time licenses. To create the license file for a project called MyLicensedComponent, use the Add New Item Wizard with the Text File template, as shown in Figure 6-78.

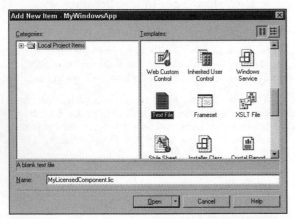

Figure 6-78: Creating a design time license file

Make sure to save the file in the `\bin\Debug` or `\bin\Release` folder (preferably in both), as shown in the Solution Explorer in Figure 6-79.

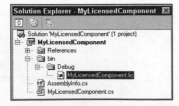

Figure 6-79: The Solution Explorer, showing the license file in the correct folder

In the Code window for the license file, I added the text shown in Figure 6-80.

Figure 6-80: The text for the license file of
MyLicensedComponent

Licenses turn into runtime licenses when they are compiled into a host component that uses
a licensed component, as described in the next section.

Using licensed components

If you include any licensed components in a project, you'll discover that VS .NET adds a file
named *licenses.licx* to the project. This is a clear text file containing a list of all the licensed
components used in the project.

To demonstrate the details of using a licensed component in an application, I created a simple licensed component called *MyLicensedWindowControl* in an assembly named
MyLicensedWindowControls (plural) and added the component to the toolbox. In a separate
Windows Forms project, called *MyLicensedComponentHost,* I dropped an instance of the
licensed control on a form. VS .NET created a *licenses.licx* file, as shown in the Figure 6-81.

Figure 6-81: The licenses.licx file
automatically created by VS .NET

The contents of the licenses.licx file are shown in Listing 6-8.

Listing 6-8: The Contents of the licenses.licx File Created by VS .NET

```
System.Windows.Forms.Form,
  System.Windows.Forms,
  Version=1.0.2411.0,
  Culture=neutral,
  PublicKeyToken=b77a5c561934e089

MyLicensedWindowsControls.MyLicensedWindowsControl,
  MyLicensedWindowsControls,
  Version=1.0.687.28096,
  Culture=neutral,
  PublicKeyToken=null
```

As you can see, the file specifies which licensed components the project uses. The file actually used one line for each component. I broke the lines into smaller pieces to make the content more legible.

When you add licensed components from the toolbar, VS .NET automatically creates or updates the licenses.licx file as needed. If you add code manually to instantiate licensed components, you'll need to create or edit the licenses.lics file by hand.

When you build a project containing a licenses.licx file, VS .NET extracts information from the file and embeds a binary form of it in the assembly executable. When the application attempts to instantiate a licensed component using code of the form

```
MyLicensedComponent comp = new MyLicensedComponent ();
```

the runtime will realize that MyLicensedComponent is licensed (because the class is marked with the `LicenseProvider` attribute. The license provider will then attempt to locate a .lic text file containing the license key. Since you won't distribute this file to end users, the license provider will then search the embedded resources of the assembly for compiled license information. If it finds it, the code in the previous listing will succeed; otherwise, a `LicenseException` will be thrown.

Summary

Try to keep setup programs as simple as possible, without presenting too many options to the user. If your software really does have lots of options, a good approach is to let users choose categories, such as Typical User or Advanced User. Each category can apply a whole series of settings, making the setup process much easier and enjoyable.

An important decision to make early-on is how your software will be deployed. If you plan for an Internet-based distribution scheme, you'll want to create small assemblies that download quickly. If you're going to ship the code on CDs, the size of the assemblies is not that important.

Deployment issues are often not contemplated in sufficient detail during the design phase. That's too bad, because the first impression people will get of your software will be affected by how fast, easy, and polished the deployment process is. Some companies assign junior programmers to create setup programs, under the pretext that little programming experience is required. Don't try to cut corners on the deployment code. You might save a few dollars on programmer salaries, but you could also set yourself up for major embarrassments. The last place you want to have problems in your software is in the deployment code. If the software fails to install correctly, you can imagine what impression your customers will have of the product, and possibly your organization.

✦   ✦   ✦

Front-End Components

Windows Form Components

We've got the best government money can buy.

—Anonymous

The best government is not the only thing money can buy. Now,
with the .NET framework, you can also buy the best Windows-
based programming tools and technology.

The Front End of any application is the place where a user interface is
shown. A user interface doesn't necessarily have to be graphical in
nature, but character-based terminal UIs are fortunately *passè*: Nobody
liked to type in commands and parameter lists in DOS boxes, or read
screens of unformatted white text on a blue background. I remember
reading a review of the first version of Microsoft Word for Windows
(as it was initially called). The reviewer actually criticized the product
for being too hard on the eyes, with its on-screen formatting. He preferred the old DOS version that couldn't show any character formatting at all, using underlines and colors to signal formatted characters.
The reviewer's reaction to Word for Windows represented a classic
behavior: Any time you introduce change, no matter how good or bad,
there will always be pockets of resistance. Funny thing, though: I can't
remember reading any other reviews by that author. The moral of the
story is that people like graphical front ends, and GUIs are here to stay.

Windows Forms

Front-end components are all about GUI components, and in this second part of the book I'll try to cover as much material as I can, without going outside the space constraints I have.

The central part of software development of Windows applications is
based on Windows Forms. The overwhelming majority of applications have a main window or form, which is displayed when the application starts up. The main form usually determines the lifetime of the
application—closing the form also terminates the application. In this
chapter, I'll show you how to create a simple Windows application,
using the tools and components available in VS .NET. To make things
interesting, I'll develop an application that highlights a number of tips
and techniques that are useful in many types of applications.

I'll create a Windows application with a main form that has a layout similar to Windows Explorer: It has a TreeView on the left, a splitter bar, and a right pane that displays information about the item selected in the TreeView. The application will demonstrate several interesting .NET features, including the following (in no particular order):

✦ Managing overlapped Panels to create rich screen layouts

✦ Using a Treeview

✦ Adding bitmaps to nodes in a Treeview

✦ MenuItems with bitmapped images

✦ Controlling the minimum and maximum size of a form

✦ Using Arrays, StringCollections, and Dictionaries

✦ Sorting

✦ Getting Win32 process and module information

✦ Accessing command-line arguments

✦ Using regular expressions

✦ Getting information about the operating system

✦ Determining the current directory

✦ Retrieving environment variables

✦ Creating text files

✦ Using Cut, Copy, and Paste

✦ Printing

✦ Determining if a mouse is attached to the system

✦ Determining if the user's system is connected to a network

✦ Getting a list of logical drives

This is quite a list of features, as you can see. I'll call the project *ProcessViewer* and design it to display a list of running processes in the TreeView. Each process will also have a list of modules under it. The right side of the form will display details about the item selected in the left pane. If the root node is selected, the right pane will display a variety of system information, as shown in Figure 7-1.

Obviously, the information displayed is system-dependent, so running ProcessViewer will produce different results on your machine. When the user selects a process from the tree in the left pane, the right pane changes to display detailed process information, as shown in Figure 7-2.

If the user drills down into a process node and selects one of the loaded modules, the right pane shows module details as shown in Figure 7-3.

For those of you unfamiliar with processes, I'll make a short digression into Win32 processes. A *process* is basically a running program. A running program is any kind of code that can be loaded by the kernel and executed, including drivers, services, applications, and even operating system code. The Windows Task Manager displays a list of the running processes, but doesn't give much information about the processes. Processes run code that is contained in files, starting with the process .exe file, and generally including code contained in numerous DLLs. In Win32 terms, any file that is loaded for execution by the kernel is referred to as a *module,* or sometimes a *process module.* While a process has details such as the Process ID and the number of owned threads, a module has details such as the filename containing the executable code, file version, and file size.

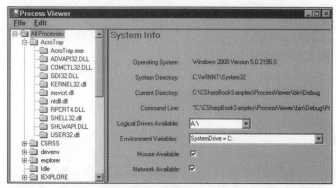

Figure 7-1: The main page of ProcessViewer, displaying a list of processes on the left and general environment information on the right

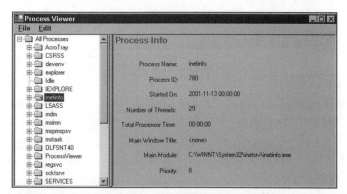

Figure 7-2: How ProcessViewer displays Win32 process details

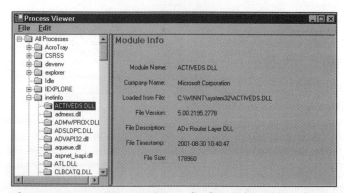

Figure 7-3: How ProcessViewer displays information about the modules loaded by a Win32 process

Designing ProcessViewer

The user interface is fairly simple, consisting of a left pane and a right pane, separated by a splitter. The left pane contains a TreeView component. The right pane contains a series of panels, of which only one is visible at a time, as shown in the previous three figures. Figure 7-4 shows the basic class diagram.

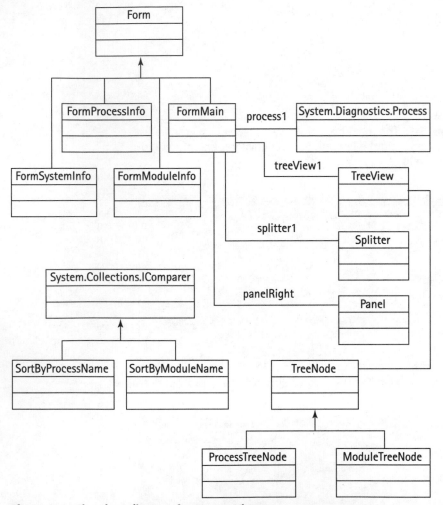

Figure 7-4: The class diagram for ProcessViewer

I didn't include the less interesting classes, like menus, printing-support classes, clipboard-support classes, and common file dialog components. I'll talk a bit more about menu items when I describe class `MyMenuItem`, which adds the ability to display images along with text.

The `System.Diagnostics.Process` component is where the list of running processes and loaded modules comes from. The component is built-in and available on the VS .NET

Components page of the toolbox. I created two classes called `SortByProcessName` and `SortByModuleName`, to sort the list of processes and modules, as described later.

ProcessViewer has a UI similar to Windows Explorer: It has a navigation control on the left side, with a content pane on the right. When developing Explorer-like user interfaces, one of the recurring issues is how to manage the detailed information about each node in the navigator. Each node has potentially lots of information to display, and there may be a lot of nodes. Think how many nodes there are in the Windows Explorer Folders pane—if you expanded each folder with all its subfolders, there could easily be thousands of nodes or more. An important question is this: When should the application load information about the nodes displayed? There are basically two methods: lazy loading and early loading.

With *lazy loading,* you only load the information for a node when the user clicks it. This is how Windows Explorer works. It would take an awfully long time for the Explorer to load if it went out and gathered a list of every file in every folder when it started up. It makes much more sense to wait for the user to select a folder, so only the contents of one folder need to be fetched at a time.

With ProcessViewer, a request is made by clicking a node in the TreeView. In a lazy-loading design, the TreeView would be used only to store the names of the processes and modules. When a node is clicked, the application could retrieve information about that one node.

With *early loading,* you read all the information about each node at startup time, and store it somewhere during the process of populating the TreeView. The information can be stored in a series of in-memory caches, in files, or in the TreeView itself.

Deciding whether to lazy load or early load depends largely on how expensive it is computationally to get information about each node, and how much information there is to keep track of. With a large or unknown amount of data, as in Windows Explorer, lazy loading is often chosen. With lazy loading, you need to make sure that each TreeView node provides enough information to identify and retrieve its details.

For ProcessViewer, I chose the early loading approach, because I know the list of processes will be fairly small, and it is relatively expensive to get detailed information about a process of module later. Moreover, the list of processes and modules shown in the tree represents a snapshot of the system at a given point in time. It is important to capture all the information immediately, because a process listed in the tree may terminate before the user selects it in the tree. By capturing it all at once, the information is guaranteed to be available.

The next design decision is where to store the detailed information. I could create a series of arrays or collections to manage the process and module details, but I already have the `TreeView` component with a list of the processes and modules neatly organized, so I'll store the details in the tree. To do so, I'll create the classes `ProcessTreeNode` and `ModuleTreeNode` to store the strings to be displayed in the tree nodes, and also to hold on to a reference to `Process` and `ProcessModule` objects respectively.

The last step is to tie together the `TreeView` with the detailed information displayed on the right side. When the user clicks an item in the tree, I want the right pane to display the details for the item clicked. Since there are three different Panels to display—one for system information, one for process details, and one for module details—I created three new forms, called *FormGeneralInfo, FormProcessInfo,* and *FormModuleInfo,* and put a Panel component with the `Docking` property set to `Fill Docking` on all three forms. I then added the necessary UI components to each window's Panel by dragging and dropping the necessary components from the toolbox. I'll show you later how to switch the form displayed at runtime in the right pane.

All of the other features listed earlier, like support for Cut and Paste, printing, and localization are fluff: They were added exclusively to show how to support them, even though an application like ProcessViewer has no need for most of them. .

Developing ProcessViewer

Let's start from the very beginning. I want ProcessViewer to be a standalone Windows application, so I'll use VS .NET's trusted New Project Wizard, selecting Windows Application as the project type. The main form is pretty simple. To achieve the desired Windows Explorer layout, I'll do the following:

1. Drop a TreeView component on the form and change its `Dock` property to `Left`.

2. Drop a Splitter component and set its `Dock` property to `Left` as well.

3. Drop a Panel component called `panelRight` on the form and set its `Dock` property to `Fill`. (I'll use this Panel later to act as the parent for the Panels that carry the system, process, and module detail information.)

4. Put a MainMenu component on the form to demonstrate how to support menu commands.

5. Add a File menu with the commands Save as, Print, and Exit. To add entries to the menu after adding the `MainMenu` component, just click the menu placeholder at the top of the form and enter the menu commands directly.

6. Add an Edit menu with the commands Copy and Paste.

I'll also need a few non-UI components to handle some of the internal ProcessViewer tasks. The most important one is the Process component, which I'll get from the Components page of the Toolbox. After adding a few other needed components, the form looks like Figure 7-5.

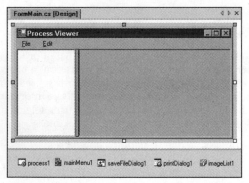

Figure 7-5: The main form of ProcessViewer

Now I need to create three more forms for the panes to display on the right side. I already showed what they look like in Figures 7-1, 7-2, and 7-3, so I won't bore you with the details. The only important thing is that the forms use a Panel to hold all the other components. It is this Panel, and not the parent form, that I'll be showing in the right pane of ProcessViewer.

Getting the process data

The `System.Diagnostics.Process` component makes it almost trivial to get a list of the processes running on a system, along with the related modules. The static method `Process.GetProcesses()` returns an array of Process objects. The `Process` objects in turn have a `Modules` property that returns an array of all their `ProcessModules`. The code to iterate over the processes and modules looks basically like Listing 7-1.

Listing 7-1: **Using System.Diagnostics.Process to Get a List of Processes and Modules**

```
Process[] allProcesses = Process.GetProcesses();
foreach (Process p in allProcesses)
{
  TreeNode processNode = new ProcessTreeNode(p);
  rootNode.Nodes.Add(processNode);


  ProcessModuleCollection allModules = p.Modules;
  foreach (ProcessModule m in allModules)
    processNode.Nodes.Add(new ModuleTreeNode(m) );
}
```

For each process and module found, the code calls `TreeNode.Add()` to add a new node to the tree.

Sorting the processes

The arrays of processes and modules returned by `System.Diagnostics.Process` are not sorted in any particular order. I want the lists I display in the TreeView to be sorted, so I'll add a couple of sorting classes to the code. `Array.Sort()` is a static method that can be used to sort any array using a custom method. This custom method must belong to a class that implements the `IComparer` interface, and the method name must have the following signature:

```
public int Compare(object x, object y)
```

`Array.Sort()` will call the `Compare()` method many times, passing it a reference to two objects to be compared. The returned value must indicate whether object *x* is less than, equal to, or greater than *y*. To sort the process names, I created the comparer shown in Listing 7-2.

Listing 7-2: **The Comparer Class Used to Sort the Process Names**

```
public class SortByProcessName : IComparer
{
  public int Compare(object x, object y)
  {
  Process a = (Process) x;
  Process b = (Process) y;

  return a.ProcessName.CompareTo(b.ProcessName);
  }
}
```

To sort the module names, I used the comparer shown in Listing 7-3.

Listing 7-3: **The Comparer Class Used to Sort the Module Names**

```
public class SortByModuleName : IComparer
{
  public int Compare(object x, object y)
  {
    ProcessModule a = (ProcessModule) x;
    ProcessModule b = (ProcessModule) y;
    return a.ModuleName.CompareTo(b.ModuleName);
  }
}
```

Populating the TreeView

To populate the TreeView, I could have just read the process and module names and stuffed them into TreeNodes, but doing so would have forced me to keep track of the process and module details separately. Instead I created two classes — ProcessTreeNode and ModuleTreeNode — and stored the detail information in them. The tree population logic looks something like Listing 7-4.

Listing 7-4: **The Code Used to Populate the TreeView with Sorted Items**

```
private void PopulateTreeView()
{
  String rootText = "All Processes";
  rootNode = new TreeNode(rootText);

  Process[] allProcesses = Process.GetProcesses();
  Array.Sort(allProcesses, new SortByProcessName() );
  foreach (Process p in allProcesses)
  {
    TreeNode processNode = new ProcessTreeNode(p);
    rootNode.Nodes.Add(processNode);

    // convert modules from a collection to an array, so
    // we can use the Array class to sort them
    ProcessModuleCollection allModules = p.Modules;
    ProcessModule[] modules = new ProcessModule[allModules.Count];
    int i = 0;
    foreach (ProcessModule m in allModules)
      modules.SetValue(m, i++);

    // Sort the modules and add them to the tree
    Array.Sort(modules, new SortByModuleName() );
    foreach (ProcessModule m in modules)
      processNode.Nodes.Add(new ModuleTreeNode(m) );
  }
```

```
        treeView1.Nodes.Add(rootNode);
        rootNode.Expand();
}
```

To keep the code clean, I left out a few details regarding regular expressions. ProcessViewer lets you enter a regular expression to choose the processes to display. In a later section, I'll describe the regular expression logic by itself.

In the previous listing, I populated the code with two custom TreeNode classes: ProcessTreeNode and ModuleTreeNode. The two classes are trivial, in effect extending the base class TreeNode only by adding a field to reference the node details. The classes are implemented as shown in Listing 7-5.

> **Listing 7-5: The Custom TreeNode Classes Created to Hold the Process and Module Detail Information**

```
public class ProcessTreeNode : TreeNode
{
  public Process processInfo;
  public ProcessTreeNode(Process theProcess) :
        base(theProcess.ProcessName)
  {
    processInfo = theProcess;
  }
}

public class ModuleTreeNode : TreeNode
{
  public ProcessModule moduleInfo;
  public ModuleTreeNode(ProcessModule theModule) :
        base(theModule.ModuleName)
  {
    moduleInfo = theModule;
  }
}
```

In both classes, the base class is passed only the string to display in the tree.

Setting bitmaps for the TreeView items

ProcessViewer, like most Windows applications, displays a small bitmap next to each item in the TreeView in the left pane. Adding bitmaps to a TreeView is really simple. You just need to add an ImageList component to the form, add some images to it, and then set the TreeView's ImageList property to reference the ImageList component. Items in the tree can use two different bitmaps from the ImageList: one for unselected items, and one for selected items. I created two small bitmaps of yellow folders, like the ones used in Windows Explorer.

To add images to the ImageList, just select the component and click the button in the Images property. You'll see the Image Collection Editor, which lets you add, arrange, and remove images. Figure 7-6 shows the Editor after I added a couple of bitmaps.

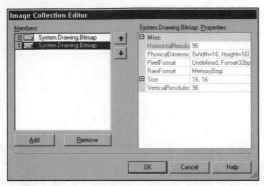

Figure 7-6: The Image Collection Editor for ImageList components

In the Property window for the TreeView, there are two fields related to bitmaps: imageIndex and selectedImageIndex. By default, they are both 0, but I want ProcessViewer to show selected items with the open folder bitmap, so I set selectedImageIndex to 1.

By setting only the TreeView's imageIndex and selectedImageIndex properties, all the nodes in the tree will be affected by default. What if you want to use different bitmaps, perhaps based on the type of item in the tree, or its level? No problem. When you add the node to the tree, just specify the index of the images to use from the ImageList. Say you wanted to use the images at index 7 and 8 in the ImageList with a certain node. You would set up the node as shown in Listing 7-6.

Listing 7-6: Setting the Bitmaps Programmatically at the Node Level

```
TreeNode node = new TreeNode ("myText");
node.ImageIndex = 7;
node.SelectedImageIndex = 8;

// assume parentNode was created earlier
parentNode.Nodes.Add(node);
```

By setting the image indexes at runtime, you can override the default bitmaps each node would use. If you have a node that requires no bitmap, just set the imageIndex and selectedImageIndex values to -1.

Note   Be sure all the images in the ImageList are the same size; otherwise, you might wind up with some bizarre vertical spacing in the tree items.

If the items in the tree are fixed, you can also add the nodes at design time. Just click the button in the TreeView's Nodes property, and you'll see the TreeNode Editor, as shown in Figure 7-7.

Figure 7-7: The Node Editor
for TreeView items

The Editor lets you edit the text and images used with each node without writing a line of code.

Setting bitmaps for the MenuItems

The standard class `MenuItem` doesn't support the display of images. Since many applications do, I'll implement a quick custom class called `MyMenuItem` that lets you specify an image contained in an ImageList. Figure 7-8 shows the File menu of ProcessViewer, on which the SaveAs entry was assigned an image.

Figure 7-8: The custom File menu, showing images as well as text

`MyMenuItem` is really easy to use. After instantiating it, you just assign it properties like ordinary `MenuItems`, as shown in Listing 7-7.

Listing 7-7: **Creating MyMenuItems Programmatically**

```
menuItemFileSaveListAs = new MyMenuItem();
menuItemFileSaveListAs.Index = 0;
menuItemFileSaveListAs.Text = "&Save List As...";
menuItemFileSaveListAs.Click +=
    new System.EventHandler(this.menuItemFileSaveListAs_Click);
menuItemFileSaveListAs.Shortcut = Shortcut.CtrlS;
menuItemFileSaveListAs.ImageList = imageList1;
menuItemFileSaveListAs.ImageIndex = 0;
```

The event handlers for `MyMenuItem` are identical to those for `MenuItem`. Listing 7-8 shows the handler for the `SaveListAs` item.

Listing 7-8: An Event Handler for MyMenuItem

```
private void menuItemFileSaveListAs_Click(object sender,
System.EventArgs e)
{
  // save info as a text file
  saveFileDialog1.InitialDirectory = Environment.CurrentDirectory;
  saveFileDialog1.FileName = "ProcessViewer.txt";
  saveFileDialog1.OverwritePrompt = true;

  if (saveFileDialog1.ShowDialog() == DialogResult.OK )
  SaveListInFile(saveFileDialog1.FileName);
}
```

By using an ImageList to manage the images, MyMenuItem avoids having to deal with the details of reading resources from image files or assemblies. Listing 7-9 shows the complete code for MyMenuItem.

Listing 7-9: The Complete Code for MyMenuItem, a Class Supporting Images in Menus

```
using System;
using System.ComponentModel;
using System.Drawing;
using System.Drawing.Text;
using System.Windows.Forms;

namespace ProcessViewer
{
  public class MyMenuItem : MenuItem
  {
    ImageList imageList;
    Font font;

    StringFormat format = new StringFormat();

    Brush unselectedBrush = SystemBrushes.Control;
    Brush selectedBrush = SystemBrushes.Highlight;
    Image image;
    int imageIndex;
    const int offsetOfShortcutText = 90;  // in pixels

    public MyMenuItem()
    {
      OwnerDraw = true;
      font = new Font("Microsoft Sans Serif", 8);
```

```
      format.HotkeyPrefix = HotkeyPrefix.Show;
      format.SetTabStops(offsetOfShortcutText, new float[] {0} );
    }

    public ImageList ImageList
    {
      get { return imageList; }
      set
      {
        imageList = value;
        setImage();
      }
    }

    public int ImageIndex
    {
      get { return imageIndex; }
      set
      {
        imageIndex = value;
        setImage();
      }
    }

    protected void setImage()
    {
      if (imageList == null)
      {
        image = null;
        return;
      }
      if (imageIndex >= imageList.Images.Count)
        imageIndex = 0;
      if (imageIndex >= imageList.Images.Count)
        image = null;
      else
        image = imageList.Images [imageIndex];
    }


    protected override void OnMeasureItem(MeasureItemEventArgs e)
    {
      e.ItemHeight = 22;

      e.ItemWidth = (int) e.Graphics.MeasureString(TextWithShortcut(),
                                                   font, 500,
format).Width;
      e.ItemWidth += 10;  // some extra space on the right
    }

    protected override void OnDrawItem(DrawItemEventArgs e)
```

Continued

Listing 7-9 *(continued)*

```
    {
      if (image != null )
        e.Graphics.DrawImage(image, e.Bounds.Left + 2, e.Bounds.Top + 2);

      Brush brush;
      Rectangle rect = e.Bounds;
      rect.X += 24;

      if ( (e.State & DrawItemState.Selected) ==
DrawItemState.Selected)
        brush = selectedBrush;
      else
        brush = unselectedBrush;

      e.Graphics.FillRectangle(brush, rect);

      brush = new SolidBrush(e.ForeColor);

      e.Graphics.DrawString(TextWithShortcut(), font, brush,
                        e.Bounds.Left + 25, e.Bounds.Top + 2,
format);
    }

    private String TextWithShortcut()
    {
      String s = Text;

      if (!ShowShortcut) return s;
      if (Shortcut == Shortcut.None) return s;


      Keys key = (Keys) Shortcut;
      return s + "\t" + keyConverter.ConvertToString(key);
    }
  }
}
```

Now for a short explanation of MyMenuItem's code. In order to change the appearance of a MenuItem, you need to set the OwnerDraw property to true. By doing so, the base class will fire two important events that you can override: OnMeasureItem and OnDrawItem.

OnMeasureItem is where the derived class computes the width and height of the menu item's screen area. My example uses the code shown in Listing 7-10.

Listing 7-10: The OnMeasureItem Event Handler for MyMenuItem

```
protected override void OnMeasureItem(MeasureItemEventArgs e)
{
  e.ItemHeight = 22;
  e.ItemWidth = (int)
             e.Graphics.MeasureString(TextWithShortcut(),
                                       font, 500,
                                       format).Width;
  e.ItemWidth += 10;  // some extra space on the right
}
```

All the method does is measure the size of the menu's text and shortcut string, and then adds a little more space to maintain a small margin on the right side. The presence of the last parameter, called format, is important. The parameter is declared and set up as shown in Listing 7-11.

Listing 7-11: The StringFormat Object Used to Format the Caption of MyMenuItem

```
const int offsetOfShortcutText = 90;  // in pixels
StringFormat format = new StringFormat();
format.HotkeyPrefix = HotkeyPrefix.Show;
format.SetTabStops(offsetOfShortcutText, new float[] {0} );
```

The format object is set up with a tab stop at the 90-pixel mark. Now look at Listing 7-12 to see how TextWithShortcut() creates the caption to be displayed:

Listing 7-12: The OnMeasureItem Event Handler for MyMenuItem

```
private String TextWithShortcut()
{
  String s = Text;

  Keys key = (Keys) Shortcut;
  return s + "\t" + keyConverter.ConvertToString(key);
}
```

The tab character is important. It lets me create the full string, without worrying about the exact positioning of the text following the tab. The OnMeasureItem handler uses the StringFormat object to determine the exact positioning and size of the text.

The last interesting piece of code is the OnDrawItem event handler, which is called when MyMenuItem needs to render itself on the screen. The code is shown in Listing 7-13.

Listing 7-13: The OnDrawItem Event Handler for MyMenuItem

```
protected override void OnDrawItem(DrawItemEventArgs e)
{
  if (image != null )
    e.Graphics.DrawImage(image, e.Bounds.Left + 2,
                                e.Bounds.Top + 2);

  Brush brush;
  Rectangle rect = e.Bounds;
  rect.X += 24;

  if ( (e.State & DrawItemState.Selected) == DrawItemState.Selected)
    brush = selectedBrush;
  else
    brush = unselectedBrush;

  e.Graphics.FillRectangle(brush, rect);

  brush = new SolidBrush(e.ForeColor);
  e.Graphics.DrawString(TextWithShortcut(), font, brush,
                        e.Bounds.Left + 25, e.Bounds.Top + 2, format);
}
```

The image is drawn first, with the method `Graphics.DrawImage()`. Then the background of the menu item is drawn with `Graphics.FillRectangle()`, using a brush whose color depends on whether the menu item is selected or not. Finally, the full text is drawn with `Graphics.DrawString()`, using the `format` parameter to lay out the text containing the tab character.

Controlling the right pane

The process and module detail windows were designed with the VS .NET Forms Designer. At runtime, I want these two windows to cover the right pane, but you can't simply drag and drop forms onto another form. An easy solution, as I mentioned earlier, is to use a *Panel* to hold all the components of the forms that need to be shown in the right pane. All you need to do is switch the parent of this Panel to the Panel covering the right pane of FormMain. I used this code in the constructor for FormMain, the window with the Explorer-like interface, as shown in Listing 7-14.

Listing 7-14: Reparenting the Child Panels at Runtime

```
public FormMain()
{
  //...

  formSystemInfo = new FormSystemInfo();
  formSystemInfo.panel1.Parent = this.panelRight;

  formProcessInfo = new FormProcessInfo();
```

```
    formProcessInfo.panel1.Parent = this.panelRight;

    formModuleInfo = new FormModuleInfo();
    formModuleInfo.panel1.Parent = this.panelRight;

    //...
}
```

When changing a Panel's parent, the Panel is effectively removed from the old window and added to the new one. The three reparented Panels then behave like any other child component of the new parent. Since the three Panels have the `Dock` property set to `Fill`, they expand to cover the entire client area of the parent Panel in the right pane. One last step is to ensure that only one of the reparented Panels is visible at a time. The `AfterSelected()` event handler for the tree is where the Panel selection logic is, and the code looks like Listing 7-15.

Listing 7-15: Choosing What to Display in the Right Pane

```
protected void treeView1_AfterSelect(object sender,
                                     System.WinForms.TreeViewEventArgs
e)
{
  if (treeView1.SelectedNode.Parent == null)
    DisplayMainPage();
  else if (treeView1.SelectedNode.Parent == rootNode)
    DisplayProcessInfo(treeView1.SelectedNode as ProcessTreeNode);
  else
    DisplayModuleInfo(treeView1.SelectedNode as ModuleTreeNode);
}

protected void DisplayMainPage()
{
  formSystemInfo.panel1.Visible = true;
  formProcessInfo.panel1.Visible = false;
  formModuleInfo.panel1.Visible = false;
}

protected void DisplayProcessInfo(ProcessTreeNode theNode)
{
  formSystemInfo.panel1.Visible = false;
  formProcessInfo.panel1.Visible = true;
  formModuleInfo.panel1.Visible = false;

  // display the process info
  formProcessInfo.DisplayInfo(theNode);
}

protected void DisplayModuleInfo(ModuleTreeNode theNode)
{
  formSystemInfo.panel1.Visible = false;
```

Continued

Listing 7-15 *(continued)*

```
formProcessInfo.panel1.Visible = false;
formModuleInfo.panel1.Visible = true;

// display the module info
formModuleInfo.DisplayInfo(theNode);
}
```

The code hides both the module and the process information Panels if the root node is selected; otherwise, one of the Panels is made visible and a method is called to display the necessary details.

Restricting the size of a form

By default, any form you create with a resizable border will let the user shrink the form down to a very small rectangle, containing only a small part of the caption bar. It doesn't make sense for ProcessViewer to have such a small size, so I added some code to restrict the minimum size. All I had to do was set the inherited property MinimumSize as shown in Listing 7-16.

Listing 7-16: Setting a Minimum Size for a Form

```
public class FormMain : System.WinForms.Form
{
  public FormMain()
  {
    InitializeComponent();

    // constructor code...

    MinimumSize = new Size(300, 200);
  }
}
```

This code sets the minimum width to 300 pixels and the minimum height to 200 pixels. There is also a property called MaximumSize that you can use to set the upper limit for the form size.

Displaying the process and module details

Let's get to the code that actually shows the data that ProcessViewer was created to show in the first place. I wrote two methods called DisplayInfo() (one in class FormProcessInfo and the other in class FormModuleInfo) to display the process and module information on the screen. I could have added the two methods to FormMain, but decided to add them to the forms whose components they need to access, as shown in Listing 7-17.

Listing 7-17: **Displaying the Process and Module Details**

```
  public FormProcessInfo()
{
  //...

  public void DisplayInfo(ProcessTreeNode theNode)
  {
    labelProcessName.Text = theNode.processInfo.ProcessName;
    labelProcessID.Text = theNode.processInfo.Id.ToString();
    labelStartedOn.Text = theNode.processInfo.StartTime.Date.ToString();


    labelNumberOfThreads.Text = theNode.processInfo.Threads.Length.ToString();

    TimeSpan t = theNode.processInfo.TotalProcessorTime;
    if (t.Days > 0)
      labelTotalProcessorTime.Text =

          String.Format("{0} Days {1:00}:{2:00}:{3:00}",
                        t.Days, t.Hours, t.Minutes, t.Seconds);
    else
      labelTotalProcessorTime.Text =
          String.Format("{0:00}:{1:00}:{2:00}",
                        t.Hours, t.Minutes, t.Seconds);


    if ( (theNode.processInfo.MainWindowTitle == null) ||
         (!theNode.processInfo.MainWindowTitle.Equals("")  ) )
      labelMainWindowTitle.Text = theNode.processInfo.MainWindowTitle;
    else
      labelMainWindowTitle.Text = "<none>";

    // Beta 2 bug workaround: can't reference Modules property for Idle process
    if (theNode.processInfo.ProcessName.Equals("Idle") )
      labelMainModule.Text = "<none>";
    else {
      if ( (theNode.processInfo.Modules != null) &&
           (theNode.processInfo.Modules.Length > 0) )
        labelMainModule.Text = theNode.processInfo.MainModule.FileName
      else
        labelMainModule.Text = "<none>";
    }

    labelPriority.Text = theNode.processInfo.BasePriority.ToString();
  }
}


public class FormModuleInfo : System.WinForms.Form
{
```

Continued

Listing 7-17 *(continued)*

```
//...

public void DisplayInfo(ModuleTreeNode theNode)
{
  labelModuleName.Text = theNode.moduleInfo.ModuleName;
  labelCompanyName.Text = theNode.moduleInfo.FileVersionInfo.CompanyName;
  labelLoadedFromFile.Text = theNode.moduleInfo.FileVersionInfo.FileName;
  labelFileVersion.Text = theNode.moduleInfo.FileVersionInfo.FileVersion;

  if (!theNode.moduleInfo.FileVersionInfo.FileDescription.Equals("") )
    labelFileDescription.Text =
theNode.moduleInfo.FileVersionInfo.FileDescription;
  else
    labelFileDescription.Text = "<none>";


  File f = new File(theNode.moduleInfo.FileVersionInfo.FileName);
  labelFileTimestamp.Text = f.CreationTime.ToString();
  labelFileSize.Text = f.Length.ToString();
  }
 }
```

It is much better to keep the DisplayInfo() methods off the main form for two reasons. First, the methods need to access Windows Form components like Label that are declared private by default on each form. Second, the main form is really a container for the right-pane windows and should be used primarily to select the right-pane window, based on which node is selected in the tree. This way, the main form remains fairly simple, regardless of how many windows there are for the right pane.

Accessing command-line arguments

When your application is run from the command line, you may want to allow users to specify one or more arguments. There are two ways to access command-line arguments at runtime: using the args parameter array passed to the Main() method, or using the Environment class.

The method Main() is a public static method, which is declared as shown in Listing 7-18.

Listing 7-18: The Main() Method of a C# Application

```
public class FormMain : System.WinForms.Form
{

  public static void Main(string[] args)
  {
    // run the application...
  }
}
```

The `args` parameter holds all the command-line arguments. Arguments entered on the command line must be separated by white space (a space or a tab). If an argument needs to contain spaces, it can be enclosed in quotes, like this: `"my    parameter"`. The system will strip the quotes from the parameter before putting it in the `args` array. If you need to embed a quote character in a command-line argument, prefix it with a backslash, like this: `\"`.

Note
The `args` parameter passed to `Main()` contains *only* arguments. If you're a C or C++ programmer, you might expect the first item in the array to be the name of the application, which would be the string "ProcessViewer" in my example. This is not the case in Visual C#. The name of the application is not included in the `args` array.

Table 7-1 gives a few examples of command entered in a Command Prompt box, with the corresponding items you would find in the `args` array.

Table 7-1: Command-Line Examples

Command-Line	Contents of the args Array
ProcessViewer red and green	args [0] = red
	args [1] = and
	args [2] = green
ProcessViewer "red and green" and blue	args [0] = red and green
	args [1] = and
	args [2] = blue
ProcessViewer \"hello\"	args [0] = "hello"

The other way to access command-line arguments is with the `Environment` class, with the static method `GetCommandLineArgs()`, which returns a String array similar to the `args` parameter passed to `Main()`, with one difference: *The first entry is the name of the executable* (as in `ProcessViewer`). To reinforce this small but significant difference, Table 7-2 shows the command-line examples listed earlier for the `args` parameter, with the corresponding array returned by `GetCommandLineArgs()`.

Table 7-2: Command-Line Examples and Environment.GetCommandLineArgs()

Command-Line	Contents of the Array Returned by GetCommandLineArgs()
ProcessViewer red and green	args [0] = ProcessViewer
	args [1] = red
	args [2] = and
	args [3] = green

Continued

Table 7-2 *(continued)*

Command-Line	*Contents of the Array Returned by GetCommandLineArgs()*
ProcessViewer "red and green" and blue	args [0] = ProcessViewer
	args [1] = red and green
	args [2] = and
	args [3] = blue
ProcessViewer \"hello\"	args [0] = ProcessViewer
	args [1] = "hello"

The name of the executable may or may not include a path. For example, on a Windows 2000 platform, with the prerelease .NET code I'm using, I get two different behaviors: The executable name includes the path when using the Debug ⇨ Start command in VS .NET, but not when running from a DOS box. In any case, if you need the directory path of the executable, you can get it with `Environment.CurrentDirectory`.

ProcessViewer uses command-line arguments to let the user specify which processes to list. If no arguments are entered, all the processes are shown; otherwise, the argument is assumed to be a regular expression that identifies the pattern of the process names to list.

Listing 7-19 shows the ProcessViewer code that reads the command-line arguments.

Listing 7-19: Reading the Command-Line Arguments with GetCommandLineArgs()

```
protected String RegularExpressionFromCommandLine()
{
  if (Environment.GetCommandLineArgs().Length <= 1)
    return "";

  String[] args = Environment.GetCommandLineArgs();
  return args [1];
}
```

For those readers who might be new to regular expressions, I'll make a short digression to discuss them.

Using regular expressions

A *regular expression* is a string containing a special type of pattern. The built-in class `System.Text.RegularExpressions.Regex` can use this pattern and tell you whether a string matches it or not. Regular expressions can get pretty esoteric, and a full discussion of them is beyond the scope of this book, but I will discuss a few commonly used expressions.

Regular expressions can specify a sequence of characters. For example the expression `abc` would match any string containing *abc,* like the strings `abcde`, `myabc`, and `1abc2`.

Regular expressions can use placeholders to match against any character. For example "`.`" matches any single character. Quantifier symbols can be used to indicate how many times a character or group of characters must appear. For example, "`*`" indicates zero or more repetitions of a character or group of characters, while "`+`" indicates one or more repetitions. The expression `a.` would match any string containing the letter *a* followed by another character. The expression `a.*` would match any string containing the letter *a* followed by zero or more characters. The expression `a.+` would match any string containing the letter *a* followed by one or more characters.

Regular expressions can also match against a set of characters, using the bracket notation. For example the expression `[e-h]` would match any string containing the lowercase letters *e, f, g,* or *h*. Sets can also be concatenated, so the expression `[e-hA-C]` would match any string containing the lowercase letters *e, f, g, h,* or the uppercase letters *A, B, C.* The special character "`^`" is used to match against characters *not* in a set, so the expression `[^s-u]` would match any string that didn't contain the characters *s, t, u.*

You can also specify where a pattern needs to be in a string for a match to be valid. The character "`^`", used outside the bracket notation, indicates the beginning of a string. The character "`$`" indicates the end of a string. For example, the expression `^a` would match any string starting with a lowercase *a;* the expression `a$` would match any string ending with the lowercase character *a.*

You can also specify alternative patterns, using the "`|`" character. For example, the expression `(before|after)` would match the strings *"before you"* and *"after you".*

Note Spaces are significant in a regular expression, so the patterns `(before|after)` and `(before | after)` are different.

Table 7-3 shows a number of examples of simple regular expressions.

Table 7-3: Simple Regular Expressions with Class Regex

Expression	Meaning	Example
abc	Any occurrence of *abc.*	abcdef 123abc 123abcdef
(abc)*def	Match any string starting with zero or more repetitions of abc followed by *def.*	abcdef def abcabcabcdef
(ab)+def	Match any string starting with one or more repetitions of *ab* followed by *def.*	abdef abababdef
[a-c]def	Match any string starting with *a, b,* or *c* followed by *def.*	adef bdef cdef

Continued

Table 7-3 *(continued)*

Expression	Meaning	Example
a.c	Match any character preceded by the letter *a* and followed by *c*.	abc azc 123ahcdd
a.*c	Match any string containing the letters *a* and *c*, *separated by zero or more characters.*	acc bacd babdc babbcd
a.+c	Match any string containing the letter *a*, followed by at least one character, and then the letter *c*.	babdc babbcd
[a-d]	Match any string containing the letters *a*, *b*, *c*, or *d*.	a straight hidden
[^a-d]	Match any string that does *not* containing the letter *a*, *b*, *c*, or *d*.	John SUPER listen
^s	Match any string starting with the letter *s*.	"sails are down!"
$s	Match any string ending with the letter *s*.	"A handful of dollars"
(a|b)	Match any string containing the letter *a* or *b* (or both).	"the best" table apple
(abc){3}	Match any string containing three repetitions of *abc*.	abcabcabc abcabcabcvvvv
(abc)?def	Match any string that starts with an optional *abc* string, followed by *def*.	abcdef def defkkkk

Table 7-4 shows a number of expressions that identify commonly used types of data.

Table 7-4: Useful Regular Expressions with Class Regex

Expression	Description
[0-9]*	An unsigned integer number (such as 1234) or a blank string.
[0-9]+	An unsigned integer number (such as 1234).
[+-]?[0-9]+	An integer number preceded by an optional + or − sign (such as −1234).
[0-9a-fA-F]*	A hexadecimal number (such as F200a), or a blank string.
[0-9a-fA-F]{8}	An 8-digit hexadecimal number (such as F200DD88).

Expression	Description
[0-9]{3}-[0-9]{3}-[0-9]{4}	A telephone number with the area code (such as 111-333-5555).
([0-9]{3}-)?[0-9]{3}-[0-9]{4}	A telephone number with optional area code (such as 111-333-5555 or 333-5555).
[0-9]{5}	A 5-digit U.S. Postal Code (such as 12345).
[0-9]{5}(-[0-9]{4})?	A 5-digit U.S. Postal Code with optional +4 digits (such as 12345-1234).

ProcessViewer interprets any command-line arguments as a regular expression and uses the expression to filter the process names displayed. The filtering code is very simple, and looks like Listing 7-20.

Listing 7-20: Using a Regex Object to Filter the Process Names Displayed

```
using System.Text.RegularExpressions;

private void PopulateTreeView()
{
  String regularExpression = RegularExpressionFromCommandLine();

  Regex regExp = new Regex(regularExpression);

  foreach (Process p in Process.GetProcesses() )
  {
    if (!regExp.IsMatch(p.ProcessName) )
      continue;  // skip this process

    // display the process...
  }
}
```

You need to import the namespace System.Text.RegularExpressions to use the regular expression classes. The code in the previous listing uses the method Regex.IsMatch(String) to test process names against the regular expression. The value returned will be true only if the string matches the expression.

Regular expressions are a very powerful tool for processing text. Regex not only will tell you if a string matches an expression, but also has a method called Matches() that returns an array of all items where a match was found. For example, the code:

```
Regex re = new Regex("o.");
String w = "what a wonderful world";
MatchCollection matches = re.Matches(w);
StringCollection sc = new StringCollection();
foreach (Match m in matches)
  sc.Add(m.ToString() );
```

will locate the strings `"on"` and `"or"` in "what a wonderful world" and store them in the `StringCollection`. Often, regular expressions are used to find and replace characters in a string. The class `Regex` has a method called that does all the work for you. For example, the code

```
Regex re = new Regex(@"^w");  // the expression to replace
String changedString = re.Replace("what a wonderful world", "W");
```

will change the first character of the string to `"W"`:

```
"What a wonderful world"
```

The "@" symbol in `new Regex(@"^w")` has nothing to do with regular expressions. It just tells the compiler to take the following string literally. To change the remaining words to start with an uppercase *W*, you could use the code

```
Regex re = new Regex(@" w");  // the expression to replace: notice the
space!
String changedString = re.Replace("What a wonderful world", " W");
```

which returns

```
What a Wonderful World
```

As I indicated earlier, regular expressions are a rich subject, requiring much more space to describe in depth than I have in this book. Hopefully the examples shown will be enough to get you interested in using them in your own applications.

Getting information about the operating system

There are times when an application needs to behave differently based on which operating system the program is running under. For example, in the previous section, I noted that the first item returned by `Environment.GetCommandLineArgs()` is the name of the executable. Under Windows 2000, the name includes the full path. Under Windows 95, it doesn't.

To get operating system information, you can read the property `Environment.OSVersion`, which returns an object of type `OperatingSystem`. The class has properties indicating which Windows platform is being used, and its version, as shown in Table 7-5.

Table 7-5: Important Properties of Class OperatingSystem

OperatingSystem Property	Value	Meaning
Platform	PlatformID.Win32NT	NT or Win2000
	PlatformID.Win32S	Win32 on Win16
	PlatformID.Win32Windows	Win95, 98, ME
Version	Windows version	Includes the major and minor version numbers, and the build number

The version of Windows 2000 I use returns `PlatformID.Win32NT` for the `Platform` property and `"5.0.0.2195"` for the `Version` property. Listing 7-21 shows the code used by ProcessViewer to retrieve the operating system type and version.

Listing 7-21: How ProcessViewer Determines the Operating System Type and Version

```
public FormGeneralInfo()
{
  // initialization code...

  labelOS.Text = GetPlatformName() + " Version " +
                 Environment.OSVersion.Version;
}

protected String GetPlatformName()
{
  OperatingSystem os = Environment.OSVersion;
  String osName;
  switch (os.Platform)
  {
    case PlatformID.Win32NT:
      if (os.Version.Major <= 4)
        osName = "Windows NT";
      else if (os.Version.Major == 5)
        osName = "Windows 2000";
      else
        osName = "New version of Windows!";
      break;

    case PlatformID.Win32S:
      osName = "Win32S";
      break;

    case PlatformID.Win32Windows:
      osName = "Windows 95, 98 or ME";
      break;

    default:
      osName = "Unknown platform";
  }
  return osName;
}
```

The `Version` object returned by `Environment.OSVersion.Version` has four properties to access the `Major`, `Minor`, `Release`, and `Build` numbers.

Determining the current directory

When an application is first started up, the current directory is the one containing the executable program. During execution, the current directory can change. For example, if your program displays a File Open or File Save common dialog box, the user can use it to change directories. The directory chosen when the OK button is clicked will become the new current directory. Finding out what the current directory is set to is trivial: Just use the property `Environment.CurrentDirectory`.

Retrieving environment variables

Environment variables are used for storing settings in memory that can be read by all applications. Back in the days of DOS batch files (which still exist, but are being increasingly displaced by Windows Scripting programs), a common way of passing parameters to DOS programs was through environment variables. The environment consists of a set of strings defined as key=value pairs. Examples of environment settings include the `PATH`, `WINDIR`, and `SystemRoot` variables. To get a list of all the environment variables in your system, open a DOS box and type the following command:

```
set
```

On my computer, I get the list shown in Listing 7-22.

Listing 7-22: A Sample List of Environment Variables

```
ALLUSERSPROFILE=C:\Documents and Settings\All Users.WINNT
APPDATA=C:\Documents and Settings\Ted.DANIELLE\Application Data
CLASSPATH=C:\PROGRA~1\Borland\vbroker\\lib\vbcpp.jar
CommonProgramFiles=C:\Program Files\Common Files
COMPUTERNAME=DANIELLE
ComSpec=C:\WINNT\system32\cmd.exe
CORPATH=C:\WINNT\Microsoft.NET\Framework\v1.0.2204\
HOMEDRIVE=C:
HOMEPATH=\
INCLUDE=C:\Program Files\Microsoft.Net\FrameworkSDK\include\
LIB=C:\Program Files\Microsoft.Net\FrameworkSDK\Lib\
LOGONSERVER=\\DANIELLE
netsamplepath=C:\PROGRA~1\MICROS~1.NET\FRAMEW~1\Samples
netsdk=C:\PROGRA~1\MICROS~1.NET\FRAMEW~1\
NUMBER_OF_PROCESSORS=1
OANOCACHE=1
OS=Windows_NT
Os2LibPath=C:\WINNT\system32\os2\dll;
Path=C:\Program Files\Microsoft.Net\FrameworkSDK\Bin\;...other
directories...
PATHEXT=.COM;.EXE;.BAT;.CMD;.VBS;.VBE;.JS;.JSE;.WSF;.WSH
PROCESSOR_ARCHITECTURE=x86
PROCESSOR_IDENTIFIER=x86 Family 6 Model 6 Stepping 5, GenuineIntel
PROCESSOR_LEVEL=6
PROCESSOR_REVISION=0605
ProgramFiles=C:\Program Files
PROMPT=$P$G
SystemDrive=C:
SystemRoot=C:\WINNT
```

```
TEMP=C:\DOCUME~1\TED~1.DAN\LOCALS~1\Temp
TMP=C:\DOCUME~1\TED~1.DAN\LOCALS~1\Temp
USERDNSDOMAIN=mydomain.local
USERDOMAIN=MYDOMAIN
USERNAME=Ted
USERPROFILE=C:\Documents and Settings\Ted.DANIELLE
VSCOMNTOOLS="C:\Program Files\Microsoft Visual
Studio.NET\Common7\Tools\"
windir=C:\WINNT
```

The .NET Framework makes it easy to access environment variables, using the method `Environment.GetEnvironmentVariables()`, as shown in Listing 7-23.

Listing 7-23: **Reading All the Environment Variables as (key, value) Pairs**

```
foreach (DictionaryEntry d in Environment.GetEnvironmentVariables() )
{
  String nextKey = d.Key;
  String nextValue = d.Value;
}
```

The key is the name of the variable. For example, the last variable in Listing 7-22 has the following settings:

```
key="windir"
value="C:\WINNT"
```

To locate a variable by key, you can use the `IDictionary` interface's default indexer, as shown in Listing 7-24.

Listing 7-24: **Looking Up the Value of a Specific Environment Variable**

```
IDictionary dictionary = Environment.GetEnvironmentVariables();
String path = (String) dictionary ["Path"];
String computerName = (String) dictionary ["COMPUTERNAME"];
```

Keep in mind that uppercase and lowercase are significant in the key string, and must match an environment variable name exactly; otherwise, you'll get a `null` for the `String` object. Also, the key may not use the same case displayed in a DOS box. For example, the `PATH` variable is shown in all-uppercase in a DOS box, but has the key "Path" in the dictionary returned by `GetEnvironmentVariables()`. If you're not sure about the case of an environment variable, you can iterate over the dictionary and use a case-insensitive compare on each key, as shown in Listing 7-25.

Listing 7-25: Using a Case-Insensitive String Compare to Find the Value of an Environment Variable

```
String path = null;

foreach (DictionaryEntry de in dictionary)
{
  if (de.Key.ToString().ToLower().Equals("path") )
  {
    path = (String) de.Value;
    break;
  }
}
```

After the `foreach` loop, you would need to see if the `path` object is `null` before using it. The object would be `null` if no environment with the desired key existed.

Determining if a mouse is attached to the system

Some types of programs, like games and other graphics applications, require a mouse to be attached to the user's computer. Some programs behave differently based on whether a mouse is available. Checking for the presence of a mouse is easy, and requires only one line of code:

```
bool mousePresent = SystemInformation.MousePresent;
```

If a mouse is detected, you can get find out whether it has a wheel and how many buttons it has using the following code:

```
int numberOfMouseButtons = SystemInformation.MouseButtons;
bool mouseWheelPresent = SystemInformation.MouseWheelPresent
```

There are few other methods in `SystemInformation` that give information about the mouse. I won't discuss them here, but if you're interested, check out the VS .NET documentation on the following `SystemInformation` properties: `MouseButtonsSwapped`, `MouseWheelScrollLines`, and `NativeMouseWheelSupport`.

Determining if the user's system is connected to a network

Getting information on whether a computer is connected to a network is another no-brainer. All you need is one line of code:

```
bool networkIsAvailble = SystemInformation.Network;
```

Getting a list of logical drives

Logical drives include both physical disk drives like A: and C:, as well as mapped drives. To get a list of the logical drives, use the code:

```
String[] drives = Environment.GetLogicalDrives();
```

The program `ProcessViewer` adds the list of logical drives to a combo box using the following code:

```
foreach (String s in Environment.GetLogicalDrives() )
  comboBoxLogicalDrives.Items.Add(s);
```

Using text files

ProcessViewer has a File Save menu command that lets you save in a text file a list of the modules associated with the first process. Like so many other things in the .NET Framework, creating a text file and writing to it is very easy. Listing 7-26 shows the code used by ProcessViewer to save the process information.

Listing 7-26: The ProcessViewer Code Used to Save Information to a Text File

```
private void menuItemFileSaveListAs_Click(object sender, System.EventArgs e)
{
  // save info as a text file
  saveFileDialog1.InitialDirectory = Environment.CurrentDirectory;
  saveFileDialog1.FileName = "ProcessViewer.txt";
  saveFileDialog1.OverwritePrompt = true;

  if (saveFileDialog1.ShowDialog() == DialogResult.OK )
    SaveListInFile(saveFileDialog1.FileName);
}

protected void SaveListInFile(String theFilename)
{
  StreamWriter stream = null;
  try
  {
    stream = File.CreateText(theFilename);
  }
  catch (Exception e)
  {

    MessageBox.Show("Error creating file: " + e.Message);
    return;
  }


  StringCollection collection = GetTextCollection();
  foreach(String s in collection)
    stream.WriteLine(s);
  stream.Close();
}

protected StringCollection GetTextCollection()
{
```

Continued

Listing 7-26 *(continued)*

```
StringCollection strings = new StringCollection();

TreeNode firstProcessNode = treeView1.Nodes [0].Nodes [0];
String header1 = String.Format("List of Modules loaded by Process [{0}]",
                               firstProcessNode.Text);
String header2 = String.Format("on the computer [{0}] as of {1}",
                               SystemInformation.ComputerName,
                               DateTime.Now);
strings.Add(header1);
strings.Add(header2);
strings.Add("");

strings.Add(firstProcessNode.Text);
foreach (TreeNode m in firstProcessNode.Nodes)
  strings.Add("      " + m.Text);
strings.Add("");
strings.Add("--- end of list");
return strings;
}
```

The code has lots of interesting details. First, to support file operations, make sure you import the namespace System.IO:

```
using System.IO;
```

To create a file for writing, you create a StreamWriter by calling File.CreateText(), and then use the StreamWriter as shown in Listing 7-27.

Listing 7-27: Saving Text in a Text File

```
StreamWriter stream = null;
try
{
  stream = File.CreateText(theFilename);
}
catch (Exception e)
{
  MessageBox.Show("Error creating file: " + e.Message);
  return;
}

// write all the lines of text
stream.WriteLine(...);

stream.Close();
```

You should always put a `try` block around the call to `File.CreateText(String)`, because exceptions can occur if the filename is invalid or the code is running with insufficient privileges to create files. Also, keep in mind that if a file already exists with the name passed to `File.CreateText(String)`, the file will be overwritten.

The method `GetTextCollection()` puts all the text to print into a StringCollection. ProcessViewer calls the method three different times: when saving to a file, when printing, and when print previewing.

Although ProcessViewer doesn't show how to read files, the procedure is straightforward. Just create a StreamReader by calling `File.OpenText()`, and then use the StreamReader as shown in Listing 7-28.

Listing 7-28: **Reading a Text File**

```
String s;
String filename = @"c:\MyTextFile.txt";
if (File.FileExists(filename) )
{
  try
  {
    StreamReader streamReader = File.OpenText(filename);
    while ( (s = streamReader.ReadLine() ) != null)
    {
 // s contains the next line of text from the file
    }
    streamReader.Close();
  }
  catch (Exception e)
  {
    MessageBox.Show("An exception occurred: " + e.Message);
  }
}
```

The method `StreamReader.ReadLine()` returns `null` when the end of the file is reached. It also strips off the end-of-line sequence, which is either \n (the ASCII linefeed character) or \r\n (carriage return followed by linefeed). Remember to call `StreamReader.Close()` when you're finished reading the file.

To check if a file exists, use the static method `File.FileExists(String)`, passing it the full path and filename of the file to check for.

Cut, Copy, and Paste

An application like ProcessViewer has no need for Cut and Paste, but many applications deal with the Windows Clipboard in one way or the other. To show how to transfer data to and from the Clipboard, I added some code to ProcessViewer to support Copy and Paste. The Copy operation is similar to a Cut, except the latter removes data from the application after copying it to the Clipboard. A Copy operation can take as little as one line of code. Listing 7-29 shows a typical Edit ⇨ Copy menu command handler.

Listing 7-29: **Copying a String to the Clipboard**

```
protected void menuItemEditCopy_Click (object sender, System.EventArgs
e)
{
  String text = "text to copy";  // get some arbitrary text
  Clipboard.SetDataObject(text); // copy it to the clipboard
}
```

You can copy other types of data just as easily, including bitmaps, HTML code, XML, and even complete objects (but only if they can be serialized).

Pasting data from the Clipboard into an application is a little more complicated than cutting or copying data, because you have to check to see if the Clipboard has data in a format you can deal with. Listing 7-30 shows the code I used in ProcessViewer.

Listing 7-30: **Getting Text from the Clipboard**

```
protected void menuItemEditPaste_Click (object sender, System.EventArgs e)
{

  IDataObject clipboardData = Clipboard.GetDataObject();
  String text;

  // see if the clipboard has any text

  if (clipboardData.GetDataPresent(DataFormats.Text) )
    // get the text

    text = (String) clipboardData.GetData(DataFormats.Text);

  else
    text = "No text available on clipboard";
  MessageBox.Show(text, "Clipboard Data");
}
```

You always use an `IDataObject` interface to get data from the Clipboard. The same interface is also used in drag and drop operations. Use the `IDataObject.GetDataPresent(DataFormats)` method to find out if a given type of data is available. If data is available, you can use the `IDataObject.GetData(DataFormats)` method to get it. You could check for different types of data, based on the order of preference of your application. You don't have to use `GetDataPresent()` before calling `GetData()`. If you omit the call to `GetDataPresent()`, make sure to check the object returned by `GetData()` to see if it is `null`.

Table 7-6 lists some of the commonly used data types that can be used with both `IDataObject.GetDataPresent()` and `IDataObject.GetData()`. The right column shows the type of object you'll get back from `IDataObject.GetData()` for each type of data requested.

Table 7-6: Common Data Types Used in Paste Operations

Data Type	Type Returned
DataFormats.Bitmap	System.Drawing.Bitmap
DataFormats.DIB	System.Drawing.Bitmap
DataFormats.FileDrop	System.String[]
DataFormats.HTML	System.String
DataFormats.MetafilePict	System.IO.Memory
DataFormats.Text	System.String
DataFormats.UnicodeText	System.String

There are other data types you can use. You might want to check the section titled "Supporting Drag-and-Drop," in Chapter 9, for additional details on DataFormats and data types available through the IDataObject interface.

Printing

Adding support for printing to an application can range in difficulty from simple to moderate. If you just need to preview and print unformatted text, the process is pretty easy. If you need to support formatted text or graphics, it gets a little harder. It gets even harder if you need to support other options, such as

✦ Scaling

✦ Panning

✦ Rotation

✦ Other graphics features

Since this is a book on general component-based development, I'll limit my discussion to the simpler and more common requirements of printing. I'll use ProcessViewer to show how to print a text document, and how to preview the document on the screen.

The .NET Framework has built-in classes to support print preview and printing, including dialog boxes for printer selection, printer setup, and page layout. The Print Preview window is a handy form that presents a fairly complete user interface, supporting zooming and multiple page previewing. Figure 7-9 shows the Print Preview form displayed by ProcessViewer.

Customizing the Print Preview dialog box is easy. Just derive a class from it, and add or change the necessary features.

The built-in Print dialog box allows the user to select a printer, choose which part of a document to print, and specify how many copies to make. The Print dialog box displayed in ProcessViewer looks like Figure 7-10.

The Print dialog box is one of the so-called *common dialogs* built-into the Windows platform. Common dialog boxes are not new — most of them have been around since Windows 3.1.

Figure 7-9: The built-in Print Preview form displayed by ProcessViewer

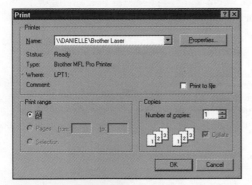

Figure 7-10: The Print dialog box displayed in ProcessViewer

Let's take a look at the component architecture used in the .NET Framework to support printing and previewing. The central class used is `System.Drawing.Printing.PrintDocument`. The interaction diagram in Figure 7-11 shows the sequence of calls between `PrintDocument` and the other classes involved in printing.

The diagram assumes the print process is initiated by calling the `Print()` method in the MainForm. The class called `MyPrintDocument` is derived from `PrintDocument`. The base class `PrintDocument` handles the `Print()` method and starts the printing process by starting a PrintController, which interacts with the Windows print engine and the printer's device driver. The PrintController then calls event handlers in `MyPrintDocument` during the various phases of printing.

`OnBeginPrint()` is called to let the application initialize variables at the last moment before printing actually starts. The event handler is passed an object of type `PrintEventArgs` that has a Cancel property. Setting it to true will abort printing before any pages are printed.

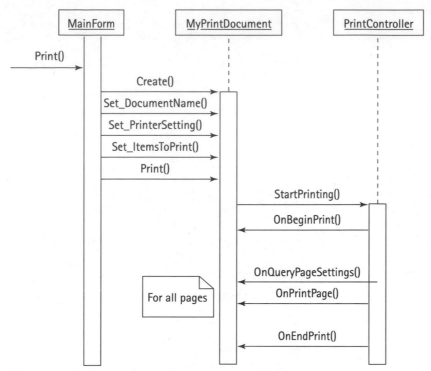

Figure 7-11: What happens when you print a document

After `OnBeginPrint()` is called, the PrintController goes into a loop, calling `OnQueryPageSettings()` and `OnPrintPage()` for each page to be printed. `OnQueryPageSettings()` is passed the usual `PrintEventArgs` object, allowing you to cancel printing on any page, as with `OnBeginPrint()`. The real purpose of `OnQueryPageSettings()` is to let you change properties of the PrintController between pages. For example, you could change the page orientation to landscape, or change the page size. Most applications don't change page settings in the middle of a print job, but the .NET Framework gives you an easy way to do so if you need to.

The real meat and potatoes of printing is the `OnPrintPage()` handler. This method is passed an object of type `PrintPageEventArgs`, which contains some very important properties. One is the `Graphics` context that your code uses to draw each page. Another is the `HasMorePages` flag that you can set to false when you want to stop printing.

`OnEndPrint()` is called when printing has finished. Since the printing process is asynchronous, once the application calls `PrintDocument.Print()`, it doesn't know when the print job is done. You could use the `OnEndPrint()` handler to notify the application that printing has finished.

Listing 7-31 shows the implementation of class `MyPrintDocument` used in ProcessViewer.

Listing 7-31: The Class Used for Printing in ProcessViewer

```
namespace ProcessViewer
{
  using System;
  using System.Drawing;
  using System.ComponentModel;
  using System.Collections;
  using System.Core;
  using System.Configuration;
  using System.Diagnostics;
  using System.Drawing.Printing;

  public class MyPrintDocument : PrintDocument
  {
    private void InitializeComponent()   { }

    Font font;
    StringCollection strings;
    int linesPerPage = 0;
    int totalLinesPrinted;
    float lineHeight;

    public MyPrintDocument(String theDocumentName,
                           StringCollection theStringsToPrint,
                           PrinterSettings thePrinterSettings)
    {
      DocumentName = theDocumentName;  // name displayed while printing
      strings = theStringsToPrint;
      PrinterSettings = thePrinterSettings;
      font = new Font("Courier New", 10);
    }

    // setup any last minute things before printing starts
    protected override void OnBeginPrint(PrintEventArgs ev)
    {
      base.OnBeginPrint(ev);

      totalLinesPrinted = 0;
    }

    // clean up after printing is finished
    protected override void OnEndPrint(PrintEventArgs ev)
    {
      base.OnEndPrint(ev);

      // nothing to do in this demo...
    }

    protected override void OnQueryPageSettings(PrintEventArgs ev)
    {
      base.OnQueryPageSettings(ev);
```

```
      // nothing to do in this demo...
    }

    // print each page
    protected override void OnPrintPage(PrintPageEventArgs ev)
    {
      base.OnPrintPage(ev);

      float y;
      float leftMargin = ev.MarginBounds.Left;
      float topMargin = ev.MarginBounds.Top;
      StringFormat format = new StringFormat

      if (lineHeight == 0)
      {
        lineHeight = font.GetHeight(ev.Graphics);
        if (lineHeight == 0)
          throw new Exception("lineHeight is zero!");
        linesPerPage = (int) (ev.MarginBounds.Height / lineHeight);
      }

      for (int lineNumber = 0; lineNumber < linesPerPage; lineNumber++)
      {
        if (totalLinesPrinted >= strings.Count)
          break;
        y = topMargin + lineNumber * lineHeight;
        String text = strings [totalLinesPrinted++];

        ev.Graphics.DrawString(text, font, Brushes.Black,
                               leftMargin, y, new StringFormat());
      }


      ev.HasMorePages = (totalLinesPrinted < strings.Count) ? true : false;
    }
  }
}
```

The class `MyPrintDocument` is used both for printing and print previewing. I set it up to print the text contained in a `StringCollection`, but it could be changed to print graphics objects, richly formatted text, or the contents of a file. Listing 7-32 shows the code in the main form that handles the File ⇨ Print menu command:

Listing 7-32: Handling the File ⇨ Print Command in ProcessViewer

```
protected void menuItemPrint_Click(object sender, System.EventArgs e)
{
  printDialog1.PrinterSettings = new PrinterSettings();
  if (printDialog1.ShowDialog() != DialogResult.OK)
```

Continued

Listing 7-32 *(continued)*

```
      return;

  StringCollection textToPrint = GetTextCollection();

  try {
    MyPrintDocument textPrinter =
        new MyPrintDocument(Text, textToPrint, printDialog1.PrinterSettings);
    textPrinter.Print();
  }
  catch(Exception ex) {
    MessageBox.Show("Exception raised while printing: " + ex.Message);
  }
}
```

The first parameter passed to the `MyPrintDocument` constructor is the string that appears in the Printing dialog box displayed by the PrintController, as shown in Figure 7-12.

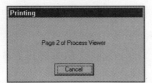

Figure 7-12: The Printing dialog box showing the name of the document being printed

The interaction diagram for Print Preview is similar to the one for printing. The same `MyPrintDocument` class is used, but there is an additional `PrintPreviewDialog` object, as shown in Figure 7-13.

Listing 7-33 shows the code used in ProcessViewer to support Print Preview.

Listing 7-33: How ProcessViewer Handles Print Preview

```
protected void menuItemFilePrintPreview_Click (object sender,
                                               System.EventArgs e)
{
  try
  {
    PrintPreviewDialog previewDialog = new PrintPreviewDialog();
    PrinterSettings printerSettings = new PrinterSettings();
    StringCollection textToPrint = GetTextCollection();
    previewDialog.Document =
        new MyPrintDocument(Text, textToPrint, printerSettings);

    previewDialog.ShowDialog();
  }
```

```
catch(Exception ex)
{
  MessageBox.Show("Exception during print preview: " + ex.Message);
}
}
```

The .NET Framework uses the same architecture to support both printing and plotting. You can find out if a printing device is a plotter by checking the property `PrinterSettings.IsPlotter`.

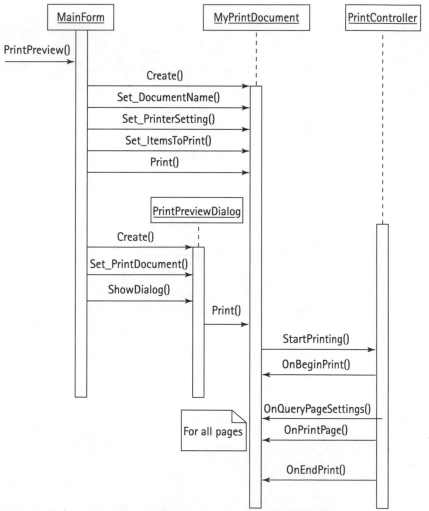

Figure 7-13: What happens when you preview a document

The Complete Code for ProcessViewer

Up to this point, I've shown a lot of fragments of the ProcessViewer code. The quasi-complete code is shown in Listings 7-34 through 7-39. Due to space limitations, I had to leave out the code that creates and initializes the various GUI controls.

Listing 7-34: The Complete Code for FormMain

```
using System;
using System.Drawing;
using System.Collections;
using System.ComponentModel;
using System.Windows.Forms;
using System.Data;
using System.Diagnostics;
using System.IO;
using System.Text.RegularExpressions;
using System.Drawing.Printing;
using System.Collections.Specialized;

namespace ProcessViewer
{
  public class FormMain : System.Windows.Forms.Form
  {
    // declare all the standardGUI controls...

    // custom MenuItems
    private MyMenuItem menuItemFileSaveListAs;
    private MenuItem   menuItemFileBreak1 = new MenuItem("-");
    private MyMenuItem menuItemFilePrintPreview;
    private MyMenuItem menuItemFilePrint;
    private MenuItem   menuItemFileBreak2 = new MenuItem("-");
    private MyMenuItem menuItemFileExit;


    private TreeNode rootNode;
    private FormSystemInfo formSystemInfo;
    private FormProcessInfo formProcessInfo;
    private FormModuleInfo formModuleInfo;

    public FormMain()
    {
InitializeComponent();

        AddCustomFileMenuItems();

MinimumSize = new Size(300, 200);

formSystemInfo = new FormSystemInfo();
formSystemInfo.panel1.Parent = this.panelRight;
```

```
formProcessInfo = new FormProcessInfo();
formProcessInfo.panel1.Parent = this.panelRight;

formModuleInfo = new FormModuleInfo();
formModuleInfo.panel1.Parent = this.panelRight;

PopulateTreeView();
  }

  protected void AddCustomFileMenuItems()
  {
    menuItemFileSaveListAs = new MyMenuItem();
    menuItemFileSaveListAs.Index = 0;
    menuItemFileSaveListAs.Text = "&Save List As...";
    menuItemFileSaveListAs.Click +=
        new System.EventHandler(this.menuItemFileSaveListAs_Click);
    menuItemFileSaveListAs.Shortcut = Shortcut.CtrlS;
    menuItemFileSaveListAs.ImageList = imageList1;
    menuItemFileSaveListAs.ImageIndex = 0;

    menuItemFileBreak1 = new MenuItem("-");
    menuItemFileBreak1.Index = 1;
    menuItemFileBreak1.Text = "-";

    menuItemFilePrintPreview = new MyMenuItem();
    menuItemFilePrintPreview.Index = 2;
    menuItemFilePrintPreview.Text = "Print Pre&view";
    menuItemFilePrintPreview.Click +=
        new System.EventHandler(this.menuItemFilePrintPreview_Click);

    menuItemFilePrint = new MyMenuItem();
    menuItemFilePrint.Index = 3;
    menuItemFilePrint.Text = "&Print...";
    menuItemFilePrint.Click +=
        new System.EventHandler(this.menuItemFilePrint_Click);

    menuItemFileBreak2 = new MenuItem("-");
    menuItemFileBreak2.Index = 4;
    menuItemFileBreak2.Text = "-";

    menuItemFileExit = new MyMenuItem();
    menuItemFileExit.Index = 5;
    menuItemFileExit.Text = "&Exit";
    menuItemFileExit.Click +=
        new System.EventHandler(this.menuItemFileExit_Click);

    menuItemFile.MenuItems.AddRange(new System.Windows.Forms.MenuItem[] {
        this.menuItemFileSaveListAs,
        this.menuItemFileBreak1,
        this.menuItemFilePrintPreview,
        this.menuItemFilePrint,
        this.menuItemFileBreak2,
```

Continued

Listing 7-34 *(continued)*

```csharp
        this.menuItemFileExit});
  }

  protected override void Dispose( bool disposing )
  {
    // standard wizard-generated code...
  }

  private void InitializeComponent()
  {// omitted code...}

  protected String RegularExpressionFromCommandLine()
  {
if (Environment.GetCommandLineArgs().Length <= 1)
  return "";

String[] args = Environment.GetCommandLineArgs();
return args [1];
  }

  private void PopulateTreeView()
  {
String regularExpression = RegularExpressionFromCommandLine();
String rootText;
if (regularExpression.Equals("") )
  // an empty expression will match anything
  rootText = "All Processes";
else
  rootText = "Processes Matching " + regularExpression;

Regex regExp = new Regex(regularExpression);

rootNode = new TreeNode(rootText);

Process[] allProcesses = Process.GetProcesses();
Array.Sort(allProcesses, new SortByProcessName() );
foreach (Process p in allProcesses)
{
  // only use processes with names matching the
  // regular expression
  if (!regExp.IsMatch(p.ProcessName) )
    continue;

  TreeNode processNode = new ProcessTreeNode(p);
  rootNode.Nodes.Add(processNode);

  // Beta 2 bug workaround: can't access Modules for the Idle process
  if (p.ProcessName.Equals("Idle") )
    continue;
```

```
// convert modules from a collection to an array, so
// we can use the Array class to sort them
ProcessModuleCollection allModules = p.Modules;
ProcessModule[] modules = new ProcessModule[allModules.Count];
int i = 0;
foreach (ProcessModule m in allModules)
  modules.SetValue(m, i++);

// Sort the modules and add them to the tree
Array.Sort(modules, new SortByModuleName() );
foreach (ProcessModule m in allModules)
  processNode.Nodes.Add(new ModuleTreeNode(m) );
}
treeView1.Nodes.Add(rootNode);
rootNode.Expand();
}

  [STAThread]
  public static void Main(string[] args)
  {
    try
    {
  if (UserNeedsHelp() )
    DisplayUsage();
  else
   Application.Run(new FormMain());
    }
    catch (Exception e)
    {
  MessageBox.Show("Exception raised: " + e.Message);
    }
}

  protected static bool UserNeedsHelp()
  {
String[] args = Environment.GetCommandLineArgs();

if (args.Length <= 1)
  return false;

if (args.Length == 2)
  return args [1].Equals("/?") ? true : false;

// regular expression provided
return false;
  }

  protected static void DisplayUsage()
  {
    String msg;
    msg = "This program shows a list of the processes running on your
          machine.\r\n";
```

Continued

Listing 7-34 *(continued)*

```
msg += "Usage:\r\n";
msg += "\r\n";
msg += "ProcessViewer [regular expression] | [/?]\r\n";
msg += "\r\n";
msg += "If no command-line arguments are supplied, ProcessViewer will
            display\r\n";
msg += "all the processes running.\r\n";
msg += "\r\n";
msg += "if a regular expression is provided, only processes that match
            the\r\n";
msg += "expression will be displayed. For example the command
            line:\r\n";
msg += "\r\n";
msg += "ProcessViewer ^[a-dA-D]\r\n";
msg += "\r\n";
msg += "will limit the list of displayed processes to those whose names
            start\r\n";
msg += "with the letters a, b, c or d (both lower and uppercase).\r\n";
msg += "\r\n";
msg += "[/?] \t Displays these Usage instructions.";

MessageBox.Show(msg, "Command-line arguments for ProcessViewer");
    }

   protected void SaveListInFile(String theFilename)
   {
  StreamWriter stream = null;
  try
     {
   stream = File.CreateText(theFilename);
     }
     catch (Exception e)
     {
  MessageBox.Show("Error creating file: " + e.Message);
  return;
     }

     StringCollection collection = GetTextCollection();
     foreach(String s in collection)
  stream.WriteLine(s);
     stream.Close();
   }

   private void treeView1_AfterSelect(object sender,
                        System.Windows.Forms.TreeViewEventArgs e)
   {
  if (treeView1.SelectedNode.Parent == null)
        DisplayMainPage();
  else if (treeView1.SelectedNode.Parent == rootNode)
    DisplayProcessInfo(treeView1.SelectedNode as ProcessTreeNode);
  else
```

```
        DisplayModuleInfo(treeView1.SelectedNode as ModuleTreeNode);
        }

    protected void DisplayMainPage()
        {
formSystemInfo.panel1.Visible = true;
formProcessInfo.panel1.Visible = false;
formModuleInfo.panel1.Visible = false;
        }

    protected void DisplayProcessInfo(ProcessTreeNode theNode)
        {
formSystemInfo.panel1.Visible = false;
formProcessInfo.panel1.Visible = true;
formModuleInfo.panel1.Visible = false;

// display the process info
formProcessInfo.DisplayInfo(theNode);
        }

    protected void DisplayModuleInfo(ModuleTreeNode theNode)
        {
formSystemInfo.panel1.Visible = false;
formProcessInfo.panel1.Visible = false;
formModuleInfo.panel1.Visible = true;

// display the module info
formModuleInfo.DisplayInfo(theNode);
        }

    private void menuItemFileSaveListAs_Click(object sender,
                                      System.EventArgs e)
        {
        // save info as a text file
        saveFileDialog1.InitialDirectory = Environment.CurrentDirectory;
        saveFileDialog1.FileName = "ProcessViewer.txt";
        saveFileDialog1.OverwritePrompt = true;

        if (saveFileDialog1.ShowDialog() == DialogResult.OK )
    SaveListInFile(saveFileDialog1.FileName);
        }

    private void menuItemFilePrint_Click(object sender, System.EventArgs e)
        {
        printDialog1.PrinterSettings = new PrinterSettings();
        if (printDialog1.ShowDialog() != DialogResult.OK)
    return;

        StringCollection textToPrint = GetTextCollection();

        try
        {
```

Continued

Listing 7-34 *(continued)*

```csharp
      MyPrintDocument textPrinter =
  new MyPrintDocument(Text, textToPrint,
                                    printDialog1.PrinterSettings);
        textPrinter.Print();
    }
    catch(Exception ex)
    {
      MessageBox.Show("Exception raised while printing: " + ex.Message);
    }
  }

  protected StringCollection GetTextCollection()
  {
    StringCollection strings = new StringCollection();

    TreeNode firstProcessNode = treeView1.Nodes [0].Nodes [0];
    String header1 = String.Format("List of Modules loaded by
                                  Process [{0}]",
                                  firstProcessNode.Text);
    String header2 = String.Format("on the computer [{0}] as of {1}",
                                  SystemInformation.ComputerName,
                                  DateTime.Now);
    strings.Add(header1);
    strings.Add(header2);
    strings.Add("");

    strings.Add(firstProcessNode.Text);
    foreach (TreeNode m in firstProcessNode.Nodes)
      strings.Add("       " + m.Text);
    strings.Add("");
    strings.Add("--- end of list");
    return strings;
  }

  private void menuItemFilePrintPreview_Click(object sender,
                                        System.EventArgs e)
  {
    try
    {
      PrintPreviewDialog previewDialog = new PrintPreviewDialog();
      PrinterSettings printerSettings = new PrinterSettings();
      StringCollection textToPrint = GetTextCollection();
      previewDialog.Document =
       new MyPrintDocument(Text, textToPrint, printerSettings);
      previewDialog.ShowDialog();
    }
    catch(Exception ex)
    {
      MessageBox.Show("Exception raised during print preview: " +
                  ex.Message);
    }
```

```
      }

      private void menuItemFileExit_Click(object sender, System.EventArgs e)
      {
        Close();
      }

      private void menuItemEditCopy_Click(object sender, System.EventArgs e)
      {
        String text = "Text placed on the clipboard by ProcessViewer";
        Clipboard.SetDataObject(text);
        String s = String.Format("The following text was copied to the
                            clipboard: [{0}]", text);
        MessageBox.Show(s, "Clipboard Data");
      }

      private void menuItemEditPaste_Click(object sender, System.EventArgs e)
      {
        IDataObject clipboardData = Clipboard.GetDataObject();
        String text;

        // see if the clipboard has any text
        if (clipboardData.GetDataPresent(DataFormats.Text) )
          // get the text
          text = (String) clipboardData.GetData(DataFormats.Text);
        else
          text = "No text available on clipboard";
        MessageBox.Show(text, "Clipboard Data");
      }
  }

  public class SortByProcessName : IComparer
  {
public int Compare(object x, object y)
{
      Process a = (Process) x;
      Process b = (Process) y;
      return a.ProcessName.CompareTo(b.ProcessName);
}
  }

  public class SortByModuleName : IComparer
  {
    public int Compare(object x, object y)
    {
      ProcessModule a = (ProcessModule) x;
      ProcessModule b = (ProcessModule) y;
      return a.ModuleName.CompareTo(b.ModuleName);
    }
  }

  public class ProcessTreeNode : TreeNode
```

Continued

Listing 7-34 *(continued)*

```
    {
      public Process processInfo;
      public ProcessTreeNode(Process theProcess) : base(theProcess.ProcessName)
      {
        processInfo = theProcess;
      }
    }

    public class ModuleTreeNode : TreeNode
    {
      public ProcessModule moduleInfo;
      public ModuleTreeNode(ProcessModule theModule) :
                            base(theModule.ModuleName)

      {
        moduleInfo = theModule;
      }
    }
  }
```

Listing 7-35: The Complete Code for MyMenuItem

```
using System;
using System.ComponentModel;
using System.Drawing;
using System.Drawing.Text;
using System.Windows.Forms;

namespace ProcessViewer
{
  public class MyMenuItem : MenuItem
  {
    ImageList imageList;
    Font font;

    StringFormat format = new StringFormat();

    Brush unselectedBrush = SystemBrushes.Control;
    Brush selectedBrush = SystemBrushes.Highlight;
    Image image;
    int imageIndex;
    const int offsetOfShortcutText = 90;   // in pixels

    public MyMenuItem()
    {
      OwnerDraw = true;
      font = new Font("Microsoft Sans Serif", 8);
      format.HotkeyPrefix = HotkeyPrefix.Show;
```

```
      format.SetTabStops(offsetOfShortcutText, new float[] {0} );
    }

    public ImageList ImageList
    {
      get { return imageList; }
      set
      {
        imageList = value;
        setImage();
      }
    }

    public int ImageIndex
    {
      get { return imageIndex; }
      set
      {
        imageIndex = value;
        setImage();
      }
    }

    protected void setImage()
    {
      if (imageList == null)
      {
        image = null;
        return;
      }
      if (imageIndex >= imageList.Images.Count)
        imageIndex = 0;
      if (imageIndex >= imageList.Images.Count)
        image = null;
      else
        image = imageList.Images [imageIndex];
    }


    protected override void OnMeasureItem(MeasureItemEventArgs e)
    {
      e.ItemHeight = 22;

      e.ItemWidth = (int) e.Graphics.MeasureString(TextWithShortcut(),
                                     font, 500, format).Width;
      e.ItemWidth += 10;   // some extra space on the right
    }

    protected override void OnDrawItem(DrawItemEventArgs e)
    {

      if (image != null )
```

Continued

Listing 7-35 *(continued)*

```
        e.Graphics.DrawImage(image, e.Bounds.Left + 2, e.Bounds.Top + 2);

    Brush brush;
    Rectangle rect = e.Bounds;
    rect.X += 24;

    if ( (e.State & DrawItemState.Selected) == DrawItemState.Selected)
      brush = selectedBrush;
    else
      brush = unselectedBrush;

    e.Graphics.FillRectangle(brush, rect);

    brush = new SolidBrush(e.ForeColor);

    e.Graphics.DrawString(TextWithShortcut(), font, brush,
                          e.Bounds.Left + 25, e.Bounds.Top + 2, format);
  }

  private String TextWithShortcut()
  {
    String s = Text;

    if (!ShowShortcut) return s;
    if (Shortcut == Shortcut.None) return s;



    Keys key = (Keys) Shortcut;
    return s + "\t" + keyConverter.ConvertToString(key);
  }
 }
}
```

Listing 7-36: **The Complete Code for FormSystemInfo**

```
using System;
using System.Drawing;
using System.Collections;
using System.ComponentModel;
using System.Windows.Forms;

namespace ProcessViewer
{
  public class FormSystemInfo : System.Windows.Forms.Form
  {
```

```
// declare GUI controls...

public FormSystemInfo()
{
  InitializeComponent();

  checkBoxNetworkAvailable.Checked = SystemInformation.Network;
  checkBoxMouseAvailable.Checked = SystemInformation.MousePresent;

  foreach (DictionaryEntry d in Environment.GetEnvironmentVariables() )
    comboBoxEnvironmentVariables.Items.Add(d.Key + " = " + d.Value);
  comboBoxEnvironmentVariables.SelectedIndex = 0;

  foreach (String s in Environment.GetLogicalDrives() )
    comboBoxLogicalDrivesAvailable.Items.Add(s);
  comboBoxLogicalDrivesAvailable.SelectedIndex = 0;

  labelOperatingSystem.Text = GetPlatformName() + " Version " +
          Environment.OSVersion.Version;

  labelCurrentDirectory.Text = Environment.CurrentDirectory;;
  labelSystemDirectory.Text = Environment.SystemDirectory;
  labelCommandLine.Text = Environment.CommandLine;
}

protected String GetPlatformName()
{
  OperatingSystem os = Environment.OSVersion;
  String osName;
  switch (os.Platform)
  {
    case PlatformID.Win32NT:
      if (os.Version.Major <= 4)
    osName = "Windows NT";
      else if (os.Version.Major == 5)
    osName = "Windows 2000";
      else
    osName = "New version of Windows!";
      break;

    case PlatformID.Win32S:
      osName = "Win32S";
      break;

    case PlatformID.Win32Windows:
      osName = "Windows 95, 98 or ME";
      break;

    default:
      osName = "Unknown platform";
      break;
```

Continued

Listing 7-36 *(continued)*

```
      }
      return osName;
   }

   protected override void Dispose( bool disposing )
   {// omitted wizard code...}

   private void InitializeComponent()
   {// omitted GUI control initialization code}
  }
}
```

Listing 7-37: **The Complete Code for FormProcessInfo**

```
using System;
using System.Drawing;
using System.Collections;
using System.ComponentModel;
using System.Windows.Forms;

namespace ProcessViewer
{
  public class FormProcessInfo : System.Windows.Forms.Form

    // declare private GUI controls...

    public FormProcessInfo()
    {
      InitializeComponent();
    }

    protected override void Dispose( bool disposing )
    {// omitted wizard code...}

    private void InitializeComponent()
    {//omitted GUI control initialization code}

    public void DisplayInfo(ProcessTreeNode theNode)
    {
      labelProcessName.Text = theNode.processInfo.ProcessName;
      labelProcessID.Text = theNode.processInfo.Id.ToString();
      labelStartedOn.Text = theNode.processInfo.StartTime.Date.ToString();

      labelNumberOfThreads.Text = theNode.processInfo.Threads.Count.ToString();

      TimeSpan t = theNode.processInfo.TotalProcessorTime;
      if (t.Days > 0)
        labelTotalProcessorTime.Text = String.Format("{0} Days
                                      {1:00}:{2:00}:{3:00}",
```

```
                                           t.Days, t.Hours, t.Minutes, t.Seconds);
        else
          labelTotalProcessorTime.Text = String.Format("{0:00}:{1:00}:{2:00}",
                                        t.Hours, t.Minutes, t.Seconds);

        if ( (theNode.processInfo.MainWindowTitle == null) ||
            (!theNode.processInfo.MainWindowTitle.Equals("")  ) )
          labelMainWindowTitle.Text = theNode.processInfo.MainWindowTitle;
        else
          labelMainWindowTitle.Text = "<none>";

        // Beta 2 bug workaround:
        // can't reference Modules property for Idle process
        if (theNode.processInfo.ProcessName.Equals("Idle") )
          labelMainModule.Text = "<none>";
        else
        {
          if ( (theNode.processInfo.Modules != null) &&
              (theNode.processInfo.Modules.Count > 0) )
            labelMainModule.Text = theNode.processInfo.MainModule.FileName;
          else
            labelMainModule.Text = "<none>";
        }

        labelPriority.Text = theNode.processInfo.BasePriority.ToString();
      }
    }
}
```

Listing 7-38: **The Complete Code for FormModuleInfo**

```
using System;
using System.Drawing;
using System.Collections;
using System.ComponentModel;
using System.Windows.Forms;
using System.IO;

namespace ProcessViewer
{
  public class FormModuleInfo : System.Windows.Forms.Form
  {
    // declare private GUI controls...

    public FormModuleInfo()
    {
      InitializeComponent();
    }

    protected override void Dispose( bool disposing )
```

Continued

Listing 7-38 *(continued)*

```
{// omitted wizard code...}

private void InitializeComponent()
{//omitted GUI control initialization code}


public void DisplayInfo(ModuleTreeNode theNode)
{
  labelModuleName.Text = theNode.moduleInfo.ModuleName;
  labelCompanyName.Text = theNode.moduleInfo.FileVersionInfo.CompanyName;
  labelLoadedFromFile.Text = theNode.moduleInfo.FileVersionInfo.FileName;
  labelFileVersion.Text = theNode.moduleInfo.FileVersionInfo.FileVersion;

  if (!theNode.moduleInfo.FileVersionInfo.FileDescription.Equals("") )
    labelFileDescription.Text =
              theNode.moduleInfo.FileVersionInfo.FileDescription;
  else
    labelFileDescription.Text = "<none>";

  DateTime timestamp =
      File.GetCreationTime(theNode.moduleInfo.FileVersionInfo.FileName);
  labelFileTimestamp.Text = timestamp.ToString();
  FileInfo fileInfo = new
                  FileInfo(theNode.moduleInfo.FileVersionInfo.FileName);
  labelFileSize.Text = fileInfo.Length.ToString();
  }
 }
}
```

Listing 7-39: The Complete Code for MyPrintDocument

```
namespace ProcessViewer
{
  using System;
  using System.Drawing;
  using System.ComponentModel;
  using System.Collections.Specialized;
  using System.Configuration;
  using System.Diagnostics;
  using System.Drawing.Printing;

  public class MyPrintDocument : PrintDocument
  {
    Font font;
    StringCollection strings;
    int linesPerPage = 0;
    int totalLinesPrinted;
    float lineHeight;
```

```
public MyPrintDocument(String theDocumentName,
                       StringCollection theStringsToPrint,
                       PrinterSettings thePrinterSettings)
{
  DocumentName = theDocumentName;  // name displayed while printing
  strings = theStringsToPrint;
  PrinterSettings = thePrinterSettings;
  font = new Font("Courier New", 10);
  QueryPageSettings += new
    QueryPageSettingsEventHandler(OnQueryPageSettings);
}

// setup any last minute things before printing starts
protected override void OnBeginPrint(PrintEventArgs ev)
{
  base.OnBeginPrint(ev);
  totalLinesPrinted = 0;
}

// clean up after printing is finished. If you had acquired any
// resources while printing, this is where you would release them
protected override void OnEndPrint(PrintEventArgs ev)
{
  base.OnEndPrint(ev);

  // nothing to do in this demo...
}

protected void OnQueryPageSettings(Object sender,
                                   QueryPageSettingsEventArgs ev)
{
  // nothing to do in this demo...
}

// print each page
protected override void OnPrintPage(PrintPageEventArgs ev)
{
  base.OnPrintPage(ev);

  float y;
  float leftMargin = ev.MarginBounds.Left;
  float topMargin = ev.MarginBounds.Top;
  StringFormat format = new StringFormat();

  if (lineHeight == 0)
  {
    lineHeight = font.GetHeight(ev.Graphics);
    if (lineHeight == 0)
 throw new Exception("MyPrintDocument.OnPrintPage:
                         lineHeight is zero!");
    linesPerPage = (int) (ev.MarginBounds.Height / lineHeight);
```

Continued

Listing 7-39 *(continued)*

```
    }

    for (int lineNumber = 0; lineNumber < linesPerPage; lineNumber++)
    {
      if (totalLinesPrinted >= strings.Count)
        break;
      y = topMargin + lineNumber * lineHeight;
      String text = strings [totalLinesPrinted++];
      ev.Graphics.DrawString(text, font, Brushes.Black, leftMargin,
                             y, new StringFormat());
    }

    ev.HasMorePages = (totalLinesPrinted < strings.Count) ? true : false;
  }
}
}
```

Localization

Before delving into the details of localization, let me back up one step and talk briefly about *globalization* (also referred to as *internationalization*). The Java folks will recognize globalization as I18N. Before you go off looking for a W3C standard called I18N, let me add that I18N is just an abbreviation for *InternationalizatioN:* the letter *I,* followed by 18 characters, then the letter *N.* As if the field of technology didn't have enough acronyms, someone had to be cute and come up with yet another meaningless word for the alphabet soup.

When you create a component that is designated for more than one locale (language or country), you need to add the capability to use different languages, images, and even form layouts at runtime, based on the locale of the end user. You also need to use code that handles dates, times, currency, and large numbers according to the end user's locale rules:

✦ When handling dates, the runtime code needs to format dates as MM-DD-YY, DD-MM-YY, YYYY-MM-DD, or other.

✦ When handling time, the runtime needs to format values using the AM/PM convention for 12-hour times, or use 24-hour values.

✦ When handling currencies, there are several locale dependencies, such as the currency symbol, the symbol used to group digits (1,000 versus 1.000 for example), the number of decimals to use, and the decimal separator symbol.

✦ When handling large numbers, the runtime needs to use the proper digit grouping and decimal separator (1,000,222.44 versus 1.000.222,44 for example).

There are other items that require localization, such as measurements, paper sizes, and others. Globalization is the infrastructure required by a component to support more than one locale. The .NET Framework contains complete support for globalization through the use of locale-specific resource files and runtime code that properly formats dates, times, currency, and large numbers according to the end user's locale. Globalization is handled completely by the .NET Framework.

Locale designations

The .NET globalization framework uses a string to represent a locale, based on the ISO 639-1 standard, which specifies designations for over 100 languages and regions. The string may contain just a two-letter language designator, or the designator plus a two-letter region code when a language has significant variations by region. The combined language-region designation is based on W3C RFC 1766. Tables 7-7 through 7-12 show the locales for some of the countries on each continent.

Table 7-7: Some of the Locales in North America

Locale Designation	Language - Country
en-CA	English - Canada
en-US	English - United States
fr-CA	French - Canada
es-MX	Spanish - Mexico

Table 7-8: Some of the Locales in South America

Locale Designation	Language - Country
pt-BR	Portuguese - Brazil
es-AR	Spanish - Argentina
es-CL	Spanish - Chile
es-CO	Spanish - Colombia
es-VE	Spanish - Venezuela

Table 7-9: Some of the Locales in Europe

Locale Designation	Language - Country
da	Danish
nl	Dutch
en-GB	English - United Kingdom
fr-BE	French - Belgium
fr-FR	French - France
de-AT	German - Austria
de-DE	German - Germany
el	Greek

Continued

Table 7-9 *(continued)*

Locale Designation	Language - Country
it	Italian
no	Norwegian
pt-PT	Portuguese - Portugal
ru	Russian
es-ES	Spanish - Spain
sv	Swedish
uk	Ukrainian

Table 7-10: Some of the Locales in Asia

Locale Designation	Language - Country
ar	Arabic
zh-HK	Chinese - Hong Kong S.A.R.
zh-CN	Chinese - China
zh-TW	Chinese - Taiwan
en-PH	English - Philippines
fa	Farsi
he	Hebrew
hi	Hindi
id	Indonesian
ja	Japanese
ko	Korean
th	Thai
tr	Turkish
vi	Vietnamese

Table 7-11: Some of the Locales in Africa

Locale Designation	Language - Country
ar-EG	Arabic - Egypt
ar-LY	Arabic - Libya
en-ZA	English - South Africa
sw	Swahili

Table 7-12: Some of the Locales in Oceania

Locale Designation	Language - Country
en-AU	English - Australia
en-NZ	English - New Zealand

Note that language designators are always lowercase, while region designators are always uppercase. For a complete list of the locale designations supported by the .NET Framework, look up the class `CultureInfo` in the online VS .NET help documentation.

Changing the locale programmatically

Like I said, the .NET framework handles all globalization details automatically. When it comes to formatting dates, times, and other items, the runtime libraries need to know the end user's locale. This information is stored in the thread of the main form. When the thread is started, the .NET Framework sets the thread's `CurrentUICulture` property to the system locale, which corresponds to the locale specified by the end user in the Regional Options applet in the Control Panel.

You can also change your component's locale at runtime by assigning a new locale to `Thread.CurrentUICulture` as shown in Listing 7-40.

Listing 7-40: Setting the Locale Programmatically

```
using System.Globalization;
using System.Threading;
// ...

Thread.CurrentThread.CurrentUICulture = new CultureInfo("nl");
```

This code would change the local to Dutch. If you attempt to set the locale using an invalid string, an exception will be thrown, so it is always a good idea to wrap the locale-setting logic in a try block and use a default locale in the catch handler, as shown in Listing 7-41.

Listing 7-41: Using a Default Locale if a Bad Locale Is Used

```
try
{
  Thread.CurrentThread.CurrentUICulture = new CultureInfo("nl");
}
catch (ArgumentException e)
{
  Console.Out.WriteLine("Invalid locale: Setting locale to US English");
  Thread.CurrentThread.CurrentUICulture = new CultureInfo("en-US");
}
```

Localized resource files

Localization is the process of generating resource files for the locales that your components need to support. Localization requires all the UI text to be translated into the various languages you want to support. It also requires locale-specific images to be created and saved in locale-specific resource files. Localization used to require a lot of work, often with third-party tools. With the .NET Framework, localization is a breeze, because all you have to do is create the necessary resource files. Of course, someone will need to produce the translations of textual material into the different locales you'll support, but at least the job is not programming-intensive. The .NET Framework's globalization infrastructure will automatically load the correct resources at runtime, based on the end user's locale.

There are two types of resource files used in the .NET globalization framework:

✦ .resx. files

✦ .resource files

The .resx files can hold both binary and XML data, and are generated by VS .NET for each localized form, as described in this section. They are also used to store localized versions of strings used in your component.

The .resource files contain XML-based text that can describe both strings and serializable objects. When you compile and link a project, VS .NET compiles the .resx files of your forms into .resource files and includes the latter in the satellite assemblies.

Localizing forms

Each form whose `Localizable` property is `true` has a .resx file to hold the localizable items, such as text and images. This file contains all the UI features of the form, including layout information. Each locale is associated with its own .resx file, and can use not only a different language, but also a different layout. When creating localized versions of components for locales in which text flows vertically instead of horizontally, it is generally necessary to change the layout of UI elements to match the text flow.

To demonstrate the details of forms localization, I created a simple application called MyLocalizedForm.exe, which has a simple form that looks like Figure 7-14.

Figure 7-14: The interface of MyLocalizedForm, when running with the English locale

After creating the form, I set its Localizable property to True and left the Language property set to (Default), as shown in Figure 7-15.

Figure 7-15: Setting the Localizable property to true with the default language

Then I added the controls to the form and set the various properties. Since I did all this work with the Default language setting, English becomes the default language for the form. At run-time, if the resources for the end user's locale are not found at runtime, the default resources are used, and the form will appear in English. Obviously, you can use any locale you want for the default.

When you build the project, VS .NET will create a .resx file containing the default language resources for each localized form. To see the .resx files in the Solution Explorer, click the Show All Files button on the toolbar. The files will be listed as shown in Figure 7-16.

Figure 7-16: The .resx file created for MyLocalizedForm

The .resx file contains XML code describing the localizable features of each form. VS.NET has a built-in tool for editing .resx files. To launch the tool, just double-click on the .resx file in the Solution Explorer. The .resx editor will appear in the code window, as shown in Figure 7-17.

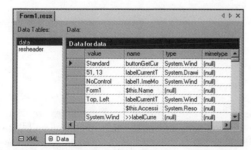

Figure 7-17: The .resX Editor in the Visual Studio code window

As you can see, the Editor has two buttons at the bottom: the one on the left selects the XML pane; the other selects the Data pane. The latter presents information in a friendly property-value format as shown in Figure 7-17. The XML pane shows the raw XML code in the .resx file, as shown in Figure 7-18.

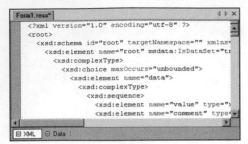

Figure 7-18: The resx Editor showing the raw XML code for a form

Now I'll create an Italian version of the form. In the Properties window of the form, I changed the Language property from Default to Italian, as shown in Figure 7-19.

Figure 7-19: Creating the Italian version of the form

After changing the Language setting, VS .NET immediately adds two more .resx files to the solution, as shown in Figure 7-20.

Figure 7-20: The Solution Explorer showing the newly added localization files

Now that I have an Italian version of the form, I'll go ahead and change all the text to Italian. In the process, because the text is of different length, I'll adjust the label positions a bit and also widen the button, to display the full Italian caption. Figure 7-21 shows the new Italian form in the Code window.

Let me reiterate the fact that the Italian version of the form has both different text and a different layout from the English version. The differences between Italian and English are not major in my example, but if you need to localize to a language that flows vertically or from right to left, you may need to make significant changes to the layout.

That's all there is to it. Just build the project and run it. If the machine's system locale is Italian, the Italian version will appear, otherwise the English one will. Figure 7-22 shows the Italian version.

Figure 7-21: The Italian version of the form

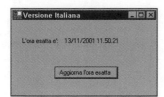

Figure 7-22: The Italian version of the application

Notice the wider button in the Italian version with respect to the English version. Also notice the formatting of the time and date, which both use Italian formats.

The whole thing is like magic. I didn't add a single line of code to explicitly support multiple languages, but everything works perfectly. It's actually all pretty simple. When the .NET Framework loads the application, it looks at the system locale. If the locale is it-IT, it looks in the folder of the program for a subfolder named it-IT. If it finds it, it looks in the subfolder for a satellite assembly containing the localized forms and resources for the application. In my example, the application is called MyLocalizedForm.exe, so the loader will look for a satellite assembly called MyLocalizedForm.resources.dll. If it finds the assembly, it loads it; otherwise, it searches for a fallback assembly and looks for a subfolder called "it". If it finds it, great; otherwise, it falls back to the default locale built into the application, which in my case was English. Like I said in the beginning, if you ignore the difficulty of translating text from one language to another, handling localization is a breeze.

Localizing strings

Forms are not the only part of a component needing localization. If your component displays messages to the end user, you probably have code that builds strings at runtime. Since these strings are not part of a form's resources, you need to handle them differently, in terms of localization. What you need to do is isolate them and put them in a resource file.

Say you have a component that needs to support two locales: the default locale is English and the other one is Italian. What you need to do is put all the locale-dependent strings in resource files whose filenames are tagged with a standard locale abbreviation. You can use any name you want for the resource file. Assuming the default resource file contained U.S. English and was named MyStrings.resx, the name of the Italian resource file would then be MyStrings.it-IT.resx.

Creating the resource files for the text in your component is easy using the VS .NET wizard. Just right-click on the project in the Solution Explorer and select Add New Item. In the dialog box that appears, select the Assembly Resource File template, as shown in Figure 7-23.

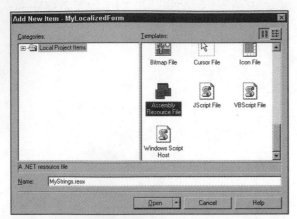

Figure 7-23: Creating a resource file to contain the strings of a component

Enter the name of the resource file to create. It can be any name you want: It doesn't have to share a common name with the project or any of its files. If you enter the name **MyStrings.resx**, the wizard creates a resource file with that name and adds it to the Solution Explorer. To edit the strings, double-click on the .resx file in the Solution Explorer and edit it, as shown in Figure 7-24.

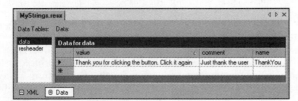

Figure 7-24: Editing localized text in a string resource file

To keep things simple, I just entered the single string with the name **ThankYou**, as shown in the figure. The value field contains the string's text. You can also enter comments that may help translators understand the context of the message. The name is the identifier you'll use in your code to reference the string. Save the file in the same folder as the other source code file.

Make a copy of the file and rename it to **MyStrings.it-IT.resx**. Put it in the same folder as MyStrings.resx. Edit the file to change the text into Italian. With the resource files, you're done. Figure 7-25 shows the Solution Explorer after creating the two text resource files.

Figure 7-25: The Solution Explorer showing the newly created text resource files

Now you need to add some code to your component to access the text stored in the resource files just created. There are two basic techniques. The first technique loads all the resource names contained in a resource file, but doesn't load the resource values until you ask for them. This technique uses class ResourceManager, as shown in Listing 7-42.

Listing 7-42: **Using ResouceManager to Load One Localized String at a Time**

```
ResourceManager rm = new ResourceManager("MyLocalizedForm.MyStrings",
                                   this.GetType().Assembly);
String s = rm.GetString("ThankYou");
MessageBox.Show(this, s);
```

ResourceManager provides an important *fallback* capability. If you look for a certain resource whose name is not present in the locale specified, the class will search in the parent locale to find the resource. For example, say you have specified the locale **it-CH** (Swiss Italian). You're looking for the string named *Hello,* but it's not in the it-CH resource file. ResourceManager will then look in the resource file for the parent locale "it" (general Italian). If it finds the string named Hello, it returns it to you automatically. If it doesn't find it, it will look in the resources for the default locale.

The second technique uses class ResourceSet to load all the localized names and values at once for subsequent rapid access, as shown in Listing 7-43.

Listing 7-43: **Using ResouceSet to Load All Strings in a Resource File at Once**

```
ResourceManager rm = new   ResourceManager("MyLocalizedForm.MyStrings",
                                   this.GetType().Assembly);
ResourceSet rs = rm.GetResourceSet(Thread.CurrentThread.CurrentUICulture,
                              true, true);
String s = rs.GetString("ThankYou");
MessageBox.Show(this, s);
```

Keep in mind that ResourceSet does *not* support fallback locales. If the resource is not found in the designated resource file, the search will return a null.

Figure 7-26 shows the two versions of the message box produced by the code in the two previous listings.

In case you're curious about how data is stored in the .resx file, Listing 7-44 shows the contents of MyStrings.resx.

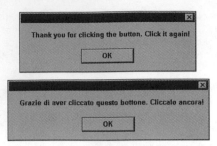

Figure 7-26: The English and Italian versions of the same message

---

Listing 7-44: **The XML Code Saved in the File MyStrings.resx**

```xml
<?xml version="1.0" encoding="utf-8" ?>
<root>
  <xsd:schema id="root" targetNamespace="" xmlns=""
      xmlns:xsd="http://www.w3.org/2001/XMLSchema"
      xmlns:msdata="urn:schemas-microsoft-com:xml-msdata">
    <xsd:element name="root" msdata:IsDataSet="true">
      <xsd:complexType>
        <xsd:choice maxOccurs="unbounded">
          <xsd:element name="data">
            <xsd:complexType>
              <xsd:sequence>
                <xsd:element name="value" type="xsd:string"
                    minOccurs="0" msdata:Ordinal="1" />
                 <xsd:element name="comment" type="xsd:string"
                    minOccurs="0" msdata:Ordinal="2" />
              </xsd:sequence>
              <xsd:attribute name="name" type="xsd:string" />
              <xsd:attribute name="type" type="xsd:string" />
              <xsd:attribute name="mimetype" type="xsd:string" />
            </xsd:complexType>
          </xsd:element>
          <xsd:element name="resheader">
            <xsd:complexType>
              <xsd:sequence>
                <xsd:element name="value" type="xsd:string"
                    minOccurs="0" msdata:Ordinal="1" />
              </xsd:sequence>
              <xsd:attribute name="name" type="xsd:string" use="required" />
            </xsd:complexType>
          </xsd:element>
        </xsd:choice>
      </xsd:complexType>
    </xsd:element>
  </xsd:schema>


  <data name="ThankYou">
```

```
    <value>Thank you for clicking the button. Click it again!</value>
    <comment>Just thank the user</comment>
  </data>

  <resheader name="ResMimeType">
    <value>text/microsoft-resx</value>
  </resheader>

  <resheader name="Version">
    <value>1.0.0.0</value>
  </resheader>

  <resheader name="Reader">
    <value>System.Resources.ResXResourceReader</value>
  </resheader>

  <resheader name="Writer">
    <value>System.Resources.ResXResourceWriter</value>
  </resheader>
</root>
```

The text is stored in Unicode, so it can contain characters from any of the major languages used throughout the world.

Phrases with parameter substitution

Not all UI text is static. Sometimes phrases need to be built on-the-fly at runtime. Consider having to build the following text for display in a message box:

The red car has been sold.

Simple enough. Let's assume the color *(red)* and the object type *(car)* are variables. Maybe your software deals with boats and airplanes besides cars. You could use the following code:

```
String s = string.Format("The {0} {1} has been sold", color,
typeOfVehicle);
```

To localize the code, you would save the entire formatting string in the resource file, like this:

```
VehicleSold=The {0} {1} has been sold
```

Then you would reference the localized string in the code like this:

```
private ResourceManager rm;


rm = new ResourceManager("MyStrings", this.GetType().Assembly);


String format = rm.GetString("VehicleSold ");
String s = string.Format(format, color, typeOfVehicle);
```

There is a problem you need to watch out for: The order of parameters may need to change for some languages. For example, in Italian the sentence would need to read:

The vettura rossa e' stata venduta.

Translated word for word, it would be: *The car red has been sold.* In Italian, and many other languages, adjectives often come after the noun they refer to. A common way to prepare localized resource files is to create a file for the default locale, and then give it to a translator for a new locale. If you just handed the English resource file to an Italian translator, he or she would come across the line:

```
VehicleSold= The {0} {1} has been sold
```

The translator might translate it like this:

```
VehicleSold= La {0} {1} e' stata venduta
```

This would produce the Italian message: *La rossa vettura e' stata venduta,* which is wrong.

There are all kinds of other variations in parameter ordering. For example, Italian sometimes puts the object before the verb, and the subject after, as in the following sentence:

La pizza l'ho ordinata io! (It was I who ordered the pizza!)

There are also cases when the subject is suppressed entirely in Italian. And don't forget that many languages have genders that apply to nouns, adjectives, and verbs. The list of differences between the structure of English and Italian phrases goes on and on. The important thing is to include in the resource file all information that may be necessary for translators. The most important is a description of the parameters in a format statement. You might want to add a comment to the string that says something like this:

```
Parameter 0: color. Parameter 1: vehicle type
```

Then the translator would know to create the correct formatting string like this:

```
VehicleSold= La {1} {0} e' stata venduta
```

Sometimes you might even want to include an example of the phrase that results from the formatting statement. Always try to give translators as much information as you can about text, including contextual information that may apply.

The code for MyLocalizedForm

Just for the sake of completeness, Listing 7-45 shows the salient code used in `MyLocalizedForm`.

Listing 7-45: **The Code for MyLocalizedForm**

```
using System;
using System.Drawing;
using System.Collections;
using System.ComponentModel;
using System.Windows.Forms;
using System.Data;
using System.Threading;
using System.Globalization;
using System.Resources;

namespace MyLocalizedForm
{
  public class Form1 : System.Windows.Forms.Form
  {
```

```
    private System.Windows.Forms.Label label1;
    private System.Windows.Forms.Button buttonGetCurrentTime;
    private System.Windows.Forms.Label labelCurrentTime;

    private System.ComponentModel.Container components = null;

    public Form1()
    {
      InitializeComponent();
    }

    protected override void Dispose( bool disposing )
    {
      //  code created by wizard...
    }

    #region Windows Form Designer generated code
    private void InitializeComponent()
    {
      // code created by designer
    }
    #endregion

    [STAThread]
    static void Main()
    {
      // show the current locale on the system console
      Console.Out.WriteLine("The locale is " +
              Thread.CurrentThread.CurrentUICulture.ToString() );

      Application.Run(new Form1());
    }

    private void buttonGetCurrentTime_Click(object sender, System.EventArgs e)
    {
      labelCurrentTime.Text = DateTime.Now.ToString();

      // create a localized message at runtime using ResourceManager
      // ResourceManager rm = new ResourceManager("MyLocalizedForm.MyStrings",
      //                                    this.GetType().Assembly);
      // String s = rm.GetString("ThankYou");
      // MessageBox.Show(this, s);

      // create a localized message at runtime using ResourceManager
      ResourceManager rm = new ResourceManager("MyLocalizedForm.MyStrings",
                                        this.GetType().Assembly);
      ResourceSet rs = rm.GetResourceSet(Thread.CurrentThread.CurrentUICulture,
                                    true, true);
      String s = rs.GetString("ThankYou");
      MessageBox.Show(this, s);
    }
  }
}
```

Localizing images

Text is not the only thing that needs localizing in a component. Your application may need to also change graphical items. If these items belong to controls placed on a Windows Form, you can just edit the resx file for the form's locale and change the image using VS .NET. If the graphical item is not part of a Windows Form control, you'll need to do some extra work outside of VS .NET.

Say you want to create a set of resource files with localized images that you'll access to create a Web page. I'll use an example that is part of the .NET framework SDK, in the folder:

```
C:\Program Files\Microsoft.NET\FrameworkSDK\Samples\tutorials\
resourcesandlocalization\graphic\cs
```

The resources in this case are bitmaps of flags for various countries. You have the images as jpeg files, and need to somehow convert them to .resx and .resource files. First, you need to create the .resx file. There are two ways to create them. Both methods work with text and image resources. The first method uses a Windows application called ResEditor; the second uses a command-line utility called ResxGen. I'll describe both in the next two sections.

Using ResEditor

ResEditor is a small tool that is included in the .NET Framework SDK as a tutorial program showing how to handle .resx files. You can find it (with its source code) in the folder:

```
C:\Microsoft Visual Studio
.NET\FrameworkSDK\Samples\tutorials\resourcesandlocalization\reseditor
```

The ResEditor program is a simple Windows Form application that lets you create resource files containing both strings and images. To use it, first you need to build the executable, using the build.bat file in the ResEditor folder. Once the application is built, run it. Figure 7-27 shows the program after opening a .resx file and adding some items to it.

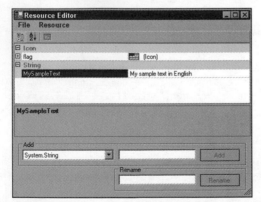

Figure 7-27: The ResEditor application that allows you to put graphics items into a .resx or .resource file

ResEditor is a fairly simple tutorial program, so don't set your expectations too high for it. Keep in mind that ResEditor is not capable of creating new .resx files. To create a new .resx file, use the VS .NET Add New Item Wizard and select the Assembly Resource File template, as shown in Figure 7-28.

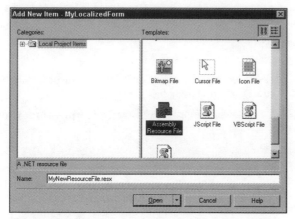

Figure 7-28: Creating a new .resx file in VS .NET

Once the .resx file is created, you can open it in ResEditor using the Open button. To add a string resource, follow these steps.

1. Select System.String as the resource type, as shown in Figure 7-29.

2. Enter a name for the resource.

3. Click the Add button. Figure 7-29 shows the UI just before adding a new string named MyNextSampleString. The grid in the top section has two columns. The left one is the name and the right one is the value of a resource.

4. To edit the value of a string, click its value cell. For example, to edit the value of MySampleString, click on the grid where it says *My sample text in English,* and enter the new text you want.

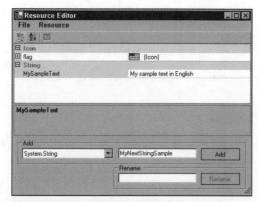

Figure 7-29: Adding a string resource to a .resx file with ResEditor

To add images to the resource file, the process is slightly different. First enter a name for the image by typing a name in the Add section. Choose an image type, and then click the Add button. The `System.Drawing.Bitmap` type can handle .bmp, .gif, and .jpg files, to name a few. When you click the Add button, a blank bitmap appears in the grid above in the value cell. To load the image, click the ellipsis button in the value cell. A File Open dialog box will appear, letting you choose the name of the image file to load. Once the file is loaded, a small thumbnail will appear in the value cell, as shown in the previous figure with the U.S. flag.

Using ResxGen

Another tool for creating .resx files is ResxGen, a command-line utility that takes a string, image, or other type of resource file and adds it to a .resx file.

Like ResEditor, ResxGen is also a .NET Framework utility that is available with source code. You can find it in the folder

```
C:\Microsoft Visual Studio .NET\FrameworkSDK\Samples\tutorials\
resourcesandlocalization\resxgen
```

Unlike ResEditor, ResXGen can also create a .resx file. The source code for ResXGen can be a valuable resource for people wanting to learn more about the structure of .resx files. You have to build ResxGen to get the executable program. Just run the batch file in the ResxGen folder. After building ResxGen, I moved it to my C:\ directory so it would be on the Windows search path, obviating the need to type in the long ResxGen path name each time I want to run the utility.

To run ResxGen, open a DOS box and go to the folder containing the resource to add to the .resx file. Type a command like this:

```
resxgen /i:mybitmap.jpg   /o:Images.resx   /n:mybitmapname
```

The `/i:` parameter designates the file containing the image, text, or other resource you want to add to the .resx file. The `/o:` parameter is the name of the .resx file to generate. The `/n:` parameter is the name you wish to assign to the resource. Remember, once items are in a resource file, your program will reference them using only their name. There are no filenames stored in .resx files.

Setting up the localized images

So far I have shown you how to create a single .resx file containing images. To complete the localization process, I need to create multiple resources for all the locales I wish to support. To do so, I need to create a number of subfolders that designate the locales. Let's assume the U.S. English locale is the default one, so all its resources will be built into the main assembly. To build the U.S. flag image into the .resx for the main assembly, you need to put the file with the image file in the folder containing the executable file for the component you're developing and use the following command:

```
resxgen /i:en-US.jpg   /o:Images.resx   /n:flag
```

The output file has no locale suffix (such as *Images.en-US.resx*) because it is the file for the default locale. To support the it-IT locale for Italian, create a new subfolder called it-IT. In this folder, put the image file you want to use, which in my example is a file called it-IT.jpg with the Italian flag. From this new folder, run ResxGen like this:

```
resxgen /i:it-IT.jpg   /o:Images.it-IT.resx   /n:flag
```

This time, the output file has the it-IT suffix. Notice how the two .resx files use the same name (in this case, *flag*) for the resource. This is essential in order for the .NET Framework global-ization code to find the localized versions of a resource. The folder structure containing the resource files is also critical. If the folder with the executable is called *Graphic\bin\Debug*, the folder structure needs to be

```
Graphic
  bin
    Debug
      it-IT
```

All the folders containing localized versions of the images are named after the locale they relate to. Remember: The base folder (*Graphic\bin\Debug*) is the folder where the executable file resides. Where the source code and other files reside is irrelevant.

I'm still not done localizing the image files. At this point, I have two .resx files. The first .resx file is in the executable folder called Images.resx and contains the default locale image for a flag. The second .resx file is in the it-IT folder and contains the Italian version of the flag image. Now I have to compile the files into .resource files. To compile the files, I'll need the command-line utility called ResGen that ships with the .NET Framework SDK. To compile the default locale resource, open a DOS box, go to the folder containing the executable file, and enter the following command:

```
resgen <input filename> <output filename>
```

To generate the U.S. resource file, I need to enter

```
resgen   images.resx   images.resources
```

This will create the file image.resources in the executable folder. To generate the Italian resource file, I need to enter

```
resgen   it-IT\images.it-IT.resx   it-IT\images.it-IT.resources
```

This command will create the file images.it-IT.resources in the it-IT folder.

The next step is to link the Italian .resource file and create a satellite assembly, like this:

```
al /out:it-IT\Graphic.resources.dll
   /c:it-IT
      /embed:it-IT\Images.it-IT.resources, Images.it-IT.resources, Private
```

Now you need to build the main assembly and reference the satellite assembly, like this:

```
csc /debug+ /target:winexe /r:System.DLL /r:System.Drawing.DLL
    /r:System.Windows.Forms.DLL /r:System.Data.DLL
    /res:Images.resources, Images.resources graphic.cs
```

That's quite a bit of work just to put some images into satellite assemblies. There is also an easier way, using VS .NET. Just add the .resx files created with ResxGen and add them to your project in the Solution Explorer. Then VS .NET will handle all the other details for you. For each .resx file whose name contains a locale designator (such as MyResxFile.en-US.resx), VS .NET will generate a satellite assembly containing the compiled resources and put the file in the proper subfolder. For example, if the .resx file is named Graphic.en-US.resx, VS .NET will create a satellite assembly with the name Graphic.resource.dll and place it in the subfolder us-US. This folder will be directly under the folder containing the executable file of your component.

Now all the parts are in place to access the localized images at runtime. To access the flag resource in your code, you would do something like what's shown in Listing 7-46.

> **Listing 7-46: Accessing a Localized Image at Runtime**

```
using System.Drawing;
//...


ResourceManager rm = new ResourceManager("Images", this.GetType().Assembly);

Image myFlag.Image = (Image) rm.GetObject("flag");
```

And that's all there is to it. As you can see, creating the localized versions of images is the hard part. Accessing them at runtime is the easy part. If you use ResourceManager to get the resources, it will provide fallback support. If a resource is not available in the requested locale, the parent locale will be searched (assuming there is one). If it's not found there either, the default locale will be searched.

For production environments, many developers prefer to use the command-line tools ResxGen and ResGen to build the image resource files. This way they can run them in batch mode and build all of the .resource satellite assemblies with a single command.

Summary

I've covered a wide range of topics in this chapter, many of which apply not just to front-end components, but to many other types of components as well. For example, regular expressions, file management, and printing are completely general topics that can be useful almost anywhere in a project.

Keep in mind that Windows Forms components need to be polished to a much higher degree than other types of components. Just because the code is debugged doesn't mean a Windows Form is ready to be shipped. The precise size, layout, color, and position of controls on a Form are very important considerations, among others. Your customers will be probably spend many an hour looking at your application's user interface, and something as simple as an incorrect tab order can be a source of irritation for many people.

✦   ✦   ✦

Creating Front Ends with the WebBrowser Component

A billion here, a billion there — sooner or later it adds up to real money.

— Former U.S. Senator Everett Dirksen on public finance

Senator Dirksen's concept of *real money* may have been slightly different from yours or mine, but one thing is certain: If you fail to take advantage of existing components when building the front end of your application, you'll find your development costs adding up to *real money*.

The Microsoft WebBrowser Component

One of the most powerful reusable UI components I know of is the `WebBrowser` ActiveX component used by Internet Explorer. Microsoft designed it to be extremely flexible in terms of the kinds of content it can display. Obviously, it can display HTML documents, but it may come as a surprise to some of you that it can also display other common file types such as Word, Excel, PowerPoint, TXT, RTF, GIF, JPEG, XML, PDF, and others. `WebBrowser` achieves this incredible flexibility by using an embedded ActiveX component to render its data. In the case of HTML documents, the component is `MsHtml`. For more complex documents like Word or Excel, `WebBrowser` acts as an Active Document host and embeds Word or Excel in the client area to handle the rendering.

Since `WebBrowser` was designed specifically to be hosted by a container application, it has a lot of features you can control. Microsoft uses the component in several different applications, and customizes its look and feel to blend in with the rest of the host application. Examples of hosts include Windows Explorer, Outlook, and even the VS .NET Start Page. In this chapter, I'll show you how to create a Windows application that hosts the `WebBrowser` component. Later, since customization is very important to many of you, I'll create a second Windows application showing how to access the various customization features that `WebBrowser` makes available.

I'll call the first browser application *MyWebBrowser* and give it a toolbar, to show how to control some of the common functions of `WebBrowser`. As I said earlier, `WebBrowser` can handle more than just HTML files. Figures 8-1 through 8-6 show MyWebBrowser displaying different types of files.

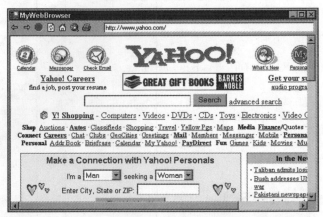

Figure 8-1: Using MyWebBrowser to display an HTML page

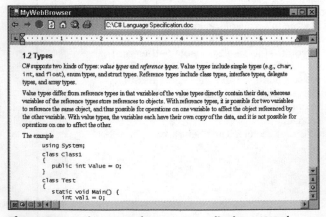

Figure 8-2: Using MyWebBrowser to display a Word document

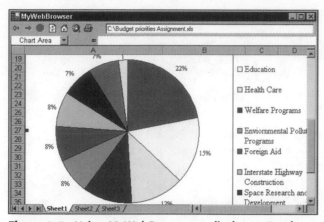

Figure 8-3: Using MyWebBrowser to display an Excel spreadsheet

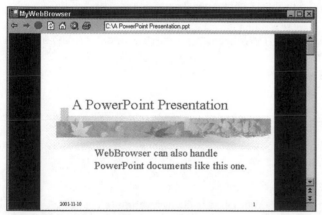

Figure 8-4: Using MyWebBrowser to display a Powerpoint document

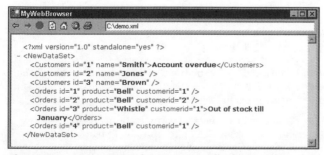

Figure 8-5: Using MyWebBrowser to display an XML document

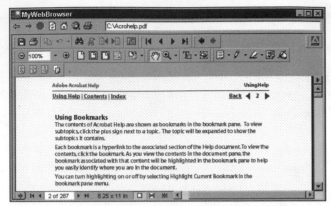

Figure 8-6: Using MyWebBrowser to display a PDF document

These screen shots hopefully give you some sense of how flexible WebBrowser really is. WebBrowser and its Active Document subcomponents do all the work behind the scenes. If you can find a more powerful reusable UI component than WebBrowser, let me know.

Not only does WebBrowser display a zillion file types, it also lets you control the way documents are presented. In the case of HTML documents, there is a whole slew of behaviors that can be changed, such as:

✦ Changing the context menu

✦ Hiding scrollbars

✦ Disabling text selection

✦ Removing the 3D border

✦ Using flat scrollbars

✦ Forcing in-place navigation

I'll show you how to make these and other kinds of customizations to MsHtml, but first, I'll get you familiar with WebBrowser by showing you a simple application called *MyWebBrowser* that can be used as a simple mini-browser without any customizations. After describing MyWebBrowser, I'll show you a customized browser in an application called *MyCustom WebBrowser*. This application will use COM interfaces and callbacks to control the way MsHtml works.

Designing MyWebBrowser

Since almost all the functionality you need is already built into WebBrowser, the design of an application based on Windows Forms that embeds the component is fairly trivial. Figure 8-7 shows the salient parts of the class diagram for MyWebBrowser.

Like I said, in this first example, I won't add any special customizations to MsHtml or WebBrowser, because doing so requires utilizing COM interoperability features. After showing a simple example, I'll show you how to use COM interfaces to customize many MsHtml features.

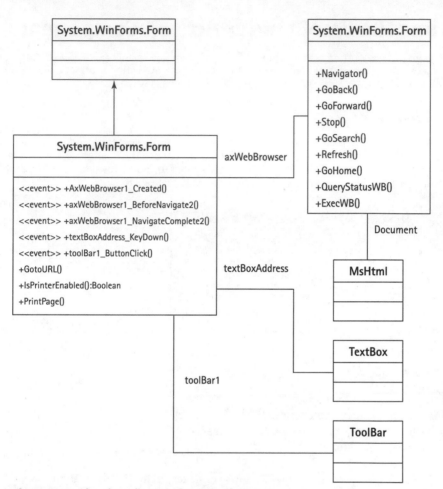

Figure 8-7: The class diagram for MyWebBrowser

Developing MyWebBrowser

Enough said about the glories of WebBrowser and MsHtml. They're built-in, they're good, they're wonderful. Great. Let's put them to work in a real program. MyWebBrowser is a simple Windows application that has just a single form, called *MainForm,* which hosts the WebBrowser component and demonstrates not only how to use it, but more generally how to access ActiveX components from managed code.

I created MyWebBrowser with the New Project Wizard, choosing Windows Application as the project type. I renamed the main form class from *Form1* to *MainForm*, and set the project name to *MyWebBrowser*. The next step was to add the WebBrowser ActiveX component to MainForm, a task that deserves a separate explanation.

Importing the WebBrowser ActiveX Component

There is no `WebBrowser` component in the Toolbox when you install VS .NET, so you have to import a .NET version of the `WebBrowser` into your project. As with just about everything in life, the import process can be done the easy way or the hard way.

The easy way

The easy way is with the Customize Toolbox dialog box. First select the Windows Forms page on the Toolbox and then right-click on the Toolbox and choose the Customize Toolbox command on the pop-up menu. Select the COM Components tab, scroll down to the Microsoft Web Browser item, and check its checkbox, as shown in Figure 8-8.

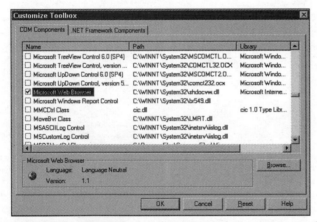

Figure 8-8: Importing the ShDocVw.WebBrowser control into the VS .NET Toolbox

The `WebBrowser` will show up on the Windows Forms tab of the Toolbox with the name *Explorer,* as shown in Figure 8-9.

Figure 8-9: The WebBrowser component after installing it on the Toolbox

Now drop an instance of `WebBrowser` on MainForm. When the component is dropped, VS .NET performs the following tasks.

1. It launches an import process that creates the two files *AxInterop.SHDocVw.dll* and *Interop.SHDocVw.dll.*

2. It puts the two files in your project's `bin\Debug` or `bin\Release` directory (depending on whether your project configuration is set to Debug or Release).

3. It adds the two files to the References node of your project in the Solution Explorer.

4. It adds an instance of *AxSHDocVw.AxWebBrowser* to your form.

A nice piece of work, saving you precious time and money — perhaps not billions, but hey, no one said life is fair.

In case you're wondering, much of the process was performed under the covers by a command-line utility called *aximp*, described later. At this point the Solution Explorer looks like Figure 8-10.

Figure 8-10: The Solution Explorer, showing the newly imported files

That was the easy way to import the `WebBrowser` component. The hard way is for those of you that like typing (and I know there are a lot of you out there).

The hard way

I always get a kick out of watching people open DOS boxes and furiously type in long commands that could be replaced with a couple of mouse clicks. Force of habit is a powerful thing. But using command-line utilities for the import process is not always a bad thing, because they create the necessary import files without adding anything to the Toolbox. Although you may want to have a useful component like `WebBrowser` in the Toolbox, you don't necessarily want every ActiveX component you'll ever use cluttering up the precious Toolbox space.

In any case, there are two command-line utilities available for converting COM types into .NET-compatible types that can be referenced in a VS .NET project. Which one to use depends on how you want to use the imported components.

Using TlbImp

The lowest level command-line utility for ActiveX importing is `TlbImp`. You'll want to use this utility when importing ActiveX components that *won't* be used in a Windows Form. `TlbImp` reads a file containing COM Type Library information — which can be a .tlb, .dll, .odl, or other file type — and produces a DLL containing .NET-compatible metadata. The DLL must then be added to the References node of your project.

For example, to use shdocvw.dll (containing the `WebBrowser` component, for those of you that jumped into this section without reading the previous ones) in the MyWebBrowser project, you would open a Command-Prompt box, go to the folder `C:\Program Files\Microsoft.NET\FrameworkSDK\Bin`, and then type the command:

```
tlbimp c:\winnt\system32\shdocvw.dll
/out:C:\MyWebBrowser\bin\Debug\Interop.shdocvw.dll
```

You can inspect the .NET metadata in the DLL generated by TlbImp with a standard .NET tool like ildasm. Open a Command-Line box and go to the folder containing the newly generated Shdocvw.dll file and then type the command:

```
"C:\Program Files\Microsoft.NET\FrameworkSDK\Bin\ildasm" shdocvw.dll
```

Figure 8-11 shows some of the contents of the metadata file displayed by ildasm.

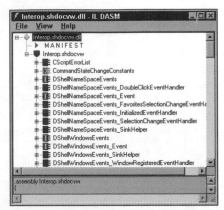

Figure 8-11: Inspecting the metadata in the DLL produced by running TlbImp on c:\winnt\system32\shdocvw.dll

The metadata makes it possible for your code to interact with the unmanaged code of COM components using exactly the same syntax you would use with native C# components.

Using AxImp

If you plan to use an ActiveX component in a Windows Form, as I did with WebBrowser, you'll need to use the AxImp command-line utility instead of TlbImp. The reason is this: To use an ActiveX component in a Windows Form, a wrapper class must also be generated. All components dropped in Windows Forms are required to be derived from the common base class System.Windows.Forms.Control. The utility AxImp creates the wrapper for you.

To create the wrapper for WebBrowser, open a Command-Line box, go to the folder where the executable code of your project will go. For the project MyWebBrowser, the folder will be MyWebBrowser\bin\debug or MyWebBrowser\bin\release. Type the following command:

```
"C:\Program Files\Microsoft.NET\FrameworkSDK\Bin\aximp"
c:\winnt\system32\shdocvw.dll
```

The utility will generate two files, called *SHDocVw.dll* and *AxSHDocVw.dll*. The first file contains the .NET metadata that describes the COM types contained in c:\winnt\system32\shdocvw.dll. The file is identical to the one produced by TlbImp in the previous section (because AxImp internally calls TlbImp to generate it). The second file is a .NET assembly containing the wrapper classes that allow you to use the ActiveX component in standard Windows Forms. Figure 8-12 shows the contents of AxSHDocVw.dll, as viewed with ildasm.

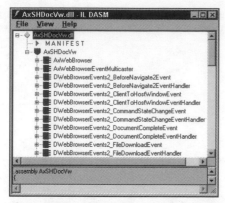

Figure 8-12: The wrapper class created for SHDocVw

Basically, `AxImp` creates a new class derived from `System.Windows.Forms.AxHost`, which is derived from `System.Windows.Forms.Control`. This new class acts as a .NET wrapper for the ActiveX component.

Runtime Callable Wrappers (RCW)

When you instantiate a COM type in your C# code, using code like this:

```
AxSHDocVw.AxWebBrowser axWebBrowser1 = new AxSHDocVw.AxWebBrowser();
```

there is more going on than meets the eye. What actually happens is this: The compiler looks at the metadata describing the class `AxWebBrowser`, in the `AxSHDocVw` assembly generated by `TlbImp` or `AxImp`. Using this metadata, it creates something called a *Runtime Callable Wrapper* (RCW), which is a proxy component that on one side is callable from your managed code and on the other side deals with the unmanaged COM code of the `WebBrowser` ActiveX component. The RCW acts as an invisible bridge between your code and the ActiveX code, as shown in Figure 8-13.

Figure 8-13: The Runtime Callable Wrapper as a proxy for COM components

The RCW manages all those pesky COM details that you don't want to deal with, such as reference counting, deleting the component when it is no longer used, marshalling parameters in method calls, and so on. If you create multiple instances of the same COM component in your code, all the instances will share a single RCW. Keep in mind that all this RCW business is generally completely transparent to you. It's there to help you, making it as easy to access an ActiveX component as any other managed component.

Adding a toolbar

Before I completely lose track of where I am, let me finish describing the code for MyWebBrowser. First I'll discuss the toolbar buttons. Most UIs containing `WebBrowser` support some means for navigating, whether it's with toolbar buttons, menu commands, or some other element.

I added a toolbar to MyWebBrowser by dropping a Toolbox component of type `ToolBar` on the main form. In the ToolBar's properties, I clicked on the `Collections` field and added seven buttons with the following functions:

✦ Back

✦ Forward

✦ Stop

✦ Refresh

✦ Home

✦ Search

✦ Print

To make the buttons look like those used by Internet Explorer, I used a screen capture utility to get the IE button images, and then saved them as bitmap files in the folder containing the source code for MyWebBrowser. I set them all to have a green background. I added an `ImageList` component to the form and added all the bitmap images to it. I set the `ImageList` `TransparentColor` property to green, so the green areas of the bitmaps would be transparent and assume the color of the button faces. Then I set the `ToolBar`'s `ImageList` property to reference the `ImageList` component. For each toolbar button, I set the following properties: `ToolTipText`, `Text`, and `ImageIndex`. To the right of the toolbar buttons, I dropped a `TextBox` control. To make the `TextBox` always stretch to the right side of the form, I set its `Anchor` property to (Top, Left, Right). Figure 8-14 shows the finished toolbar.

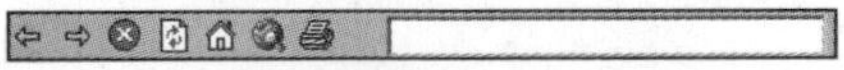

Figure 8-14: The finished toolbar

Notice the *flat* look of the toolbar, with the buttons showing no borders. This look was achieved by setting the toolbar's `Appearance` property to `Flat`. Next, I added some event handling code for the toolbar buttons, as shown in Listing 8-1.

Listing 8-1: **The Toolbar Event Handler**

```
protected void toolBar1_ButtonClick(object sender,
           System.WinForms.ToolBarButtonClickEventArgs e)
{
  Cursor.Current = Cursors.WaitCursor;

  try
  {
    if (e.button == toolBarButtonBack)
      axWebBrowser1.GoBack();


    else if (e.button == toolBarButtonForward)
      axWebBrowser1.GoForward();


    else if (e.button == toolBarButtonStop)
```

```
    {
      axWebBrowser1.Stop();
      toolBarButtonStop.Enabled = false;
    }

    else if (e.button == toolBarButtonSearch)
      axWebBrowser1.GoSearch();


    else if (e.button == toolBarButtonPrint)
      PrintPage();

    else if (e.button == toolBarButtonRefresh)
    {
      object REFRESH_COMPLETELY = 3;
      axWebBrowser1.Refresh2(ref REFRESH_COMPLETELY);
    }

    else if (e.button == toolBarButtonHome)
      axWebBrowser1.GoHome();

  }
  finally
  {
    Cursor.Current = Cursors.Default;

  }
}
```

The method `WebBrowser.GoSearch()` navigates to the Search site, which can be set up in Internet Explorer by clicking the Search toolbar button and selecting Customize in the Search pane. By default, `WebBrowser` uses the search engine at `http://search.msn.com`.

The method `WebBrowser.GoHome()` navigates to the Home site set up in Internet Explorer with the Tools ⇨ Internet Options dialog box, on the General tab.

Adding support for printing

All of the buttons except Print are handled by calling a method in the embedded `WebBrowser` component. As noted earlier, there is no `Print()` method, so printing is handled differently, with the code shown in Listing 8-2.

Listing 8-2: **Printing the HTML Page Displayed in the WebBrowser**

```
private bool IsPrinterEnabled()
{
  int response =
    (int) axWebBrowser1.QueryStatusWB(SHDocVw.OLECMDID.OLECMDID_PRINT);
  return (response & (int) SHDocVw.OLECMDF.OLECMDF_ENABLED) != 0 ?
```

Continued

Listing 8-2 *(continued)*

```
    true : false;
}

private void PrintPage()
{
  object o = "";

  // constants useful when printing
  SHDocVw.OLECMDID Print = SHDocVw.OLECMDID.OLECMDID_PRINT;

  // use this value to print without prompting
  // SHDocVw.OLECMDEXECOPT PromptUser =
  //   SHDocVw.OLECMDEXECOPT.OLECMDEXECOPT_PROMPTUSER;

  SHDocVw.OLECMDEXECOPT DontPromptUser =
    SHDocVw.OLECMDEXECOPT.OLECMDEXECOPT_DONTPROMPTUSER;

  if (!IsPrinterEnabled() ) return;

  // print without prompting user
  axWebBrowser1.ExecWB(Print, DontPromptUser, ref o, ref o);

  // to prompt the user with printer settings
  // axWebBrowser1.ExecWB(Print, PromptUser, ref o, ref o);
}
```

The last two lines in the listing show two ways to print: The first way prints silently, the second way prints after prompting the user for printer settings. I created two constants called DontPromptUser and PromptUser, which are derived from ShDocVw enumerated values. When you call WebBrowser.ExecWB(), you simply pass the constant indicating whether you want the method to display a Print dialog box or not.

Adding navigation support

To navigate to a Web site, you call the Navigate() or Navigate2() method of the WebBrowser. The first method handles navigating to ordinary URLs, including local files. The second method extends the first by supporting navigation to items in the Windows Desktop and My Computer folders. To protect the rest of the application from errors caused by invalid URLs or network problems, I wrapped the call to WebBrowser.Navigate() in a try block in a method called GotoURL(), shown in Listing 8-3.

Listing 8-3: Setting the URL of the Document to Load

```
public void GotoURL(String theURL)
{
  try
  {
    Cursor.Current = Cursors.WaitCursor;
```

```
      Object o = null;
      axWebBrowser1.Navigate(theURL, ref o, ref o, ref o, ref o);
    }
  finally {
    Cursor.Current = Cursors.Default;
    }
  }
```

To allow the user to type a URL in the `TextBox`, I added an event handler for the `TextBox` that calls `GotoURL()` as shown in Listing 8-4.

Listing 8-4: **The TextBox Event Handler**

```
protected void textBoxAddress_KeyDown (object sender,
                                       System.WinForms.KeyEventArgs e)
{
  if (e.KeyCode == Keys.Return)
    GotoURL(textBoxAddress.Text);
}
```

To display an hourglass cursor while a page is being loaded, I set the cursor in the WebBrowser's `BeforeNavigate2()` handler as shown in Listing 8-5.

Listing 8-5: **Setting the Cursor to an Hourglass during Navigation**

```
protected void axWebBrowser1_BeforeNavigate2 (object sender,
            AxSHDocVw.DWebBrowserEvents2_BeforeNavigate2Event e)
{
  toolBarButtonStop.Enabled = true;
  Cursor.Current = Cursors.WaitCursor;
}
```

Once a page is loaded, I need make sure the cursor is eventually restored to an arrow pointer. Navigation commands can end in one of two ways. If the page can't be loaded, the `NavigateError` handler is called. If the page was loaded, the `NavigateComplete` handler is called. I created a simple `NavigateError` handler, as shown in Listing 8-6.

Listing 8-6: **The NavigateError Handler that Restores the Mouse Cursor**

```
private void axWebBrowser1_NavigateError(object sender,
            AxSHDocVw.DWebBrowserEvents2_NavigateErrorEvent e)
{
  Cursor.Current = Cursors.Default;
```

Continued

Listing 8-6 *(continued)*

```
    toolBarButtonStop.Enabled = false;
    toolBarButtonHome.Enabled = true;
    toolBarButtonSearch.Enabled = true;
    toolBarButtonRefresh.Enabled = true;
}
```

If navigation to a site is successful, the `NavigateComplete2` handler is called, if available. I created a `NavigateComplete2` handler, as shown in Listing 8-7.

Listing 8-7: The NavigateComplete2 Handler

```
private void axWebBrowser1_NavigateComplete2(object sender,
        AxSHDocVw.DWebBrowserEvents2_NavigateComplete2Event e)
{
  Cursor.Current = Cursors.Default;

  toolBarButtonStop.Enabled = false;
  toolBarButtonHome.Enabled = true;
  toolBarButtonSearch.Enabled = true;
  toolBarButtonRefresh.Enabled = true;

  // update the URL displayed in the address bar
  String s = e.uRL.ToString();
  textBoxAddress.Text = s;

  // update the list of visited URLs
  int i = urlsVisited.IndexOf(s);
  if (i >= 0)
    currentUrlIndex = i;
  else
    currentUrlIndex = urlsVisited.Add(s);

  // enable / disable the Back and Forward buttons
  toolBarButtonBack.Enabled = (currentUrlIndex == 0) ? false : true;
  toolBarButtonForward.Enabled =
    (currentUrlIndex >= urlsVisited.Count-1) ? false : true;

  // set the state of the Print button
  toolBarButtonPrint.Enabled = IsPrinterEnabled();
}
```

In the `NavigateComplete2` handler, I displayed the current URL in the TextBox and updated the list of visited URLs. Each time the user goes to a new URL, I store it in an ArrayList. I used the list to support enabling and disabling the Back and Forward buttons. When the user clicks the Back button, I retrieve the previous URL in the list and navigate to it. When the user navigates all the way back to the first URL in the list, I disable the Back button. Similarly, when the user navigates forward to the end of the list, I disable the Forward button.

Disabling the Back and Forward buttons is more than just a cosmetic exercise: If you call the WebBrowser's GoBack() or GoForward() method when there is no previous or next URL to navigate to, the component will raise an exception. If you don't catch the exception, an error message will be displayed.

The last feature to add is one that will make MyWebBrowser go to the Home page when it is run. All you need to do is call the method axWebBrowser1.GoHome() in the constructor for MainForm.

The complete code

The next section will deal with ways to customize the WebBrowser component. Before I move to this new topic, I've included the full code for MyWebBrowser in Listing 8-8.

Listing 8-8: **The Code for MyWebBrowser**

```
using System;
using System.Drawing;
using System.Collections;
using System.ComponentModel;
using System.Windows.Forms;
using System.Data;

namespace MyWebBrowser
{
  public class MainForm : System.Windows.Forms.Form
  {
    private System.Windows.Forms.Panel panel1;
    private System.Windows.Forms.ToolBar toolBar1;
    private System.Windows.Forms.ImageList imageList1;
    private System.Windows.Forms.ToolBarButton toolBarButtonBack;
    private System.Windows.Forms.ToolBarButton toolBarButtonForward;
    private System.Windows.Forms.ToolBarButton toolBarButtonStop;
    private System.Windows.Forms.ToolBarButton toolBarButtonRefresh;
    private System.Windows.Forms.ToolBarButton toolBarButtonHome;
    private System.Windows.Forms.ToolBarButton toolBarButtonSearch;
    private System.Windows.Forms.ToolBarButton toolBarButtonPrint;
    private AxSHDocVw.AxWebBrowser axWebBrowser1;
    private System.Windows.Forms.TextBox textBoxAddress;
    private System.ComponentModel.IContainer components;

    ArrayList urlsVisited = new ArrayList();
    int currentUrlIndex = -1;  // no sites visited initially

    public MainForm()
    {
      InitializeComponent();

      toolBarButtonBack.Enabled = false;
      toolBarButtonForward.Enabled = false;
      toolBarButtonStop.Enabled = false;
```

Continued

Listing 8-8 *(continued)*

```
    toolBarButtonRefresh.Enabled = false;
    toolBarButtonHome.Enabled = false;
    toolBarButtonSearch.Enabled = false;
    toolBarButtonPrint.Enabled = false;

    axWebBrowser1.GoHome();
}

protected override void Dispose( bool disposing )
{
  // standard wizard-created code
}

private void InitializeComponent()
{
  // standard wizard-created code
}

[STAThread]
static void Main()
{
    Application.Run(new MainForm());
}

private void toolBar1_ButtonClick(object sender,
        System.Windows.Forms.ToolBarButtonClickEventArgs e)
{
  Cursor.Current = Cursors.WaitCursor;

  try
  {
    if (e.Button == toolBarButtonBack)
      axWebBrowser1.GoBack();


    else if (e.Button == toolBarButtonForward)
      axWebBrowser1.GoForward();


    else if (e.Button == toolBarButtonStop)
    {
      axWebBrowser1.Stop();

      toolBarButtonStop.Enabled = false;
    }

    else if (e.Button == toolBarButtonSearch)
      axWebBrowser1.GoSearch();


    else if (e.Button == toolBarButtonPrint)
```

```
        PrintPage();

      else if (e.Button == toolBarButtonRefresh)
      {
        object REFRESH_COMPLETELY = 3;
        axWebBrowser1.Refresh2(ref REFRESH_COMPLETELY);
      }

      else if (e.Button == toolBarButtonHome)
        axWebBrowser1.GoHome();
    }
    finally
    {
      Cursor.Current = Cursors.Default;
    }
}

private bool IsPrinterEnabled()
{
  int response =
    (int) axWebBrowser1.QueryStatusWB(SHDocVw.OLECMDID.OLECMDID_PRINT);
  return (response & (int) SHDocVw.OLECMDF.OLECMDF_ENABLED) != 0 ?
        true : false;
}

private void PrintPage()
{
  object o = "";

  // constants useful when printing
  SHDocVw.OLECMDID Print = SHDocVw.OLECMDID.OLECMDID_PRINT;

  // use this value to print without prompting
  // SHDocVw.OLECMDEXECOPT PromptUser =
  //   SHDocVw.OLECMDEXECOPT.OLECMDEXECOPT_PROMPTUSER;

  SHDocVw.OLECMDEXECOPT DontPromptUser =
    SHDocVw.OLECMDEXECOPT.OLECMDEXECOPT_DONTPROMPTUSER;

  if (!IsPrinterEnabled() ) return;

  // print without prompting user
  axWebBrowser1.ExecWB(Print, DontPromptUser, ref o, ref o);

  // to prompt the user with printer settings
  // axWebBrowser1.ExecWB(Print, PromptUser, ref o, ref o);
}

public void GotoURL(String theURL)
{
  try
  {
```

Continued

Listing 8-8 *(continued)*

```csharp
    Cursor.Current = Cursors.WaitCursor;
    Object o = null;
    axWebBrowser1.Navigate(theURL, ref o, ref o, ref o, ref o);
  }
  finally
  {
    Cursor.Current = Cursors.Default;
  }
}

private void textBoxAddress_KeyDown(object sender,
        System.Windows.Forms.KeyEventArgs e)
{
  if (e.KeyCode == Keys.Return)
    GotoURL(textBoxAddress.Text);
}

private void axWebBrowser1_BeforeNavigate2(object sender,
        AxSHDocVw.DWebBrowserEvents2_BeforeNavigate2Event e)
{
  toolBarButtonStop.Enabled = true;
  Cursor.Current = Cursors.WaitCursor;
}

private void axWebBrowser1_NavigateComplete2(object sender,
        AxSHDocVw.DWebBrowserEvents2_NavigateComplete2Event e)
{
  Cursor.Current = Cursors.Default;

  toolBarButtonStop.Enabled = false;
  toolBarButtonHome.Enabled = true;
  toolBarButtonSearch.Enabled = true;
  toolBarButtonRefresh.Enabled = true;

  // update the URL displayed in the address bar
  String s = e.uRL.ToString();
  textBoxAddress.Text = s;

  // update the list of visited URLs
  int i = urlsVisited.IndexOf(s);
  if (i >= 0)
    currentUrlIndex = i;
  else
    currentUrlIndex = urlsVisited.Add(s);

  // enable / disable the Back and Forward buttons
  toolBarButtonBack.Enabled = (currentUrlIndex == 0) ? false : true;
  toolBarButtonForward.Enabled =
    (currentUrlIndex >= urlsVisited.Count-1) ? false : true;

  // set the state of the Print button
```

```
      toolBarButtonPrint.Enabled = IsPrinterEnabled();
   }

   private void axWebBrowser1_NavigateError(object sender,
         AxSHDocVw.DWebBrowserEvents2_NavigateErrorEvent e)
   {
     Cursor.Current = Cursors.Default;

     toolBarButtonStop.Enabled = false;
     toolBarButtonHome.Enabled = true;
     toolBarButtonSearch.Enabled = true;
     toolBarButtonRefresh.Enabled = true;
   }
 }
}
```

In the next section, I'll switch gears and get into advanced topics with COM Interop programming. If you're not experienced in COM, you may want to skip the rest of the chapter entirely.

Creating a Customized Web Browser

MyWebBrowser has all the basic browser features, such as navigation, printing, and so on. It also has features you may want to change, such as how accelerator keys are handled or what commands are available on the context menu. To make these kinds of changes, things get a bit more complicated with WebBrowser, and you are forced to get your hands dirty with some COM interoperability programming. In this and the following sections, I'll create another Windows application called *MyCustomWebBrowser* that demonstrates how to develop a fully customized WebBrowser. To start the project, I just copied the entire MyWebBrowser solution into a new folder and renamed it to **MyCustomWebBrowser**.

Customizing the WebBrowser component is more complicated than one might think. The problem is this: Most of the customizable features of MsHtml depend on COM callbacks that must be handled by the host window—MainForm in this case. Callbacks are methods exposed through COM interfaces, so you have to make the necessary interfaces available to MsHtml. It would have been nice if MsHtml had exposed a list of properties for all its customizable features, so you could change a feature with a simple line of code like this:

```
AxWebBrowser.Use3Dborders = false;  // this won't work
```

That would have been way too simple! Besides, each time the parent WebBrowser loads a new HTML page, it creates a new instance of MsHtml, so even if you could set the properties using the previous code, the new MsHtml component wouldn't be affected. You might be thinking, *"Why didn't Microsoft store the customizable properties of MsHtml in the parent WebBrowser component? This way you could set them once, and have WebBrowser automatically reapply them each time it created a new MsHtml component."* For better or for worse, WebBrowser doesn't want anything to do with presentation of content. It was designed to act as a host for rendering components. It handles other aspects of Web browsing, like navigation. WebBrowser is an Active Document host, and it delegates all details of presentation to the hosted Active Document rendering component (MsHtml in this case).

The moral of the story is this: MainForm needs to implement a number of COM interfaces to support MsHtml customizing. Figure 8-15 shows the class diagram for MainForm.

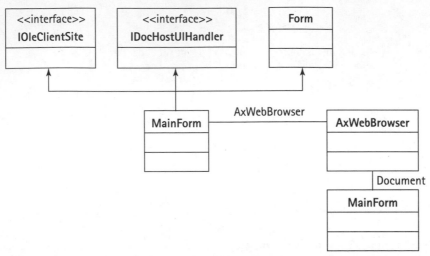

Figure 8-15: The class diagram for a fully customized WebBrowser host Windows Form

Let's take a look at what the COM interfaces are used for. The first step in any type of WebBrowser customization is to establish a component as the *controlling host*. By default, the WebBrowser has no controlling host. To set up MainForm as the new controlling host, you need to call WebBrowser through its OleClient interface as shown in Listing 8-9.

Listing 8-9: Setting Up MainForm as the Controlling Host of WebBrowser

```
object obj = axWebBrowser1.GetOcx();
IOleObject oc = obj as IOleObject;
oc.SetClientSite(this);
```

These three deceptively simple lines of code are critical. The method GetOcx() retrieves the IUnknown interface of the native COM object wrapped by axWebBrowser1. The second line implicitly issues a QueryInterface, seeking an IOleObject interface from the WebBrowser COM object. You can use the as operator like this to query for any type of interface. If the interface is not available, a null will be returned. Once the IOleObject interface is obtained from WebBrowser, the method SetClientSite() is called to set MainForm as the controlling host. Objects passed as a parameter to SetClientSite() must implement the IOleClientSite, ergo the presence of IOleClientSite in the Class Diagram previously shown in Figure 8-15.

Importing and wrapping COM interfaces

MyCustomWebBrowser implements the two COM interfaces IOleClientSite and IDocHostUIHandler, and calls methods of the interface IOleObject. Unfortunately there are no type libraries published by Microsoft that contain these interfaces, meaning you have to get your hands dirty with a bit of COM programming to work around the problem. As it turns out, most of the COM interfaces that Microsoft uses in its components are not published as type libraries. You'll either find them as .idl files, or in some cases as C++ header files.

IOleObject and IOleClientSite

You sometimes have to do a bit of digging to locate the file that declares an interface. In the case of IOleClientSite and IOleObject, I found them both declared in the file oleidl.h, which is in the following folder:

```
C:\Program Files\Microsoft Visual Studio.NET\Vc7\PlatformSDK\include
```

I created C# interfaces to wrap the two COM interfaces, as shown in Listings 8-10 and 8-11.

Listing 8-10: **The Interface that Wraps the COM Interface IOleObject**

```csharp
using System;
using System.Windows.Forms;
using System.Runtime.InteropServices;

namespace MyCustomWebBrowser
{
  [ComImport,
  Guid("00000112-0000-0000-C000-000000000046"),
  InterfaceType(ComInterfaceType.InterfaceIsIUnknown) ]

  public interface IOleObject
  {
    void SetClientSite(IOleClientSite pClientSite);
    void GetClientSite(IOleClientSite ppClientSite);
    void SetHostNames(object szContainerApp, object szContainerObj);
    void Close(uint dwSaveOption);
    void SetMoniker(uint dwWhichMoniker, object pmk);
    void GetMoniker(uint dwAssign, uint dwWhichMoniker, object ppmk);
    void InitFromData(IDataObject pDataObject, bool
                      fCreation, uint dwReserved);
    void GetClipboardData(uint dwReserved, IDataObject ppDataObject);
    void DoVerb(uint iVerb, uint lpmsg, object pActiveSite,
                uint lindex, uint hwndParent, uint lprcPosRect);
    void EnumVerbs(object ppEnumOleVerb);
    void Update();
    void IsUpToDate();
    void GetUserClassID(uint pClsid);
    void GetUserType(uint dwFormOfType, uint pszUserType);
    void SetExtent(uint dwDrawAspect, uint psizel);
    void GetExtent(uint dwDrawAspect, uint psizel);
    void Advise(object pAdvSink, uint pdwConnection);
    void Unadvise(uint dwConnection);
    void EnumAdvise(object ppenumAdvise);
    void GetMiscStatus(uint dwAspect,uint pdwStatus);
    void SetColorScheme(object pLogpal);
  };
}
```

Listing 8-11: The Interface that Wraps the COM Interface IOleClientSite

```
using System;
using System.Runtime.InteropServices;

namespace MyCustomWebBrowser
{
  [ComImport,
  Guid("00000118-0000-0000-C000-000000000046"),
  InterfaceType(ComInterfaceType.InterfaceIsIUnknown) ]

  public interface IOleClientSite
  {
    void SaveObject();
    void GetMoniker(uint dwAssign, uint dwWhichMoniker, object ppmk);
    void GetContainer(object ppContainer);
    void ShowObject();
    void OnShowWindow(bool fShow);
    void RequestNewObjectLayout();
  }
}
```

A few words of explanation are due regarding the attributes used on the interface declarations. The ComImport attribute is used to tag an interface as an existing COM interface that is being implemented in managed code. A requirement for a *ComImported* interface is that there must also be a Guid attribute providing the interface's Globally Unique ID. The InterfaceType attribute indicates the basic type of the interface. The choices are

- ✦ InterfaceIsDual. This interface supports both early and late binding.
- ✦ InterfaceIsIDispatch. This interface supports the IDispatch interface.
- ✦ InterfaceIsIUnknown. This interface just derives directly or indirectly from IUnknown.

The value ComInterfaceType.InterfaceIsIUnknown is by far the most common type of interface.

I don't have enough space here to describe all the methods exposed by the interfaces in the last two listings. For the purpose of this discussion, the only method that matters is IOleObject.SetClientSite().

When creating wrapper interfaces that will be called from native COM code, it is obviously critical that the GUID you specify matches the original one used by COM. It is also essential that the wrapper interface implements all the original COM methods, and that all methods have the same signature as the original method.

Using ICustomDoc

As stated earlier, the first step in customizing WebBrowser is to establish MainForm as the controlling host. Calling IOleObject.SetClientSite() is the way to do this. If you're not interested in working with WebBrowser, but only with MsHtml, there is another way to support customizations, without the need to use IOleObject or IOleClientSite.

Since customizing MsHtml is a fairly common operation, the component was provided with an interface called ICustomDoc that you can call to specify an IDocHostUIHandler object, which will act as a customizer. When MsHtml is about to interact with the user is some way, it checks to see if an IDocHostUIHandler object is available. If so, it calls its methods to find out how to behave. I'll talk about these methods a bit later. For the moment, what counts is how MainForm would use MsHtml's ICustomDoc interface. Listing 8-12 shows the details.

Listing 8-12: Setting a Component as the Customizer for MsHtml

```
object obj = mshtml.GetOcx();  // assume mshtml was created earlier
ICustomDoc doc = obj as ICustomDoc;
doc.SetUIHandler(this);  // 'this' must implement IDocHostUIHandler
```

Keep in mind that the interface ICustomDoc is only available on MsHtml — not on WebBrowser — so the code shown in the listing requires you to have a reference to an instance of MsHtml. There are many applications that use MsHtml by itself to render HTML pages. For example, it is increasingly common to see forms and dialog boxes containing HTML controls instead of Windows controls. By embedding MsHtml on a form, you have easy access to the powerful HTML renderer contained in MsHtml.

IDocHostUIHandler

This is the most important interface MainForm needs, in terms of customizing MsHtml. In the following sections, I'll give you a detailed description about what methods the interface has, what parameters the methods take, when MsHtml calls the methods, and what effect they have on the user interface.

Before I get ahead of myself (and I'm not talking about an out-of-body experience), let me show you how to import the interface into your managed code. As it turns out, IDocHostUIHandler references a fairly large number of other OLE interfaces and enumerations, so it isn't as easy to import as other interfaces.

Since I didn't have days or weeks to create the necessary wrapper classes and interfaces for all the items referenced in IDocHostUIHandler, I cheated and used a tool to help me. Borland's Delphi product has a very powerful and easy-to-use Type Library editor. The types used by IDocHostUIHandler are mostly defined in the file mshtmhst.idl, available on the Web and in the following folder:

```
C:\Program Files\Microsoft Visual Studio.NET\Vc7\PlatformSDK\include
```

But cutting and pasting code from the .idl file into the Delphi Type Library editor, I was able create a new type library file that I could use with TypImp. I'll spare you the gory details of my cutting and pasting adventures. Suffice it to say that I created a file called MsHtmlCustomization.tlb, which I saved in the folder "MyCustomWebBrowser\Type Libraries". Using TlbImp, I easily converted the file into a .dll that I could use with MyCustomWebBrowser. All I had to do is use the Add Reference Wizard to import the .dll and then add the following statement to class MainForm:

```
using MsHtmlCustomization;
```

In case you're curious, Figure 8-16 shows Delphi's Type Library editor with the interfaces and other items the library contains.

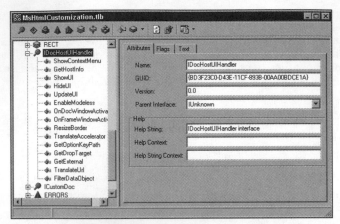

Figure 8-16: The Delphi Type Library editor, which is a convenient tool for rapidly creating type libraries

Figure 8-17 shows what the imported assembly MsHtmlCustomization.dll looks like with `ildasm`.

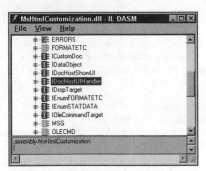

Figure 8-17: Exploring the MsHtmlCustomization contents with ILDASM

As you can see from the figure, MsHtmlCustomization contains a number of interfaces that are useful when customizing MsHtml, including ICustomDoc and IDocHostShowUI. Listing 8-13 shows how IDocHostUIHandler would look if it were declared in C#.

Listing 8-13: **The C# Implementation of IDocHostUIHandler**

```
namespace MsHtmlCustomization
{
  [ComImport,
  Guid("BD3F23C0-D43E-11CF-893B-00AA00BDCE1A"),
  InterfaceType(ComInterfaceType.InterfaceIsIUnknown) ]

  public interface IDocHostUIHandler : IUnknown
  {
```

```csharp
public void ShowContextMenu(
        MsHtmlCustomization.ContextMenuTarget dwContext,
        ref MsHtmlCustomization.POINT pPoint,
        MsHtmlCustomization.IOleCommandTarget pCommandTarget,
        object HTMLTagElement);

public void GetHostInfo(
        ref MsHtmlCustomization.DOCHOSTUIINFO theHostUIInfo);

public void ShowUI(int dwID, object pActiveObject,
        MsHtmlCustomization.IOleCommandTarget pCommandTarget,
        object pFrame, object pDoc);

public void HideUI();
public void UpdateUI();
public void EnableModeless(int fEnable);
public void OnDocWindowActivate(int fActivate);
public void OnFrameWindowActivate(int fActivate);

public void ResizeBorder(ref MsHtmlCustomization.RECT prcBorder,
            int pUIWindow, int fFrameWindow) {}
public void TranslateAccelerator(ref MsHtmlCustomization.MSG lpMsg,
            ref MsHtmlCustomization.UUID pguidCmdGroup, int nCmdID);

public void GetOptionKeyPath(ref int pchKey, int dw);

public MsHtmlCustomization.IDropTarget
        GetDropTarget(MsHtmlCustomization.IDropTarget pDropTarget);

public object GetExternal();
public int TranslateUrl(int dwTranslate, int pchURLIn);

public MsHtmlCustomization.IdataObject
        FilterDataObject(MsHtmlCustomization.IDataObject pDO);
  }
}
```

Besides `IDocHostUIHandler`, **there is another COM interface that is useful in customizing** MsHtml: `IDocHostShowUI`. **Although the limited space available prevents me from describing this interface in detail, I did include it in MsHtmlCustomization. Listing 8-14 shows how the class would look if declared in C#.**

Listing 8-14: The C# Implementation of IDocHostShowUI

```csharp
namespace MsHtmlCustomization
{
  [ComImport,
  Guid("C4D244B0-D43E-11CF-893B-00AA00BDCE1A"),
  InterfaceType(ComInterfaceType.InterfaceIsIUnknown) ]
```

Continued

Listing 8-14 *(continued)*

```
public interface IDocHostShowUI : IUnknown
{
  public void ShowMessage(int hwnd, ref int lpstrText,
                          ref int lpstrCaption, uint dwType,
                          ref int lpstrHelpFile, uint dwHelpContext,
                          out int lpResult);

  public void ShowHelp(uint hwnd, ref int pszHelpFile,
                       uint uCommand, uint dwData,
                       MsHtmlCustomization.POINT ptMouse,
                       out object pDispatchObjectHit);
  }
}
```

This interface is used to control how message boxes and help windows are handled by MsHtml. As you can see, the interface only supports two methods. In order for IDocHostShowUI methods to be called back from MsHtml, the host component (MainForm in this case) needs to implement the interfaces IOleClientSite and IOleDocumentSite. To keep my discussion as short as possible, my example MyCustomWebBrowser doesn't support IOleDocumentSite or IDocHostShowUI. Using the guidelines shown for supporting IOleObject, IOleClientSite, and IDocHostUIHandler, you should be able to add support for IDocHostShowUI if you need it.

Returning values from methods invoked through a COM interface

When you import a COM method into managed code, the imported method's signature is different from the original one. For example, Listing 8-15 shows a native COM method and its equivalent C# method.

Listing 8-15: A COM Method and Its Equivalent C# Method

```
// the IDL for a COM method
HRESULT ShowContextMenu([in]      ContextMenuTarget dwContext,
                        [in, out] POINT* pPOINT,
                        [in]      IOleCommandTarget* pCommandTarget,
                        [in]      IDispatch* HTMLTagElement);

// the C# declaration of a COM method
public void ShowContextMenu(
          MsHtmlCustomization.ContextMenuTarget dwContext,
          ref MsHtmlCustomization.POINT pPoint,
          MsHtmlCustomization.IOleCommandTarget pCommandTarget,
          object HTMLTagElement);
```

The C# method uses a more friendly notation that is much easier to deal with. A potential problem with the new C# method is the absence of an HRESULT return value. While COM methods are expected to return an HRESULT to indicate success or failure, the translated C# methods don't appear to give you access to the HRESULT. As you can see, the C# version of the method returns void, while the IDL version returns an HRESULT.

When you implement COM interfaces using managed code, there are times when you need to set the HRESULT value returned. For example, IDocHostUIHandler.ShowContextMenu uses the HRESULT to return an important value to the caller. Normally the Runtime Callable Wrapper class takes care of the HRESULT automatically like this: If a managed method throws an exception, the value S_FALSE is returned to COM; otherwise, the value S_OK is returned.

If you want to directly control the value returned back to COM, using HRESULT to return a parameter, you need to throw a special exception called COMException. When you throw this type of exception, the RCW intercepts it and uses its parameter as the HRESULT returned to COM. Listing 8-16 shows you how you use COMException.

Listing 8-16: Using COMException to Return HRESULT Values to COM

```
const int Ok = 0;
const int Error = 1;

// use one of the following statements

throw new COMException("", Ok);     // HRESULT returned: S_OK
throw new COMException("", Error);  // HRESULT returned: S_FALSE
```

Most OLE and COM methods use the HRESULT to signal success or failure of execution. In those few cases in which the HRESULT is used to return a parameters, just throw a COMException.

Common customizations

Although you can customize most user interface features of MsHtml, some customizations are in high demand, so I'll discuss them in this separate section to make them easier to find in the book. For the other types of customization, you'll need to look through the later sections of the chapter that discuss the individual callback methods that MsHtml invokes.

Removing the vertical scroll bar

This is probably the number one customization that developers ask for. When MsHtml displays a page, a vertical scroll bar is always shown, regardless of whether the page is completely visible or not. If the page fits on the screen, the vertical scroll bar appears with no thumb, as shown in Figure 8-18.

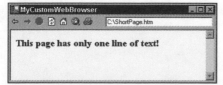

Figure 8-18: The vertical scroll bar that MsHtml shows by default on all HTML pages

Internet Explorer also exhibits this behavior, which is to be expected, since it also uses `MsHtml` internally to display HTML content. No matter how much you resize the window, the vertical scroll bar always appears. One way to remove the scroll bar, if you have control over the content displayed, involves setting an attribute of the `<body>` element of the page. Using this approach, you don't need to write any programming code at all. Just add the `scroll` attribute to the page's `<body>` tag like this:

```
<BODY scroll="NO">
```

That's it. The page will then appear with no scroll bars, as shown in Figure 8-19.

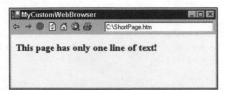

Figure 8-19: Displaying HTML pages with no vertical scroll bar

The problem with this approach is that it requires you to change the HTML code of the page displayed—something that is not always feasible. A better way to remove the vertical scroll-bar is by using one of the `IDocHostUIHandler` callbacks. When `MsHtml` interacts with the user interface, it frequently makes calls to these callback methods to see how to proceed. By implementing the method `GetHostInfo()`, you can disable the vertical scroll bar. The nice thing about this programmatic customization is that it doesn't require you to make any changes to the content of the HTML page being displayed. Listing 8-17 shows how the `GetHostInfo()` method needs to look to turn off the vertical scroll bar.

Listing 8-17: Programmatically Hiding the Vertical Scroll Bar

```
public void GetHostInfo(ref MsHtmlCustomization.DOCHOSTUIINFO
theHostUIInfo)
{
   theHostUIInfo.dwFlags |= DOCHOSTUIFLAG.DOCHOSTUIFLAG_SCROLL_NO;
}
```

The code does hide the vertical scroll bar, but is not quite sufficient to prevent users from scrolling. How could they scroll without scroll bars? All they have to do is click the mouse somewhere in the HTML page and drag it off the end of the window. `MsHtml` thinks the user wants to select text and scrolls to the right or downwards. To disable this behavior, you need to add the `DOCHOSTUIFLAG_DIALOG` flag to the value returned from `GetHostInfo()`, as shown in Listing 8-18.

> **Listing 8-18: Preventing Users from Scrolling an HTML Document**

```
public void GetHostInfo(ref MsHtmlCustomization.DOCHOSTUIINFO theHostUIInfo)
{
  // turn two flags on
  theHostUIInfo.dwFlags |= (DOCHOSTUIFLAG.DOCHOSTUIFLAG_SCROLL_NO |
                            DOCHOSTUIFLAG.DOCHOSTUIFLAG_NO3DBORDER |
                            DOCHOSTUIFLAG.DOCHOSTUIFLAG_DIALOG);
}
```

In case you're wondering, the name `DOCHOSTUIFLAG_DIALOG` comes from the fact that the flag is generally used to display an HTML page inside an ordinary dialog box. In such a case, you normally don't want users to be able to scroll around the dialog box contents.

The `GetHostInfo()` method enables you to control a wide variety of other features. For details, see the section titled "GETHOSTINFO", later in this chapter. Keep in mind that if you disable the vertical scroll bar, users won't be able to scroll downwards on HTML pages even if the documents extend beyond the bottom of the window.

Customizing the context menu

Another common request from developers is a way to hide or customize the context menu that appears when users right-click on an HTML page. Figure 8-20 shows the default context menu shown by `MsHtml`.

Figure 8-20: The default MsHtml context menu

The items listed in the menu depend on what type of element was right-clicked in the HTML page. The most popular reason for hiding the context menu is to prevent users from choosing the View Source command to gain access to the HTML code of the page. The proper way to control `MsHtml`'s context menu is through the `ShowContextMenu()` callback. This callback gives you complete control over the context menu, enabling you to do the following:

✦ Hide the context menu completely.

✦ Display your own context menu.

Let's take a look at each of these options. To hide the context menu altogether, just return `S_OK` as the `HRESULT` from `ShowContextMenu()`, as shown in Listing 8-19.

Listing 8-19: Preventing MsHtml's Context Menu from Appearing

```
public void ShowContextMenu(
            MsHtmlCustomization.ContextMenuTarget dwContext,
            ref MsHtmlCustomization.POINT pPoint,
            MsHtmlCustomization.IOleCommandTarget pCommandTarget,
            object HTMLTagElement)
{
  const int Ok = 0;
  throw new COMException("", Ok); // returns HRESULT = S_OK;
}
```

That was easy. Returning S_OK from the callback is your way of telling MsHtml that your host code handled the context menu and MsHtml is to take no further action. Whether your callback code displayed a context menu of its own or not is important to MsHtml.

To show your own context menu, you can use the pPoint parameter to get the position at which the user right-clicked the mouse. Using a standard .NET Framework ContextMenu component, you can show your custom menu at the same location where MsHtml would have displayed the default menu. Listing 8-20 shows an example.

Listing 8-20: Replacing the MsHtml Context Menu with a Custom Menu

```
public void ShowContextMenu(
            MsHtmlCustomization.ContextMenuTarget dwContext,
            ref MsHtmlCustomization.POINT pPoint,
            MsHtmlCustomization.IOleCommandTarget pCommandTarget,
            object HTMLTagElement)
{
  // show our custom context menu
  Point p = new Point(pPoint.x, pPoint.y);
  p = PointToClient(p);
  myCustomContextMenu.Show(this, p);

  // tell MsHtml that we handled the context menu ourselves
  const int Ok = 0;
  throw new COMException("", Ok);
}
```

The parameter pPoint passed to ShowContextMenu() is the location right-clicked by the user. The point is in screen coordinates, so you need to call PointToClient to convert it to client coordinates. I created a simple menu with one command labeled Print. Figure 8-21 shows how the context menu appears on the browser.

In the ShowContextMenu() callback, you may want to add logic that displays a custom menu under certain conditions, and the standard MsHtml menu in others. To make MsHtml show its own default context menu, throw a COMException as shown in Listing 8-21.

Figure 8-21: Displaying a custom context menu

Listing 8-21: **Telling MsHtml to Use Its Own Default Context Menu**

```
public void ShowContextMenu(
        MsHtmlCustomization.ContextMenuTarget dwContext,
        ref MsHtmlCustomization.POINT pPoint,
        MsHtmlCustomization.IOleCommandTarget pCommandTarget,
        object HTMLTagElement)
{
  // tell MsHtml to show its default context menu
  const int Error = 1;
  throw new COMException("", Error); // returns HRESULT = S_FALSE;
}
```

Preventing new windows from being opened

Another default behavior of MsHtml that you may want to disable is allowing a new browser window to be opened with an accelerator key. The built-in behavior of MsHtml is to open the current document in a new window when the Ctrl-N accelerator key is pressed. To disable this behavior, all you need to do is add some code to a callback method. Any time an accelerator key is pressed (while MsHtml has the input focus), it will call the callback method TranslateAccelerator(), passing a message containing the key code for the accelerator key. The value returned in the HRESULT from the callback tells MsHtml what to do. The value S_OK tells MsHtml to handle the accelerator. If you don't want MsHtml to process the accelerator, return the value S_FALSE. Listing 8-22 shows how to prevent all accelerators from being processed.

Listing 8-22: **Disabling All Accelerator Keys**

```
public void TranslateAccelerator(
        ref MsHtmlCustomization.MSG lpMsg,
        ref MsHtmlCustomization.UUID pguidCmdGroup,
        int nCmdID)
{
  // squelch all accelerators
  const int Error = 1;
  throw new COMException("", Error); // HRESULT = S_FALSE;
}
```

If you only want to disable certain accelerators, you need to use the lpMsg parameter to see which keys were pressed. Listing 8-23 shows how to disable only the Ctrl-N accelerator.

Listing 8-23: **Disabling Only the Ctrl-N Accelerator**

```
public void TranslateAccelerator(
          ref MsHtmlCustomization.MSG lpMsg,
          ref MsHtmlCustomization.UUID pguidCmdGroup,
          int nCmdID)
{
  const int WM_KEYDOWN = 0x0100;
  const int VK_CONTROL = 0x11;

  if (lpMsg.message != WM_KEYDOWN)
    // don't disable
    throw new COMException("", 1); // returns HRESULT = S_FALSE

  lpMsg.wParam &= 0xFF; // get the virtual keycode
  if (lpMsg.wParam == 'N')
  if (GetAsyncKeyState(VK_CONTROL) < 0)
    // disable the Ctrl-N accelerator
    throw new COMException("", 0); // returns HRESULT = S_OK

  // allow everything else
  throw new COMException("", 1); // returns HRESULT = S_FALSE
}
```

The code makes use of the native Windows API method GetAsyncKeyState() to get the status of the Ctrl key. The method is imported using the code shown in Listing 8-24.

Listing 8-24: **Importing the Windows API Method GetAsyncKeyState()**

```
[DllImport("User32.dll")]
public static extern short GetAsyncKeyState(int vKey);
```

I've taken you through some of the most common types of customization you can apply to MsHtml, but there are many more. In the following sections, I'll describe them in terms of the callback methods that are exposed to MsHtml through the IDocHostUIHandler interface.

IDocHostUIHandler methods in detail

In the following sections, I'll describe the various methods of the IDocHostUIHander interface. The methods appear in alphabetical order.

The `IDocHostUIHandler` methods are called when the `WebBrowser` component is showing an HTML document using `MsHtml`. If a different document type is loaded, such as a Word
or PDF file, `IDocHostUIHandler` methods won't necessarily be called.

EnableModeless

This method has the signature:

```
public void EnableModeless(int fEnable);
```

`EnableModeless()` is called at various times by `MsHtml` to tell you to disable any modeless
dialogs you might have in your host component. For example, when `MsHtml` is about to display an error message, it calls `EnableModeless` with `fEnable` set to 0. After the user closes
the error message, `MsHtml` calls `EnableModeless()` again with `fEnable` set to 1, telling you
that it's OK to enable any modeless dialog boxes you may have. Listing 8-25 is a simple example that just logs calls to `EnableModeless()` to the Trace output window.

Listing 8-25: A Simple Example with EnableModeless()

```
using System.Diagnostics;


public void EnableModeless(int fEnable) {
  int i = fEnable;
  Trace.WriteLine("EnableModeless: fEnable= " + i);
}
```

FilterDataObject

This method has the signature:

```
public MsHtmlCustomization.IDataObject
       FilterDataObject(MsHtmlCustomization.IDataObject pDO);
```

The DataObjects in question are those used typically with Clipboard operations. At various
times, `MsHtml` may call `FilterDataObject` to let the host component see what type of data
is about to be handled. To prevent handling, return the value `null`. To allow handling, return
the `pDO` object, as show in Listing 8-26.

Listing 8-26: Allowing All Data Types to Be Handled

```
public MsHtmlCustomization.IDataObject
       FilterDataObject(MsHtmlCustomization.IDataObject pDO)
{
  return pDO;
}
```

GetDropTarget

This method has the signature:

```
public MsHtmlCustomization.IdropTarget
       GetDropTarget(MsHtmlCustomization.IDropTarget pDropTarget)
```

During Drag and Drop operations, when the user drops an object on a target object, MsHtml calls GetDropTarget(). Using this method, you can supply an alternative target. It is unusual to change the drop target. Listing 8-27 shows how to just accept the default target.

Listing 8-27: Accepting the Default Drop Target

```
public MsHtmlCustomization.IdropTarget
       GetDropTarget(MsHtmlCustomization.IDropTarget pDropTarget)
{
   return pDropTarget;
}
```

GetExternal

This method has the signature:

```
public object GetExternal();
```

MsHtml calls this method to obtain the IDispatch interface of the host component (MainForm, in my case). If the host doesn't implement IDispatch, it must return null. Listing 8-28 shows how you would return the IDispatch if your host did implement it.

Listing 8-28: Returning the IDispatch Interface

```
public object GetExternal()
{
   return this as IDispatch;
}
```

If you need to implement the IDispatch interface in a class, the managed code wrapper for IDispatch is available in the file *StdOle.dll* in the folder:

```
C:\Program Files\Microsoft.NET\Primary Interop Assemblies
```

GetHostInfo

This is an important customization callback. The method has the signature:

```
public void GetHostInfo(
        ref MsHtmlCustomization.DOCHOSTUIINFO theHostUIInfo);
```

The parameter passed in is a struct that looks like the code in Listing 8-29.

Listing 8-29: The Equivalent C# Code for the DOCHOSTUIINFO struct

```
public struct DOCHOSTUIINFO
{
  public uint cbSize;
  public uint dwFlags;
  public uint dwDoubleClick;
  public uint pchHostCss;
  public uint pchHostNS;
};
```

cbSize is the length of the struct in bytes. dwFlags is the most important field, and is described later in detail. dwDoubleClick is where you specify what to show in MsHtml when the user double-clicks the mouse. Possible values are shown in Listing 8-30.

Listing 8-30: The Values that Can Be Assigned to dwDoubleClick

```
public enum DOCHOSTUIDBLCLK: uint
{
  DOCHOSTUIDBLCLK_DEFAULT          = 0,
  DOCHOSTUIDBLCLK_SHOWPROPERTIES   = 1,
  DOCHOSTUIDBLCLK_SHOWCODE         = 2
};
```

Table 8-1 describes the values.

Table 8-1: Allowed Values for DOCHOSTUIINFO.dwDoubleClick

Value	Meaning
DOCHOSTUIDBLCLK_DEFAULT	Perform the default double-click action.
DOCHOSTUIDBLCLK_SHOWPROPERTIES	Show the properties of the double-clicked item.
DOCHOSTUIDBLCLK_SHOWCODE	Show the code for the double-clicked item.

Before you get too excited about controlling the double-click action with GetHostInfo(), let me inform you that this feature appears to have been disabled in MsHtml.

Getting back to my description of DOCHOSTUIINFO, the field pchHostCss references the Cascading Style Sheet (CSS) used to layout the current HTML page.

The field pchHostNS references a semicolon-delimited list of namespaces used on the page.

By far the most useful field of DOCHOSTUIINFO is dwFlags, which defines a fairly long list of flags you can control to change MsHtml interface elements. Table 8-2 describes each flag.

Table 8-2: Flags Available in DOCHOSTUIINFO.dwFlags

Flag Name	Effect When Property Is Set
DOCHOSTUIFLAG_DIALOG	Prevents the user from selecting text. If you don't want users to be able to scroll content by dragging the mouse, use this flag.
DOCHOSTUIFLAG_DISABLE_HELP_MENU	Disables the right mouse button pop-up menu.
DOCHOSTUIFLAG_NO3DBORDER	Disables the 3D border around the HTML document displayed.
DOCHOSTUIFLAG_SCROLL_NO	Turns off both vertical and horizontal scroll bars. Users will then only be able to see the part of the HTML document that fits in the window. They will still be able to scroll the window by dragging the mouse off the document. To prevent this last behavior, include the flag DOCHOSTUIFLAG_DIALOG.
DOCHOSTUIFLAG_DISABLE_SCRIPT_INACTIVE	Disables all scripts from being run while a page is being loaded.
DOCHOSTUIFLAG_OPENNEWWIN	Forces WebBrowser to open a new Internet Explorer window if a link is clicked.
DOCHOSTUIFLAG_FLAT_SCROLLBAR	Disables the 3D look on all scroll bars. If no scroll bars are visible, the property has no effect.
DOCHOSTUIFLAG_DIV_BLOCKDEFAULT	When the user edits the HTML text on the screen and presses the Enter key, this property makes MsHtml insert a <DIV> tag in the HTML code, rather than the default <P> tag.
DOCHOSTUIFLAG_ACTIVATE_CLIENTHIT_ONLY	Tells MsHtml to take the input focus only when the user clicks the mouse in the client area. By default, the component will become focused even if the user clicks a non-client area, such as a scroll bar.
DOCHOSTUIFLAG_OVERRIDEBEHAVIORFACTORY	Disables DHTML behaviors IE 5 and later. (For a discussion of behaviors, see http://msdn.microsoft.com/library/periodic/period99/HTMLbehaviors.htm.)

Flag Name	Effect When Property Is Set
DOCHOSTUIFLAG_CODEPAGELINKEDFONTS	This flag was added only to provide a common look and feel across the two Microsoft products, Outlook Express and Internet Explorer. It applies to Outlook Express 4 and Internet Explorer 5 (or later versions). You'll probably never use this flag.
DOCHOSTUIFLAG_URL_ENCODING_DISABLE_UTF8	Disables the use of UTF8 character coding for URLs that have characters that are not in the UTF8 set. By default, MsHtml will always try to use UTF8. Applies to IE 5 and later.
DOCHOSTUIFLAG_URL_ENCODING_ENABLE_UTF8	Forces the use of UTF8 character coding with URLs that have characters that are not in the UTF8 set. By default, MsHtml will always try to use UTF8. Applies to IE 5 and later.
DOCHOSTUIFLAG_ENABLE_FORMS_AUTOCOMPLETE	Enables the AutoComplete feature for Forms, which by default is enabled. The value set for this property will be ignored if the user has disabled AutoComplete for Forms in Internet Explorer. To disable AutoComplete for Forms in IE, select the menu command Tools ⇨ Internet Options, switch to the Content tab, click the AutoComplete button and uncheck the Forms checkbox.

You can combine multiple flags, as shown in Listing 8-31.

Listing 8-31: **Setting Multiple Flags in GetHostInfo()**

```
public void GetHostInfo(
        ref MsHtmlCustomization.DOCHOSTUIINFO theHostUIInfo)
{
  // turn three flags on
  theHostUIInfo.dwFlags |=
      (DOCHOSTUIFLAG.DOCHOSTUIFLAG_SCROLL_NO |
       DOCHOSTUIFLAG.DOCHOSTUIFLAG_NO3DBORDER |
       DOCHOSTUIFLAG.DOCHOSTUIFLAG_DISABLE_SCRIPT_INACTIVE);
}
```

You can set any flags you need, by combining them with a Boolean OR operation.

GetOptionKeyPath

This method is called to retrieve the Registry path to use for storing user preferences. It is rarely used.

HideUI

If the host component draws UI elements, such as toolbars or menus, related to the MsHtml state, you need to make sure your UI elements are shown only at the proper time. When the HideUI() callback occurs, you need to hide those elements. At some later time, MsHtml will call the ShowUI() method to let you restore the hidden elements back on the screen.

OnDocWindowActivate

This method has the signature:

```
public void OnDocWindowActivate(int fActivate);
```

The method is called at various times by MsHtml to tell you when the HTML document being displayed is activated or deactivated. A document is basically considered activated when it has the input focus. Windows shows the currently active window with a different caption bar color from inactive windows. The reason MsHtml calls to inform you when the Active status changes is to allow your host component to make any necessary changes to its UI.

OnFrameWindowActivate

This method has the signature:

```
public void OnFrameWindowActivate(int fActivate);
```

The method is called at various times by MsHtml to tell you when the top-level frame window containing MsHtml is activated or deactivated. Use this callback method to change any UI elements in the host component that appear differently when the window is activated versus deactivated.

ResizeBorder

This method has the signature:

```
public void ResizeBorder(ref MsHtmlCustomization.RECT prcBorder,
                         int pUIWindow, int fFrameWindow);
```

This method is useful if your host component allows MsHtml to become *inplace-activated*. When an embedded component becomes inplace-activated, the host normally draws a hatched border around the embedded component. Inplace-activation used to be considered a really cool technology that used menu-merging and OLE-nested documents. Outside of products like Microsoft Office, inplace-activation just isn't used that much, so the requirement to support ResizeBorder() is somewhat unusual.

ShowContextMenu

This method has the signature:

```
public void ShowContextMenu(
        MsHtmlCustomization.ContextMenuTarget dwContext,
        ref MsHtmlCustomization.POINT pPoint,
        MsHtmlCustomization.IOleCommandTarget pCommandTarget,
        object HTMLTagElement);
```

This is a commonly used callback method, because it allows you to customize how pop-up menus behave with `MsHtml`. You basically have three options:

✦ Allow `MsHtml` to display its context menu.

✦ Disable context menus altogether.

✦ Hide `MsHtml`'s menu and display your own.

To allow `MsHtml` to show its normal context menu, return the value S_FALSE by throwing a `COMException` as shown in Listing 8-32.

Listing 8-32: Allowing MsHtml to Show Its Default Context Menu

```
public void ShowContextMenu(
          MsHtmlCustomization.ContextMenuTarget dwContext,
          ref MsHtmlCustomization.POINT pPoint,
          MsHtmlCustomization.IOleCommandTarget pCommandTarget,
          object HTMLTagElement)
{
  const int Error = 1;
  throw new COMException("", Error); // returns HRESULT = S_FALSE
}
```

To prevent `MsHtml` from showing its context menu, return the value S_OK by throwing a `COMException` as shown in Listing 8-33.

Listing 8-33: Disabling Context Menus Altogether

```
public void ShowContextMenu(
          MsHtmlCustomization.ContextMenuTarget dwContext,
          ref MsHtmlCustomization.POINT pPoint,
          MsHtmlCustomization.IOleCommandTarget pCommandTarget,
          object HTMLTagElement)
{
  const int Ok = 0;
  throw new COMException("", Ok); // returns HRESULT = S_OK
}
```

To show your own custom menu, use a `ContextMenu` component in the callback and return the value S_OK by throwing a `COMException` as shown in Listing 8-34.

Listing 8-34: Disabling Context Menus Altogether

```
public void ShowContextMenu(
          MsHtmlCustomization.ContextMenuTarget dwContext,
          ref MsHtmlCustomization.POINT pPoint,
```

Continued

Listing 8-34 *(continued)*

```
                MsHtmlCustomization.IOleCommandTarget pCommandTarget,
                object HTMLTagElement)
{
    Point p = new Point(pPoint.x, pPoint.y);
    p = PointToClient(p);
    myCustomContextMenu.Show(this, p);
    const int Ok = 0;
    throw new COMException("", Ok); // return HRESULT = S_OK, so MsHtml
                                    // doesn't display its own menu
}
```

Notice the call to `PointToClient()`. This call is necessary, because the `pPoint` is in screen coordinates, while `ContextMenu.Show()` requires client coordinates. By setting up your own `ContextMenu`, you can customize the pop-up menu in any way you want.

ShowUI

If the host component (MainForm in my case) needs to draw UI elements such as toolbars or menus related to `MsHtml`, this callback tells you it's okay to show them. At some later time, `MsHtml` will call the `HideUI()` and `UpdateUI()` methods where you should be prepared to hide or refresh your UI elements. You don't need to handle `ShowUI()` unless your UI elements are related to `MsHtml`'s state.

TranslateAccelerator

When the user presses an accelerator key, such as Ctrl-O or Ctrl-P, `MsHtml` calls `TranslateAccelerator()` to see what you want to do. This method has the signature:

```
public void TranslateAccelerator(
            ref MsHtmlCustomization.MSG lpMsg,
            ref MsHtmlCustomization.UUID pguidCmdGroup,
            int nCmdID);
```

Accelerator keys are keys that activate menu commands. Table 8-3 shows the important accelerator keys supported by `MsHtml`.

Table 8-3: Main Accelerator Keys Supported by MsHtml

Accelerator	Description
Ctrl-N	Opens the current HTML document in a new `WebBrowser` window.
Crtl-P	Displays a Print dialog box for printing the HTML document.
Ctrl-A	Selects the entire contents of the HTML document.
Crtl-F	Displays a Find dialog box for searching the HTML document.
F5, Ctrl-F5	Refreshes the currently loaded HTML document.

The accelerators most often disabled are Ctrl-N and Ctrl-P. Listing 8-35 shows how to disable them.

Listing 8-35: Disabling the Ctrl-N and Ctrl-P Accelerators

```
public void TranslateAccelerator(
          ref MsHtmlCustomization.MSG lpMsg,
          ref MsHtmlCustomization.UUID pguidCmdGroup,
          int nCmdID)
{
  const int Ok = 0;
  const int Error = 1;
  const int WM_KEYDOWN = 0x0100;
  const int VK_CONTROL = 0x11;

  if (lpMsg.message != WM_KEYDOWN)
    // allow message
    throw new COMException("", Error); // returns HRESULT = S_FALSE

  if (GetAsyncKeyState(VK_CONTROL) >= 0)
    // Ctrl key not pressed: allow message
    throw new COMException("", Error); // returns HRESULT = S_FALSE

  // disable the Ctrl-N and Ctrl-P accelerators
  lpMsg.wParam &= 0xFF; // get the virtual keycode
  if ( (lpMsg.wParam == 'N') || ((lpMsg.wParam == 'P')) )
    throw new COMException("", Ok); // returns HRESULT = S_OK

  // allow everything else
  throw new COMException("", Error); // returns HRESULT = S_FALSE
}
```

TranslateUrl

This method is called when the user clicks a hyperlink in an HTML document. Before passing the link's URL to the WebBrowser, MsHtml calls TranslateUrl() to allow the host component to modify the URL.

UpdateUI

If you draw UI elements that are based on the state of MsHtml, this callback tells you when to refresh those elements. This callback will occur anytime a significant state occurs in MsHtml.

The Complete Code

I've shown you lots of bits and pieces of code. Listing 8-36 shows the complete code for MainForm of MyCustomWebBrowser.

Listing 8-36: The Complete Code for MainForm of MyCustomWebBrowser

```
using System;
using System.Drawing;
using System.Collections;
using System.ComponentModel;
using System.Windows.Forms;
using System.Data;
using System.Runtime.InteropServices;
using System.Diagnostics;
using MsHtmlCustomization;

namespace MyCustomWebBrowser
{
  public class MainForm : System.Windows.Forms.Form,
                          IOleClientSite,
                          IDocHostUIHandler
  {
    private System.Windows.Forms.Panel panel1;
    private System.Windows.Forms.ToolBar toolBar1;
    private System.Windows.Forms.ImageList imageList1;
    private System.Windows.Forms.ToolBarButton toolBarButtonBack;
    private System.Windows.Forms.ToolBarButton toolBarButtonForward;
    private System.Windows.Forms.ToolBarButton toolBarButtonStop;
    private System.Windows.Forms.ToolBarButton toolBarButtonRefresh;
    private System.Windows.Forms.ToolBarButton toolBarButtonHome;
    private System.Windows.Forms.ToolBarButton toolBarButtonSearch;
    private System.Windows.Forms.ToolBarButton toolBarButtonPrint;
    private AxSHDocVw.AxWebBrowser axWebBrowser1;
    private System.Windows.Forms.TextBox textBoxAddress;
    private System.ComponentModel.IContainer components;

    ArrayList urlsVisited = new ArrayList();
    private System.Windows.Forms.ContextMenu myCustomContextMenu;
    private System.Windows.Forms.MenuItem menuItemPrint;
    int currentUrlIndex = -1;  // no sites visited initially

    public MainForm()
    {
      InitializeComponent();

      // tell WebBrowser that we are its host
      object obj = axWebBrowser1.GetOcx();
      IOleObject oc = obj as IOleObject;
      oc.SetClientSite(this);

      toolBarButtonBack.Enabled = false;
      toolBarButtonForward.Enabled = false;
      toolBarButtonStop.Enabled = false;
      toolBarButtonRefresh.Enabled = false;
      toolBarButtonHome.Enabled = false;
```

```
    toolBarButtonSearch.Enabled = false;
    toolBarButtonPrint.Enabled = false;

    axWebBrowser1.GoHome();
}

protected override void Dispose( bool disposing )
{
    // standard wizard-generated code
}

private void InitializeComponent()
{
    // standard wizard-generated code...

    this.axWebBrowser1 = new AxSHDocVw.AxWebBrowser();
    this.panel1 = new System.Windows.Forms.Panel();
    this.textBoxAddress = new System.Windows.Forms.TextBox();
    this.myCustomContextMenu = new System.Windows.Forms.ContextMenu();
    this.menuItemPrint = new System.Windows.Forms.MenuItem();

    //
    // axWebBrowser1
    //
    this.axWebBrowser1.Dock = System.Windows.Forms.DockStyle.Fill;
    this.axWebBrowser1.Enabled = true;
    this.axWebBrowser1.Location = new System.Drawing.Point(0, 28);
    this.axWebBrowser1.OcxState =
            ((System.Windows.Forms.AxHost.State)
            (resources.GetObject("axWebBrowser1.OcxState")));
    this.axWebBrowser1.Size = new System.Drawing.Size(394, 245);
    this.axWebBrowser1.TabIndex = 1;
    this.axWebBrowser1.NavigateError += new
        AxSHDocVw.DWebBrowserEvents2_NavigateErrorEventHandler(
                            this.axWebBrowser1_NavigateError);
    this.axWebBrowser1.NavigateComplete2 += new
        AxSHDocVw.DWebBrowserEvents2_NavigateComplete2EventHandler(
                            this.axWebBrowser1_NavigateComplete2);
    this.axWebBrowser1.BeforeNavigate2 += new
        AxSHDocVw.DWebBrowserEvents2_BeforeNavigate2EventHandler(
                            this.axWebBrowser1_BeforeNavigate2);
    // more wizard-generated code...
}

[STAThread]
static void Main()
{
    Application.Run(new MainForm());
}

private void toolBar1_ButtonClick(object sender,
        System.Windows.Forms.ToolBarButtonClickEventArgs e)
```

Continued

Listing 8-36 *(continued)*

```
{
  Cursor.Current = Cursors.WaitCursor;

  try
  {
    if (e.Button == toolBarButtonBack)
      axWebBrowser1.GoBack();


    else if (e.Button == toolBarButtonForward)
      axWebBrowser1.GoForward();


    else if (e.Button == toolBarButtonStop)
    {
      axWebBrowser1.Stop();

      toolBarButtonStop.Enabled = false;
    }

    else if (e.Button == toolBarButtonSearch)
      axWebBrowser1.GoSearch();


    else if (e.Button == toolBarButtonPrint)
      PrintPage();

    else if (e.Button == toolBarButtonRefresh)
    {
      object REFRESH_COMPLETELY = 3;
      axWebBrowser1.Refresh2(ref REFRESH_COMPLETELY);

    }

    else if (e.Button == toolBarButtonHome)
      axWebBrowser1.GoHome();

  }
  finally
  {
    Cursor.Current = Cursors.Default;
  }
}

private bool IsPrinterEnabled()
{
  int response =
    (int) axWebBrowser1.QueryStatusWB(SHDocVw.OLECMDID.OLECMDID_PRINT);
  return (response & (int) SHDocVw.OLECMDF.OLECMDF_ENABLED) != 0 ?
```

```csharp
      true : false;
}

private void PrintPage()
{
  object o = "";

  // constants useful when printing
  SHDocVw.OLECMDID Print = SHDocVw.OLECMDID.OLECMDID_PRINT;

  // use this value to print without prompting
  // SHDocVw.OLECMDEXECOPT PromptUser =
  //   SHDocVw.OLECMDEXECOPT.OLECMDEXECOPT_PROMPTUSER;

  SHDocVw.OLECMDEXECOPT DontPromptUser =
    SHDocVw.OLECMDEXECOPT.OLECMDEXECOPT_DONTPROMPTUSER;

  if (!IsPrinterEnabled() ) return;

  // print without prompting user
  axWebBrowser1.ExecWB(Print, DontPromptUser, ref o, ref o);

  // to prompt the user with printer settings
  // axWebBrowser1.ExecWB(Print, PromptUser, ref o, ref o);
}

public void GotoURL(String theURL)
{
  try
  {
    Cursor.Current = Cursors.WaitCursor;
    Object o = null;
    axWebBrowser1.Navigate(theURL, ref o, ref o, ref o, ref o);
  }
  finally
  {
    Cursor.Current = Cursors.Default;
  }
}

private void textBoxAddress_KeyDown(object sender,
            System.Windows.Forms.KeyEventArgs e)
{
  if (e.KeyCode == Keys.Return)
    GotoURL(textBoxAddress.Text);
}

private void axWebBrowser1_BeforeNavigate2(object sender,
      AxSHDocVw.DWebBrowserEvents2_BeforeNavigate2Event e)
{
  toolBarButtonStop.Enabled = true;
```

Continued

Listing 8-36 *(continued)*

```csharp
    Cursor.Current = Cursors.WaitCursor;
}

private void axWebBrowser1_NavigateComplete2(object sender,
        AxSHDocVw.DWebBrowserEvents2_NavigateComplete2Event e)
{
  Cursor.Current = Cursors.Default;

  toolBarButtonStop.Enabled = false;
  toolBarButtonHome.Enabled = true;
  toolBarButtonSearch.Enabled = true;
  toolBarButtonRefresh.Enabled = true;

  // update the URL displayed in the address bar
  String s = e.uRL.ToString();
  textBoxAddress.Text = s;

  // update the list of visited URLs
  int i = urlsVisited.IndexOf(s);
  if (i >= 0)
    currentUrlIndex = i;
  else
    currentUrlIndex = urlsVisited.Add(s);

  // enable / disable the Back and Forward buttons
  toolBarButtonBack.Enabled = (currentUrlIndex == 0) ? false : true;
  toolBarButtonForward.Enabled =
    (currentUrlIndex >= urlsVisited.Count-1) ? false : true;

  // set the state of the Print button
  toolBarButtonPrint.Enabled = IsPrinterEnabled();
}

private void axWebBrowser1_NavigateError(object sender,
        AxSHDocVw.DWebBrowserEvents2_NavigateErrorEvent e)
{
  Cursor.Current = Cursors.Default;

  toolBarButtonStop.Enabled = false;
  toolBarButtonHome.Enabled = true;
  toolBarButtonSearch.Enabled = true;
  toolBarButtonRefresh.Enabled = true;
}

// implement IOleClientSite methods

void IOleClientSite.SaveObject() {}
void IOleClientSite.GetMoniker(uint dwAssign,
                               uint dwWhichMoniker,
                               object ppmk) {}
```

```csharp
void IOleClientSite.GetContainer(object ppContainer)
{
  ppContainer = this;
}
void IOleClientSite.ShowObject() {}
void IOleClientSite.OnShowWindow(bool fShow) {}
void IOleClientSite.RequestNewObjectLayout() {}

// implement IDocHostUIHandler methods

public void ShowContextMenu(
          MsHtmlCustomization.ContextMenuTarget dwContext,
          ref MsHtmlCustomization.POINT pPoint,
          MsHtmlCustomization.IOleCommandTarget pCommandTarget,
          object HTMLTagElement)
{
  // use this code to show a custom menu
  const int Ok = 0;
  Point p = new Point(pPoint.x, pPoint.y);
  p = PointToClient(p);
  myCustomContextMenu.Show(this, p);
  throw new COMException("", Ok); // HRESULT = S_OK

  // use this code to let MsHtml shows its menu
  // const int Error = 1;
  // throw new COMException("", Error); // HRESULT = S_FALSE
}

public void GetHostInfo(
          ref MsHtmlCustomization.DOCHOSTUIINFO theHostUIInfo)
{
  // turn two flags on
  theHostUIInfo.dwFlags |= (DOCHOSTUIFLAG.DOCHOSTUIFLAG_SCROLL_NO |
                          DOCHOSTUIFLAG.DOCHOSTUIFLAG_NO3DBORDER);
}

public void ShowUI(int dwID, object pActiveObject,
          MsHtmlCustomization.IOleCommandTarget pCommandTarget,
          object pFrame, object pDoc) {}

public void HideUI() {}
public void UpdateUI() {}

public void EnableModeless(int fEnable) {
  int i = fEnable;
  Trace.WriteLine("EnableModeless: fEnable= " + i);
}

public void OnDocWindowActivate(int fActivate) {}
public void OnFrameWindowActivate(int fActivate) {}

public void ResizeBorder(ref MsHtmlCustomization.RECT prcBorder,
```

Continued

Listing 8-36 *(continued)*

```
            int pUIWindow, int fFrameWindow) {}


public void TranslateAccelerator(
          ref MsHtmlCustomization.MSG lpMsg,
          ref MsHtmlCustomization.UUID pguidCmdGroup,
          int nCmdID)
{
  const int Ok = 0;
  const int Error = 1;
  const int WM_KEYDOWN = 0x0100;
  const int VK_CONTROL = 0x11;

  if (lpMsg.message != WM_KEYDOWN)
    // allow message
    throw new COMException("", Error); // returns HRESULT = S_FALSE

  if (GetAsyncKeyState(VK_CONTROL) >= 0)
    // Ctrl key not pressed: allow message
    throw new COMException("", Error); // returns HRESULT = S_FALSE

  // disable the Ctrl-N and Ctrl-P accelerators
  lpMsg.wParam &= 0xFF; // get the virtual keycode
  if ( (lpMsg.wParam == 'N') || ((lpMsg.wParam == 'P')) )
    throw new COMException("", Ok); // returns HRESULT = S_OK

  // allow everything else
  throw new COMException("", Error); // returns HRESULT = S_FALSE
}

public void GetOptionKeyPath(ref int pchKey, int dw) {}

public MsHtmlCustomization.IdropTarget
      GetDropTarget(MsHtmlCustomization.IDropTarget pDropTarget)
{
  return pDropTarget;
}

public object GetExternal()
{
  return null;
}

public int TranslateUrl(int dwTranslate, int pchURLIn) {return 0;}

public MsHtmlCustomization.IDataObject
      FilterDataObject(MsHtmlCustomization.IDataObject pDO)
```

```
    {
      return pDO;
    }

    [DllImport("User32.dll")]
    public static extern short GetAsyncKeyState(int vKey);
  }
}
```

Summary

By the sheer number of ways WebBrowser can be customized, you must realize by now how important this component is, not only for Microsoft, but also for your own applications. Once you import the proper COM interfaces into your managed code, WebBrowser is your friend. Moreover, it's already installed on practically every Windows machine on the planet, is flexible beyond words, and is a pleasure to use.

✦   ✦   ✦

Custom Controls

It's like an Alcatraz around my neck!

—Boston mayor T. Menino on the shortage
of city parking spaces

For a lot of people in years past, developing custom GUI controls was also like having an albatross around their neck. Let's face it, before MFC or Visual Basic came around, the task was brutal. Just writing a *HelloWorld* control required mastering dozens of pages of obscure technical information, learning a new SDK, and using tools few people were comfortable with. In this chapter I'll show you how to create custom controls the new way, with the .NET Framework. If you have any prior experience with custom controls, you'll appreciate the simplicity and power of the new way.

Custom Controls in the Old Days

Before diving into the .NET Framework custom controls, I'll give a short history of custom controls on the Windows platform. In the early days of Windows, before Microsoft introduced Common Controls, Office Controls, and Internet Controls, the landscape of Graphical User Interface (GUI) controls was pretty bleak. Kind of like the Java world in 1995, when version 1.0 of the Java Development Kit was released. You really only had the most basic and primitive GUI elements, such as edit boxes, labels, list boxes, and combo boxes. Corporate developers were often forced to create their own GUI controls to add a minimum of pizzazz to their applications. The need for more built-in GUI controls was definitely there, and GUI Custom Control development became a blossoming industry in its own right.

Later, with the advent of products like Borland C++, and then Visual Basic, Delphi, and Visual Studio, the process became considerably easier to tackle. Microsoft finally started addressing the problem at the root by releasing groups of increasingly sophisticated GUI components. First was the Common Control package, containing familiar components like `TreeViews` and `ListViews`. Somewhat later they released many of the high-end controls used in Internet Explorer, Outlook, and Office.

These days, developers have access to a pretty substantial number of GUI components right out of the box, in addition to a large number of third-party products, so developing custom controls is not as common as it used to be. This is good, because it means that developers are spending more of their time (presumably) focusing on business-related issues. In a rich development environment, you shouldn't have to reinvent the UI wheel in each project.

In any event, Custom Controls will always be needed to solve those UI situations that are special, or that require that nonstandard look and feel. The good news is that the .NET Framework makes developing GUI controls much easier than before. You basically identify the UI class that most closely suits your needs, derive a class from it, and customize it by adding properties, methods, and events. You can forget the old days, when you had to understand weird callbacks, hooks, or other horrific gunk.

Custom-control development often requires handling tasks that are not required with other types of components, such as custom painting, keyboard handling, mouse handling, focus handling, and a slew of others. To demonstrate as many aspects of custom-control development as possible, I'll create a control that is a bit odd, and really wouldn't be marketable, but does deal with a significant number of the tasks you're likely to be faced with when developing your own custom controls.

I'll call the control *MyCustomControl*. The control will appear as a rectangle with a 3D border, with the client area divided into four quadrants with different backgrounds, as shown in Figure 9-1.

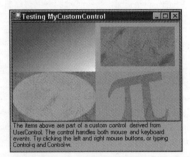

Figure 9-1: How MyCustomControl looks at runtime

The figure shows `MyCustomControl` running inside a simple form. The custom control paints the quadrants based on the current window size. If the user resizes the control, the quadrants will also resize themselves. As the user moves the mouse over the control, the targeted quadrant will respond by drawing a border around itself. I'll use some of the new GDI+ features to paint the interiors of the quadrants with gradients, textures, and partially transparent brushes. For example, the lower right quadrant uses coordinate transforms to display a rotated π (pi) character.

The control will also show how to handle the keyboard. The control will denote its focused state by drawing a focus rectangle around itself. Once focused, it will respond to two keys, arbitrarily chosen: Control-Q and Control-W.

I'll also add a number of other features that are useful not just with custom controls, but with any type of component. Overall, `MyCustomControl` will highlight the following features (in no particular order):

- ✦ Drag and drop
- ✦ Custom painting
- ✦ Keyboard handling
- ✦ Mouse handling
- ✦ Focus handling

✦ Graphics rotation and translation

✦ Using random numbers

✦ Searching the file system for a file

Choosing the Right Base Class

The easiest way to create a new custom control is with the New Project wizard, by choosing Windows Control Library as the project type. The wizard creates a class derived from `System.Windows.Forms.UserControl`. This type of control is useful when the control will be used to host other UI components, like edit boxes and labels. By having `UserControl` as the base class, your control appears as a panel, with an empty gray drawing surface in the Forms Designer. Being able to see your control in the Forms Designer is a plus, because you can see how subcomponents look, without having to run the code, and you can inspect properties at design time with the VS .NET Properties window.

Having `UserControl` as a base class is useful when you plan to embed other UI components in your control, or when your control will be providing all the code that paints the control on the screen. However, there are cases when `UserControl` is not the best choice as a base class. The most common situation is when you need to customize an existing control. Say you want to create a custom button. You could drop a `Button` control on the `UserControl` in the Forms Designer, and then set the button's `Dock` property to `DockStyle.Fill`, so the button is always the same size as the custom control. A drawback of this approach is that your component will expose the properties and events of `UserControl`, not of `Button`. If the control was dropped on a form and a `Click` handler was added to it, the handler would never get called, because it is a handler for `UserControl Click` events. The button covers the entire `UserControl` area, and intercepts all mouse events.

The solution is to use a different base class. If you're creating a customized button, it makes sense to use `Button` as the base class. First use the Windows Control Library wizard to create an empty shell for your control, and then go in and manually change the name of the base class. Any standard control like `Button`, `TreeView`, and `ListBox` can be used as a base class. Depending on which base class you choose, the Forms Designer may or may not be subsequently available for your control. If it isn't, you'll have to set up the control exclusively with code, without access to the Properties window.

`MyCustomControl` has three key features shared by many custom controls:

✦ It paints itself.

✦ It handles keyboard events.

✦ It handles mouse events

Custom controls that have these three features often use `System.Windows.Forms.UserControl` as the base class. `UserControl` is indirectly derived from `Control`, so it has the plumbing necessary to interact with a parent form. `UserControl` adds support for a number of useful UI features, such as anchoring and docking. I'll use `UserControl` for the base class of `MyCustomControl`.

Designing the Component

Many custom controls are fairly simple from an architectural point of view, and `MyCustomControl` is no exception. In many cases, the complexity of a custom control lies in the painting code, or in the mouse-handling code. The class diagram of these controls will be quite simple, even though there is a significant amount of complex graphics or event handling logic. In these cases, an interaction diagram is more useful for understanding the component than the class diagram. I'll provide both for MyCustomControl. First is the class diagram, shown in Figure 9-2.

Figure 9-2: The class diagram for MyCustomControl

As I said, the class diagram doesn't really tell much about MyCustomControl, other than the fact that the component has a lot of event handlers. To understand what makes MyCustomControl tick, you need to see the interaction diagrams for the event handlers. Many handlers are standard and don't need too much explanation. For example handlers that open files, cut and paste data, or display help would be self-explanatory. To save space, in the interaction diagram shown in Figure 9-3 for MyCustomControl, I'll only include the mouse, focus, and keyboard handlers.

As you can see, there isn't much *interaction* in the interaction diagram. MyCustomControl handles most of the events shown by simply calling Invalidate() to repaint itself. This situation is fairly typical: Custom controls often interact more with the user interface than with other components.

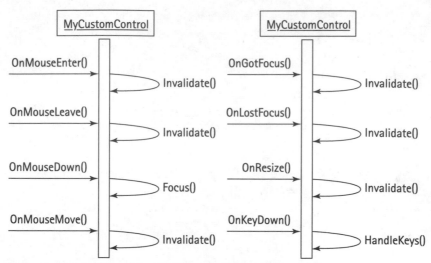

Figure 9-3: The interaction diagram for MyCustomControl

Creating a custom control library

The easiest way to create this type of library is with the New Project wizard, choosing Windows Control Library as the project type. I used the wizard to create a library called *MyCustomControls.dll,* as shown in Figure 9-4.

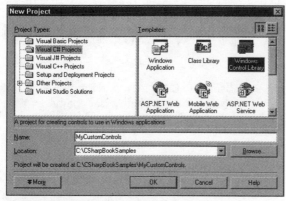

Figure 9-4: Using the New Project wizard to create my custom controls project

Keep in mind that you can put more than one control in the same DLL. The VS .NET Solution Explorer window shows the new project with a blank custom control called *Control1* in a file named *UserControl1.cs,* as depicted in Figure 9-5.

Figure 9-5: The files created by the Windows Control Library wizard

The first order of business is to change the control's filename to *MyCustomControl.cs*. The easiest way is to click directly on the filename in the Solution Explorer and edit the filename in-place, as shown in Figure 9-6.

Figure 9-6: Using the Solution Explorer to change a filename

Any filename can be changed in the Solution Explorer, including the project and solution filenames.

Changing the control's class name

If you install the control on the VS .NET Toolbox, the text that will appear next to the control's icon will be the control's class name, not its filename. There are two ways to change the class name: the hard way and the easy way. The hard way involves opening the source code file and editing all the occurrences of the class name by hand. The easy way uses the Class View window. If the window isn't already open, open it using the View ⇨ Class View command on the main menu. Select the `Control1` node. The Properties window will display the class' properties, including the class name. I changed the class name to `MyCustomControl`, as shown in Figure 9-7.

Figure 9-7: Using the Class View and Properties windows to change a component's class name

If you change the class name after having added event handlers to a class, you'll need to go and edit the handler names by hand.

Changing the control's Toolbox icon

This is an optional step, especially if you are creating a control for personal use and don't plan to reuse it frequently. By default, VS uses a built-in icon to represent your control on the Toolbox. Figure 9-8 shows the default icon used in the Toolbox for `MyCustomControl`.

Figure 9-8: The default icon used in the Toolbox for MyCustomControl

Unless you change the default icon, all your custom controls will have the same one. This not only makes it more difficult to find your control on the Toolbox, but also gives the impression that the control was developed in a hurry. Changing the Toolbox icon is fairly simple, and can be done in two different ways:

✦ By including a bitmap in the resources of the assembly

✦ By referencing a .bmp file that is located somewhere on your system

Regardless of which technique you choose, you need a .bmp file that has the image to use. The image dimensions should be 16-by-16 pixels. The file must be a .bmp file (*not* a .ico file). You can create it in VS .NET if you want, using the Add New Item project wizard and selecting Bitmap File as the file type, as shown in Figure 9-9.

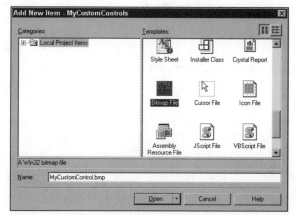

Figure 9-9: Using the Add New Item wizard to create a bitmap file

The first technique (including a bitmap in the resources of the custom control assembly) is probably the most commonly used one, and the one used by all the standard VS .NET components. I recommend this approach because the compiled .dll contains everything necessary, and doesn't rely on .bmp files to be present on your machine. There is only one requirement: Make sure the name of the .bmp file matches the class of the custom control you want to associate it with. In my case, I need the file name to be *MyCustomControl.bmp*. Since you can have multiple custom controls in the same project, this naming convention lets you associate a different Toolbox image with each control.

If you want to use an existing .bmp file, just add it to the project. To do so, right-click on the project node in the Solution Explorer, select the Add command from the menu, and then choose Add Existing Item from the next menu. In the Add Existing Item dialog box, select the .bmp file you want to use, as shown in Figure 9-10.

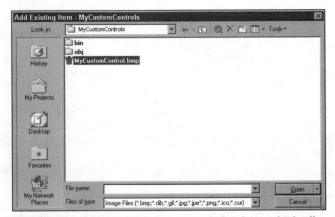

Figure 9-10: The Add Existing Item dialog box, which allows you to set the icon to display in the VS .NET Toolbox for your custom controls

Now select the .bmp file in the Solution Explorer. In the Properties window, you'll see that the Build Action property is set to Content. Change it to Embedded Resource, as shown in Figure 9-11.

Figure 9-11: The Build Action property of a bitmap file

By being an embedded resource, the .bmp file will be put into the main assembly with the rest of the executable code. If you inspect the assembly with ILDASM and open the manifest node, you'll be able to see all the embedded bitmaps resources in the assembly.

The second way to add custom Toolbox icons to a class is by referencing an external .bmp file. To use this technique, you need to tag your custom control class with a `ToolboxBitmap` attribute like this:

```
[ToolboxBitmap(@"C:\MyCustomControl.bmp")]
public class MyCustomControl : Windows.Forms.UserControl { ... }
```

The parameter passed to the `ToolboxBitmap` attribute is the absolute path to the .bmp file containing the image to use. The drawback of this second technique is that it requires your .bmp file to be present in a specific folder. Any developers using your custom control in their VS .NET environment will need to have the same folder and .bmp file on their system.

Adding the component to the Toolbox

Now you're ready to add the custom control to the VS.NET Toolbox. The Toolbox organizes its components by type, so there is a Data page, a Windows Forms page, and so on. You can also create your own page for your controls, if you want. Just right-click on the Toolbox and select the Add Tab command from the pop-up menu. At the bottom of the Toolbox, an edit box will appear, allowing you to type in the name of the new page. I created a new page called *My Controls,* as shown in Figure 9-12.

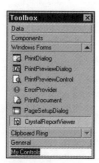

Figure 9-12: Creating a new page on the Toolbox

You can delete a page using the Delete Tab command on the Toolbox's context menu. To change the order of pages, just click on the page name and drag it to the desired location.

To add a component to the Toolbar, first select the Toolbox page you want to add the component to. You can pretty much add any component to any page. Pages are just a way to categorize components to make them easier to find. Right-click on the Toolbox and select the Customize Toolbox command. You'll get a dialog box, showing a list of the available and installed COM and .NET components. Select the .NET Framework Components tab, as shown in Figure 9-13.

Click the Browse button and you'll get another dialog box that lets you select components to load. Navigate to the directory containing the executable file of your component, as shown in Figure 9-14. Select the file and click OK.

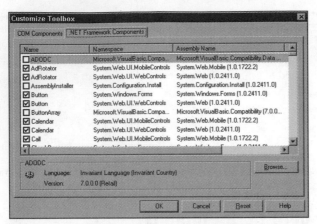

Figure 9-13: The Customize Toolbox dialog box, showing the currently available COM and .NET Framework components

Figure 9-14: Installing a component in the Toolbox

After closing the Open dialog box, you'll see the name of the component in the Customize Toolbox dialog box, as shown in Figure 9-15.

Notice the new control's icon shown near the bottom of the dialog box. The last step is to check the box next to the component and click the OK button. Now the Toolbox will be updated with the component, as shown in Figure 9-16.

The component will be added to whichever Toolbox page was selected when you chose the Customize Toolbox command. You can change the order of the component on each page using drag-and-drop, or by choosing Move Up/Move Down from the Toolbox context menu.

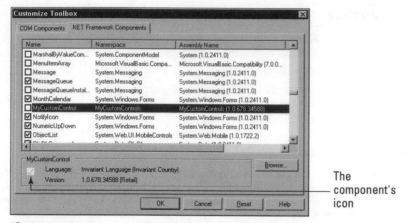

The component's icon

Figure 9-15: How a newly added component appears in the Customize Toolbox dialog box

Figure 9-16: The Toolbox showing the newly added MyCustomControl

Adding components to the Toolbox before they are stable

Even though I'm showing you how to add a component to the Toolbox immediately after creating the component with the VS .NET wizard, in practice you'll want to wait until the component is reasonably stable. The reason is this: When a component is added to the Toolbox, VS .NET caches its interface. The Properties window will display the properties and events as they were when the interface was cached. If you subsequently make changes to the component's interface, such as any of the following, the Properties window will not reflect those changes:

✦ Adding or deleting a property

✦ Changing the name of a property

✦ Changing the visibility of a property

✦ Changing the type of a property

✦ Adding or deleting an event

✦ Changing the name of an event

✦ Changing the visibility of an event

✦ Changing the signature of an event

You can recompile a component as many times as you want, but it won't make any difference. Removing and adding the component from the Toolbox is also useless. You need to exit and restart VS .NET, because VS .NET updates the cache when it starts up. For this reason, you should add components to the Toolbox until they are reasonably stable, in terms of interface elements.

Even though VS .NET caches the interface, it doesn't cache the component itself. If you rebuild the component after making a change to its code, and then run a program that uses the component, your changes will be available.

Creating a test fixture

When you develop custom controls that aren't derived from UserControl, you may not be able to see it in the Forms Designer at design time. Consequently, it will be impossible to see what the component looks like unless you actually run it. Even if the component is derived from UserControl, you still can't see what the Paint logic does until the control is run. The moral of the story is that when developing a custom control, right after creating the skeleton control with the wizard, the next thing you'll probably want to do is create a test fixture application that embeds the control in a form. Any time you need to see how the control looks, or whether its event handling logic is working correctly, you can just run the test fixture.

To test MyCustomControl, I'll use the New Project wizard to create a plain Windows application. After doing so, the Solution Explorer will show two projects, *MyCustomControls.dll* and *TestFixture.exe*, as shown in Figure 9-17.

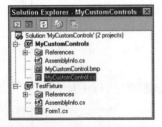

Figure 9-17: The Solution Explorer, showing the custom control project and the new test fixture

Adding a reference to the test fixture

Before you can create an instance of MyCustomControl in the test fixture's main form, you need to add a reference to its namespace in the test fixture's project. To do so, right-click on the test fixture project in the Solution Explorer and select Add Reference as shown in Figure 9-18.

Choosing the Add Reference command will display the Add Reference dialog box, shown in Figure 9-19. On the .NET Framework tab, click the Browse button and locate your custom control's DLL. Having done so, your control will appear at the bottom of the Add Reference dialog box.

Click the OK button and you're just about are ready to use MyCustomControl in the test fixture. There are two ways to add a component to the Text Fixture: the easy way and the hard way. The easy way uses the Toolbox; the hard way requires you to manually add code to the test fixture. I'll discuss both methods.

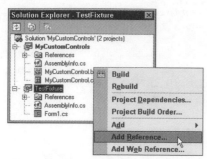

Figure 9-18: Adding a reference to MyCustomControls.dll to the test fixture project

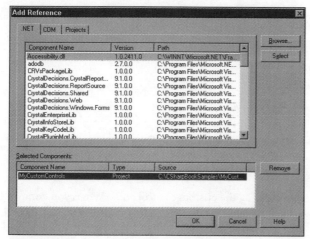

Figure 9-19: The new reference to MyCustomControls.dll added to the test fixture project

Adding the custom control using drag-and-drop

This procedure is a no-brainer. Like the heading says, just select MyCustomControl on the Toolbox and drop in on the test fixture form. Now you can configure MyCustomControl using the VS .NET Properties window. I'll change only one property, setting the Docking value to Fill. That was easy. Now let's take a look at the manual process, to see what VS .NET did behind the scenes for us.

Adding the custom control manually

First you need to add a using statement in the test fixture form that references the custom control's namespace, so you'll need the following line:

```
using MyCustomControls;
```

Then you'll need to add code to the form's constructor to create an instance of `MyCustomControl` and set its `Docking` property to `DockStyle.Fill`. Listing 9-1 shows the code.

Listing 9-1: The Code Necessary to Manually Instantiate
MyCustomControl in the Test Fixture

```
public class Form1 : System.Windows.Forms.Form
{
  // miscellaneous fields...

  MyCustomControl myControl;

  public Form1()
  {
    myControl = new MyCustomControl();
    myControl.Dock = DockStyle.Fill;
    this.Controls.Add(myControl);

    // code created by wizard...
  }
}
```

Not too complicated. Still, using drag-and-drop with the Toolbox is easier.

Running the custom control code

There is one last thing to do before running the custom control code: When you compile the custom control and click the Start button to debug it, you'll get the error message shown in Figure 9-20.

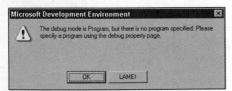

Figure 9-20: The error message displayed if you try to run MyCustomControls.dll by itself

The problem is that the system can't run a DLL by itself. What you need to do is tell VS .NET to run the test fixture any time you tell it to run the MyCustomControls.dll code. Right-click on the DLL's project name in the Solution Explorer and select the Properties menu command. In the Property Pages window, select the Debugging page under Configuration Properties, on the left side of the window, as shown in Figure 9-21.

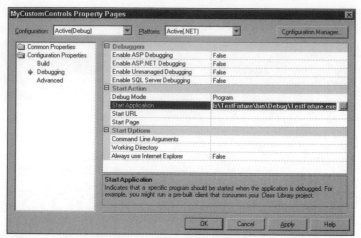

Figure 9-21: Setting the test fixture as the debug application for MyCustomControls.dll

On the right side, change the Debug Mode property to Program. For the Start Application property, enter the full path of the test fixture application. I entered a path like this:

```
C:\MyBaseFolder\MyCustomControls\TestFixture\bin\Debug\TestFixture.exe
```

After closing the dialog box with the OK button, you're ready to debug the MyCustomControls.dll code. Select the custom control project in the Solution Explorer and click the Start button. The test fixture will start up and run, but most of the form will be empty space, because MyCustomControl doesn't have a `Paint()` method. The Text Fixture form will look like Figure 9-22.

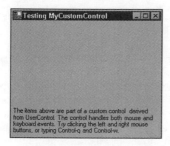

Figure 9-22: The test fixture, showing a blank area where the custom control will go

The text at the bottom of the form is a `Label` control that I put on the form to show which keys the custom control will be set up to understand. With the test fixture running, you can set breakpoints in the custom control code, step through the code, examine variables, and debug the control using ordinary debugging techniques.

Developing the Component

Testing an invisible control is not easy — you can't even be sure your control is there. The first thing I normally add to a new control is some paint logic, so I can see where the control is on the screen. For example, the code shown in Listing 9-2 will paint the control's client area in light blue.

Listing 9-2: Painting the Client Area of MyCustomControl with a Solid Color

```
public class MyCustomControl : System.Windows.Forms.UserControl
{
  protected override void OnPaint(PaintEventArgs e)
  {

    e.Graphics.FillRectangle(Brushes.LightBlue, ClientRectangle);
  }

  // other methods...
}
```

With the new OnPaint handler, I can see where the control is on the test fixture's form, making it easier to ensure the code I add later does what it's supposed to. The test fixture now displays MyCustomControl as a light blue box, as shown in Figure 9-23.

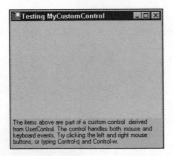

Figure 9-23: Using a plain OnPaint handler in MyCustomControl to paint the area occupied by the control

Since the figure isn't in color, it looks pretty much like the previous figure, containing empty space where the control is located. So what do I have at this point? Basically, just a component that looks like a colored rectangle that doesn't do anything. With the added color, now I can tell what area of the screen MyCustomControl occupies. The next step is to make it interact with the user. I'll need to add mouse and keyboard handlers. Not all components have handlers for both. Some components, like standard Labels don't have handlers for either. Although MyCustomControl is not the kind of control that you would do typing with, I'll add a keyboard event handler just to show how to handle keys, because the old technique of using virtual keys is obsolete in the .NET Framework.

Adding mouse event handlers

If you recall the interaction diagram from Figure 9-3, there are a number of mouse event handlers. Their main purpose is to invalidate the control's client area to force the control to repaint itself. MyCustomControl needs to repaint itself because it displays a dark border around the quadrant the mouse is in. The control also displays a focus rectangle around the client area when the user clicks the control. Listing 9-3 shows all the event handlers I added that are related to mouse events.

Listing 9-3: Event Handlers Related to Mouse Events in MyCustomControl

```csharp
protected override void OnMouseEnter(EventArgs e)
{
  if (Form.ActiveForm != FindForm() ) return;

  Invalidate();
}

protected override void OnMouseLeave(EventArgs e)
{
  if (Form.ActiveForm != FindForm() ) return;
  quadrantHighlighted = Rectangle.Empty;
  Invalidate();
}

protected override void OnMouseMove(MouseEventArgs e)
{
  if (Form.ActiveForm != FindForm() ) return;

  if (!quadrantHighlighted.Contains(PointToClient(MousePosition) ) )
    Invalidate();
}

protected override void OnMouseDown(MouseEventArgs e)
{

  Focus();
}

protected override void OnGotFocus(EventArgs e)
{
  Invalidate();
}

protected override void OnLostFocus(EventArgs e)
{
  quadrantHighlighted = Rectangle.Empty;
  Invalidate();
}

protected override void OnResize(EventArgs e)
{
  Invalidate();
}
```

The variable `quadrantHighlighted` is a rectangle denoting which of the four quadrants the mouse is over. In the `OnMouseEnter` and `OnMouseLeave` handlers, I check to see if the parent form of MyCustomControl is active before doing anything. The code `Form.ActiveForm` gives me the form of my application that is currently active. If my application is not active, it will give me a `null`. The method `FindForm()` returns the parent form of the control. Say the control is in a group box in a panel in a form. Without having to write code to iterate over the parent and the parent's parent to find the parent form, just call `FindForm()`. The method will search the parent chain until it finds a `Form`.

Knowing whether the parent form is active is important. Consider the situation in which the user has two different applications on the screen. Say Word is running on the left side of the screen, and the test fixture with the embedded `MyCustomControl` is on the right side. Assume the user has clicked on Word and is typing text. If the mouse is moved to the right side of the screen over `MyCustomControl`, without clicking anything, I don't want the control to change its appearance just because the mouse cursor was moved over it. Most controls behave this way — they react to the mouse only if their parent form is active. If the user activates the control by clicking it, things are different.

The `OnMouseDown` handler is really simple. All it does is call `Focus()` to give the input focus to `MyCustomControl`. Calling `Focus()` causes the control to receive an `OnGotFocus` event.

When the mouse is moved, I check to see if it moved outside the quadrant it was in, using this code:

```
if (!quadrantHighlighted.Contains(PointToClient(MousePosition) ) )
    Invalidate();
```

To get the current mouse cursor position, I use the property `Control.MousePosition`, which returns the cursor location in screen coordinates. The quadrant rectangle is in client coordinates, so I convert the mouse position to client coordinates with the method `Control.PointToClient(Point)`. Then I use the method `Rectangle.Contains(Point)` to see if the mouse is within the boundaries of the quadrant. If so, the control is invalidated and subsequently repainted with the dark border removed from the quadrant the mouse just left.

Adding keyboard event handlers

At any given point in time, Windows is typically displaying more than one item on the screen. Even when all applications are closed, the screen will still show the desktop, the Task Bar, and the System Tray. If the user presses a key, which item on the screen should the key be given to? Graphical User Interface systems like Windows handle this problem with the concept of *input focus:* The key will be sent to whatever control has the input focus. If no control has the focus, the key will be ignored. Only one control of one application can have the focus at any given time. A control can get the focus in the following ways:

✦ The user clicks it with the mouse.

✦ The user tabs to it with the Tab key.

✦ The user presses an accelerator or shortcut key.

In all cases, an `OnGotFocus` event will be sent to the control. When a control has the input focus, it should display a focus rectangle around itself, as feedback to the user. To make the focus rectangle appear, the `OnGotFocus` handler for `MyCustomControl` just invalidates the entire client area. The `OnPaint` handler will subsequently check to see if the control has the input focus, and draw the focus rectangle if necessary.

Once a control has the input focus, it will receive keyboard events if the user presses keys on the keyboard. Two types of keyboard events are handled by many controls:

✦ OnKeyDown

✦ OnKeyPress

What is the difference? Simple: OnKeyPress occurs when the user types a character, like *a, ?,* or *Y.* But there are several keys, like the function keys, the Caps Lock key, and the Shift key, that don't designate characters. For these keys, OnKeyPress events don't occur. The rule of thumb is this: If the key has an ASCII value, it will generate an OnKeyPress event. For example, the Escape key and the Backspace both have ASCII values and will generate OnKeyPress events. Keep in mind that ASCII defines different values for uppercase and lowercase characters. The property KeyPressEventArgs.KeyChar, which is passed to the OnKeyPress handler, will indicate not only the character, but also the case of the character.

The OnKeyDown event is much more generic. It occurs when the user presses any key or key-combination on the keyboard, including the Control key, the Alt key, a function key, a regular character like *a,* or even a combination of keys, like Control-X or Control-Shift-S. The property KeyEventArgs.KeyCode, which is passed to the OnKeyDown handler, will indicate only the character, not the case of the character. For example, both *a* and *A* use the KeyCode 65, which is the ASCII value of an uppercase *A.* To determine the case, you can check the property KeyEventArgs.Shift of the parameter passed to the event handler.

Listing 9-4 shows the code used by MyCustomControl to handle keyboard events.

Listing 9-4: **The OnKeyDown Handler for MyCustomControl**

```
protected override void OnKeyDown(KeyEventArgs e)
{
  // we only respond to Ctl-Q and Ctl-W
  if ( e.Control && (e.KeyCode == Keys.Q) )
  {
  MessageBox.Show("You pressed the Ctl-Q key!");
  e.Handled = true;
  }

  else if ( e.Control && (e.KeyCode == Keys.W) )
  {
  MessageBox.Show("You pressed the Ctl-W key!");
  e.Handled = true;
  }

  else
    e.Handled = false;
}
```

The event handler is passed a KeyEventArgs parameter that has a couple of properties. One is Handled, which you'll need to set to true if you don't want the base class to continue processing a key. The other useful field is KeyCode. It provides the code of the key that was depressed. The value of KeyCode will be one of the values listed in the Keys enumeration. Table 9-1 shows some of the most commonly used values.

Table 9-1: The Most Commonly Used Values of the Keys Enumeration

Value of the Keys Enumeration	Keyboard Key
Keys.Alt	The Alt key
Keys.A to Keys.Z	The 26 letters in the English alphabet, both uppercase and lowercase
Keys.Back	The Backspace key
Keys.CapsLock	The Caps Lock key
Keys.Control	The Ctrl key
Keys.D0 to Keys.D9	The digits 0 to 9
Keys.Delete	The Delete key
Keys.End	The End key
Keys.Enter	The Enter key
Keys.Escape	The Esc key
Keys.F0 to Keys.F24	The function keys
Keys.Home	The Home key
Keys.Insert	The Insert key
Keys.Left	The left arrow key
Keys.NumLock	The Num Lock key
Keys.NumPad0 to Keys.NumPad9	The digits 0 to 9 on the Num pad.
Keys.PageDown	The Page Down key
Keys.PageUp	The Page Up key
Keys.Right	The right arrow key
Keys.Shift	The Shift key
Keys.Space	The spacebar
Keys.Tab	The Tab key

Punctuation keys, like the period (.) and question mark (?) don't have values in the Keys enumeration. For these keys, you'll need to use the numeric value assigned to each key, as shown in Table 9-2.

Table 9-2: Numeric Values Passed to the OnKeyDown Event Handler for Special Keys

Key Pressed	Numeric Value
, or <	188
. or >	190

Key Pressed	Numeric Value
/ or ?	191
; or :	186
' or "	222
[or {	219
] or }	221
\ or |	220
` or ~ (tilde)	192
- or _	189
= or +	187

The values in the previous table are valid for U.S. keyboards. Keyboards for other locales, such as German and French, may have different key assignments.

`MyCustomControl` implements a handler for the `OnKeyPress` event, and Listing 9-5 shows some of the common character-handling techniques you might find useful.

Listing 9-5: An OnKeyPress Handler Showing Ways of Dealing with Characters

```
protected override void OnKeyPress(KeyPressEventArgs e)
{
  if (Char.IsLower(e.KeyChar) )
    MessageBox.Show("You typed a lower case character");

  else if (Char.IsUpper(e.KeyChar) )
    MessageBox.Show("You typed an upper case character");

  else if (Char.IsDigit(e.KeyChar) )
    MessageBox.Show("You typed a number key");

  else if (Char.IsPunctuation(e.KeyChar) )
    MessageBox.Show("You typed a punctuation key");

  else if (Char.IsWhiteSpace(e.KeyChar) )
    MessageBox.Show("You typed a whitespace key");

  // check for specific characters
  switch (e.KeyChar)
  {
    case 'a':
      MessageBox.Show("You typed the character: " + e.KeyChar);
      break;  // lowercase 'a'
```

Continued

Listing 9-5 *(continued)*

```
    case 'A':
      MessageBox.Show("You typed the character: " + e.KeyChar);
      break;  // uppercase 'A'
    case '.':
      MessageBox.Show("You typed the character: " + e.KeyChar);
      break;  // the period key
    case ',':
      MessageBox.Show("You typed the character: " + e.KeyChar);
      break;  // the comma key
    case '[':
      MessageBox.Show("You typed the character: " + e.KeyChar);
      break;  // the [ key
    case ']':
      MessageBox.Show("You typed the character: " + e.KeyChar);
      break;  // the ] key

    default:
      break;
  }
}
```

In Listing 9-5, I used some of the character classification methods available in the Char class, to see if a character is uppercase, lowercase, and so on. The methods of class Char are designed to behave correctly across locales and can save you some time determining what classification a character falls under.

Painting the control

Many custom controls devote a substantial amount of code to painting. The place to put painting code is normally inside the OnPaint event handler. The handler is passed a PaintEventArgs parameter that has two important properties: the ClipRectangle and the Graphics object to paint with.

The ClipRectangle tells you which area of the control needs to be repainted. Small controls often ignore the ClipRectangle and always paint the entire client area. MyCustomControl ignores the ClipRectangle, but controls that have complex painting code usually try to minimize the amount of painting by using the ClipRectangle. The section "Painting only what needs to be painted" later in this chapter provides details on using ClipRectangle.

The Graphics object referenced by the PaintEventArgs parameter is the object you use to draw on the screen. The object has methods to draw everything from lines, boxes, and text to complex shapes like Bezier curves.

A quick historical digression on Bezier curves: A lot of people are under the impression that these curves have been around for a long time, kind of like parabolas and ellipses. Not true. They were actually developed as recently as 1970 by Pierre Bezier, a mechanical engineer working for the French car manufacturer Renault, who used them to model the body designs of cars. Although young, Bezier curves are in widespread use. Just to give one example, Adobe PostScript fonts make extensive use of them.

The next section discusses painting common things like lines, rectangles, circles, and text. The .NET Framework supports a number of new advanced graphics features collectively known as GDI+. The features include textured brushes, gradient fills, alpha blending, and world transforms. *Alpha blending* allows graphics items to be partially or completely transparent, letting you draw objects that have a translucent look. *World transforms* replace the old mapping modes and enable you to support advanced graphics transforms like rotation, shearing, and scaling using matrices.

To make use of the GDI+ features, you need to import the Drawing.Drawing2D namespace in your code like this:

```
using System.Drawing.Drawing2D;
```

MyCustomControl uses a number of GDI+ features. Before diving into the painting code used in MyCustomControl, it's best to describe the painting primitives separately, so you understand how MyCustomControl works.

Pens and brushes

To paint geometric shapes on the screen, you need something to paint with. When painting lines, you need a pen. When filling an area, you need a brush. The .NET Framework comes with a large assortment of built-in pens and brushes that satisfy the most common painting requirements. The following code shows how to get a standard black pen and a standard white brush:

```
Pen pen = Pens.Black;
Brush brush = Brushes.White;
```

The Pens and Brushes classes have static properties that give instant access to all kinds of colors. A large number of hues have been assigned names, for convenience. For example, you can get a Chocolate or DeepSkyBlue pen or brush. If you need a pen or brush that isn't built-in, you can create one. To create a pen all you need to do is this:

```
Pen pen = new Pen(Color.Beige, 3);
```

This creates a solid beige pen, 3 units wide. By default, a unit translates to a pixel on the screen, but if you enable scaling for the surface the pen draws on, the number of pixels will vary.

To create a dashed pen, just choose one of the DashStyle enumerations and assign it to the pen like this:

```
pen.DashStyle = DashStyle.DashDot;
```

You can also create a pen that uses a brush to fill the strokes. Using a brush lets you create pens with complex strokes containing hatched patterns, gradient fills, and textures.

To create a solid brush with a custom color, use code like this:

```
int red = 200;
int green = 100;
int blue = 112;
Color weirdColor = Color.FromArgb(red, green, blue);
Brush brush = new SolidBrush(weirdColor);
```

There are separate classes for the various types of brushes. To create a hatched brush, use the HatchBrush like this:

```
Brush brush = new HatchBrush(HatchStyle.DiagonalCross,
                             Color.Red, Color.Violet);
```

This will create a hatched brush with red lines on a violet background. Another type of brush is the textured one, which uses an image to paint with. Here's how you would create a textured brush using the image contained in the file c:\myImage.jpg:

```
Image myImage = Image.FromFile(@"c:\myImage.jpg");
Brush brush = new TextureBrush(myImage);
```

I used the new @-literal notation with the filename, so I didn't have to use double backslashes. To create a brush that uses a gradient fill, you need to specify a rectangle and indicate the starting and ending colors. The rectangle is used internally to create a texture that fades from the starting to the ending color. The brush then uses this texture to paint with. Here is how you might create a gradient filled brush:

```
Rectangle rect = new Rectangle(0, 0, 100, 100);
Color startColor = Color.Azure;
Color endColor = Color.FromArgb(200, 201, 202);
Brush brush = new LinearGradientBrush(rect, startColor, endColor,

LinearGradientMode.ForwardDiagonal);
```

The last parameter in the LinearGradientBrush constructor call lets you determine which direction to go when fading from start to end color.

If you're drawing standard Windows objects, like menus, window frames, or windows captions, there are a few special classes that you'll need. The SystemColors class contains properties denoting all the various colors used by Windows to draw windows, buttons, scrollbars, and the like. Keep in mind that users can change the system colors by selecting a Color Scheme from the Desktop Properties window, so buttons may look gray in one scheme and pink in another. If you wanted to get the color currently selected for filling buttons and active title bars, you would use the SystemColors class like this:

```
Color buttonColor = SystemColors.Control;
Color activeCaptionColor = SystemColors.ActiveCaption;
```

If you need the colors to paint objects, you can get use a stock pen or brush that uses one of the system colors. For example, to paint the text in an active caption bar you would get a system pen like this:

```
Pen captionText = SystemPens.ActiveCaptionText;
```

To paint the scrollbar of a window, you could use a system brush like this:

```
Brush scrollbarBrush = SystemBrushes.ScrollBar;
```

There are system colors, pens, and brushes for all the standard decorations of a window and all items that appear on the desktop.

Painting basic figures

Now that you know how to create pens and brushes, it's time to do something with them. The Graphics object passed to a custom control's OnPaint handler in the PaintEventArg parameter has two sets of methods for drawing just about anything: the first set draws outlines of figures; the second set fills the interiors. Not surprisingly, methods in the first set have names starting with the word Draw and methods in the second set have names starting with the word Fill. The Draw methods use a Pen to draw lines. The Fill methods use a Brush to fill areas.

The methods that tend to be used most are shown in Table 9-3.

Table 9-3: The Most Commonly Used Painting Methods

Draw Method	Fill Method	Description
DrawEllipse	FillEllipse	Used with circles and ellipses.
DrawIcon		Used to paint icons.
DrawImage		Used to display jpeg, png, bmp, gif, or other images.
DrawLine		Used with straight lines.
DrawPolygon	FillPolygon	Used to create arbitrary polygons.
DrawRectangle	FillRectangle	Used to create boxes.
DrawString		Displays text.

The `DrawIcon()` and `DrawImage()` methods use images to paint, while the other `Draw` methods use a pen. Controls sometimes are in the disabled state and need to display images or text that looks *grayed-out*. In these cases, you'll want to use the `ControlPaint` class, which offers the methods `ControlPaint.DrawImageDisabled()` and `ControlPaint.DrawStringDisabled()`.

Once you get the hang of things, you'll find all the drawing methods quite intuitive and easy to use. I'll show a number of examples that demonstrate some of the methods. In the code, the e object will be assumed to be the `PaintEventArgs` parameter passed to the `OnPaint` handler.

To draw a dashed brown line between the points (0, 0) and (100, 100) you could use code like this:

```
Point p1 = new Point(0, 0);
Point p2 = new Point(100, 100);
e.Graphics.DrawLine(Pens.Brown, p1, p2);
```

To draw and fill a rectangle, you could use code like this:

```
Rectangle r = new Rectangle(0, 0, 100, 100);
e.Graphics.DrawRectangle(Pens.Red, r);
e.Graphics.FillRectangle(Brushes.LightBlue, r);
```

To draw and fill a circle, you could use code like this:

```
Rectangle r = new Rectangle(0, 0, 100, 100);
e.Graphics.DrawEllipse(Pens.Red, r);
e.Graphics.FillEllipse(Brushes.LightBlue, r);
```

Using the draw and fill methods is easy. Programmers familiar with graphics programming before the advent of the .NET Framework will remember the labors of using resource handles, device contexts, and calling `SelectObject` to select and deselect pens and brushes. Leakage of graphics handles, caused by using a handle and not freeing it, was a common nightmare for complex graphics applications. When running on Windows 95 or 98, these applications would eventually require the entire operating system to be restarted to free the leaked handles. All of these problems are fortunately a memory of the past, as .NET graphics programming leaves all the details to the system. Automatic garbage collection means you will never have to worry about a leaked bitmap, pen, or other resource ever again. Amen!

Painting standard objects

With the expression *standard objects,* I refer to graphics items that are used to paint windows, like caption bars, window frames, and buttons. The .NET Framework has a class called ControlPaint that has a number of methods that paint these standard objects.

Table 9-4 shows some of the commonly used methods of ControlPaint.

Table 9-4: Some of the Commonly Used Methods of Class ControlPaint

Method	Description
DrawBorder	Draws a window border with the given border style.
DrawBorder3D	Draws a window with a 3D border.
DrawButton	Draws a standard button.
DrawCaptionButton	Draws one of the buttons used in the caption bar of a window. Caption buttons include the Close, Minimize, Maximize, and Restore buttons.
DrawCheckBox	Draws a standard checkbox.
DrawComboButton	Draws the drop-down button used in standard combo boxes.
DrawFocusRectangle	Draws a dotted rectangle.
DrawImageDisabled	Draws an image that appears grayed-out.
DrawRadioButton	Draws a standard radio button.
DrawReversibleFrame	Draws a reversible rectangular frame. The frame can be erased from the screen by drawing it again. With a Thick FrameStyle, you can draw the silhouette of a window when the user is dragging the window with the mouse. With a Dashed FrameStyle, you can draw *rubberbands,* which are those dotted rectangles displayed by many applications when the user is dragging the mouse to select multiple items. (See the note on reversible methods that follows this table.)
DrawReversibleLine	Draws a reversible line. The line can be erased from the screen by drawing it again. This type of line is useful to show the silhouette of a line when the user is dragging a line with the mouse. (See the note on reversible methods that follows this table.)
DrawScrollButton	Draws a standard scroll bar button.
DrawSelectionFrame	Draws a standard selection frame, which is a rectangle with a thick border. Selection frames are often drawn around components in design-time environments to indicate they have been selected.
DrawStringDisabled	Draws a string that appears grayed-out.
FillReversibleRectangle	Draws a reversible filled rectangle on the screen. The rectangle can be erased from the screen by drawing it again. (See the note on reversible methods that follows this table.)

Note The reversible methods (DrawReversibleFrame, DrawReversibleLine, and FillReversibleRectangle) are different from the other drawing methods. First, they draw directly on the screen, without using your control's Graphics object. Second, they take a rectangle whose units must be in screen units.

Use Control.RectangleToScreen() to convert from client to screen units, as shown in Listing 9-6.

Listing 9-6: Converting Client Coordinates to Screen Coordinates with the Reversible Draw Methods

```
public class MyCustomControl : System.Windows.Forms.UserControl
{
  protected override void OnPaint(PaintEventArgs e)
  {

    Rectangle rect = new Rectangle(0, 0, 100, 100);
    rect = RectangleToScreen(rect);
    ControlPaint.FillReversibleRectangle(rect, Color.White);
  }
}
```

All of the standard objects have default dimensions that you can read using the SystemInformation class. For example, to draw a Close button in the standard size, you could use this code:

```
Size size = SystemInformation.CaptionButtonSize;
ControlPaint.DrawCaptionButton(e.Graphics, 0, 0,
                           size.Width, size.Height,
                     CaptionButton.Maximize, ButtonState.Normal);
```

Listings 9-7 through 9-21 demonstrate how you might call each of the methods in Table 9-4, and the figures that accompany these listings (Figures 9-24 through 9-38) show what the various graphics look like on the screen.

Listing 9-7: DrawBorder()

```
ControlPaint.DrawBorder(e.Graphics, rect,
                     SystemColors.ActiveBorder, style);
```

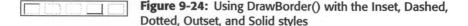

Figure 9-24: Using DrawBorder() with the Inset, Dashed, Dotted, Outset, and Solid styles

Listing 9-8: **DrawBorder3D()**

```
ControlPaint.DrawBorder3D(e.Graphics, rect, style);
```

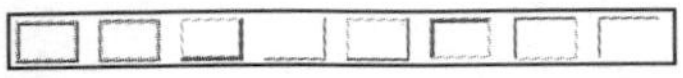

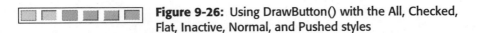

Figure 9-25: Using DrawBorder3D() with the Bump, Flat, Raised, RaisedInner, RaisedOuter, Sunken, SunkenInner, and SunkenOuter styles

Listing 9-9: **DrawButton()**

```
ControlPaint.DrawButton(e.Graphics, rect, style);
```

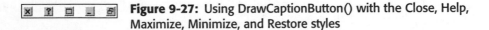

Figure 9-26: Using DrawButton() with the All, Checked, Flat, Inactive, Normal, and Pushed styles

Listing 9-10: **DrawCaptionButton()**

```
Size s = SystemInformation.CaptionButtonSize;
Rectangle rect = new Rectangle(0, 0, s.Width, s.Height);
ControlPaint.DrawCaptionButton(e.Graphics, rect, style,
ButtonState.Normal);
```

Figure 9-27: Using DrawCaptionButton() with the Close, Help, Maximize, Minimize, and Restore styles

Listing 9-11: **DrawCheckBox()**

```
Size s = SystemInformation.MenuCheckSize;
Rectangle rect = new Rectangle(0, 0, s.Width, s.Height);
ControlPaint.DrawCheckBox(e.Graphics, rect, ButtonState.ALL);
```

Figure 9-28: Using DrawCheckBox() with the All, Checked, Flat, Inactive, Normal, and Pushed styles

Listing 9-12: **DrawComboButton()**

```
Size s = SystemInformation.MenuButtonSize;
Rectangle rect = new Rectangle(0, 0, s.Width, s.Height);
ControlPaint.DrawComboButton(e.Graphics, rect, ButtonState.ALL);
```

 **Figure 9-29:** Using DrawComboButton() with the All, Checked, Flat, Inactive, Normal, and Pushed styles

Listing 9-13: **DrawFocusRectangle()**

```
ControlPaint.DrawFocusRectangle(e.Graphics, rect);
```

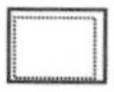

Figure 9-30: Using DrawFocusRectangle() to draw a focus rectangle

Listing 9-14: **DrawImageDisabled()**

```
Point p = new Point(20, 20);
Image image = Image.FromFile(@"c:\myImage.gif");
e.Graphics.DrawImage(image, p);
ControlPaint.DrawImageDisabled(e.Graphics, image, 60, 20,
                              Color.White);
```

Figure 9-31: An image drawn with Graphics.DrawImage() and with ControlPaint.DrawImageDisabled()

Listing 9-15: **DrawRadioButton()**

```
Size s = SystemInformation.MenuButtonSize;
Rectangle rect = new Rectangle(0, 0, s.Width, s.Height);
ControlPaint.DrawRadioButton(e.Graphics, rect, ButtonState.ALL);
```

 **Figure 9-32:** Using DrawRadioButton() with the All, Checked, Flat, Inactive, Normal, and Pushed styles

Listing 9-16: **DrawReversibleFrame()**

```
e.Graphics.FillRectangle(Brushes.LightBlue, ClientRectangle);

// screen (not client) coordinates!
Rectangle rect = new Rectangle(10, 20, 50, 45);

// if you had client coordinates, convert them to
// screen coordinates
// rect = RectangleToScreen(rect);

ControlPaint.DrawReversibleFrame(rect, Color.White,
                                 FrameStyle.Thick);
```

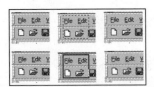

Figure 9-33: Using DrawReversibleFrame() with the Dashed and Thick styles

In the figure, the screen captures in the left column show a portion of the screen before drawing. The center column shows the effect of the first call to DrawReversibleFrame(). The right column shows the screen after calling DrawReversibleFrame() a second time. As you can see, the frame rectangle is gone and the screen looks like it did before drawing the reversible frame.

The screen captures on the top row used FrameStyle.Dashed; the ones on the bottom row used FrameStyle.Thick.

Listing 9-17: **DrawReversibleLine()**

```
// screen (not client) coordinates
Point p1 = new Point(20, 30);
Point p2 = new Point(60, 30);


// if you have client coordinates, convert to screen coordinates
//p1 = PointToScreen(p1);
//p2 = PointToScreen(p2);

ControlPaint.DrawReversibleLine(p1, p2, Color.White);
```

Figure 9-34: Using DrawReversibleLine()

In the figure, the screen capture on the left shows a portion of the screen before drawing. The center screen shows the effect of the first call to `DrawReversibleLine()`. Notice the thin horizontal line between over the File and Edit menus. The right screen capture shows the screen after calling `DrawReversibleLine()` a second time. As you can see, the line is gone and the screen looks like it did before drawing the reversible line.

Listing 9-18: DrawScrollButton()

```
int w = SystemInformation.VerticalScrollBarWidth;
int h = SystemInformation.VerticalScrollBarArrowHeight;
Rectangle rect = new Rectangle(20, 50, w, h);
ControlPaint.DrawScrollButton(e.Graphics, rect, ScrollButton.Down,
                              ButtonState.ALL);
```

 **Figure 9-35:** Using DrawScrollButton() with All, Checked, Flat, Inactive, Normal, and Pushed styles

---

Listing 9-19: DrawSelectionFrame()

```
Point p = new Point(20, 20);
Size s = new Size(40, 30);
Rectangle innerRect = new Rectangle(p, s);
Size size = SystemInformation.FrameBorderSize;
Rectangle outerRect = Rectangle.Inflate(innerRect,
                                        size.Width,
                                        size.Height);
ControlPaint.DrawSelectionFrame(e.Graphics, isActive,
                                outerRect,
                        innerRect,
                                Color.LightBlue);
```

 Figure 9-36: Using DrawSelectionFrame() with isActive set to false and then true

---

Listing 9-20: DrawStringDisabled()

```
Point p = new Point(20, 50);
String s = "Arriverderci!";
e.Graphics.DrawString(s, Font, Brushes.Black, p);

Rectangle rect = new Rectangle(150, 50, 100, 30);
```

Continued

Listing 9-20 *(continued)*

```
ControlPaint.DrawStringDisabled(e.Graphics, s, Font,
                        Color.Black rect,
                        StringFormat.GenericDefault);
```

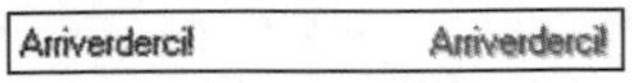

Figure 9-37: Drawing text with Graphics.DrawString() and ControlPaint.DrawStringDisabled()

Listing 9-21: FillReversibleRectangle()

```
// screen (not client) coordinates
Rectangle rect = new Rectangle(10, 20, 50, 45);

// if you have client coordinates, convert them to
// screen coordinates
//rect = RectangleToScreen(rect);

ControlPaint.FillReversibleRectangle(rect, Color.LightBlue);
```

Figure 9-38: UsingFillReversibleRectangle()

In the figure, the screen capture on the left shows a portion of the screen before drawing. The center screen shows the effect of the first call to `FillReversibleRectangle()`. The right screen capture shows the screen after calling `FillReversibleRectangle()` a second time. As you can see, the box is gone and the screen looks like it did before drawing the reversible rectangle. The color used in the call to `FillReversibleRectangle()` is XORed with each pixel painted on the screen. If a blue reversible rectangle were painted over a white area, the box's color would be (`white XOR blue`), which translates to yellow. A red rectangle over white would produce a cyan box.

Painting text

Displaying text is one of the most common painting requirements. At first glance, you might think the .NET Framework doesn't support much variety in the ways you can paint text, since it only has two paint methods that deal with text:

✦ `ControlPaint.DrawStringDisabled()`

✦ `Graphics.DrawString()`

I discussed the first method in the previous section. It only displays grayed-out text, so it isn't used that frequently. That leaves us with only one other method to handle text drawing: `DrawString()`. But if you look a little closer at the Graphics class, you'll find that

`DrawString()` has a number of overloaded methods. The simplest one just paints a given string with a given font and brush at a given location on the screen, as shown in Listing 9-22.

Listing 9-22: **Calling the Simplest Graphics.DrawString() Method**

```
String s = "Queen of Hearts";
Font font = new Font("Arial", 20, FontStyle.Bold);
Point p = new Point(20, 20);
e.Graphics.DrawString(s, font, Brushes.Black, p);
```

The code will paint a string that looks like Figure 9-39.

Queen of Hearts   **Figure 9-39:** Painting a string with a solid brush

The `Point p` designates the upper left corner of the string. The brush can be of any type, including solid, hatched, gradient, or textured, as shown in Listing 9-23.

Listing 9-23: **Painting Strings with Different Brushes**

```
String s = "B";

Font font = new Font("Arial", 75, FontStyle.Bold);
Point p = new Point(20, 5);
e.Graphics.DrawString(s, font, Brushes.Black, p);

Brush hatchBrush = new HatchBrush(HatchStyle.Cross,
                                  Color.Red, Color.White);
p = new Point(100, 5);
e.Graphics.DrawString(s, font, hatchBrush, p);

Rectangle rect = new Rectangle(0, 0, 100, 100);
Brush gradientBrush = new LinearGradientBrush(rect, Color.Red,
                                              Color.White,

LinearGradientMode.BackwardDiagonal);
p = new Point(180, 5);
e.Graphics.DrawString(s, font, gradientBrush, p);

p = new Point(260, 5);
Image texture = Image.FromFile(@"c:\alloc.gif");
Brush textureBrush = new TextureBrush(texture);
e.Graphics.DrawString(s, font, textureBrush, p);
```

The code paints the letter *B* in several ways, as shown in Figure 9-40.

Figure 9-40: The text painted with the code in Listing 9-23

You can control the placement, clipping, alignment, and other attributes of the painted text by calling one of the `DrawString()` methods that take a `StringFormat` parameter. The code in Listing 9-24 shows a few of the options.

Listing 9-24: Using StringFormat Properties to Control Attributes of Painted Text

```
String s = "yes";
Font font = new Font("Arial", 20, FontStyle.Bold);
Rectangle rect = new Rectangle(20, 20, 150, 50);
StringFormat format = new StringFormat();
format.Alignment = StringAlignment.Center;
format.LineAlignment = StringAlignment.Center;

e.Graphics.DrawRectangle(Pens.Black, rect);
e.Graphics.DrawString(s, font, Brushes.Black, rect, format);
```

The code produces the output shown in Figure 9-41.

yes

Figure 9-41: Centering a string horizontally and vertically inside a rectangular area

The property `StringFormat.Alignment` sets the horizontal alignment within the bounding rectangle. The `StringFormat.LineAlignment` property sets the vertical alignment. Check out the documentation for class `StringFormat` and you'll discover a number of locale-independent attributes. The .NET Framework supports text that reads left-to-right, right-to-left, and top-to-bottom. The various alignment properties work correctly across all locales.

Painting with transparency

Painting something that's completely transparent is a no-brainer — you don't paint it! Many UI components can be set to have a transparent background, so that images or colors from the component behind them show through. Things get a bit more interesting if you want to paint something that is partially transparent, because you need to blend the background pixels somehow with the pixels that are on top of them (in z order). Fortunately, support for partial transparency is built into all GDI+ methods. You should be familiar with the notion of RGB colors, in which a color is made up of the primary additive colors red, green, and blue. The folks who specialize in *colorimetry* (the science of color) often refer to color as being the result of primary components fed through 3 *color channels:* the red, the green, and the blue. To add support for transparency, GDI+ introduces a new channel, called the *alpha channel.* This channel is like the color channels: Its value is combined with the values of the other channels to create a resultant color. The difference is that rather than specifying a color, the alpha channel specifies the degree of *opacity.* The value 0 means a color is completely transparent; the value 255 means the color is completely opaque. The code in Listing 9-25 shows how to create a brush with varying degrees of transparency.

Listing 9-25: Drawing with Varying Degrees of Transparency

```
e.Graphics.FillRectangle(Brushes.LightBlue, ClientRectangle);

Point p = new Point(0, 0);
Font font = new Font("Times New Roman", 50);
e.Graphics.DrawString("Alpha", font, Brushes.Black, p);

Color yellow = Color.FromArgb(255, Color.Yellow);
Brush brush = new SolidBrush(yellow);
Rectangle rect = new Rectangle(30, 30, 30, 40);
e.Graphics.FillRectangle(brush, rect);

Color thickYellow = Color.FromArgb(175, Color.Yellow);
brush = new SolidBrush(thickYellow);
rect = new Rectangle(70, 30, 30, 40);
e.Graphics.FillRectangle(brush, rect);

Color mediumYellow = Color.FromArgb(125, Color.Yellow);
brush = new SolidBrush(mediumYellow);
rect = new Rectangle(110, 30, 30, 40);
e.Graphics.FillRectangle(brush, rect);

Color thinYellow = Color.FromArgb(60, Color.Yellow);
brush = new SolidBrush(thinYellow);
rect = new Rectangle(150, 30, 30, 40);
e.Graphics.FillRectangle(brush, rect);
```

The code draws a light blue background, paints some text in solid black on it, and then draws four boxes. All the boxes have the same color, but they use different alpha values. Figure 9-42 shows what the screen looks like.

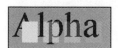

Figure 9-42: The screen produced by the code in the previous listing

Painting only what needs to be painted

When a component's OnPaint event handler is called, it means that some or all of the component needs to be redrawn. Many controls, like MyCustomControl, keep the paint code simple by always painting the entire component. If you have a control that has complex painting that may take a considerable amount of time to execute, or if the paint code needs to be as fast as possible, you should only repaint the area that needs repainting. The OnPaint handler is passed a PaintEventArgs parameter that has a ClipRectangle property. This property tells you which part of the component's UI is invalid and needs redrawing.

The easiest way to speed up the paint code is to set a clipping rectangle for the Graphics object you paint on in the OnPaint handler, as shown in Listing 9-26.

Listing 9-26: Setting a Clipping Area in a Graphics Object before Painting with It

```
protected override void OnPaint(PaintEventArgs e)
{
  Graphics g = e.Graphics;
  g.SetClip(e.ClipRectangle);  // set the clipping area

  // paint the control...
}
```

By setting a clipping area, any painting operations will be restricted to pixels inside the clipping area. Any pixels you try to paint on the area outside the clipping area will be left unchanged. As a result, the painting code runs faster.

A better, but more complicated way to exploit the clipping rectangle is to avoid painting areas of your control that are completely outside the clipping rectangle. Say your control has 4 quadrants, like MyCustomControl. It doesn't make sense to draw a quadrant if it's completely outside the clipping area. The code shown in Listing 9-27 could be used to draw the top left quadrant only if it was found to fall partially or entirely inside the clipping area.

Listing 9-27: Drawing a Portion of a Control Only If It Intersects the Clipping Area

```
protected override void OnPaint(PaintEventArgs e)
{
  Graphics g = e.Graphics;
  g.SetClip(e.ClipRectangle);  // set the clipping area

  // paint the control...

  if (e.ClipRectangle.IntersectsWith(upperLeftRect) )
  {
    // ... draw the top left quadrant
  }
}
```

The method `Rectangle.IntersectsWith()` will return `true` if any part of the two rectangles being compared overlap, even by one pixel. Note that the code in the listing still uses `g.SetClip()` to restrict painting to the clipping rectangle. This way, the graphics primitives used to paint the quadrant will skip pixels that don't need refreshing.

Using world transforms

If you look up the meaning of the word *transform* in a math textbook, you'll find a definition that goes something like this: *Transforms are mathematical functions that map one space into another.* So, what the heck does that mean? Without wanting to disappoint anyone, I'll tell you right now that a world transform won't get you into another dimension of some alien world, where the known laws of physics cease to exist. To understand what it will get you, you need to know what the *world* part means.

In the old days before .NET, Windows programmers worked with two coordinate systems: a logical system and a device system. All that stuff is gone with the .NET Framework (it's really still there, but you don't access it directly), and now we have not two, but three coordinate systems, or spaces: the world, page, and device coordinate spaces.

I don't have enough space in this book to go into all the details of the new spaces, but I will give you enough information to use common world transforms in your code for common situations. The page coordinate space is only significant in painting operations that span multiple pages, such as when printing a document or handling print preview commands. For most custom controls, you can think in terms of just the world and device spaces, so I won't be discussing the page space.

The device space represents the addressable pixels of the screen or the dots printed on a printer. If you're painting on a Graphics object associated with the screen, device coordinates represent pixels. If the screen has a resolution of 1024-by-768 pixels, the device space has an x-axis whose range is (0..1023), increasing from left to right. The y-axis range is (0..767), increasing from top to bottom, as shown in Figure 9-43.

Figure 9-43: The device coordinate space for the screen

The world space represents the logic coordinate system you use in your application. By default, the world space maps one-to-one to the device space. World transforms are operations that change the relationship between the world and device space, allowing you to translate, rotate, and scale graphics objects displayed on the screen. World transforms belong to the category of mathematical transforms known as *affine transforms,* which have the important property of maintaining parallelism. If two lines are parallel before being transformed, they will be parallel after being transformed. For example, if you translate (move) an image 20 pixels to the right, and then rotate the whole image by 10 degrees clockwise, that would not cause parallel lines to become nonparallel. Straight lines remain straight. They just wind up going in a different direction. The image still looks the same, except it's at a different location and is slightly rotated. You haven't distorted, morphed, or bent the image in any way.

Note

World transforms are *not* commutative. You may recall from college or high school geometry something about *commutative* operations. Given an operation *T* applied to two entities *a* and *b,* the operation is said to be commutative if *(a T b)* gives the same result as *(b T a)*. The order in which world transforms are applied is important. For example, translating an object to the right by 20 units and rotating it clockwise by 20 degrees gives you one result. If you perform the rotation first and then the translation, you'll get a different result.

The basic procedure for applying world transforms is to call one or more of the transform methods of class `Graphics`. To restore the default 1:1 transform, call `Graphics.ResetTransform()`. Listing 9-28 shows an example of how to perform a translation and then a rotation.

Listing 9-28: **The Basic Procedure of Applying and Resetting Transforms**

```
// do some drawing before applying any transforms
// ...

// translate and rotate
e.Graphics.TranslateTransform(35, 35);
e.Graphics.RotateTransform(20);

// do more drawing
// ...

// remove all transforms
e.Graphics.ResetTransform();

// do more drawing
// ...
```

You can call the transform methods in any order you like (as long as they produce the result you want). All operations are cumulative: Any transform you apply will be concatenated to those transforms already applied. You can call the same transform method more than once. For example, you can call TranslateTransform() once, draw something, call the method again, draw something else, and then call the method again. There are no restrictions on how many calls you can make to the translate methods. The next sections will discuss each of the basic transforms you can apply to the world space.

Translation

In mathematics, the term *translation* has nothing to do with converting words from one language to another. Translation means movement. To translate an object is to move it, without changing its orientation. When translation is used in the world space, the whole Cartesian coordinate system of the world space is shifted with respect to the device space. Consider the code in Listing 9-29 and the result shown in Figure 9-44.

Listing 9-29: **Drawing Objects with a Translated World Space**

```
// draw the cartesian axes
Point p0 = new Point(0, 0);
Point px = new Point(100, 0);
Point py = new Point(0, 100);
e.Graphics.DrawLine(Pens.Black, p0, px);
e.Graphics.DrawLine(Pens.Black, p0, py);

Rectangle rect = new Rectangle(30, 20, 25, 25);

e.Graphics.DrawRectangle(Pens.Black, rect);
```

```
e.Graphics.TranslateTransform(35, 35);
e.Graphics.DrawRectangle(Pens.Black, rect);

e.Graphics.ResetTransform();
```

Figure 9-44: The objects drawn by the code in the previous listing

The vertical and horizontal lines show the *x* and *y* axes of the world space before applying any translations. Note how the code in the listing draws the same rectangle twice: once before and once after the world space is translated. The second rectangle appears in a different area of the screen. Positive values of *x* and *y* translation shift the world space to the right and downwards. As you would expect, negative values shift to the left and upwards.

Rotation

You can rotate items on the screen with the `Graphics.RotateTransform()` method. The parameter passed to the method is a value assumed to be in degrees (not radians). Positive values cause rotation in the clockwise direction. The code in Listing 9-30 shows an example, and Figure 9-45 shows the result of running this code.

Listing 9-30: Drawing Objects with a Rotated World Space

```
// draw the cartesian axes
Point p0 = new Point(0, 0);
Point px = new Point(100, 0);
Point py = new Point(0, 100);
e.Graphics.DrawLine(Pens.Black, p0, px);
e.Graphics.DrawLine(Pens.Black, p0, py);

Rectangle rect = new Rectangle(30, 20, 25, 25);

e.Graphics.DrawRectangle(Pens.Black, rect);
e.Graphics.RotateTransform(10);
e.Graphics.DrawRectangle(Pens.Black, rect);
e.Graphics.RotateTransform(10);
e.Graphics.DrawRectangle(Pens.Black, rect);

e.Graphics.ResetTransform();
```

Figure 9-45: The objects drawn by the code in the previous listing

Note how the rectangles are rotated about the origin of the world space, which is the intersection of the x and y axes, in the top left corner. I called `RotateTransform()` twice in the code to show how rotations are cumulative.

If you want to rotate an object about its center, you need to use translations and rotation together. First you translate the origin of the world space to the object's center of rotation, then rotate the object, and then move the origin back where it was. The code in Listing 9-31 rotates a box about its center, and Figure 9-46 shows the result.

Listing 9-31: **Drawing Objects with a Translated World Space**

```
// draw the cartesian axes
Point p0 = new Point(0, 0);
Point px = new Point(100, 0);
Point py = new Point(0, 100);
e.Graphics.DrawLine(Pens.Black, p0, px);
e.Graphics.DrawLine(Pens.Black, p0, py);

Rectangle rect = new Rectangle(30, 20, 25, 25);
e.Graphics.DrawRectangle(Pens.Black, rect);

// get the coordinates of the box's center
int x = rect.Left + rect.Width / 2;
int y = rect.Top + rect.Height / 2;

e.Graphics.TranslateTransform(x, y);
e.Graphics.RotateTransform(20);
e.Graphics.TranslateTransform(-x, -y);
e.Graphics.DrawRectangle(Pens.Black, rect);

e.Graphics.TranslateTransform(x, y);
e.Graphics.RotateTransform(20);
e.Graphics.TranslateTransform(-x, -y);
e.Graphics.DrawRectangle(Pens.Black, rect);

e.Graphics.ResetTransform();
```

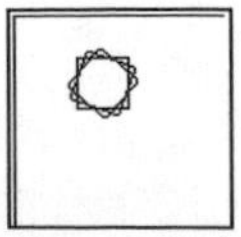

Figure 9-46: Rotating an object about its center

Note how the code in the listing draws the same rectangle twice: once before and once after the world space is translated. The second rectangle appears in a different area of the screen. Positive values of x and y translation shift the world space to the right and downwards. As you would expect, negative values shift to the left and upwards.

Scaling

Most programmers know scaling as *zooming*. The method `Graphics.ScaleTransform()` takes two doubles that indicate the amount of scaling in the *x* and *y* direction. For isotropic scaling (which changes the size of an object without otherwise distorting it), you need to use the same scaling for the *x* and *y* directions. A scaling value of 1.0 produces no change. Values between 0 and 1.0 make objects smaller. Values greater than 1.0 make objects bigger. A value of 0.5 would half the size of an object in the *x* and *y* dimensions. The resulting area would therefore be ¼ of the original size. A value of 2 would double the *x* and *y* sizes, quadrupling the area. Keep in mind that scaling is accomplished by multiplying coordinate values by the scaling factors. This means the origin — the point with coordinates (0, 0) — will not be affected, but every other point in the world space will be. Scaling values greater than 1 will cause points to move away from the origin. Values less then 1 will make points move towards the origin. The code in Listing 9-32 shows a scaling example, and Figure 9-47 shows the result.

Listing 9-32: **Drawing Objects with a Scaled World Space**

```
// draw the cartesian axes
Point p0 = new Point(0, 0);
Point px = new Point(100, 0);
Point py = new Point(0, 100);
e.Graphics.DrawLine(Pens.Black, p0, px);
e.Graphics.DrawLine(Pens.Black, p0, py);

Rectangle rect = new Rectangle(30, 20, 25, 25);

e.Graphics.DrawRectangle(Pens.Black, rect);
e.Graphics.ScaleTransform(1.2f, 1.2f);
e.Graphics.DrawRectangle(Pens.Black, rect);

e.Graphics.ResetTransform();
```

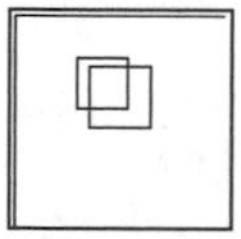

Figure 9-47: Scaling the world space

The small box is the original, unscaled box. As a result of the scaling operation, the box was both enlarged and moved. If you don't want an object to move, you need to move the world space origin to the object's center, scale the world space, and then move the origin back before drawing the object. The code in Listing 9-33 shows example code, and Figure 9-48 shows the result.

Listing 9-33: **Scaling an Object without Translating It**

```
// draw the cartesian axes
Point p0 = new Point(0, 0);
```

Continued

Listing 9-33 *(continued)*

```
Point px = new Point(100, 0);
Point py = new Point(0, 100);
e.Graphics.DrawLine(Pens.Black, p0, px);
e.Graphics.DrawLine(Pens.Black, p0, py);

Rectangle rect = new Rectangle(30, 20, 25, 25);
e.Graphics.DrawRectangle(Pens.Black, rect);

// get the coordinates of the box's center
int x = rect.Left + rect.Width / 2;
int y = rect.Top + rect.Height / 2;

e.Graphics.TranslateTransform(x, y);
e.Graphics.ScaleTransform(1.5f, 1.5f);
e.Graphics.TranslateTransform(-x, -y);
e.Graphics.DrawRectangle(Pens.Black, rect);

e.Graphics.ResetTransform();
```

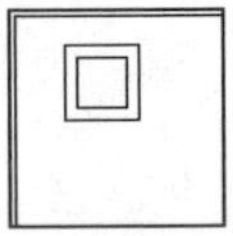

Figure 9-48: Scaling an object about its center

Using a matrix to do everything at once

When you need to apply several transforms at once, it is not only tedious to call the various transform methods, but also slow. The alternative is to use an affine transform directly. Recall from earlier that affine transforms maintain parallelism in transformed objects. An affine transform can be represented by a 3x3 matrix. If you aren't familiar with matrices, you might want to skip this section and just use the simpler transform methods. The Graphics object uses an internal affine matrix to map the world space you draw on into the device space. It does so by taking the coordinate of each pixel to draw and multiplying it by the affine matrix.

To get the matrix used by the Graphics object, use the property Graphics.Transform, like this:

```
Matrix matrix = e.Graphics.Transform;
```

Once you have the matrix, you can apply translation, rotation, scaling, and even shearing to it, and then assign the matrix back to the Graphics object. The Matrix class has a number of shortcut methods that let you apply multiple transforms at once. For example, the code in Listing 9-34 rotates the world space 40 degrees clockwise about the point (20, 30), effectively doing a translate(20, 30), rotate(40), and translate(-20, -30) all at once.

Listing 9-34: Using the Matrix Class to Perform Rotation about a Point

```
Point p = new Point(20, 30);
Matrix m = e.Graphics.Transform;
m.RotateAt(40, p);
e.Graphics.Transform = m;
```

You can also set up a matrix with all your transforms and apply it to the existing transform by using matrix multiplication. For example, the code in Listing 9-35 sets up a translation and scaling matrix, and then uses it to transform the world space.

Listing 9-35: Using a Matrix Object to Apply Multiple Transforms to the World Space at Once

```
// draw the cartesian axes
Point p0 = new Point(0, 0);
Point px = new Point(100, 0);
Point py = new Point(0, 100);
e.Graphics.DrawLine(Pens.Black, p0, px);
e.Graphics.DrawLine(Pens.Black, p0, py);

Rectangle rect = new Rectangle(30, 20, 25, 25);
e.Graphics.DrawRectangle(Pens.Black, rect);

// get the coordinates of the box's center
int x = rect.Left + rect.Width / 2;
int y = rect.Top + rect.Height / 2;

Matrix myMatix = new Matrix();
myMatix.Translate(x, y);
myMatix.Scale(1.4f, 1.4f);
myMatix.Translate(-x, -y);
Matrix m = e.Graphics.Transform;
m.Multiply(myMatix);
e.Graphics.Transform = m;
e.Graphics.DrawRectangle(Pens.Red, rect);

e.Graphics.ResetTransform();
```

The code uses the `Matrix.Multiply()` method to concatenate the `myMatrix` changes to the transform matrix already used by the Graphics object. Figure 9-49 shows the screen produced by the code.

Figure 9-49: The screen produced by the code in the previous listing

Matrix multiplication is not commutative, so using `myMatrix.Multiply(m)` will not give the same result as `m.Multiply(myMatrix)`. When you first get a `Graphics` object in an `OnPaint` handler, the matrix is set to the *identity* matrix, which produces a 1:1 mapping between world and device spaces.

Class `Matrix` has several other methods that can be handy. One of them enables you to shear objects, which basically makes them look slanted. Listing 9-36 is an example of how to shear, and Figure 9-50 shows the resulting sheared object.

Listing 9-36: **Using a Matrix Object to Shear an Object**

```
// draw the cartesian axes
Point p0 = new Point(0, 0);
Point px = new Point(100, 0);
Point py = new Point(0, 100);
e.Graphics.DrawLine(Pens.Black, p0, px);
e.Graphics.DrawLine(Pens.Black, p0, py);

Rectangle rect = new Rectangle(30, 20, 25, 25);

// get the coordinates of the box's center
int x = rect.Left + rect.Width / 2;
int y = rect.Top + rect.Height / 2;

Matrix myMatix = new Matrix();
myMatix.Translate(rect.Left, rect.Top);
myMatix.Shear(0.5f, 0.0f);
myMatix.Translate(-rect.Left, -rect.Top);

Matrix m = e.Graphics.Transform;
m.Multiply(myMatix);
e.Graphics.Transform = m;
e.Graphics.DrawRectangle(Pens.Black, rect);

e.Graphics.ResetTransform();
```

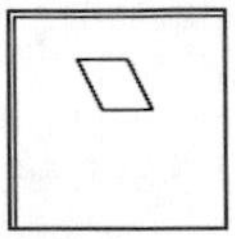

Figure 9-50: An object sheared in the *x* direction by a factor of 0.5

The *shear factor* is a floating-point number that represents the arctangent of the angle of the slant you want to get. For example, a 0 (zero) produces no slant and a value of 1.0 yields a 45-degree slant. Positive values cause a clockwise effect. Although my example only sheared along the *x*-axis, you can shear in both the *x* and *y* directions simultaneously.

Searching the File System for a File

Before you completely lose track of the topic of this chapter, let me back up and return to the discussion of MyCustomControl. This component uses an image to create a textured brush. The image is expected to be in the file c:\wint\FeatherTexture.bmp, which is a standard file that ships with Windows NT and 2000. But what if the user is running Windows ME? Or what if the file was deleted? MyCustomControl looks for an alternative file, searching the entire file system for another .bmp file. If it finds one, it uses it for the texture image; otherwise, it displays an error message and quits. Listing 9-37 shows the code that performs the search.

Listing 9-37: **Recursively Searching Directories for a File**

```
String FindAnyBitmapFileUnderFolder(String theFolder)
{
  // search the folder
  String[] files = Directory.GetFiles(theFolder);
  foreach (String f in files)
  if (f.ToLower().EndsWith(".bmp") )
    return f;

  // recursively search all the subfolders
  String[] directories = Directory.GetDirectories(theFolder);
  foreach (String d in directories)
  {
  String filename = FindAnyBitmapFileUnderFolder(d);
    if (filename != null)
      return filename;
  }

  return null;
}
```

The code is pretty simple. The static method Directory.GetFiles() returns an array of all the filenames in a given directory. If a .bmp file is not found, the subdirectories are searched recursively by calling FindAnyBitmapFileUnderFolder() again for each subdirectory until a .bmp file is found or all the subdirectories have been searched. To kick off the search for a .bmp file, MyCustomControl calls FindAnyBitmapFileUnderFolder() like this:

```
String imageFilename = FindAnyBitmapFileUnderFolder(@"c:\");
```

If you wanted to search all the logical drives for the file, and not just the C: drive, you could use EnvironmentGetLogicalDrives() to get a list of the drives. For example, you might do something like what's shown in Listing 9-38.

Listing 9-38: **Searching All the Logical Drives for a File**

```
String[] drives = Environment.GetLogicalDrives();
foreach (String drive in drives)
```

Continued

Listing 9-38 *(continued)*

```
{
   // skip the floppy drives
   if (drive.ToLower().Equals(@"a:\") ) continue;
   if (drive.ToLower().Equals(@"b:\") ) continue;

   String imageFilename = FindAnyBitmapFileUnderFolder(drive);
}
```

Adding a Context Menu

A context menu is the menu that pops up on the screen when you click the right mouse. The easiest way to add a context menu is by dropping a ContextMenu component from the Toolbox on your component in the Forms Designer. Once a menu is added, you need to set the form's ContextMenu property to reference it. Doing so automatically enables the right mouse button handler to show the pop-up menu, if your component is like MyCustomControl and is derived from UserControl.

To add menu items programmatically to the context menu, MyCustomControl uses the code shown in Listing 9-39.

Listing 9-39: Adding Items to a Menu Programmatically

```
// setup the context menu programmatically

// first a standard type of item...
MenuItem fileOpenMenuItem = new MenuItem("File &Open");
fileOpenMenuItem.Click += new
System.EventHandler(this.OnClickFileOpen);
fileOpenMenuItem.Shortcut = Shortcut.CtrlO;

// then an application-specific item
MenuItem changeColorsMenuItem =
         new MenuItem("&Change Colors Randomly");
changeColorsMenuItem.Click +=
      new System.EventHandler (this.OnClickChangeColors);
changeColorsMenuItem.Shortcut = Shortcut.CtrlF4;

contextMenu1.MenuItems.Add(fileOpenMenuItem);
contextMenu1.MenuItems.Add(new MenuItem("-") ); // menu break
contextMenu1.MenuItems.Add(changeColorsMenuItem);
```

The item `fileOpenMenuItem` is assigned the shortcut Control-O, which is a standard shortcut under Windows. The & character used in the menu caption *File & Open* tells Windows to underline the *O* of *Open* and use that character as an accelerator key, allowing users to select the menu item using the Alt-O accelerator.

The context menu also contains an application-specific command called `changeColors MenuItem` that changes the colors displayed in one of the quadrants of `MyCustomControl`. I assigned the arbitrary shortcut Control-Shift-F4 to the menu, just to give another example of using the `Shortcut` enumerations. I separated the two menu items with a menu break, which is a horizontal ruler you find on many menus. Figure 9-51 shows how the context menu looks on the screen.

Figure 9-51: The simple context menu used by MyCustomControl

When the user clicks the right mouse button, the context menu appears with its top left corner under the mouse cursor. Again, the handling of the right mouse button is built into the base class `UserControl`. The handlers for all menu items must be declared to take two parameters, like this:

```
protected void OnClickFileOpen(object sender, EventArgs e)
{
  // handle the menu command
}
```

The sender is the menu item that was selected, which in this case is the object `fileOpenMenuItem`. The `EventArgs` parameter is a standard object passed to many event handlers. It enables the sender to specify additional information about the event. In the case of menu handlers, the `EventArgs` parameter doesn't carry any useful information.

Supporting Drag-and-Drop

If you develop applications with rich user interfaces, you may want to allow users to select items, drag them on the screen, and drop them somewhere. Users might use drag-and-drop to rearrange some text, to move an object from one window to another, or even to move a list of files from the Windows Explorer into your application. Adding drag-and-drop support to an application used to require a certain amount of OLE programming, which by itself was enough to keep many programmers away. Fortunately, the .NET Framework makes drag-and-drop easy to support. You only need to do three things:

✦ Set the component's `AllowDrop` property to `true`.

✦ Add a `DragEnter` event handler.

✦ Add a `DragDrop` event handler.

I added drag-and-drop support to `MyUserControl` to show the details, allowing the user to select a list of files in the Windows Explorer and drop them on my component. `MyCustomControl` doesn't do anything with the list of files in particular. It just displays a message showing the names of the files dropped.

If your component is visible in the Forms Designer, you can use the Properties window to set the `AllowDrop` property, as shown in Figure 9-52.

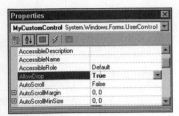

Figure 9-52: Setting a component's
AllowDrop property

Using the Events page of the Properties window, you can automatically create handlers for
the DragDrop and DragEnter events by simply double-clicking on those events, as shown in
Figure 9-53.

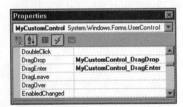

Figure 9-53: Creating event handlers
for DragEnter and DragDrop

If your component doesn't appear in the Forms Designer, you won't be able to customize it
with the Properties window. You'll have to set the AllowDrop property yourself and also add
the DragDrop and DragEnter handlers as shown in Listing 9-40.

Listing 9-40: Programmatically Adding Support for Drag-and-Drop

```
public class MyCustomControl : System.Windows.Forms.UserControl
{
  private void InitializeComponent()
  {
    // other initialization...

    this.AllowDrop = true;
    this.ContextMenu = this.contextMenu1;
    this.DragDrop +=
        new System.Windows.Forms.DragEventHandler(this.OnDragDrop);
    this.DragEnter +=
        new System.Windows.Forms.DragEventHandler(this.OnDragEnter);
  }
}
```

The DragEnter event handler looks like Listing 9-41.

Listing 9-41: The Event Handler for DragEnter

```
protected void MyCustomControl_DragEnter(object sender,
              System.Windows.Forms.DragEventArgs e)
{
  IDataObject dataObject = e.Data;
  if (dataObject.GetDataPresent(DataFormats.FileDrop) )
    e.Effect = DragDropEffects.Copy;
}
```

The DragEnter event is fired when the user drags the mouse and crosses into the MyCustomControl window. In the event handler, you tell Windows whether you accept drops. My event handler sets the DragEventArgs.Effect property to the value DragDropEffects.Copy only if the user is in the process of dropping files. The Effect property determines the type of cursor displayed during a drop when the mouse cursor is over MyCustomControl. Table 9-5 shows the possible values you can assign to DragEventArgs.Effect, along with the cursor displayed.

Table 9-5: Drop Cursors Used by Windows

DragEventArgs.Effect Value	Cursor
DragDropEffects.All	
DragDropEffects.Copy	
DragDropEffects.Link	
DragDropEffects.Move	
DragDropEffects.None	
DragDropEffects.Scroll	

Note   The DragDropEffects.Scroll cursor is the same as the DragDropEffects.None cursor.

The DragEventArgs.Effects values are self-explanatory, except for DragDropEffects.All. This value is used to convey an operation in which the data will be copied and scrolled in the drop target, and then removed from the drag source.

Although MyCustomControl only handles drops of type FileDrop, you can easily support many other types of data, like bitmaps and text. To discover what kind of data is being dropped, call the method IDataObject.GetDataPresent(DataFormats), passing it the name of the DataFormat you are interesting in handling. In the DragDrop() handler, which is called only if the user drops something on your component, you'll retrieve the data dropped using code like what's shown in Listing 9-42.

Listing 9-42: **Accepting the Dropped Data**

```
protected void MyCustomControl_DragDrop(object sender,
             System.Windows.Forms.DragEventArgs e)
{
  IDataObject droppedData = e.Data;
  if (droppedData == null) return;

  // see if there are files to drop
  if (droppedData.GetDataPresent(DataFormats.FileDrop) )
  {
    // get the names of the files
    String[] droppedFiles =
        (String[]) droppedData.GetData(DataFormats.FileDrop);
    String files = "";
    foreach (String s in droppedFiles)
      files += s + "\r\n";
    MessageBox.Show(files, "You dropped these files");
  }
}
```

My DragDrop handler just gets a list of the files being dropped and displays them with a MessageBox. The code contains a call to IDataObject.GetDataPresent(DataFormats) to verify again that the data being dropped indeed contains a list of one or more files. If you omit this call, then you might want to make sure the call to IDataObject.GetData(DataFormats. FileDrop) returns a non-null object. In all probability, GetData() should return a non-null object, because we told Windows previously in the DragEnter handler that we were interested in FileDrops, and Windows wouldn't have called our DragDrop handler unless it had files to drop.

Table 9-6 lists some of the commonly used data types that can be used with both IDataObject.GetDataPresent() and IDataObject.GetData(). The right column shows the type of object you'll get back from IDataObject.GetData() for each type of data requested.

Table 9-6: Types Returned by the Method IDataObject.GetData(DataFormats)

Data Type	Type Returned
DataFormats.Bitmap	System.Drawing.Bitmap
DataFormats.DIB	System.Drawing.Bitmap
DataFormats.FileDrop	System.String[]

Data Type	Type Returned
DataFormats.HTML	System.String
DataFormats.MetafilePict	System.IO.Memory
DataFormats.Text	System.String
DataFormats.UnicodeText	System.String

When you call GetDataPresent() or GetData() with a given data type, the system will tell you that data is available in two situations:

✦ If the data being dragged is exactly the type requested

✦ If the system knows how to convert the dragged data into the requested type

For example, if the user is dragging some unformatted text from an editor and you request the data type DataFormats.HTML, the system will give the text to you as HTML, because it knows how to make the conversion automatically.

Generating Random Numbers

Not everybody uses random numbers, and certainly a component like MyCustomControl doesn't need them, but I thought it might be useful to have at least one example of random numbers in the book. MyCustomControl used random numbers to select colors to use in the upper left quadrant, which is filled with a gradient that fades from one color to another. The code is invoked through a context menu command, and is shown in Listing 9-43.

Listing 9-43: Using Random Numbers to Generate Colors

```
protected void OnClickChangeColors(object sender, EventArgs e)
{
  // use the random number generator to select new colors for
  // the Linear Gradient used in the top left quadrant
  Random random = new Random();
  int red = random.Next(255);
  int green = random.Next(255);
  int blue = random.Next(255);
  startingColor = Color.FromArgb(red, green, blue);
  endingColor = Color.FromArgb(255-red, 255-green, 255-blue);
  Invalidate(); // repaint the whole control with the new colors
}
```

Calling the constructor for class Random automatically seeds the internal random number generator using the current date and time, so the seed will truly be random. To get random numbers, you call the Random.Next() method, indicating the max value you want. The method will return a pseudo-random integer whose value will be (0 <= value <= max). You can also get random floating point numbers in the range (0..1) by calling the method Random.NextDouble(). If you need a whole bunch of random numbers, perhaps to create a random image, call the method Random.NextBytes() passing it a Byte[] to fill with values.

Design-Time Properties

All the components on the Toolbox can be configured to various degrees using the Properties window. But exactly which members of a component show up on the Properties window? How are they grouped into categories? How is a description added? All good questions. The short answer is this: All public properties and events show up. The long answer is a bit more complicated. Let's start with the most common situation: adding a simple property.

Note   In the following sections, what is said for properties is essentially valid also for events.

Adding a simple property

If you declare a public property whose type is simple (and by simple, I mean a type that VS .NET already knows about, like `int`, `Color`, or `bool`), then the property will show up "automagically" in the Properties window. I'll add a couple of `Color` properties to `MyCustomControl` with the code shown in Listing 9-44.

Listing 9-44: Adding Three Design-Time Properties with Different Types

```
private Color topLeftQuadrantColor1 = Color.Red;
private Color topLeftQuadrantColor2 = Color.White;

public Color TopLeftQuadrantColor1
{
  get { return topLeftQuadrantColor1; }
  set { topLeftQuadrantColor1 = value; }
}

public Color TopLeftQuadrantColor2
{
  get { return topLeftQuadrantColor2; }
  set { topLeftQuadrantColor2 = value; }
}
```

As you can see, there are no magic keywords or compiler settings needed. By the simple virtue of being public, the two properties will appear in the Properties window. The properties will initially appear with their default values (`Red` and `White`), as shown in Figure 9-54.

Note   After adding, deleting, or editing properties and recompiling the component, the changes won't appear in the Properties window unless you exit and restart VS .NET.

Figure 9-54: The Properties window, showing the two new properties added to MyCustomControl

Adding descriptions to properties

In the previous figure, notice the descriptive text that appears at the bottom of the window. All properties can have their own descriptions. Adding your own description requires the use of the special attribute called `DescriptionAttribute`, or simply `Description` for short. To add a description, use the attribute with your properties as shown in Listing 9-45.

Listing 9-45: Adding a Description to a Property

```
[Description("Starting color for gradient")]
public Color TopLeftQuadrantColor1
{
  get { return topLeftQuadrantColor1; }
  set { topLeftQuadrantColor1 = value; }
}
```

And that's all there is to it. Descriptions are not meant to be displayed at runtime. They are designed for component-development tools like VS .NET.

Preventing a property from appearing in the Properties window

Since all public properties automatically show up in the Properties window, what do you do if you have a public property that can only be changed or set at runtime? You need some way to prevent the property from appearing in the Properties window. No problem. Just use the `Browsable` attribute with the argument `false`, as shown in Listing 9-46.

Listing 9-46: Preventing a Public Property from Appearing in the Properties Window

```
[Browsable(false)]
public int MyProperty
{
```

Continued

Listing 9-46 *(continued)*

```
  get { ... };
  get { ... };
}
```

Non-public properties and the Properties window

By default, all public properties of an object are listed in the Properties window. What if you have a protected or private property, but want it to appear? I'm not sure what conditions would warrant a protected or private property to appear in the Properties window, but let's assume you have your reasons. You might think you could use the Browsable attribute, this time with the argument true, as shown in Listing 9-47.

Listing 9-47: Trying to Force a Nonpublic Property to Appear in the Properties Window

```
[Browsable(true)]
private int MyProperty
{
  get { ... };
  get { ... };
}
```

Unfortunately, this doesn't work. The bottom line is this: In order for a property to appear in the Properties window, it has to be public.

Hiding an inherited property from the Properties window

By default, all public properties are listed in the Properties window, including inherited ones. What if you have an inherited property that you want to hide? There are two ways to do this, depending on how the property was declared in the base class. In most cases, properties are not declared virtual, so you would hide them as shown in Listing 9-48.

Listing 9-48: Hiding an Inherited Property from the Properties Window

```
[Browsable(false)]
public new bool Visible
{
  get {return base.Visible; }
  set {base.Visible = value; }
}
```

The new keyword makes the derived Visible property replace the inherited one. In my example, I simply call the base class implementation, but I could have implemented the derived property in any way I wanted to.

If the base class property is declared `virtual`, you need to tag the derived property with the `override` keyword, as shown in Listing 9-49.

Listing 9-49: **Hiding an Inherited Virtual Property from the Properties Window**

```
[Browsable(false)]
public override bool Visible
{
  get {return base.Visible; }
  set {base.Visible = value; }
}
```

Most properties are not `virtual`, so you probably won't need to override properties too often.

Adding a property under a category

Look at the Properties window, and notice the button in the upper left corner. This is the Categorized Properties button. When clicked, all the properties are listed by category. How do you assign a property to a category? It's simple: Just tag the property with the `Category` attribute as shown in Listing 9-50.

Listing 9-50: **Assigning a Category to a Property**

```
[Category("My Properties")]
[Description("Starting color for gradient")]
public Color TopLeftQuadrantColor1
{
  get { return topLeftQuadrantColor1; }
  set { topLeftQuadrantColor1 = value; }
}
```

Figure 9-55 shows the Properties window after assigning two properties to the `My Properties` category.

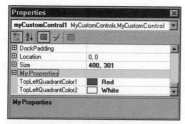

Figure 9-55: The Properties window, showing the newly added My Properties category

Any property that isn't assigned to a category will show up by default under a category named Misc.

Preventing a property from being saved

When you assign a value to an item in the Properties window, and then close the form, you expect the new value to be saved. If you later reopen the form and select your custom control, you'll expect the new value to still be there. This will indeed be the case if the property is serializable, which most properties (such as int, bool, String, and Color) are. What if you don't want the system to save a property's value? Just add a method to your custom control as shown in Listing 9-51.

Listing 9-51: Preventing a Property from Being Saved

```
public bool ShouldSerializeMyProperty() {
    return false;  // never save MyProperty
  }
```

The method uses a simple naming convention. For a property named MyProperty, the method name must be ShouldSerializeMyProperty() and return a bool. How you determine the returned value is completely up to you.

Property editors

Until now, I have described properties with common types, such as Color and bool. What if you want to create a type of property that is completely new? Say you have an audio component with a property called Volume of type VolumeLevel declared as shown in Listing 9-52.

Listing 9-52: A Custom Type to Be Used in the Properties Window

```
public class VolumeLevel
{
  private int level;

  public VolumeLevel(int theLevel)
  {
    level = theLevel;
  }

  public int Level
  {
    get {return level;}
    set {level = value;}
  }
}
```

Say MyCustomControl is equipped with a Volume property as shown in Listing 9-53.

Listing 9-53: Adding the New Property Type to MyCustomControl and Omitting the TypeConverter Attribute

```
public class MyCustomControl : System.Windows.Forms.UserControl
{
  // other stuff...

  private VolumeLevel volume = new VolumeLevel(23);

  public VolumeLevel Volume
  {
    get {return volume; }
    set {volume = value; }
  }
}
```

If you just compile MyCustomControl, exit, and then restart VS .NET, the new property will look like Figure 9-56 in the Properties window.

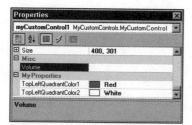

Figure 9-56: The new Volume property of type VolumeLevel

The `Volume` property is grayed out. If you try to edit its value, you won't be able to. The problem is that VS .NET has no idea how to convert the text you enter in the Properties window into a `VolumeLevel` object. There are three ways to add design-time editing support to a property:

✦ Using a Type Converter

✦ Using a UI Editor

✦ Using a Designer

You can use a Type Converter if you have a way of converting text into an object value. For example, with a `bool` property, a simple Type Converter might change the text *"true"* into the Boolean value `true`.

A UI Editor uses a small drop-down form on which the user can select property values. The Color editor is a good example of a UI Editor.

A Designer is a full-fledged mini-application that enables the user to configure a complete component.

In the following section, I'll show you how to develop a simple Type Converter. The details of UI Editors and Designers are beyond the scope of this book.

Note   VS .NET caches the executable code for Property Editors. Any time you make a change to an editor and recompile it, you need to exit and restart VS .NET to make the changes effective.

Because of the caching, you should test Property Editors with a standalone test fixture before associating them with a property using the `TypeConverter` attribute.

Implementing a Type Converter

Let's assume you want to implement the Property Editor for `VolumeLevel` as a Type Converter. First create a class that derives from `System.ComponentModel.TypeConverter`, and then add to it the following methods:

✦ `CanConvertFrom()`

✦ `ConvertFrom()`

✦ `CanConvertTo()`

✦ `ConvertTo()`

The methods are called by the Property Editor framework in VS .NET to determine which types the Type Editor can convert to and from. The code in Listing 9-54 is the Type Converter I implemented for VolumeLevel types.

Listing 9-54: The Type Converter for VolumeLevel Properties

```
public class VolumeLevelConverter : TypeConverter
{
  public override bool CanConvertFrom(ITypeDescriptorContext context,
                                      Type sourceType)
  {

    if (sourceType == typeof(string) )
      return true;

    return base.CanConvertFrom(context, sourceType);
  }

    public override object ConvertFrom(ITypeDescriptorContext context,
                                       CultureInfo culture, object value)
    {
      int level;
      if (value is String)
      {
        try
        {

          level = Int32.Parse(value as String);
        }
```

```
        catch(Exception)
        {

          throw new NotSupportedException(
                    "The text entered must be a number.");
        }

        if ( (level < 0) || (level > 100) )
          throw new NotSupportedException(
                    "The text entered must be in the range (0..100).");
        VolumeLevel volumeLevel = new VolumeLevel(level);
        return volumeLevel;
      }
      return base.ConvertFrom(context, culture, value);
    }

    public override bool CanConvertTo(ITypeDescriptorContext context,
                                        Type destinationType)
    {
      if (destinationType == typeof(String) )
        return true;
      return base.CanConvertFrom(context, destinationType);
    }

    public override object ConvertTo(ITypeDescriptorContext context,
                                       CultureInfo culture, object value,
                                       Type destinationType)
    {
      if (destinationType == typeof(String) )
        return (value as VolumeLevel).Level.ToString();
      return base.ConvertTo(context, culture, value, destinationType);
    }
  }
```

The `ConvertFrom()` method is called to convert a `String` value into a `VolumeLevel`. The method is required to throw a `NonSupportedException` if the `String` can't be converted successfully. VS .NET will catch the exception and display an error message. For example, entering the value **200** for a VolumeLevel property in the Properties window will cause the message shown in Figure 9-57 to be displayed.

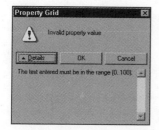

Figure 9-57: The error message displayed by VS .NET if the value "200" is entered for a VolumeLevel setting

Once you have a Type Converter, you need to tell VS .NET when to use it, or rather on which type of properties to use it. All you need to do is add the TypeConverter attributes to any `VolumeLevel` properties. In the `MyCustomControl` code, you would tag the property with the attribute shown in Listing 9-55.

Listing 9-55: Tagging a Custom Property Type with the TypeConverter Attribute

```
public class MyCustomControl : System.Windows.Forms.UserControl
{
  //...


  [ TypeConverter(typeof(VolumeLevelConverter) ) ]
  public VolumeLevel Volume
  {
    get {return volume; }
    set {volume = value; }
  }
}
```

The Source Code for MyCustomControl

Now that all the programming techniques used in `MyCustomControl` have been shown, it's time to see all the code together. Listing 9-56 shows the essential code for `MyCustomControl`.

Listing 9-56: The Source Code for MyCustomControl

```
using System;
using System.Collections;
using System.ComponentModel;
using System.Drawing;
using System.Data;
using System.Windows.Forms;
using System.IO;
using System.Drawing.Drawing2D;

namespace MyCustomControls
{
  public class MyCustomControl : System.Windows.Forms.UserControl
  {
    private System.ComponentModel.Container components = null;

    private ContextMenu contextMenu1;

    Rectangle upperLeftRect, upperRightRect;
    Rectangle lowerLeftRect, lowerRightRect;
```

```
    Rectangle quadrantHighlighted;

    Image textImage = null;

    public MyCustomControl()
    {
      // This call is required by the Windows.Forms Form Designer.
      InitializeComponent();

      // setup the context menu programmatically

      // first a standard type of item...
      MenuItem fileOpenMenuItem = new MenuItem("File &Open");
      fileOpenMenuItem.Click += new System.EventHandler (this.OnClickFileOpen);
      fileOpenMenuItem.Shortcut = Shortcut.CtrlO;  // Control-O

      // then an application-specific item
      MenuItem changeColorsMenuItem = new MenuItem("&Change Colors Randomly");
      changeColorsMenuItem.Click +=
            new System.EventHandler (this.OnClickChangeColors);
      changeColorsMenuItem.Shortcut = Shortcut.CtrlF4; // an arbitrary shortcut

      contextMenu1.MenuItems.Add(fileOpenMenuItem);
      contextMenu1.MenuItems.Add(new MenuItem("-") ); // a menu break
      contextMenu1.MenuItems.Add(changeColorsMenuItem);

      // create the four quadrants.
      // We'll set the size and position in OnPaint()
      upperLeftRect = new Rectangle(ClientRectangle.Location,
                                    ClientRectangle.Size);
      upperRightRect = new Rectangle(ClientRectangle.Location,
                                     ClientRectangle.Size);
      lowerLeftRect = new Rectangle(ClientRectangle.Location,
                                    ClientRectangle.Size);
      lowerRightRect = new Rectangle(ClientRectangle.Location,
                                     ClientRectangle.Size);

      textImage = FindTextImageFile();
      if (textImage == null)
      {
        MessageBox.Show("Can't find a bitmap file anywhere on your system." +
                    "MyCustomControl can't run.");
        FindForm().Close();
      }
    }

    protected Image FindTextImageFile()
    {
      // see if the file "FeatherTexture.bmp exists in the winnt folder
      String winntFolder = Environment.SystemDirectory;
winntFolder = winntFolder.Substring(0, winntFolder.LastIndexOf(@"\")+1 );

      // remove the system32 subfolder
```

Continued

Listing 9-56 *(continued)*

```
  String imageFilename = winntFolder + "FeatherTexture.bmp";

  if (File.Exists(imageFilename) )
    return Image.FromFile(imageFilename);
  else
  {
    // search the entire c: drive for a .bmp file
    imageFilename = FindAnyBitmapFileUnderFolder(@"c:\");
    if (imageFilename != null)
      return Image.FromFile(imageFilename);
  }
  return null;  // no bitmap files found
}

String FindAnyBitmapFileUnderFolder(String theFolder)
{
  // search the folder
  String[] files = Directory.GetFiles(theFolder);
  foreach (String f in files)
  if (f.ToLower().EndsWith(".bmp") )
    return f;

  // recursively search all the subfolders
  String[] directories = Directory.GetDirectories(theFolder);
  foreach (String d in directories)
  {
  String filename = FindAnyBitmapFileUnderFolder(d);
    if (filename != null)
      return filename;
  }

  return null;
}

protected void OnClickFileOpen(object sender, EventArgs e)
{
  MessageBox.Show("This is where you display an OpenFileDialog.");
}

protected void OnClickChangeColors(object sender, EventArgs e)
{
  // use the random number generator to select new colors for
  // the Linear Gradient used in the top left quadrant
  Random random = new Random();
  int red = random.Next(255);
  int green = random.Next(255);
  int blue = random.Next(255);
  topLeftQuadrantColor1 = Color.FromArgb(red, green, blue);
  topLeftQuadrantColor2 = Color.FromArgb(255-red, 255-green, 255-blue);
  Invalidate(); // repaint the whole control with the new colors
}
```

```
protected override void Dispose( bool disposing )
{
  /* code created by wizard... */
}


#region Component Designer generated code
private void InitializeComponent()
{
  this.contextMenu1 = new System.Windows.Forms.ContextMenu();
  //
  // MyCustomControl
  //
  this.AllowDrop = true;
  this.ContextMenu = this.contextMenu1;
  this.Name = "MyCustomControl";
  this.DragEnter += new System.Windows.Forms.DragEventHandler(
                    this.MyCustomControl_DragEnter);
  this.DragDrop += new System.Windows.Forms.DragEventHandler(
                    this.MyCustomControl_DragDrop);
}
#endregion

private void MyCustomControl_DragDrop(object sender,
                            System.Windows.Forms.DragEventArgs e)
{
  IDataObject droppedData = e.Data;
  if (droppedData == null) return;

  // see if there are files to drop
  if (droppedData.GetDataPresent(DataFormats.FileDrop) )
  {
    // get the names of the files
    String[] droppedFiles =
    (String[]) droppedData.GetData(DataFormats.FileDrop);
    String files = "";
    foreach (String s in droppedFiles)
       files += s + "\r\n";
    MessageBox.Show(files, "You dropped these files");
  }
}

private void MyCustomControl_DragEnter(object sender,
                            System.Windows.Forms.DragEventArgs e)
{
  IDataObject dataObject = e.Data;
  if (dataObject.GetDataPresent(DataFormats.FileDrop) )
    e.Effect = DragDropEffects.Copy;
}

protected override void OnMouseEnter(EventArgs e)
{
```

Continued

Listing 9-56 *(continued)*

```
    if (Form.ActiveForm != FindForm() ) return;
    Invalidate();
}

protected override void OnMouseLeave(EventArgs e)
{
  if (Form.ActiveForm != FindForm() ) return;
  quadrantHighlighted = Rectangle.Empty;
  Invalidate();
}

protected override void OnMouseDown(MouseEventArgs e)
{
  Focus();
}

protected override void OnMouseMove(MouseEventArgs e)
{
  if (Form.ActiveForm != FindForm() ) return;

  if (!quadrantHighlighted.Contains(PointToClient(MousePosition) ) )
    Invalidate();
}

protected override void OnGotFocus(EventArgs e)
{
  Invalidate();
}

protected override void OnLostFocus(EventArgs e)
{
  quadrantHighlighted = Rectangle.Empty;
  Invalidate();
}

protected override void OnResize(EventArgs e)
{
  Invalidate();
}

protected override void OnKeyDown(KeyEventArgs e)
{
  // we only respond to Ctl-Q and Ctl-W
  if ( e.Control && (e.KeyCode == Keys.Q) )
{
  MessageBox.Show("You pressed the Ctl-Q key!");
  e.Handled = true;
}

else if ( e.Control && (e.KeyCode == Keys.W) )
{
```

```
        MessageBox.Show("You pressed the Ctl-W key!");
        e.Handled = true;
    }

    else
        e.Handled = false;
    }

protected override void OnKeyPress(KeyPressEventArgs e)
{
if (Char.IsLower(e.KeyChar) )
    MessageBox.Show("You typed a lower case character");

else if (Char.IsUpper(e.KeyChar) )
    MessageBox.Show("You typed an upper case character");

else if (Char.IsDigit(e.KeyChar) )
    MessageBox.Show("You typed a number key");

else if (Char.IsPunctuation(e.KeyChar) )
    MessageBox.Show("You typed a punctuation key");

else if (Char.IsWhiteSpace(e.KeyChar) )
    MessageBox.Show("You typed a whitespace key");

// check for specific characters
switch (e.KeyChar)
{
    case 'a':
        MessageBox.Show("You typed the character: " + e.KeyChar);
        break;  // lowercase 'a'

    case 'A':
        MessageBox.Show("You typed the character: " + e.KeyChar);
        break;  // uppercase 'A'

    case '.':
        MessageBox.Show("You typed the character: " + e.KeyChar);
        break;  // the period key

    case ',':
        MessageBox.Show("You typed the character: " + e.KeyChar);
        break;  // the comma key

    case '[':
        MessageBox.Show("You typed the character: " + e.KeyChar);
        break;  // the [ key

    case ']':
        MessageBox.Show("You typed the character: " + e.KeyChar);
        break;  // the ] key
```

Continued

Listing 9-56 *(continued)*

```
    default:
      break;
    }
}

protected override void OnPaint(PaintEventArgs e)
{
  Graphics g = e.Graphics;

  g.SetClip(e.ClipRectangle);

  if (e.ClipRectangle.IntersectsWith(upperLeftRect) )
  {
    // ... draw the top left quadrant
  }

  if (e.ClipRectangle.IntersectsWith(upperRightRect) )
  {
    // ... draw the top right quadrant
  }

  if (e.ClipRectangle.IntersectsWith(lowerLeftRect) )
  {
    // ... draw the bottom left quadrant
  }

  if (e.ClipRectangle.IntersectsWith(lowerRightRect) )
  {
    // ... draw the bottom right quadrant
  }

  // recompute the size of each quadrant
  upperLeftRect.Width = ClientRectangle.Width / 2;
  upperLeftRect.Height = ClientRectangle.Height / 2;

  upperRightRect.X = ClientRectangle.Width / 2;
  upperRightRect.Width = ClientRectangle.Width / 2;
  upperRightRect.Height = ClientRectangle.Height / 2;

  lowerLeftRect.Y = ClientRectangle.Height / 2;
  lowerLeftRect.Width = ClientRectangle.Width / 2;
  lowerLeftRect.Height = ClientRectangle.Height / 2;

  lowerRightRect.X = ClientRectangle.Width / 2;
  lowerRightRect.Y = ClientRectangle.Height / 2;
  lowerRightRect.Width = ClientRectangle.Width / 2;
  lowerRightRect.Height = ClientRectangle.Height / 2;

  // paint the four quandrants
  // use a gradient fill for the top left quadrant
```

```
LinearGradientBrush gradientBrush =
    new LinearGradientBrush(upperLeftRect,
                            topLeftQuadrantColor1,
                            topLeftQuadrantColor2,
                            LinearGradientMode.ForwardDiagonal);
g.FillRectangle(gradientBrush, upperLeftRect);

// use the previously loaded bitmap to fill top right
// quadrant with a texture
TextureBrush textureBrush = new TextureBrush(textImage);
g.FillRectangle(textureBrush,
                Rectangle.Inflate(upperRightRect, -10, -10) );

// use a semi-transparent circle on a solid background for
// the lower left quadrant
g.FillRectangle(textureBrush, lowerLeftRect);
Color translucentAzure = Color.FromArgb(90, Color.Azure);
Brush myBrush = new SolidBrush(translucentAzure);
g.FillEllipse(myBrush, lowerLeftRect);

// draw a textured string in the lower right quadrant

g.FillRectangle(Brushes.LightSkyBlue, lowerRightRect);
String piText = "\x3c0";  // the greek letter pi
Font piFont = new Font("Times New Roman", 170);
SizeF stringSize = g.MeasureString(piText, piFont);
float x = lowerRightRect.Left +
          (lowerRightRect.Width - stringSize.Width) / 2;
float y = lowerRightRect.Top +
          (lowerRightRect.Height - stringSize.Height) / 2;

// rotate the lower right about its center point
float x1 = lowerRightRect.Left + lowerRightRect.Width / 2;
float y1 = lowerRightRect.Top + lowerRightRect.Height / 2;
g.TranslateTransform(x1, y1);
g.RotateTransform(-10);
g.TranslateTransform(-x1, -y1);

// draw the rotated string
g.DrawString(piText, piFont, textureBrush, x, y);

// go back to normal drawing
g.ResetTransform();

HighlightQuadrantUnderMouse(g);
if (!Focused) return;
// paint two focus rectangles, to make them more visible
ControlPaint.DrawFocusRectangle(g,
        Rectangle.Inflate(ClientRectangle, 0, 0) );
ControlPaint.DrawFocusRectangle(g,
        Rectangle.Inflate(ClientRectangle, -1, -1) );
}
```

Continued

Listing 9-56 *(continued)*

```csharp
protected void HighlightQuadrantUnderMouse(Graphics g)
{
  if (Form.ActiveForm != FindForm() ) return;

  // draw a highlight around the quadrant the mouse is in
  if (upperLeftRect.Contains(PointToClient(MousePosition) ) )
  {
    g.DrawRectangle(Pens.Black, upperLeftRect);
    quadrantHighlighted = upperLeftRect;
  }

  if (upperRightRect.Contains(PointToClient(MousePosition) ) )
  {
    g.DrawRectangle(Pens.Black, upperRightRect);
    quadrantHighlighted = upperRightRect;
  }

  if (lowerLeftRect.Contains(PointToClient(MousePosition) ) )
  {
    g.DrawRectangle(Pens.Black, lowerLeftRect);
    quadrantHighlighted = lowerLeftRect;
  }

  if (lowerRightRect.Contains(PointToClient(MousePosition) ) )
  {
    g.DrawRectangle(Pens.Black, lowerRightRect);
    quadrantHighlighted = lowerRightRect;
  }
}

private Color topLeftQuadrantColor1 = Color.Red;
private Color topLeftQuadrantColor2 = Color.White;

[Category("My Properties")]
[Description("Starting color for gradient")]
public Color TopLeftQuadrantColor1
{
  get { return topLeftQuadrantColor1; }
  set { topLeftQuadrantColor1 = value; }
}

[Category("My Properties")]
[Description("Ending color for gradient")]
public Color TopLeftQuadrantColor2
{
  get { return topLeftQuadrantColor2; }
  set { topLeftQuadrantColor2 = value; }
}

private VolumeLevel volume = new VolumeLevel(23);
```

```
    [ TypeConverter(typeof(VolumeLevelConverter) ) ]
    public VolumeLevel Volume
    {
      get {return volume; }
      set {volume = value; }
    }
  }
}
```

Listing 9-72 shows the full code for VolumeLevel.

Listing 9-72: The source code for VolumeLevel

```
using System;
using System.Windows.Forms;
using System.ComponentModel;
using System.Globalization;
using System.Drawing;

namespace MyCustomControls
{
  public class VolumeLevel
  {
    private int level;

    public VolumeLevel(int theLevel)
    {
      level = theLevel;
    }

    public int Level
    {
      get {return level;}
      set {level = value;}
    }
  }

  public class VolumeLevelConverter : TypeConverter
  {
    public override bool CanConvertFrom(ITypeDescriptorContext context,
                                 Type sourceType)
    {
      if (sourceType == typeof(string) )
        return true;
      return base.CanConvertFrom(context, sourceType);
    }
    public override object ConvertFrom(ITypeDescriptorContext context,
                                 CultureInfo culture, object value)
    {
      int level;
      if (value is String)
      {
        try
        {
```

Continued

Listing 9-56 *(continued)*

```
        level = Int32.Parse(value as String);
    }
    catch(Exception)
    {
      throw new NotSupportedException(
             "The text entered must be a number.");
    }

    if ( (level < 0) || (level > 100) )
      throw new NotSupportedException(
             "The text entered must be in the range (0..100).");
    VolumeLevel volumeLevel = new VolumeLevel(level);
    return volumeLevel;
  }
  return base.ConvertFrom(context, culture, value);
}

public override bool CanConvertTo(ITypeDescriptorContext context,
                        Type destinationType)
{
  if (destinationType == typeof(String) )
    return true;
  return base.CanConvertFrom(context, destinationType);
}

public override object ConvertTo(ITypeDescriptorContext context,
                        CultureInfo culture,
                        object value,
                        Type destinationType)
{
  if (destinationType == typeof(String) )
    return (value as VolumeLevel).Level.ToString();
  return base.ConvertTo(context, culture, value, destinationType);
}
}
}
```

Summary

The .NET Framework, with its rich hierarchy of control classes, makes it much easier than ever before to create custom controls. You no longer have to use special development environments or SDKs, and your controls can be added to the VS .NET Toolbox easily, and used like the stock components that Microsoft provides. The new tabbed architecture of the Toolbox lets you define new tabs to organize controls by function, vendor, or product type. While Visual Basic has long supported the installation of custom controls into the development environment, now all languages managed by VS .NET will benefit from the availability of large numbers of custom controls that can be used with the familiar drag-and-drop metaphor.

✦   ✦   ✦

User Controls

*It's necessary for me to establish a winner image. Therefore,
I have to beat somebody.*

—Richard M. Nixon, former U.S. president

To stay in business for the long term and prosper, your company
also needs a winner image, although perhaps not the presidential
kind. You need to beat the competition to market, and the .NET
Framework is currently the best way to do that on Windows
platforms.

User Controls versus Custom Controls

There are two different types of custom controls in the Visual C#
nomenclature: custom controls and user controls. I showed you an
example of a custom control in the previous chapter. So, what is a
user control, and how is it different from a custom control?

Both custom and user controls are components you create by
deriving a class from one of the base classes provided in the .NET
Framework. Custom controls are often derived from `UserControl`, or
one of the more specialized Windows Forms controls. User controls
are derived from the class `UserControl`. *Custom controls* are single
controls that typically have no children. *User controls* are composite
controls that have one or more child controls. User controls are
basically panels that contain other controls. You can provide
keyboard, mouse, and painting handlers in user controls, with
the advantage that the base class takes care of managing the child
controls, dispatching keyboard and mouse events to the right child.

In this chapter, I'll create a control called *MyUserControl* that will
demonstrate a whole array of interesting concepts and programming
techniques, including (in no particular order):

+ Managing rectangles

+ Drawing rubberbands

+ Checking mouse buttons and location

+ Controlling the cursor

+ Constraining the mouse cursor inside an area

+ Drawing selection frames

✦ Drawing grab handles

✦ Resizing objects on the screen

✦ Drawing shapes

✦ System icons

MyUserControl will present a user interface that is divided into two parts, as shown in Figure 10-1.

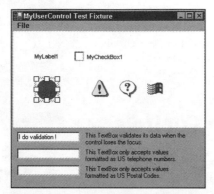

Figure 10-1: How MyUserControl looks when run inside a simple test fixture

The top part is a simple Component Designer where you can place components, select them, move them around with the mouse, resize them, and delete them. This area will demonstrate using rubberbands to select objects on the screen, and how to use selection frames with grab handles to support dragging and resizing components.

The bottom area is dedicated to something completely different. It has a panel containing three TextBox controls, and shows how to support different kinds of data validation. The first TextBox uses simple validation to verify the contents of the control. The second and third TextBoxes show other methods.

Designing a Graphics Designer Component

To support all the features required to support the simple Component Designer, I'm going to need a number of classes. To represent the items dropped in the Component Designer, I'll need a common base class, which I'll call MyComponent. I'll create a simple hierarchy of components derived from MyComponent, as shown in the class diagram in Figure 10-2.

The class MyComponent handles all the details of the Designer-compatible components, except for painting. Each component has a name, like *MyLabel1,* which can be displayed in the Designer. The bounds property is the bounding rectangle of the component. The property isSelected indicates whether the user selected the component. Components are selected in the Designer by drawing a rubberband around them, as described a later. When a component is selected, it displays itself with a selection frame and eight grab handles, as previously shown with the circle component in Figure 10-1. Grab handles are supported by their own class hierarchy, based on the class GrabHandle and referenced in Figure 10-2. The complete class hierarchy for grab handles is shown in Figure 10-3.

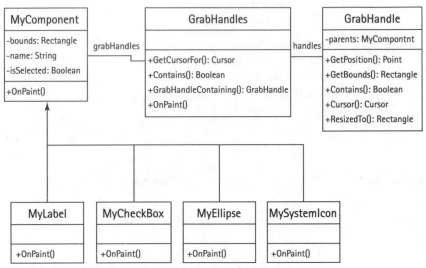

Figure 10-2: The classes associated with MyComponent

The base class GrabHandle takes care of most of details. The derived classes only override three methods. GetPosition() returns the *x* and *y* offset of the grab handle from the top left corner of the parent component's bounding rectangle. Cursor() returns the cursor to show when the mouse is over the grab handle. ResizedTo() is used to resize the parent component when the grab handle is dragged.

The last few classes are those related to the following component manipulation features:

✦ Drawing rubberbands

✦ Moving components

✦ Resizing components

These classes are associated directly with MyUserControl, as shown in Figure 10-4, the next and final class diagram for this example.

Although it is possible to incorporate all the features into the single class MyUserControl, I opted to split the code for rubberbanding, dragging and resizing into separate classes to make the code simpler and more reusable.

MyUserControl has two collections to manage the components in the Designer area: one called items and the other called selectedItems. The former stores all the components in the Designer; the other just keeps track of selected items. When an item is added to the `selectedItems` collection, the collection's `Add()` method sets the item's `isSelected` property. When a component draws itself, it checks to see if it is selected. If so, it draws a selection frame around itself and displays the grab handles.

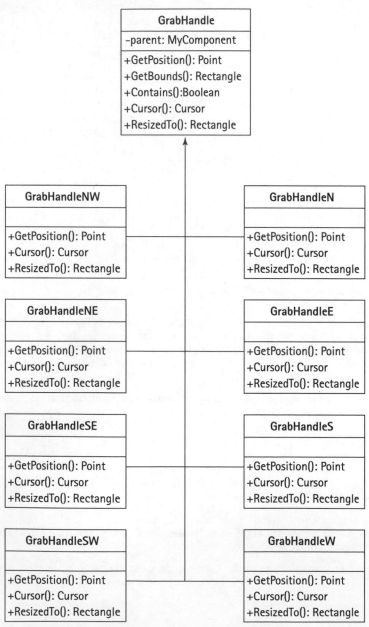

Figure 10-3: The class hierarchy for grab handles

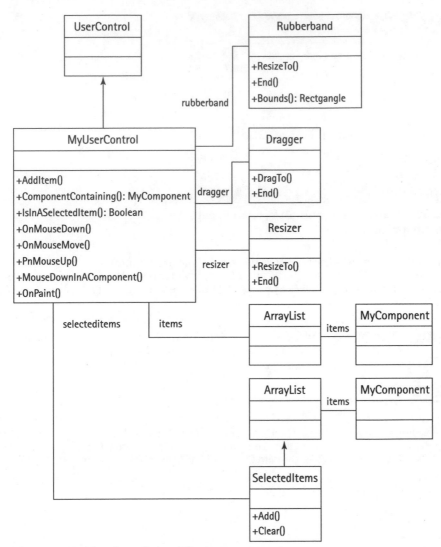

Figure 10-4: The class diagram for MyUserControl

Developing the Component

Although custom controls and user controls can be added directly to any project, I usually put them in a separate DLL, making it easier to reuse them and keeping application code out of the way. Having code for controls and applications together makes it more difficult to debug controls.

The easiest way to create a new user control is with the New Project wizard, by selecting Windows Control Library, as shown in Figure 10-5.

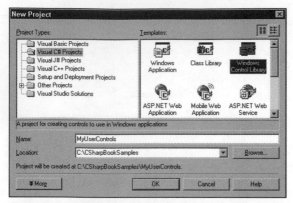

Figure 10-5: Creating the initial DLL project to put MyUserControl in

I used the Class View window to change the name of the user control class from `Control1` to `MyUserControl`, and then used the Solution Explorer window to change the control's filename from *UserControl1.cs* to *MyUserControl.cs*. At this point, the Solution Explorer looked like Figure 10-6.

Figure 10-6: The Solution Explorer, showing the newly created MyUserControl file at the bottom

Before adding any code to `MyUserControl`, I created the classes that `MyUserControl` would reference, starting with `MyComponent`. To create the new class, right-click the project name in the Solution Explorer and select the Add Class menu item as shown in Figure 10-7.

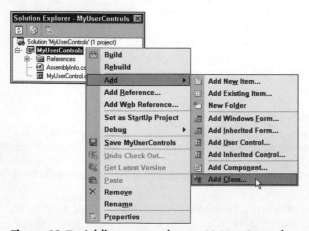

Figure 10-7: Adding a new class to MyUserControls

In the Add New Item dialog box, I chose C# Class as the item type (see Figure 10-8), to start out with an empty class and also because I don't want `MyComponent` to be derived from an existing component, such as `ListBox` or `TextBox`.

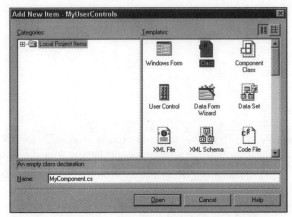

Figure 10-8: Using the Add New Item dialog box to create MyComponent

I used the same process to create all the other classes in the project. The last step is to add a bitmap to the project, to be used on the Toolbar. The process was described in the previous chapter, using the VS .NET Bitmap Designer, so I'll just summarize the steps here:

1. Create a 16 x 16 pixel bitmap.

2. Add the new bitmap to the project.

3. Rename the bitmap file to **MyUserControl.bmp.**

4. Make sure the bitmap's Build Action property is set to Embedded Resource.

After creating the classes and the bitmap, and renaming the files, the Solution Explorer looked like Figure 10-9.

Figure 10-9: The files used by MyUserControls

Before going any further, I created a test fixture project so I could test the code I would be adding. Remember, the project MyUserControls is a DLL, and can't be run by itself. I used the New Project wizard to add a Windows Application project to the solution, making the Solution Explorer look like Figure 10-10.

Figure 10-10: The Solution Explorer, showing the newly added test fixture

I set the test fixture as the startup project, and then went to the project properties for MyUserControls and set the Start Application to point to the new test fixture. I changed the Debug Mode from Project to Program, as shown in Figure 10-11.

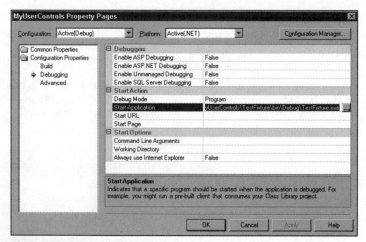

Figure 10-11: Adding the test fixture as the debug application for MyUserControls

Next, I built the two projects. Then I added a reference to MyUserControls.dll to the test fixture project. To add the reference, the easiest way is to right-click the References node of the test fixture project and select the Add Reference command. In the Add Reference dialog box, go to the Projects tab. Use the Browse button to locate the file MyUserControls.dll, and then click the Select button. Before closing the dialog box, it should look like Figure 10-12.

Now I can reference class MyUserControl in the test fixture. I opened the source code editor for class Form1 in the test fixture and imported the namespace MyUserControls with a using statement like this:

```
using MyUserControls;
```

Then, I added a few lines to the class constructor as shown in Listing 10-1.

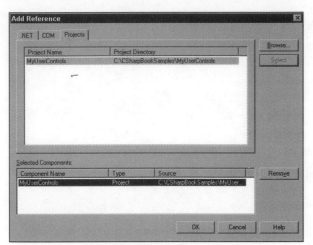

Figure 10-12: The Add Reference dialog box, after selecting MyUserControls.dll

Listing 10-1: **Using MyUserControl in the Test Fixture**

```
public Form1()
{
  InitializeComponent();

  // I added these 3 lines
  MyUserControl myUserControl = new MyUserControl();
  myUserControl.Dock = DockStyle.Fill;
  this.Controls.Add(myUserControl);
}
```

I set the DockStyle of MyUserControl to Fill, to make the component use all the available space in the test fixture. Running the test fixture by pressing F5 will display a form whose entire client area is filled by MyUserControl. Since I haven't added any code, the form will appear empty, because MyUserControl doesn't know how to draw anything yet.

Creating components for use in the Designer

You can't drop arbitrary components like TextBoxes and Labels in the Designer space of MyUserControl. The problem is that those components don't know how to interact with the Designer, in terms of user selections, user dragging, and user resizing. What I need is a custom class that is set up to handle the required interactions. Such is class MyComponent, whose code is shown in Listing 10-2. I'll subsequently derive a series of classes from MyComponent to implement the various objects shown previously in the Designer space in Figure 10-1.

Listing 10-2: The Code for MyComponent

```
public class MyComponent
{
  protected Font font;
  protected StringFormat alignVertically;

  public Rectangle bounds;
  public String name;
  public bool isSelected;

  public GrabHandles grabHandles;

  public MyComponent(Point theLocation, String theName)
  {
    name = theName;

    bounds = new Rectangle(theLocation, new Size(60, 15) );
    font = new Font("Arial", 8);

    alignVertically = new StringFormat();


alignVertically.LineAlignment = StringAlignment.Center;

    grabHandles = new GrabHandles(this);
  }

  public bool Contains(Point thePoint)
  {
    if (!isSelected)
      return bounds.Contains(thePoint);
    else
    {
      Rectangle selectionRect = bounds;
      selectionRect.Inflate(SystemInformation.FrameBorderSize);

      return selectionRect.Contains(thePoint);

    }
  }

  public bool IsInADragHandle(Point thePoint)
  {
    if (!isSelected) return false;
    return grabHandles.Contains(thePoint);
  }

  public Cursor GetCursorFor(Point thePoint)
  {
    if (isSelected)
    {
```

```
      if (IsInADragHandle(thePoint) )
        return grabHandles.GetCursorFor(thePoint);
      else

        return Cursors.SizeAll;
    }
    else
      return Cursors.Default;
  }


  public virtual void OnPaint(PaintEventArgs e)
  {
    if (!isSelected) return;

    // paint the selection box
    Rectangle outerRect = bounds;
    outerRect.Inflate(SystemInformation.FrameBorderSize);

    ControlPaint.DrawSelectionFrame(e.Graphics, true,
                                  outerRect bounds,
                                  SystemColors.ActiveBorder);


    // paint the grab handles
    grabHandles.OnPaint(e);
  }
}
```

The constructor is passed the name for the component, and the location of its top left corner. The constructor then creates a default rectangle for the initial bounds of the component. Since most derived components will display their name, the constructor instantiates Font and StringFormat objects. The latter object is set to draw text aligned vertically inside a bounding rectangle. The last thing the constructor does is instantiate the GrabHandles class, which internally creates the eight grab handles that will be displayed when a component is in the selected state.

The method MyComponent.Contains(Point) determines whether a given coordinate is inside the bounding rectangle of a component. The code is a little more complicated than you might expect, because the size of the bounding rectangle increases slightly when the selection frame and grab handles are added to a selected component. The method uses the code shown in Listing 10-3.

Listing 10-3: Using Rectangle.Inflate() to Increase the Size of the Bounding Rectangle for Selected Components

```
public bool Contains(Point thePoint)
{
  if (!isSelected)
```

Continued

Listing 10-3 *(continued)*

```
      return bounds.Contains(thePoint);

  else
  {
    Rectangle selectionRect = bounds;
    selectionRect.Inflate(SystemInformation.FrameBorderSize);
    return selectionRect.Contains(thePoint);

  }
}
```

If the component is selected, the code expands the basic bounding rectangle to account for the added size of the selection frame. The method `Rectangle.Inflate(Size)` increases the size of a rectangle by the given amount in all directions.

The method `GetCursorFor(Point)` determines which part of a component the mouse is over, and sets the cursor accordingly. If the mouse if over a grab handle, a double-headed arrow will be used for the cursor, pointing in a direction set by the grab handle. If the cursor is inside a selected component, the cursor is set to `Cursors.SizeAll`, which is a cross made up of double-headed arrows. Listing 10-4 shows the code for managing the cursor.

Listing 10-4: **Setting the Cursor**

```
public Cursor GetCursorFor(Point thePoint)
{
  if (isSelected)
  {
    if (IsInADragHandle(thePoint) )
      return grabHandles.GetCursorFor(thePoint);
    else
      return Cursors.SizeAll;

  }
  else
    return Cursors.Default;
}
```

The last method of `MyComponent` is `OnPaint()`, which draws the selection frame and grab handles, if the component is selected. This method is designed to be called by derived classes after they have painted themselves, so the grab handles and selection frame appear on top of the component. In the next section, I'll show how derived classes call `MyComponent.OnPaint()`.

Specialized classes derived from MyComponent

Let's look at the classes derived from `MyComponent`. The first one is a simple label component called `MyLabel`. Its code is shown in Listing 10-5. `MyLabel` just displays itself inside the component's bounding rectangle.

Listing 10-5: The Code for MyLabel

```
public class MyLabel: MyComponent
{
  public MyLabel(Point theLocation, String theName)
  : base(theLocation, theName) { }

  public override void OnPaint(PaintEventArgs e)
  {
    e.Graphics.DrawString(name, font, Brushes.Black, bounds,
alignVertically);


    base.OnPaint(e);  // paint the selection frame, if necessary

}

  }
```

Slightly more complicated than `MyLabel` is `MyCheckBox`, which draws a standard checkbox with the code shown in Listing 10-6.

Listing 10-6: Using ControlPaint Methods to Draw Standard Windows Controls

```
public class MyCheckBox: MyComponent
{
  public MyCheckBox(Point theLocation, String theName)
  : base(theLocation, theName)
  {
    bounds = new Rectangle(theLocation, new Size(100, 20) );
  }

  public override void OnPaint(PaintEventArgs e)
  {
    Rectangle boxBounds = new Rectangle(bounds.Location,
                          SystemInformation.MenuButtonSize);

    ControlPaint.DrawCheckBox(e.Graphics, boxBounds,
                          ButtonState.Normal);

    Rectangle textBounds = bounds;
    textBounds.Offset(boxBounds.Width + 4, 0);

    textBounds.Width -= boxBounds.Width + 4;
    e.Graphics.DrawString(name, font, Brushes.Black,
                          textBounds, alignVertically);

    base.OnPaint(e);  // paint the selection frame, if necessary
  }
}
```

The `OnPaint()` method uses `ControlPaint.DrawCheckBox()` to draw the checkbox. As described in a previous chapter, `ControlPaint` has methods for drawing all standard Windows controls and window embellishments. To draw a simple shape, you can just use one of the methods available in the `Graphics` class, as demonstrated with the class `MyEllipse` in Listing 10-7.

Listing 10-7: Drawing Simple Figures using Graphics Methods

```
public class MyEllipse: MyComponent
{
  public MyEllipse(Point theLocation, String theName)
  : base(theLocation, theName)
  {
    bounds = new Rectangle(theLocation, new Size(40, 40) );
  }

  public override void OnPaint(PaintEventArgs e)
  {
    e.Graphics.FillEllipse(Brushes.BlueViolet, bounds);

    base.OnPaint(e);  // paint the selection frame, if necessary
  }
}
```

Drawing the Windows System Icons

The last class I derived from `MyComponent` is called `MySystemIcon`. It demonstrates how to display a *System Icon,* which is just a built-in icon that Windows uses in various places, such as message boxes. Table 10-1 shows the System Icons.

Table 10-1: Standard Icons Available in Class SystemIcon

Icon Name	Appearance
SystemIcons.Application	
SystemIcons.Asterisk	
SystemIcons.Error	
SystemIcons.Exclamation	
SystemIcons.Hand	

Icon Name	Appearance
SystemIcons.Information	
SystemIcons.Question	
SystemIcons.Warning	
SystemIcons.WinLogo	

To demonstrate how to display System Icons on the screen, I created a small class called MySystemIcon, whose code is shown in Listing 10-8.

Listing 10-8: Displaying One of the System Icons

```
public class MySystemIcon: MyComponent
{
  Icon icon;
  Icon[] allIcons =
  {
    SystemIcons.Application,
    SystemIcons.Asterisk,
    SystemIcons.Error,
    SystemIcons.Exclamation,
    SystemIcons.Hand,
    SystemIcons.Information,
    SystemIcons.Question,
    SystemIcons.Warning,
    SystemIcons.WinLogo
  };

  public MySystemIcon(Point theLocation, String theName)
  : base(theLocation, theName)
  {
    // choose an icon at random
    icon = GetRandomIcon();
    bounds = new Rectangle(theLocation, icon.Size);
  }

  protected Icon GetRandomIcon()
  {
    Random r = new Random();

    return allIcons [r.Next(allIcons.Length)];
  }
```

Continued

Listing 10-8 *(continued)*

```
public override void OnPaint(PaintEventArgs e)
{
  e.Graphics.DrawIcon(icon, bounds.Left, bounds.Top);


  base.OnPaint(e);  // paint the selection frame, if necessary
}
}
```

The class uses an internal array of `SystemIcon` objects to store all the icons available. Each time `MySystemIcon` is instantiated, it calls the method `GetRandomIcon()` to randomly select an icon from the array.

Displaying and managing grab handles

When a component gets selected, it paints a selection frame around itself containing eight grab handles. For those readers who might have skipped earlier sections of this chapter, a *grab handle* is a small square that represents a visual cue for people to use to resize items on the screen. Figure 10-13 shows a selected item with a selection frame and eight grab handles.

Figure 10-13: An object displayed with a selection frame and eight grab handles

Grab handles can be displayed by calling the method `ControlPaint.DrawGrabHandle()`. Rather than have `MyComponent` call this method eight times and have to keep track of where each handle is, I created a hierarchy of classes to simplify the overall management and display of grab handles.

Let's look at the grab handle logic. The abstract base class `GrabHandle` handles many of the details, and looks like Listing 10-9.

Listing 10-9: The Base Class of all GrabHandle Classes

```
public abstract class GrabHandle
{
  protected MyComponent parent;

  public GrabHandle(MyComponent theParent)
  {
    parent = theParent;
  }

  protected abstract Point GetPosition();

  protected Rectangle GetBounds()
  {
```

```
      Rectangle rect = new Rectangle();
      rect.Location = parent.bounds.Location
  ;

      // get the location of this handle
      Point p = GetPosition();

      rect.Offset(p.X, p.Y);

      rect.Inflate(SystemInformation.FrameBorderSize);

      rect.Inflate(1, 1);

      return rect;
   }

   public virtual bool Contains(Point thePoint)
   {
      return GetBounds().Contains(thePoint);
   }

   public abstract Cursor Cursor();

   public virtual void OnPaint(PaintEventArgs e)
   {
      ControlPaint.DrawGrabHandle(e.Graphics, GetBounds(),
                                  true, true);
   }

   public abstract Rectangle ResizedTo(Rectangle theRect,
                                       Size theChange);
}
```

The base class provides the following features:

    ✦ It determines the bounding rectangle of a grab handle.

    ✦ It determines which grab handle contains a given point.

    ✦ It paints the grab handle.

The derived classes are extremely simple, and provide the following information:

    ✦ The cursor for each grab handle

    ✦ The position of each grab handle, relative to the parent's top left corner

In addition, the `ResizedTo()` method is overridden to support resizing the parent component when a grab handle is moved. Each grab handle affects the parent's bounding rectangle differently. The derived grab handle classes are shown in Listing 10-10. The class names end with the initial of a compass direction, based on the location of the handle in relationship to the center of the parent component: North, East, South, or West.

Listing 10-10: The Derived GrabHandle Classes

```
public class GrabHandleNW: GrabHandle
{
  public GrabHandleNW(MyComponent theParent): base(theParent) { }

  public override Cursor Cursor() {return Cursors.SizeNWSE;}

  protected override Point GetPosition()
  {
    return new Point(0, 0);
  }

  public override Rectangle ResizedTo(
                          Rectangle theRectangleToResize,
                          Size theChange)
  {
    theRectangleToResize.Offset(theChange.Width, theChange.Height);

    theRectangleToResize.Inflate(-theChange.Width,
                                 -theChange.Height);
    return theRectangleToResize;
  }
}

public class GrabHandleN: GrabHandle
{
  public GrabHandleN(MyComponent theParent): base(theParent) { }
  public override Cursor Cursor() {return Cursors.SizeNS;}

  protected override Point GetPosition()
  {
    return new Point(parent.bounds.Size.Width/2, 0);
  }

  public override Rectangle ResizedTo(
                          Rectangle theRectangleToResize,
                          Size theChange)
  {
  theRectangleToResize.Offset(0, theChange.Height);
  theRectangleToResize.Inflate(0, -theChange.Height);
  return theRectangleToResize;
  }
}

public class GrabHandleNE: GrabHandle
{
  public GrabHandleNE(MyComponent theParent): base(theParent) { }

  public override Cursor Cursor() {return Cursors.SizeNESW;}
  protected override Point GetPosition()
  {
```

```
          return new Point(parent.bounds.Size.Width, 0);
     }

  public override Rectangle ResizedTo(
                          Rectangle theRectangleToResize,
                          Size theChange)
  {
    theRectangleToResize.Offset(0, theChange.Height);

    theRectangleToResize.Width += theChange.Width;
    theRectangleToResize.Height -= theChange.Height;
    return theRectangleToResize;
  }
}

public class GrabHandleE: GrabHandle
{
  public GrabHandleE(MyComponent theParent): base(theParent) { }
  public override Cursor Cursor() {return Cursors.SizeWE;}
  protected override Point GetPosition()
  {
    return new Point(parent.bounds.Size.Width,
                     parent.bounds.Size.Height/2);
  }

  public override Rectangle ResizedTo(
                          Rectangle theRectangleToResize,
                          Size theChange)
  {
    theRectangleToResize.Width += theChange.Width;
    return theRectangleToResize;
  }
}

public class GrabHandleSE: GrabHandle
{
  public GrabHandleSE(MyComponent theParent): base(theParent) { }
  public override Cursor Cursor() {return Cursors.SizeNWSE;}
  protected override Point GetPosition()
  {
    return new Point(parent.bounds.Size.Width,
                     parent.bounds.Size.Height);
  }

  public override Rectangle ResizedTo(
                          Rectangle theRectangleToResize,
                          Size theChange)
  {
    theRectangleToResize.Width += theChange.Width;
    theRectangleToResize.Height += theChange.Height;
    return theRectangleToResize;
```

Continued

Listing 10-10 *(continued)*

```
    }
  }

public class GrabHandleS: GrabHandle
{
  public GrabHandleS(MyComponent theParent): base(theParent) { }
  public override Cursor Cursor() {return Cursors.SizeNS;}
  protected override Point GetPosition()
  {
    return new Point(parent.bounds.Size.Width/2,
                     parent.bounds.Size.Height);
  }

  public override Rectangle ResizedTo(
                          Rectangle theRectangleToResize,
                          Size theChange)
  {
    theRectangleToResize.Height += theChange.Height;
    return theRectangleToResize;
  }
}

public class GrabHandleSW: GrabHandle
{
  public GrabHandleSW(MyComponent theParent): base(theParent) { }
  public override Cursor Cursor() {return Cursors.SizeNESW;}
  protected override Point GetPosition()
  {
    return new Point(0, parent.bounds.Size.Height);
  }

  public override Rectangle ResizedTo(
                          Rectangle theRectangleToResize,
                          Size theChange)
  {
    theRectangleToResize.Offset(theChange.Width, 0);
    theRectangleToResize.Inflate(-theChange.Width,
                                 -theChange.Height);
    return theRectangleToResize;
  }
}

public class GrabHandleW: GrabHandle
{
  public GrabHandleW(MyComponent theParent): base(theParent) { }
  public override Cursor Cursor() {return Cursors.SizeWE;}
  protected override Point GetPosition()
  {
    return new Point(0, parent.bounds.Size.Height/2);
  }
```

```
    public override Rectangle ResizedTo(
                            Rectangle theRectangleToResize,
                            Size theChange)
    {
      theRectangleToResize.Offset(theChange.Width, 0);
      theRectangleToResize.Inflate(-theChange.Width, 0);
      return theRectangleToResize;
    }
}
```

Grab handles are managed by a collection class called (not surprisingly) `GrabHandles`. This class acts as a liaison between `MyUserControl` and the grab handles. The code for `GrabHandles` is shown in Listing 10-11.

Listing 10-11: **The Code for the Collection Class GrabHandles**

```
public class GrabHandles
{

  GrabHandle[] handles;

  public GrabHandles(MyComponent parent)
  {
    handles = new GrabHandle[]
    {
      new GrabHandleNW(parent),
      new GrabHandleN(parent),
      new GrabHandleNE(parent),
      new GrabHandleE(parent),
      new GrabHandleSE(parent),
      new GrabHandleS(parent),
      new GrabHandleSW(parent),
      new GrabHandleW(parent)
    };
  }

  public Cursor GetCursorFor(Point thePoint)
  {
    GrabHandle gh = GrabHandleContaining(thePoint);
    if (gh != null)
      return gh.Cursor();

    return Cursors.Default;
  }

  public bool Contains(Point thePoint)
  {
    return GrabHandleContaining(thePoint) != null ? true : false;
  }
```

Continued

Listing 10-11 *(continued)*

```
public GrabHandle GrabHandleContaining(Point thePoint)
{
  foreach (GrabHandle gh in handles)

    if (gh.Contains(thePoint) )
      return gh;
  return null;
}

public void OnPaint(PaintEventArgs e)
{
  // paint the grab handles
  foreach (GrabHandle gh in handles)
    gh.OnPaint(e);
}
}
```

The class manages the painting of the individual grab handles, determines which handle is located at a given position, and uses that `GrabHandle` to set the cursor.

Resizing a component with grab handles

Let's take a look at the interaction dynamics between a component and its grab handles when the user resizes a component by dragging one of the handles. The interaction diagram in Figure 10-14 shows the sequence of events following `OnMouseDown`, `OnMouseMove`, and `OnMouseUp` events.

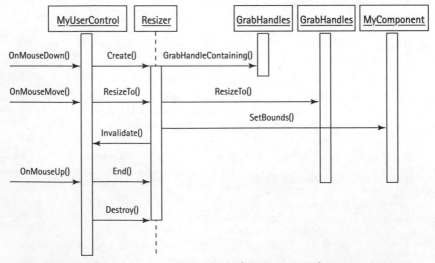

Figure 10-14: The interactions occurring when a user resizes a component

The diagram uses a class called `Resizer` to coordinate and encapsulate the details of resizing. The class is very simple and is shown in Listing 10-12.

Listing 10-12: The code for Class Resizer

```
public class Resizer
{
  Control parent = null;
  GrabHandle grabHandle = null;
  MyComponent componentToResize = null;
  Point location;

  public Resizer(Control theParent,
                 MyComponent theComponentToResize,
                 Point theStartingPoint)
  {
    if (theComponentToResize == null) return;
    componentToResize = theComponentToResize;

    parent = theParent;
    location = theStartingPoint;

    if (componentToResize.grabHandles == null) return;
    grabHandle =
      componentToResize.grabHandles.GrabHandleContaining(location);
    if (grabHandle == null) return;

    parent.Capture = true;
    Cursor.Clip = parent.RectangleToScreen(parent.ClientRectangle);


  }

  public void ResizeTo(Point p)
  {
    if (grabHandle == null) return;

    Size delta = new Size(p.X - location.X, p.Y - location.Y);
    Rectangle r =
      grabHandle.ResizedTo(componentToResize.bounds, delta);

    // don't let the rectangle get reversed
    if ( (r.Width <= 0) || (r.Height <= 0) )
      return;

    componentToResize.bounds = r;
    parent.Invalidate();

    location = p;
  }
  public void End()
```

Continued

> **Listing 10-12** *(continued)*
>
> ```
>     {
>         if (grabHandle == null) return;
>         Cursor.Clip = Rectangle.Empty;
>
>         parent.Capture = false;
>     }
> }
> ```

The constructor is passed the location of where the mouse button was pressed. It uses this location to determine which grab handle should handle subsequent mouse motion. The constructor also establishes a clipping area for the mouse, preventing the mouse from being moved outside the client rectangle of MyUserControl.

When the mouse is moved, Resizer.ResizeTo() is called by MyUserControl. This method delegates the call to GrabHandle to determine how the motion affects the bounding rectangle of the parent component, and then updates the bounding rectangle and invalidates the entire area covered by MyUserControl to cause the resized component to be repainted.

When the mouse button is released, MyUserControl calls Resizer.End(), which terminates mouse clipping and capturing.

Selecting items with a rubberband

For those readers who might have skipped earlier sections of this chapter, a *rubberband* is the dashed rectangle used by many applications to allow the user to designate rectangular regions of the screen. Rubberbands are created usually by pressing the left mouse button and dragging the mouse. When the left mouse button is released, the rubberband is erased from the screen. Figure 10-15 shows MyUserControl with a rubberband at various moments of a mouse drag.

Figure 10-15: Creating a rubberband with the mouse

Since rubberbands are designed to cover existing items on the screen, they need to restore the covered parts each time the rubberband is changed in size. If the restoration is slow, the screen will flicker each time the mouse is moved. The easiest way to draw something that can be erased quickly and without flicker is by using a paint technique that XORs the color of the drawing pen with each pixel drawn on. The Boolean XOR operation is symmetrical: XORing once will produce one value. XORing a second time will restore the original value. The rubberband shown in the previous figure used a white pen to draw with, so the rubberband shows up in black. Why? Simple. White pixels XORed with the white pen give black pixels. You can use other colors for the rubberband pen, but you may wind up with rubberbands that either have unusual colors or are hard to see on the screen. White is the most common pen color used, but it produces black pixels only against a white background. If your background is gray or a dark color, you may need to use a black pen, to get a light-colored rubberband.

So, having said all this, how do you draw with XOR operations? All you need is the ControlPaint class, which has a couple of methods that have the word *Reversible* in them, such as DrawReversibleFrame(),DrawReversibleLine(), and FillReversible Rectangle(). The first two draw outlines with a pen. The last one draws the interior of a rectangle with a brush. The important thing here is that all three methods are reversible: calling them twice with the same parameters will restore the screen to the way it was before the first call.

The code I used to draw a rubberband in class Rubberband is shown in Listing 10-13.

Listing 10-13: **Drawing a Rubberband**

```
protected void Draw()
{
  Rectangle r = parent.RectangleToScreen(rect);

  ControlPaint.DrawReversibleFrame(r, Color.White,
                                   FrameStyle.Dashed);

}
```

It's important to remember that all the reversible drawing methods of ControlPaint take screen coordinates. In Listing 10-13, the variable parent refers to MyUserControl, which inherits from Control the method RectangleToScreen(). This method converts the coordinates of a rectangle from client to screen coordinates. As I said earlier, calling Rubberband.Draw() twice produces the original screen, with no rubberband visible. Class Rubberband uses a simple strategy to draw and erase rubberbands: When the class is first created, following a mouse down event, it draws an empty rectangle. For every subsequent mouse move event, the method Rubberband.ResizeTo()is called. The method calls Rubberband.Draw() to erase the old rubberband, updates the bounds, and then calls Rubberband.Draw() again to draw the new rubberband. When the user releases the mouse, the method Rubberband.End() is called to erase the rubberband. Listing 10-14 shows the code for Rubberband.ResizeTo().

Listing 10-14: **Erasing an Old Rubberband and Drawing a New One with Different Dimensions**

```
public void ResizeTo(Point thePoint)
{
  // erase the old rubberband
  Draw();

  // get the new size of the rubberband
  rect.Width =  thePoint.X - rect.Left;
  rect.Height = thePoint.Y - rect.Top;

  // draw the new rubberband
  Draw();
}
```

The parameter `thePoint` passed to the method is the new mouse position in client coordinates. The value is used to set the new width and height of the rubberband, and then the rubberband is drawn. Listing 10-15 shows the complete code for class `Rubberband`.

Listing 10-15: **The Complete Code for Class Rubberband**

```
namespace MyUserControls
{
  using System;
  using System.WinForms;
  using System.Drawing;

  public class Rubberband
  {
    protected Control parent;
    protected Rectangle rect = Rectangle.Empty;

    public Rubberband(theParent, Point theStartingPoint)
    {
      parent = theParent;
      parent.Capture = true;
      Cursor.Clip =
        parent.RectangleToScreen(parent.ClientRectangle);
      rect = new Rectangle(theStartingPoint.X,
                           theStartingPoint.Y, 0, 0);
    }

    public void End()
    {
      Cursor.Clip = Rectangle.Empty;
      parent.Capture = false;

      // erase the rubberband
      Draw();
      rect = Rectangle.Empty;
    }

    public void ResizeTo(Point thePoint)
    {
      // erase the old rubberband
      Draw();

      // get the new size of the rubberband
      rect.Width =  thePoint.X - rect.Left;
      rect.Height = thePoint.Y - rect.Top;

      // draw the new rubberband
      Draw();
    }
```

```
      public Rectangle Bounds()
      {
        // return a normalized rectangle, i.e. a rect
        // where (left <= right) and (top <= bottom)
        if ( (rect.Left > rect.Right) || (rect.Top > rect.Bottom) )
        {
          int left = Math.Min(rect.Left, rect.Right);
          int right = Math.Max(rect.Left, rect.Right);
          int top = Math.Min(rect.Top, rect.Bottom);
          int bottom = Math.Max(rect.Top, rect.Bottom);
          return Rectangle.FromLTRB(left, top, right, bottom);
        }
        return rect;
      }

      // Reversible drawing method
      // Calling theis method the first time draws the rubberband.
      // Calling it a second time with the same rect erases the
      // rubberband

      protected void Draw()
      {
        Rectangle r = parent.RectangleToScreen(rect);
        ControlPaint.DrawReversibleFrame(r, Color.White,
                                   FrameStyle.Dashed);
      }
    }
  }
}
```

One method I haven't discussed is `Rubberband.Bounds()`. If its purpose is to return the bounding rectangle of the rubberband, why not just return `rect`? The problem with this approach is that it fails to account for *nonnormalized rectangles*. If the user draws a rubberband by moving the mouse towards the upper left of the screen, the rubberband's rectangle will be nonnormalized. Such rectangles have a width and/or height that is less than zero. You can draw nonnormalized rubberbands without any problems, but `MyUserControl`, like many applications, uses the bounds of a rubberband to locate the enclosed items. For example, to see if a component is inside the rubberband's area, you would use code like this:

```
// this will work only with normalized rubberbands
if (rubberband.rect.Contains(theComponent.rect) )
  // the component is enclosed by the rubberband
```

The problem is that a nonnormalized rectangle will always return `false` from the `Contains()` method. To avoid the problem, `MyUserControl` calls the method `Bounds()` to obtain the normalized rectangle for the rubberband, like this:

```
// this will work with any rubberband
if (rubberband.Bounds().Contains(theComponent.rect) )
  // the component is enclosed by the rubberband
```

To get a better sense of how the class `Rubberband` is used in `MyUserControl`, see the interaction diagram in Figure 10-16.

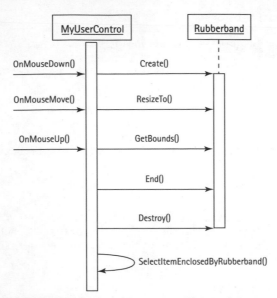

Figure 10-16: How class Rubberband interacts with MyUserControl

Although the diagram shows how a rubberband is created and controlled, it's important to remember that a rubberband is only a means to an end. Its purpose is only to allow users to designate a portion of the screen. What the application does with that information (the selected screen area) is not for the Rubberband class to worry about. The next section describes the actions generically labeled SelectItemsEnclosedByRubberband() in the previous figure.

Managing selected items

In MyUserControl, selected items have two important features: they display themselves with grab handles and can be dragged around with the mouse. I want the display logic of MyComponent to take care of all the display details, so I added a property called isSelected to the class. When painting itself, MyComponent checks this property and displays a selection frame with grab handles if the property is true. To manage groups of selected items, I used an ArrayList collection class called SelectedItems. The act of selecting an item entails two actions: putting the item in the SelectedItems collection, and setting the component's isSelected property to true. To put all this logic in one place, I derived SelectedItems from ArrayList and overrode the two methods Add() and Clear(). Listing 10-16 shows the code for SelectedItems.

Listing 10-16: **The Class that Manages Selected Items**

```
namespace MyUserControls
{
  using System;
```

```
using System.Collections;

public class SelectedItems: ArrayList

{
  public SelectedItems() {}

  public override void Clear()
  {
    foreach (MyComponent c in this)
      c.isSelected = false;
    base.Clear();
  }

  public void Add(MyComponent theComponent)
  {
    base.Add(theComponent);
    theComponent.isSelected = true;
  }
 }
}
```

Moving components around on the screen

Now that you've seen how I keep track of selected items, I can describe how selected components are moved around on the screen. The user first selects one or more items with a rubberband, and then clicks the mouse inside one of the selected items and drags them to a new
location. To keep the code simple and reusable, I put the code related to component-moving
in a class called Dragger, whose code is shown in Listing 10-17.

Listing 10-17: **The Complete Code for Class Dragger**

```
namespace MyUserControls
{
  using System;
  using System.WinForms;
  using System.Drawing;
  using System.Collections;

  public class Dragger
  {
    Control parent;
    SelectedItems items;
    Point location;
    public Dragger(Control theParent, SelectedItems theItemsToDrag,
```

Continued

Listing 10-17 *(continued)*

```
                    Point theStartingPoint)
    {
      parent = theParent;
      items = theItemsToDrag;
      location = theStartingPoint;

      parent.Capture = true;

      Cursor.Clip =
        parent.RectangleToScreen(parent.ClientRectangle);

    }

    public void DragTo(Point thePoint)
  {
      int xDelta = thePoint.X - location.X;
      int yDelta = thePoint.Y - location.Y;

      foreach (MyComponent c in items)
        c.bounds.Offset(xDelta, yDelta);


      parent.Invalidate();
      location = thePoint;
    }

    public void End()
    {
      Cursor.Clip = Rectangle.Empty;
      parent.Capture = false;
    }
  }
}
```

The class creates a clipping area for the mouse, preventing the user from dragging components outside the client area of MyUserControl. The clipping area restriction is removed when the Dragger.End() method is called after the user finishes a drag operation. The code that moves the selected components is in the method Dragger.DragTo(), which takes the list of components passed to the constructor and moves them. After changing the position of all the components, the Invalidate() method is called to refresh the screen.

Figure 10-17 shows the interactions between MyUserControl and Dragger when dragging components.

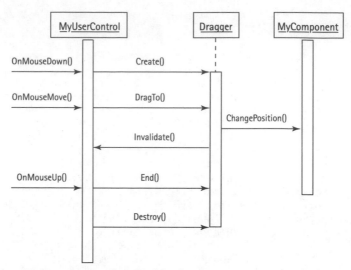

Figure 10-17: The significant events involved in dragging components on the screen

The Designer Component

I've described all the small pieces that are used by the Designer part of MyUserControl, so to demonstrate how everything fits together, I need to show the source code for class MyUserControl. Listing 10-18 shows the code related to the Designer. Remember, MyUserControl also supports three types of TextBox controls in the lower part of its client area that demonstrate data-entry validation. The validation logic is described later in the chapter.

Listing 10-18: The Code in MyUserControl Related to the Designer

```
using System;
using System.Collections;
using System.ComponentModel;
using System.Drawing;
using System.Data;
using System.Windows.Forms;
using System.Text.RegularExpressions;
using System.Runtime.InteropServices; // to call MessageBeep()

namespace MyUserControls
{
  public class MyUserControl : System.Windows.Forms.UserControl
  {
    private System.ComponentModel.Container components = null;

    Rubberband rubberband = null;
    Dragger dragger = null;
    Resizer resizer = null;

    ArrayList items = new ArrayList();
```

Continued

Listing 10-18 *(continued)*

```
SelectedItems selectedItems = new SelectedItems();

private System.Windows.Forms.ContextMenu contextMenu1;
private System.Windows.Forms.MenuItem menuItemAddLabel;
private System.Windows.Forms.MenuItem menuItemAddCheckbox;
private System.Windows.Forms.MenuItem menuItemAddEllipse;
private System.Windows.Forms.MenuItem menuItemAddIcon;
private System.Windows.Forms.MenuItem menuItem5;
private System.Windows.Forms.Panel panel1;
private System.Windows.Forms.TextBox textBoxValidated;
private System.Windows.Forms.TextBox textBoxPhoneNumber;
private System.Windows.Forms.TextBox textBoxZipCode;
private System.Windows.Forms.Label label1;
private System.Windows.Forms.Label label2;
private System.Windows.Forms.Label label3;
MenuItem menuItemDeleteSelectedItems;

public MyUserControl()
{
  // This call is required by the Windows.Forms Form Designer.
  InitializeComponent();

  // add a few items
  Point p = new Point(10, 10);
  items.Add(new MyLabel(p, "MyLabel1") );
  p.Offset(100, 40);
  items.Add(new MyCheckBox(p, "MyCheckBox1") );
  p.Offset(-50, 80);
  items.Add(new MyEllipse(p, "MyEllipse1") );
  p.Offset(100, -30);
  items.Add(new MySystemIcon(p, "MyIcon1") );
}

protected override void Dispose( bool disposing )
{
  // standard wizard-generated code...
}

private void InitializeComponent()
{
  // code generated by VS.NET Forms Designer
}

private void menuItemAddLabel_Click(object sender,
                                    System.EventArgs e)
{
  Point p = PointToClient(MousePosition);
  AddItem(new MyLabel(p, "MyLabel" +
                      items.Count.ToString() ) );
}
private void menuItemAddCheckbox_Click(object sender,
```

```csharp
                                              System.EventArgs e)
{
  Point p = PointToClient(MousePosition);
  AddItem(new MyCheckBox(p, "MyCheckBox" +
                            items.Count.ToString() ) );
}

private void menuItemAddEllipse_Click(object sender,
                                      System.EventArgs e)
{
  Point p = PointToClient(MousePosition);
  AddItem(new MyEllipse(p, "MyEllipse" +
                           items.Count.ToString() ) );
}

private void menuItemAddIcon_Click(object sender,
                                   System.EventArgs e)
{
  Point p = PointToClient(MousePosition);
  AddItem(new MySystemIcon(p, "MyIcon" +
                              items.Count.ToString() ) );
}

private void menuItemDeleteSelectedItems_Click(
                                object sender,
                                System.EventArgs e)
{
  foreach (MyComponent c in selectedItems)
    items.Remove(c);
  selectedItems.Clear();
  Invalidate();
}

protected void AddItem(MyComponent theItem)
{
  items.Add(theItem);
  Invalidate();
}

protected MyComponent SelectedComponentContaining(
                                Point thePoint)
{
  // iterate backwards over the items collection
  // if a selected item is found, return it
  for (int i = items.Count-1; i >= 0; i--)
  {
    MyComponent c = items [i] as MyComponent;
    if (selectedItems.Contains(c) )
      if (c.Contains(thePoint) )
        return c;
  }
  return null;
}
```

Continued

Listing 10-18 *(continued)*

```
protected bool IsInASelectedItem(Point thePoint)
{
  return SelectedComponentContaining(thePoint) != null ?
                                      true : false;
}

private void MyUserControl_MouseDown(
                object sender,
                System.Windows.Forms.MouseEventArgs e)
{
  if (MouseButtons == MouseButtons.Right)
    return;

  Point p = new Point(e.X, e.Y);

  if (IsInASelectedItem(p) )
    MouseDownInAComponent(p);
  else
  {
    selectedItems.Clear();
    rubberband = new Rubberband(this, p);
    Invalidate();
  }
}

protected void MouseDownInAComponent(Point thePoint)
{
  MyComponent c = SelectedComponentContaining(thePoint);
  if (c == null) return;

  if (c.IsInADragHandle(thePoint) )
    resizer = new Resizer(this, c, thePoint);
  else
    dragger = new Dragger(this, selectedItems, thePoint);
}

private void MyUserControl_MouseUp(
                object sender,
                System.Windows.Forms.MouseEventArgs e)
{
  // we're in the process of resizing an item
  if (resizer != null)
  {
    resizer.End();
    resizer = null;
    return;
  }

  // we're in the process of dragging items
  if (dragger != null)
  {
```

```
        dragger.End();
        dragger = null;
        return;
      }

    // We just created a selection area with a rubberband.
    // Select all the items enclosed.
    if (rubberband != null)
    {
      Rectangle rect = rubberband.Bounds();
      rubberband.End();
      rubberband = null;

      foreach (MyComponent c in items)
      {
        if (rect.Contains(c.bounds) )
          selectedItems.Add(c);
      }
      Invalidate();
    }
}

private void MyUserControl_MouseMove(
                    object sender,
                    System.Windows.Forms.MouseEventArgs e)
{
  Point p = new Point(e.X, e.Y);

  if (dragger != null)
    dragger.DragTo(p);

  if (resizer != null)
  {
    resizer.ResizeTo(p);
    return;
  }

  if (rubberband != null)
    rubberband.ResizeTo(p);

  // set the cursor if the mouse is over a selected item
  foreach (MyComponent c in selectedItems)
  {
    if (c.Contains(p) )
    {
      Cursor = c.GetCursorFor(p);
      return;
    }
  }

  // cursor isn't over a selected item
  Cursor = Cursors.Default;
}
```

Continued

Listing 10-18 *(continued)*

```
    private void MyUserControl_Paint(
                    object sender,
                    System.Windows.Forms.PaintEventArgs e)
    {
      // paint the items
      foreach (MyComponent c in items)
        c.OnPaint(e);
    }
  }
}
```

The class uses the method SelectedComponentContaining(Point) to locate the selected component at the mouse position. Since there can be multiple items in the same place on the screen, the method needs to account for the Z-order of items on the screen, as shown in Listing 10-19.

Listing 10-19: Iterating Backwards over the Items Collection to Find the Top Selected Item in Z-Order

```
protected MyComponent SelectedComponentContaining(Point thePoint)
{
  // iterate backwards over the items collection
  // if a selected item is found, return it
  for (int i = items.Count-1; i >= 0; i--)
  {
    MyComponent c = items [i] as MyComponent;
    if (selectedItems.Contains(c) )
      if (c.Contains(thePoint) )
        return c;
  }
  return null;
}
```

If you add two items at the same location, the second will be on top of the first, in Z-order. When determining which item is at a given location, you normally want to use the top item in Z-order. To find this item, all you need to do is iterate *backwards* over the items collection, as shown in the previous listing. For each item, see if the item is selected. If so, see if the item contains the given point.

Adding and Deleting Items

MyUserControl uses a ContextMenu to allow users to add components to the Designer, or to delete the selected items. To add a menu, drop one on MyUserControl from the Toolbox and then change MyUserControl's ContextMenu property to reference it. After setting up the menu with the VS .NET Menu Designer, the menu looks like Figure 10-18.

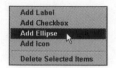

Figure 10-18: The ContextMenu used by MyUserControl to add and delete items in the Designer

When adding items, the items are dropped at the cursor position with the code shown in Listing 10-20.

Listing 10-20: **Adding Items at the Mouse Position**

```
protected void OnMenuItemAddCheckBox(object sender,
                                     System.EventArgs e)
{
  Point p = PointToClient(MousePosition);
  AddItem(new MyCheckBox(p, "MyCheckBox" +
                         items.Count.ToString() ) );
}

protected void AddItem(MyComponent theItem)
{
  items.Add(theItem);
  Invalidate();
}
```

The property `Control.MousePosition` returns the position of the mouse cursor in screen coordinates, so I need to call `Control.PointToClient()` to convert the position to client coordinates. To delete all of the selected component, I need to iterate over the components in the `selectedItems` collection, remove them from the `items` collections, and then remove everything from the `selectedItems` collection, as shown in Listing 10-21.

Listing 10-21: **Deleting Items from the Designer**

```
protected void OnMenuItemDeleteSelectedItems(
                            object sender,
                            System.EventArgs e)
{
  foreach (MyComponent c in selectedItems)
    items.Remove(c);
  selectedItems.Clear();
  Invalidate();
}
```

The handlers for mouse events in `MyUserControl` delegate most of the processing to the rubberband, dragger, and resizer objects. The last method, `OnPaint()`, just iterates over the items collection and tells each component to paint itself.

Controlling Data Entry

Data entry is the process of using the keyboard to enter data into a program. Data Entry is a big part of many applications, so I'll cover some of the important ways to control and verify the data entered. There are two general ways to control data entry:

✦ Checking keys as they are typed

✦ Checking the data only when the input control loses the focus

The first way prevents invalid keys from being entered. Most systems issue a beep or do nothing if an invalid key is typed. Checking the data only after it has all been entered may be necessary if the data has a variable or complex layout. I'll discuss both methods in the next two sections.

Checking keys as they're typed

Before writing any code to check keys, take a look at the TextBox properties in Table 10-2.

Table 10-2: TextBox Properties that Can Be Useful in Controlling Entered Data

Property	Description
CharacterCasing	Can be set to change all characters to uppercase or lowercase.
MaxLength	Can be set to limit the number of characters entered.
MultiLine	Can be set to prevent more than one line of text.

If you need further control over the data entered at the character level (which is not completely out of the question), you'll need to add a handler for the KeyPress event. This handler will be called every time the user presses a character key.

Note   Noncharacter key combinations, like Alt-F5 or Ctrl-C, will not generate KeyPress **events.**

The handler shown in Listing 10-22 accepts only characters that are part of a number.

Listing 10-22: Allowing Only Characters Used with Numbers

```
private void textBoxPhoneNumber_KeyPress(
                            object sender,
                            KeyPressEventArgs e)
{
  if (IsValidKey(e.KeyChar) )
    e.Handled = false;
  else
  {
    e.Handled = true;
```

```
      Beep();
   }
}

private bool IsValidKey(Char theKey)
{
   return  (theKey == '\b')  ||   // backspace
           (theKey == '+')   ||
           (theKey == '-')   ||
           (theKey == '.')   ||
        (  (theKey >= '0')   &&
           (theKey <= '9') ) ) ? true : false;
}
```

Notice that `IsValidKey()` allows the Backspace character as well, so users can back up and make corrections. The Backspace key is the only cursor-moving key that is included in `KeyPress` events. The other cursor-moving keys, such as the arrow keys, Home, and End are only sent in `KeyDown` and `KeyUp` events.

In the `KeyPress` handler shown in the listing, the code sets `e.Handled` to `false` if the character is acceptable. This might sound backwards, but it's not: When the handler exits, the base class will check `e.Handled` to see if we took care of the key. If the value is `false`, then the base class handles the key and puts it in the `TextBox`.

In case you're wondering, the `Beep()` method is not a built-in one. It turns out that the .NET Framework doesn't have a simple method to issue beeps (which is fairly surprising), so I implemented one myself. My code, shown in Listing 10-23, just calls the `MessageBeep()` method in the native (unmanaged) module User32.dll.

Listing 10-23: **Issuing a Beep by Calling a Method in a Native (Unmanaged) DLL**

```
using System.Runtime.InteropServices; // to call into native DLLs

[DllImport("user32.dll")]
public static extern int MessageBeep(int typeOfSound);
private void Beep()
{
   MessageBeep(0);
}
```

Not too difficult, but I consider the code a workaround. The .NET Framework should have included a method equivalent to `MessageBeep()`. I'd like to remind Microsoft of their own philosophy with the .NET Framework: Common tasks should be easy and the others should be possible. (I guess the designers thought that issuing beeps was unusual.)

Checking individual characters is a really weak way to constrain input data. The code shown in Listing 10-22 in the `KeyPress` handler just looks at each key. The problem with this type of simplistic technique is that it allows the user to type in the "+", "-", and "." keys at any time and in any combination. The code would allow such nonsense as +-+- or *9.9.9.9.*

Validating with regular expressions

Obviously, checking each key is good, but not good enough. What you usually need to do is look at the whole string entered, to see if it makes sense. By using *regular expressions*, you can define the layout of many types of input strings accurately. For example, some of the expressions described in section titled "Using regular expressions" in Chapter 7 could be handy. To save you the trouble to go back to that section, Table 10-3 shows some of the most useful expressions.

Table 10-3: Useful Regular Expressions

Regular Expression	Description
[0-9]*	An unsigned integer number (such as **1234**) or a blank string
[0-9]+	An unsigned integer number (such as **1234**)
[+-]?[0-9]+	An integer number preceded by an optional + or − sign (such as **−1234**)
[0-9a-fA-F]*	A hexadecimal number (such as **F200a**), or a blank string
[0-9a-fA-F]{8}	An 8-digit hexadecimal number (such as **F200DD88**)
[0-9]{3}-[0-9]{3}-[0-9]{4}	A telephone number with area code (such as **111-333-5555**)
([0-9]{3}-)?[0-9]{3}-[0-9]{4}	A telephone number with an optional area code (such as **111-333-5555** or **333-5555**)
[0-9]{5}	A 5-digit U.S. Postal Code, (such as **12345**)
[0-9]{5}(-[0-9]{4})?	A 5-digit U.S. Postal Code with the optional +4 digits (such as **12345-1234**)

It isn't too complicated to create regular expressions for many reoccurring formats. You could use these expressions in code as shown in Listing 10-24.

Listing 10-24: **Using Regular Expressions to Validate String Formats**

```
bool IsValidPhoneNumber(String theString)
{
  String telephoneNumberWithAreaCode =
       @"[0-9]{3}-[0-9]{3}-[0-9]{4}";

  Regex regExp = new Regex(telephoneNumberWithAreaCode);
  MatchCollection matches = regExp.Matches(theString);
  if (matches.Count == 0) return false;
  return matches [0].ToString().Equals(theString);
}
```

The code not only checks to see if the entered string matches the regular expression, it also checks to make sure the *whole* string is a match. If not, it would let the string contain arbitrary characters after the ones satisfying the regular expression.

Using built-in methods

Some data formats are difficult to express with regular expressions. Often the difficulty stems from the number of variants a valid string can have. Floating-point numbers are a good example, because they can be written in all sorts of ways. For example, these are all valid numbers:

0.4

.2

+1

+.2

Rather than using some really complicated regular expression to validate floating-point numbers, it's much easier to try to convert the string to a number and see what happens. The code shown in Listing 10-25 will work just fine.

Listing 10-25: Verifying that a String Represents a Valid Floating-Point Number

```
private bool IsValidFloatingPointNumber(String theString)
{
  try
  {

    double d = Double.Parse(theString);
  }
  catch (Exception)
  {
    return false;
  }
  return true;
}
```

You can use the same approach to check for valid integers, as shown in Listing 10-26.

Listing 10-26: Verifying that a String Represents a Valid Integer

```
private bool IsValidInteger(String theString)
{
  try
  {

    int i = Int32.Parse(theString);
  }
  catch (Exception)
  {
    return false;
  }
  return true;
}
```

Other types of strings that are fairly complex to validate with regular expressions are URIs, which are very similar to URLs. URIs are more general than URLs. While the latter indicate a physical location of a file, such as `http://myhost/myfile.html`, the former can also identify resources that don't have a file location. Think about an HTML document returned by an ASP page—you could say the document's URI is `http://myhost/myDocument.asp`. The ASP script is not the location of the HTML file. The script is just a way to identify the file. Since URIs are more flexible than URLs, they tend to be used more often. The code in Listing 10-27 could be used to validate a URI.

Listing 10-27: **Verifying that a String Represents a Valid URI**

```
private bool IsValidUri(String theString)
{
  try
  {
    Uri uri = new Uri(theString);
  }
  catch (Exception)
  {
    return false;
  }
  return true;
}
```

The constructor for class `Uri` takes a URI and throws an exception if the URI is malformed. You can also use class `Uri` to parse a string into the protocol, host name, and path, if you want. The code in Listing 10-28 displays the protocol and host name.

Listing 10-28: **Extracting the Protocol and Host Names from a URI**

```
Uri uri = new Uri(myString);
String scheme = uri.Scheme;
String host = uri.Host;
MessageBox.Show("Scheme: " + scheme + " Host: " + host);
```

If neither regular expressions nor built-in methods solve your validation problems, you have two basic choices: write the validation code yourself or buy third-party data-entry components that provide what you need. Personally, I opt for the latter choice nine times out of ten. There is a growing market for third-party components that handle every conceivable data-entry case. Most components are sold in suites at very reasonable prices, and will save you long, pointless hours of both development and debugging. Get out your component vendor catalog and check what's out there. A vendor I like in particular is Developer Express, at `www.devexpress.com`.

The validation events

If you look at the properties for a TextBox, you'll notice one called *CausesValidation*. What does this property do? It controls whether you want to enable or disable the generation of the two validation events: Validating and Validated. The former occurs when the TextBox loses focus. The latter occurs shortly afterwards, assuming Validating didn't throw an exception.

The purpose of the Validating event is to let you check the data entered into the TextBox. If the data is not acceptable, you can do one of two things. The recommended option is to set the Cancel property of the CancelEventArgs parameter to true, but you can also just throw an exception as shown in Listing 10-29.

Listing 10-29: **Validating Data in the Validating Event Handler**

```
void textBox_Validating(object sender,
                        System.ComponentModel.CancelEventArgs e)
{
  // see if the value is an integer
  if (IsValidInteger( (sender as TextBox).Text) ) return;

  // not an integer: display an error message
  MessageBox.Show("The text must be a valid number.");

  e.Cancel = true;          // either set the Cancel property

  // throw new Exception(); // or throw an exception
}
```

Setting the Cancel property or throwing an exception both tell the .NET Framework that the value entered is not valid, so the TextBox control is prevented from losing the focus.

If you don't set the Cancel property, it defaults to false. If the Validating handler accepts the data (by not setting Cancel and not throwing an exception), the .NET Framework will shortly afterwards fire a Validated event. This event is the place where you take the data entered and use it. For example, you could save it in a database or look up the values of other UI controls that contain related information. Listing 10-30 shows a trivial Validated handler.

Listing 10-30: **A Simple Validated Event Handler**

```
private void textBoxValidated_Validated(object sender,
                                        System.EventArgs e)
{
  MessageBox.Show("You entered the text: " +
                  (sender as TextBox).Text);
}
```

For some reason, Microsoft completely left formatted data-entry components out of the .NET Framework. It's particularly interesting if you consider that in the early Beta 1 code, there were traces of it. For example, I came across vestiges of a NumericFormat class, now extinct. A preBeta version of TextBox also had a Format property that you could presumably assign a mask string to. Unfortunately, that property is also gone.

Maybe Microsoft deliberately left formatted input controls out to give the third-party component vendors more room. Whatever the reasons were, I personally would have preferred getting at least minimal input formatting capability, or hooks that let you easily add in custom formatters.

Summary

In this chapter, I've shown how to create a typical user control. One of the key features of user controls is their ability to be shown graphically in the VS .NET Forms Designer, allowing you to add components to them as you would with Windows Forms.

I also touched briefly on data validation, showing a few simple ways to check entered data. Because the stock TextBox component is very weak in the data-validation department, my advice is to either develop your own specialized validation components, or to purchase one of the excellent third-party products, available at reasonable prices.

✦   ✦   ✦

Database Front Ends

I've never had major knee surgery on any other part of my body.

— Winston Bennett, college basketball player

My advice to Winston is: *Don't give up your day job!* On the other hand, he's lucky. I hear that having knee surgery on your lower back can cause all kinds of problems.

It is increasingly common to find applications that deal with databases. In this chapter I'll discuss how to create so-called *fat client* front ends. They're called *fat* because they require a number of database support files to be resident on the user's machine, even though the database service may be running somewhere else. Fat clients represent the *client* part of traditional client-server architectures.

When you expect the database service to be running on a different machine from the end user's, a *thin client* approach is often a much better choice. Thin clients are a lot easier to deploy, load quicker, and in some ways are more flexible than fat clients. To develop thin client front ends, you may want to consider using a Web service on the middle tier or back end that gets the data from the database and makes the record sets available to the front end using XML packets. For information on how to create this type of Web service, check out Chapter 19, which is entirely dedicated to database Web services.

In this chapter, I'll focus mostly on ways to display data in Windows Forms. VS .NET has a number of really spectacular wizards that drastically reduce the amount of hand-coding needed to set up database front ends. I won't spend too much time describing the underlying ADO.NET components that move data in and out of the database. For more detailed information regarding the database components and architecture, see Chapter 18, titled "The ADO.NET Architecture."

This chapter covers four major types of database user interfaces based on Windows Forms:

✦ Navigator-based forms

✦ Grid-based forms

✦ Master-detail forms

✦ Database report forms

Each type of user interface has its own structure and idiosyncrasies. The good news is that VS .NET has wizards for each type, reducing the amount of hand-coding to a minimum. There is no bad news. Before jumping into the details for each type of user interface, I need to set up a database connection that I'll use in each of the later examples.

Setting Up a Database Connection

One of the first things you'll need in all database projects is a *Data Connection,* which specifies which server and database to access, and which user name and password to use to log into the database. VS .NET has a wizard that walks you through the steps needed to set up a Data Connection. Once a connection is created, it can be used in any project.

To start the wizard, right-click the Data Connections component in the Server Explorer window and select Add Connection from the context menu, as shown in Figure 11-1.

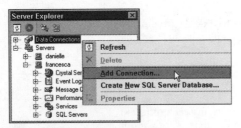

Figure 11-1: The Server Explorer tool for adding data connections to the VS .NET environment

When the wizard finishes, the connection will appear in the Server Explorer under the Data Connections folder. Figure 11-2 shows a newly create data connection on a computer named *Francesca* and the SQL Server Pubs database.

Figure 11-2: A Data Connection component with a default name

By default, the name of the connection component is set to *computername.database.* To change the name, just right-click on the component and select Rename from the context menu. Or just click in the name field and edit it in-place. Once you have a Data Connection, you can use it in a VS .NET project.

Let's take a look at the details of the Add Connection wizard. When the wizard starts up, it prompts you for database connection information. I entered the data shown in Figure 11-3.

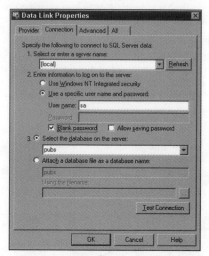

Figure 11-3: The Data Link Properties window shown by the Add Data Connection wizard

After entering the requested information, you can check immediately if the information entered is valid or not. Just click the Test Connection button. If everything is okay, you'll get a *"Test connection succeeded"* message; otherwise, you'll get an error message describing the problem encountered.

A few words are in order for the fields in the Data Link Properties window: For the *server name,* you can choose the name of a specific computer from the drop-down list, leave the field blank, or use *(local).* If you leave the server name blank, the Data Connection component will prompt at runtime for the name of the server. Different database vendors have their own Login window. Figure 11-4 shows the Login window displayed by SQL Server.

Figure 11-4: The Login window displayed at runtime by SQL Server if you don't supply all the login information necessary in the Data Link Properties window

If you enter *(local)* for the server name in the Data Link Properties window, the Data Connection component will connect to the database service running on the same computer as the Data Connection component. If you develop code on one computer and access data from a remote database server, you may want to use (local) for the server name and do all the development on a test machine. Obviously, you'll need to have a database service installed on your test machine. When you're done coding and testing, you can change the server name and switch over to the production database server.

The Password fields (shown previously in Figure 11-3) deserve some attention. If the *User name* specified is set up by the database administrator with a blank password, which is extremely unusual for production environments but quite common for development environments, check the *Blank password* box and leave the *Allow saving password* check box unchecked. In Figure 11-3, I used the user name *sa*, which is a default name configured with a blank password when you initially install SQL Server.

If you configure the Data Link Properties with a user name that requires a password, the Data Connection component will automatically prompt for the password at runtime, unless you check the *Allow saving password* box (and provide a valid password). With the check box checked, the password will be saved in the source code with the connection string, looking something like Listing 11-1.

Listing 11-1: How the Password Is Embedded in the Connection String When You Check the Allow Saving Password Check Box in the Datalink Properties Window

```
sqlConnection1.ConnectionString = "data source=(local); initial
catalog=Pubs; password=sa; persist security info=true; user id=sa;";
```

If the user name you select is configured for a blank password, be sure to leave the Password field blank and check the *Blank password* check box. If you don't check the check box, at runtime the Data Connection component will see you didn't supply a password and prompt the user for one with a Login dialog box like the one shown previously in Figure 11-4.

Once a Data Connection is created, it is added to the Server Explorer. If you select the Data Connection in the Server Explorer, the Properties window will show you how it is configured, as shown in Figure 11-5.

Figure 11-5: The properties of the newly created Data Connection component

To disconnect a Data Connection from the database, right-click on it in the Server Explorer and select Close Connection from the pop-up menu, as shown in Figure 11-6.

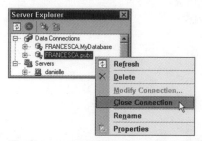

Figure 11-6: Closing the connection of a Data Connection component

The prerelease version of VS .NET that I used didn't allow the properties of a Data Connection to be changed, even after closing the connection, but I expect this problem to have been resolved in the release software. To reopen the connection for a Data Connection, right-click on it and choose Refresh on the pop-up menu. The state of a Data Connection is indicated by a small green or red arrow next to its icon in the Server Explorer.

Navigator-Based Forms

Now that a Database Connection is available, I can move on with the discussion on navigator-based forms. With the expression *navigator-based form,* I refer to forms that display fields for one record at a time. A *navigator* is a control or set of controls that appear on the form to let users select the current record, or move from record to record. There are two popular formats for navigator controls:

✦ The VCR-button format, with buttons to allow moving to the first, next, previous, or last record

✦ The list or combo box format, in which the list or records is displayed allowing the user to randomly select any record

In this section, I'll show you how to use the VS .NET Data Form Wizard to rapidly create a navigator-based form with default VCR-like navigator buttons. I'll call the program FrontEnd_DBNavigatorForm. To create the application, I used the VS .NET Windows Application Project Wizard, which sets up a new project containing a blank form with the default name *Form1*.

Then I added a DataForm using the Data Form Wizard. To run the wizard, right-click on the project and select Add New Item from the pop-up menu. In the Add New Item dialog box, select the Data Form Wizard template, as shown in Figure 11-7.

I used the name *MyNavigatorForm* for the new form and clicked the Open button. Next, the wizard started and prompted me for the name of the DataSet component to create for the form, as shown in Figure 11-8.

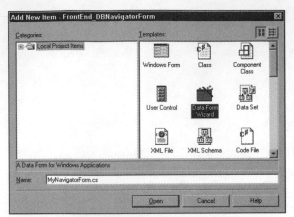

Figure 11-7: The Data Form Wizard, for rapidly configuring database front ends

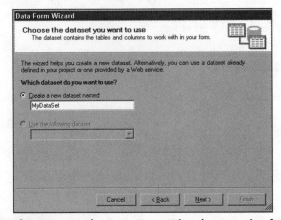

Figure 11-8: The Data Form Wizard, prompting for the name of a new DataSet component to create

If you had previously added one or more DataSets to the project, the radio button labeled *Use the following dataset* would be enabled and you could select an existing Dataset. For my example, I'll create a new Dataset called *MyDataSet* and then click the Next button. The next screen allows me to choose the database connection to use with the form, as shown in Figure 11-9.

I'll just use the default connection and click the Next button. The next screen lets you specify which tables the data will be coming from. I'll just choose the Authors table, as shown in Figure 11-10.

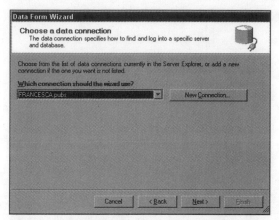

Figure 11-9: The Data Form Wizard screen that enables you to specify the database connection to use with the form

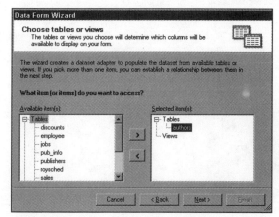

Figure 11-10: Choosing the tables to access on the form

In a later section, I'll show how to use multiple tables on the same form and set up a master-detail relationship between tables. Clicking the Next button in the Wizard dialog box brings up a screen on which you choose the names of the fields you want to show on the form, as shown in Figure 11-11.

I'll leave all the fields checked. The next screen is where you tell the wizard whether you want a grid-style or navigator-style form to be generated. I'll click the Single-record button to select a navigator-style, and I'll leave all the boxes checked in the lower section, as shown in Figure 11-12.

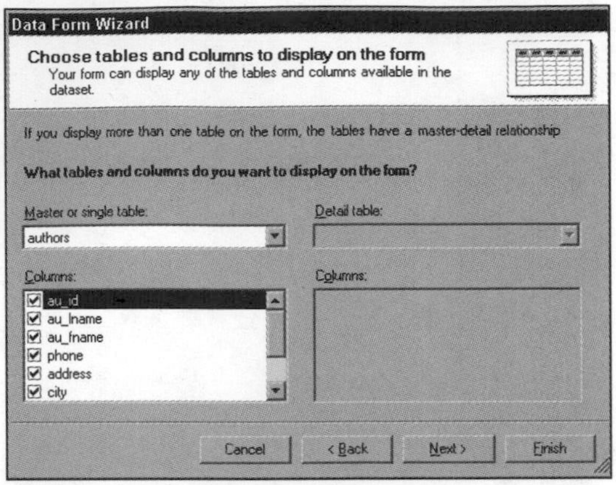

Figure 11-11: The screen that enables you to select the database fields to display on the form

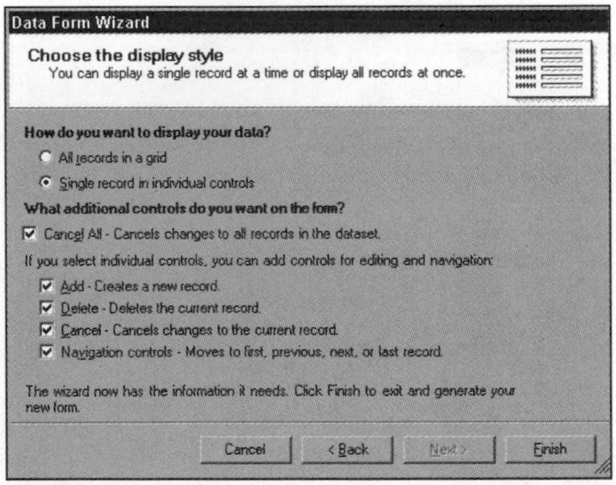

Figure 11-12: The wizard screen on which you indicate the style of the form to generate

The wizard gives you the option of adding or removing a number of buttons that control data entry and navigation. The bottom check box controls whether a set of VCR-style navigation buttons are added or not. Clicking the Finish button allows the wizard to create the new Data Form, as shown in Figure 11-13.

Not bad for a few minutes of work. This is the kind of productivity developers not only enjoy in VS .NET, but should also expect. If you find yourself spending a lot of time creating some type of item, such as a derived component, an XSL style sheet, an HTML file — whatever — you might want to check to see if there is a wizard somewhere to do a lot of the grunt work for you. You'll be surprised by the number of wizards buried here and there in VS .NET.

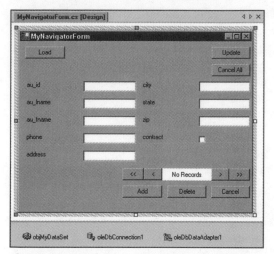

Figure 11-13: The new Data Form created by the wizard

Getting back to the Data Form Wizard, you can see from the previous figure that it created a number of database components in the bottom part of the screen. The component named oleDbConnection1 handles the database connection with SQL Server. There are two types of connection components currently supported by the ADO.NET, the framework that deals with database connectivity: SqlConnection and OleDbConnection. The former type is exclusively for Microsoft SQL Server 7 and later databases. The latter handles everything else, including Oracle, Sybase SQL Server, Access, and earlier versions of Microsoft SQL Server. When using Microsoft SQL Server 7 and later, SqlConnection has significantly better performance that the equivalent OleDb component.

The prerelease version of VS .NET I used to write this book generated the OleDb version of the components, even though the database I'm using is SQL Server 2000. I would expect the released code to use the more efficient Sql version of the components with SQL Server 2000. The difference between the two types of components is described in more detail in Chapter 18, titled "The ADO.NET Architecture."

Before trying out the newly generated Data Form, I need to eliminate the Form1 component created by the Windows Application Project Wizard and replace it with the new Data Form. That job is easy: I just need to cut the Main() method in Form1, paste it into MyNavigatorForm, replace the reference to Form1 with MyNavigator, and then delete Form1 from the project. The new Main() method in MyNavigatorForm will look like Listing 11-2.

Listing 11-2: The Edited Main() Method Added to MyNavigatorForm

```
[STAThread]
static void Main()
{
    Application.Run(new MyNavigatorForm());
}
```

Now the project can be compiled and run. The result is the form shown in Figure 11-14.

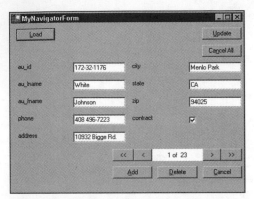

Figure 11-14: The new Data Form created with the wizard

As described earlier, you can tell the wizard which of the various buttons you want on the form. The Load button causes the form to query the Authors table and get a *navigatable* result set. Once a result set is available, you can change the current record with the navigator buttons at the bottom of the form The Add and Delete buttons enable you to insert and remove records. To change an existing record, select it and use the UI controls to change its fields. The Cancel button rolls back any edits you made to the current record which haven't been posted to the database yet. The Cancel All button rolls back all changes made to the result set that haven't been posted yet. The Update button takes all the changes you've made and posts them to the database. Let's take a look at some of the code our good wizard generated for us. I'll start with the code that loads the record set.

Loading records

The Data Form Wizard loads records from the database in the `Click` event handler of the Load button. If you want your form to load records immediately, move this code in the form's constructor. The code to load records looks like Listing 11-3.

Listing 11-3: The Click Handler for the Load Button

```
private void btnLoad_Click(object sender, System.EventArgs e)
{
  try
  {
    this.LoadDataSet();
  }
  catch (System.Exception eLoad)
  {
    System.Windows.Forms.MessageBox.Show(eLoad.Message);
  }
  this.objMyDataSet_PositionChanged();
}
```

The interesting part is the method LoadDataSet(), whose code looks like Listing 11-4.

Listing 11-4: The Code that Loads the Record Set

```
public void LoadDataSet()
{
  FrontEnd_DBNavigatorForm.MyDataSet objDataSetTemp;
  objDataSetTemp = new FrontEnd_DBNavigatorForm.MyDataSet();
  try
  {
    // Execute the SelectCommand on the DatasetCommmand and fill the
dataset
    this.FillDataSet(objDataSetTemp);
  }
  catch (System.Exception eFillDataSet)
  {
    // Add exception handling code here.
    throw eFillDataSet;
  }
  try
  {
    // Merge the records that were just pulled from the
    // data store into the main dataset
    objMyDataSet.Merge(objDataSetTemp);
  }
  catch (System.Exception eLoadMerge)
  {
    // Add exception handling code here
    throw eLoadMerge;
  }
}
```

As you can see, the record set is loaded into a DataSet component of type MyDataSet, which was created with the Data Form wizard. Listing 11-5 shows the code for the component's FillData() method.

Listing 11-5: The Code that Makes MyDataSet Load a Record Set into Its Cache

```
public void FillDataSet(FrontEnd_DBNavigatorForm.MyDataSet dataSet)
{

  this.oleDbConnection1.Open();

  dataSet.EnforceConstraints = false;
```

Continued

Listing 11-5 *(continued)*

```
  try
  {

    this.oleDbDataAdapter1.Fill(dataSet);
  }
  catch (System.Exception fillException)
  {
    throw fillException;
  }
  finally
  {
    dataSet.EnforceConstraints = true;

    this.oleDbConnection1.Close();
  }
}
```

The `DataSet` component manages an in-memory cache of a record set, but has no idea about how to get this record set. It calls a database adapter component to get the set, and then uses the set to populate the cache. So `DataSet`s manage in-memory record sets and `DataAdapter`s take care of moving data from the database to the `DataSet` and vice versa.

Notice how the `DataSet.EnforceConstraints` property is temporarily set to `false` while loading data. This is necessary, because during the course of loading the cache, there may be moments (before all data is loaded) during which some database constraints are violated. Once all the data is available, constraint checking can be turned back on.

The `DataAdapter` is responsible for getting the record set to populate the `DataSet`. It's also responsible for the SQL code to perform database edits, updates, and deletes. These operations are closely related to SQL statements, and in fact, a `DataAdapter` has four properties holding SQL statements. The component `oleDbDataAdapter1` generated in my code by the Data Form Wizard has the SQL statements listed in Table 11-1.

Table 11-1: SQL Statements Used by the DataAdapter Component Generated by the Data Form Wizard

Property Name	Property Value
InsertCommand	INSERT INTO dbo.authors(au_id, au_lname, au_fname, phone, address, city, state, zip, contract) VALUES (?, ?, ?, ?, ?, ?, ?, ?, ?); SELECT au_id, au_lname, au_fname, phone, address, city, state, zip, contract FROM dbo.authors WHERE (au_id = ?)

Property Name	Property Value
UpdateCommand	UPDATE dbo.authors SET au_id = ?, au_lname = ?, au_fname = ?, phone = ?, address = ?, city = ?, state = ?, zip = ?, contract = ? WHERE (au_id = ?) AND (address = ? OR ? IS NULL AND address IS NULL) AND (au_fname = ?) AND (au_lname = ?) AND (city = ? OR ? IS NULL AND city IS NULL) AND (contract = ?) AND (phone = ?) AND (state = ? OR ? IS NULL AND state IS NULL) AND (zip = ? OR ? IS NULL AND zip IS NULL); SELECT au_id, au_lname, au_fname, phone, address, city, state, zip, contract FROM dbo.authors WHERE (au_id = ?)
DeleteCommand	DELETE FROM dbo.authors WHERE (au_id = ?) AND (address = ? OR ? IS NULL AND address IS NULL) AND (au_fname = ?) AND (au_lname = ?) AND (city = ? OR ? IS NULL AND city IS NULL) AND (contract = ?) AND (phone = ?) AND (state = ? OR ? IS NULL AND state IS NULL) AND (zip = ? OR ? IS NULL AND zip IS NULL)
SelectCommand	SELECT au_id, au_lname, au_fname, phone, address, city, state, zip, contract FROM dbo.authors

You can tweak the SQL statements by hand, if you need to, by editing the SQL properties of the DataAdapter in the Properties window. A better way is to use the Data Adapter Configuration Wizard, available by right-clicking on the DataAdapter and choosing Generate Data Adapter from the pop-up menu. Later, I'll show how to use this wizard.

Navigating the record set

Let's take a peek at the code that performs the record set navigation. Listing 11-6 shows the code for the First, Last, Next, and Previous record buttons.

Listing 11-6: **The Wizard-Generated Code for Record Set Navigation**

```
private void mfp_btnNavNext_Click(object sender, System.EventArgs e)
{
  this.BindingContext[objMyDataSet,"authors"].Position =
    (this.BindingContext[objMyDataSet,"authors"].Position + 1);
  this.objMyDataSet_PositionChanged();
}

private void mfp_btnNavPrev_Click(object sender, System.EventArgs e)
{
  this.BindingContext[objMyDataSet,"authors"].Position =
    (this.BindingContext[objMyDataSet,"authors"].Position - 1);
```

Continued

Listing 11-6 *(continued)*

```
    this.objMyDataSet_PositionChanged();
}

private void mfp_btnNavLast_Click(object sender, System.EventArgs e)
{
  this.BindingContext[objMyDataSet,"authors"].Position =
    (this.objMyDataSet.Tables["authors"].Rows.Count - 1);
  this.objMyDataSet_PositionChanged();
}

private void mfp_btnNavFirst_Click(object sender,
                                      System.EventArgs e)
{
  this.BindingContext[objMyDataSet,"authors"].Position = 0;
  this.objMyDataSet_PositionChanged();
}

private void objMyDataSet_PositionChanged()
{
  this.mfp_lblNavLocation.Text =
 ((((this.BindingContext[objMyDataSet,"authors"].
     Position +1)).ToString() +  " of  ") +
     this.BindingContext[objMyDataSet,"authors"].Count.ToString());
}
```

The code is almost self-explanatory. The BindingContext component is called to retrieve the first, last, next, and previous records, after which a `PositionChanged` event is fired, to synchronize any other components that need updating when the current record changes. In this case, the only component that is updated in the `PositionChanged` handler is the label displaying the number of the current record.

Inserting a new record

At a minimum, inserting a new record requires a call to `BindingContext.AddNew()` method. Before doing so, call `EndCurrentEdit()` to post any edits in progress. The wizard-generated code looks like Listing 11-7.

Listing 11-7: The Wizard-Generated Code for Inserting a New Record

```
private void mfp_btnAdd_Click(object sender, System.EventArgs e)
{
  try
  {
    this.BindingContext[objMyDataSet,"authors"].EndCurrentEdit();
    this.BindingContext[objMyDataSet,"authors"].AddNew();
```

```
   }
   catch (System.Exception eEndEdit)
   {
      System.Windows.Forms.MessageBox.Show(eEndEdit.Message);
   }
   this.objMyDataSet_PositionChanged();
}
```

After adding a new record, a DataSet.PositionChanged event is fired to allow the other controls on the form to refresh themselves. The newly added record will only exist in MyDataSet, so the database won't know about your new records until you post your changes to MyDataSet to the database, as described later, in the section titled "Posting changes to the database."

Deleting records

To delete the current record, find its location in the result set, and then call the RemoveAt() method. The code shown in Listing 11-8 was generated by the Data Form wizard.

> **Listing 11-8: The Wizard-Generated Code for Deleting the Current Record**
>
> ```
> private void mfp_btnDelete_Click(object sender, System.EventArgs e)
> {
>    if ((this.BindingContext[objMyDataSet,"authors"].Count > 0))
>    {
>       this.BindingContext[objMyDataSet,"authors"].RemoveAt(
>          this.BindingContext[objMyDataSet,"authors"].Position);
>       this.objMyDataSet_PositionChanged();
>    }
> }
> ```

Again, the record is only removed from the local MyDataSet recordset cache. The database isn't affected until you post your changes to the database using the code in the next section.

Posting changes to the database

To update fields in the current record, just use the user interface controls. Since they are bound to database fields, they will automatically update the current record when you make changes to them. For example, typing text in a TextBox or clicking a CheckBox will both change the current if those controls are data-bound.

Keep in mind that the changes are only made to the result set maintained by the DataSet bound to the controls. If you closed the application at this point, your changes would be lost, because they weren't posted to the database. To post the changes, you need to call the code that the good wizard put in the Click handler for the Update button, which looks like Listing 11-9.

Listing 11-9: **Posting Changes to the Database**

```
private void btnUpdate_Click(object sender, System.EventArgs e)
{
  try
  {
    this.UpdateDataSet();
  }
  catch (System.Exception eUpdate)
  {
    System.Windows.Forms.MessageBox.Show(eUpdate.Message);
  }
  this.objMyDataSet_PositionChanged();
}
```

Canceling edits to the current record

When you begin to change the current record, the DataSet component saves the old values. If the user changes his mind, he can roll the record back to the original values by calling the BindingContext's CancelCurrentEdit() method, as shown in Listing 11-10.

Listing 11-10: **The Wizard-Generated Code for Canceling Edits to the Current Record**

```
private void mfp_btnCancel_Click(object sender, System.EventArgs e)
{
  this.BindingContext[objMyDataSet,"authors"].CancelCurrentEdit();
  this.objMyDataSet_PositionChanged();
}
```

Canceling all edits

You can also back out of all the changes made to a DataSet, assuming these changes haven't been posted to the database yet. Listing 11-11 shows how.

Listing 11-11: **The Wizard-Generated Code for Canceling Edits Made to All Records**

```
private void btnCancelAll_Click(object sender, System.EventArgs e)
{
  this.objMyDataSet.RejectChanges();
}
```

I'll be discussing the process of posting and rejecting changes made to a `DataSet` in subsequent sections in this chapter, and in Chapter 18, titled "The ADO.NET Architecture."

Data Binding in Windows Forms

The way that user interface controls are bound to data sources is fairly straightforward in the .NET Framework. If you look back at the previous five or six listings, you'll notice the code is almost self-explanatory.

The presence of that `BindingContext` property suggests there is more at work than meets the eye. The property is inherited from `Control`. It returns the *BindingManager* component responsible for synchronizing all the UI components connected to the same DataSet. The BindingManager returns a component called a *CurrencyManager* that manages a given data source. For each data source used in a form, there is one CurrencyManager. In my example, there is only one data source (`MyDataSet`), but you could have more than one. Figure 11-15 shows the relationship between the various components.

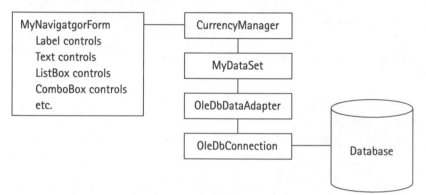

Figure 11-15: The components used in Windows Forms Data Binding

The Data Binding architecture of the .NET Framework is extremely powerful. Any property of any component derived from Control can be bound to a data source. In object-oriented and component-based systems prior to the .NET Framework, such as MFC and Delphi, there used to be separate UI controls for normal and data-bound controls. In the .NET Framework, all controls have the ability to be data-bound. For example, you could tie any of these properties to a database field:

✦ The color of a Text control

✦ The font of a Label control

✦ The image shown by a PictureBox

Keep in mind that when I say *database* field, I really mean any *data source*. The data source doesn't necessarily need to be a database. The data might be in an Array, or in a file. As long as there is a way to get data in and out of a DataSet (using a DataAdapter), you're in business.

Binding properties to a data source

Let's take a quick look at how you might bind an arbitrary property to a data source. To save time, I'll bind a property to an existing database field. — I'll bind the `Visible` property of the Zip Code edit box to the Contract field of the Authors table. The value of the Contract field will then control whether the Zip Code edit box is visible or not.

Using VS .NET, it's pretty easy to bind properties to data sources. Select the Zip Code edit box in the Forms Designer. In the Properties window, scroll to the very top property, which is designed by (DataBindings). Expand the list of DataBindings by clicking the small + sign. Select the (Advanced) property, as shown in Figure 11-16.

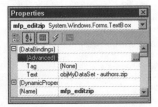

Figure 11-16: Binding an arbitrary property of a control to a data source

Click the ellipsis button to display the full list of bindable properties. Scroll down to the Visible property, as shown in Figure 11-17.

Figure 11-17: The Visible property, before binding it to a data source

Open the drop-down list for the Visible property. You'll see a list of data sources that are available through the form's BindingContext. In my case, the only data source is the component MyDataSet, which is populated with records from the authors table, as shown in Figure 11-18.

Figure 11-18: The list of data sources available for data binding

Scroll down in the list to the Contract field and select it. The drop-down list will close and show the property's new data source, as shown in Figure 11-19.

Figure 11-19: The Visible property, after binding it to a data source

That's really all there is to it. As with so many other tasks in VS .NET, you don't have to write any code. Now when you run `FrontEnd_DBNavigatorForm`, the Zip Code edit control will disappear for records whose Contract field is false and reappear for records whose Contract field is true. Not too complicated.

Let's take a look at the components and infrastructure involved in binding a property to a data source. You already know the process is based on a CurrencyManager. There are two ways to bind a component to a data source: Simple Binding, which ties an object to a single field of a single row, and Complex Binding, which ties an object to multiple fields and multiple rows. I'll discuss Complex Binding a bit more in later sections of this chapter, and also in Chapter 18, titled "The ADO.NET Architecture."

Simple data binding

Most controls can only handle one value at a time. Examples of such controls are `Labels`, `TextBoxes`, `PictureBoxes`, `RadioButtons`, and `CheckBoxes`. These types of controls use *Simple Binding*. To set up a control with Simple Binding, all you need to do is call the control's `DataBindings.Add()` method, specifying a data source. The code in Listing 11-12 shows how to bind the property `Label.Text` to the `au_lname` field of the `Authors` table:

Listing 11-12: Binding a Label to a Database Field

```
Label myLabel = new Label();
Binding binding = new Binding("Text", objMyDataSet,
"authors.au_lname");
myLabel.DataBindings.Add(binding);
```

The procedure is the same for other types of controls. For example, to bind the `CheckBox.Checked` property to the `Contract` field of the `Authors` table, you would use the code shown in Listing 11-13.

Listing 11-13: Binding a CheckBox to a Database Field

```
CheckBox myCheckBox = new CheckBox();
Binding binding = new Binding("Checked", objMyDataSet,
                              "authors.contract");
myCheckBox.DataBindings.Add(binding);
```

You get the idea. Using the same technique, you can bind any property of a control to any database field, assuming the property type and field type are compatible. A couple of lines of code and the entire plumbing infrastructure is set up for you.

VS .NET tips

There are a lot of features in VS .NET, but the program keeps them discretely tucked away, to avoid overwhelming inexperienced users with them. In the following sections, I'll describe a few features that can save you time when working with database front-end forms.

Dragging tables from the Server Explorer

If you have a form that wasn't generated with the Data Form Wizard, there are various ways to "data-enable" it. Basically, you need to add the following components to the form:

✦ DataConnection

✦ DataAdapter

✦ DataSet

One way to add a DataConnection and DataAdapter is with drag-and-drop. Open the Server Explorer and select the fields of the tables you will use on the form, as shown in Figure 11-20.

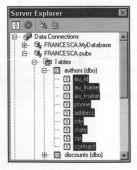

Figure 11-20: Selecting table fields to drag and drop onto a form

When you drag the fields to a form, VS .NET adds a DataConnection component to the form and then adds a DataAdapter configured with the fields you selected. What if you don't know which tables to use? VS .NET can show you the contents of any database table or other data source listed in the Server Explorer. Just right-click on the desired table and select *Retrieve Data from Table* on the pop-up menu, as shown in Figure 11-21.

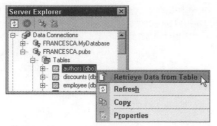

Figure 11-21: Fetching the contents of a database table using the Server Explorer

A new tab will be added to the Code window, showing you a grid with the contents of the table, as shown in Figure 11-22.

Figure 11-22: Using VS .NET to view the contents of a database table

You can use the same technique to select a Stored Procedure from the Server Explorer and open a window showing the procedure's result set.

If you are uncertain what type of data is stored in each field, you can use the Server Explorer window again to find out. Just select a database field, and its properties will be shown in the Properties window. Figure 11-23 shows the properties of the au_lname field of the authors table.

Figure 11-23: Showing the attributes of a database field in the Properties window

You can't change the properties shown for a field, because they ultimately depend on the database schema. If you need to change a column type, you would have to do so using the database-management tools for your database, such as SQL Server Enterprise Manager.

Configuring SQL statements with a wizard

Once you have a DataConnection and DataAdapter on a form, you still need to hook a DataSet up to the DataAdapter. You also may need to change the configuration of the

DataAdapter, if you changed your mind about something after dragging the component from the Server Explorer. The easy way to reconfigure the DataAdapter is with (what else?) a wizard. Right-click on the DataAdapter and choose Configure Data Adapter from the pop-up menu, as shown in Figure 11-24.

Figure 11-24: Invoking the Data Adapter wizard in VS .NET

The wizard allows you to change the DataConnection used with the Adapter. You won't be changing the DataConnection very often, but you will want to tweak the SQL expressions or stored procedures used by the DataAdapter. Figure 11-25 shows the important pages of the wizard that help build SQL expressions.

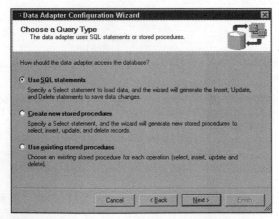

Figure 11-25: The wizard page on which you can choose the type of SQL item to configure

Clicking the Next button shows the Select statement currently set up for the DataAdapter, as shown in Figure 11-26.

You can type in a new expression, or use the Query Builder Wizard. I'll talk about the Query Builder in the next section.

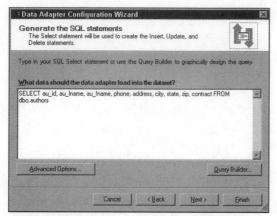

Figure 11-26: The SQL Select statement used
by the DataAdapter

Click the Finish button and the wizard will generate Insert, Update, and Delete expressions
based on the Select statement you entered, and using schema information regarding the
tables referenced. Listing 11-14 shows all the statements generated by the Query Builder.

**Listing 11-14: The SQL Statements Produced by the Data Adapter
                Configuration Wizard**

```
SELECT au_id,  au_lname,  au_fname,  phone,
       address,  city,  state,  zip,  contract
FROM authors


INSERT INTO authors( au_id,  au_lname,  au_fname,  phone,
                     address,  city,  state,  zip,  contract )
VALUES( ?,  ?,  ?,  ?,  ?,  ?,  ?,  ?,  ? ) ;


UPDATE authors
SET au_id = ?,  au_lname = ?,  au_fname = ?,  phone = ?,
    address = ?,  city = ?,  state = ?,  zip = ?,  contract = ?
WHERE (au_id = ?) ;


DELETE FROM authors WHERE (au_id = ?)
```

The wizard then generates a small report showing the results of its activities, as shown in
Figure 11-27.

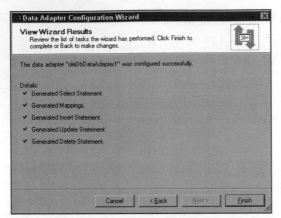

Figure 11-27: The Results page of the wizard

Using the Query Builder

You don't always have to get your hands dirty doing SQL programming. SQL Query Builders have been available for some time in Microsoft products such as Access and SQL Server. These Builders enable you to specify the rows to fetch using drag-and-drop actions and some easy-to-understand conditions. Most developers are unaware of the sheer power a Query Builder puts in their hands. Since most developers are not experts in SQL, having a tool like the Query Builder can enable them to create expert SQL code with little effort.

Here's a simple example showing how to use the Query Builder. Let's say you want a list of all the authors, along with all their publications. But you only want the authors whose last names start with letters between *B* and *D* or between *S* and *V.* You also want to sort the list by last name, first name, and title.

Using the *pubs* database, you'll need to include three tables in the query: the `authors`, `titleauthor`, and `sales` tables. You can add tables into the Query Builder and build most `Select` statements without writing a line of code. Figure 11-28 shows what a Query Builder screen looks like after adding the *titleauthor* and *title* tables to the upper pane and running the generated `Select` statement.

To add the tables, I just right-clicked in the top pane and chose Add Table from the pop-up menu. The wizard automatically joins the tables on the proper fields and generates all the necessary SQL code for the `Select` statement. I deselected all the table columns except for `authors.au_lname`, `authors.au_fname`, and `titles.title`. I added the following two constraints in the Criteria and Or columns for the au_lname row in the top grid:

```
>= 'B%' AND <= 'D%'

>= 'S%' AND <= 'V%'
```

I set the sorting criteria for the result set using the Sort Type and Sort Order columns in the top grid. To see the result of the `Select` statement, I right-clicked in the upper pane and chose Run from the pop-up menu.

If you need more power, such as `Select` statements with multiple outer joins or subqueries, you may want to use the Query Builders that come with Microsoft Access or Microsoft SQL Server.

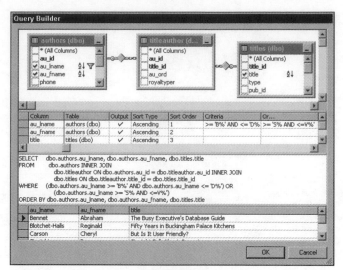

Figure 11-28: The Query Builder, showing the result set created by the Select statement created

Previewing the rows fetched by a DataAdapter

Whether you generate the SQL statements for your `DataAdapter` using a wizard or enter them by hand, you need a simple way to check the set of records that is fetched. The hard way is to open a client session with your database and cut and paste the SQL code into it. The easy way is to use the data previewer built right into VS .NET. To see the previewer, right-click the `DataAdapter` component and select the Preview Data command from the pop-up menu, as shown in Figure 11-29.

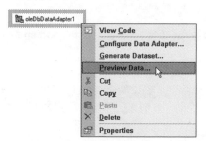

Figure 11-29: Previewing the result set returned by a DataAdapter component

The Data Adapter Preview window will appear, as shown in Figure 11-30.

As you know, `DataAdapters` are responsible for pumping data back and forth between a `DataSet` and a data source, which is typically a database. The `Select` statement or stored procedure used by a `DataAdapter` may take parameters. If it so, a description for each parameter would be shown in the Parameters list at the top of the Preview window.

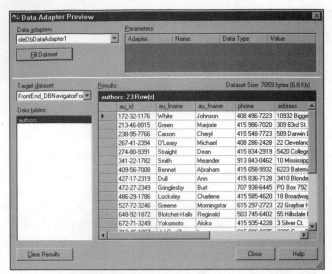

Figure 11-30: The Data Adapter Preview window, showing the result set returned by the Select statement set up in a Data Adapter

The Target dataset drop-down list lets you select which DataSet in your project the DataAdapter connects the data source to. The *Data tables* list shows the tables handled by the DataSet. A DataSet can be thought of as an in-memory mini database, containing tables, relationships, and constraints.

The complete source code

Listing 11-15 shows the source code for FrontEnd_DBNavigatorForm.

Note   I omitted some of the standard code generated by the Data Form Wizard, to concentrate on the code discussed in the text.

Listing 11-15: **The Source Code for FrontEnd_DBNavigatorForm**

```
using System;
using System.Drawing;
using System.Collections;
using System.ComponentModel;
using System.Windows.Forms;

namespace FrontEnd_DBNavigatorForm
{
   public class MyNavigatorForm : System.Windows.Forms.Form
   {
      private System.Data.OleDb.OleDbCommand oleDbSelectCommand1;
```

```csharp
private System.Data.OleDb.OleDbCommand oleDbInsertCommand1;
private System.Data.OleDb.OleDbCommand oleDbUpdateCommand1;
private System.Data.OleDb.OleDbCommand oleDbDeleteCommand1;
private FrontEnd_DBNavigatorForm.MyDataSet objMyDataSet;
private System.Data.OleDb.OleDbConnection oleDbConnection1;
private System.Data.OleDb.OleDbDataAdapter oleDbDataAdapter1;

// declare other GUI controls...

private System.ComponentModel.Container components = null;

public MyNavigatorForm()
{
      InitializeComponent();
}

protected override void Dispose( bool disposing )
{
  // standard Wizard-generated code
}

private void InitializeComponent()
{
  // standard Wizard-generated code
}

public void FillDataSet(MyDataSet dataSet)
{
  this.oleDbConnection1.Open();

  dataSet.EnforceConstraints = false;
  try
  {
    this.oleDbDataAdapter1.Fill(dataSet);
  }
  catch (System.Exception fillException)
  {
    throw fillException;
  }
  finally
  {
    dataSet.EnforceConstraints = true;
    this.oleDbConnection1.Close();
  }
}

public int UpdateDataSource(MyDataSet dataSet)
{
  this.oleDbConnection1.Open();

  System.Data.DataSet UpdatedRows;
  System.Data.DataSet InsertedRows;
```

Continued

Listing 11-15 *(continued)*

```csharp
    System.Data.DataSet DeletedRows;
    int AffectedRows = 0;

    UpdatedRows =
      dataSet.GetChanges(System.Data.DataRowState.Modified);
    InsertedRows =
      dataSet.GetChanges(System.Data.DataRowState.Added);
    DeletedRows =
      dataSet.GetChanges(System.Data.DataRowState.Deleted);
    try
    {
      if ((UpdatedRows != null))
      {
        AffectedRows = oleDbDataAdapter1.Update(UpdatedRows);
      }
      if ((InsertedRows != null))
      {
        AffectedRows = (AffectedRows +
                      oleDbDataAdapter1.Update(InsertedRows));
      }
      if ((DeletedRows != null))
      {
        AffectedRows = (AffectedRows +
                      oleDbDataAdapter1.Update(DeletedRows));
      }
    }
    catch (System.Exception updateException)
    {
      throw updateException;
    }
    finally
    {
      this.oleDbConnection1.Close();
    }

    return AffectedRows;
}

public void LoadDataSet()
{
    FrontEnd_DBNavigatorForm.MyDataSet objDataSetTemp;
    objDataSetTemp = new FrontEnd_DBNavigatorForm.MyDataSet();
    try
    {
      // Execute the SelectCommmand on the DatasetCommmand
      // and fill the dataset
      this.FillDataSet(objDataSetTemp);
    }
    catch (System.Exception eFillDataSet)
    {
      // Add exception handling code here.
```

```
      throw eFillDataSet;
    }
    try
    {
      // Merge the records that were just pulled from the
      // data store into the main dataset
      objMyDataSet.Merge(objDataSetTemp);
    }
    catch (System.Exception eLoadMerge)
    {
      // Add exception handling code here
      throw eLoadMerge;
    }

}

public void UpdateDataSet()
{
  // Get a new dataset that holds only the changes
  // that have been made to the main dataset
  MyDataSet objDataSetChanges = newMyDataSet();
  System.Data.DataSet objDataSetUpdated  = new MyDataSet();

  // Clear out the current edits
  this.BindingContext[objMyDataSet,"authors"].EndCurrentEdit();

  // Get a new dataset that holds only the changes
  // that have been made to the main dataset
  objDataSetChanges = ((MyDataSet)(objMyDataSet.GetChanges()));

  // Check to see if the objCustomersDatasetChanges
  // holds any records
  if ((objDataSetChanges != null))
  {
    try
    {
      // Call the update method passing inthe dataset
      // and any parameters
      this.UpdateDataSource(objDataSetChanges);
    }
    catch (System.Exception eUpdate)
    {
      // If the update failed and is part of a transaction,
      // this is the place to put your rollback
      throw eUpdate;
    }
    // If the update succeeded and is part of a transaction,
    // this is the place to put your commit
    // Add code to Check the returned dataset
    // (objCustomersDataSetUpdate) for any errors
    // that may have been
    // pushed into the row object's error
```

Continued

Listing 11-15 *(continued)*

```csharp
      // Merge the returned changes back into the main dataset
      try
      {
        objMyDataSet.Merge(objDataSetUpdated);
      }
      catch (System.Exception eUpdateMerge)
      {
        // Add exception handling code here
        throw eUpdateMerge;
      }
      // Commit the changes that were just merged
      // This moves any rows marked as updated, inserted or
      // changed to being marked as original values
      objMyDataSet.AcceptChanges();
    }
}

private void btnCancelAll_Click(object sender,
                                System.EventArgs e)
{
  this.objMyDataSet.RejectChanges();
}

private void objMyDataSet_PositionChanged()
{
  this.mfp_lblNavLocation.Text =
    ((((this.BindingContext[objMyDataSet,"authors"].
        Position + 1)).ToString() + " of  ") +
        this.BindingContext[objMyDataSet,"authors"].
        Count.ToString());
}

private void mfp_btnNavNext_Click(object sender,
                                  System.EventArgs e)
{
  this.BindingContext[objMyDataSet,"authors"].Position =
    (this.BindingContext[objMyDataSet,"authors"].Position + 1);
  this.objMyDataSet_PositionChanged();
}

private void mfp_btnNavPrev_Click(object sender,
                                  System.EventArgs e)
{
  this.BindingContext[objMyDataSet,"authors"].Position =
    (this.BindingContext[objMyDataSet,"authors"].Position - 1);
  this.objMyDataSet_PositionChanged();
}

private void mfp_btnNavLast_Click(object sender,
                                  System.EventArgs e)
{
```

```
     this.BindingContext[objMyDataSet,"authors"].Position =
        (this.objMyDataSet.Tables["authors"].Rows.Count - 1);
     this.objMyDataSet_PositionChanged();
}

private void mfp_btnNavFirst_Click(object sender,
                                   System.EventArgs e)
{
   this.BindingContext[objMyDataSet,"authors"].Position = 0;
   this.objMyDataSet_PositionChanged();
}

private void btnLoad_Click(object sender, System.EventArgs e)
{
   try
   {
     this.LoadDataSet();
   }
   catch (System.Exception eLoad)
   {
     System.Windows.Forms.MessageBox.Show(eLoad.Message);
   }
   this.objMyDataSet_PositionChanged();
}

private void btnUpdate_Click(object sender, System.EventArgs e)
{
   try
   {
     this.UpdateDataSet();
   }
   catch (System.Exception eUpdate)
   {
     System.Windows.Forms.MessageBox.Show(eUpdate.Message);
   }
   this.objMyDataSet_PositionChanged();
}

private void mfp_btnAdd_Click(object sender, System.EventArgs e)
{
   try
   {
     // Clear out the current edits
     this.BindingContext[objMyDataSet,"authors"].
                       EndCurrentEdit();
     this.BindingContext[objMyDataSet,"authors"].AddNew();
   }
   catch (System.Exception eEndEdit)
   {
     System.Windows.Forms.MessageBox.Show(eEndEdit.Message);
   }
```

Continued

Listing 11-15 *(continued)*

```
      this.objMyDataSet_PositionChanged();
   }

   private void mfp_btnDelete_Click(object sender,
                                    System.EventArgs e)
   {
     if ((this.BindingContext[objMyDataSet,"authors"].Count > 0))
     {
       this.BindingContext[objMyDataSet,"authors"].
           RemoveAt(this.BindingContext[objMyDataSet,"authors"].
                Position);
       this.objMyDataSet_PositionChanged();
     }
   }

   private void mfp_btnCancel_Click(object sender,
                                    System.EventArgs e)
   {
     this.BindingContext[objMyDataSet,"authors"].
                  CancelCurrentEdit();
     this.objMyDataSet_PositionChanged();
   }

   [STAThread]
   static void Main()
   {
     Application.Run(new MyNavigatorForm());
   }
 }
}
```

Grid-Based Forms

Navigator-type front ends let you work with only one record at a time. Using a data-bound grid, you can see multiple records. In this section, I'll create a small application called FrontEnd_DBGridForm to show the details of building such interfaces. To create a grid-based form, the process is similar to the one shown in the previous section: Right-click on the project in the Solution Explorer and select Add New Item from the pop-up menu. On the Add New Item screen, select the Data Form Wizard, as shown in Figure 11-31.

I used the name *MyGridForm* for the form. Follow the same steps described in the previous section until you get to the wizard screen shown in Figure 11-32.

Make sure the radio button labeled *All records in a grid* is checked. This is the default selection for the wizard. Click the Finish button and you're done. The form generated is shown in Figure 11-33.

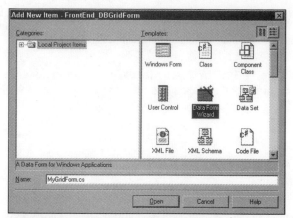

Figure 11-31: Invoking the Data Form Wizard

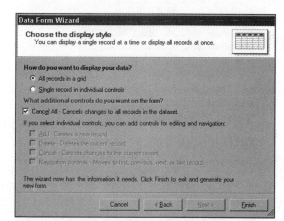

Figure 11-32: Selecting a grid-based form in the Data Form Wizard

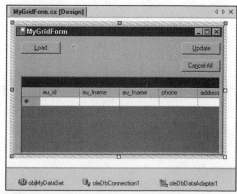

Figure 11-33: The form generated by the Data Form Wizard

If you don't like the grid's style, you can change it using the AutoFormat Wizard. To start this wizard, click the link named AutoFormat. The link is displayed at the bottom of the Properties window when the grid is selected in the Forms Designer, as shown in Figure 11-34.

Figure 11-34: The AutoFormat Wizard button, for customizing database grids the easy way

The AutoFormat Wizard has a number of built-in styles you can choose from. Figure 11-35 shows some of the styles you can choose.

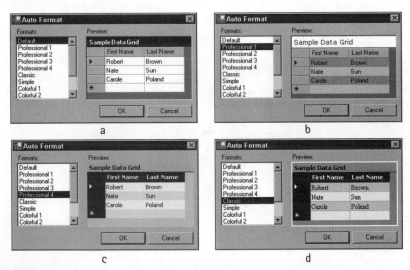

Figure 11-35: Some of the styles available using the AutoFormat Wizard

I chose the Professional #1 style. Figure 11-36 shows how MyGridForm looks at runtime after loading some records. The white area above the column headers of the grid is the caption bar.

That's really all there is to it, if you only want to show a grid on your UI form. You can display text in the caption bar by editing the CaptionText property of the grid, in the Property window. If don't want a caption bar to be shown, set the CaptionVisible property to false.

You can insert new rows by scrolling to the last row of the grid and clicking in a column, as shown in Figure 11-37.

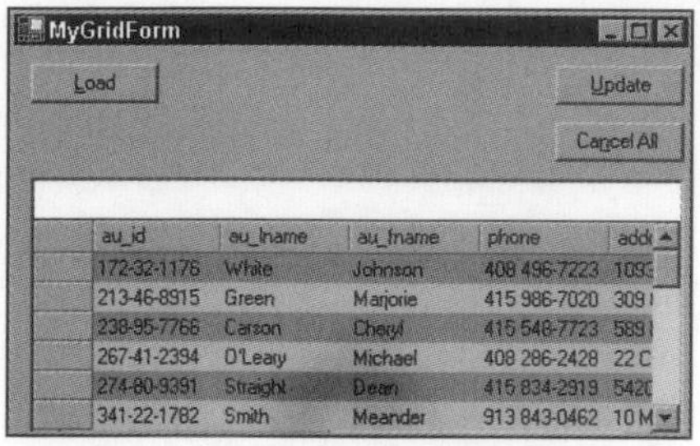

Figure 11-36: The appearance of MyGridForm after selecting the Professional #1 style

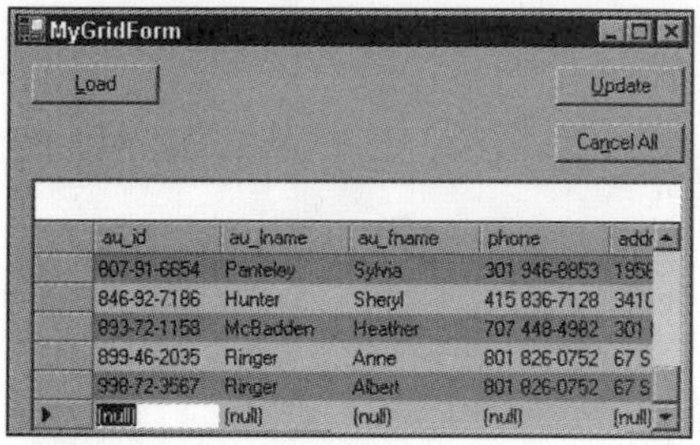

Figure 11-37: Adding a new record with the grid

To delete a row, just select it and press the Delete key. To change a row, click on a field and edit its contents.

> **Note**
>
> Keep in mind that all your changes are made to the records stored in MyDataSet. To post the changes to the database, you need to click the Update button. If you click the Cancel All button, all the changes are discarded. The database is not involved in discarded local records managed by MyDataSet.

Customizing the grid

The built-in functionality of the default grid is impressive, but you'll probably never ship an application without some degree of customization. Let's customize the UI of my grid-based form. First, I'll add a title for the grid by setting the CaptionText property in the Property window to My Customized Grid.

The captions displayed in each column also need some work. By default, the grid will use the raw column names as defined in the MyDataSet, which inherits the names from the underlying database. The problem is that database column names like au_lname don't mean much to end-users. To change the column headers and other column-related information, the process is simple and doesn't require any programming. Access the grid's TableStyles property in the Property window, as shown in Figure 11-38.

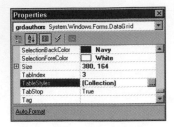

Figure 11-38: The TableStyles property, which is the starting point for customizing data-bound grids

Clicking the ellipsis button opens the DataGridTableStyle Collection Editor. Customizations to a grid are handled by `DataGridTableStyle` components. The Data Form Wizard doesn't add any `DataGridTableStyle` components to a grid, so the DataGridTableStyle Collection Editor is initially blank. You can add a customization to a grid by clicking the Add button. Figure 11-39 shows what the Collection Editor will look like.

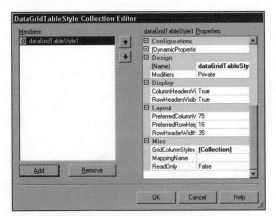

Figure 11-39: The DataGridTableStyles Collection Editor

This dialog box controls styles that apply to the grid as a whole. You can show or hide column and row headers, make the grid read-only, select the alternating row colors, and more.

 Note   Before proceeding any farther, set the `MappingName` to the name of the table the grid is showing data for, which in my case is *authors*.

To customize columns, click the ellipsis button for the `GridColumnStyles` property to open the DataGridColumnStyle Collection Editor, A grid initially has no customizations for column styles, so the Collection Editor starts out blank. To add a new style, click the small drop down image located on the Add button, as shown in Figure 11-40.

By default, the Collection Editor creates text columns, but you can also set up Boolean columns. Let's start by changing the au_lname and au_fname column headers to say *Last Name* and *First Name,* and make the First Name appear before the Last Name. I clicked the Add button, selecting the `DataGridTextBoxColumns` style for the first column that will show the First Name. In the properties on the right, I set the `HeaderText` to **First Name** and then increased the Width to **100.** To make this column show the data from the au_fname column, I set the `MappingName` property to **au_fname.** Figure 11-41 shows the various properties in the Collection Editor.

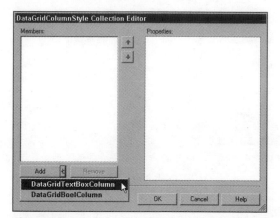

Figure 11-40: Selecting the type of column style to set up

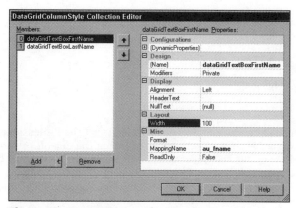

Figure 11-41: Setting up the First Name column in the grid

The `ReadOnly` property lets you prevent users from editing the data in the column. I used similar steps to set up the Last Name column. In the last column, I want to display the Boolean value of the Contract column. I created a Boolean column by selecting `DataGridBoolColumn` from the Add button's drop down list, and then set the column's properties as shown in Figure 11-42.

Sometimes Boolean columns in databases use values other than true and false. They may use Yes and No, or 1 and 0, or Up and Down, or whatever. To accommodate these types of columns, just set the `FalseValue` and `TrueValue` properties accordingly. Running the program with these customizations yields the screen shown in Figure 11-43.

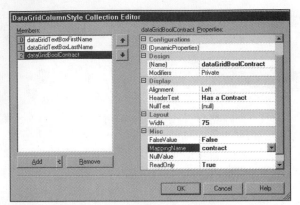

Figure 11-42: Setting up the Contract column
in the grid

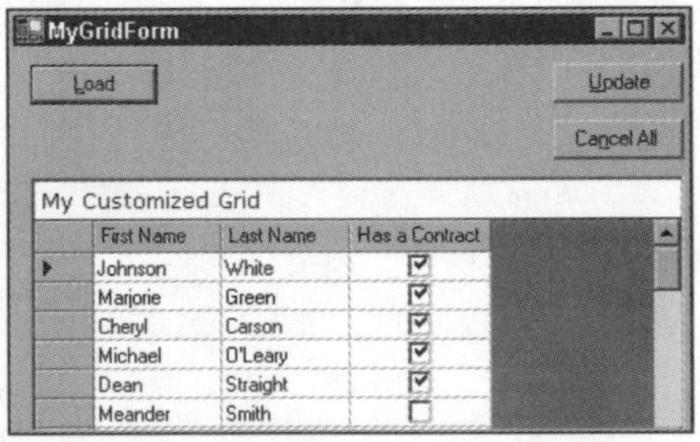

Figure 11-43: The appearance of the
customized grid

Not too bad, since I didn't write a line of code. You may have noticed that the Professional #1
style I picked in the AutoFormat Wizard is gone. What happened is that the default properties
set up by the wizard were overridden by the customizations I applied. To get alternating colors on rows, just click the ellipsis button of the `TableStyles` property to bring up the
DataGridTableStyle Collection Editor, select the style to customize (dataGridtableStyle1 in my
case), and change the `AlternatingBackColor` and `BackColor` properties, as shown in
Figure 11-44.

With these latest customizations, the grid appears as shown in Figure 11-45.

The CheckBoxes in the last column can be in one of three states: checked, unchecked, or
undefined. To force the CheckBoxes to have only the states (checked and unchecked), use
the DataGridColumnStyle Collection Editor and set the property `AllowNull` to false for the
Has a Contract column.

By using the procedures described, and also changing other grid properties and styles, you
can make considerable changes in the appearance of a grid.

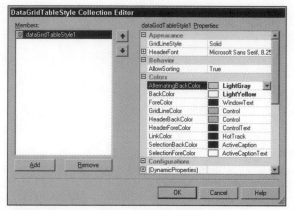

Figure 11-44: Setting up the alternating row colors for the grid

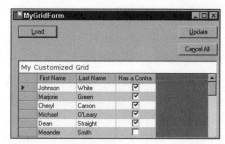

Figure 11-45: The customized grid with alternating row colors

Formatting numbers, dates, and times

One last customization worth mentioning is setting the format of the data in a text column. The format will then be used to display the column data according to the format string rules. The nice thing about formatting strings is that they follow the conventions of the end user's locale.

There are currently two classes of formatting strings: number formats and date/time formats. Table 11-2 describes the number formats. Keep in mind that the Windows Regional Options on my machine use the following settings:

✦ A period (.) to separate the whole and fractional parts of a number (for example, 1.52)

✦ A comma (,) to group a number by thousands (for example, 2,000,000 for two million)

✦ A dollar sign ($) as the currency symbol

Table 11-2: Number-Formatting Characters

Format Character	Description	Example
C or c	Currency	$23,567.95
		($23,567,95)
D or d	Decimal	123456789
		-123456789
E or e	Exponential	0.234523E+012
		-0.234523E+012
		0.234523E-012
		-0.234523E-012
F or f	Fixed point	1234.3334
		-1234.3334
G or g	General	The system automatically uses the Number or Exponential format, depending on which format yields the shortest string.
N or n	Number	123,345.4568
		-123,345.4568
P or p	Percent	23.43%
		-7932.32%
R or r	Roundtrip	The system formats the number into a string such that no loss in precision will occur when converting it back to a number.
X or x	Hexadecimal	FA2C
		a0ff23ce
		Using an uppercase X produces uppercase hex digits. Lowercase x produces lowercase hex digits.

Internally, the grid uses the Format property to call the `ToString()` method of numeric data types. Listing 11-16 shows some formatting examples.

Listing 11-16: Some Examples of Numeric Formatting

```
string s;
int i = 234567;
int h = 64204;
double d = 234.5678;
double p = 0.7623;
s = i.ToString("n3");   // produces 234,567.000
s = h.ToString("x6");   // produces 00ffac
```

```
s = h.ToString("X6");    // produces 00FFAC
s = d.ToString("n10");   // produces 234.5678000000
s = d.ToString("f2");    // produces 234.57
s = p.ToString("p");     // produces 76.23 %
s = d.ToString("e8");    // produces 2.34567800e+002
s = d.ToString("E8");    // produces 2.34567800E+002
s = d.ToString("g");     // produces 234.5678
```

Table 11-3 describes the Date/Time formats.

Table 11-3: Date/Time-Formatting Characters

Format Character	Description	Example
d	Short date	2001-09-01
D	Long date	Saturday, September 01, 2001
f	Full date	Saturday, September 01, 2001 8:56 AM
F	Full date	Saturday, September 01, 2001 08:56:51
g	General date	2001-09-01 8:56 AM
G	General date	2001-09-01 08:56:51
m	Month day	September 01
r	RFC1123 format	Sat, 01 Sep 2001 08:56:51 GMT
s	Sortable date, ISO 8601.	2001-09-01T08:56:51
t	Short time	8:56 AM
T	Long time	08:56:51
u	Universal time	2001-09-01 08:56:51Z (Zulu)
U	UTC time.	Saturday, September 01, 2001 15:56:51
y	Year month	September, 2001

Listing 11-17 shows examples of date/time formatting.

Listing 11-17: **Some Examples of Date/Time Formatting**

```
String s;
DateTime n = DateTime.Now;
s = n.ToString("d");  // produces 2001-09-01
s = n.ToString("D");  // produces Saturday, September 01,2001
s = n.ToString("f");  // Saturday, September 01,2001 8:56 AM
s = n.ToString("F");  // Saturday, September 01,2001 08:56:51
s = n.ToString("g");  // produces 2001-09-01 8:56 AM
s = n.ToString("G");  // produces 2001-09-01 08:56:51
```

Continued

Listing 11-17 *(continued)*

```
s = n.ToString("m");  // produces September 01
s = n.ToString("M");  // produces September 01
s = n.ToString("r");  // produces Sat, 01 Sep 2001 08:56:51 GMT
s = n.ToString("R");  // produces Sat, 01 Sep 2001 08:56:51 GMT
s = n.ToString("s");  // produces 2001-09-01T08:56:51
s = n.ToString("t");  // produces 8:56 AM
s = n.ToString("T");  // produces 08:56:51
s = n.ToString("u");  // produces 2001-09-01 08:56:51Z
s = n.ToString("U");  // Saturday, September 01, 2001 15:56:51
s = n.ToString("Y");  // produces September, 2001
```

Remember that the Format string is used by grids only when displaying data. The user is not in any way constrained to entering data in the same format, so you'll need your own validation code to check data entered.

Managing Data in a Grid

So far I've shown you how to use the various wizards and grid properties to customize the look and feel of a grid. Now it's time to look under the hood, to see how a grid loads records, and what it does when you insert, update and delete rows.

Loading records

Listing 11-18 shows the code generated by the Data Form Wizard for the Load button's Click handler.

Listing 11-18: The Click Handler for the Load Button

```
private void btnLoad_Click(object sender, System.EventArgs e)
{
  try
  {
    this.LoadDataSet();
  }
  catch (System.Exception eLoad)
  {
    System.Windows.Forms.MessageBox.Show(eLoad.Message);
  }
}
```

All the interesting stuff is tucked away in the LoadDataSet() method, which is shown in Listing 11-19.

Listing 11-19: The Code to Get Records from the Database

```
public void LoadDataSet()
{
  MyDataSet objDataSetTemp;
  objDataSetTemp = new MyDataSet();
  try
  {
    // Execute the SelectCommand on the DatasetCommmand
    // and fill the dataset
    this.FillDataSet(objDataSetTemp);
  }
  catch (System.Exception eFillDataSet)
  {
    // Add exception handling code here.
    throw eFillDataSet;
  }
  try
  {
    // Merge the records that were just pulled from
    // the data store into the main dataset
    objMyDataSet.Merge(objDataSetTemp);
  }
  catch (System.Exception eLoadMerge)
  {
    // Add exception handling code here
    throw eLoadMerge;
  }
}
```

This code calls yet another method — FillDataSet() — to get the records, using a temporary DataSet object, and then uses DataSet.Merge() to transfer the records into the main DataSet. Listing 11-20 shows the code for the FillDataSet() method.

Listing 11-20: The Code to Populate a Grid with Records

```
public void FillDataSet(FrontEnd_DBGridForm.MyDataSet dataSet)
{
  this.oleDbConnection1.Open();

  dataSet.EnforceConstraints = false;
  try
  {

    this.oleDbDataAdapter1.Fill(dataSet);
  }
  catch (System.Exception fillException)
  {
```

Continued

Listing 11-20 *(continued)*

```
    throw fillException;
  }
  finally
  {
    dataSet.EnforceConstraints = true;
    this.oleDbConnection1.Close();
  }
}
```

As you may recall, a DataSet is like an in-memory database, but it doesn't know how to move its records in or out of a database. A DataSet relies entirely on its associated DataAdapter to read and write records from and to the database. To get data, you need to call the DataAdapter.Fill() method, passing it a DataSet component to fill will records. FillDataSet() turns off the DataSet's EnforceConstraints property momentarily, to prevent exceptions while data is being loaded.

Notice the Open() and Close() calls to the OleDbConnection component. DataSets are designed to work without a continuous database connection. A connection is established only briefly, when loading data, or while posting changes to the database.

Posting changes to the database

Inserts, updates, and deletes are handled internally by the DataGrid component. Basically, all changes are made to the local in-memory database managed by MyDataSet. When you want the changes to be recorded in the database, you need to post the changed records in MyDataSet to the database. The Data Form Wizard adds the posting code to the Click handler of the Update button. The code is shown in Listing 11-21.

Listing 11-21: The Click Handler for the Update Button

```
private void btnUpdate_Click(object sender, System.EventArgs e)
{
  try
  {
    this.UpdateDataSet();
  }
  catch (System.Exception eUpdate)
  {
    System.Windows.Forms.MessageBox.Show(eUpdate.Message);
  }
}
```

As you can see, the real work is not here, but in the UpdateDataSet() method, whose code is shown in Listing 11-22.

Listing 11-22: The Click Handler for the Update Button

```
public void UpdateDataSet()
{
  MyDataSet objDataSetChanges = new MyDataSet();
  DataSet objDataSetUpdated = new MyDataSet();

  // Close edits in progress
  this.BindingContext[objMyDataSet,"authors"].EndCurrentEdit();

  // Get a new dataset that holds only the changes
  // that have been made to the main dataset
  objDataSetChanges = (MyDataSet) (objMyDataSet.GetChanges());

  // See if any changes were made
  if ((objDataSetChanges != null))
  {
    try
    {
      // Call the update method
      this.UpdateDataSource(objDataSetChanges);
    }
    catch (System.Exception eUpdate)
    {
      // If the update failed and is part of a transaction,
      // this is the place to put your rollback
      throw eUpdate;
    }

    // If the update succeeded and is part of a transaction,
    // this is the place to put your commit

    // Add code to Check the returned dataset
    // (objCustomersDataSetUpdate) for any errors that
    // may have been pushed into the row object's error

    // Merge the returned changes back into the main dataset
    try
    {
      objMyDataSet.Merge(objDataSetUpdated);
    }
    catch (System.Exception eUpdateMerge)
    {
      // Add exception handling code here
      throw eUpdateMerge;
    }
    // Commit the changes that were just merged
    // This moves any rows marked as updated, inserted
    // or changed to being marked as original values
    objMyDataSet.AcceptChanges();
  }
}
```

This method creates a temporary DataSet object and calls objMyDataSet.GetChanges() to get a list of all the modified records in MyDataSet. The temporary DataSet will then contain only inserted, updated, or deleted records that need to be posted to the database. For the actual posting, the method UpdateDataSource() is called. Its code is shown in Listing 11-23.

Listing 11-23: Posting All Changed Records to the Database

```
public int UpdateDataSource(MyDataSet dataSet)
{
  this.oleDbConnection1.Open();

  DataSet UpdatedRows;
  DataSet InsertedRows;
  DataSet DeletedRows;
  int AffectedRows = 0;

  UpdatedRows = dataSet.GetChanges(DataRowState.Modified);
  InsertedRows = dataSet.GetChanges(DataRowState.Added);
  DeletedRows = dataSet.GetChanges(DataRowState.Deleted);
  try
  {
    if ((UpdatedRows != null))
    {
      AffectedRows += oleDbDataAdapter1.Update(UpdatedRows);
    }
    if ((InsertedRows != null))
    {
      AffectedRows += oleDbDataAdapter1.Update(InsertedRows);
    }
    if ((DeletedRows != null))
    {
      AffectedRows += oleDbDataAdapter1.Update(DeletedRows));
    }
  }
  catch (System.Exception updateException)
  {
    throw updateException;
  }
  finally
  {
    this.oleDbConnection1.Close();
  }

  return AffectedRows;
}
```

The code creates separate `DataSet` objects to segregate the inserted, updated, and deleted records. Then the `DataAdapter` is called with each set of records to post the changes. Notice that the database connection is kept open only while posting changes to the database.

Rolling back all records

Since all changes you make to rows in the grid are stored locally in a `DataSet` component, it is trivial to roll all records back to their previous, unedited state. Listing 11-24 shows the `Click` handler for the Cancel All button.

> **Listing 11-24: The Click Handler for the Update Button**
>
> ```
> private void btnCancelAll_Click(object sender, System.EventArgs e)
> {
>    this.objMyDataSet.RejectChanges();
> }
> ```

The DataSet component will throw all the changes out and restore the original row values that it cached away. The database is not involved at all in this type of rollback operation.

For information regarding data validation, reconciliation errors during posting operations, and other details, see Chapter 18.

Prepopulating rows with default values

In many situations, adding a new row to a grid requires adding some default values to some or all of the fields. For example, let's say that when a new row is added to the *authors* table using MyGridForm, you want to set the default values shown in Table 11-4.

Table 11-4: Default Values Used in the authors Table

Field Name	Default Value
au_fname	<first name>
au_lname	<last name>
contract	false
address	<no address>

You can set default values for any column in a table, even if the `DataGrid` doesn't show that column. This can be particularly useful for ID fields used as keys or foreign keys, which are often not shown on the screen. The first three fields (`au_fname`, `au_lname`, and `contract`) are visible in `MyDataGrid`. The last one (`address`) is not. To set the default values shown in the table, the code in Listing 11-25 can be used:

Listing 11-25: Posting All Changed Records to the Database

```
public MyGridForm()
{
  InitializeComponent();

  objMyDataSet.Tables["authors"].Columns["au_fname"].DefaultValue =
    "<first name>";
  objMyDataSet.Tables["authors"].Columns["au_lname"].DefaultValue =
    "<last name>";
  objMyDataSet.Tables["authors"].Columns["contract"].DefaultValue =
    false;
  objMyDataSet.Tables["authors"].Columns["address"].DefaultValue =
    "<no address>";
}
```

Figure 11-46 shows how a newly added row appears before making any changes to it.

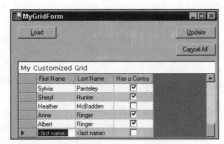

Figure 11-46: A newly added row
with default values

To complete this section on grid-based forms, Listing 11-26 shows the entire code for the sample program called `FrontEnd_DBGridForm`.

Listing 11-26: The Complete Code for FrontEnd_DBGridForm

```
using System;
using System.Drawing;
using System.Collections;
using System.ComponentModel;
using System.Windows.Forms;

namespace FrontEnd_DBGridForm
{
  public class MyGridForm : System.Windows.Forms.Form
  {
    private System.Data.OleDb.OleDbCommand oleDbSelectCommand1;
    private System.Data.OleDb.OleDbCommand oleDbInsertCommand1;
```

```
private System.Data.OleDb.OleDbCommand oleDbUpdateCommand1;
private System.Data.OleDb.OleDbCommand oleDbDeleteCommand1;
private FrontEnd_DBGridForm.MyDataSet objMyDataSet;
private System.Data.OleDb.OleDbConnection oleDbConnection1;
private System.Data.OleDb.OleDbDataAdapter oleDbDataAdapter1;

private System.Windows.Forms.DataGrid grdauthors;
private DataGridTableStyle dataGridTableStyle1;
private DataGridTextBoxColumn
        dataGridTextBoxColumnFirstName;
private DataGridTextBoxColumn
        dataGridTextBoxColumnLastName;
private DataGridBoolColumn
        dataGridBoolColumnContract;
private DataGridTextBoxColumn
        dataGridTextBoxColumnTelephone;
private DataGridTextBoxColumn
        dataGridTextBoxColumnPhone;

// other controls...

public MyGridForm()
{
  InitializeComponent();

  objMyDataSet.Tables ["authors"].Columns
    ["au_fname"].DefaultValue = "<first name>";
  objMyDataSet.Tables ["authors"].Columns
    ["au_lname"].DefaultValue = "<last name>";
  objMyDataSet.Tables ["authors"].Columns
    ["contract"].DefaultValue = false;
  objMyDataSet.Tables ["authors"].Columns
    ["address"].DefaultValue = "<no address>";
}

protected override void Dispose( bool disposing )
{
  // standard wizard-generated code...
}


private void InitializeComponent()
{
  // standard wizard-generated code...
}

public void FillDataSet(MyDataSet dataSet)
{
  this.oleDbConnection1.Open();

  dataSet.EnforceConstraints = false;
  try
```

Continued

Listing 11-26 *(continued)*

```
      {
        this.oleDbDataAdapter1.Fill(dataSet);
      }
      catch (System.Exception fillException)
      {
        throw fillException;
      }
      finally
      {
        dataSet.EnforceConstraints = true;
        this.oleDbConnection1.Close();
      }
    }

  public int UpdateDataSource(MyDataSet dataSet)
  {
    this.oleDbConnection1.Open();

    System.Data.DataSet UpdatedRows;
    System.Data.DataSet InsertedRows;
    System.Data.DataSet DeletedRows;
    int AffectedRows = 0;

    UpdatedRows =
      dataSet.GetChanges(System.Data.DataRowState.Modified);
    InsertedRows =
      dataSet.GetChanges(System.Data.DataRowState.Added);
    DeletedRows =
      dataSet.GetChanges(System.Data.DataRowState.Deleted);
    try
    {
      if ((UpdatedRows != null))
      {
        AffectedRows = oleDbDataAdapter1.Update(UpdatedRows);
      }
      if ((InsertedRows != null))
      {
        AffectedRows += oleDbDataAdapter1.Update(InsertedRows);
      }
      if ((DeletedRows != null))
      {
        AffectedRows += oleDbDataAdapter1.Update(DeletedRows);
      }
    }
    catch (System.Exception updateException)
    {
      throw updateException;
    }
    finally
    {
```

```
      this.oleDbConnection1.Close();
  }

  return AffectedRows;
}

    public void LoadDataSet()
    {
      FrontEnd_DBGridForm.MyDataSet objDataSetTemp;
      objDataSetTemp = new FrontEnd_DBGridForm.MyDataSet();
      try
      {
        // Execute the SelectCommand on the
        // DatasetCommmand and fill the dataset
        this.FillDataSet(objDataSetTemp);
      }
      catch (System.Exception eFillDataSet)
      {
        // Add exception handling code here.
        throw eFillDataSet;
      }
      try
      {
        // Merge the records that were just pulled
        // from the data store into the main dataset
        objMyDataSet.Merge(objDataSetTemp);
      }
      catch (System.Exception eLoadMerge)
      {
        // Add exception handling code here
        throw eLoadMerge;
      }
    }


    public void UpdateDataSet()
    {
      // Get a new dataset that holds only the changes
      // that have been made to the main dataset
      FrontEnd_DBGridForm.MyDataSet objDataSetChanges =
              new FrontEnd_DBGridForm.MyDataSet();
      System.Data.DataSet objDataSetUpdated =
              new FrontEnd_DBGridForm.MyDataSet();

      // Clear out the current edits
      this.BindingContext[objMyDataSet,"authors"].EndCurrentEdit();

      // Get a new dataset that holds only the changes
      // that have been made to the main dataset
      objDataSetChanges =
          ((MyDataSet)(objMyDataSet.GetChanges()));

      // Check to see if the objCustomersDatasetChanges
```

Continued

Listing 11-26 *(continued)*

```csharp
      // holds any records
      if ((objDataSetChanges != null))
      {
        try
        {
          // Call the update method passing inthe
          // dataset and any parameters
          this.UpdateDataSource(objDataSetChanges);
        }
        catch (System.Exception eUpdate)
        {
          // If the update failed and is part of a
          // transaction, this is the place to put
          // your rollback
          throw eUpdate;
        }

        // If the update succeeded and is part of a
        // transaction, this is the place to put your commit

        // Add code to Check the returned dataset
        // (objCustomersDataSetUpdate) for any errors that may
        // have been pushed into the row object's error

        // Merge the returned changes back into the main dataset
        try
        {
          objMyDataSet.Merge(objDataSetUpdated);
        }
        catch (System.Exception eUpdateMerge)
        {
          // Add exception handling code here
          throw eUpdateMerge;
        }
        // Commit the changes that were just merged
        // This moves any rows marked as updated, inserted
        // or changed to being marked as original values
        objMyDataSet.AcceptChanges();
      }
    }

    private void btnCancelAll_Click(object sender,
                                    System.EventArgs e)
    {
      this.objMyDataSet.RejectChanges();
    }

    private void btnLoad_Click(object sender,
```

```
                                      System.EventArgs e)
    {
      try
      {
        this.LoadDataSet();
      }
      catch (System.Exception eLoad)
      {
        MessageBox.Show(eLoad.Message);
      }
    }

    private void btnUpdate_Click(object sender,
                                  System.EventArgs e)
    {
      try
      {
        this.UpdateDataSet();
      }
      catch (System.Exception eUpdate)
      {
        MessageBox.Show(eUpdate.Message);
      }
    }

    [STAThread]
    static void Main()
    {
      Application.Run(new MyGridForm() );
    }
  }
}
```

There are numerous other topics regarding grid-based front-end components that may be useful, but I don't have enough room in this book to discuss them in detail. A few topics you may be interested in are the following:

✦ Using a computed value (instead of a database field) in a column

✦ Setting required fields that must be filled in

✦ Handling exceptions caused by duplicate rows, bad data, or other conditions

For these and other details, see Chapter 18, titled "The ADO.NET Architecture."

Master-Detail Forms

Master-detail relationships are quite common in business applications. An example would be an invoice, which may have many line items. The invoice is the master record, the line items the details. Using the authors table in the SQL Server database, an author may be associated to multiple book titles. The author is the master record, the titles are the detail records.

In the .NET Framework documentation, you find master-detail relationships often called *parent-child* relationships. The two expressions are entirely equivalent.

Tables related by a master-detail relationship must have a way to associate the detail records with their master. The Master table generally defines a primary key, which is a foreign key for the Detail table. Figure 11-47 shows a simple relationship between the `authors` table and the `titleauthor` table, in the SQL Server sample `Pubs` database.

Figure 11-47: The master-detail relationship between the authors and titleauthor tables in the Pubs database

The table `authors` acts as a Master table for the `titleauthor` table records. The relationship in this example is *one-to-many:* For each `author` record there can be any number of `titleauthor` records. The association is through the `au_id` fields present in both tables. The field `au_id` is a primary key in the `authors` table and a foreign key in the `titleauthor` table.

It should be clear in your mind at this point that a master-detail relationship requires two separate tables, joined by one or more columns. There are several ways to present master-detail relationships at the user-interface level. One method, which I'll use in my sample program called `FrontEnd DBMasterDetail` shown in Figure 11-48, displays the Master table as a grid in the upper part of a form and the Detail records in a grid in the bottom part.

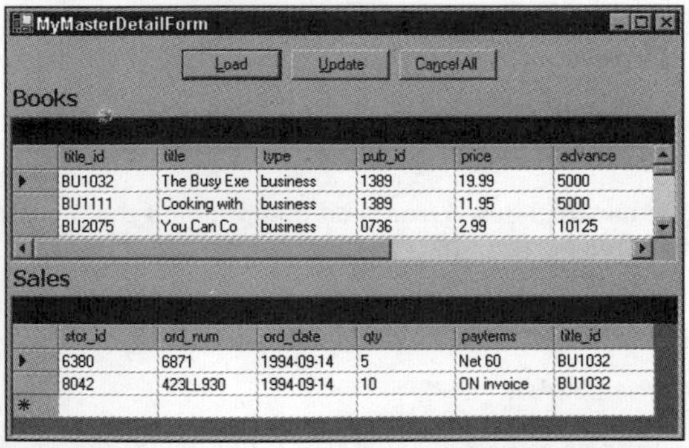

Figure 11-48: The master-detail form of my sample program, showing the Master table at the top and the Detail table at the bottom

When you select a record in the Master grid at the top, the associated Detail records are shown in the bottom grid. If you read the previous sections on creating grid-based forms, you'll need to add very little more to support master-detail forms. What is new is the use of multiple tables simultaneously. The interesting part is how the tables are linked together, so that selecting a new row in the top grid automatically displays the detail records in the bottom grid.

Creating the form

To create a master-detail form, start by running the Data Form Wizard. In case you skipped the previous sections of this chapter, here's how:

1. Right click on the project in the Solution Explorer and select Add New Item from the pop-up menu.

2. In the Add New Item dialog box, select Data Form Wizard from the templates in the right pane.

3. Enter a name for the new DataSet to be used on the form. (For my example program, I used the name MyDataSet.)

4. Choose a database connection component, and then press the Next button.

The new screen lets you select the tables to be handled by the DataAdapter component. I selected the titles and sales tables, as shown in Figure 11-49.

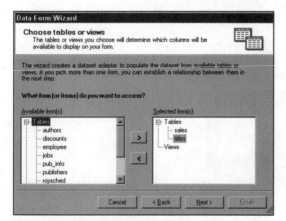

Figure 11-49: Selecting multiple tables to set up a master-detail relationship

The titles table will be the Master table, the sales table the Detail table. Master-detail relationships often entail only two tables. Click the Next button to go to the Relationship screen of the wizard. Enter a name for the relationship. I used the name *Titles_Sales_Relationship*. Select the Master and Detail tables, plus the column they are joined on. At this point, the screen should look like Figure 11-50.

Click the > button to add Titles_Sales_Relationship to the Relations list on the right. Click the Next button. On the new screen, select the Master and Detail tables, plus the columns of each table you want to show in the form, as shown in Figure 11-51.

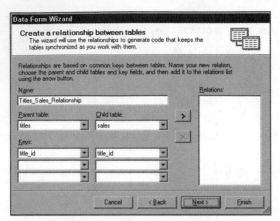

Figure 11-50: Creating the first relationship between tables

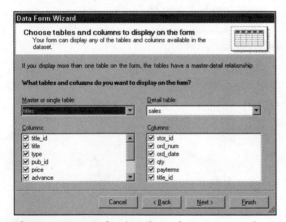

Figure 11-51: Selecting the columns to use for the Master and Detail tables

Click the Next button. On the next screen, select *All records in a grid,* as shown in Figure 11-52.

After clicking the Finish button, the Forms Designer will display the newly created master-detail form, as shown in Figure 11-53.

Notice the two OleDbDataAdapters. The first one transfers the Master records, the second the Detail records. A single DataSet component manages the in-memory database containing both tables. I enlarged the form a bit so I could increase the size of the two grids. Then I repositioned the buttons and added a couple of labels to describe the grids. When I ran the program, the master-detail form appeared as shown in Figure 11-54.

As you change the book selected in the top grid, the bottom grid automatically refreshes with details about the new book selected. You can edit both the top and bottom grids at any time. When you click the Update button, all changes made to the two grids are posted to the database.

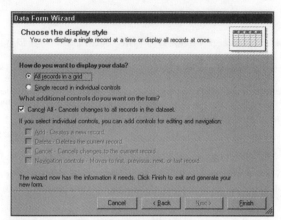

Figure 11-52: Telling the wizard to generate a grid-based master-detail form

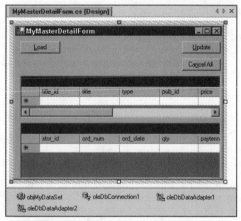

Figure 11-53: The master-detail form created by the wizard

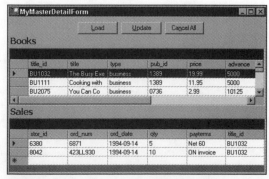

Figure 11-54: The master-detail form

How it works

The basic operation of a `DataGrid` was described previously in the section titled "Grid-Based Forms." What's new in master-detail front ends is the relationship between the two tables, which is managed *automagically* by the `DataSet` created by the Data Form Wizard.

The .NET Framework handles the master-detail relationship with a minimal amount of code. Basically all you have is a form with two grids on it, each connected to a different table. The `DataSet` with the two tables is populated with the following code:

```
this.oleDbDataAdapter1.Fill(dataSet);
this.oleDbDataAdapter2.Fill(dataSet);
```

The first `DataAdapter` fetches data for the Master table (`titles`). The other one fetches data for the Detail table (`sales`). The relationship between the two tables is managed internally by the `DataSet`.

The two grids are connected to different tables in the common `DataSet`. The titles grid is connected to the titles table, but the sales grid is connected to the Detail records managed through a special table relationship: the one I set up using the Data Form Wizard. Listing 11-27 shows the code that connects the grids to data sources.

> **Listing 11-27: Connecting the Master and Detail Grids to Their Respective Data Sources**
>
> ```
> grdtitles.DataMember = "titles";
> grdtitles.DataSource =objMyDataSet;
>
> grdsales.DataMember = "titles.Titles_Sales_Relationship";
> grdsales.DataSource =objMyDataSet;
> ```

There's no other code involved in the master-detail relationship management. What's going on here? There has to be code somewhere, to set up the relationship. That's true, and the code is not C# code but XML code, tucked away in the .xsd (for *xml schema definition*) file created by the Data Form Wizard. Let's take a look at this code. Double-click on the file MyDataSet.xsd in the Solution Explorer, and you'll see a graphic representation of the database schema in the Code window, as shown in Figure 11-55.

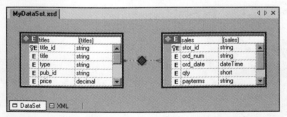

Figure 11-55: The master-detail relationship stored in the file MyDataSet.xsd

The dotted line and diamond linking the two tables tells you there is some kind of relationship between the tables. The funny looking character at the end of the dotted line on the sales table indicates the presence of a *many* cardinality in the relationship: For each title's record, there may be many sales records. To see the XML code defining the relationship, click the XML button at the lower left of the screen. Listing 11-28 shows the complete XML code.

Listing 11-28: The XML Code Defining the Titles and Sales Tables, Including Their Relationship

```
<xsd:schema id="MyDataSet"
targetNamespace="http://www.tempuri.org/MyDataSet.xsd"
xmlns="http://www.tempuri.org/MyDataSet.xsd"
xmlns:xsd="http://www.w3.org/2001/XMLSchema"
            xmlns:msdata="urn:schemas-microsoft-com:xml-msdata"
            attributeFormDefault="qualified"
            elementFormDefault="qualified">
  <xsd:element name="MyDataSet" msdata:IsDataSet="true">
    <xsd:complexType>
      <xsd:choice maxOccurs="unbounded">
        <xsd:element name="sales">
          <xsd:complexType>
            <xsd:sequence>
              <xsd:element name="stor_id" type="xsd:string" />
              <xsd:element name="ord_num" type="xsd:string" />
              <xsd:element name="ord_date" type="xsd:dateTime" />
              <xsd:element name="qty" type="xsd:short" />
              <xsd:element name="payterms" type="xsd:string" />
              <xsd:element name="title_id" type="xsd:string" />
            </xsd:sequence>
          </xsd:complexType>
        </xsd:element>
        <xsd:element name="titles">
          <xsd:complexType>
            <xsd:sequence>
              <xsd:element name="title_id" type="xsd:string" />
              <xsd:element name="title" type="xsd:string" />
              <xsd:element name="type" type="xsd:string" />
              <xsd:element name="pub_id" type="xsd:string"
                          minOccurs="0" />
              <xsd:element name="price" type="xsd:decimal"
                          minOccurs="0" />
              <xsd:element name="advance" type="xsd:decimal"
                          minOccurs="0" />
              <xsd:element name="royalty" type="xsd:int"
                          minOccurs="0" />
              <xsd:element name="ytd_sales" type="xsd:int"
                          minOccurs="0" />
              <xsd:element name="notes" type="xsd:string"
                          minOccurs="0" />
              <xsd:element name="pubdate" type="xsd:dateTime" />
```

Continued

Listing 11-28 *(continued)*

```
          </xsd:sequence>
        </xsd:complexType>
      </xsd:element>
    </xsd:choice>
  </xsd:complexType>
  <xsd:unique name="Constraint1" msdata:PrimaryKey="true">
    <xsd:selector xpath=".//sales" />
    <xsd:field xpath="stor_id" />
    <xsd:field xpath="ord_num" />
    <xsd:field xpath="title_id" />
  </xsd:unique>
  <xsd:unique name="titles_Constraint1"
              msdata:ConstraintName="Constraint1"
        msdata:PrimaryKey="true">
    <xsd:selector xpath=".//titles" />
    <xsd:field xpath="title_id" />
  </xsd:unique>
  <xsd:keyref name="Titles_Sales_Relationship"
              refer="titles_Constraint1">
    <xsd:selector xpath=".//sales" />
    <xsd:field xpath="title_id" />
  </xsd:keyref>
  </xsd:element>
</xsd:schema>
```

You'll notice that I put three lines in bold, to emphasize their importance. The first is where the `sales` table is declared. The second is where the `titles` table is declared. The third is where the relationship between the tables is declared. `DataSet` components manage relationships using `DataRelation` components, stored in the `DataRelationCollection` object. You can inspect the relations managed by a `DataSet` by right-clicking on the `DataSet` and selecting DataSet Properties from the pop-up menu. Figure 11-56 shows some of the relationship properties.

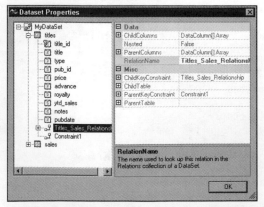

Figure 11-56: Inspecting properties of relationships used internally by a DataSet

The `ChildColumns` and `ParentColumns` properties contain a list of the columns the Master and Detail tables are joined on. To show how all the pieces fit together, Listing 11-29 shows the source code for `MyMasterDetailForm`. To keep the listing short, I removed some of the standard code generated by the various wizards.

Listing 11-29: The Source Code for MyMasterDetailForm

```
using System;
using System.Data;
using System.Windows;

// other imports...

namespace FrontEnd_DBMasterDetail
{
  public class MyMasterDetailForm : System.Windows.Forms.Form
  {
    private MyDataSet objMyDataSet;
    private OleDb.OleDbConnection oleDbConnection1;
    private OleDb.OleDbDataAdapter oleDbDataAdapter1;
    private OleDb.OleDbDataAdapter oleDbDataAdapter2;
    private Button btnLoad;
    private Button btnUpdate;
    private Button btnCancelAll;
    private DataGrid grdtitles;
    private DataGrid grdsales;

    // other standard controls...

    public MyMasterDetailForm()
    {
      InitializeComponent();
    }

    protected override void Dispose( bool disposing )
    {
      // standard wizard-generated code...
    }

    private void InitializeComponent()
    {
      // wizard-generated code...
      this.objMyDataSet = new MyDataSet();
      this.btnCancelAll = new Button();
      this.grdtitles = new DataGrid();
      this.oleDbDataAdapter1 = new OleDb.OleDbDataAdapter();
      this.oleDbDataAdapter2 = new OleDb.OleDbDataAdapter();
      this.btnUpdate = new Button();
      this.btnLoad = new Button();
      this.grdsales = new DataGrid();

      //
```

Continued

Listing 11-29 *(continued)*

```csharp
// oleDbConnection1
//
this.oleDbConnection1.ConnectionString =
   @"Provider=SQLOLEDB.1;Integrated Security=SSPI;
      Persist Security Info=False;User ID=Ted;
      Initial Catalog=pubs;
      Data Source=(local);Use Procedure for Prepare=1;
      Auto Translate=True;Packet Size=4096;
      Workstation ID=FRANCESCA;
      Use Encryption for Data=False;
      Tag with column collation when possible=False";

//
// grdtitles
//
this.grdtitles.AllowNavigation = false;
this.grdtitles.DataMember = "titles";
this.grdtitles.DataSource = this.objMyDataSet;

// other UI-related properties...

//
// grdsales
//
this.grdsales.AllowNavigation = false;
this.grdsales.DataMember = "titles.Titles_Sales_Relationship";
this.grdsales.DataSource = this.objMyDataSet;
// other UI-related properties...

// other controls...
}

public void FillDataSet(MyDataSet dataSet)
{
  this.oleDbConnection1.Open();

  dataSet.EnforceConstraints = false;
  try
  {
    this.oleDbDataAdapter1.Fill(dataSet);
    this.oleDbDataAdapter2.Fill(dataSet);
  }
  catch (System.Exception fillException)
  {
    throw fillException;
  }
  finally
  {
    dataSet.EnforceConstraints = true;
```

```csharp
      this.oleDbConnection1.Close();
   }
}

public int UpdateDataSource(MyDataSet dataSet)
{
  this.oleDbConnection1.Open();

  DataSet UpdatedRows;
  DataSet InsertedRows;
  DataSet DeletedRows;
  int AffectedRows = 0;

  UpdatedRows = dataSet.GetChanges(DataRowState.Modified);
  InsertedRows = dataSet.GetChanges(DataRowState.Added);
  DeletedRows = dataSet.GetChanges(DataRowState.Deleted);
  try
  {
    if ((UpdatedRows != null))
    {
      AffectedRows = oleDbDataAdapter1.Update(UpdatedRows);
      AffectedRows += oleDbDataAdapter2.Update(UpdatedRows);
    }
    if ((InsertedRows != null))
    {
      AffectedRows += oleDbDataAdapter1.Update(InsertedRows);
      AffectedRows += oleDbDataAdapter2.Update(InsertedRows);
    }
    if ((DeletedRows != null))
    {
      AffectedRows += oleDbDataAdapter1.Update(DeletedRows);
      AffectedRows += oleDbDataAdapter2.Update(DeletedRows);
    }
  }
  catch (System.Exception updateException)
  {
    throw updateException;
  }
  finally
  {
    this.oleDbConnection1.Close();
  }

  return AffectedRows;
}

public void LoadDataSet()
{
  MyDataSet objDataSetTemp;
  objDataSetTemp = new MyDataSet();
  try
```

Continued

Listing 11-29 *(continued)*

```
      {
        // Execute the SelectCommand on the
        // DatasetCommmand and fill the dataset
        this.FillDataSet(objDataSetTemp);
      }
      catch (System.Exception eFillDataSet)
      {
        // Add exception handling code here.
        throw eFillDataSet;
      }
      try
      {
        // Merge the records that were just pulled from
        // the data store into the main dataset
        objMyDataSet.Merge(objDataSetTemp);
      }
      catch (System.Exception eLoadMerge)
      {
        // Add exception handling code here
        throw eLoadMerge;
      }
    }

    public void UpdateDataSet()
    {
      // Get a new dataset that holds only the changes
      // that have been made to the main dataset
      MyDataSet objDataSetChanges = new MyDataSet();
      DataSet objDataSetUpdated = new MyDataSet();

      // Clear out the current edits
      this.BindingContext[objMyDataSet,"titles"].EndCurrentEdit();
      this.BindingContext[objMyDataSet,"sales"].EndCurrentEdit();

      // Get a new dataset that holds only the changes
      // that have been made to the main dataset
      objDataSetChanges = ((MyDataSet)(objMyDataSet.GetChanges()));

      // see if any changes made
      if ((objDataSetChanges != null))
      {
        try
        {
          // Call the update method passing inthe
          // dataset and any parameters
          this.UpdateDataSource(objDataSetChanges);
        }
        catch (System.Exception eUpdate)
        {
          // If the update failed and is part of a transaction,
          // this is the place to put your rollback
```

```
         throw eUpdate;
       }
       // If the update succeeded and is part of a transaction,
       // this is the place to put your commit. Add code to Check
       // the returned dataset for any errors that may have been
       // pushed into the row object's error.
       // Merge the returned changes back into the main dataset
       try
       {
          objMyDataSet.Merge(objDataSetUpdated);
       }
       catch (System.Exception eUpdateMerge)
       {
          // Add exception handling code here
          throw eUpdateMerge;
       }
       // Commit the changes that were just merged
       // This moves any rows marked as updated, inserted
       // or changed to being marked as original values
       objMyDataSet.AcceptChanges();
    }
}

private void btnCancelAll_Click(object sender,
                               System.EventArgs e)
{
  this.objMyDataSet.RejectChanges();
}

private void btnLoad_Click(object sender,
                          System.EventArgs e)
{
  try
  {
    this.LoadDataSet();
  }
  catch (System.Exception eLoad)
  {
    System.Windows.Forms.MessageBox.Show(eLoad.Message);
  }
}

private void btnUpdate_Click(object sender,
                            System.EventArgs e)
{
  try
  {
    this.UpdateDataSet();
  }
  catch (System.Exception eUpdate)
  {
    MessageBox.Show(eUpdate.Message);
```

Continued

Listing 11-29 *(continued)*

```
        }
    }

    [STAThread]
    static void Main()
    {
      Application.Run(new MyMasterDetailForm() );
    }
  }
}
```

Master-detail grids with nested rows

Instead of using two grids to show the Master and Detail tables separately, you can use a single grid to show both. When doing so, the rows of the Master table appear with plus (+) signs next to them, as shown in Figure 11-57.

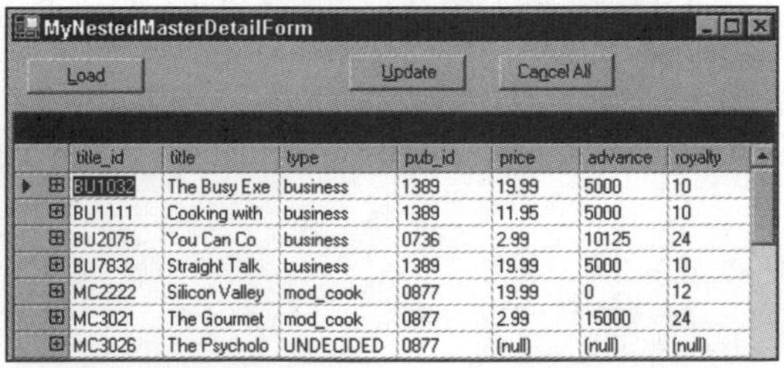

Figure 11-57: A master-detail grid with details listed hierarchically under their master records

The figure represents the main form of a project called *FrontEnd_DBMasterDetailWithNesting* that I'll describe in this section. Notice the + signs on the row header columns. If you click on one, the row expands to give you the option of displaying Detail records, as shown in Figure 11-58.

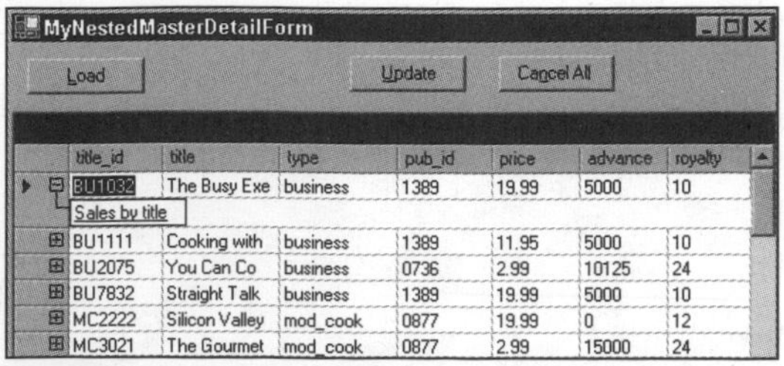

Figure 11-58: Expanding a Master row

A hyperlink is shown, with the caption Sales Details. The text used in the hyperlink is simply the name of a `DataRelation` object that you can create programmatically, as shown later. If you click the hyperlink, the grid navigates to the Detail records and keeps a copy of the Master record displayed at the top of the grid, as shown in Figure 11-59.

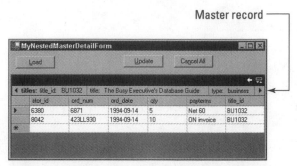

Figure 11-59: The Detail records for the selected Master record, which is shown at the top of the grid

Now you can navigate up and down in the grid to see all the sales records for the given title. To switch the grid back to showing the Master table, click the left-arrow as shown in Figure 11-60.

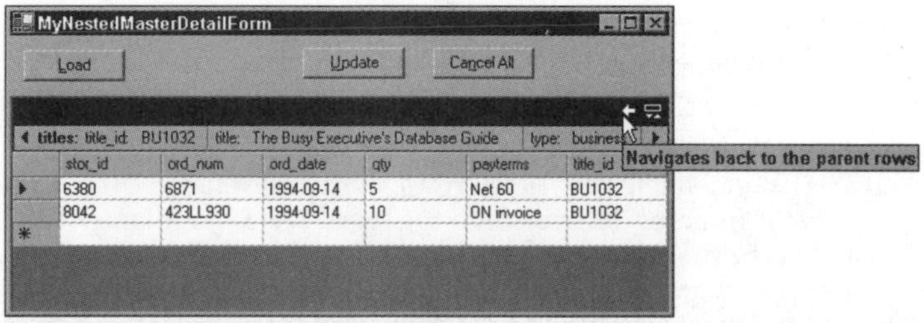

Figure 11-60: Returning to the Master records

The small left- and right-pointing triangles shown on the top row on the left and right sides shown in the figure let you scroll through the various fields on the Master record. The look and feel of the grid's UI is intended to be reminiscent of an Internet Explorer browsing session. The button to return to the Master table is like the Back button in Internet Explorer.

Nested grids are pretty cool, so I'll show you how to set them up. This time we're going to have to get our hands dirty with some coding. Can you create a master-detail relationship programmatically? Absolutely. Does it require you to write XML code and create a .xsd file? No. Although in my previous example I showed the .xsd that contains the complete schema used by a `DataSet`, the .xsd file is just an initialization file that is used to tell a `DataSet` component how to configure itself. Anything you can do with a .xsd file can be done with C# code. In fact, there is a utility program that ships with the Framework SDK called xsd.exe. This utility can take a .xsd file and generate a C# class for it. The utility can also generate Visual Basic or JavaScript classes.

I created a new project called *FrontEnd_DBMasterDetailWithNesting* to show how to set up a nested grid from scratch. I just created a plain old application with the Windows Application Project Wizard.

To create a nested master-detail grid, start from the Data Form Wizard. The first two wizard screens ask for the name of the `DataSet` and `DataConnection` to use. The next page lets you choose the tables to include in the form. Instead of telling the wizard to use both the `titles` and `sales` table, as in the normal master-detail case, just select the Master table (the `titles` table), as shown in Figure 11-61.

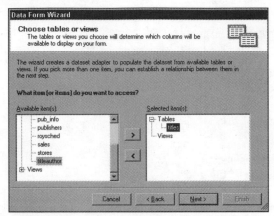

Figure 11-61: Selecting only the Master table, when you want to set up a nested master-detail grid

That's it. On the next two wizard pages, use the defaults and then click the Finish button. The Data Form Wizard will set up a form with a single grid, looking much like the form shown back in Figure 11-33.

Now you need to set up a `DataAdapter` for the Detail rows, in the sales table. Drop an `OleDbDataAdapter` component from the Toolbox onto the form. The Data Adapter Wizard will start up automatically. On the first page, select the Data Connection used with the Data Form Wizard. The next page asks whether to use an SQL statement or a Stored Procedure. For my example, I'll use an SQL statement. The next page lets you enter the SQL statement. I'll use the Query Builder Wizard by clicking the Query Builder button. The next screen is where the Query Builder prompts for the tables to use. I'll just select the sales table, as shown in Figure 11-62, by clicking the Add button and then the Close button.

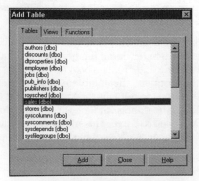

Figure 11-62: Telling the Query Builder to use the sales table

Back in the Query Builder, I selected All Columns at the top, and then right-clicked and chose the Run command on the pop-up menu, to populate the bottom grid with some rows. Figure 11-63 shows the Query Builder screen at this point.

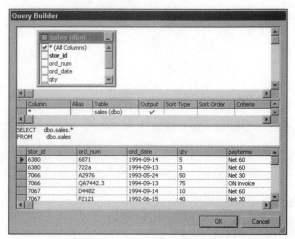

Figure 11-63: The Query Builder, showing the SQL Select statement used to fetch rows from the sales table

After closing the Query Builder and letting the Data Adapter Wizard finish, a new `OleDbDataAdapter` will be added to the form. Now you need to update the existing DataSet on the form, to include the data generated by the new `DataAdapter`. Right-click on the new `DataAdapter`, and select the command Generate DataSet from the pop-up menu, as shown in Figure 11-64.

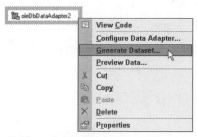

Figure 11-64: Updating an existing DataSet after adding a new DataAdapter

The Generate DataSet Wizard lets you specify whether to update an existing DataSet or to create a brand new one. By default, it will use an existing DataSet. The wizard then checks the configuration of the existing DataSet, and finds that it needs to by configured for the sales table, as shown in Figure 11-65.

Just click the OK button, and the wizard will add support for the sales table to the `DataSet`. You're not done yet. You need to add calls in the existing code to the new `DataAdapter`, to handle filling, inserting, updating, and deleting records. Add the second `DataAdapter` to the `FillDataSet()` method as shown in Listing 11-30.

Figure 11-65: Selecting which tables to add to the DataSet

Listing 11-30: **Adding the New DataAdapter to the Fill Logic**

```
public void FillDataSet(MyDataSet dataSet)
{
  this.oleDbConnection1.Open();

  dataSet.EnforceConstraints = false;
  try
  {
    this.oleDbDataAdapter1.Fill(dataSet);
    this.oleDbDataAdapter2.Fill(dataSet);
  }
  catch (System.Exception fillException)
  {
    throw fillException;
  }
  finally
  {
    dataSet.EnforceConstraints = true;
    this.oleDbConnection1.Close();
  }
}
```

Without adding the line shown in bold font, no sales records would show up in the form. To populate the DataSet correctly, you have to fill it using both the Master and Detail DataAdapters. To handle inserts, updates, and deletes of child records, the method UpdateDataSource() must also be updated, as shown by the bolded lines in Listing 11-31.

Listing 11-31: The Changes Made to Support Inserting, Updating, and Deleting Records from the Detail (Sales) Table

```
public int UpdateDataSource(MyDataSet dataSet)
{
  this.oleDbConnection1.Open();

  System.Data.DataSet UpdatedRows;
  System.Data.DataSet InsertedRows;
  System.Data.DataSet DeletedRows;
  int AffectedRows = 0;

  UpdatedRows =
    dataSet.GetChanges(System.Data.DataRowState.Modified);
  InsertedRows =
    dataSet.GetChanges(System.Data.DataRowState.Added);
  DeletedRows =
    dataSet.GetChanges(System.Data.DataRowState.Deleted);
  try
  {
    if ((UpdatedRows != null))
    {
      AffectedRows =  oleDbDataAdapter1.Update(UpdatedRows);
      AffectedRows += oleDbDataAdapter2.Update(UpdatedRows);
    }
    if ((InsertedRows != null))
    {
      AffectedRows += oleDbDataAdapter1.Update(InsertedRows);
      AffectedRows += oleDbDataAdapter2.Update(InsertedRows);
    }
    if ((DeletedRows != null))
    {
      AffectedRows += oleDbDataAdapter1.Update(DeletedRows);
      AffectedRows += oleDbDataAdapter2.Update(DeletedRows);
    }
  }
  catch (System.Exception updateException)
  {
    throw updateException;
  }
  finally
  {
    this.oleDbConnection1.Close();
  }

  return AffectedRows;
}
```

The last step is to tell the DataSet about the master-detail relationship between the titles and sales tables. In the constructor of the form, I added the code shown in Listing 11-32.

Listing 11-32: **Programmatically Setting Up a Master-Detail Relationship between Tables**

```
using System.Data;

public MyMasterDetailFormWithNesting()
{
  InitializeComponent();

  DataColumn titles_titleID =
            objMyDataSet.Tables["titles"].Columns["title_id"];
  DataColumn sales_titleID =
            objMyDataSet.Tables["sales"].Columns["title_id"];

  DataRelation relation;
  relation = new DataRelation("Sales by title",
                              titles_titleID,
                              sales_titleID,
                              true); // add foreign key constraint
  objMyDataSet.Relations.Add(relation);
}
```

The relationship is specified using a DataRelation object. The last parameter in the constructor call is set to true, indicating that I want the relationship to handle foreign key constraints automatically. This constraint will set up the following actions:

✦ Deleting a record in the Master table will delete all the related Detail records.

✦ Updating the title_id field of a record in the Master table will propagate the changes to the title_id field of all the related Detail records.

To change these default constraints, you can create a ForeignKeyConstraint object, set the new constraint rules, and add it to the DataSet as shown in Listing 11-33.

Listing 11-33: **Adding a New Constraint to the Master-Detail Relationship**

```
public MyMasterDetailFormWithNesting()
{
  // other code...
  objMyDataSet.Relations.Add(relation);

  // remove an existing foreign key constraints than
  // may have already be setup for the title_id column

  ForeignKeyConstraint keyConstraint;
```

```
      ForeignKeyConstraint constraintToRemove = null;
      foreach (Constraint c in objMyDataSet.Tables["sales"].Constraints)
      {
        if (c is ForeignKeyConstraint)
        {

          keyConstraint = c as ForeignKeyConstraint;
          if (keyConstraint.Table.TableName != "sales") continue;
          if (!keyConstraint.Table.Columns.Contains("title_id") )
            continue;
          constraintToRemove = keyConstraint;
          break;
        }
      }

      if (constraintToRemove != null)
        objMyDataSet.Tables["sales"].Constraints.
                                Remove(constraintToRemove);

      // setup a new custom constraint and add it to the DataSer
      ForeignKeyConstraint constraint =
              new ForeignKeyConstraint(titles_titleID, sales_titleID);
      constraint.DeleteRule = Rule.SetNull;
      constraint.UpdateRule = Rule.Cascade;

      objMyDataSet.Tables["sales"].Constraints.Add(constraint);
      objMyDataSet.EnforceConstraints = true;
    }
```

Notice how I searched the `DataSet` constraints and removed any existing
`ForeignKeyConstraint` that may have already been set on the title_id column. If you
try to add a new constraint that conflicts with an existing one, an exception will be thrown.

With the `DeleteRule` used (`Rule.SetNull`), deleting a record in the Master table will cause
all the Detail records to be set to null. If you don't want the Detail records to be changed at all,
use the value `Rule.None`. With the `UpdateRule` used, changing the foreign key (`title_id`)
field in a record of the Master table will also change the Detail records to use the new value for
title_id.

Once you set up a master-detail relationship between tables in a `DataSet`, any `DataGrids`
that use the Master table will automatically discover the relationship with the Detail table
and show the nested rows. If you don't want nested rows to be displayed in a grid, you can
disable them as shown in Listing 11-34.

Listing 11-34: **Disabling the Display of Detail Records in a Master-Detail Grid**

```
grdtitles.AllowNavigation = false;
```

To fetch rows programmatically from the Master table and Detail tables, the code shown in Listing 11-35 will do.

> **Listing 11-35: Programmatically Iterating over Master and Detail Records**

```
void FetchRows()
{
  DataTable masterTable = objMyDataSet.Tables["titles"];
  foreach (DataRow masterRow in masterTable.Rows)
  {
    // get a value from the Master Table
    String title = masterRow ["title"].ToString();

    DataRow[] detailRows = masterRow.GetChildRows("Sales by title");
    foreach (DataRow detailRow in detailRows)
    {
      // get some values from Detail Table
      DateTime d = (DateTime) detailRow ["ord_date"];
      String date = d.ToString("d");  // e.g. 2001-09-01
      String paymentTerms = detailRow ["ord_date"].ToString();
    }
  }
}
```

Running the program with the changes just described, the main form appears as shown in Figure 11-66.

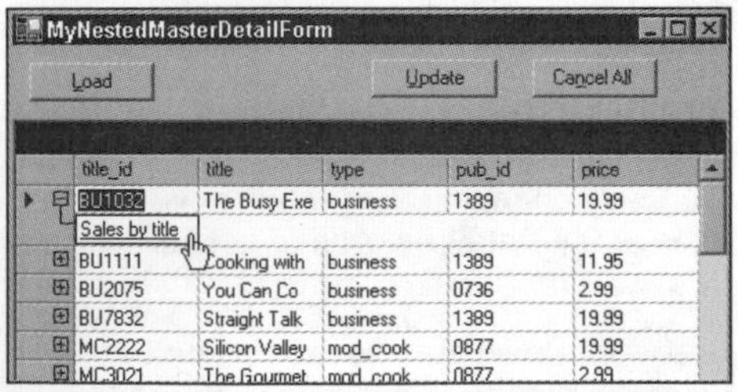

Figure 11-66: The master-detail grid with nested rows

Clicking the plus sign (+) switches the grid to display the Detail sales records for the given book. I'll omit showing the full code for MyMasterDetailFormWithNesting, since it is very similar to the code in the previous master-detail example.

Database Report Forms

When you deal with databases, you often manage large amounts of data. User interfaces are fine for looking at individual records, or small numbers of records. A common requirement is the ability to create reports from the data, showing relationship between tables, trends, summaries, or a filtered subset of the data. Reports are often the only way upper management sees the database data.

VS .NET now comes with full support for creating database-reporting front ends using a number of Crystal Report components that are completely integrated into the product and very easy to use. Reports can be generated both on the screen and in printed form. I'll try to compress as much information about reporting front-end components in the next few sections, even though I'm way over my page quota for this chapter. I'll create a couple different kinds of reports related to the Pubs database that ships with SQL Server 2000.

Creating a simple report

I'll just cut to the chase and show you what the first report will look like. As you can see in Figure 11-67, the report shows a list of all the books in the titles table, along with their prices.

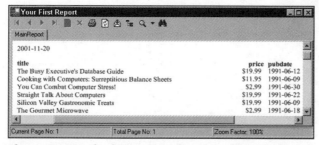

Figure 11-67: The first report, showing a list of books and prices

Nothing too spectacular, but adequate for introducing you to the Crystal Report components and wizards. To create the report, there are a number of steps to follow, none of which require any hand-coding. I created a project called *FrontEnd_DBReport1* to show you how to set up a simple report. Right-click on the Solution Explorer and choose Add New Item from the pop-up menu. In the Add New Item dialog box, select Crystal Report in the Templates section, as shown in Figure 11-68.

The first thing the wizard does is prompt you for the type of report to create, as shown in Figure 11-69.

I selected the first option—*Using the Report Expert*—although you can create a blank report or open an existing one. I also chose the Standard report type, and then clicked the OK button. The Report Expert starts up and takes you through the rest of the report-setup process. Think of the Report Expert as a wizard inside a wizard. The first thing the Expert needs to know is where the data in the report will be coming from. In other words it needs the name of the DataConnection component to use in the report.

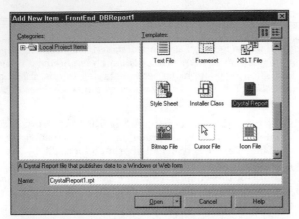

Figure 11-68: Launching the Crystal Report Wizard to create a new report

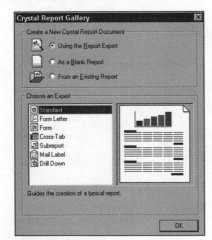

Figure 11-69: Choosing the type of report to generate

I added a `DataConnection` called `sqlConnection1` to the main form of the project before running the Crystal Report Wizard. In the Report Expert, I opened the Current Connections folder under the Project Data folder, expecting to find `sqlConnection1`, but the list was empty, as shown in Figure 11-70.

I believe that in the final released VS .NET software the Data Connections added to your project will show up in the list. Since they didn't show up on my computer, I resorted to Plan B. I clicked on the OLE DB (ADO) folder to launch the OLE DB Wizard, and selected SQL Server as the data provider, as shown in Figure 11-71.

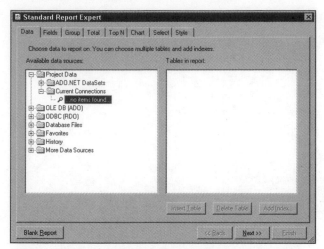

Figure 11-70: The folder under which you should find existing Data Connections used in your project

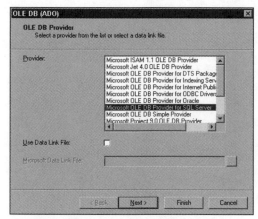

Figure 11-71: Selecting SQL Server as the data provider for the report

Clicking the Next button takes you to a screen where you specify the database to use and the login data. I chose the Pubs database on my (local) computer and then selected Integrated Security, as shown in Figure 11-72.

Clicking the Next button takes you to the last screen of the OLE DB Wizard, as shown in Figure 11-73. I left all the default selections and clicked the Finish button.

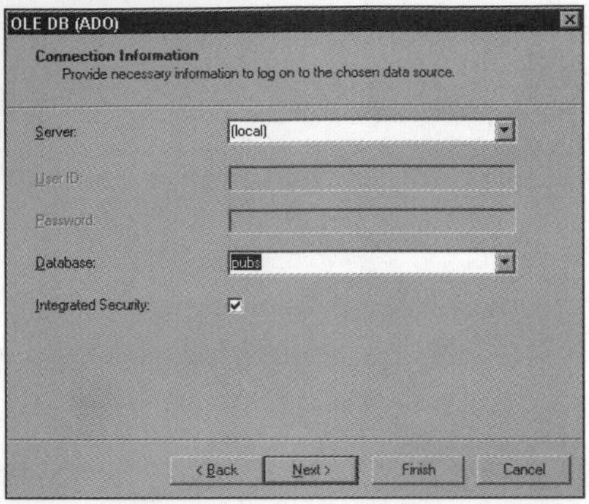

Figure 11-72: Selecting the database and login information

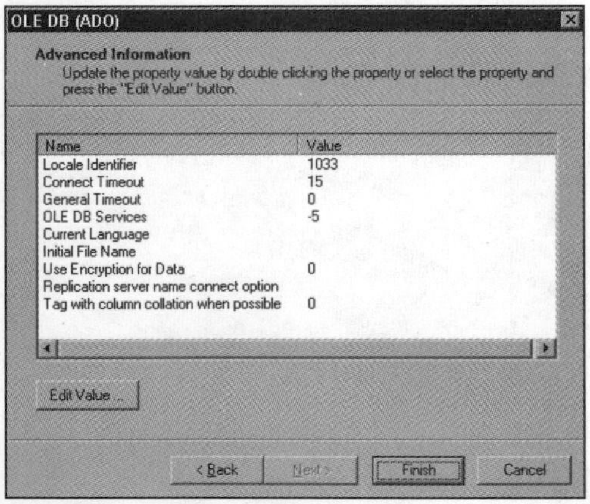

Figure 11-73: The Advanced Information page of the OLE DB Wizard

Clicking the Finish button took me back to the Standard Report Expert. Now that I set up a database connection, the Expert needs to know which table or tables will be used. I selected the `titles` table, as shown in Figure 11-74.

You can select any number of tables. For this first report, I'll only use one. Clicking the Next button takes you to the Fields tab, on which you tell the Expert which column or columns in the selected tables you want on the report. I chose the `title`, `price`, and `pubdate` fields, as shown in Figure 11-75.

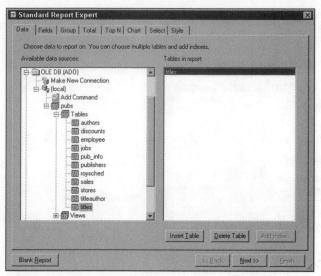

Figure 11-74: Selecting the titles table for the report

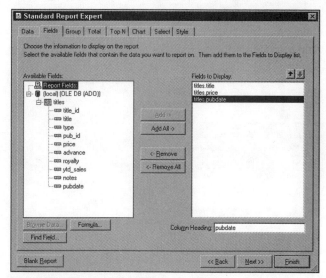

Figure 11-75: Specifying which columns your report will use

Clicking the Next button takes you to the Group tab, where you tell the Expert how you want the records to be grouped. In this simple report, I won't use grouping, so I just skipped to the next tab. (I'll use grouping in the next report.) Clicking the Expert's Next button takes you to the Chart tab (if no grouping options were set). I won't include any charts in my reports, so I skipped this tab as well. The next tab lets you select a subset of information to display in the report. I'll skip this page, too. The last page lets you choose a style for the report. I chose the Shading style, as shown in Figure 11-76.

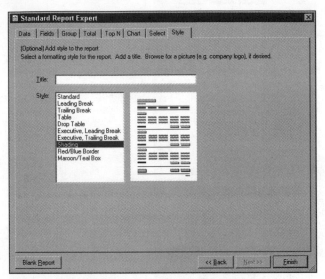

Figure 11-76: Choosing a style for the report

After you click the Finish button, the Report Expert generates the template for the report and displays it in the Forms Designer, as shown in Figure 11-77.

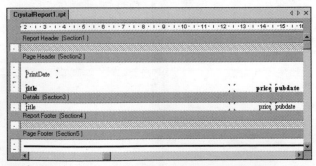

Figure 11-77: The report template created by the Standard Report Expert

I'll leave everything the way it is and run the report. To run it, you need a report viewer. Remember, the report created with the Report Export only sets up a template for the runtime Crystal Report engine to use. To set up a Report Viewer, follow these simple steps. From the Windows Forms page of the Toolbox, select the CrystalReportViewer component, as shown in Figure 11-78.

Figure 11-78: Selecting the component to view Crystal Report with

Drop the component on the main form of the application. The main form will then look like Figure 11-79.

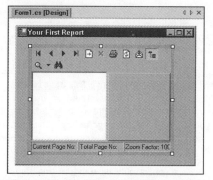

Figure 11-79: The CrystalReportViewer component in a Windows Form

Using the Properties window, I changed the `Dock` property to `Fill`. The single most important property of the viewer is the name of the report to display. In the Properties window, select the `ReportSource` property, and then choose the Browse command, as shown in Figure 11-80.

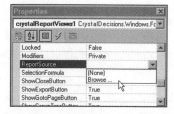

Figure 11-80: Browsing for the report to display in the Report Viewer

In the Browse dialog box, navigate to the folder containing the report file. In my example, the file name is *CrystalReport1.rpt*. Select the file and close the Browse dialog box. The `ReportSource` property should show the selected file. Build and run the application. The report will appear in the main form, as shown in Figure 11-81.

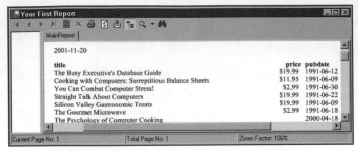

Figure 11-81: The appearance of the first simple report

The various categories of toolbar buttons have the functions described in Table 11-5.

Table 11-5: CrystalReportViewer Buttons

Button Function	Description
Page Navigation Controls	Reports are organized into pages. While an HTML page is one continuous document, reports are divided into pages and can display page headers and footers. The buttons on the left side of the toolbar allow you to navigate from page to page. The buttons in my simple report example are grayed out because my report only has one page.
Close Viewer	If the viewer is shown in a separate modal window, this button closes the Viewer and returns to the main application.
Print Report	Lets you select a printer, set the printer settings, and print the report.
Refresh Report	Refreshes the report with new data from the database.
Export Report	Lets you export the report to a number of different file types, including PDF, Excel, Word, and RTF. You can also create a custom exporter to support other file types.
Show/Hide Group Tree	The Group Tree is like the table of contents of your report. Groups are major sections of a report, and can be set up with the Report Expert. This first report doesn't use grouping, so the tree is empty.
Zooming	You can zoom in or out of the report, using a number of standard settings (for example, Zoom to Page Width) or custom settings.
Search Report	You can use this button search the report for words or phrases.

As mentioned in the table, the Export Report button can save a report in a number of different file formats. I saved the report as an Excel file, and then opened it with Excel. Figure 11-82 shows the report opened with Excel.

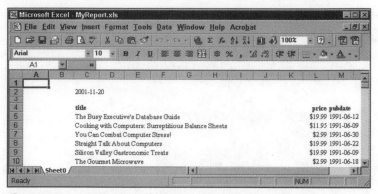

Figure 11-82: An exported report opened with Excel

Keep in mind that I didn't write a line of code to create this report. That's what component-based development is all about: using high-powered tools and Wizards to set up the majority of the basic plumbing and adding your own code only to support nonstandard or special features. Let's move on to a more complicated type of report.

Creating a more complex report

With the first report, I got your feet wet with a real simple report. Still, the previous report used quite of few of the Crystal Report features. But there's much, much more you can do, so I'll show another example. This time, I'll create a report with a more complex structure. I'll add a title page, grouping, group headers, group summaries, and report summaries. Just to add a little spice, I'll throw in a calculated column, using the values of other columns. Figure 11-83 shows the finished report.

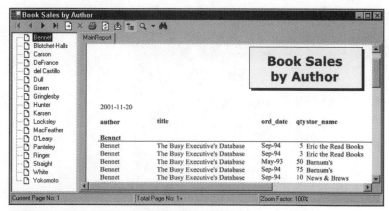

Figure 11-83: A more complicated report

I created the report in a project named *FrontEnd_DBReport2*. As with the previous report, I launched the Crystal Report Wizard by right-clicking on the project in the Solution Explorer and choosing Add New Item from the pop-up menu. To start the Crystal Report Wizard, I chose Crystal Report from the Templates list in the Add New Item dialog box. For the Report Type, I selected Standard. Once the Standard Report Expert started, I selected the five tables in the SQL Server Pubs database, as shown in Figure 11-84.

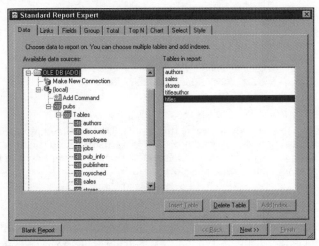

Figure 11-84: Specifying the tables to use in the report

On the next page, the Expert shows the links it automatically set up between the tables selected, as shown in Figure 11-85.

Delete these links

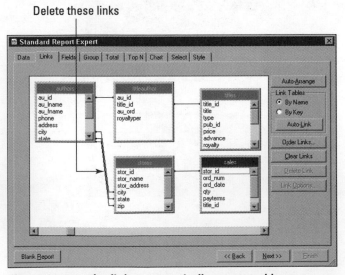

Figure 11-85: The links automatically generated by the Report Expert

Note The Expert automatically joins the authors and stores tables on the city, state, and zip columns. When looking for columns to join tables on, the Expert uses the heuristic of joining columns with the same name. In the case of the authors and sales tables, the city, state, and zip columns have nothing to do with each other, so you must delete the joins by hand: Just click each of the three links and press the Delete key.

Figure 11-86 shows the final links I left.

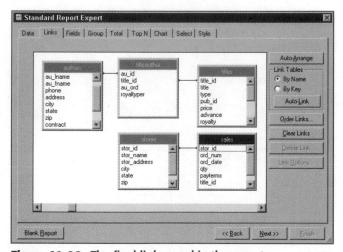

Figure 11-86: The final links used in the report

On the next page, I selected the fields to use in the report, as shown in Figure 11-87.

To make things a little more interesting, I'll add a calculated field to show the revenue for each book. To create the field, I clicked the Formula button shown in the previous figure. In the Formula Name dialog box, I entered the string **Revenue**, as shown in Figure 11-88.

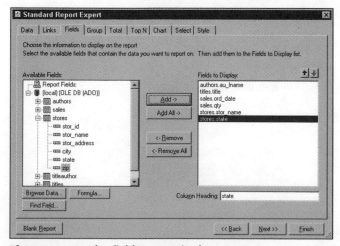

Figure 11-87: The fields to use in the report

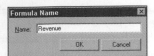

Figure 11-88: Assigning a name to a calculated field

Closing the box with the OK button launched the Formula Editor. I entered the expression to calculate book revenues, as shown in Figure 11-89.

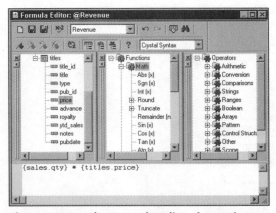

Figure 11-89: The Formula Editor, for setting up calculated fields

I closed the Formula Editor using the Save button on the toolbar. Back in the Report Expert, I selected the new Revenue formula and added it to the Fields to Display, as shown in Figure 11-90.

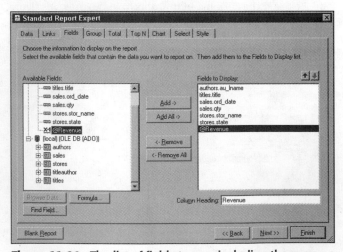

Figure 11-90: The list of fields to use, including the new calculated field

Calculated fields are shown with an @ character in front, to distinguish them from database columns. On the next page, I selected the field au_lname as the *Group By* criterion listbox, as shown in Figure 11-91.

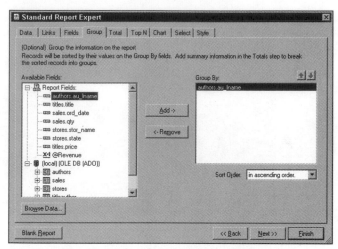

Figure 11-91: Specifying the grouping criterion

Each time the `au_lname` changes in the result set, the report will display the detail items for that author in a separate grouping. You can add more than one field to the Group By listbox. On the next page, I specified the Summarized Fields I wanted. These fields will show up in the Group Footer. Summarized fields are used for subtotals or statistical information. I selected the sales.qty field, as shown in Figure 11-92.

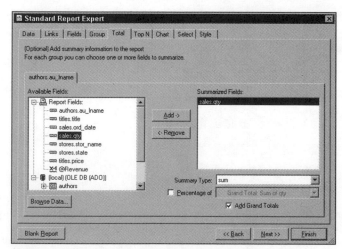

Figure 11-92: Selecting the summarized fields for the Group Footers

By clicking on the Add Grand Totals checkbox, the sales.qty total will also appear as a grand total at the end of the report. On the next and last page of the Report Expert, I selected the report style, as shown in Figure 11-93.

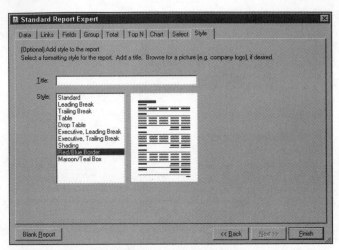

Figure 11-93: Selecting the report style

After closing the Expert, the report appeared as shown in Figure 11-94 in the Forms Designer.

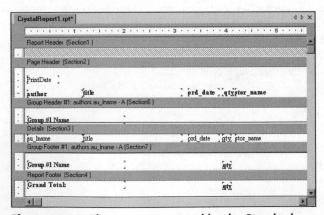

Figure 11-94: The report generated by the Standard Report Expert

I then made some changes to the report. I expanded the size of the Report Header section, and then enabled it by right-clicking inside it and choosing Format Section from the pop-up menu. In the Format Section dialog box, I unchecked the Suppress box, as shown in Figure 11-95. By default, Crystal Report doesn't print the Report Header on a separate page. To force a page break, click on the Report Header band in the Forms Designer. In the Properties window, set the property NewPageAfter to true.

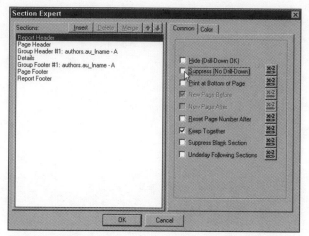

Figure 11-95: Enabling the Report Header by clearing the Suppress checkbox

From the Crystal Reports page of the Toolbox, I dragged a Box Object to the Report Header. I set the Box's `HasDropShadow` property to true and set the `Fill` color to light yellow.

From the Crystal Reports page of the Toolbox, I dragged a Text Object to the Report Header and dropped it inside the Box Object. I double-clicked the Text Object and used in-place editing to enter the text **Book Sales by Author.** I set the text font to Verdana 18 Bold. I also set the `HorAlignment` to `crHorCenterAlign`. The Report Header then looked like Figure 11-96.

Figure 11-96: Adding a Report Header with a shaded box

Page headers contain the repeating text that is shown on every page. In the Page Header section, I changed the first Text Object to display the string *Author,* instead of *au_lname*. I also rearranged some of the field widths to make them fit.

In the Details section, I aligned the fields with the corresponding fields in the Page Header. I changed the format used to display the `ord_date` field by right-clicking on the field and choosing Format from the pop-up menu. On the Format Editor, I chose the date format Mar-99, as shown in Figure 11-97.

In the Group Footer #1 section: I turned off underlining on the `qty` field by setting the `BottomLineStyle` to `crLSNoLine`. I moved the field to align it with the qty field in the Page Header. I added a subtotal field for Revenues like this: I right-clicked in the Group Footer section and selected Insert ⇨ Subtotal from the pop-up menu. In the Insert Subtotal dialog box, I chose the Revenue field. I also checked the Insert grand total field box, as shown in Figure 11-98, to make the Revenue total appear at the end of the report.

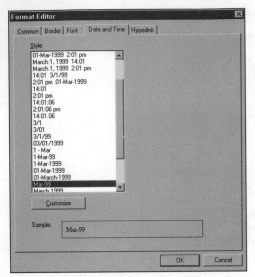

Figure 11-97: The Format Editor for setting data and time formats

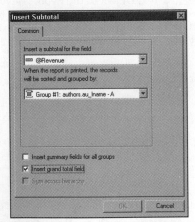

Figure 11-98: Adding a group subtotal field

In the Report Footer section, I also turned off underlining for the qty field. I moved the field to align it with the qty field in the Page Header.

In the Page Footer section, I added a Text Box with the caption, *Book Sales by Author,* and then added a Date field to show the Print Date. To add this field, I right-clicked in the section, and chose Insert ➪ Special Field ➪ Print Date from the pop-up menus.

That's it for the report. To display it, I dropped a CrystalReportViewer component from the Toolbox onto Form1 and set the viewer's `ReportSource` property to my report file CrystalReport1.rpt.

When I ran the application, the report looked like Figure 11-99.

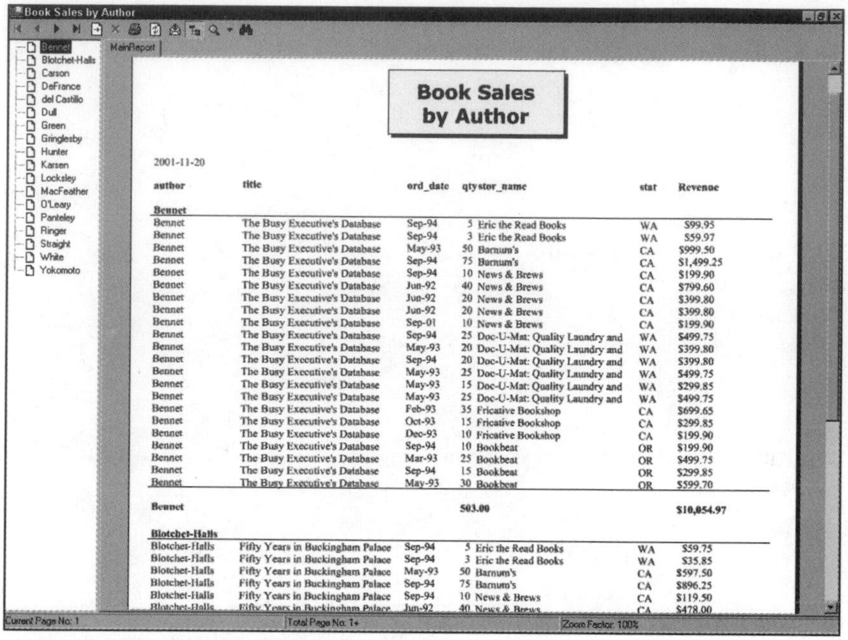

Figure 11-99: The final report, as shown at runtime

The Group Tree on the left side lets you quickly jump to the group describing the given author. The bold column headers (author, title, and so on) appear at the top of each page, because they were added to the Page Header. The Group name (showing the author name) is printed in bold blue text just above a line break. The sales for each of the author's book titles are shown next. Notice the Revenue column, which calculates the book sales by multiplying the book price by the number of items ordered. Although not visible in the figure, the last page of the report also shows the grand totals for the number of books sold and revenue.

I barely scratched the surface of what you can do with Crystal Report, but hopefully I have shown enough to give you an idea of the some of the things you can accomplish. There are wizards for all of the common report types, including Form Letters, Cross Tabs, and Mailing Labels.

Summary

In this chapter, I showed a number of ways to present database information on the screen. Looking over the contents of this chapter, you may have noticed the abundance of figures and the relative scarcity of code listings. The prominent use of figures was no accident. One of the goals of component-based development is to shift the development emphasis from manual coding to the use of tools. VS .NET has a slew of spectacular wizards to accomplish most of the mundane tasks that used to require extensive manual coding. To make good use of the VS .NET development environment is to understand and use the wizards, ergo the copious figures.

✦　　✦　　✦

Tips for the Front End

*I didn't have time to write a short letter, so I wrote a long one
instead.*

— Mark Twain

In this chapter, I'll discuss some of those little tasks that seem to
be noticed only towards the end of a project. Even though they're
little, handling these tasks elegantly can put a nice polish on your
application.

Originally, this chapter was just supposed to be a short section at the
end of Chapter 8, but like Mark said, I wound up not having enough
time to write a small section, so I wrote a whole new chapter instead.
You'll find the material in this chapter to be somewhat of a hodge-
podge of topics, but the common thread is that they all apply to
front-end components.

Displaying a Splash Window

A Splash window is a simple form that is displayed while an application loads, and before a program's main user interface appears. Splash
windows have been in vogue for quite some time now. They aren't just
a fashion. They display useful information, such as a program's name
and version, while indicating that an operation (loading a program) is
in progress.

If you develop an application that takes a long time to load, users may
be confused about what is happening during this time. The system
might be showing an hourglass cursor, but not necessarily. Expert
users may notice increased disk activity and realize the program is
loading, but others may think nothing is happening and try to start
the application again.

To display an hourglass, you might be tempted to use the code
shown in Listing 12-1.

Listing 12-1: This Approach Won't Display a Busy Cursor Correctly While Your Application Loads

```
public MainForm()
{
  InitializeComponent();

  try
  {
   Cursor.Current = Cursors.WaitCursor;

    // TODO: Do other timeconsuming initialization...
  }
  finally
  {
      Cursor.Current = Cursors.Default;
  }
}
```

The problem with the code in the listing is that the hourglass cursor will only be displayed when the mouse cursor is in a window owned by your application. Since no windows of your application are visible yet, no hourglass cursor will appear.

What you need is to display a simple window, often called a *Splash window,* which informs the user that your application is loading. If the load time is expected to be more than a few seconds, you should also include a ProgressBar in the Splash window. I created a simple application called *SplashWindow* that shows the details. The application uses a Splash window that looks like Figure 12-1.

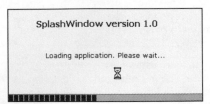

Figure 12-1: An example of a Splash window

Listing 12-2 shows some of the important properties of the form.

Listing 12-2: The Important Properties of the Splash Window

```
Cursor = System.Drawing.Cursors.WaitCursor;
Text = "Name of your Application";
StartPosition = System.WinForms.FormStartPosition.CenterScreen;
BorderStyle = System.WinForms.FormBorderStyle.None;
```

The hourglass cursor is set for the Splash window's cursor. When the loading process ends and the Splash windows is hidden, the cursor automatically reverts to the default cursor.

The Text property is important, because it determines what is displayed in the Windows Task Bar while the application loads.

I set the Splash Window's BorderStyle to None, to hide the caption bar and to prevent the user from moving or resizing the window.

The Splash window is created and managed in the constructor for the application's MainForm, with the code shown in Listing 12-3.

Listing 12-3: **Creating and Managing a Splash Window**

```
public Form1()
{
  InitializeComponent();

  MySplashForm splash = new MySplashForm();
  splash.Show();
  splash.Update();

  splash.progressBar1.Maximum = 100;
  splash.progressBar1.Value = 0;
  for (int i = 0; i < 20; i++)
  {
    // update the progress bar
    splash.progressBar1.Value = i * 100 / 20 ;

    // simulate a timeconsuming operation...
    Thread.Sleep(200);
  }
  splash.Hide();
}
```

The code is inside the constructor for the application's MainForm. The call to splash.Update() is important, because otherwise the window will not appear immediately. In fact, it may not appear at all, depending on how intensive your subsequent initialization code is. Notice how the code directly accesses the ProgressBar component of SplashForm. I changed the ProgressBar's Modifier property to public to make the ProgressBar accessible from the main form. The SplashForm is hidden when the load process is finished.

Note There are cases in which the bulk of your initialization code is in someone else's code. In these cases, it is possible that their code doesn't return until the entire initialization process is complete. If so, you may need to create a secondary thread to run the initialization code on. A timer on the primary thread could then be used to update the ProgressBar periodically.

You can get fairly creative with Splash windows. For example, you could show animated GIF images in it, or even host an MSHTML component and display fancy HTML documents. No matter how rich your Splash window is, the bottom line is that people don't like to wait very long for programs to start. Any delay longer than 5 or 10 seconds is probably too much for many users. If your application takes a really long amount of time to come up, you may want to consider breaking the initialization code into small increments. Then you could bring up the UI of the application in a short amount of time, with a minimally initialized system, and run the additional initialization fragments on a background thread.

Managing User Settings

In this section, I'll be discussing how and where to save application-specific data using files and the Windows registry. Many programs allow users to set options. Often there is a Tools ⇨ Options menu command that lets users change options for display attributes, default directories, screen colors, and any number of other things. I'll group all these things under the category *user settings* and show a few techniques for managing them. What I don't include in user settings are two important items: most recently used files and user data. The former are described in later sections, and managing user data is often too application-dependent to be of general interest.

The first question to answer about user settings is: Are they kept in the registry or in a file? In these last few years, there has been a tendency to move away from the registry and toward the use of files. Does that mean we're back to using .ini files as we did years ago? Not quite. The problem with .ini files wasn't really that they did a poor job of storing information. The problem was that they were put in one of two places — the Windows folder or the application folder — forcing all users of your program to share the same settings. Problems also occurred when there were multiple .ini files in different directories that happened to be on the Windows search path.

The special folders

The uncontrolled use of .ini files quickly turned into a mess. Fortunately, a solution was fairly simple: Create a special folder for each user that logged on to Windows and keep the user's settings and other private files there.

Windows 2000 has a number of folders that are considered *special*. They are special either because of the nature of the information they store, or because their name is tied to system information, such as the user name or the domain name. In case you're interested, you can obtain the user name, domain name, computer name, and other useful system information through the SystemInformation object like this:

```
String userName = SystemInformation.UserName;
String domain = SystemInformation.UserDomainName;
String computerName = SystemInformation.ComputerName;
```

Table 12-1 shows the special folder paths for a user named Ted and a computer named Danielle.

Table 12-1: SpecialFolder Enumeration Values

SpecialFolder Name	Example of SpecialFolder Path
ApplicationData	C:\Documents and Settings\Ted.DANIELLE\ Application Data
CommonApplicationData	C:\Documents and Settings\All Users.WINNT\ Application Data

SpecialFolder Name	Example of SpecialFolder Path
CommonProgramFiles	`C:\Program Files\Common Files`
Cookies	`C:\Documents and Settings\Ted.DANIELLE\Cookies`
DesktopDirectory	`C:\Documents and Settings\Ted.DANIELLE\Desktop`
Favorites	`C:\Documents and Settings\Ted.DANIELLE\Favorites.`
History	`C:\Documents and Settings\Ted.DANIELLE\` `Local Settings\History`
InternetCache	`C:\Documents and Settings\Ted.DANIELLE\` `Local Settings\Temporary Internet Files`
LocalApplicationData	`C:\Documents and Settings\Ted.DANIELLE\` `Local Settings\Application Data`
Personal	`C:\Documents and Settings\Ted.DANIELLE\` `My Documents`
ProgramFiles	`C:\Program Files`
Programs	`C:\Documents and Settings\Ted.DANIELLE\` `Start Menu\Programs`
Recent	`C:\Documents and Settings\Ted.DANIELLE\Recent`
Sendto	`C:\Documents and Settings\Ted.DANIELLE\SendTo`
StartMenu	`C:\Documents and Settings\Ted.DANIELLE\Start Menu`
Startup	`C:\Documents and Settings\Ted.DANIELLE\Start Menu\` `Programs\Startup`
System	`C:\WINNT\System32`
Templates	`C:\Documents and Settings\Ted.DANIELLE\Templates`

The `SpecialFolder` names listed in the left column belong to the enumeration `Environment.SpecialFolder`.

To retrieve the folder path for a special folder, use the method

```
String folderPath = Environment.GetFolderPath(SpecialFolder);
```

with one of the `SpecialFolder` names shown in table like this:

```
String systemPath =
    SystemInformation.GetFolderPath(Environment.SpecialFolder.System);
```

Most of the `SpecialFolder` names are self-explanatory. The only two that deserve a few extra words are `ApplicationData` and `LocalApplicationData`. How are they different and which one should you use? To understand the difference, you need to know about the *roaming user* concept. A roaming user is one that can log in to an account from different computers. Say you have an office network which your computer is part of. You also have a home computer, which can access the office network. You normally work on the office computer, but also work from home. If your office computer is set up with a roaming user account, you can use the same login account in the office and at home.

`ApplicationData` is the folder that stores user settings for a roaming user. This type of folder is stored on a computer that can be accessed from other computers in a network. Besides Microsoft applications, there aren't too many other commercial applications that are prepared to handle roaming users.

`LocalApplicationData` is the folder used by the user logged in locally on this machine. This is the SpecialFolder you are most likely to use for user settings, and the one I'll use in the following sections.

Using a binary file

I wrote a simple application that shows how to use a Special Folder to manage user settings. The program is called *UserSettings_UsingBinaryFiles* and loads and saves a number of variables in a binary file called *MyUserSettings.data* in the `LocalApplicationData` Special Folder. The program uses the built-in serialization and deserialization methods provided by the `BinaryFormatter` component.

I created a separate class called `MyUserSettings` to manage all the user settings. The class also provides `Load()` and `Save()` methods for the application to call when starting and terminating. Listing 12-4 shows the code for `MyUserSettings`.

Listing 12-4: The Class for Handling User Settings

```
using System;
using System.Drawing;
using System.Windows.Forms;
using System.IO;
using System.Runtime.Serialization.Formatters.Binary;

namespace UserSettings_UsingBinaryFiles
{
  [Serializable]
  public class MyUserSettings
  {
    public static String userSettingsFolder =
            Environment.GetFolderPath(Environment.SpecialFolder.
            LocalApplicationData) +
            @"\My Company\My Product";

    public static String userSettingsFile =
          userSettingsFolder + @"\My User Settings.data";

    // the private versioning string
    private static String version = "1.0";

    public String aString = "Default Text";
    public int aInt = 0;
    public bool aBool = false;
    public Color aColor = Color.White;

    public void Save()
```

```
        {

            if (!Directory.Exists(userSettingsFolder) )

                Directory.CreateDirectory(userSettingsFolder);


            Stream myStream = File.Open(userSettingsFile, FileMode.Create,
                                        FileAccess.ReadWrite);

            BinaryFormatter formatter = new BinaryFormatter();

            // save the version explicity, so we can check it
            // before trying to load the file
            formatter.Serialize(myStream, version);
            formatter.Serialize(myStream, this);

            myStream.Close();
        }

        public static MyUserSettings Load()
        {

            if (!File.Exists(userSettingsFile) )
                // use default settings
                return new MyUserSettings();

            Stream myStream = File.Open(userSettingsFile, FileMode.Open);
            BinaryFormatter formatter = new BinaryFormatter();

            // see if the version of MyUserSettings stored
            // in the file matches the version expected

            String savedVersion = (String) formatter.Deserialize(myStream);

            if (!savedVersion.Equals(MyUserSettings.version) )
            {
                // can't use file: use defaults
                myStream.Close();
                return new MyUserSettings();
            }

            // read the settings from the file
            MyUserSettings settings =
                    (MyUserSettings) formatter.Deserialize(myStream);
            myStream.Close();
            return settings;
        }
    }
}
```

I used the standard @-literal notation to define the directory and file names, to avoid having to use double backslashes. Notice the `Serializable` attribute used with the class, just before the class declaration. By default, classes are not serializable. Most of the built-in classes in the .NET Framework are serializable.

Using a formatter to serialize an object allows you to save an arbitrarily complex object. If the object contains or references other serializable objects, those are serialized too. Class `MyUserSettings` demonstrates this with the two fields of type `String` and `Color`. You could serialize an entire application if you wanted to.

Apart from the code that actually reads and writes the user setting data to a file, the only other interesting part of class `MyUserSettings` is how it handles versioning. When you save an object to a stream using the `BinaryFormatter`, the stream will have a certain binary image. If you change the layout of the class (for example, by changing one or more fields) and subsequently try to restore the new class from the binary image of the old class, an exception will occur in the `Load()` method on the following code due to an invalid typecast:

```
MyUserSettings settings =
            (MyUserSettings) formatter.Deserialize(myStream);
```

To prevent exceptions, it is a good idea to store a version string at the beginning of the stream, indicating what version of the class is in the file. Before attempting to read the file back and deserialize it, the version string is checked. If the version is not the same, the binary file is ignored. Another way is to use reflection on the object returned by `formatter.Deserialize (myStream)` and gain access to the properties by name.

To demonstrate the use of `MyUserSettings`, I wrote a small application called *UserSettings_UsingBinaryFiles* with a main form that looks like Figure 12-2.

Figure 12-2: The main form of UserSettings_UsingBinaryFiles

When the application starts up, it calls `MyUserSettings.Load()` to initialize the controls on the form. The user can then enter arbitrary values into the form. When the application shuts down, the form's `Closing` event handler calls `MyUserSettings.Save()`. Listing 12-5 shows the code for the test fixture.

Listing 12-5: Loading and Saving User Settings with MyUserSettings

```
using System;
using System.Drawing;
using System.Collections;
using System.ComponentModel;
```

```csharp
using System.Windows.Forms;
using System.Data;

namespace UserSettings_UsingBinaryFiles
{
  public class Form1 : System.Windows.Forms.Form
  {
    private System.ComponentModel.Container components = null;
    private System.Windows.Forms.Label label1;
    private System.Windows.Forms.Label label2;
    private System.Windows.Forms.Label label3;
    private System.Windows.Forms.Label label4;
    private System.Windows.Forms.TextBox textBoxString;
    private System.Windows.Forms.CheckBox checkBoxBoolean;
    private System.Windows.Forms.Label labelColor;
    private System.Windows.Forms.NumericUpDown numericUpDown1;
    private System.Windows.Forms.Button buttonChooseColor;
    private System.Windows.Forms.ColorDialog colorDialog1;
    protected MyUserSettings myUserSettings;

    public Form1()
    {
      InitializeComponent();

      myUserSettings = MyUserSettings.Load();

      // get the saved settings
      textBoxString.Text = myUserSettings.aString;
      numericUpDown1.Value = myUserSettings.aInt;
      checkBoxBoolean.Checked = myUserSettings.aBool;
      labelColor.BackColor = myUserSettings.aColor;
    }

    protected override void Dispose( bool disposing )
    {
      // standard wizard-generated code...
    }

    private void InitializeComponent()
    {
      // standard wizard-generated code...
    }


    [STAThread]
    static void Main()
    {
      Application.Run(new Form1());
    }

    private void buttonChooseColor_Click(object sender,
                                        System.EventArgs e)
```

Continued

Listing 12-5 *(continued)*

```
    {
      if (colorDialog1.ShowDialog() != DialogResult.OK) return;
      labelColor.BackColor = colorDialog1.Color;
    }

    private void Form1_Closing(object sender,
                              ComponentModel.CancelEventArgs e)
    {
      myUserSettings.aString = textBoxString.Text;
      myUserSettings.aInt = (int) numericUpDown1.Value;
      myUserSettings.aBool = checkBoxBoolean.Checked;
      myUserSettings.aColor = labelColor.BackColor;

      myUserSettings.Save();
    }
  }
}
```

The class `MyUserSettings` is called in two places. Its `Load()` method is called in the constructor, and its `Save()` method is called in the `Closing` event handler.

Using a text file

The original way for developers to store user settings employed .ini files, which are now considered obsolete in the .NET Framework. You won't find classes like `IniFile` or `IniFileSection` in the framework to support .ini files directly. If you want to store user settings in a text file a la .ini file, you'll need to do the work yourself. In this section, I'll show how to use a `DictionaryEntry` to facilitate reading and writing key-value pairs to a flat text file. A `DictionaryEntry` item associates two objects: a key and a value. I'll use the key to store the name of a user setting and the value to store the value of the setting as a string so it can be stored in a text file.

I created a small application called *UserSettings_UsingTextFiles* to demonstrate saving and restoring user settings with text files. The application uses a class called `MyTextUserSettings`, similar to `MyUserSettings` developed in the previous section, except that it uses strings to store all values. Listing 12-6 shows the code for `MyTextUserSettings`.

Listing 12-6: The Source Code for MyTextUserSettings

```
using System;
using System.Drawing;
using System.Collections;
using System.ComponentModel;
using System.Windows.Forms;
using System.Data;
```

```
using System.IO;
using System.Reflection;

namespace UserSettings_UsingTextFiles
{
  public class MyTextUserSettings
  {

    public static String userSettingsFolder =
    Environment.GetFolderPath(
      Environment.SpecialFolder.LocalApplicationData) +
      @"\My Company\My Product";

    public static String userSettingsFile =
        userSettingsFolder + @"\My User Settings.properties";

    public String aString = "Default Text";
    public int aInt = 0;
    public bool aBool = false;
    public Color aColor = Color.Black;

    public void Save()
    {

      if (!Directory.Exists(userSettingsFolder) )

        Directory.CreateDirectory(userSettingsFolder);

      StreamWriter stream = null;
      try
      {

        stream = File.CreateText(userSettingsFile);

        SaveProperty(stream, "aString", aString);
        SaveProperty(stream, "aInt", aInt);
        SaveProperty(stream, "aBool", aBool);
        SaveProperty(stream, "aColor", aColor.ToArgb() );
      }
      catch(Exception e)
      {

        MessageBox.Show(
          "Couldn't create file for the User Settings: " +
          e.Message);
      }

      stream.Close();
```

Continued

Listing 12-6 *(continued)*

```csharp
  }

  protected void SaveProperty(StreamWriter theStream,
                             String theName,
                             Object theValue)
  {


    theStream.WriteLine(theName + "=" + theValue.ToString() );
  }

  public void Load()
  {
    ArrayList dictionary = new ArrayList();
    if (ReadUserSettingsIntoDictionary(dictionary) == false)
      return;

    aString = ValueOfKey(dictionary, "aString");


    aInt = Int32.Parse(ValueOfKey(dictionary, "aInt") );


    aBool = Boolean.Parse(ValueOfKey(dictionary, "aBool") );

    aColor = Color.FromArgb(Int32.Parse(ValueOfKey(dictionary,
                                                   "aColor") ) );
  }

  protected bool ReadUserSettingsIntoDictionary(
                   ArrayList theDictionary)
  {
    if (!File.Exists(userSettingsFile) ) return false;



    StreamReader stream = File.OpenText(userSettingsFile);

    String nextLine;

    while ( (nextLine = stream.ReadLine() ) != null)
    {

      int i = nextLine.IndexOf("=");
      if (i < 0) continue;  // no "=" found

      String nextKey = nextLine.Substring(0, i).Trim();
```

```
            String nextValue = nextLine.Substring(i+1).Trim();

            DictionaryEntry de = new DictionaryEntry(nextKey,
                                                     nextValue);

            theDictionary.Add(de);
        }

        stream.Close();
        return true;
    }

    protected String ValueOfKey(ArrayList theDictionary,
                                String theKey)
    {
        foreach (object o in theDictionary)
        {
            DictionaryEntry de = (DictionaryEntry) o;

            if (de.Key.ToString().Equals(theKey) )
                return de.Value.ToString();
        }
        return null;
    }
  }
}
```

The properties file containing the user settings file is stored in a special folder. As mentioned earlier, the two special folders you can use with user settings are

✦ `Environment.SpecialFolder.LocalApplicationData`

✦ `Environment.SpecialFolder.ApplicationData`

I put the `File.CreateText()` call in a `try` block, to protect the code from exceptions that might occur if the user doesn't have permission to create files, or if a bad filename is used.

To facilitate access to the user settings stored in the text file, the code first uses the method `ReadUserSettingsIntoDictionary()` to read all the lines of the file into an `ArrayList`. Each item in the `ArrayList` is a string of the type

```
Key=Value
```

Then the method `ValueOfKey()` is called for each user setting. The method searches the `ArrayList` for an item with the given key and returns its value as a string. The `Load()` and `Save()` methods shown in Listing 12-6 become somewhat tedious if the list of user settings is really long.

To avoid having to specify which user settings to read and write, you can resort to reflection. With reflection, you can get a list of all the fields of `MyUserSettings` at runtime, as shown in Listing 12-7.

Listing 12-7: Using Reflection to Save the Fields of an Object

```
void SaveObjectInTextFile(object theObjectToSave,
                          String theFilename)
{
  StreamWriter sr = File.CreateText(theFilename);
  Type t = theObjectToSave.GetType();

  FieldInfo [] fields = t.GetFields();
  foreach (FieldInfo f in fields)
  sr.WriteLine(f.Name + "=" + f.GetValue(theObjectToSave) );

  sr.Close();
}
```

One drawback of the reflection approach with text files is that it really only works with data types that can be expressed in text form, such as strings, Booleans, and numbers. If you need to save more complex items like Fonts, Pens, or other object types, you'll need to store them as serialized objects in binary files.

To test MyTextUserSettings, I wrote a small Windows application like the one in the previous section. The code is simple: It calls MyTextUserSettings.Load() when creating the main form, and calls the Save() method in the Closing event handler. Listing 12-8 shows the code.

Listing 12-8: A Simple Windows Application that Uses MyTextUserSettings

```
using System;
using System.Drawing;
using System.Collections;
using System.ComponentModel;
using System.Windows.Forms;
using System.Data;

namespace UserSettings_UsingTextFiles
{
  public class Form1 : System.Windows.Forms.Form
  {
    private System.ComponentModel.Container components = null;
    private System.Windows.Forms.Label label1;
    private System.Windows.Forms.Label label2;
    private System.Windows.Forms.Label label3;
    private System.Windows.Forms.Label label4;
    private System.Windows.Forms.TextBox textBoxString;
    private System.Windows.Forms.CheckBox checkBoxBoolean;
    private System.Windows.Forms.Label labelColor;
    private System.Windows.Forms.NumericUpDown numericUpDown1;
```

```
private System.Windows.Forms.Button buttonChooseColor;
private System.Windows.Forms.ColorDialog colorDialog1;

protected MyTextUserSettings myUserSettings =
                           new MyTextUserSettings();

public Form1()
{
  InitializeComponent();

  myUserSettings.Load();

  // get the saved settings
  textBoxString.Text = myUserSettings.aString;
  numericUpDown1.Value = myUserSettings.aInt;
  checkBoxBoolean.Checked = myUserSettings.aBool;
  labelColor.BackColor = myUserSettings.aColor;
}

protected override void Dispose( bool disposing )
{
  // standard wizard-generated code ...
}

private void InitializeComponent()
{
{
  // standard wizard-generated code ...
}


[STAThread]
static void Main()
{
  Application.Run(new Form1());
}

private void buttonChooseColor_Click(object sender,
                                System.EventArgs e)
{
  if (colorDialog1.ShowDialog() != DialogResult.OK) return;
  labelColor.BackColor = colorDialog1.Color;
}

private void Form1_Closing(object sender,
                      ComponentModel.CancelEventArgs e)
{
  myUserSettings.aString = textBoxString.Text;
  myUserSettings.aInt = (int) numericUpDown1.Value;
```

Continued

Listing 12-8 *(continued)*

```
        myUserSettings.aBool = checkBoxBoolean.Checked;
        myUserSettings.aColor = labelColor.BackColor;

        myUserSettings.Save();
      }
   }
}
```

Using the registry

To demonstrate the use of the Windows registry for storing user settings, I created a project similar to the one in the previous section and called it *UserSettings_UsingRegistry*. I created a new class called `MyRegistryUserSettings` to load and save fields in the Windows registry.

It is important to realize that the registry is a repository that doesn't handle binary data well. While it is completely possible to serialize an object into a binary stream and then save the stream in the registry, the practice should be avoided. Serialized object streams not only tend to get big, in registry terms, but are also completely opaque when viewed with a tool like RegEdit. A user has no clue what the binary data means. Moreover, if the data gets corrupted and requires manual editing in the registry, it is nearly impossible for an administrator to fix it. While presenting unfathomable data in RegEdit can be an advantage if you're storing proprietary information, user settings are not normally in this category.

One of the first decisions you need to make after selecting the registry as your repository of user settings is which registry hive and key to store the settings under. Most applications use the `HKEY_CURRENT_USER` hive, using keys under a path of the type

```
HKEY_CURRENT_USER\Software\My Company\My Product\Product
Version\Settings
```

One of the limitations of this type of key is that all users that log onto the system will share it. To save settings on a per-user basis, use the `HKEY_USERS` hive with a path of this form:

```
HKEY_ USERS\User Name\Software\My Company\My Product\Product
Version\Settings
```

If you check the `HKEY_USERS` hive on your system, you'll find that in practice very few applications use it. To protect the privacy of user data, some applications use a hashed name rather than the actual user name, and some applications even encrypt the data. I won't go to these extremes, because user settings don't typically expose sensitive data.

Listing 12-9 shows the code for `MyRegistryUserSettings`.

Listing 12-9: Saving and Restoring User Settings Using the Registry

```
using System;
using System.Drawing;
using Microsoft.Win32;

namespace UserSettings_UsingRegistry
```

```
{
  public class MyRegistryUserSettings
  {
    String userSettingsPath =
      @"Software\My Company\My Product\1.0\Settings";

    public String aString = "Default Text";
    public int aInt = 0;
    public bool aBool = false;
    public Color aColor = Color.Black;

    public void Save()
    {

      RegistryKey userSettingsKey =
          Registry.CurrentUser.CreateSubKey(userSettingsPath);


      userSettingsKey.SetValue("aString", aString);
      userSettingsKey.SetValue("aInt", aInt);
      userSettingsKey.SetValue("aBool", aBool);
      userSettingsKey.SetValue("aColor", aColor.ToArgb() );


      userSettingsKey.Close();
    }

    public void Load()
    {
      RegistryKey userSettingsKey =
          Registry.CurrentUser.OpenSubKey(userSettingsPath);
      if (userSettingsKey == null) return;


      aString = userSettingsKey.GetValue("aString").ToString();
      aInt = (int) userSettingsKey.GetValue("aInt");
      aBool = Boolean.Parse(userSettingsKey.
              GetValue("aBool").ToString() );
      aColor = Color.FromArgb(
              (int) userSettingsKey.GetValue("aColor") );

      userSettingsKey.Close();
    }
  }
}
```

The code is really short. The Load() and Save() methods use registry classes that are in the Microsoft.Win32 namespace, so I needed to add the following statement at the top of the file:

```
using Microsoft.Win32;
```

Figure 12-3 shows how the user settings look in the registry using RegEdit.

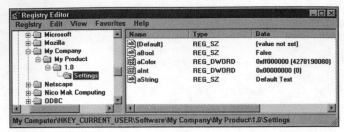

Figure 12-3: The registry, showing the saved user settings

Both the Load() and Save() methods access information in the registry by first calling OpenSubKey() to get a RegistryKey object. After reading or writing the user settings with the RegistryKey, the Close() method is called. Calling Close() is essential if you make any changes to the registry, because it writes the changes back to the registry. Failing to call Close() may result in your changes being partially or completely lost.

To test MyRegistryUserSettings, I created a simple application called *UserSettings_UsingRegistry* that has the interface shown in Figure 12-4.

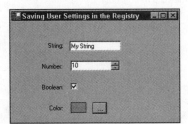

Figure 12-4: The test fixture used with MyRegistryUserSettings

The code is shown in Listing 12-10.

Listing 12-10: The Code for the Test Fixture for MyRegistryUserSettings

```
using System;
using System.Drawing;
using System.Collections;
using System.ComponentModel;
using System.Windows.Forms;
using System.Data;

namespace UserSettings_UsingRegistry
{
  public class Form1 : System.Windows.Forms.Form
  {
    private System.ComponentModel.Container components = null;
    private System.Windows.Forms.Label label1;
    private System.Windows.Forms.Label label2;
```

```csharp
private System.Windows.Forms.Label label3;
private System.Windows.Forms.Label label4;
private System.Windows.Forms.TextBox textBoxString;
private System.Windows.Forms.CheckBox checkBoxBoolean;
private System.Windows.Forms.Label labelColor;
private System.Windows.Forms.NumericUpDown numericUpDown1;
private System.Windows.Forms.Button buttonChooseColor;
private System.Windows.Forms.ColorDialog colorDialog1;

protected MyRegistryUserSettings myUserSettings =
        new MyRegistryUserSettings();

public Form1()
{
  InitializeComponent();

  myUserSettings.Load();

  // get the saved settings
  textBoxString.Text = myUserSettings.aString;
  numericUpDown1.Value = myUserSettings.aInt;
  checkBoxBoolean.Checked = myUserSettings.aBool;
  labelColor.BackColor = myUserSettings.aColor;
}

protected override void Dispose( bool disposing )
{
  // standard wizard-generated code
}

private void InitializeComponent()
{
  // standard wizard-generated code
}

[STAThread]
static void Main()
{
  Application.Run(new Form1());
}

private void buttonChooseColor_Click(object sender,
                                     System.EventArgs e)
{
  if (colorDialog1.ShowDialog() != DialogResult.OK) return;
  labelColor.BackColor = colorDialog1.Color;
}

private void Form1_Closing(object sender,
                           ComponentModel.CancelEventArgs e)
{
  myUserSettings.aString = textBoxString.Text;
```

Continued

Listing 12-10 *(continued)*

```
        myUserSettings.aInt = (int) numericUpDown1.Value;
        myUserSettings.aBool = checkBoxBoolean.Checked;
        myUserSettings.aColor = labelColor.BackColor;

        myUserSettings.Save();
      }
    }
  }
```

Managing Most Recently Used Files

If your application allows users to open files, it is often convenient to save a list of Most Recently Used (MRU) files. Most applications that support this feature display the list under the File menu, either at the bottom of the menu or in a separate submenu called Recent Files or something similar. There are three popular ways to keep track of recently used files:

✦ By storing them in the registry

✦ By storing them in a text file

✦ By storing them as Shell Shortcuts

In the following sections, I'll create three separate components to support the three approaches. I decided to use a different component for each approach not only to keep the code lightweight, but also because you'll probably never use more than one approach in the same project.

Using the registry

With the advent of .NET assemblies and metadata, the Windows registry has suddenly declined in importance. Most of the information that applications stored in the registry is now in assemblies, but there are still certain things that the registry is good for. One of them is storing program preferences and settings. Although Microsoft applications like Word and Excel don't use the registry to save MRU lists (using shortcuts instead), many companies do. The path used to store the list is generally of the following form:

```
HKEY_CURRENT_USER\Software\Your Company Name\Your Product Name\Your
Product Version\Recent Files
```

For example, the company Borland stores the MRU list for their Delphi 5.0 product using the following path:

```
HKEY_CURRENT_USER\Software\Borland\Delphi\5.0\Closed Files
```

I created a simple program called *MRU_UsingRegistry* to show how to use the registry with MRU lists. The program displays the files in the Recent Files menu as shown in Figure 12-5.

There are four places in your code where you normally hook in support for the MRU list:

✦ When the program starts.

✦ When the program ends.

✦ When a new file is opened.

✦ When the Tools ⇨ Clear List of Recently Used Files menu command is selected.

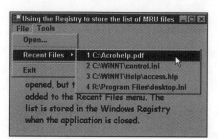

Figure 12-5: The Most Recently Used
file list displayed by MRU_UsingRegistry

Let's take a look at what my demo program does in each of these cases. When the program
loads, it reads the list of files from the registry as shown in Listing 12-11.

**Listing 12-11: Reading the List of Most Recently Used Files from the
Registry**

```
//...
using Microsoft.Win32;

public class MainForm : System.WinForms.Form
{
  String pathMRU =
    @"Software\My Company\My Product\1.0\Recently Used Files";

  public MainForm()
  {
    InitializeComponent();

    LoadMRUs();

    // other initialization...
  }

  private void LoadMRUs()
  {


    RegistryKey MRUkey = Registry.CurrentUser.OpenSubKey(pathMRU);
    if (MRUkey == null) return;


    foreach (String keyName in MRUkey.GetValueNames() )
```

Continued

Listing 12-11 *(continued)*

```csharp
  {
     String filename = MRUkey.GetValue(keyName).ToString();
     AddMRUtoMenu(filename);
  }

  MRUkey.Close();
}

protected void AddMRUtoMenu(String theFilename)
{
  // add the filename to the list

  System.Windows.Forms.MenuItem newMenuItem =
       new System.Windows.Forms.MenuItem();

  // don't add more than 9 items
  int numberOfFiles = menuItemRecentFiles.MenuItems.Count;
  if (numberOfFiles >= 9) return;


  newMenuItem.Text = String.Format("&{0} {1}", numberOfFiles+1,
                                 theFilename);

  if (!MenuContainsFile(theFilename) )
    menuItemRecentFiles.MenuItems.Add(newMenuItem);
}

private bool MenuContainsFile(String theFilename)
{
  foreach (MenuItem m in menuItemRecentFiles.MenuItems)

    if (m.Text.EndsWith(theFilename) )
      return true;
  return false;
}
}

// ... the rest of the class...
}
```

The registry path under which the MRUs are located is

```csharp
String pathMRU =
  @"Software\My Company\My Product\1.0\Recently Used Files";
```

Note the use of the @-literal notation to define the string. By prefixing a literal string with the @ character, you can enter strings containing backslashes without having to use the double-backslash notation. I frequently use @-literals with file paths to keep the string a bit more readable.

The code uses the `Registry` and `RegistryKey` classes to access the registry. To use these classes, you must add the following statement to the code:

```
using Microsoft.Win32;
```

Each MRU item added to the menu is accompanied by a numeric shortcut, starting with the value 1. The demo only saves up to nine filenames, to avoid problems with double-digit short-cuts 10 and above.

When `MRU_UsingRegistry` is closed, it saves all the filenames in the Recent Files menu back in the registry, using the code shown in Listing 12-12.

Listing 12-12: **Saving the List of Most Recently Used Files in the Registry**

```
private void Form1_Closing(object sender,
                           ComponentModel.CancelEventArgs e)
{
  SaveMRUs();
}


private void SaveMRUs()
{
  RegistryKey MRUkey =
    Registry.CurrentUser.CreateSubKey(pathMRU);

  int i = 0;
  foreach (MenuItem m in menuItemRecentFiles.MenuItems)
  {
    String keyName = String.Format("File_{0}", i++);

    int index = m.Text.IndexOf(" "); // skip over the &1 chars

    String keyValue = m.Text.Substring(index+1);

    MRUkey.SetValue(keyName, keyValue);
  }

  MRUkey.Close();
}
```

What is saved in the registry is the complete filename and path for each file in the Recent Files menu. I stripped the shortcut key off the menu text before storing the string in the registry. Figure 12-6 shows how the MRU list looks in the registry with RegEdit.

`MRU_UsingRegistry` updates the list of MRUs each time a new file is opened. Listing 12-13 shows the code.

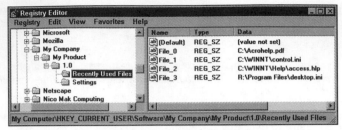

Figure 12-6: The list of Most Recently Used files stored in the registry

---

Listing 12-13: Adding a New File to the Most Recently Used Files List

```
private void menuItemFileOpen_Click(object sender,
                                    System.EventArgs e)
{
  if (openFileDialog1.ShowDialog() != DialogResult.OK)
    return;

  AddMRUtoMenu(openFileDialog1.FileName);
}

protected void AddMRUtoMenu(String theFilename)
{
  // add the filename to the list
  System.Windows.Forms.MenuItem newMenuItem =
    new System.Windows.Forms.MenuItem();

    // don't add more than 9 items
    int numberOfFiles = menuItemRecentFiles.MenuItems.Count;
    if (numberOfFiles >= 9) return;

    newMenuItem.Text = String.Format("&{0} {1}",
                                     numberOfFiles+1,
                                     theFilename);

    if (!MenuContainsFile(theFilename) )
      menuItemRecentFiles.MenuItems.Add(newMenuItem);
}

  private bool MenuContainsFile(String theFilename)
  {

    foreach (MenuItem m in menuItemRecentFiles.MenuItems)
      if (m.Text.EndsWith(theFilename) )
        return true;
    return false;
  }
```

As I indicated earlier, the method `AddMRUtoMenu()` stores no more than nine items in the Recent Files menu. It also checks to see if a given file is already in the list, to avoid adding duplicate entries. The following code adds a numeric accelerator to each filename in the menu, by prefixing the file number with the ampersand (&) character:

```
newMenuItem.Text = String.Format("&{0} {1}",
                                 numberOfFiles+1,
                                 theFilename);
```

The last feature of `MRU_UsingRegistry` to describe is how to clear the list of MRUs. The program has a menu command on the Tools menu called *Clear List of Recently Used Files*. This command clears the list of files from both the menu and the registry. Listing 12-14 shows the code.

Listing 12-14: Clearing the List of Recently Used Files

```
private void menuItemClearMRUList_Click(object sender,
                                        System.EventArgs e)
{
  // clear the list in the File menu
  menuItemRecentFiles.MenuItems.Clear();

  ClearMRUsInRegistry();
}

protected void ClearMRUsInRegistry()
{

  Registry.CurrentUser.DeleteSubKeyTree(pathMRU);
  RegistryKey MRUkey = Registry.CurrentUser.CreateSubKey(pathMRU);
  MRUkey.Close();
}
```

By storing the MRU list in the registry in the `Current_User` hive, all users that log onto the system will share the same list.

Using shortcuts

An elegant way of storing MRU file lists is by using *Shell Shortcuts*. I'm talking about those special files that you can create with Windows Explorer by right-clicking on a file and selecting the Create Shortcut command. Shell Shortcuts can be distinguished from normal (nonshortcut) files by a small pointer in their icon. Figure 12-7 shows a folder containing a normal .txt file and a shortcut file.

Shortcuts are special files that the Windows Shell understands. The files have the (generally hidden) suffix .lnk (for *link*). Polished applications like Microsoft Word and Excel use shortcuts for MRUs.

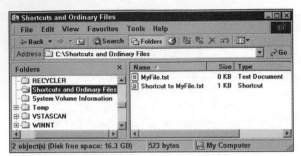

Figure 12-7: A folder containing both a .txt file and a shortcut to a .txt file

In this section, I'll take you through the steps of creating and managing Shell Shortcuts, and in the process I'll make incursions into COM territory—an interesting subject in its own right. The reason for COM is the fact that you can't just create a file and set some attribute to denote it as a shortcut file. That would have been way too simple. Besides, shortcuts need more than a simple attribute: for one thing, they need to store a path to the target file. For example, a shortcut to a .txt file needs to store the full path to `C:\winnt\Notepad.exe` and also the name of the .txt file to launch Notepad with. If you inspect a shortcut file with Windows Explorer, you'll see a number of properties that belong only to shortcut files. Figure 12-8 shows a typical Explorer Properties dialog box for a shortcut file.

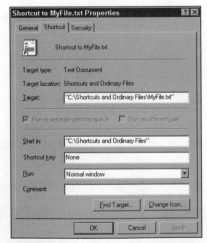

Figure 12-8: The special properties of Shell Shortcut files

Table 12-2 describes the shortcut file properties.

Table 12-2: Shell Shortcut File Properties

Property	Description
Name	This string is the filename of the shortcut file (for example "Shortcut to MyFile.txt").
Icon	The icon is shown immediately to the left of the shortcut name. If the target file is a registered file type in Windows, by default the icon will show the icon for the application registered to handle the file type.
Target Type	This is the string description of the file type. If the file type is not registered, this property will just show the file type.
Target	This is the full path to the target file (for example, `c:\winnt\notepad.exe`). You can also add arguments after the target path. The arguments will be automatically passed to the target when it is run.
Target Location	This is the folder containing the target program referenced.
Start In	This is the working directory that is set just before running the target program.
Shortcut key	Don't confuse shortcut keys with shortcut files. Shortcut keys are hotkeys or accelerators that you can assign to a shortcut. Shortcut keys must use the Ctl-Alt key modifiers. For example, the combination Ctrl-Alt-F5 would be valid. A hotkey allows you to start the target program directly, without needing to go to the Start button or to click a filename in the Windows Explorer.
Run	This property lets you specify the initial window size of the target. You can select Maximized, Minimized, or Normal.
Comment	You can add some descriptive text to a shortcut, perhaps indicating its purpose or the meaning of the arguments the shortcut passes to the target.
Change Icon	This is a button, not a property, but it allows you to change the default icon used in the shortcut. Clicking the button displays a list of icons available in the standard Windows file `c:\winnt\system32\shell132.dll`, as shown in Figure 12-9.

Figure 12-9: Some of the standard icons available in the Windows file Shell32.dll

For the icon used with shortcut files, you can reference an icon in any file you want, in the case that Shell32.dll doesn't have an icon of your liking.

Now it's time to implement a class that lets you manage Shell Shortcuts. Regarding this code, I wish to express my special thanks to Mattias Sjögren for his invaluable assistance. Let's jump right into the details.

The first difficulty I ran into was that Shell Shortcuts can only be created or set up using COM interfaces. No problem, you might think—you just use `TlbImp` to import Shell32.dll into your project and instantiate a `ShellLinkObject`. Nice try, but `ShellLinkObject` is not an instantiable object. You need to create an `IShellLink` object with a `ShellLink` CoClass, but both are missing from Shell32.dll. What you need to do is forget about Shell32.dll and manually define the interfaces, CoClasses, and data types required by IShellLink.

Declaring COM interfaces

So the problem now is how to define an interface in C# that mirrors an existing COM interface with a predefined Globally Unique Identifier (GUID). Just finding out the GUID of a COM interface can be challenging at times. A good place to look is in the following Visual Studio folder:

```
C:\Program Files\Microsoft Visual Studio.NET\Vc7\include
```

Check out the following files for some of the more common interfaces:

✦ ObjIdl.h

✦ ShlObj.h

✦ ComDef.h

These three files define hundreds of interfaces and CoClasses. Both the `IShellLink` interface and `ShellLink` CoClass are defined in ShlObj.h. Their GUIDs can be found in ComDef.h. `IShellLink` is declared in C++ as shown in Listing 12-15.

Listing 12-15: **The C++ Declaration of IShellLink in ShlObj.h**

```
//================================================================
//
// IShellLink Interface
//
//================================================================

#ifdef UNICODE
#define IShellLink        IShellLinkW
#define IShellLinkVtbl    IShellLinkWVtbl
#else
#define IShellLink        IShellLinkA
#define IShellLinkVtbl    IShellLinkAVtbl
#endif

// IShellLink::Resolve fFlags
typedef enum {
    SLR_NO_UI          = 0x0001,
```

```
        SLR_ANY_MATCH          = 0x0002,
        SLR_UPDATE             = 0x0004,
        SLR_NOUPDATE           = 0x0008,
} SLR_FLAGS;

// IShellLink::GetPath fFlags
typedef enum {
        SLGP_SHORTPATH         = 0x0001,
        SLGP_UNCPRIORITY       = 0x0002,
        SLGP_RAWPATH           = 0x0004,
} SLGP_FLAGS;

#undef  INTERFACE
#define INTERFACE     IShellLinkA

DECLARE_INTERFACE_(IShellLinkA, IUnknown)
{
    // *** IUnknown methods ***
    STDMETHOD(QueryInterface) (THIS_ REFIID riid,
                                LPVOID * ppvObj) PURE;
    STDMETHOD_(ULONG,AddRef) (THIS)  PURE;
    STDMETHOD_(ULONG,Release) (THIS) PURE;

    // *** IShellLink methods ***
    STDMETHOD(GetPath)(THIS_ LPSTR pszFile, int cchMaxPath,
                        WIN32_FIND_DATAA *pfd, DWORD fFlags) PURE;

    STDMETHOD(GetIDList)(THIS_ LPITEMIDLIST * ppidl) PURE;
    STDMETHOD(SetIDList)(THIS_ LPCITEMIDLIST pidl) PURE;

    STDMETHOD(GetDescription)(THIS_ LPSTR pszName,
                                int cchMaxName) PURE;
    STDMETHOD(SetDescription)(THIS_ LPCSTR pszName) PURE;

    STDMETHOD(GetWorkingDirectory)(THIS_ LPSTR pszDir,
                                    int cchMaxPath) PURE;
    STDMETHOD(SetWorkingDirectory)(THIS_ LPCSTR pszDir) PURE;

    STDMETHOD(GetArguments)(THIS_ LPSTR pszArgs,
                                int cchMaxPath) PURE;
    STDMETHOD(SetArguments)(THIS_ LPCSTR pszArgs) PURE;

    STDMETHOD(GetHotkey)(THIS_ WORD *pwHotkey) PURE;
    STDMETHOD(SetHotkey)(THIS_ WORD wHotkey) PURE;

    STDMETHOD(GetShowCmd)(THIS_ int *piShowCmd) PURE;
    STDMETHOD(SetShowCmd)(THIS_ int iShowCmd) PURE;

    STDMETHOD(GetIconLocation)(THIS_ LPSTR pszIconPath,
                                int cchIconPath,
                                int *piIcon) PURE;
```

Continued

Listing 12-15 *(continued)*

```
    STDMETHOD(SetIconLocation)(THIS_ LPCSTR pszIconPath,
                               int iIcon) PURE;

    STDMETHOD(SetRelativePath)(THIS_ LPCSTR pszPathRel,
                               DWORD dwReserved) PURE;

    STDMETHOD(Resolve)(THIS_ HWND hwnd, DWORD fFlags) PURE;

    STDMETHOD(SetPath)(THIS_ LPCSTR pszFile) PURE;
};

#undef  INTERFACE
#define INTERFACE    IShellLinkW

DECLARE_INTERFACE_(IShellLinkW, IUnknown)
{
    // *** IUnknown methods ***
    STDMETHOD(QueryInterface) (THIS_ REFIID riid,
                               LPVOID * ppvObj) PURE;
    STDMETHOD_(ULONG,AddRef) (THIS)  PURE;
    STDMETHOD_(ULONG,Release) (THIS) PURE;

    // *** IShellLink methods ***
    STDMETHOD(GetPath)(THIS_ LPWSTR pszFile, int cchMaxPath,
                       WIN32_FIND_DATAW *pfd, DWORD fFlags) PURE;

    STDMETHOD(GetIDList)(THIS_ LPITEMIDLIST * ppidl) PURE;
    STDMETHOD(SetIDList)(THIS_ LPCITEMIDLIST pidl) PURE;

    STDMETHOD(GetDescription)(THIS_ LPWSTR pszName,
                              int cchMaxName) PURE;
    STDMETHOD(SetDescription)(THIS_ LPCWSTR pszName) PURE;

    STDMETHOD(GetWorkingDirectory)(THIS_ LPWSTR pszDir,
                                   int cchMaxPath) PURE;
    STDMETHOD(SetWorkingDirectory)(THIS_ LPCWSTR pszDir) PURE;

    STDMETHOD(GetArguments)(THIS_ LPWSTR pszArgs,
                            int cchMaxPath) PURE;
    STDMETHOD(SetArguments)(THIS_ LPCWSTR pszArgs) PURE;

    STDMETHOD(GetHotkey)(THIS_ WORD *pwHotkey) PURE;
    STDMETHOD(SetHotkey)(THIS_ WORD wHotkey) PURE;

    STDMETHOD(GetShowCmd)(THIS_ int *piShowCmd) PURE;
```

```
    STDMETHOD(SetShowCmd)(THIS_ int iShowCmd) PURE;

    STDMETHOD(GetIconLocation)(THIS_ LPWSTR pszIconPath,
                                int cchIconPath,
                                int *piIcon) PURE;
    STDMETHOD(SetIconLocation)(THIS_ LPCWSTR pszIconPath,
                                int iIcon) PURE;

    STDMETHOD(SetRelativePath)(THIS_ LPCWSTR pszPathRel,
                                DWORD dwReserved) PURE;

    STDMETHOD(Resolve)(THIS_ HWND hwnd, DWORD fFlags) PURE;

    STDMETHOD(SetPath)(THIS_ LPCWSTR pszFile) PURE;
};
```

Ugh! Just the type of code we're all trying to keep away from! The header file declares two versions of the interface: one for Unicode and one for ANSI. I'm going to forget about the ANSI version here, because the .NET Framework uses Unicode internally.

From ComDef.h, the GUID for IShellLinkW is

```
000214F9-0000-0000-C000-000000000046
```

The GUID for the ShellLink CoClass is

```
00021401-0000-0000-c000-000000000046
```

To declare an interface that mirrors a COM interface with an existing GUID, you need a number of special attributes. To declare the IShellLinkW interface, which I'll rename to just IShellLink, I used the code shown in Listing 12-16.

Listing 12-16: **Declaring an Interface to Use an Existing COM GUID**

```
[
  ComImport(),
  InterfaceType(ComInterfaceType.InterfaceIsIUnknown),
  Guid("000214F9-0000-0000-C000-000000000046")
]
public interface IShellLink    { /*... */ }
```

The ShellLink CoClass is declared in a similar manner. From the header file in Listing 12-15, you can see there are all kinds of data types that C# doesn't understand, like LPWSTR, LPCWSTR, int*, and WIN32_FIND_DATAW*. You'll need to set up equivalent C# types, classes, structures, or enumerations for all these types. Table 12-3 shows how some of the more common C++ COM types translate into C#.

Table 12-3: Equivalence between Some C++ and C# Types Used in COM

C++ Type	C# Equivalent Type
WORD value	short value
DWORD value	int value
WCHAR buffer [100]	[MarshalAs(UnmanagedType.ByValTStr, SizeConst=100)] public string buffer;
LPWSTR name	[MarshalAs(UnmanagedType.LPWStr)] StringBuilder name
LPCWSTR name	[MarshalAs(UnmanagedType.LPWStr)] string name
int* myInteger	One of the following: out myInteger ref myInteger
WORD* myWord	One of the following: out myWord ref myWord
FILETIME	FILETIME

Note the use of the MarshalAs attribute when dealing with strings. Using the C# equivalent types and a few standard attributes, I can now finish the declaration of IShellLink as shown in Listing 12-17.

Listing 12-17: The Complete C# Declaration for the COM Interface IShellLink

```
[
  ComImport(),
  InterfaceType(ComInterfaceType.InterfaceIsIUnknown),
  Guid("000214F9-0000-0000-C000-000000000046")
]

public interface IShellLink
{
  void GetPath(
    [Out(), MarshalAs(UnmanagedType.LPWStr)] StringBuilder pszFile,
    int cchMaxPath,
    out WIN32_FIND_DATA pfd,
    SLGP_FLAGS fFlags);

  void GetIDList(
    out IntPtr ppidl);
```

```
void SetIDList(
  IntPtr pidl);

void GetDescription(
  [Out(), MarshalAs(UnmanagedType.LPWStr)] StringBuilder pszName,
  int cchMaxName);

void SetDescription(
  [MarshalAs(UnmanagedType.LPWStr)] string pszName);

void GetWorkingDirectory(
  [Out(), MarshalAs(UnmanagedType.LPWStr)] StringBuilder pszDir,
  int cchMaxPath);

void SetWorkingDirectory(
  [MarshalAs(UnmanagedType.LPWStr)] string pszDir);

void GetArguments(
  [Out(), MarshalAs(UnmanagedType.LPWStr)] StringBuilder pszArgs,
  int cchMaxPath);

void SetArguments(
    [MarshalAs(UnmanagedType.LPWStr)] string pszArgs);

void GetHotkey(
  out short pwHotkey);

void SetHotkey(
  short wHotkey);

void GetShowCmd(
  out int piShowCmd);

void SetShowCmd(
  int iShowCmd);

void GetIconLocation(
  [Out(), MarshalAs(UnmanagedType.LPWStr)]
        StringBuilder pszIconPath,
  int cchIconPath,
  out int piIcon);

void SetIconLocation(
  [MarshalAs(UnmanagedType.LPWStr)] string pszIconPath,
  int iIcon);

void SetRelativePath(
  [MarshalAs(UnmanagedType.LPWStr)] string pszPathRel,
  int dwReserved);

void Resolve(
```

Continued

Listing 12-17 *(continued)*

```
    IntPtr hwnd,
    SLR_FLAGS fFlags);

  void SetPath(
    [MarshalAs(UnmanagedType.LPWStr)] string pszFile);
}
```

There are still a few items to talk about. The GetPath() method uses two nonstandard items: a WIN32_FIND_DATA struct and a SLGP_FLAG enumeration. The first is declared in C++ as shown in Listing 12-18.

Listing 12-18: The C++ Declaration of the struct WIN32_FIND_DATAW

```
// in Windef.h
#define MAX_PATH 260

// in Winbase.h
typedef struct _WIN32_FIND_DATAW {
    DWORD dwFileAttributes;
    FILETIME ftCreationTime;
    FILETIME ftLastAccessTime;
    FILETIME ftLastWriteTime;
    DWORD nFileSizeHigh;
    DWORD nFileSizeLow;
    DWORD dwReserved0;
    DWORD dwReserved1;
    WCHAR   cFileName[ MAX_PATH ];
    WCHAR   cAlternateFileName[ 14 ];
} WIN32_FIND_DATAW;
```

The WIN32_FIND_DATA struct can be redeclared in C# as shown in Listing 12-19.

Listing 12-19: Redeclaring a C++ struct in C#

```
[StructLayoutAttribute(LayoutKind.Sequential,
                       CharSet=CharSet.Unicode)]
public struct WIN32_FIND_DATA
{
  public int dwFileAttributes;
  public FILETIME ftCreationTime;
  public FILETIME ftLastAccessTime;
  public FILETIME ftLastWriteTime;
```

```
  public int nFileSizeHigh;
  public int nFileSizeLow;
  public int dwReserved0;
  public int dwReserved1;
  [MarshalAs(UnmanagedType.ByValTStr, SizeConst=MAX_PATH)]
  public string cFileName;
  [MarshalAs(UnmanagedType.ByValTStr, SizeConst=14)]
  public string cAlternateFileName;
  private const int MAX_PATH = 260;
}
```

Notice the `StructureLayout` attribute in front of the declaration. It controls the physical layout of the fields in memory. To mimic a COM struct, you need to make sure all the fields stay in exactly the same order as declared, so you need the `LayoutKind.Sequential` value. Since the struct holds character data encoded in Unicode, the `CharSet.Unicode` flag is also used. By default, characters are always Unicode in the .NET Framework, so you don't strictly need `CharSet` unless you're *not* using Unicode.

The last items to describe are enumerations. `GetPath()` uses the `SLGP_FLAG` enumeration, which is declared in C++ as shown in Listing 12-20.

Listing 12-20: The C++ Declaration of the Enumeration SLGP_FLAGS

```
// in Shl0bj.h
typedef enum {
    SLGP_SHORTPATH      = 0x0001,
    SLGP_UNCPRIORITY    = 0x0002,
    SLGP_RAWPATH        = 0x0004,
} SLGP_FLAGS;
```

To declare an equivalent enum in C#, you need to use the code shown in Listing 12-21.

Listing 12-21: Redeclaring a C++ enum in C#

```
[Flags()]
public enum SLGP_FLAGS
{
  SLGP_SHORTPATH   = 0x1,
  SLGP_UNCPRIORITY = 0x2,
  SLGP_RAWPATH     = 0x4,
}
```

The `Flags` attribute tells the compiler to consider the fields of the enumeration to be bit flags that can be used alone or ORed together.

Now that all the basic pieces have been shown individually, I can show you the entire C# file that declares the necessary IShellLink interfaces, CoClasses, and related items. I called the file *UCOMIShellLink.cs*. The UCOM prefix is used in the .NET Framework to designate wrapper files for unmanaged COM code. The complete code is shown in Listing 12-22.

Listing 12-22: The Complete Source Code for UCOMIShellLink

```csharp
using System;
using System.Text;
using System.Runtime.InteropServices;

namespace MRU_UsingShortcuts
{
  // This file implements the Unicode versions of various
  // interfaces.

  [Flags()]
  public enum SLR_FLAGS
  {
    SLR_NO_UI = 0x1,
    SLR_ANY_MATCH = 0x2,
    SLR_UPDATE = 0x4,
    SLR_NOUPDATE = 0x8,
    SLR_NOSEARCH = 0x10,
    SLR_NOTRACK = 0x20,
    SLR_NOLINKINFO = 0x40,
    SLR_INVOKE_MSI = 0x80
  }

  [Flags()]
  public enum SLGP_FLAGS
  {
    SLGP_SHORTPATH = 0x1,
    SLGP_UNCPRIORITY = 0x2,
    SLGP_RAWPATH = 0x4
  }

  [StructLayoutAttribute(LayoutKind.Sequential,
                         CharSet=CharSet.Unicode)]
  // Unicode version
  public struct WIN32_FIND_DATA
  {
    public int dwFileAttributes;
    public FILETIME ftCreationTime;
    public FILETIME ftLastAccessTime;
    public FILETIME ftLastWriteTime;
    public int nFileSizeHigh;
    public int nFileSizeLow;
    public int dwReserved0;
    public int dwReserved1;
    [MarshalAs(UnmanagedType.ByValTStr, SizeConst=MAX_PATH)]
```

```
  public string cFileName;
  [MarshalAs(UnmanagedType.ByValTStr, SizeConst=14)]
  public string cAlternateFileName;
  private const int MAX_PATH = 260;
}

[
ComImport(),
InterfaceType(ComInterfaceType.InterfaceIsIUnknown),
Guid("000214F9-0000-0000-C000-000000000046")
]
// Unicode version
public interface IShellLink
{
  void GetPath(
    [Out(), MarshalAs(UnmanagedType.LPWStr)]
            StringBuilder pszFile,
    int cchMaxPath,
    out WIN32_FIND_DATA pfd,
    SLGP_FLAGS fFlags);

  void GetIDList(
    out IntPtr ppidl);

  void SetIDList(
    IntPtr pidl);

  void GetDescription(
    [Out(), MarshalAs(UnmanagedType.LPWStr)]
            StringBuilder pszName,
    int cchMaxName);

  void SetDescription(
    [MarshalAs(UnmanagedType.LPWStr)] string pszName);

  void GetWorkingDirectory(
    [Out(), MarshalAs(UnmanagedType.LPWStr)]
            StringBuilder pszDir,
    int cchMaxPath);

  void SetWorkingDirectory(
    [MarshalAs(UnmanagedType.LPWStr)] string pszDir);

  void GetArguments(
    [Out(), MarshalAs(UnmanagedType.LPWStr)]
            StringBuilder pszArgs,
    int cchMaxPath);

  void SetArguments(
    [MarshalAs(UnmanagedType.LPWStr)] string pszArgs);

  void GetHotkey(
```

Continued

Listing 12-22 *(continued)*

```
        out short pwHotkey);

    void SetHotkey(
        short wHotkey);

    void GetShowCmd(
        out int piShowCmd);

    void SetShowCmd(
        int iShowCmd);

    void GetIconLocation(
        [Out(), MarshalAs(UnmanagedType.LPWStr)]
                StringBuilder pszIconPath,
        int cchIconPath,
        out int piIcon);

    void SetIconLocation(
        [MarshalAs(UnmanagedType.LPWStr)] string pszIconPath,
        int iIcon);

    void SetRelativePath(
        [MarshalAs(UnmanagedType.LPWStr)] string pszPathRel,
        int dwReserved);

    void Resolve(
        IntPtr hwnd,
        SLR_FLAGS fFlags);

    void SetPath(
        [MarshalAs(UnmanagedType.LPWStr)] string pszFile);
    }

    [
    ComImport(),
    Guid("00021401-0000-0000-C000-000000000046")
    ]
    // This is a creatable class. It implements
    // IPersistFile and IShellLink
    public class ShellLink
    {
    }
}
```

Passing strings to and from COM methods

Many of the IShellLink methods use strings. Consider for example the declaration of GetDescription() shown in Listing 12-23.

Listing 12-23: A COM Wrapper Method Using Strings

```
void GetDescription(
  [Out(), MarshalAs(UnmanagedType.LPWStr)]
        StringBuilder pszName, int cchMaxName);
```

The method returns a string using a `StringBuilder` representing a `WChar` array with a specific size. A `MarshalAs` attribute is used to tell the .NET Framework how to handle the native unmanaged type. To call `GetDescription()` from C#, you need to set up a `StringBuilder` object with the required size and call the method as shown in Listing 12-24.

Listing 12-24: Getting a Returned String from a COM Wrapper Method

```
StringBuilder buffer = new StringBuilder(5000);
shellLink.GetWorkingDirectory(buffer, buffer.Capacity);
workingDirectory = buffer.ToString();
```

`StringBuilder.Capacity` denotes the size of the `WChar` buffer. The value is passed to the class constructor, and you can use any value you need. In my case, 5000 characters is more than enough space for any strings that `GetWorkingDirectory()` will be returning.

To pass a string to a method, such as with `SetWorkingDirectory()`, you can just use a plain String object as shown in Listing 12-25.

Listing 12-25: Passing a String to a COM Wrapper Method

```
String workingDirectory = "MyDirectory";
shellLink.SetWorkingDirectory(workingDirectory);
```

A wrapper for the COM object ShellLink

To make it easy to call the `ShellLink` methods, I created a wrapper class called `FileShortcut`. The class basically exposes the `IShellLink` methods as simple properties, calling the underlying `IShellLink` methods at two specific times: when loading and saving Shell Shortcut files. The class is shown in Listing 12-26.

Listing 12-26: The Complete Code for FileShortcut, a Wrapper Class for IShellLink

```
using System;
using System.Drawing;
using System.Diagnostics;
```

Continued

Listing 12-26 *(continued)*

```csharp
using System.IO;
using System.Text;
using System.Windows.Forms;
using System.Runtime.InteropServices;

namespace MRU_UsingShortcuts
{
  public class FileShortcut
  {
    private const String shortcutSuffix = ".lnk";

    private const int SW_SHOWNORMAL = 1;
    private const int SW_SHOWMINIMIZED = 2;
    private const int SW_SHOWMAXIMIZED = 3;
    private const int SW_SHOWMINNOACTIVE = 7;

    private       StringBuilder buffer = new StringBuilder(5000);

    // shortcut name, such as  c:\MyFolder\MyName.txt.lnk
    private String shortcutFilepath;

    private IShellLink shellLink = (IShellLink) new ShellLink();
    private UCOMIPersistFile file;

    // All the following fields are stored in the Shortcut file.
    // Note: the target is the file that this shortcut is a link to

    // arguments to pass to target file
    public String arguments = "";

    // shows up in Comment field on Windows Explorer
    // Property dialog
    public String description = "";

    // hotKey to invoke this shortcut with, e.g. Alt-F6
    public Keys hotKey = Keys.None;

    // the path of a file containing the icon,
    // e.g. c:\WinNT\System32\Shell32.dll
    public String iconPath = "";

    // the index of the icon in the iconPath file, e.g. 14
    public int iconIndex = 0;

    // path to the target file, e.g. "c:\WinNT\Notepad.exe"
    public String path = "";

    // initial size of target window
    public ProcessWindowStyle
          showCommand = ProcessWindowStyle.Normal;
```

```csharp
      // starting Working Directory for target
      public String workingDirectory = "";

      // theShortcutName is something like:
      // "C:\Winnt\Notepad.exe"
      public FileShortcut(String theShortcutFilepath)
      {
        shortcutFilepath = theShortcutFilepath;
        if (!shortcutFilepath.EndsWith(shortcutSuffix) )
          shortcutFilepath += shortcutSuffix;

        file = shellLink as UCOMIPersistFile;

        if (Exists() )
          // initialize fields from Shortcut file
          Load();
      }

  public String Arguments
  {
    get { return arguments; }
    set { arguments = value; }
  }

  public String Description
  {
    get { return description; }
    set { description = value; }
  }

  public Keys Hotkey
  {
    get { return hotKey; }
    set { hotKey = value; }
  }

  public int IconIndex
  {
    get { return iconIndex; }
    set { iconIndex = value; }
  }
}

  public String IconPath
  {
    get { return iconPath; }
    set { iconPath = value; }
  }

  public String Path
  {
    get { return path; }
```

Continued

Listing 12-26 *(continued)*

```
  set {
    if (value.EndsWith(shortcutSuffix) )
      throw new ArgumentException(
        "A shortcut can't point to another shortcut.");
    path = value; }
}

public ProcessWindowStyle ShowCommand
{
  get { return showCommand; }
  set { showCommand = value; }
}

public String WorkingDirectory
{
  get { return workingDirectory; }
  set { workingDirectory = value; }
}

public bool Exists()
{
  return File.Exists(shortcutFilepath);
}

public void Save()
{
  SaveAs(shortcutFilepath);
}

public void SaveAs(String theFilename)
{
  shellLink.SetArguments(arguments);
  shellLink.SetDescription(description);
  shellLink.SetWorkingDirectory(workingDirectory);
  shellLink.SetPath(path);
  shellLink.SetIconLocation(iconPath, iconIndex);

  switch (showCommand)
  {
    case ProcessWindowStyle.Minimized:
      shellLink.SetShowCmd(SW_SHOWMINNOACTIVE);
      break;

    case ProcessWindowStyle.Maximized:
      shellLink.SetShowCmd(SW_SHOWMAXIMIZED);
      break;

    default:
      shellLink.SetShowCmd(SW_SHOWNORMAL);
```

```
      break;
  }

  // convert 32-bit .NET format to native 16-bit key code
  int modifiers = (int) (hotKey & Keys.Modifiers) >> 8;
  int keyCode= (int) (hotKey & Keys.KeyCode);
  keyCode += modifiers;
  short wHotkey = (short) keyCode;
  shellLink.SetHotkey(wHotkey);

  if (!theFilename.EndsWith(shortcutSuffix) )
    theFilename += shortcutSuffix;

  FileInfo fi = new FileInfo(theFilename);
  String folderPath = fi.DirectoryName; // e.g. c:\winnt

  if (!Directory.Exists(folderPath) )
    Directory.CreateDirectory(folderPath);

    file.Save(theFilename, false);
}

public void Load()
{
  file.Load(shortcutFilepath, 0);

  shellLink.GetArguments(buffer, buffer.Capacity);
  arguments = buffer.ToString();

  shellLink.GetDescription(buffer, buffer.Capacity);
  description = buffer.ToString();

  short wHotkey;
  int dwHotkey;
  shellLink.GetHotkey(out wHotkey);
  // convert native 16-bit key code to 32-bit .NET format
  dwHotkey = ((wHotkey & 0xFF00) << 8) | (wHotkey & 0xFF);
  hotKey = (Keys) dwHotkey;

  shellLink.GetIconLocation(buffer, buffer.Capacity,
                            out iconIndex);
  iconPath = buffer.ToString();

  WIN32_FIND_DATA wfd = new WIN32_FIND_DATA();
  shellLink.GetPath(buffer, buffer.Capacity, out wfd,
                    SLGP_FLAGS.SLGP_UNCPRIORITY );
  path = buffer.ToString();

  shellLink.GetWorkingDirectory(buffer, buffer.Capacity);
  workingDirectory = buffer.ToString();

  int windowStyle;
```

Continued

Listing 12-26 *(continued)*

```
      shellLink.GetShowCmd(out windowStyle);
      switch (windowStyle)
      {
        case SW_SHOWMINIMIZED:
        case SW_SHOWMINNOACTIVE:
          showCommand = ProcessWindowStyle.Minimized;
          break;

        case SW_SHOWMAXIMIZED:
          showCommand = ProcessWindowStyle.Maximized;
          break;

        default:
          showCommand = ProcessWindowStyle.Normal;
          break;
      }
    }
  }
}
```

There are several parts of the code that are of particular interest. First, the wrapper instantiates a COM ShellLink object with the following code:

```
IShellLink shellLink = (IShellLink) new ShellLink();
UCOMIPersistFile file;
```

The COM `ShellLink` object implements two interfaces: `IShellLink` and `IPersistFile`. The interface `IPersistFile` is used to load and save shortcut files. The class constructor is passed a file shortcut name. The code looks like Listing 12-27.

Listing 12-27: The Complete Code for FileShortcut, a Wrapper Class for IShellLink

```
public FileShortcut(String theShortcutFilepath)
{

  shortcutFilepath = theShortcutFilepath;
  if (!shortcutFilepath.EndsWith(shortcutSuffix) )
    shortcutFilepath += shortcutSuffix;

  file = shellLink as UCOMIPersistFile;

  if (Exists() )
    // initialize fields from Shortcut file
    Load();
}
```

If the file exists, it calls the Load() method to read the shortcut attributes and set all the initial values of the FileShortcut properties. The IPersistFile interface is retrieved from the ShellLink COM object and assigned to the field named file, for the Load() and Save() methods to use. When retrieving shortcut attributes from a ShellLink COM object, some of the properties are converted from native COM types to .NET Framework types. For example, the Hotkey property is retrieved and used as shown in Listing 12-28.

> **Listing 12-28: Converting the ShellLink's Hotkey Property to a .NET Framework Value**

```
short wHotkey;
int dwHotkey;
shellLink.GetHotkey(out wHotkey);
// convert native 16-bit key code to 32-bit .NET format
dwHotkey = ((wHotkey & 0xFF00) << 8) | (wHotkey & 0xFF);
hotKey = (Keys) dwHotkey;
```

The native COM encoding for key codes uses a 16-bit word. The upper 8 bits contain the modifier (such as Ctrl or Alt), while the lower 8 bits contain the key code (such as "A"). In the .NET Framework, key codes are 32-bit values. The modifier is stored in bits (16..23), while the 16-bit key code is stored in bits (0..15).

Another property that requires conversion from native to .NET Framework format is showCommand. The native COM values use the values

```
int SW_SHOWNORMAL      = 1;
int SW_SHOWMINIMIZED   = 2;
int SW_SHOWMAXIMIZED   = 3;
int SW_SHOWMINNOACTIVE = 7;
```

The .NET Framework uses the ProcessWindowStyle enumeration that has equivalent, but different, values.

Using the FileShortcut class to manage MRU files

I can finally get back to the original purpose of all this COM and wrapper business: saving and retrieving Most Recently Used file lists. I created an application called *MRU_UsingShortcuts* that has a main form that looks like Figure 12-10.

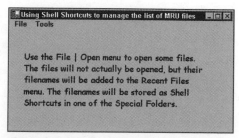

Figure 12-10: The user interface of MRU_UsingShortcuts

When you open a file, its filename is added to the MRU menu. When the program ends, it stores a list of the recently used files in Shell Shortcut files stored in the folder

```
C:\Documents and Settings\Ted.FCI.000\Local Settings\Application
Data\My Company\My Product\Recent
```

One of the nice things about shortcut files is their timestamp, because you not only get to know the name of a recently used file, but also the date it was last used. Knowing the date gives you more flexibility. For example, you could use the shortcut timestamps to display files in reverse chronological order, or to delete shortcuts that were older than a certain date.

Listing 12-29 shows the code that saves a list of Shell Shortcuts.

Listing 12-29: **Using the Class FileShortcut to Save a List of MRU Files**

```csharp
private void SaveMRUs()
{
  foreach (MenuItem m in menuItemRecentFiles.MenuItems)
  {
    int i = m.Text.IndexOf(" "); // skip over the &1 chars

    // fullpath is something like 'c:\winnt\notepad.exe'
    String fullPath = m.Text.Substring(i+1);

    // parse the filepath into directory and filename



    FileInfo fi = new FileInfo(fullPath);
    String folderPath = fi.DirectoryName; // e.g. c:\winnt
    String filename = fi.Name;         // e.g. notepad.exe

    if (filename.Equals("") ) continue;
    FileShortcut shortcut = new FileShortcut(fullPath);
    shortcut.Path = fullPath;
    shortcut.WorkingDirectory = folderPath;
    shortcut.Hotkey = Keys.Alt | Keys.F12;
    shortcut.Arguments = "My Arguments";
    shortcut.Description = "My Description";

    // don't set the IconPath or IconIndex if
    // you want to use the default icon
    // shortcut.IconPath = @"c:\winnt\shell32.dll";
    // shortcut.IconIndex = 15;

    shortcut.SaveAs(pathMRU + @"\" + filename);
  }
}
```

At the end of the method, notice the two commented-out lines:

```
// shortcut.IconPath = @"c:\winnt\shell32.dll";
// shortcut.IconIndex = 15;
```

Shortcut files use a default icon if you don't specify one. If the shortcut references a file type for which an application is registered, that application's icon will be used. By uncommenting the two lines, you can pick a file containing icons and choose an icon from that file.

One last item of interest is how the .NET Framework handles filename parsing. If you have a filename containing a complete path, there are built-in methods you can use to parse out the directory path, the filename, and the file extension. Listing 12-30 shows an example.

Listing 12-30: Parsing a Filepath into its Constituent Components

```
String filename = @"C:\WINNT\system32\perfmon.exe";
FileInfo fi = new FileInfo(fullPath);
String folderPath = fi.DirectoryName;  // C:\WINNT\system32
String filename = fi.Name;                  // perfmon.exe

String extension = fi.Extension;      //.exe
```

Summary

Like I said at the beginning of this chapter, many of the tips and techniques described here are applicable to not just the front end, but also the middle tier and the back end. The COM Interoperability code is probably the best example. Even though some developers will elect not to use Shell Shortcuts in their applications, the COM tips I provided should be helpful in many other situations.

✦   ✦   ✦

Middle-Tier Components

Web Forms

I never could make out what those damn dots meant.

—Lord Randolph Churchill, speaking about
decimal points in a national budget proposal

Those pesky little dots can be important, especially if you're putting together your country's national budget proposal. But, hey, nobody's perfect. As programmers, we use dots all over the place, so we had better *make out what those damn dots mean.* The object-dot-method notation is the basis of most object-oriented programming languages, including C#.

In this chapter, I'll discuss .NET Web Forms, one of the most exciting new aspects of the ASP.NET Framework. After looking at the ASP.NET approach to Web applications, you'll realize how simplistic the ASP model is in comparison. Who knows, you might even wonder how something as primitive as ASP technology ever got off the ground. You'll also discover how familiar the ASP.NET programming model is, if you ever worked with RAD tools like Delphi or Visual Basic.

What Was Wrong with ASP?

The short answer is: Nothing. The longer answer is: ASP worked, but was fairly primitive, and needed improving in several areas. The ASP architecture became increasingly problematic with large Web applications and under conditions of high traffic. It needed a serious face-lift. Let's take a look briefly at how Web applications were developed on IIS servers before the advent of ASP.NET. In the former Active Server Pages (ASP) model, you worked with a single .asp file for each page the user could request. The ASP page contained ordinary HTML code, that was returned intact to the user, and special ASP tags that enabled you to embed ASP script.

And here is the first problem: using a single file to hold both HTML code and executable script. The problem is that the people working on HTML code tend to have a graphics background, with limited or even no programming experience. The folks that work on the script code usually have more programming experience, often with little interest in Web graphics and page layout. Forcing both groups to share a single file for each HTML page made it difficult to manage development of medium to large Web sites.

The purpose of the ASP script code was to generate dynamic content for the page, in the form of HTML. When a user entered an ASP page's URI in his or her browser, the ASP runtime would run the ASP script on the page, gather up all the static and dynamic HTML code for the page, and ship it back to the user.

And here is another problem: the use of script to generate dynamic content. Scripted languages like ECMAScript and VBScript may be easy to use, but they have significant drawbacks in the performance department. Scripted languages are interpreted at runtime, so each line is translated into executable code on the fly and then executed. Because of the extra translation step, scripted code can be orders of magnitude slower than compiled code.

The ASP model satisfied the requirement for dynamic page content, and did so using server-side script. Since the client never saw a line of ASP script, ASP pages could also be viewed with browsers other than Internet Explorer.

And here is yet another problem: Since browsers differ considerably in their support for HTML features, developers had to spend a significant amount of time to create browser-specific ASP code. It became standard to add browser-detection code to many pages, and ASP pages tended to contain different versions of the same functions, to support different browsers.

The ASP.NET Innovations

Let's see how Microsoft attacked each problem area. The first problem was the requirement to keep both UI code (HTML) and scripted code in the same .asp file. The obvious solution was to separate the presentation logic from the business logic, which is what ASP.NET is all about. When you create a Web application using VB .NET, the project wizard automatically creates a default Web Form, which appears as a .aspx file in the Solution Explorer. This is the file containing the UI elements like text, buttons, and so forth.

What you don't see immediately is the *code-behind* file. This file, with the suffix .aspx.cs (when using C#), contains no UI elements, XML, or HTML code at all. It consists entirely of event-handling code. Each Web Form has both a .aspx file and a .aspx.cs file. The files can be worked on simultaneously by different development groups, so the graphics people work solely with .aspx files and the coders with .aspx.cs files.

What was done regarding the second problem, the use of scripted code? Microsoft made a fairly dramatic decision in this regard: They added support for compiled code on the server side. Languages like JScript and VBScript are now considered obsolete for server-side programming. ASP.NET applications must be coded with one of the .NET languages, such as Visual C#, VB .NET, or another language. Code developed with these languages is very close to native binary code in terms of performance. As a result, ASP.NET pages have a huge performance advantage over ASP pages, so a given Web server can support a much larger number of users than before.

What about the last problem: browser-dependencies? As long as you develop pages using low-level HTML tags like `<input>` or `<table>`, you need to make your code browser-specific. Browsers support different sets of attributes with each tag, and some tags (tables, in particular) are not rendered in exactly the same way on different browsers. Some older browsers may not even support all the HTML 3.2 or 4.0 tags. To solve the headaches caused by browser differences, Microsoft developed a new library of controls *(WebControls)* that perform the same tasks as ordinary HTML controls, but do so in a browser-independent way. For example, if you need to put a table in a Web Form, you have two choices: You can drop a Table component from the HTML page of the Toolbox, or you can drop a Table component from the Web Forms page. The first component simply adds a `<table>` tag to the HTML code of the page. The second component adds a WebControl Table component, which not only can be customized using the standard Properties window, but is also smart enough to produce browser-specific HTML code, based on the end user's browser.

The .aspx files containing HTML controls and WebControls can be viewed in two modes using VS .NET: Design mode and HTML mode. Design mode just shows the page layout graphically, as it will appear on the end user's browser. HTML mode shows all the XML text of the page, containing a number of ⟨asp⟩ tags with the asp namespace, representing the WebControls on the page. When a user directs his browser to your .aspx page, the ⟨asp⟩ elements are invoked by the HTTP runtime engine to render themselves in terms of standard HTML code. Then the code-behind logic is called to add dynamic content. When the page is complete, the final HTML document is sent back to the user.

At this point you're probably thinking, "That's going to take a lot of coding effort on my behalf." Wrong. The logic to produce the HTML is built into the HTTP runtime, the Web Form, and the WebControls classes. You design the page layout graphically and add the code-behind logic. You're done. The good news doesn't end here. If you use the new WebControls, as opposed to the plain vanilla HTML controls, you finally have a way to create really rich Web pages that work with all Web browsers, with little or no logic in your code to check the user's browser type and version.

In the next section, I'll show you the way the various facets of the ASP.NET architecture come together to support a superior development environment.

The Basics

Web Forms are used in the context of Web applications. In many ways, Web Forms are similar to Windows Forms, not only because they appear on the client computer's display, but also because they are developed using the same tools and techniques as Windows Forms. Like Windows Forms, Web Forms are created using VS .NET (goodbye Visual InterDev) by dragging and dropping standard components from the Toolbox. Like Windows Forms, Web Forms can be viewed in VS .NET in different ways: using the Forms Designer or using the Code window. Just as the similarities are important, so are the differences. There are two important differences between Web and Windows Forms: the way they render themselves and the way they handle events.

Before diving into the details of Web Forms, it may be useful to discuss the basic architecture of a typical ASP.NET Web application, shown in Figure 13-1.

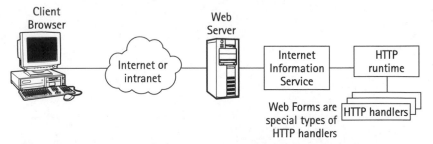

Figure 13-1: The basic architecture of an ASP.NET Web application

ASP.NET Web applications consist of Web Form components that run on the server in response to a URI request from a client browser such as Internet Explorer. When the HTTP runtime is invoked by IIS, it builds an HTTPContext object that encapsulates the HTTP parameters for the current request. Using information stored in the Config.web file for the Web site, the runtime tries to locate a handler for the request. *Handlers* are classes that implement the interface IHttpHandler. Web Forms are special types of handlers: They derive from the base class System.Web.UI.Page, which implements IHttpHandler. Once a handler is located, the HTTP runtime invokes it and passes an HttpContext object to it, with all the connection information available, including the HTTP headers, the request, information identifying the end user's browser, and more. The Web Form invoked to handle a request generates HTML code that is returned to the client and rendered on the client browser.

Note   Although I mostly use Internet Explorer in the examples in this book, Web Forms are compatible with any browser compatible with HTML 3.2, such as Netscape 4.x and later.

Goodbye include files, hello classes

If you have experience with ASP programming, you'll remember that code shared across multiple ASP pages required the use of server-side include files. Say you had a function called MySharedFunction() that you wanted to use on two different pages: Page1.asp and Page2.asp. You had to create a common file, called something like MyCommon.asp, and include it on Page1.asp and Page2.asp, as shown in Listing 13-1.

Listing 13-1: Using Include Files to Share Code in ASP

```
<!-- MyCommon.asp -->

Function MySharedFunction(MyParameter)
  '' body of function ...
End Function

<!-Page1.asp -->

<!-- #INCLUDE FILE="MyCommon.asp" -->
Sub Page1Stuff()
  ''  Call the shared function
  MySharedFunction("Hello")
End Sub

<!-Page2.asp -->

<!-- #INCLUDE FILE="MyCommon.asp" -->
Sub Page2Stuff()
  ''  Call the shared function
  MySharedFunction("Hello")
End Sub
```

To an object-oriented programmer, this kind of inline code causes an immediate sense of nausea. In the ASP.NET world, the reuse of code through include files is unnecessary and completely obsolete. The new way to share code is the object-oriented way: Put common code in a class and either access that class from your code-behind pages or derive the page itself from the common class, as shown in the class diagram in Figure 13-2.

Using the first technique, you would create a class called something like CommonCode, and reference it on two code-behind pages as shown in Listing 13-2.

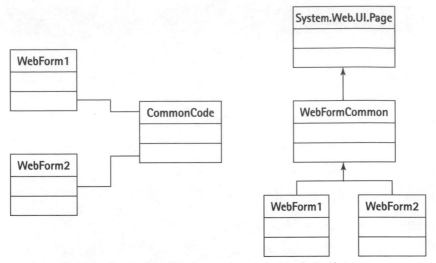

Figure 13-2: Reusing code with classes, instead of include files

---

Listing 13-2: Sharing Code in ASP.NET, Using a Public Class

```
public class CommonCode
{
  public void MySharedMethod() {}
}

public class WebForm1 : System.Web.UI.Page
{
  private void SomeWebForm2Method()
  {
    CommonCode commonCode = new CommonCode();
    commonCode.MySharedMethod();
  }
}

public class WebForm2 : System.Web.UI.Page
{
  private void SomeWebForm3Method()
  {
    CommonCode commonCode = new CommonCode();
    commonCode.MySharedMethod();
  }
}
```

With the second technique, the common code is put in a WebForm class, which is then used as the base class for other Web Forms, as shown in Listing 13-3.

Listing 13-3: Accessing Shared Code in ASP.NET, Using Inheritance

```
public class WebFormCommon : System.Web.UI.Page
{
  public void MySharedMethod() {}
}

public class WebForm1 : WebFormCommon
{
  private void SomeWebForm2Method()
  {
    MySharedMethod();
  }
}

public class WebForm2 : WebFormCommon
{
  private void SomeWebForm3Method()
  {
    MySharedMethod();
  }
}
```

What if you want to share variables? With ASP code, you created global variables and saved them in a file called global.asa. With ASP.NET, you can use the Application object of your Web application. You can add any number of named variables to the Application object. All the Web Forms in the same Web application have access to the Application object, and can share variables through it. Listing 13-4 shows a simple example of writing and reading a global string variable named MySharedVariable.

Listing 13-4: Sharing Global Variables and Methods with Class Global

```
public class WebForm1 : System.Web.UI.Page
{
  private void SomeWebForm1Method()
  {
    // access global variable

    Application.Contents ["MySharedVariable"] = "Hello";
    String hello = Application.Contents ["MySharedVariable"]
                  as String;
  }
}
```

Variables shared through the Application object can be of any type and size.

How Web Forms are rendered

Web Forms are developed using drag and drop controls in VS .NET. As you develop a Web Form, you can see how it looks in the Forms Designer. If you select a control, you can see its properties in the Properties window. At this stage, Web Forms are pretty much like Windows Forms. At runtime, however, Web and Windows Forms are quite different, especially in terms of rendering. Windows Forms have an OnPaint() event handler that draws pixels on the screen. Web Forms can't do this, because they run on the server side, which is not where the user is. Instead, Web Forms render themselves using XML. This XML code is picked up by the ASP.NET engine and converted into HTML code. When returned to the client machine's browser, this HTML code produces a deferred rendering of the server-side Web Form and the Web Controls it contains.

Assume you have a Web Form containing a standard HTML control and a Web Control. Let's say you drop two components on a Web Form: a Table component from the HTML page and a Table component from the Web Forms page of the Toolbox. Figure 13-3 shows how the Web Form looks in the Forms Designer in Design mode.

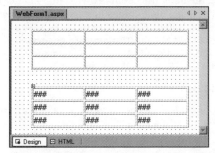

Figure 13-3: How a native HTML table and a Web Control Table look in the Forms Designer

The top grid is the HTML table. To see the HTML code generated for this Web Form, click the HTML button at the bottom of the Forms Designer. Listing 13-5 contains highlights of the XML code produced by the Web Forms Designer.

Listing 13-5: **The XML Code Generated for the Web Form**

```
<%@ Page language="c#" Codebehind="WebForm1.aspx.cs"
    AutoEventWireup="false" Inherits="MyWebForm.WebForm1" %>
<HTML>
  <HEAD>
    <meta name="CODE_LANGUAGE" Content="C#">
    <meta name="vs_defaultClientScript"
          content="JavaScript (ECMAScript)">
  </HEAD>
  <body>
    <P>
      <TABLE cellSpacing="1" cellPadding="1" width="300" border="1">
        <TR>
          <TD></TD>
```

Continued

Listing 13-5 *(continued)*

```
        <TD></TD>
        <TD></TD>
      </TR>
      <!-other rows ... --!>
    </TABLE>
  </P>
  <asp:Table id="Table1" runat="server"
          Width="68px" Height="41px">
  </asp:Table>
</body>
</HTML>
```

The code shown in this listing is server-side code, meaning the client browser doesn't get to see it. What happens is the HTTP runtime scans the page. As it comes across HTML elements, like <P> or <TABLE> tags, it copies them to an internal buffer. When it encounters a Web Control, with a tag using the asp namespace (like <asp:table>), the runtime generates browser-dependent HTML code so the control is rendered correctly on the end user's browser. To see the client HTML code, I used IE 6 to load the Web Form. In IE, I entered the URI:

```
http://localhost/MyWebForm/WebForm1.aspx
```

Since the Web Forms contains only two blank tables, the page I got was blank. More interesting is the HTML code it contained, which is shown in Listing 13-6.

Listing 13-6: The HTML Code for the Web Form, As Delivered to an IE 6 Client

```
<HTML>
  <HEAD>
    <meta name="CODE_LANGUAGE" Content="C#">
    <meta name="vs_defaultClientScript"
      content="JavaScript (ECMAScript)">
  </HEAD>
  <body>
    <P>
      <TABLE cellSpacing="1" cellPadding="1" width="300" border="1">
        <TR>
          <TD></TD> <TD></TD>  <TD></TD>
        </TR>
        <!-other rows ... --!>
      </TABLE>
    </P>

    <table id="Table1" border="0"
          style="height:41px;width:68px;">
    </table>
  </body>
</HTML>
```

As you can see, the native HTML table on the Web Form is rendered with a standard `<table>` tag with a few support attributes. In the listing, I put the HTML code generated for the Table Web Control in boldface. Like its HTML cousin, this table is also rendered with a standard `<table>` tag, but using absolute positioning attributes, which are supported by IE 6.

If I view the same ASP.NET page using a different browser, the Web Control HTML code will change, depending on the HTML capabilities of my browser. For example, viewing the page with Netscape Navigator 4.78, which doesn't support absolute positioning on tables, the salient HTML code is shown in Listing 13-7.

Listing 13-7: The HTML Code for the Web Form Delivered to a Netscape Navigator 4.78 Client

```
<HTML>
  <HEAD> same code as before...</HEAD>
  <body>
    <P>
      <TABLE cellSpacing="1" cellPadding="1"
             width="300" border="1">
        <!—same code as before --!>
      </TABLE>
    </P>
    <table id="Table1" border="0" height="41" width="68">
    </table>
  </body>
</HTML>
```

As you can see, the HTML code is the same as before, except for the Table Web Control, which no longer has absolute positioning. All Web Controls generate browser-dependent code, allowing you to spend more of your time focusing on the business aspects of your code and less on browser differences. For more information on where and how Web Controls generate browser-dependent code, see Chapter 14, which deals specifically with Web Controls.

The interaction diagram in Figure 13-4 shows the basic events that occur in the page rendering process.

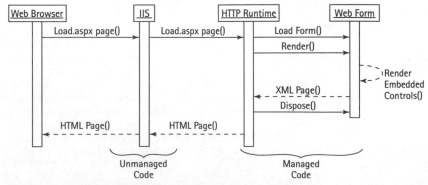

Figure 13-4: The basic components in a Web application

Note the switching from unmanaged to managed code between IIS and the HTTP runtime. There is a small cost in processing time to accomplish this switch, but for the great majority of Web applications, the cost is negligible.

How Web Form events are handled

In a Windows Form, controls can fire events. For example, when you click a button in a typical form, the button fires a `Click` event, which is usually handled by the parent form. The consumer of the event (the parent form) is part of the same program as the originator (the button) of the event. Both the producer and consumer code run on the same machine in the same process space.

In a Web Form, events are handled differently, because the event originator and consumer are on different machines. The originator is the end user's browser, while the consumer is the Web Form server-side code. When the user clicks a button in a Web Form, a `Click` event is fired, but the event isn't handled by the parent window, because this window is really just an HTML document window sitting inside the end user's Web browser. Instead, the event is sent all the way back to the server, where the Web Form code resides. The event is passed through layers of IIS code, then HTTP runtime code, and finally into the Web Form event handler. Figure 13-5 illustrates the basic idea.

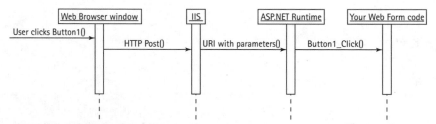

Figure 13-5: The interaction diagram showing how events triggered on the client side are propagated back to the server

When the user clicks a button in a browser, the button's `Click` handler fires an HTTP POST message to the server. The post message carries a URI with it, containing parameters and information the HTTP runtime uses to determine which event was fired, and by which control. With this information, the ASP.NET framework determines which Web Form event handler to call, and calls the `Button1_Click` handler correctly. From the viewpoint of the developer writing event handling code for the button, the event appears to have originated right on the Web server machine.

Button click events are somewhat special types of events, because they immediately generate an HTTP `POST` message, which requires a roundtrip to the server. In response, the server code usually responds by returning a new page. Most events are different: Since roundtrips to the server are slow, attempting to handle many types of events immediately would produce unacceptable delays in the user interface running on the client browser. Instead, these events are cached on the client side, and only when a `POST` operation occurs (by clicking a Submit button) are they sent to the server. When the HTTP runtime receives the `Click` event, it checks some of the parameters sent with the `POST` message to determine which cached events were fired. Those cached events (if any) are handled first, and then the `Click` event is handled.

When a POST operation occurs, the hidden binary information is sent back to the server. The HTTP runtime receives all the current values of the controls, and uses the binary information to determine what kind of changes the user made. Using this knowledge, the HTTP runtime can determine which events to fire and which event handlers to call.

For example, say you have a Web Form with a TextBox, a CheckBox, and a Submit button. Assume the Web Form has a TextChanged handler for the TextBox and a CheckChanged handler for the CheckBox. If you bring up the Web Form in a browser and type something in the TextBox, you'll find that no events are fired on the server. If you check the CheckBox, still no events are fired. When you click the Submit button, a string of events will fire on the server side: first the TextChanged and CheckChanged events, and then the button's Click event. The order in which cached events, like TextChanged and CheckChanged, are fired is fixed, rather than depending on the order in which the events actually took place on the client side. Basically, the HTTP runtime examines the binary data returned with the form's submitted data. For each client control, the runtime checks a list of possible events and fires them in the order found.

Some events that Windows Forms programmers deal with are not practical with Web Forms. In particular are events that occur at high speed, such as mouse events. These types of events would never work correctly if they had to be processed on the server every time the mouse was moved, due to the length of time it takes to effect a roundtrip operation to the server. The solution is to handle the events on the client side, using traditional script code such as ECMAScript or VBScript.

Looking at the details

I've mentioned the presence of event handling code on the server side. Where does this code reside? For each Web Form you create, there are two files — just like with Windows Forms. One file stores the graphical features of the form, including the HTML code, Web Controls, and optional client-side script. This file has the suffix *.aspx*. The other file is called the *code-behind* file and has the suffix *.aspx.cs*. The code-behind file contains all the C# code for the Web Form. As stated earlier, code-behind code is always compiled before being used, so it is considerably faster than VBScript of JScript code.

A short example will help you understand how events are handled by Web Forms. Assume you have a form that has a couple of Web Controls on it: a Label and a Button control. Figure 13-6 shows the form in the VS.NET Forms Designer.

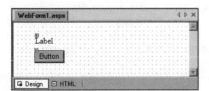

Figure 13-6: A simple Web Form in the Forms Designer

The server-side XML code for the form (with some of the nonessential code removed) is shown in Listing 13-8.

Listing 13-8: The ASP.NET HTML Code for a Simple Web Form

```
<%@ Page language="c#" Codebehind="WebForm1.aspx.cs"
    AutoEventWireup="false" Inherits="MyWebForm.WebForm1" %>
<HTML>
  <body MS_POSITIONING="GridLayout">
    <form id="Form1" method="post" runat="server">
      <asp:Button id="Button1" style="Z-INDEX: 101; LEFT: 63px;
                  POSITION: absolute; TOP: 69px" runat="server"
                  Text="Button">
      </asp:Button>
      <asp:Label id="Label1" style="Z-INDEX: 104; LEFT: 62px;
                  POSITION: absolute; TOP: 32px" runat="server">
        Label
      </asp:Label>
    </form>
  </body>
</HTML>
```

This code is not delivered directly to the end user's browser. The code is fed back to the HTTP runtime, which replaces some of the code before sending the page back to the end user. The Page directive tells the HTTP runtime what language will be used in the code-behind file, and also the name of that file. The HTTP runtime needs this information to correctly bind events it fires to event handler code in the code-behind file.

There are a couple of attributes of the Page directive, at the beginning of the XML file, that need some explanation:

✦ AutoEventWireup

✦ Inherits

Exactly what do these two attributes do?

The purpose of the AutoEventWireup attribute tends to be confusing for a lot of people. When you create a Web Form with VS .NET, the Properties window can be used to set its properties and events, as with other visual components. But Web Forms have a small twist: If you select an unassigned Web Form event and press the Enter key, you would expect VS .NET to automatically create an event handler with a default name, switch to the Code window, and place you on the new event handler method. If the AutoEventWireup attribute is false, this won't happen. The attribute is false by default. To create an event handler, you'll need to type in the name of the handler method and then press the Enter key.

The Inherits attribute is much more important. When the HTTP runtime loads a Web Form's .aspx page to handle a request, the runtime uses the Codebehind attribute to locate the file containing the form's event handling code. But not all of the form's code is in the code-behind file. Some of the code is inherited from the base class System.Web.UI.Page, or some other class derived from Page. Since the HTTP runtime compiles your code on-the-fly before loading it, you need to specify where the base class is, so it can be compiled along with the code-behind file. The Inherits attribute in the .aspx file tells the HTTP runtime the name of the Web Form's base class.

Listing 13-9 shows the contents of the code-behind file for the simple Web Form shown in Listing 13-8.

> ### Listing 13-9: **The Contents of the Code-Behind File for a Simple Web Form**

```
using System;
using ...

namespace MyWebForm
{
  public class WebForm1 : System.Web.UI.Page
  {
    protected System.Web.UI.WebControls.Label Label1;
    protected System.Web.UI.WebControls.Button Button1;

    public WebForm1()
    {
      Page.Init += new System.EventHandler(Page_Init);
    }

    private void Page_Load(object sender, System.EventArgs e)
    {
      // Put user code to initialize the page here
    }

    private void Page_Init(object sender, EventArgs e)
    {
      InitializeComponent();
    }

    private void InitializeComponent()
    {
      this.Button1.Click +=
        new System.EventHandler(this.Button1_Click);
    }

    private void Button1_Click(object sender, System.EventArgs e)
    {
      Label1.Text = "You clicked the button!";
    }
  }
}
```

As you can see in the code, I added a simple Click event handler for the button. When the button is clicked, the Label1's text is changed. A new HTML page is returned to the user, showing the new text for the label, as shown in Figure 13-7.

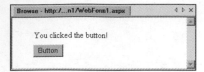

Figure 13-7: The page displayed
after clicking the button

Let's look at how the button's Click event got from the client's browser to the server and
then morphed into a call to the method Button1_Click() of the class MyWebForm. Keep in
mind that the code shown in the HTML Pane in VS .NET (see Figure 13-6) is actually XML, and
is not the code that gets sent back to the client. To see the client code, you need to open a
browser, type in the URI of the Web Form, which in my case is

```
http://localhost/CSharpBook/MyWebForm/WebForm1.aspx
```

and then view the source code for the page. Listing 13-10 shows the source code.

> **Listing 13-10: The Source Code of the HTML Page Delivered to the
> Client Browser for the Simple Web Form**

```
<!DOCTYPE HTML PUBLIC "-//W3C//DTD HTML 4.0 Transitional//EN" >
<HTML>
  <body MS_POSITIONING="GridLayout">
    <form name="Form1" method="post" action="WebForm1.aspx"
        id="Form1">
      <input type="hidden" name="__VIEWSTATE"
            value="dDwtNjI3MTUONjQyOzs+" />
      <input type="submit" name="Button1" value="Button"
          id="Button1"
              style="Z-INDEX: 101; LEFT: 63px;
              POSITION: absolute; TOP: 69px" />
      <span id="Label1" style="Z-INDEX: 104; LEFT: 62px;
          POSITION: absolute; TOP: 32px">
        Label
      </span>
    </form>
  </body>
</HTML>
```

The button is tagged as the "submit" button for a form. The form's method is "post" and
the action is "WebForm1.aspx". When you click the button, the contents of the form's controls are sent to the Web server using a post message summarized in Listing 13-11.

Listing 13-11: A Fragment of the HTTP Message Sent by the Client Browser When the Web Form's Button Is Clicked

```
POST /CSharpBook/MyWebForm/WebForm1.aspx HTTP/1.1
Host: localhost
__VIEWSTATE=dDwtNjI3MTUONjQyOzs%2B&Button1=Button
```

The `POST` message's query string, shown in the last line of the previous listing, is passed intact to the HTTP runtime. The runtime parses all the `property=value` expressions. The `__VIEWSTATE` property contains the initial state of the Web Form's controls, such as the captions of Labels, the state of CheckBoxes, and so on. The HTTP runtime takes the following actions:

1. It loads `WebForm1.aspx`.

2. It compiles `WebForm1.aspx.cs`, along with the base class file.

3. It parses the contents of the query string, sent in the post message.

4. It uses the ViewState data to initialize the state of all the Web Form controls.

5. It invokes the `Button1_Click` event handler, passing it appropriate event arguments.

The ASP.NET Framework does a remarkable job of helping wire up events originating on the end user's browser with event handling code on the server side, and all the details are hidden from view. You actually have to go out of your way to see the state-management infrastructure.

Global event handlers

Certain types of events are of a global nature, and affect all the Web Forms in a Web application. These events are associated with the Application object that is part of the context of all Web Forms. The global events for a Web Form are as follows:

✦ `AcquireRequestState`

✦ `AuthenticateRequest`

✦ `AuthorizeRequest`

✦ `BeginRequest`

✦ `EndRequest`

✦ `Error`

✦ `PostRequestHandlerExecute`

✦ `PreRequestHandlerExecute`

✦ `PreSendRequestContent`

✦ `PreSendRequestHeaders`

✦ `ReleaseRequestState`

✦ `ResolveRequestCache`

✦ `UpdateRequestCache`

To create a handler for these events, you can use code like what's shown in Listing 13-12.

Listing 13-12: Creating an Event Handler for a Global Application Event

```
public class WebForm1 : System.Web.UI.Page
{
  long startTime;

  public WebForm1()
  {
    // ...
    Application.BeginRequest +=
                 new System.EventHandler(BeginRequest);
    Application.EndRequest += new System.EventHandler(EndRequest);
  }

  private void BeginRequest(object sender, System.EventArgs e)
  {

    startTime = DateTime.Now.Ticks;
  }

  private void EndRequest(object sender, System.EventArgs e)
  {
    // get elapsed time in ticks (100 ns increments)
    double processingTime = DateTime.Now.Ticks - startTime;

    // convert ticks to milliseconds
    processingTime /= 10000;

    Response.Write("<br>Processing time: " +
                   processingTime + " ms");
  }
}
```

The listing shows how to set up handlers for the BeginRequest and EndRequest events. My code just displays the page processing time on the page returned. In addition to the global events listed previously, there are also a few global methods defined that act like event handlers. All the global events and methods are contained in the file Global.cs. Table 13-1 lists and describes the global methods.

Table 13-1: Global Methods Accessible in the Global.cs File

Method Name	Description
Application_Start	Called when the application is first loaded into memory. You might use this method to initialize a database connection pool, or to write something to the Windows Event Log.
Application_End	Called when the application is unloaded from memory. You might add code to this method to free a database connection pool, stop dependent services, and so on.

Method Name	Description
Session_Start	Called each time a session starts. You might add code to keep track of the number of sessions processed each day, or the number of times a specific user visits your site.
Session_End	Called each time a session ends.
Application_BeginRequest	Called when a request is received from a user, just before your Web Form code is activated.
Application_EndRequest	Called after your Web Form's event handlers. This method gives you a chance to add code to the page returned, or do other processing, such as computing the amount of time the request took.

Getting user information

When your Web Form code-behind page is called by the HTTP runtime, you have access to a very important object that encapsulates information about the end user's browser and the request sent to you: the *Request* object, which is an instance of the class HttpRequest. This object contains numerous properties that you'll find useful. Some of the more important properties are listed and described in Table 13-2.

Table 13-2: Important Properties in the Request Object

Property	Description
AcceptTypes	Lists the types of files the browser can handle, such as image/gif, image/jpeg, and so on.
Browser	Provides access to the browser properties, as shown in Table 13-3.
Cookies	A list of the cookies submitted by the browser.
Files	A collection of the files uploaded from the browser to the server using a file-upload button. This button is called File Field in VS.NET, and can be found on the HTML page of the Toolbox.
Headers	A list of the HTTP headers submitted with the request.
IsAuthenticated	Returns true if the user was authenticated using one of the ASP.NET authentication methods. Returns false if authentication is not used with the requested Web Form. (See Chapter 17, titled "Security," for more details on authentication.)
Params	A list of the HTTP parameters submitted with the request. Parameters may consist of ViewState data and query strings.
QueryString	A string consisting of all the (name=value) variables found at the end of the URI of the current request. For example, if the full URI was http://localhost/WebForm1.aspx?id=123, then the QueryString would be id=123.

Continued

Table 13-2 *(continued)*

Property	Description
RawUrl	The URL of the requested Web Form; for example, /CSharpBook/MyWebForm/WebForm1.aspx.
RequestType	The HTTP request type, such as GET or POST.
UrlReferrer	If the current request originated from another page, this field will contain the URI of that page. If the request comes directly from a user, the field will contain the URI of the Web Form requested (for example, http://localhost/CSharpBook/MyWebForm/WebForm1.aspx).

Of all the Request properties, probably the most accessed one is Browser, which has a list of important properties of its own. The Browser object is an instance of the class HttpBrowserCapabilities. Table 13-3 lists and describes some of the most important properties of the Request.Browser object.

Table 13-3: Salient Properties of the Request.Browser Object

Property	Description
Type	Type of browser. Includes the name and major version of the browser. The following list shows the value for some major browsers:
	Internet Explorer 6: IE6
	Internet Explorer 5: IE5
	Netscape Navigator 4.78: Netscape4
Name	Browser name, such as IE or Netscape.
Version	Complete version number, such as 6.0b or 4.78.
Major Version	The version number without the decimal part, such as 6 for IE 6.0b.
Platform	Operating system name, such as WinNT for Windows NT and 2000.
IsAOL	True if the request came from an AOL browser.
SupportsFrames	Indicates whether the browser can handle HTML frames.
SupportsTables	Indicates whether the browser can handle HTML tables.
SupportsCookies	Indicates whether the browser allows HTTP cookies.
SupportsVBScript	Indicates whether the browser can handle VB Script.
SupportsJavaScript	Indicates whether the browser can handle JavaScript (ECMAScript).
SupportsJavaApplets	Indicates whether the browser can handle Java applets.
SupportsActiveXControls	Indicates whether the browser can handle ActiveX controls.

Using the information in the `Request.Browser` object, you can determine what type of HTML to return, if you are creating the HTML code yourself. Keep in mind that WebControls all generate code based on the capabilities of the user's browser. Other browser properties, such as the ability to handle Java applets or ActiveX controls may impact the type of page you return to the end user.

A Web Application Example

Web Forms don't live in a vacuum, but exist in the context of a Web application. I'll create a small but complete Web application, to show how the various Web Form pieces fit together, such as code-behind pages, postbacks, ViewState management, server-side controls, and other items. I created an application called *MyWebForm* that shows a list of names and telephone numbers, as illustrated in the Figure 13-8.

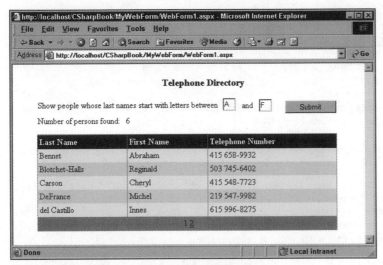

Figure 13-8: The user interface of MyWebForm

The data is stored in the `authors` table of the SQL Server Pubs database, a standard database example installed automatically with SQL Server. The list of names and telephone numbers can be filtered to include only names in a given range. MyWebForm is rather simple, but is still useful to drive home many of the interesting aspects of Web development with ASP.NET Web Forms. Notice the grid style, with its alternating row background colors, the column caption formatting, the vertical column dividers, and the page selection links on the bottom row. The grid style and a range of other attributes are easy to set up using the VS .NET wizards, as I'll show later.

Designing the Web Application

The application consists of two main parts: a Web Form and a Web Service. The Web Form represents the HTML page that will ultimately be returned to client browsers. The Web

Service is a separate component that provides connectivity with a database and supplies the data shown in the Web Form grid. Web Services are not always present in Web applications for a couple of reasons. First, not all Web Forms use data stored in a database. Second, even when a database is used, you may want to embed the database components directly in the Web Form, to simplify the application and obviate the need for a separate Web Service component.

The design I chose for MyWebForm uses a separate Web Service to show you the more general design of medium-to-high-end Web applications. Figure 13-9 shows the overall architecture.

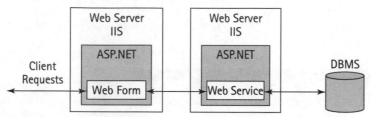

Figure 13-9: The architecture of my simple Web application

 Note   For details regarding the design and implementation of the Web Service, see Chapter 19, titled "Database Web Services."

Both the machine running the Web Form code and the machine running the Web Service need to have IIS installed. For my example, I ran both on the same machine.

Regarding the Web Form, there are two things to design: the page layout and the event-handling logic. I'll start with the page layout. This isn't a book about Web page design, so I kept the layout really simple, using the tools built into VS .NET, especially to take advantage of the new Web Controls. These controls are the answer to ASP programmers' prayers. They support rich features, are simple to use, work with all browsers, and save you a ton of work.

As shown back in Figure 13-8, the Web Form in my example has two TextBox controls to select a range of names, a Submit button, and a DataGrid showing a list of names and phone numbers. The class diagram of the Web Form is shown in Figure 13-10.

The DataSet component is loaded at runtime with a list of all the names and telephone numbers in the authors table of the SQL Server Pubs database. The list is obtained from the Web Service. To support filtering of names, I could have used two different techniques:

✦ A Where clause in the SQL Select statement used to populate the DataSet

✦ A DataView component to filter out the required rows from a DataSet

Although I haven't described DataView components in the book yet, I cover DataViews as well as DataBinding with DataGrids in Chapter 18, "The ADO.NET Architecture." For my example, I chose to use a DataView to accomplish row filtering.

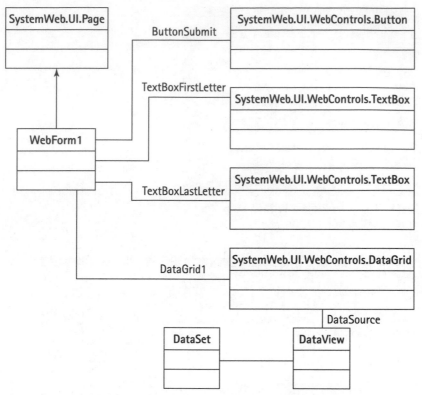

Figure 13-10: The basic design of the Web Form used in MyWebForm

Implementing the Web Application

Having decided on the basic design of the Web application and Web Form, I can start on the implementation. I created a blank application using the New Project Wizard in VS .NET, and selecting ASP.NET Web application for the project template, as shown in Figure 13-11.

The wizard contacts the Web server using the URI supplied, and sets up the necessary folders and files. To be successful, you need to have Administrator privileges on the Web server machine. This can be either your local computer or a remote Web server. Obviously, IIS must be configured and running on the machine you create the Web application on.

After creating the Web application project, the VS .NET environment looked like Figure 13-12.

The project needs a reference to the Web Service that generates the resultset needed by the Web Form. The resultset comes from a Database Web Service that basically runs the following SQL `Select` statement:

```
Select * from authors Order by au_lname
```

This statement produces a resultset, which is used to populate the `DataGrid`'s `DataSet`. I'll skip the design and implementation of the Web Service in this chapter, to concentrate on the Web Form aspects of Web application development. As stated earlier, the Database Web Service used in my example is described in detail in the Chapter 19, titled "Database Web Services."

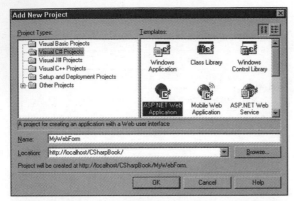

Figure 13-11: The New Project Wizard, showing how to create a Web application

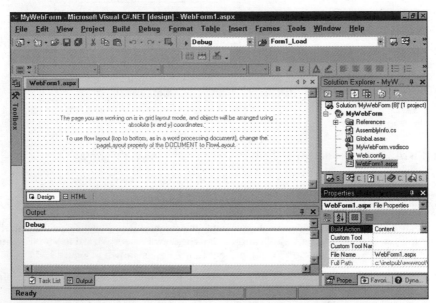

Figure 13-12: The VS .NET development environment, showing the Forms Designer for Web Forms

To access the Web Service, called *DatabaseWebService,* I had to add a Web Reference to it. To add the Web Reference, I right-clicked on the `MyWebForms` project in the Solutions Explorer and selected Add Web Reference from the pop-up menu. In the Add Web Reference Wizard, I entered the URI of the Web Service, as shown at the top of Figure 13-13.

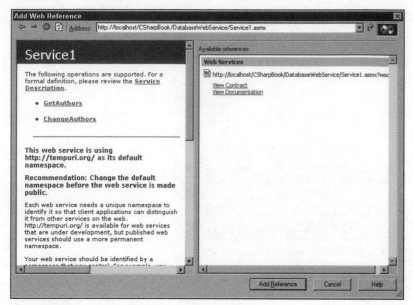

Figure 13-13: The Add Web Reference Wizard, which enables you to locate both local and remote Web Services

Then I clicked the Add Reference button to add the reference to my project. After adding the reference, the Solution Explorer was updated to show the new reference, as shown in Figure 13-14.

Figure 13-14: The Solution Explorer after adding the Web Reference

I need a few more things before starting the implementation of WebForm1. First I added a reference to the Web Service DLL to the project, and then I added the following statement at the top of WebForm1.aspx:

```
using DatabaseWebService;
```

To add a reference to the DLL, I right-clicked on the MyWebForm project and selected Add Reference from the pop-up menu. In the Add Reference Wizard, I navigated to the folder containing the Web Service DLL and clicked the Select and then the OK buttons. Figure 13-15 shows the wizard after I selected the DLL.

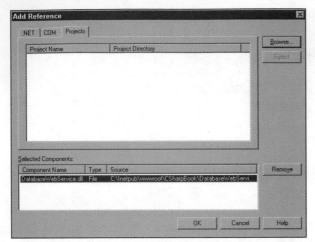

Figure 13-15: The Add Reference Wizard

The next step is to add the UI elements to the Web Form. Although I could have used either HTML or WebControls, I chose to use the latter because they have more features than their plain HTML counterparts. I used WebControls.Label for the static text areas, WebControls.Button for the Submit button, and WebControls.DataGrid for the grid. Figure 13-16 shows the final layout of the Web Form.

WebForm1.aspx	◁ ▷ ×

Telephone Directory

Show people whose last names start with letters between [A] and [H]   [Submit]

Number of persons found: 0.

Last Name	First Name	Telephone Number
abc	abc	abc
abc	abc	abc
abc	abc	abc
abc	abc	abc
abc	abc	abc

1 2

□ Design   ⊟ HTML

Figure 13-16: The design-time layout of the Web Form used in MyWebForm

You can always recognize WebControls in the Forms Designer, because they appear with a small light-green box in the upper left corner. The only control that required customizing was the DataGrid. I used a number of different properties to customize the look and feel of the grid. First I used the Auto Format Wizard to get the alternate-row-coloring scheme. One way to run the wizard is by right-clicking on the DataGrid and selecting Auto Format from the pop-up menu. The wizard is shown in Figure 13-17.

I selected the Professional 1 style and closed the wizard. Next, I needed to customize the columns and column headers displayed by the DataGrid. Before achieving this type of customization, I had to populate the DataSet used by the DataGrid with the schema and data for the authors table. I dropped a DataSet component from the Data page of the Toolbox onto the Web Form. The Add DataSet Wizard automatically started. In the Name field under the Typed DataSet radio button, I selected DatabaseWebServices.MyDataSet from the drop-down list, as shown in Figure 13-18.

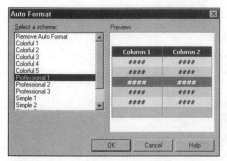

Figure 13-17: The DataGrid Auto Format Wizard

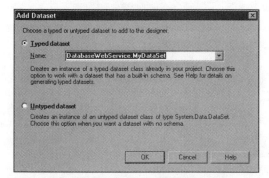

Figure 13-18: The Add Dataset Wizard

After closing the wizard, a new component named *myDataSet1* appeared in the Component Tray under the Web Form. The last component I need is a DataView, to filter the requested names and phone numbers from the complete list of records in the authors table. After dropping the DataView component on the Web Form, I set its table property to reference the authors table contained in the MyDataSet.

With the database components set up, I then proceeded to customize the columns of the DataGrid. I right-clicked on the grid and selected Property Builder from the pop-up menu. Although you can use the Properties Window to set up a DataGrid, the Property Builder has a much richer interface. In the Property Builder window, the first page is for General properties. On this page, I set the DataGrid's DataSource to the DataView component, and then set the Key Field to au_id, as shown in Figure 13-19.

Next, I switched to the Columns page and selected the following three columns from the authors table: au_lname, au_fname, and phone. By default, DataGrid columns use the raw field names as captions. I edited the column headers to use the text Last Name, First Name, and Telephone Number, as shown in Figure 13-20.

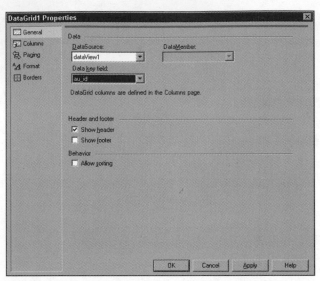

Figure 13-19: The General screen of the DataGrid Property Builder windows

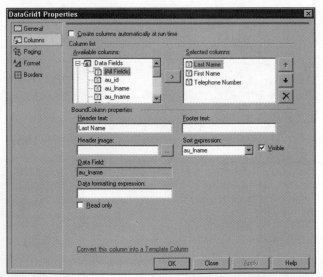

Figure 13-20: The Columns screen of the DataGrid Property Builder windows

Next, I switched to the Paging page. Paging is the way a DataGrid splits long lists into multiple pages. By default, each page shows ten rows. I change the Paging value to five. When using Paging, special page navigation links appear on the DataGrid when there are multiple pages. I set up the Paging page as shown in Figure 13-21.

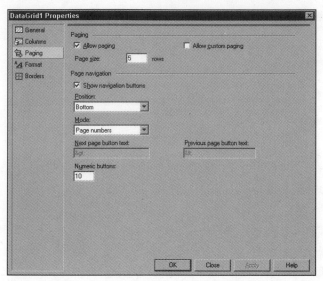

Figure 13-21: The Paging screen of the DataGrid Property
Builder window

That's all for my customizations in MyWebForm. I didn't need to add any more changes,
because I had used the Auto Format Wizard to set the basic style of the DataGrid. In case
you're curious, Figures 13-22 and 13-23 show the last two pages of the Property Builder
window.

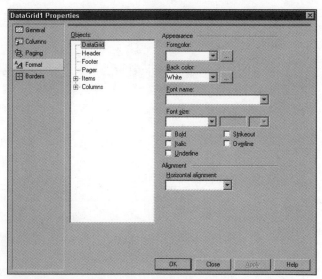

Figure 13-22: The Format screen of the DataGrid Property
Builder

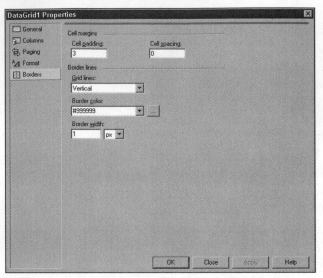

Figure 13-23: The Borders screen of the DataGrid Property Builder

With all the basic database plumbing and `DataGrid` properties set up, I needed to add a `PopulateGrid()` method to get a list of names and phone numbers and add them to the `DataGrid`. The method shown in Listing 13-13 will do.

Listing 13-13: The Method to Populate the DataGrid with Rows

```
private void PopulateGrid()
{
  MyDatabaseWebService myService = new MyDatabaseWebService();
  myDataSet1 = myService.GetAuthors() as MyDataSet;

  dataView1.Table = myDataSet1.authors;

  string s = String.Format("(au_lname >= '{0}%') and " +
                           " (au_lname <= '{1}%')",
                           TextBoxFirstLetter.Text,
                           TextBoxLastLetter.Text);

  dataView1.RowFilter = s;

  DataGrid1.DataBind();

  LabelNumberOfAuthors.Text = dataView1.Count.ToString();
}
```

The method calls the Web Service's GetAuthors() method to obtain a DataSet containing all the rows in the authors table in the SQL Server Pubs database. After populating the local DataSet named myDataSet1 with records, the DataView is hooked up to the DataSet's authors table. You need to repeat this hookup process every time you repopulate the DataSet, because DataSets discard all associations when being repopulated. After hooking up the DataView, the component's RowFilter property is set up to use the filtering characters entered in the two TextBoxes. After setting up the DataSet and DataView, the DataGrid's DataBind() method is called to load the grid with a page worth of records. The last line in PopulateGrid() displays the total number of records in the filtered DataView.

If you just add the PopulateGrid() method to WebForm1 and run the Web application, you'll find that the form appears with no data. The problem is that no one called PopulateGrid(), so I'll need to call it in an event handler. The first event handler to deal with is the Page_Load handler. Each time an end user requests a Web Form, three essential methods are always called in the following order:

1. The WebForm constructor

2. The Page_Init handler

3. The Page_Load handler

The Page_Load handler is where you typically add code to change the values of a Web Form's controls. I added a call to PopulateGrid() in it, like this:

```
private void Page_Load(object sender, System.EventArgs e)
{
  if (!IsPostBack)
    PopulateGrid();
}
```

Almost trivial, if not for the presence of that obscure property called IsPostBack. Let me make a brief digression into PostBacks to explain what's going on.

PostBacks

For some reason, the PostBack concept tends to be confusing to new ASP.NET programmers. A PostBack is simply the action that occurs when a user does something on a Web page that causes an event to be fired on the server side. When a user first navigates to your Web page, the Web server sends the initial page to the user's browser. To produce the page, the ASP.NET had to call the following standard WebForm methods:

1. The WebForm constructor

2. The Page_Init handler

3. The Page_Load handler

When users request your Web Form for the first time (by entering the Web Form's URI in their browser), the HTTP runtime calls the Web Form constructor and then immediately sets the IsPostBack property to false, indicating that the user has just arrived at your site. Shortly afterwards, the runtime calls the Page_Init and Page_Load handlers.

Once the Web Form is sent back to the user, it will probably contain controls that can be clicked on. Some of the controls, such as Submit buttons, cause a Button_Click event to be fired back on the server. To process the `Click` event, the HTTP runtime needs to reload the Web Form code, reinitialize it, and then handle the `Click` event. The following methods would be called in order:

1. The `WebForm` constructor

2. The `Page_Init` handler

3. The `Page_Load` handler

4. The `Button_Click` handler

Right after the constructor is called, the `IsPostBack` property is set to `true`, indicating that the user is already in your Web Form. When the `Page_Load` handler is called, it doesn't make sense for it to do anything, because shortly after the handler is done, the `Button_Click` handler will be called. This handler will in all likelihood assign new values to the various controls on the page. The `IsPostBack` property allows the `Page_Init` and `Page_Load` handlers to skip code whose effects would be overwritten by a subsequent event handler.

Note

`IsPostBack` is set to `false` each time the user accesses a Web Form for the *first time*. Contrary to most situations in life, there can be more than one *first time*. Let me clarify: A *first time* occurs when a user requests your Web Form by entering a URI. The user can even cause two *first time* events to occur back-to-back: All he or she has to do is enter the URI of the Web Form, wait for the form to load, and then click the browser's Refresh button. Each click of the Refresh button causes the Web Form handlers to be invoked with `IsPostBack` set to `false`.

What about the case in which a user leaves your site and then returns? To return to your Web Form, the user has to enter its URI, so the `IsPostBack` property will be `false`.

Adding event handlers

If a Web Form reacts to a user action, such as a button click, it does so through event handlers. For each control on a Web Form, you can use the Properties window to see a list of its possible event handlers. The events MyWebForm needs to handle are the following:

✦ `Page_Load` events

✦ `PageIndexChanged` events for the `DataGrid`

✦ `TextChanged` events for the name-filtering `TextBoxes`

✦ `Click` events for the Submit button

`Page_Load` events are only necessary to populate the `DataGrid` when users first enter the site.

`PageIndexChanged` events occur when users click the page links in a `DataGrid` to navigate to a new page of records. To support page navigation, I added the code shown in Listing 13-14 to the handler.

Listing 13-14: **The PageIndexChanged Event Handler**

```
private void DataGrid1_PageIndexChanged(object source,
        System.Web.UI.WebControls.DataGridPageChangedEventArgs e)
```

```
  {
    DataGrid1.CurrentPageIndex = e.NewPageIndex;
    PopulateGrid();
  }
```

By changing the value of `CurrentPageIndex`, the grid loads a different set of records from its `DataSource`, which in my case is a `DataView`.

`TextChanged` events occur when a user types something into a `TextBox` control. In my case, I need the event handler to switch the grid's current page back to the first page. I used the code shown in Listing 13-15 for the handler.

Listing 13-15: **The TextChanged Handlers**

```
private void TextBoxFirstLetter_TextChanged(object sender,
                                            System.EventArgs e)
{
  DataGrid1.CurrentPageIndex = 0;
}

private void TextBoxLastLetter_TextChanged(object sender,
                                           System.EventArgs e)
{
  DataGrid1.CurrentPageIndex = 0;
}
```

Remember that `PageIndexChanged` and `TextChanged` events are cached on the client side, so they don't fire immediately. In contrast, `Click` events for buttons are fired immediately on the server side. To process `Click` events on the server side, I added the code in Listing 13-16 to the `Click` handler.

Listing 13-16: **The Click Handler for the Web Form Button**

```
private void ButtonSubmit_Click(object sender, System.EventArgs e)
{
  PopulateGrid();
}
```

Writing event handlers can be challenging at times, because some events fire immediately and some don't. Events don't all fire handlers in the same place: Some fire only on the client side, others on either the client side or the server side, and others only on the server side.

Before moving on the test my Web application, you're probably interested in seeing its complete code. Listing 13-17 shows the main code in WebForm1.aspx.cs.

Listing 13-17: The Main Code for MyWebForm

```csharp
using System;
using System.Web.SessionState;
using System.Web.UI.WebControls;
using System.Web.UI.HtmlControls;
// other using directives...

using DatabaseWebService;

namespace MyWebForm
{
  public class WebForm1 : System.Web.UI.Page
  {
    protected System.Web.UI.WebControls.DataGrid DataGrid1;
    protected System.Web.UI.WebControls.TextBox TextBoxFirstLetter;
    protected System.Web.UI.WebControls.TextBox TextBoxLastLetter;
    protected System.Web.UI.WebControls.Label LabelNumberOfAuthors;
    protected System.Web.UI.WebControls.Button ButtonSubmit;
    protected DatabaseWebService.MyDataSet myDataSet1;
    protected System.Data.DataView dataView1;
    // other controls...

    public WebForm1()
    {

      Page.Init += new System.EventHandler(Page_Init);
    }

    private void Page_Load(object sender, System.EventArgs e)
    {
      if (!IsPostBack)
        PopulateGrid();
    }

    private void Page_Init(object sender, EventArgs e)
    {
      InitializeComponent();
    }

    private void InitializeComponent()
    {
      // code generated automatically...
    }

    private void PopulateGrid()
    {
      MyDatabaseWebService myService = new MyDatabaseWebService();
      myDataSet1 = myService.GetAuthors() as MyDataSet;
      dataView1.Table = myDataSet1.authors;
      string s = String.Format("(au_lname >= '{0}%') and
                                (au_lname <= '{1}%')",
```

```
                           TextBoxFirstLetter.Text,
                           TextBoxLastLetter.Text);
    dataView1.RowFilter = s;
    DataGrid1.DataBind();
    LabelNumberOfAuthors.Text = dataView1.Count.ToString();
  }

  private void DataGrid1_PageIndexChanged(object source,
     System.Web.UI.WebControls.DataGridPageChangedEventArgs e)
  {
    DataGrid1.CurrentPageIndex = e.NewPageIndex;
    PopulateGrid();
  }

  private void TextBoxFirstLetter_TextChanged(object sender,
                                       System.EventArgs e)
  {
    DataGrid1.CurrentPageIndex = 0;
  }

  private void TextBoxLastLetter_TextChanged(object sender,
                                       System.EventArgs e)
  {
    DataGrid1.CurrentPageIndex = 0;
  }

  private void ButtonSubmit_Click(object sender,
                             System.EventArgs e)
  {
    startTime = DateTime.Now.Ticks;

    PopulateGrid();

    Application_EndRequest(this, null);
  }
  }
}
```

Testing a Web Form

ASP developers used to have a hard time debugging their code, for a couple of reasons. For one thing, they didn't have the luxury of Visual Studio to work in. They had to work in a different environment, such as Visual InterDev, which had nowhere near the power that Visual C++, Visual Basic, or Delphi programmers are used to.

Second, a high percentage of Web developers had trouble setting up a proper debugging environment. What you want to do in the debugging stage is load your code, set breakpoints, and run the code under a debugger. While doing this sounds straightforward, I know of many Web developers that tried and simply gave up. They had no idea how to run a Web page in a debugging environment, how to step across process boundaries when client-side code called server-side code, and all kinds of other problems. As a result, sadly, the most common debugging tool for ASP developers was the `Response.Write()` call, which is equivalent to a C++ programmer using `printf()` calls to debug a C++ program. Help! To paraphrase Moe from The Three Stooges, if you're testing ASP code using `Response.Write()` calls, *"you're going nowhere fast."*

With VS .NET, testing and debugging Web Forms is a breeze. If your Web application is on a remote Web Server, make sure you have sufficient rights on that machine. Basically, your login account must make you a direct or indirect member of the Debugging Users group on the server. Once you have the proper rights, you can test and debug a Web Form using ordinary techniques. There are no special tools to use or settings to configure.

To test a Web Form, the easiest way is the click the Start button on the main VS .NET toolbar. This will display your Web Form in the default browser, which is normally Internet Explorer. If your Web application has multiple Web Forms, the form configured as the Start Page will appear. To designate a Web Form as the Start Page, right-click on its .aspx file in the Solution Explorer and select Set As Start Page from the pop-up menu, as shown in Figure 13-24.

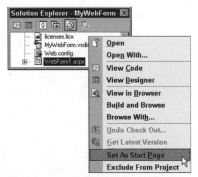

Figure 13-24: Designating a Web Form as the Start Page for testing

You can set breakpoints in the code-behind files of your Web application. You can't set breakpoints in the aspx files, because those don't contain executable code.

The Start button displays your Web Forms in a separate browser window. VS .NET also has an internal browser window. To view your Web Forms with the Internal Web Browser, right-click on the form's aspx file in the Solution Explorer and select the View in Browser command, as shown in Figure 13-25.

Figure 13-25: The View in Browser command for launching the built-in browser

The command will add a new page to the editor window, containing the Web page dynamically generated for the Web Form, as shown in Figure 13-26.

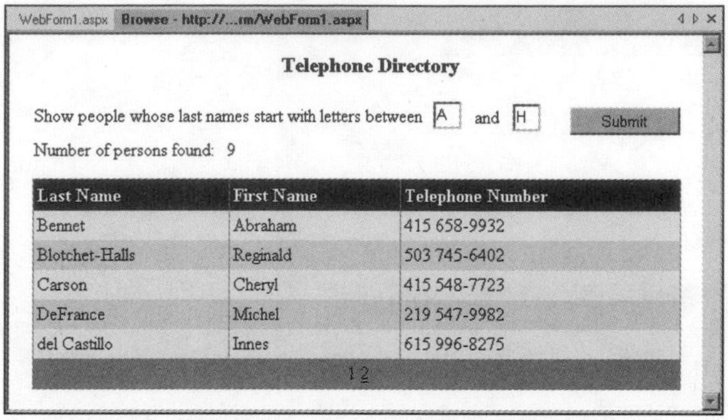

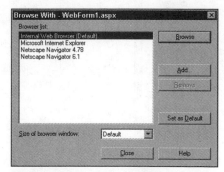

Figure 13-26: The Web Form, as it appears inside the VS .NET Internal Web Browser

As you can see, the DataGrid is now populated with data. The grid uses a number of default properties, such as the white/gray alternating colors for the row backgrounds, the blue caption bar, and the column names. The HTML code generated for the DataGrid uses a standard HTML <table> tag.

If you have more than one browser installed on your machine, you can see how the Web Form will appear with them as well. To select a browser other than the Internal Web Browser, right-click on the form's aspx file in the Solution Explorer and select the Browse With command, shown previously in Figure 13-25. A dialog box will appear, displaying a list of the browsers installed on your system, as shown in Figure 13-27.

Figure 13-27: Using the Browse With dialog box to select different browsers

Double-click on the browser you want to use. The selected browser will be opened in a separate window. Figures 13-28 and 13-29 show how WebForm1 appears with Netscape Navigator 4.78 and 6.1.

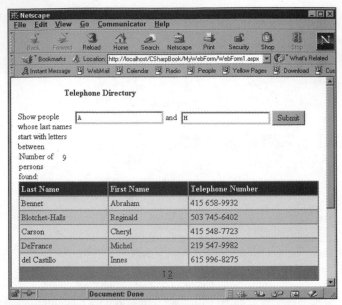

Figure 13-28: How WebForm1 appears in Netscape Navigator 4.78

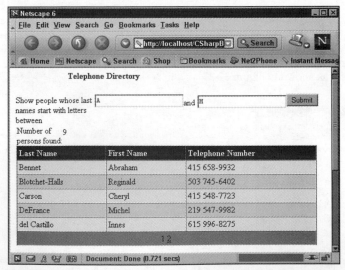

Figure 13-29: How WebForm1 appears in Netscape Navigator 6.1

You can install any browser you want into VS .NET, using the Browse With command. You can control the type of schema you want the HTML page for a Web Form to use, by setting the `targetSchema` property of the Web Form's `DOCUMENT` object in the Properties window. If you select the "Internet Explorer 3.02 / Navigator 3.0" setting, the HTTP runtime will create pages using embedded styles.

Other settings, such as Navigator 4.0 or Internet Explorer 5.0, will enable the use of Cascading Style Sheets and other features.

If you set breakpoints in your code-behind files, you can stop execution of the Web application and browse the execution context. You can inspect local variables, the stack, the `Request` and `Response` objects, and just about anything else you may need to see. As an example, I set a breakpoint in the button's `Click` handler and clicked the button. The breakpoint was triggered on the breakpoint line. I then used the Watch window to inspect the `Request` object, as shown in Figure 13-30.

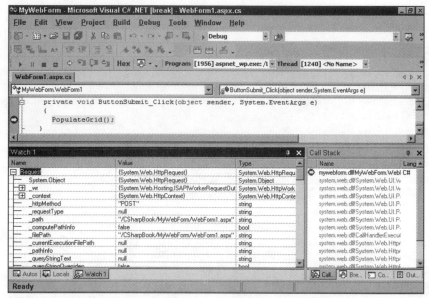

Figure 13-30: Inspecting the Request object after a breakpoint was triggered

While your code is stopped, you can not only look at variables, but also change their values before resuming execution. If you make any changes to the code, you'll need to stop the debugger and rebuild the Web application. The Call Stack window, in the lower right part of the screen, can be used to see what chain of method calls led to your breakpoint.

Using the Response object

Not every HTML page you generate has WebControls or HTML controls on it. There are plenty of situations in which you just want to return a simple message to the user, maybe informing them of an order received or giving them some sort of confirmation. In these cases, rather than assigning values to controls, you may want to access the ASP.NET Response object directly and add text to it.

If you have experience developing ASP code, you would probably consider changing the `Click` handler for the Submit button to look like Listing 13-18.

Listing 13-18: An Event Handler that Doesn't Produce the Results You Might Think

```csharp
public void Button1_Click (object sender, System.EventArgs e)
{
        Response.Write("There are " + dataView1.Count.ToString() +
                      " authors that match your selection");
}
```

This will indeed send a string back to the user, but you need to think with your new ASP.NET hat on. When the user clicks the Submit button, it actually triggers a postback operation, during which the form's ViewState (described later) is completely regenerated, with the DataGrid and the Submit button. After the Click handler is called, the HTTP runtime tells the Web Form Controls and elements to render themselves, causing a lot of additional HTML code to be added to the Response object. As a result, the page returned to the user will look like Figure 13-31.

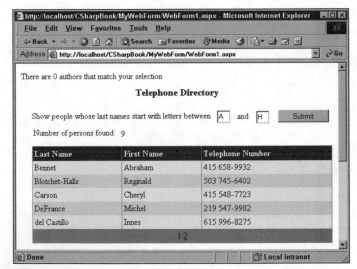

Figure 13-31: The response message, appearing with the original form

But I don't want the code to redisplay the original form; I just want my response string to show up. Is there a solution? Of course—in fact, there are several. The easiest is to generate the response text in the event handler as shown previously in Listing 13-18, and then tell the HTTP runtime to forget everything else. All you have to do is add the call to Response.End() in the event handler, as shown in Listing 13-19.

Listing 13-19: **Using Response.End() to Terminate Event Handling
for a Page**

```
public void Button1_Click (object sender, System.EventArgs e)
{
  Response.Write("Thanks for for order.");
  Response.End();
}
```

This code will produce the correct HTML page, as shown in Figure 13-32.

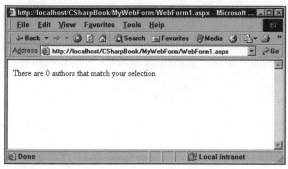

Figure 13-32: The HTML page containing only the
desired response string

Using Redirect to return a completely different page

The use of `Response.End()` works well only in the simplest cases, when a trivial page needs
to be returned with a limited amount of text on it. If you need to return more than a simple
string, it is often easier to create a whole new Web Form and send it back to the user. If this
Web Form already exists, you just have to redirect the request to the new form. Switching to a
different Web Form is easy, and all you have to do is call the `Redirect()` method of the
Response object. You can also pass parameters to the `Redirect()` method. For example, say
you have a Web Form called *WebForm2* that takes a parameter called *MyCount*. The Web Form
might look like Figure 13-33.

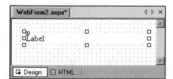

Figure 13-33: A simple Web
Form to redirect users to

The PageInit handler for WebForm2 could be set up to display the value of the parameter MyCount in the Label control, as shown in Listing 13-20.

Listing 13-20: Retrieving the Value of a Parameter from the Request Object

```
Label1.Text = "The number of items is: " + Request["MyCount"];
```

To redirect users who click the Submit button in WebForm1 to the new page WebForm2, the Click handler for WebForm1 would need to have the code shown in Listing 13-21.

Listing 13-21: Redirecting Users to a Different Page

```
private void ButtonSubmit_Click(object sender, System.EventArgs e)
{
  Response.Redirect("WebForm2.aspx?MyCount=" +
                    dataView1.Count.ToString() );
}
```

Using Response.Redirect(), you can send users to any page of your site or another site, and pass any parameters you need.

Using trace statements

The most direct way to test and debug Web Form code is by using breakpoints in the code-behind logic, but the approach isn't appropriate for all situations. For example, you may want to run tests on your Web site, without stopping it. Rather than adding a bunch of Response.Write() calls to your Web application, you can use *trace commands*. You can even leave the commands in the code when you deploy the application, because tracing is disabled by default, so no trace output will be generated. You add trace commands to code-behind pages, using the methods Trace.Write() or Trace.Warn() like this:

```
Trace.Write("MyCategory", "My trace message");
Trace.Warn(("MyCategory", "My next trace message");
```

When viewed later, trace messages produced by Trace.Write() are in black, while messages produced by Trace.Warn() are in red. Trace messages are also tagged with a category. The category has no meaning to the ASP.NET Framework. It's just meant to help you organize the trace output into groups. For example, you could use a different category for the output produced for each Web Form in your application, or you could use categories to separate messages into warnings and errors. You can create as many categories as you want.

Trace statements generate debugging information for a Web Form, but only if tracing is enabled. You can turn it on or off for individual Web Forms or for the entire application. To control tracing for the entire application, you need to access the attributes of the <trace> element in the Web.Config file. Listing 13-22 shows the default trace settings for a Web application.

> ### Listing 13-22: **The Default Trace Settings for a Web Application**
>
> ```
> <trace
>   enabled="false"
>   requestLimit="10"
>   pageOutput="false"
>   traceMode="SortByTime"
>   localOnly="true" />
> ```

Table 13-4 describes the attributes of the `<trace>` element.

Table 13-4: Attributes of the <trace> Element in Web.Config

Attribute	Description
`enabled`	Controls whether tracing is on or off. The value must be true or false. The default value is false.
`requestLimit`	The number of page requests for which tracing output is stored. The default value is 10, meaning that only the trace output for the 10 most recent requests for the Web application will be stored. Each time the Web application is started, the trace output cache is cleared. The cache is also cleared in another situation, while your application is running. Each time a request arrives, the ASP.NET Framework checks to see if the configuration was changed since the previous request. If so, the trace cache is cleared and the new trace settings are applied to the new request.
`pageOutput`	Indicates where the trace output will go. It true, the output is appended to the HTML page returned to the end user. Regardless of the pageOutput value, the trace output is always added to the trace cache (when tracing is enabled).
`traceMode`	Indicates how to sort the trace information. The default mode is SortByTime, but you can also set it to SortByCategory. The latter mode is useful if you have different categories of trace output.
`localOnly`	Controls whether the trace cache is viewable on the server only or not.

All tracing output is stored in a *trace cache*. To view the trace cache, you have two options: You can set the `pageOutput` attribute to `true`, or you can use the ASP.NET Trace Viewer. If `pageOutput` is `true`, all the tracing data is appended to the Web Form and is sent back with the form to the end user's browser. Figures 13-34 shows some of the trace information sent back with a Web Form request.

Notice the trace output in the section titled Trace Information. The third line is the output produced by my `Trace.Write()` statement. The trace output is ordered chronologically by default. To change the sort order for all the trace output of the entire Web application, set the `tracemode` attribute in the Web.Config file. To change the sort order for only a specific Web Form, change its `traceOrder` property using the Properties window. Figure 13-35 shows other trace information returned to the end user's browser.

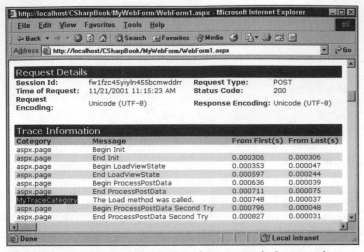

Figure 13-34: Some of the tracing data appended to a Web Form when pageOutput is true

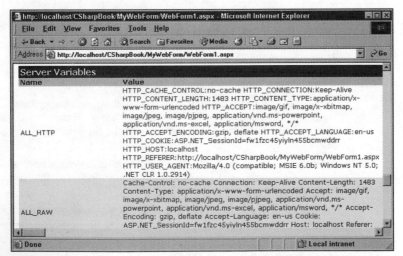

Figure 13-35: More of the tracing data appended to a Web Form when pageOutput is true

I mentioned the use of the Trace Viewer to inspect trace date. The Trace Viewer is not a standalone utility. To use the ASP.NET Trace Viewer, you need a browser. To see the trace output for a Web application named `MyWebForm`, use the following URI:

```
http://localhost/CSharpBook/MyWebForm/trace.axd
```

Figure 13-36 shows how trace.axd appears in a browser.

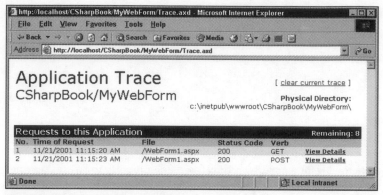

Figure 13-36: Using the ASP.NET Trace Viewer to browse the trace output for a Web application

If localOnly is set to false in the Web.Config file, end users will be able to browse the trace.axd from their remote computer. The default setting for localOnly is true, meaning only a browser running on the Web Server will have access to the Trace Viewer.

Don't go looking for a file called *trace.axd* in the root folder of your Web application — you won't find one. The URI entered to access the Trace Viewer suggests that there should be a file called *trace.axd*. In reality, the trace information is cached internally by the ASP.NET Framework. There is no file named *trace.axd*. The Trace Viewer is really just an HTTP handler that is activated by ASP.NET when a file named *trace.axd* is requested. To see how ASP.NET knows what HTTP handler to load with files named *trace.axd*, look at the machine.config file, in the following folder:

```
C:\WINNT\Microsoft.NET
```

There you'll find the code shown in Listing 13-23.

Listing 13-23: The Trace Viewer Module, Referenced in the machine.config File

```
<httpHandlers>
  <add verb="*"
       path="trace.axd"
       type="System.Web.Handlers.TraceHandler,
             System.Web, Version=1.0.2411.0,
             Culture=neutral,
             PublicKeyToken=b03f5f7f11d50a3a" />
</httpHandlers>
```

As you can see, the Trace Viewer is not associated with all files having the suffix .axd: The filename must be *trace.axd*, and is not case-sensitive.

You can turn tracing on for the whole application using the <trace> element in the Web.Config file. You can also turn tracing on for a single Web Form. To do so, display the form in the Forms Designer. Select the DOCUMENT object in the Properties window and set the trace property to True, as shown in Figure 13-37.

Figure 13-37: Enabling tracing for a specific Web Form

You can also disable tracing for a page, by setting the trace property to False. Leaving the property blank makes it dependent on the enabled attribute of the <trace> element in the Web.Config file for the Web application. If you change the DOCUMENT.trace property, you need to rebuild the Web application for the change to take effect. When enabling or disabling tracing for the entire application, using the Web.Config file, you don't have to rebuild anything. Changes take effect immediately. As you can see, the ASP.NET Framework makes available a number of ways to control and produce trace output. Tracing can be an invaluable debugging or monitoring tool, so you should give it a try.

Managing State

Interactions between client browsers and Web Forms often require knowledge about past actions and responses. For example, if you require users to log in to your site, your site will somehow need to record when a login occurs and keep the information for later. Besides login information, there may be other items to remember for a user, such as names, shopping carts, preferences, and so on. All this information is part of what is normally called the *state* of a user session. There are also state variables that are global in nature and shared across all sessions in the Web application, such as database connections.

Without a way to track state for each user, your Web site would have to keep asking users for the same information over and over again. State management is essential for Web applications, and the ASP.NET framework has a number of ways to automatically maintain Session and Application state, including

✦ Using cookies

✦ Using hidden data

✦ Using query strings

✦ Using ViewState

✦ Using Session variables

The restoration of state in Web Forms is essentially automatic, and is accomplished behind the scenes by the ASP.NET Framework. The diagram in Figure 13-38 shows some of the actions that take place when a user visits a site that uses Web Forms.

When a Web Form is loaded, all its controls are automatically put back in the state they were in when the page was last delivered to the end user. Any changes made on the client side are also applied. The fact that a page is loaded and destroyed with every user request is transparent to developers writing server-side code. From the programmer's perspective on the server side, Web Forms behave as if they were created once when the user first entered the site, remained in memory during the user session, and then were destroyed when the user left the site. State management is a really big deal for Web applications, and ASP.NET handles it very well. In the next few sections, I'll quickly go over basic state management techniques available under ASP.NET.

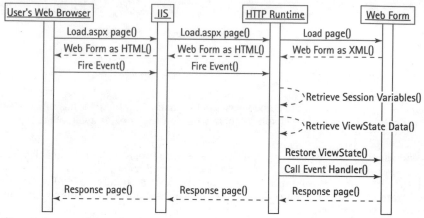

Figure 13-38: The activation sequence for event handlers configured to run on the server side

Using cookies

Cookies are small objects (strings, actually) that a Web site may send back to a browser along with a page. Browsers store cookies either in files or in memory. A Web server has no control over where cookies are stored on client machines. When you request a page from a Web site, the browser automatically checks to see if a cookie exists for the given site. If so, the cookie is automatically sent to the Web site along with the request.

Cookies can be given expiration dates, and when a cookie expires, the browser deletes it. Cookies can be used to store items like UserIDs or other information, but can only handle small amounts of information. Most browsers limit the size of cookies to 8 KB or less. What a cookie stores is entirely dependent on what the server needs. Browsers make no assumptions about what is stored in a cookie. Because browsers guarantee that a cookie is only sent to the Web site from which it came, cookies are fairly safe — in terms of preventing information obtained from one Web site from going anywhere else. Nevertheless, many people disable cookies in the browser, to maintain a certain degree of anonymity when visiting sites. Because the availability of cookies is user-selectable, you can't always count on cookies for state management. Listing 13-24 shows how to send a cookie back with a Web Form.

Listing 13-24: **Returning a Cookie from a Web Form**

```
cookie = new HttpCookie("UserID");
cookie.Value = DateTime.Now.Ticks.ToString();
Response.Cookies.Add(cookie);
```

The code uses the current time, expressed in 100 nanosecond units, as the UserID. You can return more than one cookie with a page, but try not to make your pages rely on cookies too heavily, since they can be disabled on the user's browser. To retrieve the value of a cookie saved on a user machine, use the code shown in Listing 13-25.

Listing 13-25: Retrieving a Cookie Previously Saved on a User Machine

```
HttpCookie cookie = Request.Cookies ["UserID"];
if (cookie != null)
  Label1.Text = cookie.Value;  // use the cookie
```

Make sure you check to see if the cookie exists before using it. If the user has never visited your site, or if their cookies have expired, there won't be any cookies available in the Request.Cookies collection.

Just as end users sometimes distrust cookies, server-side programmers should also be somewhat careful with them. Cookies can easily be tampered with and modified on the client side, so using them to store critical or proprietary information is definitely a bad idea. Cookies are mostly used to store information related to user preferences and session Ids to maintain state information on the server.

Using hidden data

You can place hidden controls on a Web Form that don't show up on client browsers. While cookies can be disabled on the browser side, hidden controls can't, so you can always count on them for storing data. The idea of hidden fields is this: Rather than storing user state information somewhere on the server, you embed it in a hidden control and send it back to the user. If the user subsequently clicks a Submit button, the information in the hidden control is sent back to the server. A small drawback of hidden fields is the fact that they are transferred back and forth between client and server, so they may have a certain impact on performance if they contain a lot of information.

The standard technique for managing the state of the controls on a Web Form is with a special hidden field named __VIEWSTATE. If you look at the source code for a .aspx page loaded by your browser, you'll see code that looks something like Listing 13-26.

Listing 13-26: The Hidden Field Used by Web Forms to Manage the State of Controls

```
<form name="Form1" method="post" action="WebForm1.aspx" id="Form1">
  <input type="hidden" name="__VIEWSTATE" value="...gONOz4+Oz4=" />
</form>
```

The data contained in the __VIEWSTATE hidden field is not in clear text, so you can't easily tell what it means. Hidden fields are great, but remember they can always be inspected by end users, by viewing the source code for your aspx page. Early Web developers sometimes forgot this.

I remember reading about a Web site that had a shopping cart that used hidden fields to store the items and unit prices in clear text. It doesn't take a genius to figure out that someone would notice this data and take advantage of it. A number of people exploited the loophole to modify the data and post orders with ridiculously low unit prices. The moral of the story is this: If you do put sensitive information in a hidden field, at least encrypt it, so end users can't infer what the data means or otherwise exploit it.

Using query strings

Query strings consist of a list of (name=value) pairs that may optionally follow the URL in an HTTP request. These pairs allow you to pass named arguments to the server. The following example will help you understand how this works. Say you want to pass two parameters to the server: MyParameter1 with value MyValue1, and MyParameter2 with value MyValue2. The query string you would need is this:

```
WebForm1.aspx?MyParameter1=MyValue1&MyParameter2=MyValue2
```

Multiple parameters are separated using the character "&". To demonstrate how to use the example query string in a Web Form, I dropped a WebControls.HyperLink component on a Web Form and set its NavigateUrl property with the string. When you click the hyperlink, the string is sent to the server. In the Web Form code, you need to extract the parameters and values from the query string. To do so, I added the following code to the Page_Load event handler:

```
private void Page_Load(object sender, System.EventArgs e)
{
  Object obj = Request.Params ["MyParameter1"];
  String value1, value2;
  if (obj != null)
    value1 = obj.ToString();

  obj = Request.Params ["MyParameter2"];
  if (obj != null)
    value2 = obj.ToString();
}
```

Query strings are easy to use and almost universally supported in the Web world, but keep in mind that most browsers limit the length of a URI to 255 characters. Also remember that Query strings are plainly visible in the Address Bars of browsers, so you don't want to use the strings for confidential or critical information, unless the data is encrypted.

If you need to embed spaces, punctuation, or control characters in the query string, make sure to use escape sequences with them. If you're unfamiliar with HTTP escape sequences, they are just three-character sequences that denote a hexadecimal value. The sequence starts with the character % and then has two hex characters. For example, the string "a b", which contains a space between the letters, can be represented as an escaped string by "a%20b", because a space character has the hexadecimal code 20 in ANSI or ASCII encoding.

You don't have to memorize the escape sequences for characters. Use the Uri class to convert a character into an escape sequence like this:

```
// returns "%20"
String escapedSequenceForSpace = Uri.HexEscape(' ');
```

To convert an escaped sequence back into a character, use the following code:

```
int index = 0;
char unescapedChar = Uri.HexUnescape("%20", ref index);
```

The method `Uri.HexUnescape` decodes the sequence starting at the character with a given index in the string. If the character is not the beginning of an escaped sequence, but just a regular character, that character is returned as it is. The value of `index` is adjusted to the next position to decode in the string.

Using ViewState

The ViewState of a Web Form includes the set of properties and variables required to correctly display the contents of the form. By default, Web Forms embed ViewState information, using a hidden field named __VIEWSTATE. The following is a fragment of the HTML code returned to the client browser, showing the hidden field in boldface:

```
<form name="Form1" method="get" action="WebForm1.aspx" id="Form1">
    <input type="hidden" name="__VIEWSTATE"
            value="dDwtMTE0ODQ0NzgyMjs7Pg==" />
    <input type="submit" name="ButtonSubmit" value="Submit" />
</form>
```

When the user clicks the Submit button of the form, the contents of the __VIEWSTATE field are automatically sent back to the server, along with the values of all the other controls in the form. The ViewState basically encodes the state of all the controls on a page, such as the state of a CheckBox, the text in a TextBox, or the rows displayed in a DataGrid.

Some controls, like CheckBoxes, require a minimal amount of ViewState information. Others, like DataGrids, may require much more data. You can disable ViewState support for any control, if necessary. You might want to do this if you always recalculate the control's state information when the Web Form is reloaded, making it futile to store the state. You might also need to disable a control's ViewState if it requires an excessive amount of ViewState data. To disable ViewState support for a control, select the control in the Forms Designer, and then go to the Properties window and set the value of the `EnableViewState` property to `False`, as shown in Figure 13-39.

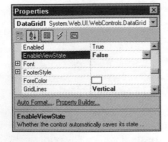

Figure 13-39: Disabling ViewState support for a control

ViewState management on the server-side is completely automatic. When ViewState data is received by the HTTP runtime, it is parsed and used to restore the controls to the state they were in when the Web Form was last returned to the end user.

Using Session variables

Session variables are objects that you can define on your Web Forms to store information for each user visiting your site. The Session State includes all the Session variables in your Web application, allowing your code to work seamlessly across a stateless HTTP link with the user. Back in the days of ASP, Session State was tracked using cookies and Session variables. Basically, a Session ID was stored in an HTTP cookie on the user machine. Each time the user returned to your site, the cookie was used to locate the user's Session variables on the server.

The use of cookies to track Session State is a simple technique, but it doesn't work with *Web farms,* which are Web sites made up of multiple Web servers that share the load of a Web site's traffic. By default, the ASP.NET Framework uses cookies to track Session IDs, but it also supports cookieless techniques that work with Web farms. The Session State management technique is specified in the Web.config file of your Web application. The file contains XML code that indicates the configuration settings used in a Web application, including the Session State. Listing 13-27 shows the XML element of interest in the file:

Listing 13-27: The Default SessionState Settings for a Web Application

```
<sessionState
  mode="InProc"
  stateConnectionString="tcpip=127.0.0.1:42424"
  sqlConnectionString="data source=127.0.0.1;user id=sa;password="
  cookieless="false"
  timeout="20"
/>
```

Each attribute is described in Table 13-5.

Table 13-5: sessionState Parameters Stored in the Config.web File

Attribute Name	Description
Mode	Determines how Session States are managed. Possible values are
	Off: Session State management is disabled.
	InProc: Managed automatically by ASP.NET code that stores Session information in a cache. This is the default value.
	SQLServer: Session variables are stored using SQL Server.
	StateServer: Session variables are stored by a separate ASPState component running as a Windows NT Service.
StateConnectionString	Indicates the protocol, IP address, and port to use to access the Windows NT Service managing the Session state. The default value is the address of the ASPState service running on the local machine. To manage Session State across Web farms, you can have all the servers access the same ASPState service on a remote machine.
SqlConnectionString	Indicates the login credentials to use when storing Session State in an SQL Server database. The default address assumes SQL Server is running on the local machine. To manage Session State across Web farms, you can have all the servers access a common SQL Server machine.
Cookieless	Indicates whether to use cookies or not to identify Session States. The default value is `false`, meaning cookies are enabled.
Timeout	The number of minutes before an idle session is closed. When a session is closed, all its session variables are deleted.

Let's take a closer look at how the Session-State-management logic works. In the default mode, cookies are used. When a user requests a page from your site, a cookie is returned with the page and stored on the user's machine. The cookie is called "ASP.NET_SessionId" and contains a 24-character base-64-encoded value that looks like this:

```
ASP.NET_SessionId=llnvsr45by2f3u45vcrttx45
```

The cookie's value represents a 120-bit Session ID. The value is similar to a GUID (Globally Unique ID) used in the COM world, and is generated automatically by the ASP.NET Framework in a way that prevents two users from having the same ID. The Session ID values include a number of error-checking redundancy bits, to allow the detection of fake values that malicious users may have submitted in an attempt to gain access to Session variables of other users.

When the user returns to your site, the SessionId cookie will be returned and used by the HTTP runtime to locate and load the variables of that Session. The ASP.NET component responsible for managing Session State is called sessionState in the HTTPContext, and is of class System.Web.SessionState.SessionStateSectionHandler. You don't normally access the sessionState component directly in your code. Just use the Session.Contents collection, passing it name of the Session variable you want. To store a value in a Session variable named MyVariable, use this code:

```
Session.Contents["MyVariable"] = "What a yo-yo!";
```

To read the Session variable back, use this code:

```
string s = Session.Contents["MyVariable"] as string;
```

Variables returned are of type Object, so you need to typecast them when reading them. If you try to access a variable that doesn't exist in the Session.Contents collection, you'll get a null value back. You can store any type of CLR variable in the Session State, because all managed types are derived from Object. Other types, such as ints and chars are transparently boxed and unboxed when saved and retrieved. The code in Listing 13-28 shows how to read and write different types of variables to the Session State.

Listing 13-28: Reading and Writing Different Types of Data to the Session State

```
int i = 1;
string s = "string";
bool b = true;
DateTime now = DateTime.Now;

Session.Contents["MyInteger"]  = i;
Session.Contents["MyString"]   = s;
Session.Contents["MyBoolean"]  = b;
Session.Contents["MyDateTime"] = now;

Object obj;
obj = Session.Contents["MyInteger"];
if (obj != null)
  i = Convert.ToInt32(obj);

obj = Session.Contents["MyString"];
```

```
  if (obj != null)
    s = obj as String;

  obj = Session.Contents["MyBoolean"];
  if (obj != null)
    b = Convert.ToBoolean(obj);

  obj = Session.Contents["MyDateTime"];
  if (obj != null)
    now = Convert.ToDateTime(obj);
```

There is a very important type of data you can't store in the Session.Contents collections: references to COM objects. But don't despair: there is a separate collection called Session.StaticObjects for COM and other types of components. You can't programmatically add components to this collection. You add items indirectly, using XML code in the Global.asax file for your Web Form, like this:

```
<OBJECT
  RUNAT="SERVER"
  SCOPE="SESSION"
  ID="MyCOMObject"
  PROGID="MyDLL.MyObjectName" />
```

You can also reference COM objects directly by ClassID like this:

```
<OBJECT
  RUNAT="SERVER"
  SCOPE="SESSION"
  ID="MyCOMObject"
  CLASSID="22D6F312-B0F6-10E0-94AB-0080C74C7E95" />
```

The <OBJECT> tag lets you create CLR objects too. The following code adds a CLR component to the Session.StaticObjects collection:

```
<OBJECT
  RUNAT="SERVER"
  SCOPE="SESSION"
  ID="MyCollection"
  CLASS="System.Collections.ArrayList" />
```

The RUNAT attribute must always be SERVER, and the SCOPE attribute must always be SESSION. The ID attribute is the name of the variable in the Session.StaticObjects collection.

To access objects set up with <object> tags from your Web Form code-behind file, you can use the code shown in Listing 13-29.

Listing 13-29: Accessing COM and CLR Objects Stored in the Session State

```
object obj = Session.StaticObjects["MyComObject"];
ArrayList myCollection =
  Session.StaticObjects["MyCollection"] as ArrayList;
```

The ASP.NET Framework is one of the most extensive areas of the entire .NET Framework, so there is no way I could cover it all in one chapter. The following two chapters deal with different aspects of Web programming, describing Web Controls and Web User Controls. Developing ASP.NET Web Forms is quite different than writing ASP pages. For one thing, ASP.NET requires you to understand and use object-oriented programming. Beyond that, you can now use a high-powered development language like C# to code all the components in your multitier applications, including Web Forms. VBScript and ECMAScript have not been rendered obsolete by the ASP.NET Framework, but have been relegated primary to the client-side.

Summary

Developing Web Forms can be pretty simple, if all you want to do is display static content. If you need to handle postback events or manage Session State, things get a little more complicated. In this chapter, I concentrated on the big picture of Web application development, focusing on the ASP.NET Framework and the HTTP runtime workings. In the next two chapters, I'll show you how to use different kinds of custom components to add power to your Web Forms.

✦   ✦   ✦

Web Controls

I have opinions of my own — strong opinions — but I don't always agree with them.

— Former U.S. President George H.W. Bush

I like people who question their beliefs, but George may have gone a bit too far. If he doesn't always agree with his own opinions, I'd hate to ask him what he thinks about someone else's.

Leaving George behind to mull on his opinions, what are Web Controls? The short answer is: They are simply components you can place on a Web Form. They don't work on Windows Forms. Web Controls usually have a user interface, meaning they are visible when their parent Web Form is loaded with a browser. I said *usually,* because there are times when you want them to be hidden, perhaps to carry out some task behind the scenes.

The Built-in Web Controls

VS .NET comes with over 20 built-in Web Controls, available on the Web Forms page of the Toolbox. The controls provide the standard features for creating rich Web pages. Web Controls are part of the larger ASP.NET Framework, and run in the managed environment of the ASP.NET runtime.

All Web Controls share basic features to support their rendering, managing postback data, handling events, and so on. The built-in Web Controls are mostly defined in the namespace `System.Web.UI.WebControls` and generally share the common base class `WebControl`, as shown in Figure 14-1.

I didn't use a UML class diagram in the figure to save space. Instead, I used indentation to show inheritance. For example, class `RadioButton` is indented under `CheckBox` because it is derived from `CheckBox`.

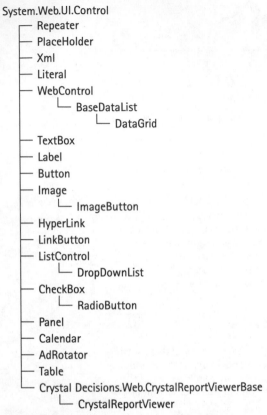

```
System.Web.UI.Control
    ├── Repeater
    ├── PlaceHolder
    ├── Xml
    ├── Literal
    ├── WebControl
    │       └── BaseDataList
    │               └── DataGrid
    ├── TextBox
    ├── Label
    ├── Button
    ├── Image
    │       └── ImageButton
    ├── HyperLink
    ├── LinkButton
    ├── ListControl
    │       └── DropDownList
    ├── CheckBox
    │       └── RadioButton
    ├── Panel
    ├── Calendar
    ├── AdRotator
    ├── Table
    └── Crystal Decisions.Web.CrystalReportViewerBase
            └── CrystalReportViewer
```

Figure 14-1: The class hierarchy of Web Controls

Why Were Web Controls Created?

If you have any experience as a Web developer, you know that HTML defines only a small set of UI controls, which handle only the most basic interface requirements. For example, the standard <table> tag produces read-only tables, so many database-oriented Web pages have special buttons to support editing of table data. HTML doesn't define many types of controls that Windows programmers take for granted, such as TreeViews, Tabbed controls, and others.

Another problem with HTML controls is with event-handling code. The code is run on the client side, putting its execution at the mercy of the client browser: If the browser doesn't support the scripting features or languages you use, the page won't run correctly. Also, if you download script code to the user's machine, you may expose sensitive details of your Web application.

A really big problem with HTML controls is browser-compatibility: Not all browsers support the same features. Some browsers don't even support HTML 4.0. If you use tables in your pages, but the end user's browser doesn't support tables, you have a problem. There are several differences between the various versions of popular browsers in use today, and adding support for each browser requires adding a lot of browser-checking code in ASP pages.

To solve these and other problems, Microsoft came up with the idea of *Web Controls,* which are reminiscent of the old *Design Time Controls* of ASP. Web Controls are components that are (mostly) derived from the common base class `WebControl` in the namespace `System.Web.UI.WebControls.`

But Web Controls are very different from controls based on simple HTML tags. The ASP.NET engine generates HTML code dynamically for each Web Control, based on the user's browser type and version. The generated code uses one or more standard HTML controls to emulate the features of each Web Control. Web Controls take the pain out of having to keep track of browser characteristics in your code, and ensure that your HTML pages always look the same (or almost) on different browsers.

How Web Controls Work

The easiest way to use a Web Control is by dropping it on a Web Form in the VS .NET Forms Designer. Just by being on a Web Form, a Web Control automatically participates in a series of events connected to the Web Form's Page lifecycle. The interaction diagram in Figure 14-2 shows the salient events in this lifecycle.

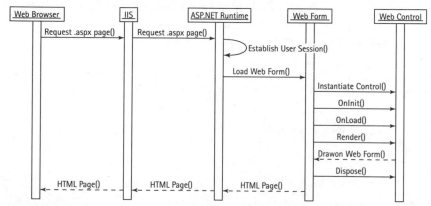

Figure 14-2: The lifecycle of a Web Control when its parent Web Form is initially loaded

The diagram shows the dynamics of a Web Control when its parent Web Form is loaded for the first time. As the user interacts with the HTML page returned, there will usually be postback events, which require Web Controls to deal with ViewState data, discussed in the previous chapter.

Developing a Custom Web Control

Creating your own customized Web Control is a fairly straightforward process, consisting of the following steps:

1. Define a namespace for the control. You can put any number of controls or other components in the namespace.

2. Derive a class from `System.Web.UI.Control` or `System.Web.UI.WebControl`.

3. Define properties, methods, and events.

4. Override the `Render()` method.

5. Add runtime attributes.

6. Add design-time attributes.

7. Test the control with a test fixture.

8. Optionally, add the control to VS .NET Toolbox.

The Add New Item Wizard in VS .NET can be used to set up a plain Web Control class that you can then customize. The default base class, `WebControl`, has the entire infrastructure needed to wire controls into the ASP.NET framework.

In this section, I'll create a simple Web Control, which I'll call *MyWebControl,* to show the overall process of design, development, and testing. The control will demonstrate how Web Controls render themselves on a Web Form, how they look on the HTML page delivered back to the user's browser, and how to handle events.

Before we talk design, we need to have some requirements. I'll keep the requirements simple: `MyWebControl` will behave like an ordinary `LinkButton` control, but I want its color to change each time it is clicked, and I want a ToolTip window to appear, showing the color of the control.

Designing the Web Control

Since `MyWebControl` needs to behave like a `LinkButton` control, I derived it from the built-in class `LinkButton`, as shown in the class diagram in Figure 14-3.

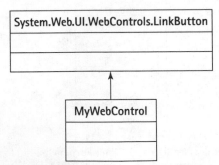

Figure 14-3: The class diagram for MyWebControl

That's really all there is to it. The next step is implementation. Obviously a real-world Web Control will be more complicated than MyWebControl, but I kept my example simple to focus on the essential steps.

There are two ways to package Web Controls: in a Web application or in a separate DLL. If you only plan to use the controls in a single Web application, it might make sense to add them directly to the application project. If you plan to reuse the controls in many Web applications, or want to distribute them to other people, you'll want to package them as a DLL. In the next section I'll show you how to implement and package Web Controls in both ways: first as part of a Web application and then as a separate DLL.

Developing the Control

I created a Web application called *MyWebControlApplication* to show you how to create a Web Control as part of an application. To create the application, I used the New Project Wizard and selected the ASP.NET Web Application template, as shown in Figure 14-4.

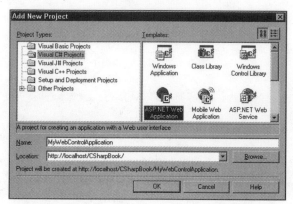

Figure 14-4: Using the New Project Wizard to create a Web application to manage and test a Web Control

The wizard creates an empty Web application with a form called WebForm1. My next step was to add a new Web Control to the project. The simplest way is to right-click the project node in the Solutions Explorer and select Add ➪ Add New Item from the pop-up menu. On the Add New Item Wizard screen, I selected the Web Custom Control Template and entered the name **MyWebControl.cs,** as shown in Figure 14-5.

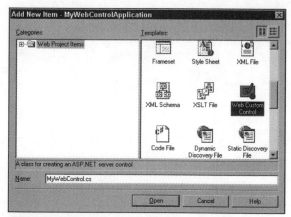

Figure 14-5: Using the Add New Item Wizard to create a Web Control

At this point the Solution Explorer had the files shown in Figure 14-6.

Figure 14-6: The Solution Explorer, showing the newly created Web Control

Before I added any code of my own, the default Web Control looked like Listing 14-1 (with the comments removed).

Listing 14-1: The Web Control Class Created by the VS .NET Wizard

```
using System;
using System.Web.UI;
using System.Web.UI.WebControls;
using System.ComponentModel;

namespace MyWebControlApplication
{
  [DefaultProperty("Text"),
   ToolboxData("<{0}:MyWebControl
                 runat=server>
               </{0}:MyWebControl>")]
  public class MyWebControl : System.Web.UI.WebControls.WebControl
  {
    private string text;

    [Bindable(true), Category("Appearance"), DefaultValue("")]
    public string Text
    {
      get { return text; }
      set { text = value; }
    }

    protected override void Render(HtmlTextWriter output)
    {
      output.Write(Text);
    }
  }
}
```

As you can see, the Wizard created a class derived from WebControl. This base class is useful if you are creating fairly rich UI controls, because you inherit a number of useful properties from it, such as Font, FontColor, BackColor, and others. If your control uses graphics without text, you may want to change the base class to System.Web.UI.Control, to avoid all the extra baggage of WebControl.

Before customizing the code of MyWebControl, it's a good idea to put it on a Web Form, to see what it looks like both at design-time and runtime. Since MyWebControl wasn't available on the Toolbox, I couldn't drag and drop it onto the Web Form, so I had to add code the hard way: by hand. No big deal, I just needed to add a few lines to the Web Form's .aspx file. To do so, I selected WebForm1.aspx in the Forms Designer, and then switched to the HTML pane. First, I added a Register tag to the file, using the code shown in Listing 14-2.

Listing 14-2: **Registering a Web Control on a Web Form**

```
<%@ Register TagPrefix= "MyStuff"
             Namespace= "MyWebControlApplication"
             Assembly=  "MyWebControlApplication"
%>
```

You must always register controls before referencing them in a Web Form. The Register tag tells the ASP.NET runtime where to find the code for MyWebControl. Note that I used the namespace and assembly name of my Web application, because MyWebControl is part of the application. Most of the time, Web Controls are distributed in DLLs with their own namespace, so you'll need to change the Register attributes accordingly. (Later, I'll show you how to reference Web Controls that are packaged in their own DLL.)

Having added the Register tag, I added MyWebControl to the Web Form, using the code shown in Listing 14-3.

Listing 14-3: **The XML Code Used to Add MyCustomControl to a Web Form**

```
<form id="Form1" method="post" runat="server">

  <MyStuff:MyWebControl Text="MyWebControl"
                        runat="server"
                        ID="MyWebControl1"
                        NAME="MyWebControl1" />
</form>
```

The <form> tag is part of all Web Forms, so I just added the control to it. Notice the use of the namespace MyStuff, which acts as a shorthand for the namespace of the Web control (in this case, MyWebControlApplication). Listing 14-4 shows the significant code of WebForm1.aspx after the custom control is added.

Listing 14-4: The WebForm1.aspx Code after Adding MyWebControl

```
<%@ Register TagPrefix="MyStuff"
             Namespace="MyWebControlApplication"
             Assembly= "MyWebControlApplication" %>

<%@ Page Language="c#"
         Codebehind="WebForm1.aspx.cs"
         AutoEventWireup="false"
         Inherits="MyWebControlApplication.WebForm1" %>

<HTML>
  <body MS_POSITIONING="GridLayout">
    <form id="Form1" method="post" runat="server">
      <MyStuff:MyWebControl Text="MyWebControl"
                            runat="server"
                            ID="MyWebControl1"
                            NAME="MyWebControl1" />

    </form>
  </body>
</HTML>
```

When I added the `<MyStuff:MyWebControl>` tag to the aspx code, VS .NET automatically added a variable called `MyWebControl1` to the form's code-behind page, as shown in boldface in Listing 14-5.

Listing 14-5: The Member Added to the Web Form's Code-Behind File

```
public class WebForm1 : System.Web.UI.Page
{
    protected MyWebControlApplication.MyWebControl MyWebControl1;
}
```

To see what the control looked like, I switched the Forms Designer to the Design pane. Figure 14-7 shows how the Web Form appeared with `MyWebControl`.

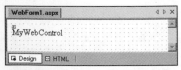

Figure 14-7: The design-time appearance of MyWebControl in WebForm1

Selecting `MyWebControl` in the Forms Designer makes all its public properties show up in the VS .NET Properties window, as shown in Figure 14-8.

Figure 14-8: Browsing the properties of MyWebControl in the Properties window

Most of the properties are inherited from `System.Web.UI.Control`, but some come from `System.Web.UI.WebControl`. Notice how I modified only one property: I changed `Text` to the string `"Click me"`.

I customized `MyWebControl` by adding a simple `Click` handler. The handler just toggles the text color from black to green. Listing 14-6 shows the event handling code for the control.

Listing 14-6: A Simple Web Control with a Click Handler

```
using System;
using System.Drawing;
using System.Web.UI;
using System.Web.UI.WebControls;
using System.ComponentModel;

namespace MyWebControlApplication
{
  public class MyWebControl : System.Web.UI.WebControls.LinkButton
  {
    protected override void OnClick(EventArgs e)
    {
      if (ForeColor == Color.Black)
        ForeColor = Color.Green;
      else
        ForeColor = Color.Black;
    }
  }
}
```

Very simple, as you can see. I loaded WebForm1.aspx with Internet Explorer and viewed the source code to see how `MyWebControl` was rendered. Listing 14-7 shows the HTML code produced after clicking the control once.

Listing 14-7: **The HTML Code Rendered for MyWebControl**

```
<a id="MyWebControl1"
   title="Now I'm Green!"
   NAME="MyWebControl1"
   href="javascript:__doPostBack('MyWebControl1','')"
   style="color:Green;">Click me</a>
```

MyWebControl is rendered by the base class LinkButton, using an HTML anchor tag. The tooltip is supported through the title attribute of the anchor. Figure 14-9 shows how WebForm1 appears at runtime in a browser, with the custom tooltip.

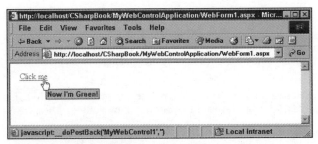

Figure 14-9: How MyWebControl looks at runtime in a browser

You might be wondering one thing: Where is the code that produced the HTML code for MyWebControl? It certainly isn't in MyWebControl.cs. To produce HTML output, a Web Control needs to have a Render() method. Since I didn't provide one, it follows that MyWebControl used the Render() method inherited from the base class LinkButton.

Custom rendering

Most custom Web Controls supply their own rendering code, so I'll tweak MyWebControl to generate the HTML code itself, rather that relying on its base class. All you need to do is override the Render() method. This method is invoked by the ASP.NET runtime while it composes the final marked up code to return for a Web Form. The Render() method has the following signature:

```
protected override void Render(HtmlTextWriter output) {...}
```

To send marked up code to the page being rendered by the ASP.NET engine, you must use the HTMLTextWriter object passed to the method. The object has a multitude of methods and properties that can be used. Listing 14-8 shows how to produce the markup text for the anchor tag.

Listing 14-8: **A Custom Rendering Method**

```
protected override void Render(HtmlTextWriter output)
{
  const string anchor = "a";
```

```
    output.WriteBeginTag(anchor);
    output.WriteAttribute("id", "WebControl1");
    output.WriteAttribute("title", ToolTip);
    output.WriteAttribute("name", "WebControl1");
    output.WriteAttribute("style", "color:Green;");
    output.Write(HtmlTextWriter.TagRightChar);
    output.Write(Text);
    output.WriteEndTag(anchor);
    output.WriteLine();
}
```

In Listing 14-8, I omitted rendering the JavaScript code to handle mouse clicks on the ⟨anchor⟩ element. Table 14-1 shows the HTML output produced by the various HtmlTextWriter methods used in the listing.

Table 14-1: The Markup Produced in Listing 14-8

Statement	*Output*
`output.WriteBeginTag(anchor);`	`<a`
`output.WriteAttribute("id", "WebControl1");`	`id="MyWebControl1"`
`output.WriteAttribute("title", ToolTip);`	`title="Now I'm Green!"`
`output.WriteAttribute("name", "WebControl1");`	`NAME="MyWebControl1"`
`output.WriteAttribute("style", "color:Green;");`	`style="color:Green;"`
`output.Write(HtmlTextWriter.TagRightChar);`	`>`
`output.Write(Text);`	`Click me`
`output.WriteEndTag(anchor);`	`</a>`

The complete markup code produced is shown in Listing 14-9.

Listing 14-9: **The Complete Marked-Up Code Produced by the Custom Render() Method**

```
<a id="MyWebControl1"
title="Now I'm Green!"
NAME="MyWebControl1"
href="javascript:__doPostBack('MyWebControl1','')"
style="color:Green;">
Click me
</a>
```

I split the code into multiple lines, for clarity. The actual markup code is all on one line.

Browser-dependent rendering

When you render markup code in a Web Control, you may need to know what type of browser the user has, before using advanced HTML features or XML. For example, if you're rendering a page for IE6 browsers, you might use features that depend on DHTML. The same page rendered for Netscape Navigator 4.x browsers would have to be different, possibly using layers to achieve the same result. To verify the browser version, check the `Context.Request.Browser` object. To check what specific types of advanced features are supported, use the `Context.Request.Browser` properties, as shown in Listing 14-10.

Listing 14-10: Rendering Output Based On the Capabilities of the User's Browser

```
protected override void Render(HtmlTextWriter output)
{
  if (Context.Request.Browser.Type == "IE6")
    output.WriteLine("OK to use DHTML");
  else if (Context.Request.Browser.Type == "NS4")
    output.WriteLine("Can use DHTML limited to <layers>");

  if (Context.Request.Browser.Tables)
    output.WriteLine("OK to use tables");
  else
    output.WriteLine("use layout without tables");

  if (Context.Request.Browser.VBScript)
    output.WriteLine("OK to use VBScript");

  if (Context.Request.Browser.JavaScript)
    output.WriteLine("OK to use ECMAScript");
}
```

Table 14-2 lists and describes the browser properties exposed by the `Context.Request.Browser` object.

Table 14-2: Browser Properties Exposed by the Context.Request.Browser Object

Attribute	Description
ActiveXControls	Indicates whether the browser can handle ActiveX controls.
AOL	True if the request came from an AOL (America Online) browser.
BackgroundSounds	Indicates whether the browser can handle sounds being played in the background while a page is being viewed.

Attribute	Description
Beta	Indicates whether the browser is a test (Beta) version.
Browser	Gets the string submitted by the last request in the User-Agent header.
CDF	Indicates whether the browser can handle Channel Definition Format (CDF). CDF is an XML-based format used in webcasting.
Cookies	Indicates whether the browser accepts cookies.
Crawler	Indicates whether the browser is a Web crawler. Crawlers are typically used by Web Search Engines.
Frames	Indicates whether the browser can handle HTML frames.
JavaApplets	Indicates whether the browser can handle Java Applets.
JavaScript	Indicates whether the browser can handle ECMAScript.
MajorVersion	The browser version number without the decimal part, such as 6 for IE 6.0b.
MinorVersion	The decimal part of the browser version number, such as .0 for IE 6.0b.
MSDomVersion	The version of the Microsoft XML DOM (if any) supported by the browser.
Platform	Operating System name, such as WinNT for Windows NT and 2000.
Tables	Indicates whether the browser can handle Tables.
Type	Type of browser. Includes the name and major version of the browser. The following list shows the value for some major browsers:
	Internet Explorer 6: IE6
	Internet Explorer 5: IE5
	Netscape Navigator 4.78: Netscape4
VBScript	Indicates whether the browser can handle VBScript.
Version	Complete browser version number, such as 6.0b or 4.78.
Win16	Indicates whether the browser is running under a 16-bit version of Windows (such as Win 3.1).
Win32	Indicates whether the browser is running under a 32-bit version of Windows (such as Win XP or 2000).

Browser attributes don't include all the possible properties that affect HTML code generation, because not all properties are sent with HTTP requests. Two essential properties that impact the type of HTML code a Web Control can generate are:

✦ The version of HTML the browser supports

✦ Whether the browser supports Cascading Style Sheets (CSS)

These properties can be inferred, based on the browser name and version. Table 14-3 lists the salient features of the most important browsers on the market.

Table 14-3: Features Supported by the Most Common Web Browsers

Browser	HTML	ActiveX	Frames	Java	Tables	CSS
IE 4	4	Yes	Yes	JDK 1.1	Yes	CSS1
IE 5	4	Yes	Yes	JDK 1.1	Yes	CSS2
IE 6	4	Yes	Yes	No*	Yes	CSS2
NN 4.7	4	No**	Yes	JDK 1.1	Yes	CSS1
NN 6	4	No**	Yes	JDK 1.3	Yes	CSS2
AOL 5***	4	Yes	Yes	JDK 1.1	Yes	CSS2

* JDK 1.1 support is installed just-in-time

** Requires a plug-in

*** Based on IE5

A constant source of headaches for ASP developers was differences in browser support for scripting languages. Each vendor and browser version is different. The closest thing to a universal standard appeared fairly recently, under the name ECMAScript. Table 14-4 shows the scripting features supported by the most popular browsers.

Table 14-4: Scripting Features Supported by Major Browsers

Browser	ECMAScript-262 compatibility	VBScript
IE 4	Partial compliance	Yes
IE 5	Full support	Yes
IE 6	Full support	Yes
NN 4.7	Partial compliance	No
NN 6	Full support	No
AOL 5*	Full support	Yes

* Based on IE5

In terms of Web page content supported, the ASP.NET Framework divides browsers into two categories:

✦ Those that support fairly recent HTML innovations, including

- HTML version 4
- ECMAScript (any version)
- Microsoft XML Document Object Model version 4

✦ Those that support only HTML 3.2

Browsers in the first category are called *uplevel* browsers, and include IE4, IE5, and IE6. Browsers in the second category are called *downlevel* browsers, and include IE3 (or earlier) and NN3 (or earlier).

Netscape Navigator versions 4 and 6 fall into a gray area, somewhere between *uplevel* and *downlevel,* because they support HTML 4 (to various extents) and ECMAScript, but don't support Microsoft XML DOM version 4.

To control the type of HTML code generated for a Web Form and its Web Controls, every Web Form has a property called *targetSchema*. The property has three possible values:

- ✦ Internet Explorer (IE) 3.02 or Netscape Navigator 3
- ✦ Netscape Navigator 4
- ✦ Internet Explorer (IE) 5

The default is IE 5. If you change the `targetSchema` to one of the other values, some of the properties of the HTML and Web Controls on that form may become grayed out or disappear, if they are not supported under the schema. For example, say you have a Web Form with an image tag `<IMG>`. HTML 4 supports absolute alignment of images, HTML 3.2 doesn't. If you set a Web Form's `targetSchema` to IE 5, the `Alignment` property for `<IMG>` elements will have a drop-down list with the following choices: left, right, top, texttop, middle, absmiddle, baseline, bottom, and absbottom.

If you set the targetSchema to IE 3.02, the following choices in the Alignment property for <IMG> elements become invalid: absmiddle, baseline, absbottom, and texttop.

Adding a custom event

Most nontrivial Web Controls fire events of some type. To show how to add customized events to a Web Control, I'll add a `TurnedGreen` event to `MyWebControl`. Any time the color of the control turns to green, the event will fire. Note that custom events are fired on the server side, and only during the processing of a postback.

The first step in adding support for events is to create a new event type. The base class `System.Web.UI.Control` has a built-in framework for handling standard and custom events. To use this framework, I declared a custom event type and added an `add/remove` method for it, as shown in Listing 14-11.

Listing 14-11: **Declaring a Custom Event in a Web Control**

```
// declare a single object to act as the key for event delegates stored
// in the Control.Events collection for TurnedGreen event handlers.

private static readonly object TurnedGreenEvent = new object();

// methods to add/remove event handlers
public event EventHandler TurnedGreen
{
   add    { Events.AddHandler(TurnedGreenEvent, value);    }
   remove { Events.RemoveHandler(TurnedGreenEvent, value); }
}
```

The static `TurnedGreenEvent` object is used as a key for the event handler delegate stored in the `Control.Events` collection. Having created a `TurnedGreen` event, the next step is to add an event-management method. This method checks to see if an event handler is available for `TurnedGreen` events, and if so, it calls the handler. Listing 14-12 shows the method.

Listing 14-12: An Event-Management Method Responsible for TurnedGreen Events

```
protected virtual void OnTurnedGreen(EventArgs e)
{
  EventHandler handler = (EventHandler) Events[TurnedGreenEvent];
  if (handler != null) handler(this, e);
}
```

The last step is to add an event-firing mechanism. My event is very simple, and is triggered by clicking the Web Control. Each time the control is clicked, it changes color. When the control turns green, MyWebControl calls `OnTurnedGreen()` in the `Click` event handler as shown with the boldface code in Listing 14-13.

Listing 14-13: Firing an Event When the Control's Color Turns Green

```
protected override void OnClick(EventArgs e)
{
  if (ForeColor == Color.Black)
    ForeColor = Color.Green;
  else
    ForeColor = Color.Black;

  ToolTip = String.Format("Now I'm {0}!", ForeColor.Name);

  if (ForeColor == Color.Green)
    OnTurnedGreen(EventArgs.Empty);
}
```

Having added the new `TurnedGreen` event to MyWebControl, you can use the Properties window in VS .NET to add an event handler to the parent Web Form. Select the control in the Forms Designer. In the Properties window, select the event and press the Enter key to create an event handler, as shown in Figure 14-10.

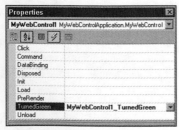

Figure 14-10: The new TurnedGreen event shown in the Properties window

I added a Label control named *Label1* to the Web Form. In the code-behind file for WebForm1.aspx, I added a line of code to handle the TurnedGreen event, as shown in Listing 14-14.

Listing 14-14: Handling the TurnedGreen Event in the Parent Web Form

```
private void MyWebControl1_TurnedGreen(object sender,
                                       System.EventArgs e)
{
  Label1.Text = "TurnedGreen event fired at " + DateTime.Now.Ticks;
}
```

And that's all there is to it. When you click MyWebControl and make it turn green, the event will fire. Custom events like TurnedGreen behave just like standard server side ones, such as Click or Init.

Adding a custom property

You can add any number of custom properties to a Web Control. The process is almost trivial. To show you how, I'll add a couple of properties to MyWebControl: an Integer property and a Boolean property. Adding properties with other types, such as Strings and Colors, uses the same process I describe here.

Basically, all you have to do is declare a public property, using standard C# notation, as shown in Listing 14-15.

Listing 14-15: Adding Two Properties to a Web Control

```
public class MyWebControl : System.Web.UI.WebControls.LinkButton
{
  // ...
  int numberOfColors;
  public int MyProperty_NumberOfColors
  {
    get { return numberOfColors; }
    set { numberOfColors = value; }
  }

  bool allowColorChanges;
  public bool MyProperty_AllowColorChanges
  {
    get { return allowColorChanges; }
    set { allowColorChanges = value; }
  }
}
```

Once you compile the code, you can use the VS .NET Properties window to see the new properties. Just add the custom Web Control to a Web Form and then select the control in the Forms Designer. The Properties window will display the custom properties along with all the other properties, as shown in Figure 14-11.

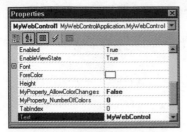

Figure 14-11: The Properties window, showing the newly added properties

There are absolutely no differences in the way you access custom versus built-in properties. In fact, there really is no such thing as a built-in property. All properties added to a .NET class use the same standard C# notation.

The complete code for MyWebControl

So far, I've only shown bits and pieces of MyWebControl. Before moving on to the topic of packaging Web Controls in DLLs, I'll show the whole picture by providing the complete code in Listing 14-16.

Listing 14-16: The Complete Code for MyWebControl

```
using System;
using System.Drawing;
using System.Web.UI;
using System.Web.UI.WebControls;
using System.ComponentModel;

namespace MyWebControlApplication
{
  public class MyWebControl : System.Web.UI.WebControls.LinkButton
  {
    protected override void OnClick(EventArgs e)
    {
      if (ForeColor == Color.Black)
        ForeColor = Color.Green;
      else
        ForeColor = Color.Black;

      ToolTip = String.Format("Now I'm {0}!", ForeColor.Name);
```

```
      if (ForeColor == Color.Green)
        OnTurnedGreen(EventArgs.Empty);
    }

    protected virtual void OnTurnedGreen(EventArgs e)
    {
      EventHandler handler =
        (EventHandler) Events[TurnedGreenEvent];
      if (handler != null) handler(this, e);
    }

    protected override void Render(HtmlTextWriter output)
    {
      base.Render(output);
    }

    private static readonly object TurnedGreenEvent = new object();
    public event EventHandler TurnedGreen
    {
      add    { Events.AddHandler(TurnedGreenEvent, value);    }
      remove { Events.RemoveHandler(TurnedGreenEvent, value); }
    }

    int numberOfColors;
    public int MyProperty_NumberOfColors
    {
      get { return numberOfColors; }
      set { numberOfColors = value; }
    }

    bool allowColorChanges;
    public bool MyProperty_AllowColorChanges
    {
      get { return allowColorChanges; }
      set { allowColorChanges = value; }
    }
  }
}
```

Porting the control to a DLL

In the first part of this chapter, I showed you how to create a Web Control in the context of a Web application. Keeping the control in an application makes it easy to test the Web Control code, because you only have to rebuild one piece of code (the Web application). You can then place breakpoints in the Web Control code and debug it as part of the application. Once you're done testing the control, you may want to repackage it, especially if you plan to use the control on other projects or make it available to other people.

The normal way to distribute Web Controls is as special DLLs known as *Web Control DLLs*. There really isn't anything special about these DLLs, except for the fact that the VS .NET New Project Wizard has a special template to create them. To create a Web Control DLL using the VS .NET New Project Wizard, select Web Control Library as the template type, as shown in Figure 14-12.

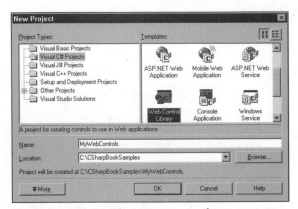

Figure 14-12: Creating a DLL to package custom Web Controls

Once the project has been created, follow these steps:

1. Copy MyWebControl.cs to the project folder.

2. Add the file to the project.

3. In MyWebControl.cs, change the namespace to **MyWebControls.**

4. Remove the superfluous file WebCustomControl1.cs from the project.

5. Build the new Web Control Library.

Testing the DLL

Before creating a test fixture for the Web Controls, you'll want to add `MyWebControl` on the VS .NET Toolbox, to make the control easier to use on Web Forms. To add the control, select the Web Forms page of the Toolbox, right-click on the Toolbox, and then select the command Customize Toolbox from the pop-up menu. In the Customize Toolbox dialog box, select the .NET Framework Components tab and then click the Browse button. Locate the file *MyWebControls.dll* and click the Open button. The component `MyWebControl` will appear in the list of .NET Framework Components. Click the selection box to select `MyWebControl`, as shown in Figure 14-13.

Click the OK button, and `MyWebControl` will appear on the Toolbox, at the bottom of the Web Forms page, as shown in Figure 14-14.

You can also add your custom controls to a different page of the Toolbox, or even to a brand new page. To create a new Toolbox page, right-click on the Toolbox and select Add Tab from the pop-up menu. You can select any name you want for the new tab.

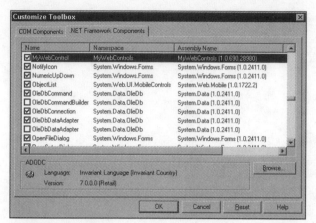

Figure 14-13: Adding MyWebControl to the VS .NET Toolbox

Figure 14-14: The VS .NET Toolbox after adding MyWebControl

Customizing the icon shown in the Toolbox

You'll notice that the icon shown for MyWebControl on the Toolbox is a standard one, used with all components that don't specify a custom icon. To make your own icon appear on the Toolbox, the procedure is quite simple. If you read Chapter 9, titled "Custom Controls," you already know it. For those who skipped that chapter, I'll recap the procedure briefly, adding a couple of extra details.

To use an existing icon, just add the file to the project. The file must contain a 16 x 16 pixel bitmap and have the suffix *.bmp* (not *.ico*).

To create the bitmap in VS .NET, right-click on the MyWebControls project, and then select Add ➪ Add New Item from the pop-up menu. In the Add New Item Wizard, select the Bitmap template, as shown in Figure 14-15.

Make sure the name of the .bmp file is the same as the Web Control. A single Web Controls Library can hold any number of controls, so VS .NET uses a simple naming pattern to locate bitmaps for each control. Using the Properties window, set the Width and Height of the bitmap to 16. To draw the bitmap, use the drawing tools on the VS .NET main toolbar. Figure 14-16 shows what the drawing toolbar looks like after undocking it from the top toolbar.

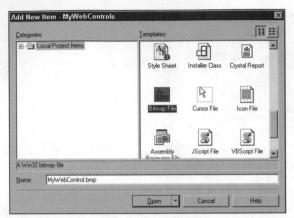

Figure 14-15: Using the Bitmap template to create a bitmap file

Figure 14-16: The drawing tools shown on the Image Editor toolbar in VS .NET

If the color palette doesn't appear automatically with the Bitmap Designer, right-click on the Bitmap Designer and select Show Colors Window from the pop-up menu. I created a simple bitmap in the Bitmap Designer, as shown in Figure 14-17. I'll use this bitmap as the Toolbox icon for `MyWebControl`.

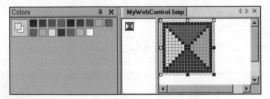

Figure 14-17: The Bitmap Designer in VS .NET

Once the bitmap is complete, save it. Then select the .bmp file in the Solution Explorer and set its Build Action to Embedded Resource, as shown in Figure 14-18.

To make the new bitmap show up on the Toolbox, you need to remove the old version of MyWebControl from the Toolbox and add the new one. After doing so, the Toolbox will show the newly added bitmap, as shown in Figure 14-19.

Although Figure 14-19 is not printed in color, you may have noticed that part of the icon is missing. I colored the right quadrant in bright green. The exact RGB color was (0, 255, 0). The Toolbox uses this color to denote transparent regions, so any areas of icons appearing with this color will assume the color of the Toolbox background, which is usually gray.

Figure 14-18: Setting the bitmap's Build Action

Figure 14-19: The Toolbox, showing the new customized icon

Creating a test fixture

Now I need a test fixture to act as a container and test bed for MyWebControl. I created a new Web application to act as the test fixture. I called the project *TestFixture* and put it in the TestFixture folder under MyWebControls folder, as shown in Figure 14-20.

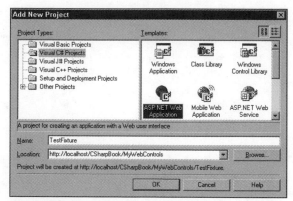

Figure 14-20: Using the Add New Project Wizard to create a test fixture for Web Controls

Figure 14-21 shows the Solution Explorer after the test fixture project is added.

Figure 14-21: The Solution Explorer, showing the Web Controls project and the test fixture

The next step is to add an instance of `MyCustomControl` to the Web Form in the test fixture. From the Toolbox, drag and drop a `MyWebControl` component onto WebForm1.aspx of the test fixture. The Forms Designer will show the component, as you can see in Figure 14-22.

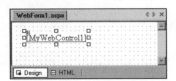

Figure 14-22: How MyWebControl looks in the Forms Designer

If you test the Web Form now, the Web Control won't show up. The problem is that the `Text` property is initially blank. I selected `MyWebControl1` and set the Text property to

```
This is my new web control.
```

If you switch to the HTML pane, you'll see that VS .NET automatically added the `<%@Register%>` tag at the top of the XML document, and also added `MyWebControl` to the `<form>` element, as shown in Figure 14-23.

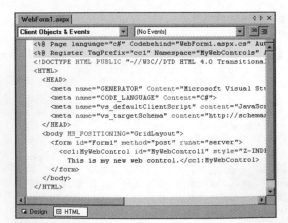

Figure 14-23: The Code window, showing the XML code generated for the test fixture Web Form

To set the test fixture as the Startup project, I right-clicked on the test fixture project in the Solution Explorer and choose Set As Startup Project from the pop-up menu. Then I built and ran the test fixture to see MyWebForm1.aspx, as shown in Figure 14-24.

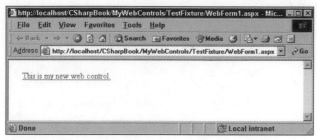

Figure 14-24: How MyWebControl appears in the Web Form of the test fixture, when viewed with a browser

Clicking on the Web Control made it change colors, as expected. Even though `MyWebControl` is in a DLL, it is still easy to debug. You can set breakpoints in the DLL code and single-step through it. All the normal debugging windows are available to you, such as the Watch window, the Call Stack window, and others.

Validating User Input

And now for something (almost) entirely different. Getting input from the user is one of the basic requirements for Web applications, and a function many Web Controls are devoted to. With ASP, a significant amount of code was required to make sure that data entered was valid, according to some business criteria. With ASP.NET, validation was moved up in status from a task to be rediscovered by each developer to a function handled by built-in classes. The built-in components provided by the ASP.NET Framework do most of the validation work for you behind the scenes.

The ASP.NET validation scheme requires special validation controls to be placed on the Web Form. These controls are normally hidden, and become visible at some point in time if invalid data is entered. There are three basic types of validation components:

✦ In-place validation components

✦ Summary validation components

✦ Custom validation components

In-place components validate the data of a single data-entry component, and display an error if the data doesn't satisfy a certain criterion. *Summary components* look at the data entered by the user, and display a summary of all the errors found. *Custom components* can do anything you want them to do.

The validation components work solely in conjunction with Web Controls. If you have HTML controls on a Web Form, those controls will need to be validated separately with your own code. Also keep in mind that some validation controls are client-side, some are server-side, and some are both. Client-side validation is supported automatically only for uplevel browsers, such as IE 4.x and later or Navigator 6.x and later. Client-side validation is performed using a combination of ECMAScript and DHTML, and you have the option of customizing the client-side validation code.

There are six built-in validation controls that you can put on a Web Form, as listed and described in Table 14-5.

Table 14-5: ASP.NET Classes Used for Data Validation

Name	Type of Validation	Description
RequiredFieldValidator	In-Place	Used to indicate which fields on a Web Form are required to be filled in.
CompareValidator	In-Place	Used to compare the contents of a field with a value or another field on the Web Form.
RangeValidator	In-Place	Used to ensure that a numeric value entered in a field is within a given range.
RegularExpressionValidator	In-Place	Used to verify that the text entered in a field matches a pattern defined with a regular expression.
CustomValidator	Custom	Used to add your own custom validation code to any field on a Web Form.
ValidationSummary	Summary	Displays a list of the ErrorMessages of the in-place validators in a single place.

All of the validator components except ValidationSummary have three essential properties:

✦ ControlToValidate, which binds a validator to a specific component

✦ ErrorMessage, which is the text to display in a summary validation message

✦ Text, which is the text to display in-place when a validation error is found

The class diagram in Figure 14-25 shows the hierarchy of built-in validators, and their relationship to Web Controls.

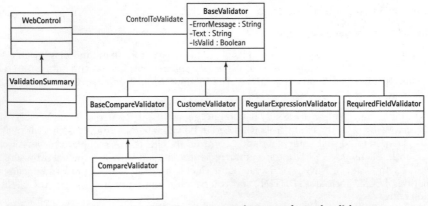

Figure 14-25: The relationship between Web Controls and validators

You can't bind a validator to more than one control in order to share validation logic. Besides ControlToValidate, ErrorMessage, Text, and IsValid, each validator class has its own set of properties and/or events that you may need to set.

When processing a page on the server side, you can find out if a Web Control attached to a validator has valid data. Just access the validator's IsValid property as shown in Listing 14-17.

Listing 14-17: **Checking the Validation State of a Single Validator**

```
private void Button1_Click(object sender, System.EventArgs e)
{
  if (RangeValidator1.IsValid)
  {
    // the data checked by RangeValidator1 is not out of range
  }
}
```

To see if all of the controls on the page contain valid data, use IsValid at the page level, as shown in Listing 14-18.

Listing 14-18: **Checking the Validation State of an Entire Page**

```
private void Button1_Click(object sender, System.EventArgs e)
{
  if (IsValid)
  {
    // all the data validated on the page is OK
  }
}
```

Determining where error messages are displayed

There are three ways to set up in-place validators, in terms of display error messages, using the Display property. The possible values are

✦ None

✦ Static

✦ Dynamic

The value *None* means that the validator will not display an error message. Why would you want to do this? When using a ValidationSummary component. When a ValidationSummary component is added to a Web Form, it collects all the ErrorMessages from the various in-place validators and shows all the messages in a single list.

The value *Static* forces a validator to show its ErrorMessage (if a validation error occurs), even if a ValidationSummary component is available. The default value for Display is Static, meaning error messages will appear twice if the form has a ValidationSummary component.

The value *Dynamic* is used when you attach more than one in-place validator to the same control. Say you want to attach a RequiredFieldValidator and a RangeValidator to a control. You'll want both validators to be next to the same input control, so both of their validation error messages appear next to the control. Both validator components will need to be at the same place on the Web Form, one on top of the other. Using the Dynamic setting makes only one of the validation `ErrorMessages` show up in a given place, so the end user will never see two messages on top of each other.

Text versus ErrorMessage

If you peruse the properties of the in-place validation components, you'll notice they have two properties that would appear to do the same thing: `Text` and `ErrorMessage`. Not to worry: There is no mistake. The `Text` property determines what string is displayed in-place when an error is detected. The `ErrorMessage` is the text shown in a `ValidationSummary` component (if available on the page). If `Text` is blank, by default it will show the text assigned to `ErrorMessage`. Why would you ever want the two strings to be different? When using `ValidationSummary` components to summarize all the errors found on a page, it is common to display a mark next to each offending control. Exclamation marks, asterisks, or small glyphs are common choices. To display an asterisk, just set the `Text` property to `*`. Just remember that you'll want to use a `ValidationSummary` component somewhere on the page; otherwise, the only indication the user will get about an error will be an asterisk next to a field.

Each type of validator has its own properties and characteristics. Since user input validation is very important to most Web developers, I'll describe each validation component in detail in the following sections.

RequiredFieldValidator

This validator is essentially trivial. All it does is verify that its associated control is not blank. Even so, it is used a lot because the other validators allow blank fields as valid data.

CompareValidator

This validator lets you compare the value of one control with another value. This other value may either be another control or a fixed value. Table 14-6 lists and describes the salient properties.

Table 14-6: Key Properties for CompareValidator Components

Key Properties	Property Description
ControlToCompare	If this property is used, the value of the `ControlToValidate` will be compared with the value of `ControlToCompare`.
Operator	The operator to use in the comparison. Allowable operators are: Equal NotEqual GreaterThan GreaterThanEqual LessThan LessThanEqual DataTypeCheck The last operator is used to see if the value entered into `ControlToValidate` has the type entered in the Type property.

Key Properties	Property Description
`Type`	How to interpret the data entered into `ControlToValidate`. Allowable values are String Integer Double Date Currency
`ValueToCompare`	A fixed value to compare against.

All but the last type of Operator are *collating* operators, because they allow you to determine the sort (collation) order of two items. But the sort order also depends on the type of data being compared. For example, if `Type` is set to `String`, the following statement is true:

```
"6" > "5999"
```

What makes this statement true is the fact that the string `"6"` comes after the string `"5999"` in string collating order. Note that string comparisons return the expected result for all Unicode characters, so locale-specific characters will be treated correctly.

If `Type` is set to `Integer` or `Currency` or `Double`, numeric comparisons are used, with obvious results.

If `Type` is set to `Date`, you have to be a little careful, because date formats are locale-specific. Does the date 8/3/01 refer to August 3rd or March 8th? You can't really tell. Hey, the date might even refer to March 1st 2008. And don't laugh — YYYY-MM-DD is actually the world standard for date formatting (ISO 8601), and the official format adopted by the U.S. Department of Defense, among other government agencies. The moral of the story is this: If you're comparing dates, you might want the Web Form to display the date format you expect, as shown in Figure 14-26.

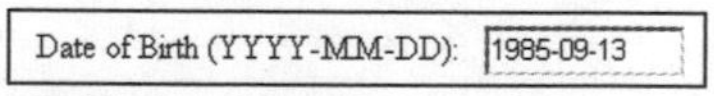

> Date of Birth (YYYY-MM-DD): 1985-09-13

Figure 14-26: Showing the expected date format with Date controls

A better alternative in some cases is to use a drop-down calendar, like the one shown in Figure 14-27.

Figure 14-27: Using a drop-down calendar to facilitate entering dates on a Web Form

The drop-down calendar in the figure can be implemented in various ways, including DTHML with ECMAScript or with a Web Control. Many implementations of drop-down calendars can be found both on the Web and from third-party component vendors.

If you're only interested in checking the type (and not the value) of data entered, choose the value `DataTypeCheck` for `Operator`, and indicate the data type in the `Type` property. Make sure the `ValueToCompare` and `ControlToCompare` properties are left blank. With type-checking, the validator does limited checking with dates. Since the validator doesn't know what date format to use, it just checks to make sure there are three fields separated by a / or other separator. For example, the validator accepts the following date formats:

✦ 01-12-20

✦ 02.11.01

✦ 2001-10-3

✦ 2/29/2000

The validator tries to infer the date format from the data itself, and usually does a pretty good job guessing the correct format. Still, with a date like 02.11.01, you can't be sure what date was intended.

RangeValidator

This validator performs client-side validation, so it can save unnecessary roundtrips to the server. The validator is activated when `ControlToValidate` loses focus. The validator can be used not just with numeric values, but also with String and Date values. Just set the Type property to indicate the kind of collation result you want. When comparing strings, the same things I said for `CompareValidator` apply here to, in terms of collating order. When comparing dates, the validator assumes that the date format of the value in `ControlToValidate` is the same as the format used in `MaximumValue` and `MinimumValue`.

A common error made by programmers using `RangeValidator` with numeric values is to forget to set the `Type` property to `Integer`, `Double`, or `Currency`. The default value is `String`. When comparing values as `Strings`, you won't get results you might expect. For example the string `"2"` is greater than the string `"1999"`.

CustomValidator

This component lets you use your own code to perform validation. The code may validate the value of one control, a group of controls, or all the controls on the page. The code may run on the client side or the server side. I'll discuss each case separately.

Client-side validation

To create a client-side validator, set the property `ClientValidationFunction` to the name of the VBScript or ECMAScript function to call on the client side. Obviously, the page you return to the end user will have to contain this function. The function must have the following ECMAScript signature (or equivalent VBScript signature):

```
function MyClientSideValidator(source, arguments) {}
```

The first parameter is the `CustomValidator` that triggered the validation. The second argument is the value of the control to validate.

As an example of a client-side validation function, consider the simple Web Form at design-time shown in Figure 14-28.

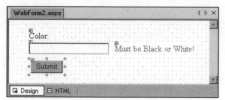

Figure 14-28: A simple Web Form using a custom client-side validation function

I'll add a client-side validation function called `ValidateColor()` to the page, as shown by the boldface code in Listing 14-19.

Listing 14-19: Highlights of the XML for the Form Containing a Client-Side Validator. As Shown on the HTML Tab of the Forms Designer

```
<%@ Page language="c#" Codebehind="WebForm2.aspx.cs"
         AutoEventWireup="false"
         Inherits="UsingValidationWebControls.WebForm2" %>

<HTML>
  <HEAD> ... </HEAD>
<body>
  <form id="WebForm2" method="post" runat="server">
  ...
  </form>

  <script>

  function ValidateColor(source, arguments)
  {
    if (arguments.Value == 'White') return true;
    if (arguments.Value == 'Black') return true;
    return false;
  }

  </script>

</body>
</HTML>
```

The method must return `true` only if the arguments are valid. To use this function, you need to set the property `CustomValidator.ClientValidatorFunction` to the string `ValidateColor`, with no arguments, as shown in Figure 14-29.

Setting the `ClientValidationFunction` property makes the ASP.NET runtime automatically generate client-side code that calls the validator when the associated control loses focus.

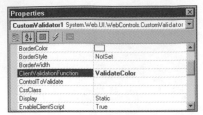

Figure 14-29: Setting the client-side validator with the Properties window

If the client-side validator function returns `false`, indicating an incorrect value, no postback will occur, so the server-side will never know about the error. If you have server-side validators, they will not be triggered. In order for a postback to be allowed, the client-side validator must return `true`. With judicious use of client-side validation, you can significantly reduce the number of roundtrips to the server, thus boosting server performance.

Server-side validation

Adding validation code on the server side is easy. Just select the `CustomValidator` in the Forms Designer, go to the Properties window, and select the Events page. Select the `ServerValidate` event and press the Enter key. A new event handler will automatically be created and appear in the Properties window, as shown in Figure 14-30.

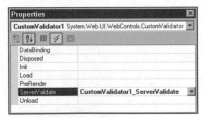

Figure 14-30: Adding a server-side custom validator

VS .NET switches to the Code window and positions the cursor on the newly added event handler. The initial handler looks something like Listing 14-20.

Listing 14-20: The Default Handler for ServerValidate Events

```
private void CustomValidator1_ServerValidate(object source,
        System.Web.UI.WebControls.ServerValidateEventArgs args)
{
}
```

The method's signature is a bit different from that of client-side validators. The first argument is a reference to the `CustomValidator` that fired the event. The second argument is an object that holds the value to validate. If the value is found to be valid according to your validation rules, you must set `args.IsValid` to `true`, as shown in Listing 14-21.

> Listing 14-21: **Setting the Validation Result in a Server-Side Validation Handler**

```
private void CustomValidator1_ServerValidate(object source,
        System.Web.UI.WebControls.ServerValidateEventArgs args)
{

  if (TextBox1.Text == "White") args.IsValid = true;
  else if (TextBox1.Text == "Black") args.IsValid = true;
  else
    args.IsValid = false;
}
```

ValidationSummary

If a Web Form contains only one or two errors, it might make sense to flag them with in-place validators like `RangeValidator` or `RequiredFieldValidator`. If many errors are detected, you might want to group all the error messages together, so the end user doesn't have to scroll up and down the page to see them all. With a `ValidationSummary` component, you can validate all the controls on a page at once and list all the errors found in a list. The error message can appear either on the Web Form or in a separate MessageBox. This last option is only available on uplevel browsers, supporting DHTML and ECMAScript 1.2, such as IE version 4 or later.

To use a `ValidationSummary` component on a page, you need to use in-place validation components to validate the individual fields. The `ErrorMessages` generated by the in-place validators will be used by the `ValidationSummary` component. To avoid having error messages appear twice, set all the `Display` properties of the in-place validators to `None`. This way, they will not show the string saved in their `Text` property, relying instead on the `ValidationSummary` component to render errors.

An example will help. I'll start with a Web Form with two controls on it, as shown in Figure 14-31.

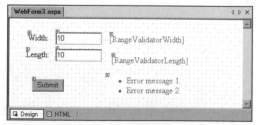

Figure 14-31: A Web Form with two in-place validators and a ValidationSummary component

I want to constrain the values entered for Width and Height to the range (1..99). The values for Width and Height can easily be validated using two RangeValidators, as shown. Both validators are set up with the following properties:

```
MinimumValue = 1
MaximumValue = 99
```

To display a summary error message, I added a ValidationSummary component to the page. I changed the Display property of the two RangeValidators to None. Figure 14-32 shows how the page looks in a browser when incorrect information is entered.

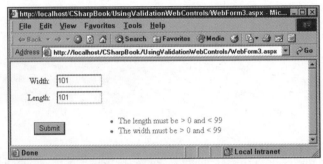

Figure 14-32: Showing ValidationSummary errors in BulletList mode

As you can see, both range validation error messages are shown in the ValidationSummary control. By default, the messages are shown as a bulleted list. Using the property ValidationSummary.DisplayMode, you can set the following options:

✦ BulletList

✦ List

✦ SingleParagraph

Figure 14-33 shows the List mode, and Figure 14-34 shows the SingleParagraph mode.

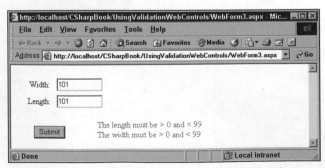

Figure 14-33: Showing ValidationSummary errors in List Mode

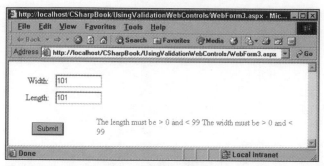

Figure 14-34: Showing ValidationSummary errors in SingleParagraph Mode

Can you customize the error message, rather than just showing a list of the ErrorMessages of each in-place validator? Absolutely. Let's say you want the Width × Length product to be no greater than 50. I'll add a CustomValidator to the form, set its Display property to None, and set up a server-side validator event as shown in Listing 14-22.

Listing 14-22: A Server-Side Custom Validator

```
private void CustomValidator1_ServerValidate(object source,
        System.Web.UI.WebControls.ServerValidateEventArgs args)
{
  int width = Int32.Parse(TextBoxWidth.Text);
  int length = Int32.Parse(TextBoxLength.Text);
  int area = width * length;

  args.IsValid = (area > 50) ? false : true;

  if (area > 50)
    // create a custom message
    CustomValidator1.ErrorMessage =
      String.Format("The total area is {0}. " +
                    "It must be less than 50", area);
}
```

The ValidationSummary component will use whatever string is assigned to ErrorMessage, so the code programmatically sets ErrorMessage to the appropriate text. The event handler checks the product of Width × Length and sets IsValid to false if the area exceeds 50. The handler then changes the ErrorMessage. Figure 14-35 shows what the Web Form looks like when viewed with a browser after values that trigger a validation error have been entered.

Notice the nicely formatted error message, showing the total area problem. But where did that string "The following errors occurred:" come from? ValidationSummary components have a property called HeaderText that shows up as the first line of the ErrorMessage. By default, HeaderText is blank.

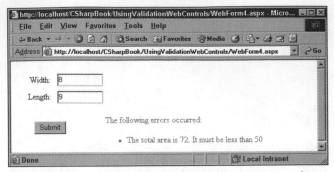

Figure 14-35: A programmatically changed message shown in a ValidationSummary component

Displaying error messages in a MessageBox

Another way to show error messages with `ValidationSummary` components is with a MessageBox. This option is available only if the client browser supports DHTML and ECMAScript 1.2 or better. IE4 and later browsers qualify. Only client-side validation errors can be shown in MessageBoxes, such as `RangeValidator` messages.

To show `SummaryValidation` errors in a MessageBox, set the component's `ShowMessageBox` to `true`. If you leave the `ShowSummary` property set to `true`, the validation errors will be displayed both with a MessageBox and on the Web Form.

When viewing the Web Form shown in the previous figure, entering an incorrect value causes the MessageBox in Figure 14-36 to appear in the client browser:

Figure 14-36: A ValidationSummary message displayed in a MessageBox

Tagging fields containing errors

When you use `ValidationSummary` components to display all the error messages in one place, it can be hard for end users to locate the fields that need to be corrected. A common technique is to put an exclamation mark, an asterisk, or a small image next to offending fields. All you need to do is change the `Text` property of the appropriate in-place validator to the text you want. Remember to set the `Display` property of the validator to a value other than `None`.

If you display characters, like exclamation marks or asterisks, you can easily format the text using the `Font` and `ForeColor` properties of the in-place validator. To display an image, use an `<IMG>` tag in the `Text` property. For example, if you have a file called *redcircle.gif* with the image of a small red circle, you could display the image in a `RangeValidator` component by adding the text shown in Listing 14-23 to the `Text` property.

Listing 14-23: Using an Image for the Text of an In-Place Validator

```
<IMG
src="http://localhost/CSharpBook/UsingValidationWebControls/redcircle10
.gif">
```

You can set the Text property using the Properties window, as shown in Figure 14-37.

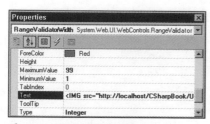

Figure 14-37: Setting the Text property with an image, using the Properties window

Figure 14-38 shows how the Web Form looks in a browser, after a validation error occurs.

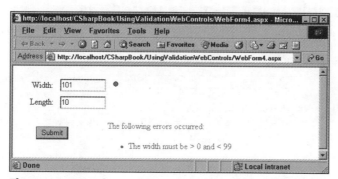

Figure 14-38: Using an image to tag controls with invalid data

You can reference any image you want in the Text property of in-place validators. Just keep in mind that images that are too big may disrupt the layout of your Web Form. You can also use any other valid HTML code in the Text property. For example, to display a large blue asterisk, you could set the Text property with the HTML code shown in Listing 14-24.

Listing 14-24: The HTML Code Required to Display a Large Blue Asterisk as an In-Place Validation Error Message

```
<span style="color:Blue;font-size:Large">*</span>
```

RegularExpressionValidator

Many types of information have an inherent layout. For example, U.S. telephone numbers have the pattern ###-####, where the character # represents a digit. One way to validate data that has a given pattern is with a CustomValidator. An even better way is to use a RegularExpressionValidator. This component has a property named ValidationExpression where you can set the regular expression to validate ControlToValidate against. You can enter the regular expression by hand, or click the ellipsis button and select a prebuilt expression for common data formats, as shown in Figure 14-39.

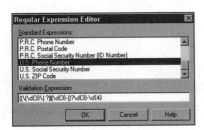

Figure 14-39: Using the built-in regular expressions with RegularExpressionValidator

Having described many of the details regarding validation components, I'll show a complete example to give you a feel for how all the pieces fit together. Both examples are part of a Web application called *UsingValidationWebControls,* described in the following two sections.

A complete example using in-place validators

I designed a Web Form called *WebForm1.aspx* that uses all the various types of in-place validators. Figure 14-40 shows the form in the VS .NET Forms Designer.

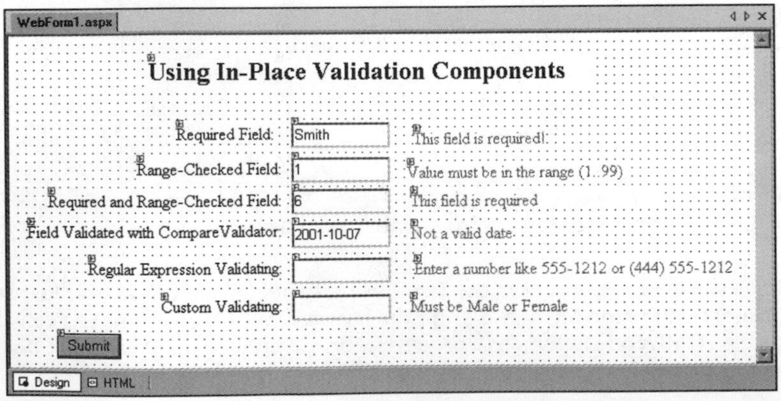

Figure 14-40: The appearance of a Web Form, demonstrating the use of in-place validators

The third field from the top, labeled Required and Range-Checked Field, is associated with two validators: RequiredFieldValidator and RangeValidator. Both validators occupy the same screen location. Their Display properties are set to Dynamic, to make their error messages appear correctly.

The fourth field, which uses a `CompareValidator`, verifies that the entered data is a date. The validator has the following properties set:

✦ **Operator:** DataTypeCheck

✦ **Type:** Date

The next field uses a `RegularExpressionValidator`, whose `ValidationExpression` property is set to the string:

```
((\(\d{3}\) ?)|(\d{3}-))?\d{3}-\d{4}
```

The string was entered automatically by choosing the U.S. Phone Number option from the dialog box shown previously in Figure 14-39.

The last field uses a `CustomValidator` with a server-side `ServerValidate` event handler that checks the entered string for the values "`Male`" or "`Female`".

Listing 14-25 shows the complete code for the Web Form.

Listing 14-25: The Complete Code for the Web Form Shown in Figure 14-40

```
using System;
using System.Collections;
using System.ComponentModel;
using System.Data;
using System.Drawing;
using System.Web;
using System.Web.SessionState;
using System.Web.UI;
using System.Web.UI.WebControls;
using System.Web.UI.HtmlControls;

namespace UsingValidationWebControls
{
  public class WebForm1 : System.Web.UI.Page
  {
    protected System.Web.UI.WebControls.Label Label1;
    protected System.Web.UI.WebControls.Label Label2;
    protected System.Web.UI.WebControls.Label Label3;
    protected System.Web.UI.WebControls.Label Label4;
    protected System.Web.UI.WebControls.RequiredFieldValidator
                                        RequiredFieldValidator1;
    protected System.Web.UI.WebControls.RangeValidator
                                        RangeValidator1;
    protected System.Web.UI.WebControls.RangeValidator
                                        RangeValidator2;
    protected System.Web.UI.WebControls.TextBox
                                        TextBoxRequiredField;
    protected System.Web.UI.WebControls.TextBox
                                        TextBoxRangeCheckedField;
    protected System.Web.UI.WebControls.TextBox
            TextBoxRequiredAndRangeCheckedField;
```

Continued

Listing 14-25 *(continued)*

```csharp
protected System.Web.UI.WebControls.TextBox
         TextBoxWithCompareValidator;
protected System.Web.UI.WebControls.CompareValidator
                                   CompareValidator1;
protected System.Web.UI.WebControls.RequiredFieldValidator
                                   RequiredFieldValidator2;
protected System.Web.UI.WebControls.Button Button1;
protected System.Web.UI.WebControls.Label Label6;
protected System.Web.UI.WebControls.Label Label7;
protected System.Web.UI.WebControls.TextBox
                                   TextBoxRegularExpression;
protected System.Web.UI.WebControls.RegularExpressionValidator
                                   RegularExpressionValidator1;
protected System.Web.UI.WebControls.CustomValidator
                                   CustomValidator1;
protected System.Web.UI.WebControls.TextBox
                                   TextBoxCustomValidating;
protected System.Web.UI.WebControls.Label Label8;

public WebForm1()
{
  Page.Init += new System.EventHandler(Page_Init);
}

private void Page_Load(object sender, System.EventArgs e)
{
  // Put user code to initialize the page here
}

private void Page_Init(object sender, EventArgs e)
{
  InitializeComponent();
}

private void InitializeComponent()
{
  this.CustomValidator1.ServerValidate +=
    new System.Web.UI.WebControls.ServerValidateEventHandler(
        this.CustomValidator1_ServerValidate);
  this.Load += new System.EventHandler(this.Page_Load);
}

private void CustomValidator1_ServerValidate(object source,
      System.Web.UI.WebControls.ServerValidateEventArgs args)
{
  if (args.Value == "Male") args.IsValid = true;
  if (args.Value == "Female") args.IsValid = true;
  args.IsValid = false;
}
  }
}
```

Since the properties of the validation controls don't appear in the code, Figures 14-41 through 14-43 show you how the properties for each control appear in the Properties window.

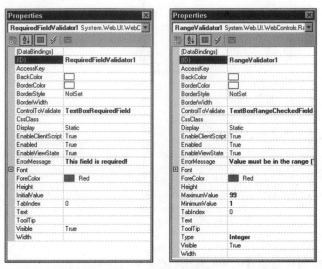

Figure 14-41: The properties for the first two validators in WebForm1.aspx

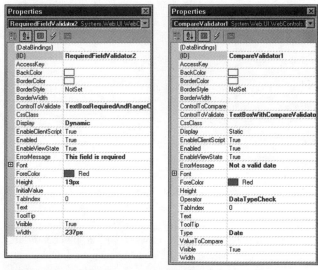

Figure 14-42: The properties for the third and fourth validators in WebForm1.aspx

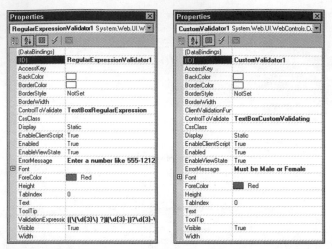

Figure 14-43: The properties for the fifth and sixth validators in WebForm1.aspx.

A complete example using ValidationSummary

The next example uses a Web Form, called *WebForm2.aspx,* to demonstrate the combined use of in-place and summary validators. Figure 14-44 shows the form in the Forms Designer.

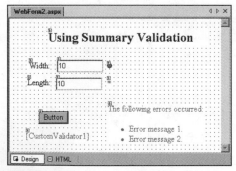

Figure 14-44: The second Web Form example in the Forms Designer

The Width and Length fields use RangeValidators to make sure the values entered are between 0 and 99. Figure 14-45 shows the Web Form in a browser, with in-place validator messages.

In addition to in-place validators, the Web Form also uses a CustomValidator to see if the Width × Length product is less than 50. The validator has a server-side validation handler that generates a message to display in the SummaryValidation component. Figure 14-46 shows the Web Form when the area exceeds 50.

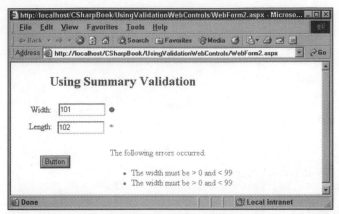

Figure 14-45: Using in-place and summary validation messages on a Web Form

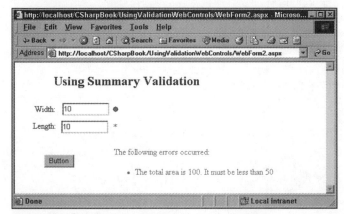

Figure 14-46: The error message produced by a CustomValidator component

Listing 14-26 shows the complete code for the Web Form.

Listing 14-26: **The Complete Code for the Web Form Shown in Figure 14-46**

```
using System;
using System.Collections;
using System.ComponentModel;
using System.Data;
using System.Drawing;
using System.Web;
```

Continued

Listing 14-26 *(continued)*

```csharp
using System.Web.SessionState;
using System.Web.UI;
using System.Web.UI.WebControls;
using System.Web.UI.HtmlControls;

namespace UsingValidationWebControls
{
  public class WebForm2 : System.Web.UI.Page
  {
    protected System.Web.UI.WebControls.Label Label1;
    protected System.Web.UI.WebControls.Label Label2;
    protected System.Web.UI.WebControls.TextBox TextBoxWidth;
    protected System.Web.UI.WebControls.ValidationSummary
                         ValidationSummary1;
    protected System.Web.UI.WebControls.RangeValidator
                         RangeValidatorLength;
    protected System.Web.UI.WebControls.RangeValidator
                         RangeValidatorWidth;
    protected System.Web.UI.WebControls.TextBox TextBoxLength;
    protected System.Web.UI.WebControls.CustomValidator
                         CustomValidator1;
    protected System.Web.UI.WebControls.Label Label6;
    protected System.Web.UI.WebControls.Button Button1;

    public WebForm2()
    {
      Page.Init += new System.EventHandler(Page_Init);
    }

    private void Page_Load(object sender, System.EventArgs e)
    {
      // Put user code to initialize the page here
    }

    private void Page_Init(object sender, EventArgs e)
    {
      InitializeComponent();
    }

    private void InitializeComponent()
    {
      this.CustomValidator1.ServerValidate +=
        new System.Web.UI.WebControls.ServerValidateEventHandler(
            this.CustomValidator1_ServerValidate);
      this.Load += new System.EventHandler(this.Page_Load);
    }

    private void CustomValidator1_ServerValidate(object source,
            System.Web.UI.WebControls.ServerValidateEventArgs args)
    {
      int width = Int32.Parse(TextBoxWidth.Text);
```

```
int length = Int32.Parse(TextBoxLength.Text);
int area = width * length;

args.IsValid = (area > 50) ? false : true;

if (area <= 50) return;

// to make the Text string appear
RangeValidatorWidth.IsValid = false;

// so no message appears in the SummaryValidation
RangeValidatorWidth.ErrorMessage = "";

// to make the Text string appear
RangeValidatorLength.IsValid = false;

// so no message appears in the SummaryValidation
RangeValidatorLength.ErrorMessage = "";

// create a custom message
CustomValidator1.ErrorMessage =
    String.Format("The total area is {0}. " +
                  "It must be less than 50", area);
        }
    }
}
```

Figures 14-47 and 14-48 show the complete properties for the validators used on the Web Form.

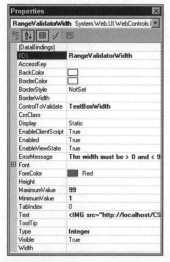

Figure 14-47: The properties for the first two validators in WebForm2.aspx

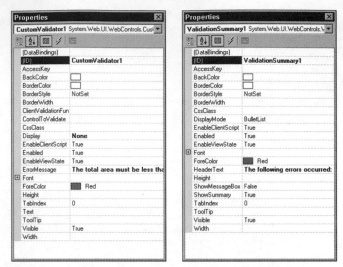

Figure 14-48: The properties for the third and fourth validators in WebForm2.aspx

Summary

I've taken you through a lot of territory from the Web Controls map in this chapter. Web Controls are on the front line in Web applications, so understanding how to use them, what they are, and how to handle validation with them is of interest to all Web Forms developers.

User Controls

My supply of brain cells is finally down to a manageable size.

—Charlie Walker

You might feel like Charlie after reading this book. There's just so
much depth and breadth to the .NET Framework that it is truly
a daunting task to try to master all of its features at once.

What's next? Another chapter on User Controls? Has my supply
of brain cells fallen into the red zone already? Not yet. The User
Controls described back in Chapter 10 were Windows Forms controls;
the controls in this chapter are Web User Controls. Same name, same
idea, different controls.

What Are User Controls?

Web User Controls (which I'll simply call *User Controls* in the rest of
the chapter) are part of a new ASP.NET technology that helps simplify
the development of complex Web pages. While a Web Control is
designed to represent a single component on a Web page, a User
Control manages a group of Web Controls, acting like a nested Web
Form. Think of a User Control like a panel containing Web and HTML
controls. The panel can be used on other Web pages any number of
times. ASP.NET User Controls are used often in frame-based pages.

What are User Controls good for? You could use them to implement
things like menu bars, banners, navigators, tabs, or anything else
that requires multiple HTML elements. These User Controls could
then be used with many of the Web Forms on your site, to achieve
a common look and feel. Figure 15-1 shows how User Controls are
used on Microsoft's ASP.NET sample Web site at `http://www.`
`ibuyspy.com`.

IBuySpy is a Web site for a fictitious online company. The site is
a fairly large Web application developed solely with ASP.NET technology by Microsoft, to demonstrate many of the high-end features of
ASP.NET. I highly recommend visiting the site. You can download the
entire VS .NET project with full source code and run it on your own
system.

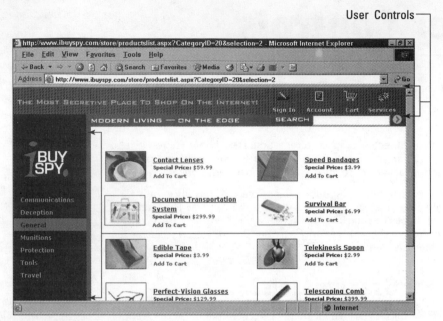

Figure 15-1: A complex Web page that demonstrates User Controls

The Basics

User Controls have an anatomy similar to Web Forms, because they have two faces: a graphical one and a code-behind one. You create User Controls graphically using standard drag-and-drop with Web Controls and HTML Controls. In the Forms Designer, you can use the HTML page to inspect the XML code produced. To add event handing code, you use a code-behind file. The main file of a User Control has the suffix *.ascx*. The code-behind file has the suffix *.ascx.cs*.

The class diagram in Figure 15-2 shows the inheritance tree for class `UserControl`.

`TemplateControl` is a *mix-in* class that provides common functionality to the classes `System.Web.UI.UserControl` and `System.Web.UI.Page`. You create a `UserControl` by deriving a class from `System.Web.UI.UserControl`, and then adding your own Web Controls and HTML Controls to it, to achieve the necessary layout. You can add all the properties, methods, and events to your `UserControl` class by editing the code-behind file, just like you would with Web Controls or other .NET classes.

User Controls are never used alone. For example, if you have a `UserControl` in the file MyUserControl.ascx, you can't use your browser to retrieve the control with a URI like:

```
http://localhost/MyUserControl.ascx.
```

If you try, IIS will return an error page, with the message *"This type of page is not served."* In case you're interested, the error message is generated by the default HTTP Handler set up for .ascx files in the machine.config file, as shown by the fragment in Listing 15-1.

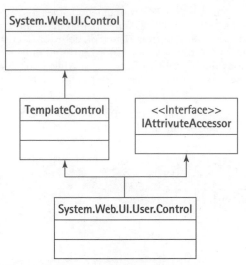

Figure 15-2: The inheritance tree for
System.Web.UI.UserControl

Listing 15-1: Configuring the Default Handler for .ascx Files on a Web Server

```
<configuration>
  <httpHandlers>
    <add verb="*" path="*.ascx"
         type="System.Web.HttpForbiddenHandler, .../>
  </httpHandlers>
</configuration>
```

The XML code for a User Control contains an @ Control directive at the top, and then a list of the Web Controls, HTML Controls, and HTML tags that make up the graphical layout of the control. Listing 15-2 shows a User Control that contains a single Label Web Control.

Listing 15-2: The XML Code for a Simple User Control

```
<%@ Control Language="c#"
            AutoEventWireup="false"
            Codebehind="MyUserControl.ascx.cs"
            Inherits="MyNamespace.MyUserControl"%>

  <asp:Label id="MyLabel" runat="server">
    It's a new world
  </asp:Label>
```

The @ `Control` directive tells the HTTP runtime that the XML document defines a `UserControl`. Following the directive are the XML and HTML elements that make up the User Control. Tags starting with the word `asp` denote Web Controls. The XML code for User Controls is reminiscent of the code used in Web Forms. User Controls represent only a fragment of the code used in a Web Form, so they don't contain `<form>` tags. While User Controls use an @ `Control` directive, Web Forms use an @ `Page` directive. Later in the chapter, I'll discuss the process of morphing a Web Control into a User Control.

When you add a User Control to a Web Form, an @`Register` directive is required at the beginning of the Web Form .aspx page, which looks something like Listing 15-3.

Listing 15-3: The @ Register Tag Needed for User Controls on a Web Form

```
<%@ Register TagPrefix="myNamespace"
             TagName="MyUserControl"
             Src="MyUserControl.ascx" %>
```

The `TagPrefix` attribute is used later on the Web Form to denote the XML namespace for the User Control. In general, you can use any string you want for this namespace, as long as it doesn't collide with an existing namespace. The `TagName` attribute is the class name of the User Control. When referencing a User Control in a code-behind file, the class name used there *must* match the name used in the `TagName` attribute. The `Src` attribute tells the HTTP runtime where the code for the code-behind file is located. Most often, the code-behind file is in the same folder as the .ascx file.

The easiest way to add a User Control to a Web Form is to drag the control's .ascx file from the Solution Explorer and drop it on the Web Form in the Forms Designer. You can achieve the same result programmatically, by adding an XML element to the .aspx file, as shown by the bolded code in Listing 15-4.

Listing 15-4: Adding a User Control to the XML Code of a Web Form

```
<HTML>
  <body>
    <form id="MyWebForm" method="post" runat="server">
      <myNamespace: MyUserControl id="MyControl" runat="server" />
    </form>
  </body>
</HTML>
```

Creating a Web Application with User Controls

User Controls are never designed to be used as standalone components. They need to be used in the larger context of other User Controls, Web Forms, and Web applications. When it comes to showing an example of User Control development, you really need to see the complete picture; otherwise, some of the details may seem to not make any sense, or to be completely unnecessary. To aid my discussion, I created a small sample Web application that uses two User Controls: One acts as a table of contents, in the left part of the window; the other displays content on the right side. Figure 15-3 shows the application's main page.

Figure 15-3: A Web page that uses frames, Web Forms, and User Controls

The page uses a frameset to create a Navigator frame on the left side and a Content frame on the right side. Both frames host User Controls. Operation of the Web page is fairly intuitive. The Navigator control lists a number of World regions. When you click on one of the links, the region name is passed to the Content User Control, which responds by displaying the headlines for that region.

Why did I go to the trouble of creating an example using more than one User Control? There is a good reason. User Controls tend to come in two varieties: those that originate events, and those that consume events. The Navigator is an example of the first kind, while the Content page is an example of the other. In my example, the headlines are shown in the Content frame using a DataList Web Control that is bound to a data source. To keep things simple, the data source is just a static array of strings, but it could easily be a database table containing headlines based on geographic region.

The example also demonstrates a couple of techniques that are simple, but also very common: how to invoke properties and methods of User Controls from a Web Form, and how to control the contents of one HTML frame from another frame.

I called the application *DiscoverTheWorld_WithUserControls,* and structured it as a monolithic Web application containing all the Web Forms and User Controls. In a later section, I'll show how to take a User Control and add it to the Toolbox, so you can reuse it easily on other Web projects.

To create the application, I just used the VS .NET New Project Wizard and selected the Web Application template. The wizard automatically created an application with a blank Web Form. I'll use this Web Form a bit later.

Designing a Navigator User Control

The Navigator User Control is quite simple, because it just contains a static list of hyperlinks. Most navigators in real Web sites display lists of items obtained from a database. Using ASP.NET components, you could use a `DataList` component to support this approach. I'll show you how to use a `DataList` component this way in the second User Control that is embedded in the Content frame. Figure 15-4 shows the class diagram for the `Navigator` User Control class.

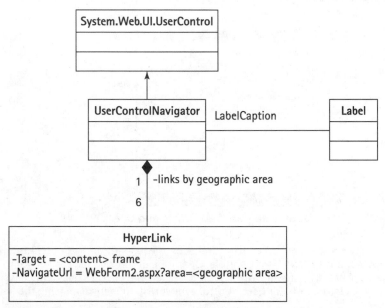

Figure 15-4: The class diagram for the Navigator User Control

The component uses six `HyperLink` controls to select a geographic area. All of the `Hyperlinks` have their `Target` property set to the Content frame. The `Target` property indicates which frame (in a multiframe page) the `NavigateUrl` value is sent to. Since the `Target` property is set to the Content frame, that frame's source URI will change when the `HyperLinks` are clicked.

Developing the Navigator

There are two general ways to create User Controls: using the VS.NET Wizard and using a Web Form. In this section I'll demonstrate the first approach. I'll discuss the second approach a bit later, in the section titled "Converting a Web Form into a User Control." With the second approach, you create a Web Form using the standard Web Form tools and techniques and then turn the form into a User Control by manually making changes to the Web Form code.

To create the Navigator control with a wizard, right-click on the Web application project in the Solution Explorer and select Add ➪ Add New Item from the pop-up menu. In the Add New Item Wizard, select the Web User Control template, as shown in Figure 15-5.

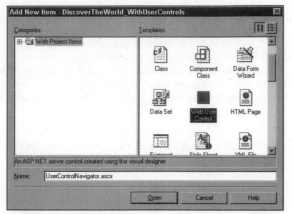

Figure 15-5: Using the Add New Item Wizard to create a Web User Control

The wizard creates a new .ascx file, adds it to the Solution Explorer, and opens the Forms Designer on the (initially empty) User Control. From the Web Forms page of the Toolbox, I dropped a Label and six `HyperLink` components into the Forms Designer, as shown in Figure 15-6.

Figure 15-6: The Navigator User Control in the Forms Designer, after adding the required controls

I customized the `Label` control by changing its `ForeColor` to `Blue`, setting its `Font` to `Bold`, and changing its `Text` to **Get Today's Headlines.**

I customized the `HyperLink`s by changing all their `Target` properties to the string `Content`, which is the name I'll use later for the frame on the right side of the main page, containing the list of headlines. For the `NavigateURL` property, I used a string of the form:

```
WebForm2.aspx?area=<geographic area>
```

For example, the first `HyperLink` uses the following string:

```
WebForm2.aspx?area=North America
```

This string is sent to the Web server when the `HyperLink` button is clicked. Since the `Target` property references the Content frame, that frame will display the page returned from the server. Later, I'll show you how the Web application processes the URIs sent by the `HyperLink` components.

Adding the Navigator to a Web Form

You can't fully test UserControlNavigator until the Content frame is set up, because the actions of the HyperLink controls on the Navigator affect that frame. For the moment, testing the Navigator only entails adding it to a WebFormNavigator.aspx. To add it, select the Web Form in the Forms Designer and then drag and drop the file UserControlNavigator.ascx from the Solution Explorer over to the Forms Designer. Figure 15-7 shows the Forms Designer after the User Control is added.

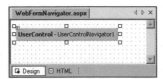

Figure 15-7: How the Navigator User Control appears on a Web Form

As you can see, the contents of UserControlNavigator don't show up in the Forms Designer for the Web Form. That's too bad, but all isn't lost. If you create a Frameset page and add the Web Form to one of the frames, as I'll show later, then the full contents of the Web Form with the User Control will show up.

When adding a User Control to a Web Form, the PageLayout for the form is automatically set to GridLayout. For my example, I changed the layout to FlowLayout, so the various controls on the page will rearrange themselves appropriately as the Web Form is resized. Since the Web Form will be put inside a resizable frame, I already know that the Web Form size will be changeable by the end user.

To make WebFormNavigator a bit more interesting, I customized it a bit. First, I changed its background color to a pale yellow. Then I added Image and Label controls. For the Image component, I created a folder named *images* under the main project folder and added the file world.gif to it. Then I set the ImageUrl property for the Image to images\world.gif. With the Label component, I changed the Text, Font Size, and ForeColor properties. I also added a horizontal line, to separate the two controls from the User Control. With these new changes, the Web Form appears as shown in Figure 15-8.

Figure 15-8: The fully customized Navigator Web Form

You can test the form immediately by running the Web application. Since WebFormNavigator.aspx is the Start Page for the application, it will appear in a Web Browser, showing the list of HyperLink components.

Creating a FrameSet

The main page of the Web application is not a simple Web Form, but an HTML page containing a Frameset. To create this page, you can obviously use a text editor like Notepad to enter the <frameset> and <frame> HTML tags by hand. A much better way is to use (guess what?) a VS .NET wizard. To run the wizard, right-click on the project in the Solutions Explorer and select Add ➪ Add New Item from the pop-up menu. In the Add New Item Wizard, select the Frameset template, as shown in Figure 15-9.

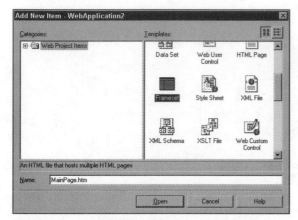

Figure 15-9: Using the Add New Item Wizard to create an HTML page containing a Frameset

After clicking the Open button, another dialog box appears to let you quickly choose from a list of common Frameset layouts. For my Web application example, I chose the Contents layout, as shown in Figure 15-10.

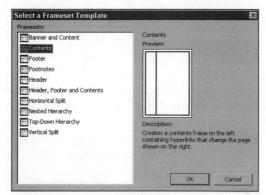

Figure 15-10: Choosing the Frameset layout to create

By splitting the contents of a complicated Web page into smaller frames, it's easier to partition the work across multiple developers. `Framesets` also make it easier to establish a common look and feel for a Web site, because you can use some of the frames to always show the same element or group of elements. For example, you might always want to show your company's logo, with a menu bar, on a header frame, on every page of the site. No matter what page users go to on your site, the top frame stays pretty much the same.

After creating the `Frameset` for the site's main page, the next step is to make this page the Start Page for the Web application. Just right-click on the HTML file in the Solution Explorer and select Set as Start Page from the pop-up menu. Figure 15-11 shows how the Frameset page appears in the Forms Designer.

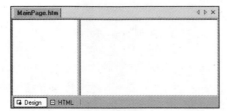

Figure 15-11: How a Frameset page appears initially in the Forms Designer

The Frameset Wizard automatically names each frame it creates. If you recall, my Navigator control uses the name *Content* for the frame on the right side. The wizard named this frame *main,* so I need to change the name. Another easy task: Just select the frame in the Forms Designer, and then go to the Properties window and change the `name` property, as shown in Figure 15-12.

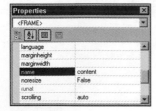

Figure 15-12: Changing the name of a frame

The next step is to add Web Forms to the left and right frames. At the moment, I only have the Web Form for the Navigator form. To add it to the left frame, right-click on that frame and choose Set Page for Frame from the pop-up menu, as shown in Figure 15-13.

A Select Page dialog box appears, allowing you to select items from the list of files in the Solution Explorer. For the left frame, I chose the file WebFormNavigator.aspx, as shown in Figure 15-14.

One of the nice things about `Frameset` pages is that VS .NET shows them in the Forms Designer with their complete content, including User Controls, as shown in Figure 15-15.

That's all there is to setting up a frame. VS .NET also has a series of menu commands you can use to make changes to your `Framesets`, as shown in Figure 15-13. You can add or delete frames without ever writing a line of HTML code.

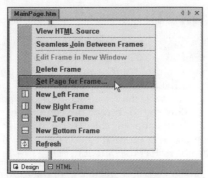

Figure 15-13: Adding a Web Form
to a frame

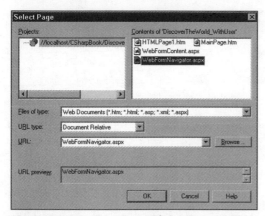

Figure 15-14: Selecting which item to add
to a frame

Figure 15-15: How the Forms Designer shows
the complete contents of frames

Developing a Content User Control

So far, I've only shown half of the Web application's Main Page. The other piece of the Main Page is the Content frame. I created another User Control to fill in this frame, using the same steps used to create the Navigator control. I called the control *UserControlContent*. For this control, I used a `Label` to display the date and geographic area, and a `DataList` component to list the headlines read from a data source. `DataLists`, with their cousins `DataGrid` and `Repeater`, are frequently used on Web Forms. They allow you to display the contents of multiple rows of data from a data source. While `DataGrids` support the display of text fields, `DataLists` let you place not only text, but also Web Controls on each row. `Repeater` is not as powerful as `DataGrid`, but it allows you to place arbitrary HTML content in every row.

To customize the `DataList`, I used a shortcut: I right-clicked on it and selected the Auto Format Wizard from the pop-up menu. In the wizard, I chose the Colorful 1 style, as shown in Figure 15-16.

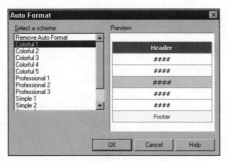

Figure 15-16: Using the Auto Format Wizard to quickly configure a DataList

The Auto Format Wizard can also be used to configure a `DataGrid`. The way you tell the `DataList` what controls to put on each row is with *templates*. There are templates for every possible row, including the header, the actual data rows, optional blank rows between data rows, and the footer.

For my `DataList`, I want the rows to contain HyperLink components, so I had to set up the Data Items template. To do so, right-click on the `DataLink` and select Edit Template ➪ Item Templates from the pop-up menu, as shown in Figure 15-17.

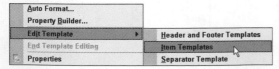

Figure 15-17: Configuring the items to display on each data row of a DataList component

After you select the Item Templates command, the VS .NET Forms Designer switches to the Edit Template mode and displays the Template Editor. The only item I added in the Editor is a `HyperLink` component, as shown in Figure 15-18.

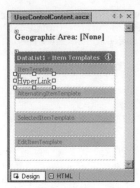

Figure 15-18: The Template Editor, which enables you to configure the contents of data rows shown in a DataList

As you can see in the figure, the Editor also lets you specify a template for alternating data rows, the selected row, and the row being edited. I left these templates empty. To set up the caption bar of the `DataList`, I selected the Header and Footer Templates command shown in Figure 15-18. I then added the text for the Header row, as shown in Figure 15-19.

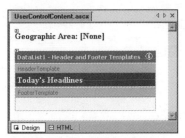

Figure 15-19: Editing the Header and Footer rows for a DataList

I left the Footer Template empty. To close the Template Editor, right-click on it and select End Template Editing from the pop-up menu. Returning to the Forms Editor, the User Control now appears as shown in Figure 15-20.

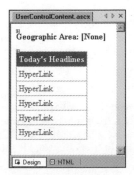

Figure 15-20: The fully configured User Control in the Forms Designer

The only thing left to do is to set up the behavior of the individual `HyperLink` controls displayed in the DataList. Each `HyperLink` needs to show a headline retrieved from a data source. Clicking on the headline should take the user to a new page with the full story.

To set up the items on data rows, display the Template Editor using the Item Templates command shown back in Figure 15-17. Select the HyperLink component in the Template Editor. In the Properties window, bind the Text property to the data source. To do so, click the ellipsis button on the (DataBindings) row, as shown in Figure 15-21.

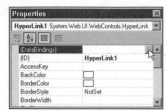

Figure 15-21: Opening the Data Binding wizard from the Properties window

Once the Data Bindings Wizard is displayed, I need to bind the Text property to the data source. I selected the Text property in the Bindable Properties list and selected DataItem in the Simple Binding list on the right, as shown in Figure 15-22.

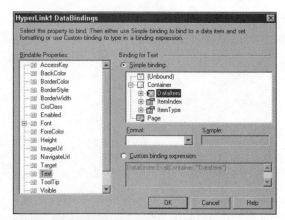

Figure 15-22: Binding the Text property of a HyperLink component to a data source

That's all you need to do to set up the data binding. Not even a line of code to write. The last step in configuring the HyperLink component is to specify the NavigateUrl property, indicating the name of the HTML document containing the full news story. For the NavigateUrl property, I just entered the following string:

```
HTMLPage1.htm
```

This is just a simple HTML page I created containing some fixed text. In a real application, you would probably want to fetch the news story, as an XML document, from a data source and use XSL to format it into an HTML document to return to the end user. The XML and XSL parts are beyond the scope of this User Control chapter. A bit later in this chapter, I'll show you how to use a wizard to create HTML pages.

Adding properties

The Content Web Form expects a Geographic Area parameter in the URI of the HTTP request. The Geographic Area is then used to set the `GeographicArea` property of the Content User Control. Adding a property to a User Control is no different than adding a property to any other type of class. The code shown in Listing 15-5 declares a read/write property named *GeographicArea*.

Listing 15-5: Declaring a Property in a User Control

```
public abstract class UserControlContent : System.Web.UI.UserControl
{

  private String geographicArea;

  public String GeographicArea
  {
    get { return geographicArea; }
    set { geographicArea = value; }
    }
}
```

The setter property for `UserControlContent` is slightly more complicated than shown in the listing, because it needs to use the `GeographicArea` value to select a set of headlines. (For the complete code for class `UserControlContent`, see Listing 15-8, later in the chapter.)

Adding event handlers

Adding an event handler to a User Control is just like adding a handler to a Web Control, as described in the previous chapter. As with Web Controls, events fired on the client side must produce a postback operation to the server. The events are handled with server-side code. Events fired on the client side are handled on the server side while processing a postback. Events fired on the server side are processed immediately.

Responding to page requests

When the end user clicks on a geographic area link in the Navigator frame in my sample Web application, the link sends out the following request to the server:

```
WebFormContent.aspx?area=<geographic area>
```

The Content Web Form processes this request in its `Page_Load` handler and passes along the geographic area parameter to `UserControlContent`. This control reacts by fetching the headlines for the given area, which are returned as an HTML page. The page is used to fill the Content frame, on the right side of the main page. The interaction diagram in Figure 15-23 shows the main events.

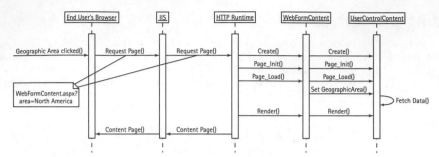

Figure 15-23: The main events to process a user click on the Navigator form

The diagram is fairly busy, but the code is simple. I only added code for the Page_Load method of WebFormContent.aspx and the setter method of the GeographicArea property of UserControlContent. Listing 15-6 shows the Page_Load method of WebFormContent.

Note When you access User Controls in code-behind files, you need to manually add a public or protected declaration of a field, as highlighted in the next listing. The instance name must match the name used in the .aspx file. You can use any name you want, as long as the code-behind and XML names match.

Listing 15-6: **The Page_Load Event Handler of WebFormContent**

```
public class WebFormContent : System.Web.UI.Page
{
  // declare this field manually, so we can access the
  // User Control programmatically. Class name must match ID
  // field of component shown in Forms Designer, and must be
  // protected or public

  protected UserControlContent UserControlContent1;

  private void Page_Load(object sender, System.EventArgs e)
  {
    String geographicArea = Request.QueryString ["area"];
    if (geographicArea == null)
      UserControlContent1.GeographicArea = "";
    else
      UserControlContent1.GeographicArea = geographicArea;
  }
}
```

The Page_Load handler simply retrieves the value of the area property passed in the URI, and uses it to set the GeographicArea property of UserControlContent.

The previous listing declares a protected field with the name UserControlContent1. This is the same name used in the .aspx XML file, summarized in Listing 15-7. (I put the XML code where the User Control is declared in boldface.)

Listing 15-7: Highlights from the XML Code for WebFormContent.aspx

```
<%@ Page language="c#"
        Codebehind="WebFormContent.aspx.cs"
        AutoEventWireup="false"
        Inherits="DiscoverTheWorld_WithUserControls.WebFormContent" %>

<%@ Register TagPrefix="uc1"
            TagName="UserControlContent"
            Src="UserControlContent.ascx" %>

<HTML>
  <body MS_POSITIONING="GridLayout">
    <form id="WebFormContent" method="post" runat="server">
      <uc1:UserControlContent id="UserControlContent1"
                              runat="server">
      </uc1:UserControlContent>
    </form>
  </body>
</HTML>
```

Listing 15-8 shows the complete code for UserControlContent.ascx.

Listing 15-8: The Complete Code for UserControlContent.ascx

```
using System;
using System.Data;
using System.Drawing;
using System.Web;
using System.Web.UI.WebControls;
using System.Web.UI.HtmlControls;

namespace DiscoverTheWorld_WithUserControls
{
  public abstract class UserControlContent : System.Web.UI.UserControl
  {
    String [] northAmericanHeadlines = new String [] {
      "Dow Jones Industrial Average Surges",
      "Hurricane Flora downgraded to Tropical Storm",
      "Congress Approves Budget for next Fiscal Year",
      "Flooding in Iowa displaces Thousands",
      "Los Angeles Lakers lead Pacific Division"};

    String [] europeanHeadlines = new String [] {
      "Euro Rises To New Levels",
      "NATO Leaders put Further Expansion Plans on Hold",
      "France Recovering from Wettest Winter in History",
      "Italian Elections Update",
```

Continued

Listing 15-8 *(continued)*

```
      "Russian President Praises Allies"};

  String [] noHeadlines = new String [] {
    "no headlines available"};

  protected System.Web.UI.WebControls.Label LabelGeographicArea;
  protected System.Web.UI.WebControls.DataList DataList1;

  public UserControlContent()
  {
    this.Init += new System.EventHandler(Page_Init);
  }

  private void Page_Load(object sender, System.EventArgs e)
  {
    // Put user code to initialize the page here
  }

  private void Page_Init(object sender, EventArgs e)
  {
    InitializeComponent();
  }

  private void InitializeComponent()
  {
    this.Load += new System.EventHandler(this.Page_Load);
  }

  private String geographicArea;
  public String GeographicArea
  {
    get { return geographicArea; }
    set
    {
      geographicArea = value;
      if (value != "")

        LabelGeographicArea.Text =
            DateTime.Today.ToString("yyyy-MM-dd") +
                               "  " + geographicArea;
      else
        LabelGeographicArea.Text =
        "Select a geographic area in the list on the left";

      if (geographicArea == "North America")
      {
        DataList1.DataSource = northAmericanHeadlines;
        DataList1.DataBind();
      }

      else if (geographicArea == "Europe")
        DataList1.DataSource = europeanHeadlines;
```

```
        else if (geographicArea != "")
          DataList1.DataSource = noHeadlines;

        if (DataList1.DataSource != null)
          DataList1.DataBind();
      }
    }
  }
}
```

The only part of the code requiring some explanation is the setter method for the
`GeographicArea` property. The setter uses the area name to locate the headlines. I put all the
headlines in a series of `String` arrays, to avoid all the overhead of setting up and using a
database. In a real application, the data source for the `DataList` component would be a
database table.

Adding the Content Control to a Web Form

Having created the second User Control, I created a new Web Form called
WebFormContent.aspx and added the User Control to it. I just dragged the file
UserControlContent.ascx from the Solution Explorer to the Content Web Form in the Forms
Designer. Then I added the Content Web Form to the Content Frame, using the menu com-
mand shown back in Figure 15-13.

Creating an HTML Page

Although not specifically related to User Controls, I'll show you how I created the page
HTMLPage1.htm referenced by the headline links in UserControlContent.ascx. All I did was
use a VS .NET wizard. To run the wizard, right-click on the project in the Solution Explorer
and select Add ➪ Add New Item from the pop-up menu. In the Add New Item Wizard, select
the HTML template as shown in Figure 15-24.

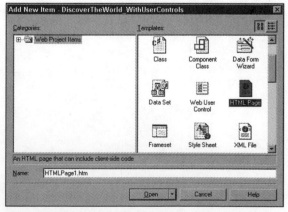

Figure 15-24: Using the Add New Item Wizard
to create an HTML page

Once the page is created, you can use the Forms Designer to add text and HTML controls to it, such as listboxes, dropdown lists, tables, buttons, and so on. The Designer lets you work either graphically with drag and drop, or at the HTML tag level, using the HTML window. Figure 15-25 shows the new HTML page after I added a bit of text to it.

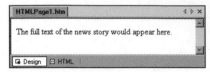

Figure 15-25: Editing an HTML page in the Forms Designer

Note   You can't add Web Controls to HTML pages, because the latter lack the XML directives needed by the ASP.NET runtime to process Web Forms and Web Controls.

Converting a Web Form into a User Control

Rather than creating a User Control from scratch, another approach is to take a Web Form and convert it into a User Control. After all, both Web Forms and User Controls represent an area of the screen that can hold literal text, Web Controls, and/or HTML Controls. Converting a Web Form into a User Control is fairly easy, but the procedure has to be done manually. You get so used to doing everything with wizards that you almost expect VS .NET to have a wizard to do the conversion. No such luck.

Listing 15-9 shows the XML code for a simple Web Form containing a Label control.

Listing 15-9: The XML Code for a Simple Web Form

```
<%@ Page language="c#"
        Codebehind="MyWebForm.aspx.cs"
        AutoEventWireup="false"
        Inherits="WebApplicationWithUserControls.MyWebForm" %>
<HTML>
  <body>
    <form id="MyWebForm" method="post" runat="server">
      <asp:label id="MyLabel" runat="server">
        What's you name?
      </asp:label>
    </form>
  </body>
</HTML>
```

Listing 15-10 shows the XML code for a User Control containing a Label control.

> **Listing 15-10: The XML Code for a Simple User Control**
>
> ```
> <%@ Control Language="c#"
>             AutoEventWireup="false"
>             Codebehind="MyWebUserControl.ascx.cs"
>             Inherits="WebApplicationWithUserControls.MyUserControl"%>
>   <asp:label id="MyLabel" runat="server">
>     What's you name?
>   </asp:label>
> ```

The first difference between Web Forms and User Controls is the @ `Page` directive in the Web Form, which is instead replaced by an @ `Control` directive in a User Control.

The second difference is that a Web Form represents a complete HTML page, with <HTML>, <HEAD>, and <BODY> tags. Since a User Control is designed to be placed on a Web Form, it does away with all the tags except for those of the controls it contains.

Testing User Controls

You can't run a User Control by itself. It has to be added to a Web Form, and the Web Form has to be part of a Web application. The bottom line is that you need a Web application to do any testing. User Controls are often used as navigators, tab controls, and menu bars, and clicking on them causes something to happen to another component. In cases like these, where one User Control affects other parts of an application, you may need to create a multi-frame Web application for the test fixture, and possibly include more that one User Control in the application. What you'll wind up with is a mini-application, much like the example DiscoverTheWorld_WithUserControls I outlined in this chapter.

Keep in mind that components that are tightly bound to others are difficult or impossible to test by themselves. Rather than have one User Control directly invoke methods of other controls or Web Forms, use events and event handlers to loosely couple components. For example, say you have two controls, UserControl1 and UserControl2. When the former is clicked, you want to call `Method2()` of UserControl2. To avoid embedding calls and references to UserControl2 in UserControl1, make UserControl1 fire an event. If an event handler is present, it will be called. In the parent Web Form, you can add an event handler and make it call `UserControl2.Method2()`. The Web Form then acts as a liaison between the two User Controls, allowing the controls to be developed and tested separately.

Packaging User Controls as DLLs

If you plan to reuse User Controls on multiple Web applications, you might want to package them as a DLL and place them on the VS .NET Toolbox. This way, developers can use simple drag-and-drop operations to add them to their Web Forms.

To create the DLL package, use the New Project Wizard with the template Web Controls Library, as shown in Figure 15-26.

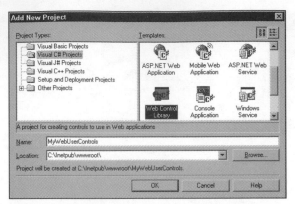

Figure 15-26: Creating a DLL to package User
Controls in

Now perform the following steps:

1. Delete the file WebCustomControl1.cs from the Solution Explorer.

2. Copy the User Controls into the new project's folder. Be sure to copy the .ascx, .ascx.cs, and .ascx.resx files for each control.

3. Add the copied .ascx, .ascx.cs, and .ascx.resx files to the new project. To do so, right-click on the project in the Solution Explorer and use the Add ➪ Add Existing Item dialog box. You can add all the files in a single operation.

4. In the code-behind files, manually change the namespace to match the new DLL project's namespace.

You'll probably want to add the User Controls to the VS .NET Toolbox. To do so, follow these steps:

1. For each User Control added to the new project, create a new 16x16 bit bitmap file. The bitmaps must be saved with filenames that match the User Controls in the project.

2. For each bitmap added, select its filename in the Solution Explorer. In the Properties window, set the Build Action to Embedded Resource.

3. To create a new tab on the Toolbox, right-click on the Toolbox and select the Add Tab command from the pop-up menu. You can use any name you want for tabs.

4. To add the User Controls to the Toolbox, select the Toolbox page you want to add the controls to, and then right-click and select Customize Toolbox from the pop-up menu. In the Customize Toolbox window, select the .NET Framework Components tab. Click the Browse button and locate the DLL containing the controls to install. Put a check-mark next to the DLL filename, as shown in Figure 15-27.

When you click the OK button, the Web User Controls in the DLL will appear on the VS .NET Toolbox.

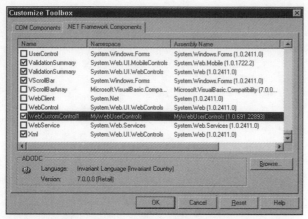

Figure 15-27: Adding a DLL with Web User Controls to the Toolbox

The Complete Code

As usual, before closing out the chapter, I'll show you all the important code used in the example I created. Figure 15-28 shows the Solution Explorer for the Web application DiscoverTheWorld_WithUserControls.

Figure 15-28: The Solution Explorer for the Web application discussed in this chapter

Listings 15-11 through 15-18 show the XML and C# code used in the Web application.

Listing 15-11: The XML Code for UserControlNavigator.ascx

```
<%@ Control
    Language="c#"
    AutoEventWireup="false"
    Codebehind="UserControlNavigator.ascx.cs"
```

Continued

Listing 15-11 *(continued)*

```
    Inherits="DiscoverTheWorld_WithUserControls.UserControlNavigator"%>
<P>
  <asp:Label id="Label1" runat="server"
             Font-Bold="True" ForeColor="Blue">
    Get Today's Headlines
  </asp:Label>
</P>
<P>
  <asp:HyperLink id="HyperLink1"
                 runat="server"
                 Target="Content"
                 NavigateUrl="WebFormContent.aspx?
                             area=North America">
    North America
  </asp:HyperLink>
</P>
<P>
  <asp:HyperLink id="HyperLink6"
                 runat="server"
                 Target="Content"
                 NavigateUrl="WebFormContent.aspx?
                             area=South America">
    South America
  </asp:HyperLink>
</P>
<P>
  <asp:HyperLink id="HyperLink2"
                 runat="server"
                 Target="Content"
                 NavigateUrl="WebFormContent.aspx?
                             area=Europe">
    Europe
  </asp:HyperLink>
</P>
<P>
  <asp:HyperLink id="HyperLink3"
                 runat="server"
                 Target="Content"
                 NavigateUrl="WebFormContent.aspx?
                             area=Middle East">
    Middle East
  </asp:HyperLink>
</P>
<P>
  <asp:HyperLink id="HyperLink4"
                 runat="server"
                 Target="Content"
                 NavigateUrl="WebFormContent.aspx?
                             area=Asia">
    Asia
```

```
      </asp:HyperLink>
</P>
<P>
   <asp:HyperLink id="HyperLink5"
                  runat="server"
                  Target="Content"
                  NavigateUrl="WebFormContent.aspx?
                               area=Australia">
      Australia
   </asp:HyperLink>
</P>
```

Listing 15-12: The Code-Behind File UserControlNavigator.ascx.cx

```
using System;
using System.Data;
using System.Drawing;
using System.Web;
using System.Web.UI.WebControls;
using System.Web.UI.HtmlControls;

namespace DiscoverTheWorld_WithUserControls
{
  public abstract class UserControlNavigator :
                        System.Web.UI.UserControl
  {
    protected System.Web.UI.WebControls.HyperLink HyperLink1;
    protected System.Web.UI.WebControls.HyperLink HyperLink2;
    protected System.Web.UI.WebControls.HyperLink HyperLink3;
    protected System.Web.UI.WebControls.HyperLink HyperLink4;
    protected System.Web.UI.WebControls.HyperLink HyperLink5;
    protected System.Web.UI.WebControls.Label Label1;
    protected System.Web.UI.WebControls.HyperLink HyperLink6;

    public UserControlNavigator()
    {
      this.Init += new System.EventHandler(Page_Init);
    }

    private void Page_Load(object sender, System.EventArgs e)
    {
    }

    private void Page_Init(object sender, EventArgs e)
    {
      InitializeComponent();
    }

    private void InitializeComponent()
```

Continued

Listing 15-12 *(continued)*

```
    {
        this.Load += new System.EventHandler(this.Page_Load);
    }
  }
}
```

Listing 15-13: The XML Code WebFormNavigator.aspx

```
<%@ Page language="c#"
        Codebehind="WebFormNavigator.aspx.cs"
        AutoEventWireup="false"
        Inherits="DiscoverTheWorld_WithUserControls.WebForm1" %>

<%@ Register TagPrefix="uc1"
            TagName="UserControlNavigator"
            Src="UserControlNavigator.ascx" %>

<HTML>
  <body bgColor="#ffffcc">
    <form id="Form1" method="post" runat="server">
      <asp:Image id="Image1" runat="server"
                ImageUrl="images\world.gif"
                Width="41px" Height="41px"/>
      <asp:Label id="Label1" runat="server"
                Width="115px" Height="52px"
                ForeColor="Blue" Font-Bold="True"
                Font-Size="Large">
        Discover the World
      </asp:Label>
      <HR width="100%" SIZE="1">

      <uc1:UserControlNavigator id="UserControlNavigator1"
                                runat="server"/>

    </form>
  </body>
</HTML>
```

Listing 15-14: The Code-Behind File WebFormNavigator.ascx.cx

```
using System;
using System.Collections;
using System.ComponentModel;
using System.Data;
```

```
using System.Drawing;
using System.Web;
using System.Web.SessionState;
using System.Web.UI;
using System.Web.UI.WebControls;
using System.Web.UI.HtmlControls;

namespace DiscoverTheWorld_WithUserControls
{
  public class WebForm1 : System.Web.UI.Page
  {
    protected System.Web.UI.WebControls.Label Label1;
    protected System.Web.UI.WebControls.Image Image1;

    public WebForm1()
    {
  Page.Init += new System.EventHandler(Page_Init);
    }

    private void Page_Load(object sender, System.EventArgs e)
    {
    }

    private void Page_Init(object sender, EventArgs e)
    {
      InitializeComponent();
    }

    private void InitializeComponent()
    {
      this.Load += new System.EventHandler(this.Page_Load);
    }
  }
}
```

Listing 15-15: **The XML Code for UserControlContent.ascx**

```
<%@ Control Language="c#"
           AutoEventWireup="false"
           Codebehind="UserControlContent.ascx.cs"

Inherits="DiscoverTheWorld_WithUserControls.UserControlContent"%>
<P>
  <asp:Label id="LabelGeographicArea"
             runat="server" Font-Bold="True">
    Geographic Area: [none]
  </asp:Label>
</P>
```

Continued

Listing 15-15 *(continued)*

```
<P>
   <asp:DataList id="DataList1" runat="server" BorderColor="#CC9966"
                 BorderStyle="None" BackColor="White" CellPadding="4"
                 GridLines="Both" BorderWidth="1px">
      <SelectedItemStyle Font-Bold="True" ForeColor="#663399"
                         BackColor="#FFCC66"/>
      <HeaderTemplate>
        Today's Headlines
      </HeaderTemplate>
      <ItemStyle ForeColor="#330099" BackColor="White"/>
      <FooterStyle ForeColor="#330099" BackColor="#FFFFCC"/>
      <ItemTemplate>
        <asp:HyperLink id="HyperLink1" runat="server"
             NavigateUrl="HTMLPage1.htm"
             Text='<%# DataBinder.Eval(Container, "DataItem") %>'
             Target="_blank">
        </asp:HyperLink>
      </ItemTemplate>
      <HeaderStyle Font-Bold="True" ForeColor="#FFFFCC"
                   BackColor="#990000"/>
   </asp:DataList>
</P>
<P>
   
</P>
<P>
   
</P>
```

Listing 15-16: The Code-Behind File UserControlContent.ascx.cx

```
using System;
using System.Data;
using System.Drawing;
using System.Web;
using System.Web.UI.WebControls;
using System.Web.UI.HtmlControls;

namespace DiscoverTheWorld_WithUserControls
{
  public abstract class UserControlContent :
                        System.Web.UI.UserControl
  {
    String [] northAmericanHeadlines = new String [] {
      "Dow Jones Industrial Average Surges",
      "Hurricane Flora downgraded to Tropical Storm",
```

```
        "Congress Approves Budget for next Fiscal Year",
        "Flooding in Iowa displaces Thousands",
        "Los Angeles Lakers lead Pacific Division"};

    String [] europeanHeadlines = new String [] {
      "Euro Rises To New Levels",
      "NATO Leaders put Further Expansion Plans on Hold",
      "France Recovering from Wettest Winter in History",
      "Italian Elections Update",
      "Russian President Praises Allies"};

    String [] noHeadlines = new String [] {
      "no headlines available"};

    protected System.Web.UI.WebControls.Label LabelGeographicArea;
    protected System.Web.UI.WebControls.DataList DataList1;

    public UserControlContent()
    {
this.Init += new System.EventHandler(Page_Init);
    }

    private void Page_Load(object sender, System.EventArgs e)
    {
// Put user code to initialize the page here
    }

    private void Page_Init(object sender, EventArgs e)
    {
      InitializeComponent();
    }

    private void InitializeComponent()
    {
      this.Load += new System.EventHandler(this.Page_Load);
    }

    private String geographicArea;

    public String GeographicArea
    {
      get { return geographicArea; }
      set
      {
        geographicArea = value;
        if (value != "")
          LabelGeographicArea.Text =
            DateTime.Today.ToString("yyyy-MM-dd") +
                                " " + geographicArea;
        else
          LabelGeographicArea.Text =
```

Continued

Listing 15-16 *(continued)*

```
            "Select a geographic area in the list on the left";

        if (geographicArea == "North America")
        {
          DataList1.DataSource = northAmericanHeadlines;
          DataList1.DataBind();
        }

        else if (geographicArea == "Europe")
          DataList1.DataSource = europeanHeadlines;

        else if (geographicArea != "")
          DataList1.DataSource = noHeadlines;

        if (DataList1.DataSource != null)
          DataList1.DataBind();
      }
    }
  }
}
```

Listing 15-17: The XML Code WebFormContent.aspx

```
<%@ Page language="c#"
        Codebehind="WebFormContent.aspx.cs"
        AutoEventWireup="false"
        Inherits="DiscoverTheWorld_WithUserControls.WebFormContent" %>

<%@ Register TagPrefix="uc1"
        TagName="UserControlContent"
        Src="UserControlContent.ascx" %>

<HTML>
  <body MS_POSITIONING="GridLayout">
    <form id="WebFormContent" method="post" runat="server">
     <uc1:UserControlContent id="UserControlContent1"
                              runat="server"/>
    </form>
  </body>
</HTML>
```

Listing 15-18: The Code-Behind File WebFormContent.ascx.cx

```csharp
using System;
using System.Collections;
using System.ComponentModel;
using System.Data;
using System.Drawing;
using System.Web;
using System.Web.SessionState;
using System.Web.UI;
using System.Web.UI.WebControls;
using System.Web.UI.HtmlControls;

namespace DiscoverTheWorld_WithUserControls
{
  public class WebFormContent : System.Web.UI.Page
  {
    // declare this field manually, so we can access the
    // User Control programmatically. Class name must match ID
    // field of component shown in Forms Designer, and must be
    // protected or public
    protected UserControlContent UserControlContent1;

    public WebFormContent()
    {
      Page.Init += new System.EventHandler(Page_Init);
    }

    private void Page_Load(object sender, System.EventArgs e)
    {
      String geographicArea = Request.QueryString ["area"];
      if (geographicArea == null)
        UserControlContent1.GeographicArea = "";
      else
        UserControlContent1.GeographicArea = geographicArea;
    }

    private void Page_Init(object sender, EventArgs e)
    {
      InitializeComponent();
    }

    private void InitializeComponent()
    {
      this.Load += new System.EventHandler(this.Page_Load);
    }
  }
}
```

Summary

Web User Controls are a great way to subdivide the content used in multiframe Web pages. They work with Web Forms and share many features with Web Controls. If you develop large or complex Web applications, you'll definitely want to incorporate Web User Controls into your projects. Doing so will enable you to better partition work between developers, reduce or eliminate duplicated code, and make it easier to achieve a common look-and-feel across Web pages.

✦   ✦   ✦

Services

No issue is so small that it can't be blown out of proportion.

—Stuart Hughes

I have certainly blown my share of small issues out of proportion in the past. Although services are no small issue in the computing world, I wouldn't want to be accused of *not* blowing them out of proportion here, so I'll dedicate an entire chapter to them.

Before getting too wrapped up in details, I want to make sure we're all on the same page here. What is a service, in the software sense? A *service* is an application created primarily or solely to be called by other programs, usually designated as clients. A service may accept calls from clients running on the same machine, or on a different machine. In the latter case, it doesn't make sense for the service to have a user interface, because the client is remote, and the user will never see the computer monitor connected to the server. Services are often started automatically when the computer boots up, because they are required to perform their function regardless of what else the computer is doing and who is logged on.

For the purposes of this book, I'll discuss two classes of services: remote and local. A remote service is one that runs on a computer to which a client has a network connection. IIS is a good example of such a service. *Remote services* are often required to support large numbers of clients simultaneously, and therefore must have very good performance and be scalable. *Local services,* on the other hand, are generally designed to support only the applications running on the same machine, and therefore have different loading characteristics by clients. An example of a local service could be the Microsoft Distributed Transaction Coordinator. Another example could be the Date/Time service that displays the current time in the system tray.

VS .NET supports two basic types of services: those that are invoked over the Internet, and those that run under control of the Windows Service Control Manager. The first type is called a *Web Service;* the second is called a *Windows Service (previously known as NT Service).* In this chapter, I'll describe both types, showing you how to design, develop, and debug them.

Web Services

There are many technologies out there to connect clients to servers, including DCOM, CORBA, Java RMI, and others. I will focus on a new and much simpler type of connectivity, based on open standards such as XML and SOAP, that is very well supported in the .NET Framework: Web Services. Simply put, a Web Service is a component that exposes its interface via the Web. Clients invoke methods of the service using standard HTTP, and get responses back in the same way. Most computers are already set up to handle HTTP networking, so the additional overhead of using the Web as the component interconnection fabric is minimal, in terms of complexity. To see a really cool example of Web Services, check out Microsoft's site at `TerraServer.Microsoft.net`. The site has Web Services that return aerial maps, topographic maps, census information, and other interesting things. You can also download the complete source code for the Web Services from this site. Figure 16-1 shows a satellite image of San Francisco returned by the site.

Figure 16-1: A satellite image of San Francisco returned by a freely accessible Microsoft Web Service

By showing a Microsoft Web Service as an example, I don't want to give you the impression that Web Services are a proprietary Microsoft technology: Many companies support them, including, IBM, HP, Borland, and a slew of others. Conspicuously missing from the list is Sun Microsystems, which is offering Web Services based on an architecture called ONE, for Open Net Environment. ONE Web Services offer features similar to .NET Web Services, but unfortunately ONE is incompatible with the .NET Web Services supported by the Microsoft camp. Among the many reasons is ONE's use of a dialect of XML called ebXML.

Programmers that developed distributed components in the past with technologies like DCOM and CORBA will probably cringe at the thought of debugging a .NET Web Service. On the contrary, Web Services actually make it much easier, even enjoyable, to build and debug distributed components with the .NET Framework. At this point, many of you may be wondering about what kind of performance hit you take for using HTTP and regular text for transferring data over the wire. Rest assured that in a very significant number of cases, users will see no noticeable difference when using HTTP compared to other techniques, such as DCOM. As with all distributed computing technologies, it is also important to design your distributed components to minimize the amount of wire traffic, and keep calls between client and server to a minimum.

The Basics

Think of a Web Service as a component whose methods you can invoke using an Internet or intranet connection. From the client machine, the Web Service appears as a URI that returns an XML page. For example, consider a simple Web Service in a class called `MyDateService`, with a method called `GetDateAndTime()` that returns the time of day. If the class were stored in the file Service1.asmx on the localhost server, you could invoke `GetDateAndTime()` by entering a URI like this:

```
http://localhost/MyWebFolder/TestWebService/Service1.asmx/GetDateAndTime?
```

The request would be converted to an HTTP POST message with a header looking something like this:

```
POST /CSharpBook/TestWebService/Service1.asmx HTTP/1.1
Host: localhost
Content-Type: text/xml; charset=utf-8
Content-Length: length
SOAPAction: http://tempuri.org/GetDateAndTime
```

Following the header would be the SOAP payload for the request, looking something like this:

```
<?xml version="1.0" encoding="utf-8"?>
<soap:Envelope .../>
  <soap:Body>
    <GetDateAndTime xmlns="http://tempuri.org/" />
  </soap:Body>
</soap:Envelope>
```

I'll be discussing SOAP and the layout of SOAP messages a bit later. The complete message would be sent to IIS on the local server, which would forward it to the ASP.NET runtime. The runtime would create an instance of `MyDateService`, invoke the `GetDateAndTime()` method, get a serialized XML document back containing the date and time, and return an HTTP response message to the browser looking something like this:

```
HTTP/1.1 200 OK
Content-Type: text/xml; charset=utf-8
Content-Length: length

<?xml version="1.0" encoding="utf-8"?>
<soap:Envelope .../">
  <soap:Body>
    <GetDateAndTimeResponse xmlns="http://tempuri.org/">
      <GetDateAndTimeResult>
        2001-10-18T09:16:39.1357981-07:00
      </GetDateAndTimeResult>
    </GetDateAndTimeResponse>
  </soap:Body>
```

Between the time the request went out and the response came back, a number of things happened that merit some explanation. How did the ASP.NET runtime know that the request indicates a Web Service method? It just looks at the file suffix .asmx, and then looks in the machine.config file to see if an HTTP handler is defined for this type of file. The machine.config file on the server contains mappings between file types and ASP.NET handlers. The code fragment in Listing 16-1 shows the mapping for .asmx files.

Listing 16-1: The machine.config Entry that Ties .asmx File Types with the Web Service Handler

```
<configuration>
  <httpHandlers>
    <add verb="*"
         path="*.asmx"
         type="System.Web.Services.
             Protocols.WebServiceHandlerFactory,
             System.Web.Services, Version=1.0.2411.0,
             Culture=neutral,
             PublicKeyToken=b03f5f7f11d50a3a"
         validate="false" />
</configuration>
```

So any time the ASP.NET runtime receives a request for a page with the .asmx suffix, it delegates the request to the Web Service handler. This handler then checks the request for the name of the method to invoke and the parameters to pass to the method. The Web Service handler looks at the signature of the method to invoke, to determine the number and type of the parameters the method takes. The runtime then deserializes the XML data representing the parameters into .NET object types and invokes the Web Method. The data returned by the Web Method is serialized back into an XML document, which is then returned to the client machine. Figure 16-2 shows a super-simplified summary of how clients call Web Services.

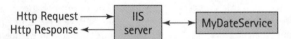

Figure 16-2: A simple way to envision Web Services from the perspective of a client machine

Although Web Services are easy to call from a client machine, there are a number of intermediate components and services that take part in a typical Web Service call, as shown in Figure 16-3.

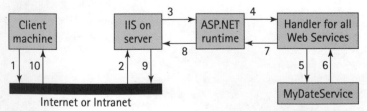

Figure 16-3: How a Web Service is invoked from a client machine

The following is a description of the numbered events in the figure:

1. The client machine establishes a connection with IIS on the server machine, using port 80, and issues a request with a URI identifying the Web Service. By using port 80, the requests can penetrate firewalls that allow Web traffic to enter.

2. IIS receives the request.

3. IIS delegates handling of the request to the ASP.NET runtime.

4. ASP.NET determines that the page type being requested is .asmx and delegates the request to the Web Services handler.

5. The Web Services handler creates an instance of `MyDateService` and invokes the method `GetDateAndTime()`. Any parameters required by the method are deserialized from the SOAP packet and passed to the method call as regular .NET objects.

6. `MyDateService` returns the date to the Web Services handler, which serializes the data into an XML document that is wrapped in a SOAP packet.

7. The SOAP packet is returned to the ASP.NET runtime.

8. The ASP.NET runtime returns the SOAP packet to IIS as the response page.

9. IIS returns the response.

10. The client receives the response.

Routing Web Service requests to the correct Web Service component is only part of the work, and a fairly simple part at that. The other part is converting data to and from SOAP packets. The ASP.NET Framework takes care of this for you. As long as you use built-in types, or custom types that are serializable, you won't have any problems getting data to and from your Web Services.

Declaring Web Methods

A Web Service component may have lots of methods, but usually only some of these methods are designed to be Web Methods, which are callable from remote clients. Since Web Methods require serialization of parameters and returned values, while ordinary methods don't, a special attribute is used to denote Web Methods to the compiler. Almost incredibly, the attribute is called `WebMethod`. To denote a method as a Web Method, add the attribute in front of the method declaration, as shown in Listing 16-2.

Listing 16-2: **Declaring a Web Method**

```
[WebMethod]
public string MyWebMethod()
{
  return "yikes!";
}
```

There are no restrictions on the names you can use with Web Methods. Just remember to declare the method `public` and to use the `WebMethod` attribute. This attribute supports a number of parameters that can be useful. Table 16-1 describes these parameters.

Table 16-1: Parameters Supported by the WebMethod Attribute

Parameter	Default	Description
BufferResponse	true	Tells the ASP.NET Framework to buffer returned data and send it back in a single block.
CacheDuration	0	Number of seconds to cache the return value for a Web Service.
Description	" "	Optional text that will appear on the automatically generated page returned by the ASP.NET Framework when the Web Service's .asmx page is requested (as illustrated later in this chapter in Figure 16-7).
EnableSession	false	Enables state management by session.
MessageName	method name	Useful when a Web Method name is overloaded. The MessageName can help users distinguish between the different versions of methods with the same name.
TransactionOption	Disabled	Indicates whether the Web Method participates in a transaction.

When the CacheDuration property is true, the system will cache returned values. The arguments used to call the Web Service are used as a key to look up the cached return value, so the values returned by invoking the service with different parameters will be cached separately.

When EnableSession is set to true, the Web Method can store and retrieve state variables for each session using the Session property. Each session has its own variables.

When TransactionOption is set to Required or RequiresNew (both have the identical effect), the Web Method automatically starts a new transaction, using the distributed transaction model supported by the .NET Framework COM+ services.

Data in, data out

The simple Web Service described earlier, MyDateService, didn't take any parameters, and only returned a single object. Most of the time, Web Services need parameters and return one or more results. When a method call has arguments, the .NET Framework assumes they are input parameters by default. Listing 16-3 shows an example of a Web Method taking a single parameter.

Listing 16-3: A Simple Web Method

```
[WebMethod]
public string GetUpperCaseFor(string theName)
{
   return theName.ToUpper();
}
```

The parameter `theName` is used as an input parameter to the method. If you change the value of `theName` inside the method, the change will not be sent back to the client. The only thing the client will see is the returned value, which will be the uppercase version of the string submitted. Why doesn't a Web Method behave in the *normal* way? If you call a normal method passing a string value, a reference to the string is passed. Since the method and the caller reference the same string object, any changes made to the string inside the method will be visible to the caller.

Web Services work differently because any time you pass an object to a Web Method, the object is serialized, sent over the wire, and deserialized on the other end. Object references have no meaning once you cross a process boundary.

The .NET Framework is somewhat optimistic in terms of parameter passing. If you don't indicate otherwise, any parameters are assumed only to be inputs to the Web Method. The default mechanism for returning data from a Web Method is with a return value and a `return` statement. The object returned can be arbitrarily complex. The only requirement is that the object be serializable.

Since methods can only return a single object in their `return` statement, to pass multiple values back to the client you need to use the parameters in the method's argument list. By declaring parameters with the `ref` or `out` modifiers, it is possible to return any parameter in the argument list back to the client. Parameters using the `ref` modifier are assumed to contain a valid value on input, and a valid input on output to send back. Parameters using the `out` modifier are assumed to contain no information on input, but valid information on output. Listing 16-4 shows an example of how to use the `ref` and `out` modifiers.

Listing 16-4: Using ref Modifiers to Pass Multiple Values Back to the Client

```
[WebMethod]
public void ParseName(string theName,
                      ref string theFirstName,
                      ref string theLastName)
{
  theFirstName = "";
  theLastName = "";
  int i = theName.IndexOf(' ');
  if (i < 0) return;
  theFirstName = theName.Substring(0, i);
  theLastName = theName.Substring(i+1);
}
```

To call a method like this, you need to initialize the parameters `theFirstName` and `theLastName`, because the compiler expects them to contain data when calling the Web Method. You might call the method from the client application as shown in Listing 16-5.

Listing 16-5: Calling a Web Method Using ref Parameters

```
string firstName = "", lastName = "";
myService.ParseName("Bill Gates", ref firstName, ref lastName);
```

With the `ref` modifier, the .NET Framework passes the values of `firstName` and `lastName` to the Web Method. In the previous listing, this is a waste of time, since the Web Method over-writes the values when it returns. The `out` modifier solves the problem. Consider the Web Method declared in Listing 16-6.

Listing 16-6: A Web Method with out Parameters

```
[WebMethod]
public void ParseName(string theName,
                      out string theFirstName,
                      out string theLastName)
{
  theFirstName = "";
  theLastName = "";
  int i = theName.IndexOf(' ');
  if (i < 0) return;
  theFirstName = theName.Substring(0, i);
  theLastName = theName.Substring(i+1);
}
```

This method can be called without initializing the second and third parameters, as shown in Listing 16-7.

Listing 16-7: Calling a Web Method Using out Parameters

```
string firstName, lastName;
myService.ParseName("Bill Gates", out firstName, out lastName);
```

Since the compiler knows how the Web Method parameters are declared in the Web Service, is it possible to just omit the `ref` and `out` modifiers and let the compiler take care of the details? No. The C# folks decided that modifiers were too dangerous, so if a method is declared with arguments using `ref` or `out` modifiers, the caller must explicitly show the same modifiers on the call statement, to confirm knowledge about the presence of the modifiers, along with side effects the modifiers may entail.

The supporting cast

Web Services represent a quantum leap forward in terms of cross-vendor support and sim-plicity of deployment. At a minimum, Web Services only need a server running IIS, a client with a Web browser, a network connection between the two machines, and support for XML. Web Services can deliver any type of information to a client machine, and use standard HTTP and XML to do so. The overwhelming majority of machines these days have Internet or intranet connectivity and a Web browser, so little else is needed to support Web Services.

But there is a small problem. If Web Services are the answer to simplified distributed comput-ing, pretty soon we'll be up to our ears in Web Services. The challenge then will be how to locate a Web Service that solves a particular type of problem. Where do you look for the Web

Services providing data like geographic maps, census information, satellite imaging data, stock quotes, directory services, and so on? We need some kind of specialized Internet Search Engine to go out and locate Web Services using some criteria.

Before we can even think about searching for services, we need a way to describe Web Services, so there is something meaningful to search for. The goal is a simple Web Service description language, based on existing standards, that can describe the methods, arguments, and return values of the published methods of a Web Service. The description needs to be precise, leaving no room for interpretation. During the late 1990s and up to the first part of 2001, a number of competing languages were proposed, such as Soap Contract Language (SCL), Service Description Language (SDL), Web Services Description Language (WSDL), and a host of others. Major industry players such as Microsoft, IBM, Sun, and others have thrown their weight behind WSDL, so this language is the de facto standard for describing and advertising the features of Web Services.

The following sections describe WSDL and some of the related technologies used to make Web Services work.

SOAP

SOAP, an abbreviation for *Simple Object Access Protocol,* is an XML-based specification for making remote procedure calls over the Internet or an intranet. SOAP packets contain elements that specify the name of the method to invoke and the input parameters for that method. The returned data is passed back to the caller in a response SOAP packet. All data for input and output is serialized into characters suitable for transmission of the wire. While SOAP packets generally travel over TCP/IP networks using the HTTP protocol, the SOAP specification in no way restricts you to using just HTTP. In theory, you can send SOAP packets using raw TCP, or any other protocol, if you want.

Note Although SOAP messages can in principle travel over any wire protocol, .NET Web Services require the use of HTTP.

Listing 16-8 shows an example of a SOAP packet invoking a simple Web Service.

Listing 16-8: **A Simple SOAP Request Message**

```
<?xml version="1.0" encoding="utf-8"?>

<soap:Envelope xmlns:xsi="http://www.w3.org/2001/XMLSchema-instance"
               xmlns:xsd="http://www.w3.org/2001/XMLSchema"
               xmlns:soap="http://schemas.xmlsoap.org/soap/envelope/">
  <soap:Body>
    <GetDateAndTime xmlns="http://tempuri.org/" />
  </soap:Body>
</soap:Envelope>
```

The <Body> element contains the name of the method to invoke, plus any input parameters that may be needed. The response packet has a similar layout. The value returned by the method is put in an element with the name <%sResponse>, where %s is the name of the method. Listing 16-9 shows a simple SOAP response message.

Listing 16-9: A Simple SOAP Response Message

```xml
<?xml version="1.0" encoding="utf-8"?>

<soap:Envelope xmlns:xsi="http://www.w3.org/2001/XMLSchema-instance"
               xmlns:xsd="http://www.w3.org/2001/XMLSchema"
               xmlns:soap="http://schemas.xmlsoap.org/soap/envelope/">
  <soap:Body>
    <GetDateAndTimeResponse xmlns="http://tempuri.org/">
      <GetDateAndTimeResult>2001-10-18</GetDateAndTimeResult>
    </GetDateAndTimeResponse>
  </soap:Body>
</soap:Envelope>
```

Any data type that is serializable can be used in a SOAP message. Since most data types in the .NET Framework are serializable, you can use SOAP almost anywhere.

WSDL

What is WSDL? Simply put, it's an XML-based language that uses standard XMLSchema to describe the methods supported by a Web Service, including a detailed description of all the parameters required by each method and the values returned. WSDL is the Web equivalent of IDL, used with DCOM, and CORBA. Listing 16-10 shows highlights of the WSDL file associated with a Web Service that has a single GetDateAndTime() method.

Listing 16-10: The WSDL File for a Simple Web Service

```xml
<?xml version="1.0" encoding="utf-8"?>

<definitions xmlns:s="http://www.w3.org/2001/XMLSchema"
             xmlns:http="http://schemas.xmlsoap.org/wsdl/http/"
             xmlns:mime="http://schemas.xmlsoap.org/wsdl/mime/"
             xmlns:tm="http://microsoft.com/wsdl/mime/textMatching/"
             xmlns:soap="http://schemas.xmlsoap.org/wsdl/soap/"
             xmlns:soapenc="http://schemas.xmlsoap.org/soap/encoding/"
             xmlns:s0="http://tempuri.org/"
             targetNamespace="http://tempuri.org/"
             xmlns="http://schemas.xmlsoap.org/wsdl/">
  <types>
    <s:schema attributeFormDefault="qualified"
              elementFormDefault="qualified"
              targetNamespace="http://tempuri.org/">
      <s:element name="GetDateAndTime">
        <s:complexType />
      </s:element>
      <s:element name="GetDateAndTimeResponse">
        <s:complexType>
          <s:sequence>
            <s:element minOccurs="1" maxOccurs="1"
```

```
                        name="GetDateAndTimeResult"
                        type="s:dateTime" />
        </s:sequence>
      </s:complexType>
    </s:element>
    <s:element name="dateTime" type="s:dateTime" />
  </s:schema>
</types>

<message name="GetDateAndTimeSoapIn">
  <part name="parameters" element="s0:GetDateAndTime" />
</message>
<message name="GetDateAndTimeSoapOut">
  <part name="parameters" element="s0:GetDateAndTimeResponse" />
</message>
<message name="GetDateAndTimeHttpGetIn" />
<message name="GetDateAndTimeHttpGetOut">
  <part name="Body" element="s0:dateTime" />
</message>
<message name="GetDateAndTimeHttpPostIn" />
<message name="GetDateAndTimeHttpPostOut">
  <part name="Body" element="s0:dateTime" />
</message>
<portType name="MyDateServiceSoap">
  <operation name="GetDateAndTime">
    <input message="s0:GetDateAndTimeSoapIn" />
    <output message="s0:GetDateAndTimeSoapOut" />
  </operation>
</portType>
<portType name="MyDateServiceHttpGet">
  <operation name="GetDateAndTime">
    <input message="s0:GetDateAndTimeHttpGetIn" />
    <output message="s0:GetDateAndTimeHttpGetOut" />
  </operation>
</portType>
<portType name="MyDateServiceHttpPost">
  <operation name="GetDateAndTime">
    <input message="s0:GetDateAndTimeHttpPostIn" />
    <output message="s0:GetDateAndTimeHttpPostOut" />
  </operation>
</portType>

<binding name="MyDateServiceSoap" type="s0:MyDateServiceSoap">
  <soap:binding transport="http://schemas.xmlsoap.org/soap/http"
                style="document" />
  <operation name="GetDateAndTime">
    <soap:operation soapAction="http://tempuri.org/GetDateAndTime"
                    style="document" />
    <input>
      <soap:body use="literal" />
    </input>
    <output>
```

Continued

Listing 16-10 *(continued)*

```
        <soap:body use="literal" />
      </output>
    </operation>
  </binding>

  <binding name="MyDateServiceHttpGet"
           type="s0:MyDateServiceHttpGet">
    <http:binding verb="GET" />
    <operation name="GetDateAndTime">
      <http:operation location="/GetDateAndTime" />
      <input>
        <http:urlEncoded />
      </input>
      <output>
        <mime:mimeXml part="Body" />
      </output>
    </operation>
  </binding>

  <binding name="MyDateServiceHttpPost"
           type="s0:MyDateServiceHttpPost">
    <http:binding verb="POST" />
    <operation name="GetDateAndTime">
      <http:operation location="/GetDateAndTime" />
      <input>
        <mime:content type="application/x-www-form-urlencoded" />
      </input>
      <output>
        <mime:mimeXml part="Body" />
      </output>
    </operation>
  </binding>

  <service name="MyDateService">
    <port name="MyDateServiceSoap" binding="s0:MyDateServiceSoap">
      <soap:address
          location="http://localhost/MyWebService/Service1.asmx" />
    </port>
    <port name="MyDateServiceHttpGet"
          binding="s0:MyDateServiceHttpGet">
      <http:address
          location="http://localhost/MyWebService/Service1.asmx" />
    </port>
    <port name="MyDateServiceHttpPost"
          binding="s0:MyDateServiceHttpPost">
      <http:address
          location="http://localhost/MyWebService/Service1.asmx" />
    </port>
  </service>
</definitions>
```

Reading a WSDL file is about as interesting as watching grass grow. WSDL files were designed to be read by component-based development tools like VS .NET — not by people. WSDL files are also known as *service contracts,* because they declare exactly what a service will do, what inputs are required, and what information is returned. WSDL is only part of the Web Services infrastructure. In order to use WSDL files that describe a Web Service, you obviously have to locate the server that offers the service. If your software only uses Web Services that you develop, no problem: You already know where the services are. The real power of Web Services as a distributed computing technology will be achieved only if there is a way to make your Web Services available to others outside your organization.

DISCO

Assuming you know the name or IP address of a machine that contains Web Services, how do you determine which Web Services are available on the machine? The answer is with DISCO, a discovery document format that can be easily accessed by automatic discovery tools such as VS .NET. DISCO files are XML documents stored in files with the suffix *.disco*. They don't contain descriptions of Web Services, but rather have references to other XML files where further Web Service descriptions are available. The most important references are the WSDL files for each Web Service available on the server.

A single DISCO file can reference any number of Web Services. Listing 16-11 shows a DISCO file that supports the automated discovery of three Web Services.

Listing 16-11: **An Example of a DISCO File Referencing Three Web Services**

```xml
<?xml version="1.0" ?>

<disco:discovery xmlns:disco="http://schemas.xmlsoap.org/disco"
                 xmlns:scl="http://schemas.xmlsoap.org/disco/scl">

  <scl:contractRef ref="http://MyWebServer/WebService1.asmx?WSDL"/>
  <scl:contractRef ref="http://MyWebServer/WebService2.asmx?WSDL"/>
  <scl:contractRef ref="http://MyWebServer/WebService3.asmx?WSDL"/>

  <disco:discoveryRef ref="SomeFolder/default.disco" />

</disco:discovery>
```

One DISCO document can also reference others. For example, Listing 16-12 shows a DISCO document that references one Web Service and two other DISCO documents.

Listing 16-12: **Referencing Web Services and Other DISCO Documents**

```xml
<?xml version="1.0" ?>

<disco:discovery xmlns:disco="http://schemas.xmlsoap.org/disco"
```

Continued

Listing 16-12 *(continued)*

```
                     xmlns:scl="http://schemas.xmlsoap.org/disco/scl">

   <scl:contractRef ref="http://MyWebServer/WebService1.asmx?WSDL"/>

   <disco:discoveryRef ref=" http://MyOtherWebServer/GoodStuff.disco" />
   <disco:discoveryRef ref=" http://MyOtherWebServer/OldStuff.disco" />

   </disco:discovery>
```

I'll show how to use DISCO files a bit later in the chapter, in the section titled "Publishing dynamic-discovery information."

UDDI

DISCO is useful when you know which server has the Web Services you're interested in, and when you just want to locate the Service Contracts (WSDL files) for them. When you don't have any idea what servers might contain them, or you don't even know if the Web Services you're looking for even exist, DISCO is of no help. What is needed is a way to publish Web Services on the Web, and some tools to locate Web Services of interest. A bonus would be to have a tool-based way to integrate Web Services into your applications.

Enter UDDI, for *Universal Description, Discovery, and Integration,* an XML-based specification that solves all these problems. The idea behind UDDI is to have a way to publish information in a standard format for businesses to use to find Web Services and companies supporting a given type of service. The UDDI specification is supported by a wide variety of industry leaders, such as IBM, Microsoft, Sun Microsystems, HP, Oracle, Software AG, SAP, and a long list of others. The latest specification (2.0) was published in June 2001.

While UDDI is a specification, there is also a Web site at www.uddi.org that acts as a world-wide registry of Web Services that use UDDI. The site contains a Business Directory that is electronically searchable, allowing you to quickly and easily locate published Web Services, based on business sector, features, and other searchable items. UDDI is the equivalent of the Yellow Pages for Web Services.

UDDI describes Web Services using five main categories:

- ✦ Business Information
- ✦ Service Information
- ✦ Binding Information
- ✦ Service Specification Information
- ✦ Publisher Assertions

Details of the UDDI specification are beyond the scope of this book, but to give you just a taste of it, Listing 16-13 shows a UDDI code fragment describing Business Information.

Listing 16-13: XML Code Providing Business Information

```
<businessDetail generic="2.0"
                operator="uddi.sourceOperator"
                truncated="true"
                xmlns="urn:uddi-org:api_v2">
   <businessEntity businessKey="F5E654748C383A94BE933A45B70698CF"
                authorizedName="Jonathan Swift"
                operator="uddi.MyCompany" >
                ... other attributes ...
   </businessEntity>
   ... other businessEntity elements ...
</businessDetail>
```

Registered businesses and services are assigned a unique ID by the UDDI Organization. These IDs are similar to the GUIDs (Globally Unique Identifiers) used to uniquely identify COM interfaces and objects. In the previous listing, the businessKey attribute provides the ID assigned to a published business.

A very important part of UDDI is the description of published services, in terms of interfaces, methods, and parameters. WSDL can and should be used for this part, allowing tools (such as VS .NET) to automatically generate proxy components to bind to the services without requiring any manual coding.

Developing a Web Service

It's time to leave specifications, languages, and standards behind, and to look at how to build a real Web Service. In this section, I'll create a simple Web Service that returns the date and time, as a DateTime object. Any serializable type can be passed to and returned from a Web Service, so types like Integers, Strings, Booleans, and Chars can all be used. Arrays are also allowed, as long as the array elements are serializable. As stated earlier, most of the types in the .NET Framework are serializable, so you should be able to use Web Services in a wide range of scenarios.

I'll call the service *MyWebService*. Keep in mind that Web Services are bona fide components, so they are instantiated by calling a constructor and garbage-collected when no longer used. All Web Services are derived from the standard class System.Web.Services.WebService. Figure 16-4 shows the class diagram for MyWebService.

In terms of implementation, the easiest way to create a Web Service is with the VS .NET New Project Wizard, by selecting the ASP.NET Web Service template, as shown in Figure 16-5.

The wizard sets up an empty Web Service. Notice how I used *localhost* for the server name of the Web Service. You can develop Web Services on remote hosts, but it's usually easier to work on your own machine and deploy the Web Service to the production machine when you're done. I'll show how to do this a bit later in the chapter.

The Web Service Wizard creates a new project containing the file called Service1.asmx, which contains the Web Service class and its Web Methods. Figure 16-6 shows the files generated by the wizard.

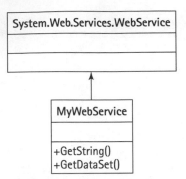

Figure 16-4: The simple class diagram for MyWebService

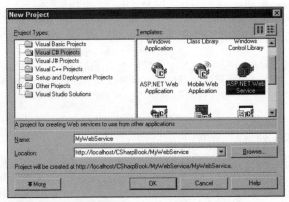

Figure 16-5: Using the New Project Wizard to create a new Web Service

Figure 16-6: The files created by the wizard for a Web Service project

The only job left is to add the Web Methods for clients to call. I'll just add one method, `GetDateAndTime()`, as shown in Listing 16-14.

Listing 16-14: Adding a Simple Web Method to a Web Service

```
[WebMethod]
public string GetDateAndTime(string theUserName)
{
  return "Hi " + theUserName +
         ". The current time is " +
         DateTime.Now;
}
```

The Web Method was added to the Web Service's .asmx.cs file. The wizard creates a dummy Web Method for you in a comment section. The dummy method shows how to declare a Web Method, with the WebMethod attribute. Other than this attribute, Web Methods are exactly like ordinary methods. Just remember that data types used in the argument list and the return value of a Web Method must be serializable.

Testing the Web Service

There are three basic ways to test Web Services:

✦ Using VS .NET's internal Web browser

✦ Using a custom Web application

✦ Using a custom Windows application

Each method has pros and cons, so the one you should choose depends on what you need to test on the Web Service. It's not that Web Services are hard to test. It's just interesting to see how to access Web Services from the three types of applications you are most likely to use. I'll discuss all three methods in the following sections.

Testing with the VS .NET internal Web browser

VS .NET has the ability to dynamically generate HTML pages to test Web Services. The pages enable you to invoke each exposed method, passing parameters to it, and then see the data returned from the method as an XML document. VS .NET uses the service's .wsdl file to get a description of each method exposed by the service. With this information, it discovers what parameters the methods use, plus the parameter names and types. No matter how simple or complex your Web Service is, you should always use the built-in browser to test every method exposed, because you can do preliminary testing without the need to create a separate test fixture.

To start the built-in browser, right-click on the Service1.asmx file in the Solution Explorer and select the View In Browser command. A browser tab will appear in the project tab, displaying an automatically generated HTML page describing the Web Service, as shown in Figure 16-7.

Notice the line I highlighted near the top of the page. The text comes from the WebService attribute I used with the Web Service class declaration. The attribute was used as shown in Listing 16-15.

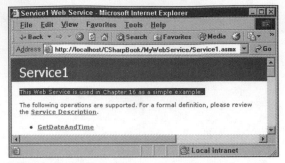

Figure 16-7: The HTML test page listing the Web Methods available in a Web Service

Listing 16-15: **Adding a Custom Description for a Web Service**

```
[WebService(Description="This Web Service is used in Chapter
                        16 as a simple example.")]
public class Service1 : System.Web.Services.WebService
{
    ...
}
```

Back in Figure 16-7, also notice the text right under the GetDateAndTime hyperlink. This text also comes from an attribute, but this time from a WebMethod attribute. The attribute was used as shown in Listing 16-16.

Listing 16-16: **Adding a Custom Description for a Web Method**

```
[WebMethod(Description="Returns your name with the current time") ]
public string GetDateAndTime(string theUserName)
{
    ...
}
```

The HTML page shown previously in Figure 16-7 has a hyperlink for each method exposed. Clicking on the link takes you to another automatically generated test page where you can enter parameters to pass to the method. For example, clicking on the GetDateAndTime link displays the page shown in Figure 16-8.

The custom description for the Web Method is also displayed on this page, as shown by the highlighted text in the figure. Entering the value **Ted** for the input parameter theUserName and clicking the Invoke button displays the results of the method call as an XML document, as shown in Figure 16-9.

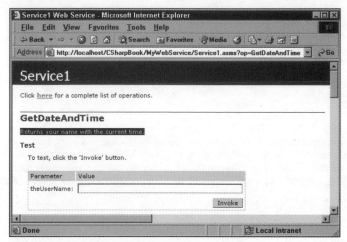

Figure 16-8: The HTML test page for testing Web Service methods

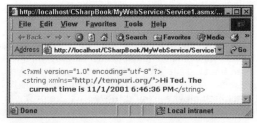

Figure 16-9: The results of the Web Method call, displayed as an XML document

To invoke the method, the browser simply takes the parameter entered and then issues an HTTP GET message with the following URI (I split the URI into two lines to make it easier to read):

```
http://localhost/CSharpBook/MyWebService/Service1.asmx/
GetDateAndTime?theUserName=Ted
```

Where the browser test pages come from

You might be wondering something: Where the heck did the HTML pages shown in Figures 16-7 and 16-8 come from? I said they were automatically generated, but by which program? Did VS .NET generate them? No, the ASP.NET Framework did, using the HTTP Handler devoted to .asmx page requests. Check out the machine.config file and you'll find the code shown in Listing 16-17.

> **Listing 16-17: A Fragment of the machine.config File, Defining the HTTP Handler for .asmx Page Requests**

```
<configuration>
  <httpHandlers>
    <add
      verb="*"
      path="*.asmx"
      type="System.Web.Services.Protocols.WebServiceHandlerFactory,
          ... />
</configuration>
```

As you can see, the `WebServiceHandlerFactory` component processes all requests for .asmx pages. When a request for a .asmx page is received without any parameters, the handler returns a dynamically built page with the Web Service methods listed as hyperlinks, as shown previously in Figure 16-7. Clicking on one of these hyperlinks causes a new URI to be requested, like this:

```
http://localhost/CSharpBook/MyWebService/Service1.asmx?
op=GetDateAndTime
```

When `WebServiceHandlerFactory` sees the `op` parameter in the request, it returns a dynamically generated page that enables you to enter the method's input parameters to test the method with, as shown previously in Figure 16-8.

Debugging with the built-in browser

You can not only call Web Methods, but also debug them with the built-in browser, without the need to create a separate test fixture. First set breakpoints in the Web Service code and then run the code using the built-in browser. Clicking the Invoke button will activate your Web Service and trigger any breakpoints you may have set. Whether the Web Service is running on your own local machine or on a machine halfway around the world, the procedure is the same. If the Web Service is on a remote machine, just make sure you have the necessary privileges to update and run code on that machine.

Testing with a Web application

In this section, I'll show you how to access a Web Service from a Web application. I created a simple Web application called *MyWebApplication*. I added a Button component on its main Web Form, with the caption *Invoke,* and a Label field for displaying the text returned from the Web Service. The Web Form is shown in Figure 16-10.

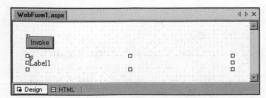

Figure 16-10: The simple Web Service test page in the Web application

Before adding code to call MyWebService, you need to create a local proxy of the Web Service. The proxy lets you call the remote Web Service methods using a local component. To add the proxy to the Web application, right-click on the application in the Solution Explorer and select Add Web Reference from the pop-up menu. The Add Web Reference Wizard will appear. Enter the URI of the Web Service you want to add, as shown in Figure 16-11.

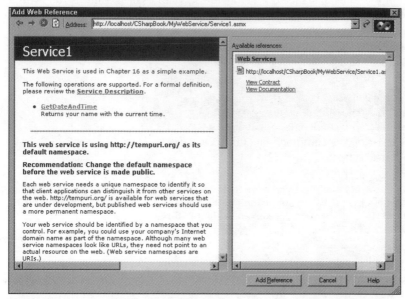

Figure 16-11: Using the Add Web Reference Wizard to automatically create a local proxy for a remote Web Service

You'll need to use the Add Web Reference Wizard even if the Web Service is running on your local machine. Once you have located the Web Service you want to use, click the Add Reference button. The wizard will add a number of files to the Solution Explorer, as shown in Figure 16-12.

Figure 16-12: The Web Reference files added to the Solution Explorer

An important file is the .wsdl file, which is the service contract describing the methods and parameters of the Web Service. Using this file, a local proxy class is created and stored in the file Service1.cs. This class is a regular C# class that you access from the client application.

Any methods of it that you invoke are invisibly passed over a network connection to the remote Web Service component. The local proxy component completely hides the fact that the Web Service is not a local object.

There is a command-line utility you can use to convert .wsdl or .xsd files into proxy classes. The utility is called *wsdl.exe*. When running it, you need to supply the URI of the .asmx, .wsdl, or .xsd file. For example, to manually generate the Service1.cs file created earlier with the Add Web Reference Wizard, you could use wsdl.exe with the URI as shown in Figure 16-13.

Figure 16-13: Using the command-line utility wsdl.exe to create local proxy classes

After adding the Web Reference, you have to add a Web Service reference to the Web application. Just right-click on the Web application in the Solution Explorer and choose Add Reference from the pop-up menu, as shown in Figure 16-14.

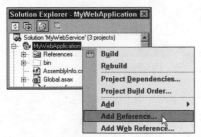

Figure 16-14: Adding a Web Service reference to the Web application

The Add Reference Wizard will start. Go to the Projects tab. If the Web Service is not listed at the top, click the Browse button and locate it. Then click the Select button. The Web Service will then be added to the Selected Components list, as shown in Figure 16-15.

Before you can call the Web Service from the Web application, there is one last step: You have to import its namespace into any files that reference the Web Service. In the WebForm1.aspx file of MyWebApplication, I added the following line:

```
using MyWebService;
```

Then I created a Click handler for the Invoke button. In the handler, I added a couple of lines of code to call the Web Service, as shown in Listing 16-18.

Running the Web application code, you get a simple Web page with an Invoke button. Clicking the button provokes a call to the Web Service. The response is displayed on the page, as shown in Figure 16-16.

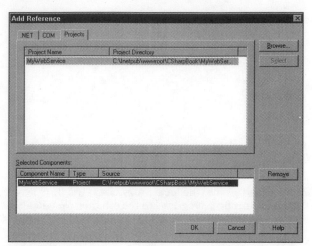

Figure 16-15: Using the Add Reference Wizard to add a reference to a Web Service

---

Listing 16-18: Invoking MyWebService from a Web Application

```
private void Button1_Click(object sender, System.EventArgs e)
{
  Service1 service = new Service1();
  LabelResponse.Text = service.GetDateAndTime("Ted");
}
```

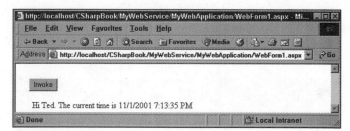

Figure 16-16: The response from the Web Service, displayed on a Web Form

That's all there is to it. You can set breakpoints in the Web application code and step seamlessly across process boundaries into the Web Service code. All the normal debugging tools, such as stack traces, watches, and variable browsing, are available.

If you make changes to the interface of a Web Service, you'll need to also update the local proxy object. To do so, right-click on server in the Solution Explorer and select Update Web Reference from the pop-up menu, as shown in Figure 16-17.

Figure 16-17: Using the Solution Explorer to update a Web Reference

A new .wsdl file (the Service Contract) and .cs file (the local proxy class) will be generated in the client application. Changes that require client programs to refresh their Web References include the following:

✦ Adding, renaming, or deleting a Web Method

✦ Changing the argument list of a Web Method

Keep in mind that VS .NET doesn't automatically generate a new Service Contract when you make changes to a Web Service — even if the service is part of a solution that also contains the test fixture. It's up to you to know when a Web Reference needs to be updated, based on the changes made to the service.

Testing with a Windows Application

Using a Windows Application to test a Web Service is also quite straightforward. I created a simple program called *MyWindowsApplication*. As with Web applications, you have to add a couple of references to a Windows Application before you can call any Web Service methods.

Using the guidelines outlined in the previous section, add a Web Reference to the application and then add a Reference to the Web Service's DLL. To the Windows Form of the application, I added a Button and Label, as in the previous example. At the top of the file Form1.cs, I added the following line:

```
using MyWebService;
```

I created a `Click` handler for the button and added the code shown in Listing 16-19.

Listing 16-19: Calling the Web Service from a Windows Application

```
private void button1_Click(object sender, System.EventArgs e)
{
  Service1 service = new Service1();
  labelResponse.Text = service.GetDateAndTime("Ted");
}
```

As you can see, the code is virtually identical to the code used in the Web application. When you click the Invoke button, the form shows the Web Service results, as shown in Figure 16-18.

Figure 16-18: How the Web
Service results look in a
Windows Application

There are no weird rules to remember when accessing Web Methods. Once the local proxy object is created for the Web Service (using the Add Web Reference command), calling Web Methods is just like calling ordinary local methods. The expression *"Vive la différence"* may apply to many things in this world, but not software and component architectures. In the software world, conformance is good, because it reduces the number of things you need to remember. In the .NET world of Web Services, the way you call a method is always the same, whether the method is local or remote.

Maintaining state

Many Web Services need to track state information for each client. Web Services can use `Session` and `Application` variables to store state information, in much the same way as Web applications. The `Session` and `Application` objects themselves are inherited from the base class of all Web Service components, `WebService`, as shown in the class diagram in Figure 16-19.

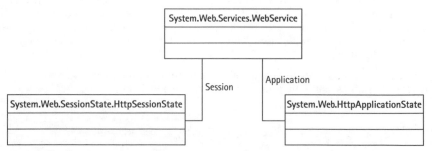

Figure 16-19: The Session and Application objects in the WebService base class

By default, all Web Methods have access to `Application` variables. To get access to `Session` variables, you need to declare a method with the `MebMethod` attribute and set the `EnableSession` parameter, as shown in Listing 16-20.

Listing 16-20: Enabling a Web Method to Access Session Variables

```
[WebMethod(EnableSession=true) ]
public string MyWebMethod()
{
   ...
}
```

With `Application` or `Session` variables, I highly recommend encapsulating read and write access to them using properties, because all variable stored are assumed to be of type `Object` (or derived from it). Properties not only reduce the amount of typecasting in your code, but also let the compiler help check for type errors, since the properties return typed information. Listing 16-21 shows how you might store and retrieve a `DateTime Session` variable using properties.

Listing 16-21: Using Properties to Protect Session Variables from Direct Access

```
private DateTime LastTimeUserInvokedMethod
{
  get
  {
    if (Session ["LastInvocationTime"] == null)
      return DateTime.Now;
    else
      return (DateTime) Session ["LastInvocationTime"];
  }
  set {Session ["LastInvocationTime"] = value;}
}
```

You don't normally need to take any special precautions to protect against simultaneous access to `Session` variables, since the ASP.NET Framework assigns a different session to each calling client. However, if clients are multithreaded, and can originate requests from concurrent threads, then you will have to use thread-locking mechanisms around operations that write `Session` variables. See Chapter 20, titled "Multithreaded Components," for details on thread synchronization techniques.

Listing 16-22 shows how a Web Service might use a session-enabled Web Method to read and write `Session` variables using the properties shown previously in Listing 16-21.

Listing 16-22: A Web Method Using Session Variables

```
[WebMethod(EnableSession=true) ]
public string GetDateAndTime(string theUserName)
   {
     string s = "You previously invoked this method at " +
                LastTimeUserInvokedMethod.ToString();
     LastTimeUserInvokedMethod = DateTime.Now;
     return s;
}
```

You can also store variables at the `Application` level, which gives them global scope. These types of variables are shared across all calls to your Web Service, from any client machine. Since concurrent access to a Web Service is possible from different clients, code that writes `Application` variables must be wrapped using `Lock()` and `UnLock()` calls. Listing 16-23 shows how you might use properties to protect `Application` variables from direct access.

Listing 16-23: Using Properties to Protect Application Variables from Direct Access

```
private int NumberOfHits
{
  get
  {
    if (Application ["NumberOfHits"] == null)
      return 1;
    else
      return (int) Application ["NumberOfHits"];
  }
  set
  {
    Application.Lock();
    Application ["NumberOfHits"] = value;
    Application.UnLock();
  }
}
```

By using properties to wrap access to Application variables, the only place you need to put the locking mechanism is in the set methods. The rest of the code is not affected. Listing 16-24 shows how you might use Application variables in a Web Method, using the properties defined earlier.

Listing 16-24: A Web Method Using Application Variables

```
[WebMethod]
public string Ping()
{
  string s = "Number of hits = " + NumberOfHits;
  NumberOfHits = NumberOfHits + 1;
  return s;
}
```

You don't have to declare Web Methods with any special attributes, because all Web Methods have access to Application variables.

Security

You may have reasons to restrict the use of a Web Service to a group of people. Maybe you only want a limited number of trusted people to access it, or maybe you only let registered users or paying customers access it. What you need is some sort of security model that can keep unwanted people out. To this end, Web Services support a number of authentication and authorization techniques. For more details, see Chapter 17, titled "Security."

Publishing dynamic-discovery information

When using the Add Web Reference Wizard, it would be nice to simply type in a Web site address and obtain a listing of all the Web Services available on that site. Such a mechanism would facilitate dynamic-discovery of Web Services. Sure, UDDI is one way to find Web Services, but your organization may publish Web Services for internal use without publishing them in a UDDI registry. What you need is a simple way to just get a list of the Web Services available on a given server or Web site. As it turns out, the folks at Microsoft gave thought to this type of dynamic discovery and came up with a couple ways to support it. Both methods use DISCO files, described earlier in the section titled "DISCO."

The first method requires prospective clients to know the URI of your DISCO file. Let's say you have a Web site at `http://localhost/MyWebSite` that has two Web Services in different folders that you want to publish for dynamic discovery. Say the two Web Service URIs are

```
http://localhost/MyWebSite/WebService1/Service1.asmx
http://localhost/MyWebSite/WebService2/Service2.asmx
```

To enable automated DISCO discovery of the services, you need to create a file with the .disco suffix and put it in the root folder of the Web site, which in my example is `http://localhost/MyWebSite`. Listing 16-25 shows the contents of the .disco file.

Listing 16-25: The .disco File that Enables Dynamic Discovery of Two Web Services

```
<?xml version="1.0" ?>

<disco:discovery xmlns:disco="http://schemas.xmlsoap.org/disco"
                 xmlns:scl="http://schemas.xmlsoap.org/disco/scl">
   <scl:contractRef ref="http://localhost/MyWebSite/
                         WebService1/Service1.asmx?WSDL"/>
   <scl:contractRef ref="http://localhost/MyWebSite/
                         WebService2/Service2.asmx?WSDL"/>
</disco:discovery>
```

If the .disco file is named AvailableServices.disco, then clients will need to use the following URL to discover the Web Services on your Web site:

```
http://localhost/MyWebSite/AvailableServices.disco
```

While this .disco file works in terms of supporting dynamic Web Service discovery, it doesn't represent a perfect solution, because it requires prospective customers to know the name of your .disco file.

The second DISCO method allows clients to discover the Web Services on your Web site without knowing the name of the .disco file: All they need to know is the URL of the server. The idea is to embed a reference to your .disco file on the default page of the Web site. If the default page is an HTML document, which is the typical case, then add the boldface lines in Listing 16-26 to the document's HEAD section.

Listing 16-26: Adding a Reference to a DISCO File to an HTML Page

```
<HEAD>
<link type='text/xml'
      rel='alternate'
      href='AvailableServices.disco'/>
</HEAD>
```

If the default page for your Web site is an XML document, then add the lines in Listing 16-27 to the document.

Listing 16-27: Adding a Reference to a DISCO File in an XML Page

```
<?xml-stylesheet type="text/xml"
                 alternate="yes"
                 href="'AvailableServices.disco" ?>
```

The `href` attribute used in both HTML and XML documents can be a relative path, as shown in the listing, or a complete URL, such as `http://www.acme.com/services.disco`.

The .NET Framework includes a command-line utility you can use to extract Web Services published in .disco files. Almost incredibly, the utility is called disco.exe. To use it, you need to enter the URL of a .disco file using commands like the ones shown in Listing 16-28.

Listing 16-28: Using the Command-Line Utility to Discover Web Services

```
disco http://www.acme.com/services.disco
disco http://localhost/CSharpBook/AvailableServices.disco
```

Remember that .disco files can also reference other .disco files. In such cases, disco.exe will recursively search the referenced .disco files as well.

Transferring a Web Service to a production machine

Once you're finished testing your Web Service on a development computer, you may want to move it to the production server. There are three ways to do this:

✦ Manually copying the necessary files

✦ Using the Copy Project command

✦ Deploying the project on the production machine

The manual process requires you to identify all the files and folders of the Web Service and to copy them to the production machine. Not all the files listed in the VS .NET Solution Explorer need to be copied, if all you want to do is run the Web Service on the production machine. For example, you may not want to copy the VS .NET solution file and project file (that have the suffixes .sln and .csproj, respectively). These two files are only required to manage and build the Web Service executable. If you're not sure which files to copy, just copy them all.

A better way is to use the Copy Project command. To run the command, select the Web Service project in the Solution Explorer, and then click the Copy Project button on the Solution Explorer toolbar, as shown in Figure 16-20.

Figure 16-20: The Copy Project button on the Solution Explorer toolbar

The Copy Project dialog box will appear. In the Destination project folder edit box, enter the name of the production server, as shown in Figure 16-21.

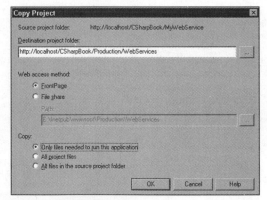

Figure 16-21: Copying an entire Web Service to a production machine

Make sure the production server has ASP.NET installed, in addition to FrontPage Extensions. The three radio buttons at the bottom of the Copy Project dialog box let you specify which files to copy. The first option is probably the one you'll use most often. It just copies the files that client machines will need to run the Web Service, such as the DLL file and a few other support files. The All project files option copies all the files and folders listed in the Solution Explorer, including the .sln and .csproj files. The last option copies everything in the project folder, including temporary files, documentation files, and anything else that might be there.

After copying the Web Service to the production server, make sure to update the client programs, so they reference the new machine. For each client, delete both the Web Reference and the reference to the old Web Service, and then run the Add Web Reference and Add Reference wizards again, indicating the Web Service on the new production server.

If the Web Service requires changing Registry, IIS, security, or other settings, the Copy Project command won't be sufficient to set up the Web Service on the new production machine. What you'll need to do is deploy the Web Service, rather than copy it, to the new machine. See Chapter 6, titled "Deployment," for further details.

Windows Services

Most programmers are familiar with Windows Services (formally called NT Services), not because they ever developed one, but by having used them in the Windows environment. To UNIX programmers, services are better known as *daemons*. Simply put, a *service* is an application that can be started in three different ways:

- ✦ By the system, for example at startup time
- ✦ By an application, via calls to the Windows Service Control Manager
- ✦ By a user, using the Microsoft Management Console Services snap-in

Services are different from normal applications in many ways. For starters, they tend to run for a long time, often for the entire duration of a Windows session. They don't appear on the TaskBar when they are running, but they sometimes show up in the Service Tray, which is the little box in the lower right corner of the screen where the time-of-day is usually displayed. In fact, the time-of-day program is a service.

Services are usually programs that are run in the background, to carry out tasks that don't involve interaction with a user. For this reason, they generally don't have a user interface, and don't display message boxes or other information on the screen. If a service needs to inform the system of unusual events or errors, it normally logs a message in the Windows Event Log, which administrators can view with the Windows Event Viewer.

Because Windows Services have the ability to be started before anyone is logged into the system, they run in their own Windows session, using either a built-in system account or a predetermined user account. A session might be set up to run with Administrator privileges, if it needs to access sensitive information on the computer. If a user logs on to the system using a different user account, perhaps one with limited privileges, Windows will treat the new user and the running service differently, maintaining the required limits on the user while letting the service run with unlimited privileges. Programs running on servers, designed only to handle requests from local or remote client programs, are often run as services. The Microsoft Internet Information Service is a well-known Windows Service of this type.

Since Windows Services are .exe application programs (albeit with special features), the executable programs containing them are also known currently as *Windows Service Applications (WSA)*. Figure 16-22 shows the inheritance diagram for a simple service.

The `ServiceName` property contains the name to be displayed in the Services snap-in. The `AutoLog` property, which defaults to `true`, allows the service to automatically log important events to the Application Log in the Windows Event Log. Important events include starting a service, stopping a service, and errors detected when starting and stopping a service.

The remaining `ServiceBase` properties determine which types of events the service can handle. `Power` events occur when the computer's power situation changes, such as low-battery conditions, changing from normal power to backup power, and so on. `CanHandlePauseAndContinue` indicates the service can be put into a `Paused` state. Set the property `CanShutdown` to `true` if you want the service to receive notification when power is about to be shutdown. `CanStop` indicates if the service is allowed to be stopped.

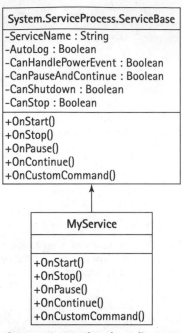

Figure 16-22: The class diagram for a simple service

The main events that apply to services are OnStart, OnPause, OnStop, and OnContinue. OnCustomCommand allows additional commands to be sent to the service. The event carries an integer argument, indicating which of 128 possible custom commands to execute.

As stated earlier, Windows Services are activated and run by the Windows Service Control Manager (SCM), which makes a call to the .NET Framework, which in turn calls the Main() method of the WSA. This method contains the code that instantiates the service component and loads the component into the SCM. If the service's StartupType is set to automatic, the OnStart handler is called shortly afterwards. When a service needs to be shut down, the SCM calls into the .NET Framework, which calls the service's OnStop handler. The UML interaction diagram in Figure 16-23 shows the details.

Note   Loading and starting a service are two entirely different things. When a service is loaded, it isn't started unless its StartupType is set to automatic. If the StartupType is manual, the service is usually started by opening the MMC Services snap-in and clicking the Start button for the service.

Listing 16-29 shows the Main() method of a simple Windows Service Application. Before you spend a lot of time memorizing the code, I should point out that this code is generated automatically using the VS .NET New Project Wizard.

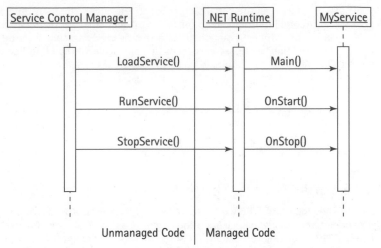

Figure 16-23: How a Windows Service is activated, run, and stopped

---

Listing 16-29: **The Main() Method of a Simple Windows Service Application**

```
public class WinService1 : System.ServiceProcess.ServiceBase
{
  static void Main()
  {
    System.ServiceProcess.ServiceBase[] ServicesToRun;
    ServicesToRun = new System.ServiceProcess.ServiceBase[]
                { new WinService1() };
    System.ServiceProcess.ServiceBase.Run(ServicesToRun);
  }
}
```

It isn't unusual for a WSA to contain more than one service. In this case, all the services can be instantiated at once and run together. If you had a WSA that contained three services, its Main() method might look like this:

```
public class WinService1 : System.ServiceProcess.ServiceBase
{
  static void Main()
  {
    System.ServiceProcess.ServiceBase[] ServicesToRun;
    ServicesToRun = new System.ServiceProcess.ServiceBase[]
                { new WinService1() };
                { new WinService2() };
                { new WinService3() };
    System.ServiceProcess.ServiceBase.Run(ServicesToRun);
  }
}
```

When you call `ServiceBase.Run()`, all the constructors for the services you identified are called. The SCM poses a 30 second limit on startup for each service. Most services can be started and stopped any number of times. The constructor is only called once, when the service is initially loaded. If you plan to release resources in a service's `OnStop` handler, then allocate those resources in the `OnStart` handler. If you allocate them in the constructor, you'll run into trouble when the service is stopped and then restarted, because the resources will be gone.

If your service initialization may take a while, you might want to use a second thread to do the lengthy part. The `OnStart` handler's thread would then start a background worker thread to perform all the service initialization and return immediately. Most services use one or more worker threads to carry out their work in the background.

Designing the service

In this section and the following ones, I'll lay out the whole development process for a simple service called *MyBeeperService*. As always, I'll keep the example as small as possible, to focus on the overall process without getting too caught up in the details. I'll design the service to issue a beep once a second. I'll also show you how to display an icon in the System Tray, indicating the status (running, paused, or stopped) of the service. I'll even throw in a custom Service Control Program (SCP) that lets you control the service through a custom interface. Figure 16-24 shows how MyBeeperService shows up in the Services snap-in.

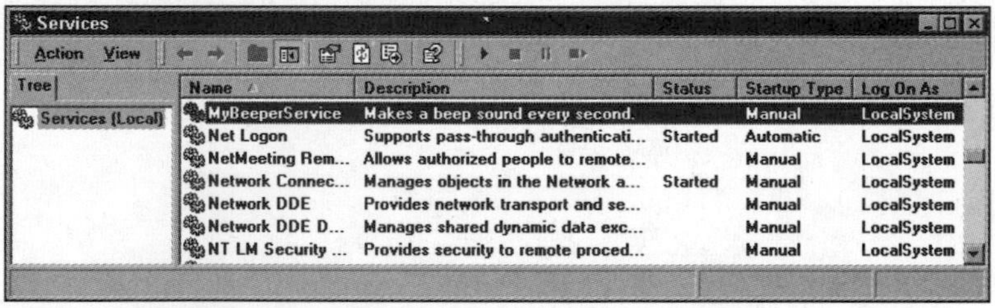

Figure 16-24: How MyBeeperService appears in the Services snap-in

While beeping is certainly not an earth-shattering breakthrough, the example should be useful as a point of departure for those of you who are interested in developing your own services.

Debugging components running as services can be challenging, because you can't run the service from the VS .NET environment. You need to install the service and start it with SCM. To simplify debugging, a simple design strategy is to put all service's core functionality into a separate component (not derived from any of the Service classes), so you can test it with a simple test fixture application. The class diagram in Figure 16-25 shows the design for MyBeeperService, in which the class `MyBeeper` implements the core functionality of the service.

As you can see, the service will respond to `OnStart`, `OnPause`, `OnStop`, `OnContinue`, and `OnCustomCommand` events. For each of these events, it simply delegates to `MyBeeperComponent`. The `OnCustomCommand` handler calls `UseBeepType1()`, passing it a parameter. The main idea here is for MyBeeperService to do as little as possible, since it is difficult to debug. `MyBeeperComponent` contains the real code, and can be tested easily with a simple test fixture.

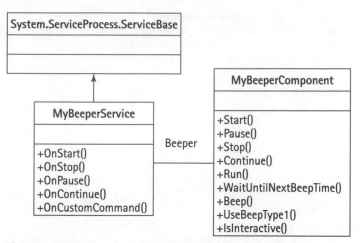

Figure 16-25: The class diagram for MyBeeperService

In the next section, I'll set up a Windows Service project for MyBeeperService and create `MyBeeperComponent`. Later, for testing purposes, I'll create a separate test fixture application to test `MyBeeperComponent` by itself.

Developing the service

To create a new service, I used the Windows Service template of the New Project Wizard, as shown in Figure 16-26.

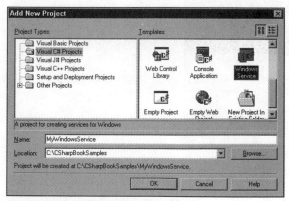

Figure 16-26: Creating a new Windows Service using the New Project Wizard

The New Project Wizard creates a service class named `Service1`, and uses the same name for the `ServiceName` property. I used the Properties window to change both the `Name` and `ServiceName` properties to `MyBeeperService`, and to enable the `CanPauseAndContinue` property, as shown in Figure 16-27.

Figure 16-27: Using the Properties window to change the ServiceName

The New Project Wizard also creates event handlers for `OnStart` and `OnStop`. I added handlers for `OnPause`, `OnContinue`, and `OnCustomCommand`. Since the core functionality of the service must be in `MyBeeperComponent`, the next step was to create its class. To do so, I right-clicked the project node in the Solution Explorer and selected Add ➪ Add New Item from the pop-up menu. In the Add New Item Wizard, I chose the Component Class template, as shown in Figure 16-28.

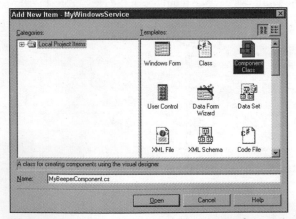

Figure 16-28: Creating a new class to put the service's core functionality in

I added methods to start, pause, stop, and continue the beeping process. The beeping is produced by a background thread that runs continuously, even when the service is paused or stopped. Figure 16-29 shows how the background thread is created and run immediately as soon as the service is loaded.

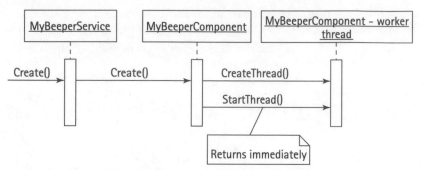

Figure 16-29: Creating the background worker threaded when the service is initially loaded

Listing 16-30 shows the constructor for `MyBeeperComponent`.

Listing 16-30: **The Constructor for MyBeeperComponent**

```
public MyBeeperComponent()
{
  InitializeComponent();

  workerThread = new Thread(new ThreadStart(Run) );
  workerThread.Start();
}
```

Don't confuse the `Thread.Start()` method called in the constructor with the `Start()` method of `MyBeeperComponent`. When the worker thread's `Start()` method is called, the thread's startup method is called, which I designated as the method `MyBeeperComponent.Run()`. This method is the worker thread's main loop, and looks like Listing 16-31.

Listing 16-31: **The Main Loop for the Worker Thread**

```
  public void Run()
  {
    while (true)
    {
      WaitUntilNextBeepTime();
      if (isRunning)
        Beep();
    }
  }
```

The field isRunning is initially false and set to true when MyBeeperComponent.Start() is called. The Pause() and Stop() methods change isRunning to false.

To produce the beeps, I called the Windows API function MessageBeep(), using a small wrapper method called Beep() that looks like Listing 16-32.

Listing 16-32: **The Beep() Method**

```
[DllImport("user32.dll")]
public static extern int MessageBeep(int typeOfSound);
private void Beep()
{
  const int NormalBeep = 0;
  const int ExclamationBeep = 0x30;

  if (UseBeep1)
    MessageBeep(NormalBeep);
  else
    MessageBeep(ExclamationBeep);
}
```

The Beep() method calls the Windows API method MessageBeep(), passing a value to determine the type of beep to issue. By default, MyBeeperComponent issues a NormalBeep, but if UseBeep1 is set to true, a different kind of beep is issued.

Being able to issue two kinds of beeps is not that big of a deal. I added this feature to MyBeeperComponent to show you how to use a service's OnCustomCommand handler to change your own custom properties in a service. UseBeep1 is a public property that is called by MyBeeperService in response to OnCustomCommand. Listing 16-33 shows the OnCustomCommand handler.

Listing 16-33: **The OnCustomCommand Handler for MyBeeperService**

```
// values below 128 are reserved by the system
public const int Beep1 = 128;
public const int Beep2 = 129;

protected override void OnCustomCommand(int command)
{
  if (command == Beep1)
    beeper.UseBeepType1(true);
  else if (command == Beep2)
    beeper.UseBeepType1(false);
}
```

The integer values you can pass to OnCustomCommand must be in the range 128..255. Values below 128 are reserved by the system. As you can see in the code, I use the value 128 to select one type of beep and the value 129 to select another type. The values are entirely arbitrary. Using `OnCustomCommand`, you can control quite a few properties. The only catch is that `OnCustomCommand` is limited to the one integer parameter.

I've pretty much described all the features for the `MyBeeperComponent`. Listing 16-34 shows its entire code.

Listing 16-34: The Code for MyBeeperComponent

```csharp
using System;
using System.ComponentModel;
using System.Collections;
using System.Diagnostics;
using System.Runtime.InteropServices;
using System.Threading;
using Microsoft.Win32;

namespace MyWindowsService
{
  public class MyBeeperComponent : System.ComponentModel.Component
  {
    private bool isRunning = false;
    Thread workerThread;


    public MyBeeperComponent(IContainer container) : this()
    {
      container.Add(this);
    }

    public MyBeeperComponent()
    {
      InitializeComponent();

      workerThread = new Thread(new ThreadStart(Run) );
      workerThread.Start();
    }

    public override void Dispose()
    {
      base.Dispose();

      // get rid of any resources allocated in
      // the constructor
    }

    private void InitializeComponent()  {  }

    public void Run()
    {
      while (true)
```

Continued

Listing 16-34 *(continued)*

```
    {
      WaitUntilNextBeepTime();
      if (isRunning)
        Beep();
    }
  }

  private void WaitUntilNextBeepTime()
  {
    const long OneSecond = 10000000; // in 100 ns increments
    const int TenMilliseconds = 10;

    long startTime = DateTime.Now.Ticks;
    while ( (DateTime.Now.Ticks - startTime) < OneSecond)
      Thread.Sleep(TenMilliseconds);
  }

  public void Start()
  {
    isRunning = true;
  }

  public void Pause()
  {
    isRunning = false;
  }

  public void Stop()
  {
    isRunning = false;
  }

  [DllImport("user32.dll")]
  public static extern int MessageBeep(int typeOfSound);
  private void Beep()
  {
    const int NormalBeep = 0;
    const int ExclamationBeep = 0x30;

    if (UseBeep1)
      MessageBeep(NormalBeep);
    else
      MessageBeep(ExclamationBeep);
  }

  private bool UseBeep1 = true;
  public void UseBeepType1(bool doUseType1)
  {
    if (doUseType1)
```

```
        UseBeep1 = true;
      else
        UseBeep1 = false;
    }
  }
}
```

The only part of the service left to describe is class MyBeeperService, which really represents the infrastructure of the service. All it does is pass along Start, Stop, and other commands to MyBeeperComponent. Listing 16-35 shows the complete code for MyBeeperService.

Listing 16-35: The Code for MyBeeperService

```
using System;
using System.Collections;
using System.ComponentModel;
using System.Data;
using System.ServiceProcess;

namespace MyWindowsService
{
  public class MyBeeperService : System.ServiceProcess.ServiceBase
  {
    private System.ComponentModel.IContainer components = null;
    MyBeeperComponent beeper;

    public MyBeeperService()
    {
      // This call is required by the Windows.Forms
      // Component Designer.
      InitializeComponent();
      beeper = new MyBeeperComponent();
    }

    // The main entry point for the process
    static void Main()
    {
      System.ServiceProcess.ServiceBase[] ServicesToRun;

      ServicesToRun = new System.ServiceProcess.ServiceBase[] {
                        new MyBeeperService() };

      System.ServiceProcess.ServiceBase.Run(ServicesToRun);
    }

    private void InitializeComponent()
    {
      this.CanPauseAndContinue = true;
```

Continued

Listing 16-35 *(continued)*

```
    this.ServiceName = "MyBeeperService";
  }

  protected override void Dispose( bool disposing )
  {
    // standard wizard-generated code...
  }


  protected override void OnStart(string[] args)
  {
    beeper.Start();
  }

  protected override void OnPause()
  {
    beeper.Pause();
  }

  protected override void OnStop()
  {
    beeper.Stop();
  }

  protected override void OnContinue()
  {
    beeper.Start();
  }

  // values below 128 are reserved by the system
  public const int Beep1 = 128;
  public const int Beep2 = 129;

  protected override void OnCustomCommand(int command)
  {
    if (command == Beep1)
      beeper.UseBeepType1(true);
    else if (command == Beep2)
      beeper.UseBeepType1(false);
  }
 }
}
```

Interactive services

Most services don't interact with users by displaying error messages and dialog boxes. By
default, services are forbidden from displaying anything on the screen. For example, if you
add a call to MessageBox.Show() to MyBeeperComponent, nothing will show up on the

screen. To enable interaction with the screen, a service must explicitly be enabled to do so. How? Using a registry key. The *registry* contains the properties and attributes for each service. To make MyBeeperService interactive, you need to locate the Type key stored in the following path:

```
\\HKEY_LOCAL_MACHINE\SYSTEM\CurrentControlSet\Services\MyBeeperService
```

The Type key contains flags that control the service. Bit 8 (0x100) is the Interactive flag. After installing MyBeeperService, just turn bit 8 on. The code in Listing 16-36 will do.

Listing 16-36: Enabling the Interactive Bit in the Registry

```csharp
using Microsoft.Win32;  // to use the Registry classes


private void MakeServiceInteractive()
{
  // read the current service type from the registry
  string keyPath;
  keyPath = @"System\CurrentControlSet\Services\MyBeeperService";
  const bool MakeWritable = true;
  RegistryKey key;
  key = Registry.LocalMachine.OpenSubKey(keyPath, MakeWritable);
  if (key == null) return;

  string s = key.GetValue("type").ToString();


  Int32 newValue = Int32.Parse(s);

  // turn on the Interactive flag
  const int InteractiveTypeFlag = 0x100;
  newValue |= InteractiveTypeFlag;
  key.SetValue("type", newValue);
  key.Close();
}
```

If you want to check whether a service has the Interactive flag set, you could use the method shown in Listing 16-37.

Listing 16-37: Checking the Registry to See if a Service Has the Interactive Flag Set

```csharp
private bool IsInteractive()
{
  // read the service's current service type from the registry
  string keyPath;
  keyPath = @"System\CurrentControlSet\Services\MyBeeperService";
```

Continued

Listing 16-37 *(continued)*

```
RegistryKey key = Registry.LocalMachine.OpenSubKey(keyPath);
if (key == null) return false;

string s = key.GetValue("type").ToString();
Int32 newValue = Int32.Parse(s);

// check service type flag
const int InteractiveTypeFlag = 0x100;
return (newValue & InteractiveTypeFlag) ==
       InteractiveTypeFlag ? true : false;
}
```

Before displaying any kind of messages or dialog boxes, make sure you check whether the service has interactive privileges, otherwise the output will go to an invisible window. Consequently, the service will hang, waiting for someone to click an invisible OK or Cancel button.

Testing the service

You can't just run a service like you would an application. It isn't sufficient to create a separate test fixture for it like you would with a DLL. Services are harder to test, because they are run and controlled by the Service Control Manager (SCM), which is a Windows program over which you have absolutely no control. So, to test a service, you need to install it on the machine as a Windows Service, and then load it into the SCM and run it. To debug it, you'll need to attach the VS .NET debugger to the service's running process.

Like I said earlier, a much simpler approach is to put most or all of the core functionality of a service into a separate component, and test that component using a simple test fixture application. Once you have finished this first round of testing, you can install the component as a service and debug it further, if necessary.

In order to test MyBeeperComponent, I used the New Project Wizard to create a new Windows application. (I'll spare you the details of creating this application.) On the main form, I added three buttons with the captions Start, Pause and Stop, as shown in Figure 16-30.

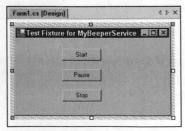

Figure 16-30: The main form of the test fixture for MyBeeperService

I added `MyBeeperComponent` to the test fixture project. To do so, just right-click on the test fixture project in the Solution Explorer and choose Add ➪ Add Existing Item in the pop-up menu. Navigate to the folder MyWindowsService and select the file MyBeeperComponent. The Add New Item Wizard will copy the file into the test fixture folder and add the file to the project.

Note Since the test fixture contains a separate copy of `MyBeeperComponent`, any changes you make to the file will not affect MyWindowsService. After testing `MyBeeperComponent`, copy it back to the MyWindowsService folder if you made any changes to it.

I hooked up the `Click` handlers of the buttons to `MyBeeperComponent`, as shown in Listing 16-38.

Listing 16-38: The Code for the Main Form of the Test Fixture

```
using System;
using System.Drawing;
using System.Collections;
using System.ComponentModel;
using System.Windows.Forms;
using System.Data;

using MyWindowsService;

namespace MyBeeperFormTestFixture
{
  public class Form1 : System.Windows.Forms.Form
  {
    private System.Windows.Forms.Button buttonStart;
    private System.Windows.Forms.Button buttonPause;
    private System.Windows.Forms.Button buttonStop;

    private System.ComponentModel.Container components = null;

    MyBeeperComponent beeper;

    public Form1()
    {
      InitializeComponent();
      beeper = new MyBeeperComponent();
    }

    protected override void Dispose( bool disposing )
    {
      if( disposing )
      {
        beeper.Stop();
        beeper.Dispose();  // immediately kill worker thread

        if (components != null)
```

Continued

Listing 16-38 *(continued)*

```
        components.Dispose();
    }

    base.Dispose( disposing );
}

private void InitializeComponent()
{
  // wizard-generated code
}

[STAThread]
static void Main()
{
  Application.Run(new Form1());
}

private void buttonStart_Click(object sender,
                               System.EventArgs e)
{
  beeper.Start();
}

private void buttonPause_Click(object sender,
                               System.EventArgs e)
{
  beeper.Pause();
}

private void buttonStop_Click(object sender,
                              System.EventArgs e)
{
  beeper.Stop();
}
  }
}
```

I added the namespace MyWindowsService to the code, to allow access to
MyBeeperComponent. In the Dispose() method, I called MyBeeperComponent.Stop()
and MyBeeperComponent.Dispose() to make sure MyBeeperComponent's worker thread
goes away when the test fixture is closed down.

Adding a System Tray icon

Some services use the System Tray to display a small icon that in some way represents the
state of the service. For example, Windows network connections can be configured to display
a set of tiny terminals that change color when data is sent or received. Adding a System Tray

icon to a regular .exe or .dll is easy: Just add a `NotifyIcon` component to its main form and set the component's Icon property with the icon to display. Unfortunately, a service doesn't typically have a main form, or any forms for that matter. If you add a form to a service, it won't be displayed, unless the service's `Interactive` flag is enabled.

To add a System Tray icon to a service, the recommended way is via a separate Service Control Program (SCP). This type of program is a plain Windows Form application that is started when the service is loaded and terminated when the service is unloaded. The application can not only display icons in the System Tray, but also attach a context menu to the icons to let users control or configure a service. Figure 16-31 shows the System Tray icon displayed by the SCP described in the next section.

 Figure 16-31: The System Tray, showing the icon representing the state of MyBeeperService

In the figure, the icon for MyBeeperService is the one on the right. The following section describes how to create an SCP for MyBeeperService that not only supports System Tray icons, but also sports a Windows Form to control customized service features.

Adding a Service Control Program

I used the trusted New Project Wizard to create the SCP. I won't bore you with the details, but Figure 16-32 shows how I set up the main form.

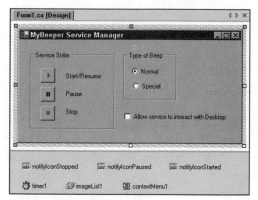

Figure 16-32: The main form for MyBeeperServiceController

As you can see, the program not only lets you start, pause, and stop the service, but also control the custom feature I called *Type of Beep*. I want the program to display a small colored box in the System Tray: red for the stopped state, yellow for the paused state, and green for the started state. I could have used a single `NotifyIcon` component and changed its Icon property to select one of three icons. Instead, I used three separate `NotifyIcon` components.

For the images to display with each `NotifyIcon` component, I created three icon files. To create the icons, I used the VS .NET Add New Item Wizard and selected the Bitmap template, as shown in Figure 16-33.

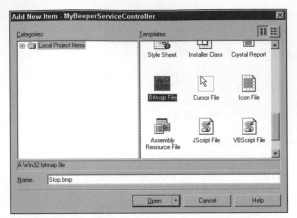

Figure 16-33: Creating bitmaps to display in the System Tray

Using the Properties window, I set the Width and Height of the bitmap to 16 pixels, which is the standard size used in the System Tray. Figure 16-34 shows the stop.bmp image in the VS .NET Bitmap Designer.

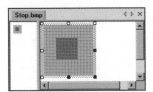

Figure 16-34: The bitmap for the Stopped state, as shown in the Bitmap Designer

The icons show a gray rectangle with a colored square in the center. The three images differ only in the color of the center square.

To display the small images shown on the Start, Pause, and Stop buttons, I added three images to an `ImageList` component on the main form. Then I set each button's `ImageList` and `ImageIndex` properties to reference one of the images.

In the `Click` handlers for the buttons, I added a few lines of code to change the state of MyBeeperService. Listing 16-39 shows the code for the Start button's `Click` handler.

Listing 16-39: The Click Handler for the Start Button

```
private void buttonStart_Click(object sender, System.EventArgs e)
{
  if (beeperService == null) return;
  if (beeperService.Status == ServiceControllerStatus.Stopped)
    beeperService.Start();
  else
    beeperService.Continue();
  buttonStart.Enabled = false;
}
```

Since the service can be started, paused, and stopped by a program other than the SCP, such as the Services snap-in, I added a timer to the main form to periodically poll the service's status. I set the timeout value for the timer to 100 milliseconds. Listing 16-40 shows part of the timer's `Elapsed` handler.

Listing 16-40: A Fragment of the Main Form's Timer.Elapsed Handler

```
ServiceController beeperService;
ServiceControllerStatus status;

private void timer1_Elapsed(object sender,
                            System.Timers.ElapsedEventArgs e)
{
  beeperService = BeeperService; // refresh beeperService, to get
                                 // any changes in status
  if (beeperService == null)
  {
    timer1.Enabled = false;
    Application.Exit();
    return;
  }

  if (beeperService.Status == status) return;

  status = beeperService.Status;

  switch (beeperService.Status)
  {
    case ServiceControllerStatus.Stopped:
      notifyIconStarted.Visible = false;
      notifyIconPaused.Visible = false;
      notifyIconStopped.Visible = true;
      buttonStart.Enabled = true;
      buttonPause.Enabled = false;
      buttonStop.Enabled = false;
      menuItemStart.Enabled = true;
      menuItemPause.Enabled = false;
      menuItemStop.Enabled = false;
      break;

  // other cases...
  }
}
```

At the beginning of the handler, I used the property BeeperService. The getter method for the property scans the list of running services to get a new reference to a ServiceController object. You can use a ServiceController object to change the state of a service, but if the service changes state in response to commands from other programs, the `ServiceController.Status` property is not refreshed with the new state. By always getting a new ServiceController reference, the `Elapsed` handler always knows the current state of the service. If the service is not found, the SCP can't run, so it self-terminates using `Application.Exit()`.

In the `Elapsed` handler, you probably noticed the menuItem objects. These objects appear on the context menu for the System Tray icons. When the user right-clicks an icon, the context menu appears. Figure 16-35 shows how the menu appears in the VS .NET Menu Designer.

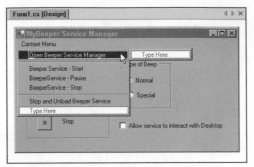

Figure 16-35: The context menu for the System Tray icons

When MyBeeperService is loaded, the SCP is started up. Since the SCP is used only occasionally, it is started with a hidden main form. (I'll show the startup code in the next section.) While the SCP is running, the System Tray icons show the status of MyBeeperService using the colored icons. To display the SCP, use the context menu's first menu command. The menu's handler just calls `Form.Show()` to make the SCP's main form appear on the screen. When the user clicks the Close box for the form, I don't want the SCP to terminate, but to hide itself. To achieve this, I added a handler for the `Closing` event and disabled the window-closing with the code shown in Listing 16-41.

Listing 16-41: **Preventing the SCP Form from Being Closed**

```
private void Form1_Closing(object sender,
                           System.ComponentModel.CancelEventArgs e)
{
  // don't shutdown: just hide the window
  e.Cancel = true;
  Hide();
}
```

To really shut down the SCP, I added the command *Stop and Unload Beeper Service* to the pop-up menu. The handler for this command is shown in Listing 16-42.

Listing 16-42: **Terminating the Service Control Program**

```
private void menuItemStopAndUnload_Click(object sender,
                                         System.EventArgs e)
{
  buttonStop_Click(null, null);
```

```
    notifyIconStopped.Visible = false;
    notifyIconPaused.Visible = false;
    notifyIconStarted.Visible = false;

    Application.Exit();
}
```

The handler stops the service, removes all its icons from the Service Tray, and terminates the program. The handlers for the Start, Pause, and Stop buttons and menu commands call the service's Start(), Pause(), and Stop() methods. Listing 16-43 shows the handler for the Start button.

Listing 16-43: **The Click Handler for the Start Button and Menu**

```
private void buttonStart_Click(object sender, System.EventArgs e)
{
  if (beeperService == null) return;
  if (beeperService.Status == ServiceControllerStatus.Stopped)
    beeperService.Start();
  else
    beeperService.Continue();
  buttonStart.Enabled = false;
}
```

Support for custom commands is demonstrated with the Type of Beep radio buttons. The handlers for these buttons just call the service's ExecuteCommand() method with an integer value to indicate which custom command to execute. Listing 16-44 shows the code.

Listing 16-44: **Calling ExecuteCommand to Run Custom Commands**

```
public const int Beep1 = 128;
public const int Beep2 = 129;

private void radioButtonBeepNormal_CheckedChanged(object sender,
            System.EventArgs e)
{
  if (beeperService == null) return;

  if (beeperService.Status == ServiceControllerStatus.Stopped)
  {
    MessageBox.Show("The service must be running " +
                    "or paused to use these radiobuttons.");
    return;
  }

  if (radioButtonBeepNormal.Checked)
    beeperService.ExecuteCommand(Beep1);
}
```

The service must be running or paused when you invoke `ExecuteCommand()`, otherwise an exception will be thrown. The integer values passed to `ExecuteCommand()` must obviously have meaning to the service.

Just because `ExecuteCommand()` accepts only a single integer doesn't necessarily mean you can't pass parameters to your service. A simple technique is to create your own custom registry values under the key:

```
\\HKEY_LOCAL_MACHINE\SYSTEM\CurrentControlSet\Services\MyBeeperService
```

You can have the SCP assign values to the custom keys, and have the service read these values when executing custom commands. Using this technique, you can pass as many parameters as you want to the service.

That pretty much wraps up the description for the SCP. Listing 16-45 shows the code for the main form.

Listing 16-45: The Code for the Main Form of the Service Control Program

```
using System;
using System.Drawing;
using System.Collections;
using System.ComponentModel;
using System.Windows.Forms;
using System.Data;
using System.ServiceProcess;

namespace MyBeeperServiceController
{
  public class Form1 : System.Windows.Forms.Form
  {
    private System.Windows.Forms.NotifyIcon notifyIconPaused;
    private System.Windows.Forms.NotifyIcon notifyIconStarted;
    private System.Windows.Forms.NotifyIcon notifyIconStopped;

    // declare other visual components...

    ServiceController beeperService;
    ServiceControllerStatus status;

    public Form1()
    {
      InitializeComponent();

      beeperService = BeeperService;

      if (beeperService == null) return;
      checkBoxInteractiveService.Checked =
              IsServiceInteractive(beeperService.ServiceType);
    }

    private bool IsServiceInteractive(ServiceType theType)
    {
```

```
      return (theType & ServiceType.InteractiveProcess) ==
              ServiceType.InteractiveProcess ? true : false;
  }

  protected override void Dispose( bool disposing )
  {
    // standard wizard-generated code
  }

  private void InitializeComponent()
  {
    // wizard-generated code...
  }

  [STAThread]
  static void Main()
  {
Application.Run(new Form1());
  }

  private ServiceController BeeperService
  {
    get
    {
      ServiceController [] services =
                        ServiceController.GetServices();
      foreach (ServiceController service in services)
      {
        if (service.ServiceName == "MyBeeperService")
          return service;
      }
      return null;
    }
  }

  private void timer1_Elapsed(object sender,
                        System.Timers.ElapsedEventArgs e)
  {
    beeperService = BeeperService; // refresh beeperService,
                                   // to get any changes in status
    if (beeperService == null)
    {
      timer1.Enabled = false;
      Application.Exit();
      return;
    }

    if (beeperService.Status == status) return;

    status = beeperService.Status;

    switch (beeperService.Status)
```

Continued

Listing 16-45 *(continued)*

```
    {
      case ServiceControllerStatus.Stopped:
        notifyIconStarted.Visible = false;
        notifyIconPaused.Visible = false;
        notifyIconStopped.Visible = true;
        buttonStart.Enabled = true;
        buttonPause.Enabled = false;
        buttonStop.Enabled = false;
        menuItemStart.Enabled = true;
        menuItemPause.Enabled = false;
        menuItemStop.Enabled = false;
        break;

      case ServiceControllerStatus.Paused:
        notifyIconStarted.Visible = false;
        notifyIconPaused.Visible = true;
        notifyIconStopped.Visible = false;
        buttonStart.Enabled = true;
        buttonPause.Enabled = false;
        buttonStop.Enabled = true;
        menuItemStart.Enabled = true;
        menuItemPause.Enabled = false;
        menuItemStop.Enabled = true;
        break;

      case ServiceControllerStatus.Running:
        notifyIconStarted.Visible = true;
        notifyIconPaused.Visible = false;
        notifyIconStopped.Visible = false;
        buttonStart.Enabled = false;
        buttonPause.Enabled = true;
        buttonStop.Enabled = true;
        menuItemStart.Enabled = false;
        menuItemPause.Enabled = true;
        menuItemStop.Enabled = true;
        break;
    }
  }

  private void buttonStart_Click(object sender,
                                 System.EventArgs e)
  {
    if (beeperService == null) return;
    if (beeperService.Status == ServiceControllerStatus.Stopped)
      beeperService.Start();
    else
      beeperService.Continue();
    buttonStart.Enabled = false;
  }

  private void buttonPause_Click(object sender,
```

```
                            System.EventArgs e)
{
  if (beeperService == null) return;
  beeperService.Pause();
  buttonPause.Enabled = false;
}

private void buttonStop_Click(object sender, System.EventArgs e)
{
  if (beeperService == null) return;
  if (beeperService.Status == ServiceControllerStatus.Stopped)
    return;
  beeperService.Stop();
  buttonStop.Enabled = false;
}

public const int Beep1 = 128;
public const int Beep2 = 129;

private void radioButtonBeepNormal_CheckedChanged(object sender,
                                System.EventArgs e)
{
  if (beeperService == null) return;

  if (beeperService.Status == ServiceControllerStatus.Stopped)
  {
    MessageBox.Show("The service must be running or paused " +
                    "to use these radiobuttons.");
    return;
  }

  if (radioButtonBeepNormal.Checked)
    beeperService.ExecuteCommand(Beep1);
}

private void radioButtonBeepSpecial_CheckedChanged(
            object sender,
            System.EventArgs e)
{
  if (beeperService == null) return;
  if (beeperService.Status == ServiceControllerStatus.Stopped)
  {
    MessageBox.Show("The service must be running or paused " +
                    "to use these radiobuttons.");
    return;
  }
  if (radioButtonBeepSpecial.Checked)
    beeperService.ExecuteCommand(Beep2);
}

private void Form1_Closing(object sender,
                System.ComponentModel.CancelEventArgs e)
```

Continued

Listing 16-45 *(continued)*

```csharp
{
  // don't shutdown: just hide the window
  e.Cancel = true;
  Hide();
}

private void menuItemStart_Click(object sender,
                                 System.EventArgs e)
{
  buttonStart_Click(null, null);
}

private void menuItemPause_Click(object sender,
                                 System.EventArgs e)
{
  buttonPause_Click(null, null);
}

private void menuItemStop_Click(object sender,
                                System.EventArgs e)
{
  buttonStop_Click(null, null);
}

private void menuItemOpenManagser_Click(object sender,
                                        System.EventArgs e)
{
  Show();
}

private void notifyIconStopped_DoubleClick(object sender,
                                           System.EventArgs e)
{
  Show();
}

private void notifyIconPaused_DoubleClick(object sender,
                                          System.EventArgs e)
{
  Show();
}

private void notifyIconStarted_DoubleClick(object sender,
                                           System.EventArgs e)
{
  Show();
}

private void menuItemStopAndUnload_Click(object sender,
                                         System.EventArgs e)
```

```
  {
    buttonStop_Click(null, null);

    notifyIconStopped.Visible = false;
    notifyIconPaused.Visible = false;
    notifyIconStarted.Visible = false;

    Application.Exit();
  }
  }
}
```

Installing the service

Once the service has been sufficiently tested using the test fixture, it's time to rock and roll and install it as a bona fide Windows Service. The process is not trivial, so VS .NET comes to the rescue with a Service Install Project Wizard you can use to easily create an installation program. The installation can then set the service up correctly so it can be managed using the Service Control Manager.

To add the Installer, display the service's main file in the Forms Designer. Right-click on the form and select Add Installer from the pop-up menu, as shown in Figure 16-36.

Figure 16-36: Adding a Service Installer to a Service component

The command will add the file ProjectInstaller.cs to the Solution Explorer. The file contains the class ProjectInstaller, which appears in the Component Tray as shown in Figure 16-37.

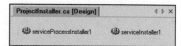

Figure 16-37: How the ProjectInstaller appears in the Component Tray

What exactly does the ProjectInstaller do, and how do you use it? And what are those two installer components that appear in the Component Tray? For starters, take a look at the class diagram in Figure 16-38.

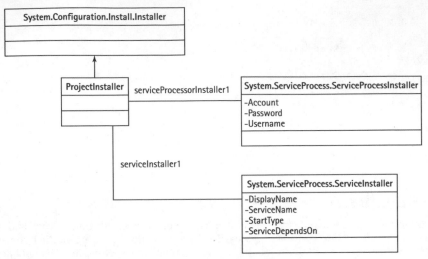

Figure 16-38: The class diagram for ProjectInstaller

ProjectInstaller is the central component for the installation process, but it doesn't really do much by itself. It acts more like a coordinator, using methods inherited from Installer, to control the ServiceProcessInstaller and ServiceInstaller components. Class ProjectInstaller is declared with the RunInstaller attribute set to true, like this:

```
[RunInstaller(true)]
public class ProjectInstaller : System.Configuration.Install.Installer
{ ... }
```

By setting the RunInstaller attribute to true, an installation program, such as InstallUtil.exe, can automatically discover that ProjectInstaller is an installation component.

The reason there are two separate classes (ServiceProcessInstaller and ServiceInstaller) can be explained like this: Services are not contained in their own DLLs; instead, they are contained in a larger executable program called a Windows Service Application (WSA), as explained earlier. A single WSA may host any number of Windows Service components. The ServiceProcessInstaller is the component that oversees the overall service loading process. The ServiceInstaller component handles the installation of individual services. For each service you put in a WSA, there needs to be a corresponding ServiceInstaller.

The SCM loads a service by running the WSA that hosts the service. When the SCM runs the WSA, it uses a specific user account, as opposed to the account of the person currently logged on. You can specify a specific user account by supplying data for the Username and Password properties of ServiceProcessInstaller. Alternatively, you can enter data into the Account property, to specify a built-in system account, such as LocalService, NetworkService, LocalSystem, or User. Most services run under the LocalService account.

When each service hosted in a WSA is loaded, there are a number of parameters that you can set that are used by the SCM. Figure 16-39 shows the items you can customize using the Properties window for ServiceInstaller components.

The DisplayName is the name of the service that will appear in the Services snap-on in the Name column. If you leave the DisplayName blank, the Services snap-in will display the ServiceName instead.

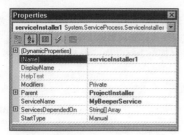

Figure 16-39: Using the Properties window to customize ServiceInstaller properties

The `ServicesDependedOn` property contains a list of service names that indicate services that must be started by the SCM before this service.

The `StartType` tells the SCM how you want it to start the service. The `StartType` value will appear in the Services snap-in, in the Startup Type column. By default, services have the Manual StartupType. If you set the `StartupType` to `Automatic`, the service will be started every time the computer restarts. The other option is `Disabled`, which will prevent the service from being started.

Once all ProjectInstaller settings are entered, build the MyWindowsService project to generate the file MyWindowsService.exe. You can't just run this file to activate it. Remember, it is a special type of .exe that must be installed as a service and controlled by the SCM. To install the .exe as a service, open a Command Prompt box, go to the directory where the .exe is located, and type the following command:

```
InstallUtil MyWindowsService.exe
```

The command will install the service and generate two log files in the directory you executed the command in. The files have the suffix .InstallLog and contain lots of details regarding the installation process, with a list of errors and problems encountered — if any.

To uninstall the services, run `Install` with the /u option, like this:

```
InstallUtil MyWindowsService.exe /u
```

Once the service is installed, run the Services snap-on, or click the Refresh button if the snap-on is already running. In the list of services on the right side, you should see the new service, as shown in Figure 16-40.

Tree	Name	Description	Status	Startup Type	Log On As
Services (Local)	MyBeeperService			Manual	LocalSystem
	Net Logon	Supports pass-through authenticati...	Started	Automatic	LocalSystem
	NetMeeting Rem...	Allows authorized people to remote...		Manual	LocalSystem
	Network Connec...	Manages objects in the Network a...	Started	Manual	LocalSystem
	Network DDE	Provides network transport and se...		Manual	LocalSystem
	Network DDE D...	Manages shared dynamic data exc...		Manual	LocalSystem

Figure 16-40: The new service displayed in the Services snap-on

As you can see, there is no description for MyBeeperService. For some reason, the folks developing the .NET Services components didn't provide a Description property for ServiceInstaller components. To create a description, you have to add some code that stores the description string in the registry. I'll show you how to do this in the next section.

Customizing the service installation

Both the ServiceProcessInstaller and the ServiceInstaller components have hooks for running your own customization code, in the form of event handlers. The most interesting events are shown in the following list and apply to both ServiceProcessInstaller and ServiceInstaller:

✦ AfterInstall

✦ AfterRollback

✦ AfterUninstall

✦ BeforeInstall

✦ BeforeRollback

✦ BeforeUninstall

✦ Committed

✦ Committing

The events are for the most part self-explanatory. The Rollback and Commit events deserve a few words. The .NET Framework supports *transacted* installations, meaning that if any errors occur during an installation, the installer aborts and the installation is rolled back. The rollback undoes everything done up to that point. If no errors occur, the installation is committed, meaning it's finalized. The Committing event is fired just before the commit process is executed. The Committed event is fired just after.

To show how to use one of the installer events, I added a handler for the ServiceInstaller's AfterInstall event. The AfterInstall handler launches the SCP and stores a description for the service in the registry. Listing 16-46 shows the code.

Listing 16-46: Customizing a Service Installation with an AfterInstall Handler

```
private void serviceInstaller1_AfterInstall(object sender,
          System.Configuration.Install.InstallEventArgs e)
{
  string filename = @"C:\CSharpBookSamples\MyWindowsService\" +
                @"MyBeeperServiceController\bin\Debug\" +
                @"MyBeeperServiceController.exe";
  if (!File.Exists(filename) )
  {
    EventLog.WriteEntry("MyBeeperService",
                "Controller not found: " + filename);
    return;
  }

  ProcessStartInfo ps = new ProcessStartInfo(filename);
```

```
ps.WindowStyle = ProcessWindowStyle.Hidden;
Process controller = Process.Start(ps);

SetDescription("Makes a beep sound every second.");
}
```

The handler checks to see if the SCP exists. If not, an error message is written to the Windows Event Application log. If the program is found, it is launched with a hidden main form, using the `ProcessStartInfo` and `Process` classes.

The method `SetDescription` creates an entry in the registry as shown in Listing 16-47.

Listing 16-47: **Adding a Description for a Service**

```
private void SetDescription(string theDescription)
{
  // read the service's current service type from the registry
  string keyPath;
  keyPath = @"System\CurrentControlSet\Services\MyBeeperService";
  const bool MakeWritable = true;
  RegistryKey key;
  key = Registry.LocalMachine.OpenSubKey(keyPath, MakeWritable);
  if (key == null) return;

  key.SetValue("Description", theDescription);
  key.Close();
}
```

Using this new customization, MyBeeperService will show up in the Services snap-in with its description, as shown in Figure 16-41.

Figure 16-41: The description added to MyBeeperService

If your service needs additional registry entries, the best place to add them is in the `BeforeInstall` handler, to guarantee that the entries will be available when the service is loaded.

When a service in uninstalled, it's a good idea to undo anything done during installation. In the case of MyBeeperService, I could remove the Description key from the registry, but since the key does no harm if left there, I decided to leave it.

I didn't need to add an `AfterUninstall` handler to stop the SCP, because the SCP runs a timer that periodically checks to see if MyBeeperService is loaded. As soon as it discovers the service is no longer loaded, the SCP terminates by itself.

A few last notes

Once you install your service, you can access it from your .NET applications using two different methods: the easy way and the hard way. The easy way is by dragging the component from the Server Explorer onto your forms or components. Figure 16-42 shows how the `MyBeeperService` component appears in the Server Explorer.

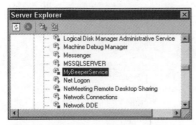

Figure 16-42: How MyBeeperService appears in the Server Explorer

When dropping `MyBeeperService` onto a form, VS .NET automatically adds a ServiceController component to your code and creates an instance of the service that you can use to interact with the service. Figure 16-43 shows how a form looks after the `ServiceController` is added.

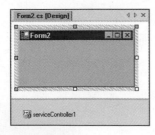

Figure 16-43: How a form appears after dropping a MyBeeperService component on it from the Server Explorer

The `ServiceController` is automatically set up with the properties shown in Figure 16-44.

Figure 16-44: The properties assigned to the ServiceController component

The MachineName is just the name of your computer. If you want the component to work on any computer, use a period (.) as the name.

The hard way to add a service to your code is by writing all the code yourself. Using the manual approach, you have to declare and instantiate the service component with your own code. Whether you use the easy way or the hard way is, of course, up to you. Keep in mind that the ServiceController component is just a wrapper to access the real service with. The property ServiceController.Status is not updated if someone changes the state of the service using an external program, like the Services snap-in. To get up-to-date status information, you need to create a new ServiceController instance bound to MyBeeperService.

Summary

Web Services are one of the hottest tickets of the .NET Framework. They promise to greatly simplify the architecture of distributed systems, enabling you to replace legacy technologies like DCOM and CORBA with simple object-oriented code that hides all the networking issues.

Windows Services are now easier than ever to develop. If you use a separate test fixture to test them, as shown in this chapter, you'll save yourself a considerable amount of time and effort in debugging your services.

✦   ✦   ✦

Security

Fidarsi è bene, non fidarsi è meglio.

—Italian adage

The saying loosely translates into *"Trust is good, distrust is better"* — an aphorism that defines the world of security. The Italian adage may sound a bit Machiavellian, but it applies perfectly to people developing Internet-accessible systems. The bottom line is: *trust no one*. Security is all about finding out who people are — authenticating them to be who they say they are. Only once the identity of a person is verified, can you determine what privileges they can be given, what authority they have to execute commands, and what areas of your applications they should have access to.

This chapter deals with security in the context of Web applications. I'll spend more time describing configuration settings in Windows and IIS than showing code. Most books that cover software development avoid dealing with security issues, because security is considered more a system administration issue than a programming one. Security policies, configurations, and system monitoring are rarely developer issues. Because of this, most developers know little about securing Web applications, and find the whole subject of security rather boring, viewing it as someone else's problem.

The truth is that in today's day of Internet computing and global systems, users can get into your Web servers from almost anywhere. Not all users are benign. It's almost scary to discover how many people devote substantial amounts of their time to find ways of getting into other people's systems. While on one hand, security may be boring for programmers; on the other hand, you just can't ignore it anymore. I'm going to approach the subject from a developer's perspective and be as pragmatic and direct as possible, sparing you the hundreds of pages that would be necessary to describe what security is and why it's good. I will focus on some very narrow specifics, to show you how to secure Web applications by walking you through the various Windows configuration steps.

Security is a big subject that entire books are devoted to. The field of security is populated by a cast of characters with varying backgrounds, skills, and inclinations. Criminals, terrorists, and law enforcement agents are sometimes encountered. You'll find paranoia to be fairly common, which shouldn't come as a surprise. If you feel overcome by a mystic experience about security while reading this chapter and want to know more, there are dozens of excellent books on the subject. A very approachable and concise one is *Securing Windows NT/2000 Servers for the Internet* [Norberg 2000]. A more comprehensive book, dealing with Windows 2000 specifically is *Microsoft Windows 2000 Security Handbook* [Schmidt 2000]. If you feel really safe, try taking a look at security from the hacker's perspective by

◆ ◆ ◆ ◆

In This Chapter

IIS security settings

Authentication techniques

Forms-based authentication

Web application security

◆ ◆ ◆ ◆

reading *Hacking Exposed: Network Security Secrets and Solutions* [McClure 1999]. It's almost incredible to see how many utilities exist in the public domain for cracking passwords, footprinting a system, finding weaknesses, penetrating defenses, and gaining access to administrative privileges. It's almost equally surprising to see how straightforward it is to protect yourself from the most common attacks.

Security for Web Applications

A .NET Web application is made up of Web Forms that optionally call components developed in one or more .NET languages, like C# and VB .NET. End users execute a Web application by pointing their browser at a URL that defines an entry point into the application. Many Web applications are open to the public, and allow any user from any country to access it. For example, the home page for Microsoft at `www.microsoft.com` represents the home page of the Microsoft corporate Web application that is accessible to the public. Anyone can visit this site as many times as they like (unless the purpose of their visit is to disrupt the normal operation of the site).

Not all Web sites are open to the general public. Some Web applications need to be restricted to a limited number of people, computers, or businesses. Restricting access to a Web application requires the application or Web site to implement a security policy to protect itself or its data from unauthorized users. Any security policy will need to address the following two problems:

✦ *Authentication:* The ability to determine the identity of a user and verify that users are indeed who they say they are.

✦ *Authorization:* The ability to refuse or limit access to the application or its data, based on the security privileges granted to the user by the Systems Administrator.

In this chapter, I'll present some of the essential notions and techniques that are common to many applications, with the hope of bringing you up-to-speed on some of the basics. If you are developing a Web application in which security is crucial, such as one that deals with private financial information, government secrets, or sensitive company data, you'll want to use stronger security methods than those I cover in this book. I won't cover the authorization aspect of security in much detail here, because it is too complicated for me to address in the limited space available.

Authentication

As I said earlier, authentication is the process by which you verify the user's identity. There are several ways to accomplish this task, and the one that is right for you depends on how sensitive or valuable the information you are protecting is, the level of effort that malicious users may be willing to resort to, and how much effort and money you are willing to commit to protect your information.

Authentication based on IP addresses

One of the easiest and most effective authentication methods involves setting up your system so that only users with certain IP addresses can access them. This method utilizes information contained at the Internet Protocol (IP) packet level, and doesn't require you to make any changes to your application code. This method is actually classified as an *access control* method rather than an *authentication* method, but I don't want to get lost in discussions of semantics here. This type of authentication is based on identifying the computer from which requests come, rather than the identity of the person using that computer. The obvious assumption is that only a certain known person (or group of known persons) has access to the computer.

To understand how the method works, you need to know a little about IP (as in *TCP/IP*). IP defines the low-level format of the packets that travel around on the Internet. IP packets contain a header portion, in which the IP address of the source and destination are specified (among other things). To digress briefly, an IP packet has the structure shown in Figure 17-1.

bit 0   bit 31

IP Version	Header Length	Type of Service	Length of Packet
Indentification	Flags		Fragment Offset
Time to Live	Protocol		Header Checksum
Source IP Address			
Destination IP Address			
Options			
Data			

Figure 17-1: The basic layout of an IP (version 4) packet, showing the IP Source and Destination Address fields

Each row represents a 32-bit word. A good source of detailed information about the structure of IP packets is "TCP/IP: Architecture, Protocols, and Implementation With IPV6 and IP Security" [Feit 1999]. The source address tells routers and servers where the packet came from, and where to send responses. The source and destination addresses are stored as 32-bit values. The next version of IP (known as IPv6) has a different header structure, and uses 128-bit addresses.

You can apply restrictions based on IP source addresses at three levels in IIS:

✦ At the Web server level

✦ At the Web site level

✦ At the Web application level

Let's see how you would restrict access to a Web site based on the source IP address. To do so, you'll need to change a few IIS configuration settings.

Note   To change the settings of your Web server, you'll need administrative rights on the computer.

Assume you have a Web site called MyWebSite that you want to secure. Say you want only users with the IP addresses 100.100.100.1 or 100.100.100.2 to be able to access it. To secure the site with IIS 5, open the Internet Services Manager (ISM) snap-in, and select the MyWebSite node in the left pane, as shown in Figure 17-2.

Right-click MyWebSite and select Properties. In the Properties dialog box that appears, go to the Directory Security tab, shown in Figure 17-3.

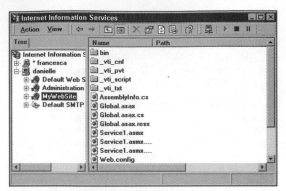

Figure 17-2: Selecting MyWebSite in the Internet Services Manager

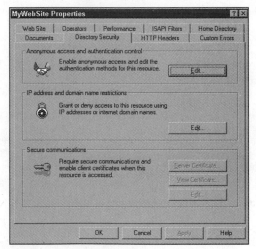

Figure 17-3: The Directory Security tab for MyWebSite

Click the Edit button in the middle portion of the dialog box, in the section titled "IP address and domain name restrictions." In the dialog box that appears, click the Denied Access radio button and add the two IP addresses you want to grant authorization to, as shown in Figure 17-4.

After closing the various dialog boxes, IIS will prevent users from accessing MyWebSite unless they have one of the two IP addresses listed. Unauthorized users will get the page shown in Figure 17-5.

There are ways to customize the HTML page shown in the figure, but that's beyond the scope of this book. Authenticating users based on their IP address is fairly secure, but sophisticated hackers may be able to get around it using IP spoofing. To increase the level of protection offered by restricted IP addresses, you can install leased TCP/IP lines between the clients and Web server. These lines are not used by general traffic and are essentially fixed connections between secured locations. Many secure sites use this approach, so that only authorized users have physical access to the Web server. With leased lines, a Web server can run in an Intranet environment, and may not be accessible at all from the public Internet. The lines connect a number of known users to the server. Of course, there is no such thing as perfect security, and even leased lines can be hacked by someone with enough incentive and resources.

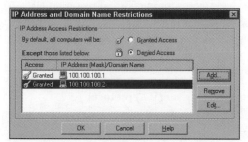

Figure 17-4: Restricting access to MyWebSite to all users except those with specific IP addresses

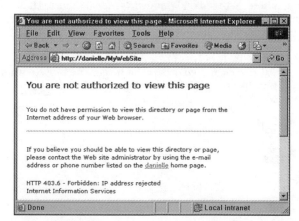

Figure 17-5: The page returned by IIS when unauthorized users try to visit MyWebSite

Although I discussed how to secure a single Web site, you can use basically the same technique to secure an entire Web server or a particular Web application.

Verifying the user through credentials

The most common way to verify a user's identity is to ask for information that only the user should know. Financial institutions often ask for your mother's maiden name, your social security number, your date of birth, or other information to verify that you are who you say you are. This information is used to augment traditional methods of identity verification, such as ID cards, driver licenses, or passports.

In the computer world, photo IDs and driver licenses are often of little use. The most common approach today for authentication is the use of passwords. Passwords are only one line of defense against intruders, but are remarkably effective if used properly. I always get a kick out of Hollywood movies that portray crackers breaking easily into a highly secured computer system. The cracker is invariably running some sort of password-breaking program that shows each cracked character of the password, one at a time, until the complete password is found. The whole process takes just seconds. Ludicrous. If it were that easy to crack passwords, then even my cat could crack into secure systems. The real problem with password security is that most people use easily guessable words, or even no password at all.

User authentication with passwords can be supported in a number of ways with Web applications. The most common ways rely on authentication methods supported directly by IIS. The following are the most common ones:

✦ Basic Authentication

✦ Basic Authentication with the Secure Sockets Layer (SSL) protocol

✦ Integrated Windows Authentication

✦ Digest Access Authentication (DAA)

Each method has pros and cons, and is discussed briefly in the following sections.

Basic Authentication

This type of authentication, like the others, is based on Windows NT/2000 security. It is also based on a standard HTTP authentication scheme, known as *RFC 2616*. With this scheme, a Web server can designate a resource to protect. The resource can be a single file, a folder, a Web site, or all the Web sites on a given machine. Collectively, the protected resource is called a *Protected Realm*. When users point their browser to a Protected Realm, the Web server responds with an HTTP error 401 *(Unauthorized access)* message. The browser then automatically displays a login dialog box, like the one shown in Figure 17-6.

Figure 17-6: The standard login dialog box displayed by Internet Explorer when a site protected by Basic Authentication is accessed

To gain access to the site, users must enter information that corresponds to a valid user account on the Web server. A weakness of Basic Authentication is that the password is sent to the Web server in clear text (albeit with Base64 encoding), making the information available for eavesdroppers to steal. The advantage of Basic Authentication is that it's compatible with practically all browsers, because it's supported at the HTTP level. Even with its security risks, Basic Authentication is widely used by sites all over the world.

Basic Authentication with SSL

If the idea of sending unencrypted security credentials over a network is unacceptable for your Web applications, consider using a Secure Sockets Layer (SSL). With SSL, all exchanges between clients and the Web server are made with HTTPS, the secure version of HTTP. SSL uses a very strong encryption algorithm that is adequate for 99.9% of secured Web sites. Financial institutions have been using SSL routinely to send highly confidential information over the public Internet for years.

One good aspect of SSL is that it works across proxy servers and firewalls. But there are two drawbacks with the SSL approach, which may or may not be acceptable for your Web applications. First, the method has a fairly heavy impact on performance, because the Web pages returned to users are all encrypted. It takes time to encrypt pages on the server and decrypt them on the client. Second, the Web server needs to be set up with an SSL Server Certificate, which requires you to obtain SSL credentials from a third-party certification authority such as VeriSign. Contact your Web or System Administrator to see if SSL is available on your organization's Web servers.

The details of setting up and managing SSL are beyond the scope of this book. A good source of information on setting up SSL with IIS 5 can be found in the online IIS documentation at `http://localhost/iishelp/iis/htm/core/iisslsc.htm`.

Integrated Windows Authentication

This authentication method is only available to users connected to a Windows NT or 2000 domain. Users must be running Internet Explorer 2 or later. The method was formerly called *Windows NT Challenge/Response* authentication in IIS 4. Before that, it was known as *NT LAN Manager (NTLM)* Authentication. Different names, similar technology. The authentication method uses a special Challenge/Response protocol, with optional Kerberos v5 authentication. Through the exchange of hashed messages representing the user name, password, and other information, the client can prove its identity without divulging anything to potential eavesdroppers.

A significant drawback of the method is that it doesn't work across proxy servers or firewalls, so it is usually used in intranet environments. The nice thing about this type of authentication is that it's transparent to users, because it uses the credentials entered when the user logged in to the Windows client machine. Users aren't prompted to log in when they go to your site, unless their user account has insufficient privileges to access it. Because Integrated Windows Authentication is restricted to Windows client machines, the method is not in widespread use on public Web sites. However, it is an excellent method to use in corporate intranet environments, and is quite popular.

Digest Access Authentication (DAA)

This authentication method is supported by IIS version 5 and later. Other types of Web servers, such as Apache, also support it. The method was introduced with HTTP version 1.1 and is based on RFC 2069 and RFC 2617. Although a full-fledged HTTP standard, Digest Access Authentication (DAA) currently works only with Internet Explorer 5 or later browsers. As of this writing, the latest version of Netscape (6.3) still doesn't support DAA, to the best of my knowledge.

With DAA, the password is hashed before being sent to the server. The hashing algorithm used is a one-way function, meaning there are no known ways to decode it from the hash. The default hashing algorithm is MD5, but others can be specified. MD5 hashes are 128-bit values. All the Web server has to do is compare the hashed value received with the hashed value generated locally, using the algorithm specified by the client. All this is done without ever sending user names or passwords over the wire.

At this point, you might think that all a cracker has to do is capture the user's hash value to hijack his or her account. Nice try, but that won't work. When a user initially accesses a site protected with DAA, the server returns a block of session-unique data. The user's browser then creates a hash that includes not only the password, but also the user name and the session-unique data. If someone captured this information and tried to play it back to the server at a later time, to impersonate the original user, they would fail, because the unique session-data hashed in the request would be incorrect.

Since DAA only uses hashing during the user-authentication phase, there is no performance degradation when sending ordinary data to the client, compared with Basic Authentication.

Let me make a really brief digression on passwords under Windows. Passwords are managed by the Security Account Manager (SAM) service on a network's Domain Controller. The service stores all passwords in hashed form in a security database. Hashed passwords are not decodable, because hashing is performed with a *one-way* algorithm. Given a password, the hashing algorithm computes a bit sequence to represent it. Hashing is not the same as encrypting, because encrypting is a *two-way* affair: Given an encrypted value, you can decrypt it if you have the necessary codes. With hashing, there are no known ways to recover the original information.

If the system is configured as an Active Directory (AD) domain, the passwords are stored with the user account information in the AD database. In case you're interested, this database is in the file `C:\WinNt\NTDS\ntds.dit`. If the system doesn't use AD, the database is managed by the system registry and stored in the folder `c:\WinNt\System32\Config`.

Now for the bad news. Passwords aren't sent over the network from the client browser to the Web server, to avoid exposing them to eavesdroppers. The only things exchanged are hash values. In order for the Web server to compute a local hash value to match the client's hash against, the server needs to have access to the user's password in clear text. These passwords must be stored on the Web server's Domain Controller. Storing unencrypted password lists on any machine may be an unacceptable risk for many organizations. If you consider the risk acceptable, the Domain Controller will have to be protected very carefully from unauthorized access.

Regardless of its weaknesses and strengths, DAA is not in widespread use, primarily due to its restriction to Internet Explorer 5 browsers. Personally, I discourage the use of DAA.

Other methods

There are other authentication methods available in IIS 5, such as certificate-based client authentication and others. Most of these methods are very strong, but also complex to set up and manage. Some even require special hardware. For example the Fortezza authentication method uses smart cards with client certificates. Since each client machine must be set up with a smart card reader, the method is used mostly in military, commercial, or government installations where security is paramount and cost is secondary. For even greater security, retinal scanners or other biometric devices can also be used.

A common problem with all these authentication techniques is that if the user is authenticated on one Web server and then follows a link to another site, he or she is confronted with a new login screen. It would be nice if the login credentials entered the first time could somehow be used to silently and automatically log in the user at each new site visited. This type of one-stop authentication is what Microsoft Passport is about. I'll discuss Passport very briefly in a later section. For a look at a different type of one-stop authentication proposal, check the paper "A National-Scale Authenticaton Infrastructure" [Butler 2000].

Securing a Web application with Basic Authentication

Let's take a look at how you would protect an IIS Web site with Basic Authentication. Keep in mind that you can use this and other types of authentication listed previously at five different levels:

+ At the Web server level

+ At the Web site level

+ At the Web application level

+ At the folder level

+ At the file level

In the sections that follow, I'll show you how to protect a Web application called *MyWebApp* with Basic Authentication. This method is based on Windows 2000 user accounts, so the first step will be to create a use account with the necessary rights.

Creating a user account

To use any of the Windows authentication schemes, such as Basic Authentication or Digest Access Authentication, the user account must permit the remote user to act like a locally logged-on user, as if the remote user were sitting in front of the Web server machine trying to log on to Windows. Once the user is authenticated, you want the ASP.NET Framework code to run with the privileges set for the user's account. In other words, you want the ASP.NET runtime to *impersonate* the security context set up for the remote user.

To support any of the Windows authentication schemes, a user account at a minimum must include the *Log On Locally* privilege. Unfortunately, when IIS is installed, it doesn't automatically create such a user account for generic remote users, for security reasons, so I'll show you how to set a new account up. To support impersonation, you have to tweak a parameter in your Web application's web.config file.

I'll assume you are running a Windows 2000 Active Directory domain, and therefore have a Windows 2000 Domain Controller somewhere running a Windows 2000 Server. You need access to this server, with administrative privileges, to create and manage user accounts.

Note   Think carefully before using a Windows Domain Controller as a Web server for public traffic. In the past, crackers have managed to compromise Web servers using a variety of techniques, including the so-called *buffer overflow* hack. Once a domain server is compromised, the entire domain is potentially threatened. For a brief overview of buffer-overflow attacks, see the article "Introducing the Web Application Manager, Client Authentication Options, and Process Isolation" [Brown 2000]. There are patches posted on the Microsoft Web site to protect IIS against buffer-overflow and other types of attacks. If you're running IIS on the public Internet, I recommend that you periodically check the Microsoft Windows Update site at http://windowsupdate.microsoft.com for security patches.

Let's get the account set up for the users of a secured Web site. On the Windows 2000 Domain Controller, select Programs from the Start menu, and then select Administrative Tools ⇨ Active Directory Users and Computers. In the left pane of the snap-in that appears, right-click on the Users folder, and then select New ⇨ User from the pop-up menu, as shown in Figure 17-7.

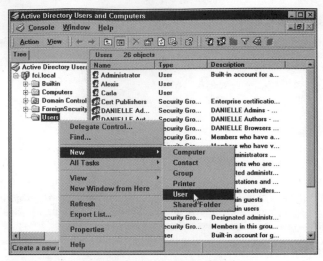

Figure 17-7: Creating a new user account

In the New Object dialog box that appears, enter the user information. Enter any name you want. I used the name *MyWebAppUser* for the user name, as shown in Figure 17-8.

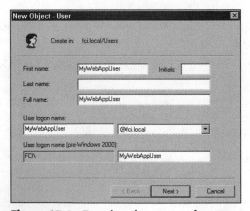

Figure 17-8: Entering the name of a new user

In the combo box next to the User logon name edit box, you'll see the name of the DNS domain the user is being added to. My domain is *FCI*. Domain names are not case-sensitive. The *local* suffix indicates that my domain is private, because the domain is not accessible from the public Internet. When you click the Next button, you can enter the password-related information for the user, as shown in Figure 17-9.

If you plan to allow more than one person to access your Web site with the same user account, it's a good idea to check the "User cannot change password" box, to prevent one user from changing the password and locking out all the other users. You may want to also check the "Password never expires" box; otherwise you'll need to change the password when it expires, and possibly need to notify a zillion users. Once the new user account is created, it will show up at the bottom of the list of users, as shown in Figure 17-10.

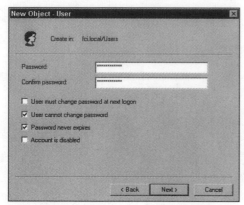

Figure 17-9: Setting the password for the MyWebAppUser

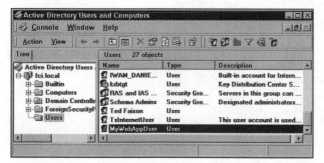

Figure 17-10: The newly created user account that will be used with MyWebAppUser

By double-clicking on the new user name in the right pane, you can enter a description to more easily identify the user account. By default, new user accounts are members of the Domain Users account, as shown in Figure 17-11.

You can configure the new user's membership as appropriate to your needs. Just remember that certain minimum privileges are required. For example, the account must have the Log On Locally right enabled. The Domain Users group includes this right, but other groups may not. To enable the Log On Locally right for an account, select Programs ➪ Administrative Tools ➪ Local Security Policy from the Start menu. In the snap-in that appears, select the folder named User Rights Assignment in the left pane. In the right pane, scroll down to the entry Log On Locally, as shown in Figure 17-12.

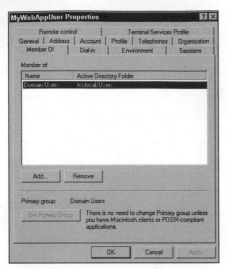

Figure 17-11: The groups a user belongs to, for security purposes

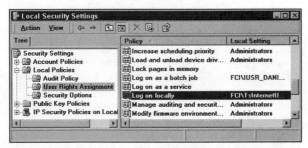

Figure 17-12: The Local Security Settings window

Double-click the Log On Locally item in the right pane. You'll see a dialog box containing of list of the accounts to which the Log On Locally right was assigned, as shown in Figure 17-13.

Click the Add button. In the upper part of the dialog box, scroll down to locate MyWebAppUser. Select it and click the Add button. MyWebAppUser will be added to the list in the bottom part of the dialog box, as shown in Figure 17-14.

Close all of the dialog boxes and you're done. If you need to assign multiple rights to a user, or need multiple users to share the same security settings, the recommended procedure is to create a new Group Account, assign the necessary rights to it, and then add users as members of the group.

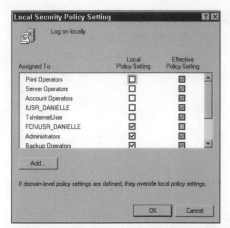

Figure 17-13: A list of the accounts to which the Log On Locally right is assigned

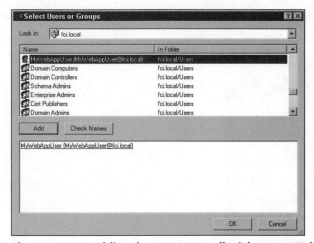

Figure 17-14: Adding the Log On Locally right to MyWebAppUser

Securing a Web application

Now that you have a user account with limited rights, you can use it to secure access to your Web application. Remember that you can apply security not just to a Web application, but also to a Web site or the entire Web server.

To secure a Web application, open the Internet Services Manager (ISM) snap-in. Right-click on the name of the application you want to secure in the left pane and select Properties from the pop-up menu, as shown in Figure 17-15.

Figure 17-15: Displaying the properties of MyWebApp

Select the Directory Security tab and click the Edit button near the top, in the section named "Anonymous access and authentication control," as shown in Figure 17-16.

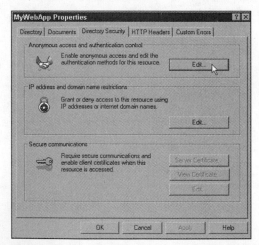

Figure 17-16: The Directory Security page for MyWebApp

The Authentication Methods dialog box will appear, as shown in Figure 17-17.

Uncheck all the boxes and then check the box labeled "Basic authentication (password is sent in clear text)." A warning box will appear, as shown in Figure 17-18.

Click Yes, and the Authentication Methods dialog box should look like Figure 17-19.

Figure 17-17: The Authentication Methods dialog box, with the default settings

Figure 17-18: The warning box that appears when you enable Basic Authentication

Figure 17-19: The Authentication Methods dialog box, with Basic Authentication selected

Click OK to close all of the dialog boxes, and MyWebApp is ready for testing. Open a browser and navigate to the MyWebApp site. You'll get a login dialog box. Figure 17-20 shows how you would fill it in.

Figure 17-20: The login dialog box shown when a site is secured with Basic Authentication

Notice that the User Name includes the domain name in front of it. The name of my domain happens to be *FCI*. You may recall that domain and user names are not case-sensitive. If you don't want to force users to enter the domain name when logging on, you can set up a default domain name. To do so, reopen the dialog box previously shown in Figure 17-19 and click the Edit button on the right of and slightly below the Basic Authentication check box. Enter the domain name, as shown in Figure 17-21.

Figure 17-21: Entering a default domain, so users don't have to specify one when logging on to MyWebApp

Now users can log in to MyWebApp with the plain user name MyWebAppUser, omitting the domain name. For security reasons, it's better for users not to know the name of the domain your Web server is running on. The less information you make public, the better. (Remember the Italian adage at the beginning of this chapter.)

Authorization with NTFS file access permissions

Once you have established a way to authenticate users, you can use NTFS permissions to restrict the files and folders they can access. This is the part of security that has to do with authorization. A security policy that doesn't include authorization is a flawed policy. Once users are validated, you need to establish what they can and can't do, possibly based on who they are or what role they have.

The simplest way to create an authorization policy is based on permissions at the NTFS file access level. Obviously, your system's hard disks will have to be formatted as NTFS drives to use this type of policy. NTFS permissions can be set at the file or folder level and can be set for individual users or groups of users.

A short example will help. Let's say MyWebApp has two folders called *FolderGeneric* and *FolderRestricted.* The two folders are under the main folder *MyWebApp,* as shown in Figure 17-22.

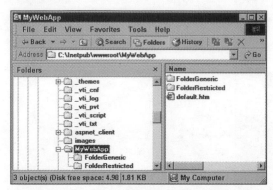

Figure 17-22: Two subfolders that will be set up with different authorization privileges

You want the first folder to be accessible to all validated users, while the second folder must be available only to users in the Payroll department. What you need is a Windows Security Group that will contain the necessary NTFS permissions. I'll call this group *Payroll* and grant access to FolderRestricted to all Payroll members.

You can setup a Payroll group using the basic guidelines shown in the previous section titled "Creating a user account." Instead of creating a user account, create a Security Group, as shown in Figure 17-23.

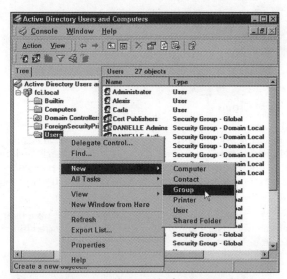

Figure 17-23: Creating a Windows Security Group

When the New Object - Group dialog box appears, enter a name for the group and select the group's scope and type, as shown in Figure 17-24.

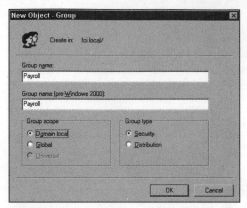

Figure 17-24: Setting up a Security Group

By setting the Group scope to *Domain local,* the group will be valid only on the domain your Domain Controller is responsible for. The Group type should be set to *Security.* Click OK to create the new group, which will appear in the Active Directory Users and Computers snap-in, as shown in Figure 17-25.

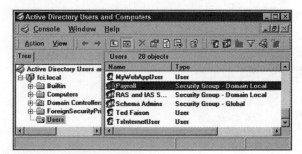

Figure 17-25: A newly created Security Group

Now that the Payroll group has been set up, you need to enable its members to access FolderRestricted. To do so, open Windows Explorer, and right-click on the FolderRestricted folder and choose Properties from the context menu. In the top list of the Properties dialog box, remove all the users and groups except *Administrators* and *SYSTEM.* Add the Payroll group and set its permissions as shown in Figure 17-26.

Close the dialog box with the OK button and you're done. The last step is to set up a user as a member of the Payroll group. I created a new user named *John Anderson* and added him as a member of the Payroll group, as shown in Figure 17-27.

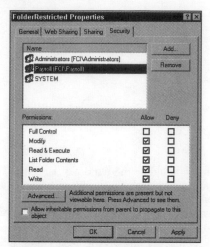

Figure 17-26: Granting limited privileges to FolderRestricted

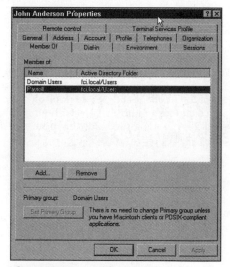

Figure 17-27: Adding a user to the Payroll Security Group

With the settings I entered for FolderRestricted, the only user (besides the Administrator and the SYSTEM account) allowed to access the folder is John Anderson, because he is the only member of the Payroll group. If any other user tries to access the folder, he or she will get the error message shown in Figure 17-28.

If unauthorized users tried to access the folder over the Web, they would get a HTTP 401 *(Unauthorized Access)* response back. If they're using a browser, they wouldn't see the error message, but would be prompted with a username/password login dialog box.

Figure 17-28: The error message displayed when unauthorized users attempt to access FolderRestricted

Don't underestimate the power of NTFS security. It is applied by the Windows Security Subsystem, so it's handled completely outside of any application. It also doesn't require any code changes in your application, and is easily configured to handle individual users or groups of users. The beauty of it is that it can be administered and adjusted using standard Windows tools, without requiring your applications to be rebuilt.

The only proviso for relying on NTFS security is that all of the information accessible from a Web application be in files. If the application code allows access to database tables, NTFS is obviously not going to able to help you prevent unauthorized access. In these cases, you can apply security settings at the database level, using the tools of the DBMS. Or you can set up your own security arrangements using custom code.

ASP.NET Security

Now that you know the basics of IIS authentication and NTFS file access security, I can move on to .NET specifics. The ASP.NET Framework supports an extremely flexible security policy, which enables you to use and extend the authentication model of IIS, set up your own security model, or use a model that lets users login once and visit multiple sites without having to log in at every new site. ASP.NET Framework security is based on the following three schemes:

✦ Impersonation

✦ Forms Authentication

✦ Passport Authentication

I'll discuss each one separately, but I'll provide only a glimpse at Passport Authentication, because I consider it a technology beyond the scope of this book and component-based development in general.

Impersonation

In everyday language, *impersonation* is the act of assuming the identity of another person. In the context of computer security, impersonation has a similar meaning: A process or thread is set up to run with the security context of another user process or thread. In a Web environment, impersonation is essential, because remote users typically have different privileges than IIS (the process that handles users requests). Just because IIS is able to access any file or folder in the system doesn't mean you want to grant those rights to remote users. In practice, you'll almost never want IIS threads handling user requests to run with IIS's privileges.

All of the standard IIS authentication models rely on impersonation to achieve security: When a user accesses a secured resource, such as a Web page, IIS prompts for a user name and password. Using this information, IIS accesses the user's account information, creates a security access token for this account, and gives the token to the ASP.NET runtime. The runtime then runs your Web application code using the security token that identifies the user. All restrictions that were established for the user's account will be enforced at the Windows Security Subsystem level. All file accesses will be constrained by NTFS file access permissions on the user's account. Figure 17-29 shows how security is implemented using impersonation.

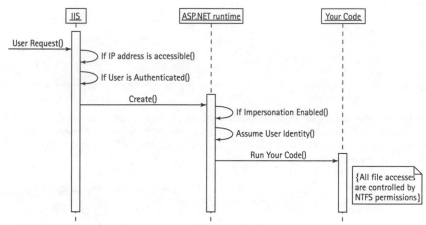

Figure 17-29: How IIS impersonation works

To enable impersonation-based security, you have to do four things, none of which entail making any changes to source code:

1. Create a user account for your clients to use.

2. Assign the required security privileges to the account.

3. Set the NTFS permissions on the files and folders accessible to users.

4. Enable impersonation for your application.

The first three steps were described previously. The last one requires you to edit your project's web.config file. To do this, go to the ⟨authentication⟩ element and set its mode attribute to Windows. Then add an ⟨identity⟩ element with its impersonate attribute set to true, as shown in Listing 17-1.

> **Listing 17-1: Enabling Impersonation-Based Security Using the web.config File**

```
<authentication mode="Windows" />
<identity impersonate="true" />
```

You can also add entries in the web.config file to add further user restrictions, in addition to those already applied at the IIS level. Add one or more `<allow>` or `<deny>` elements to specify your needs, as shown in Listing 17-2.

Listing 17-2: Enabling Specific Users and Groups Using the web.config File

```
<authorization>
  <allow users="Ted, Homer, Susan"
         roles="Payroll, Domain Users"/>
  <deny  users="John, Frank"
         roles="[roles to deny]"/>
</authorization>
```

You can specify individual user names that are allowed or restricted from accessing your Web code. You can also allow or restrict access based on what role or group a user belongs to. To indicate all users or roles, use the string "*". To denote an empty list, use the string "". Listing 17-3 shows an example.

Listing 17-3: Enabling Only Payroll Users with the web.config File

```
<authorization>
  <allow users=""
         roles="Payroll"/>
  <deny  users="*"
         roles=""/>
</authorization>
```

This example grants access privileges only to users in the Payroll group. Note the `<deny>` node with the users attribute set to "*". Without this setting, all users would be allowed access to the application. Be careful not to specify conflicting information in the web.config file. When ASP.NET is checking the file after a user request arrives, it reads the `<allow>` and `<deny>` elements in the order they appear. As soon as an element is found that applies to the user, that element is used (either allowing or denying the user) and the remaining elements are skipped.

Note   Always add a list of users or roles to deny in the `<authorization>` element, otherwise all anonymous users will be allowed to access your site. The most common practice is to add a `<deny users="*">` element. Be sure this element appears *after* the `<allow>` element; otherwise, *all* users will be excluded.

Like I said, you don't have to make any other changes in your code to support impersonation-based security. The IIS configuration determines whether Basic Authentication, Digest Access Authentication, or Integrated Windows Authentication will be used.

Forms Authentication

The *Forms* part of Forms Authentication refers to a custom Web Form you create to gather user credentials. This type of authentication completely ignores IIS authentication settings, allowing your code to take full responsibility for user authentication. Don't infer from this statement that IIS settings are completely irrelevant with Forms Authentication. To prevent IIS from interfering with Forms Authentication, make sure its Authentication Method is set to Anonymous Access, as shown in Figure 17-30.

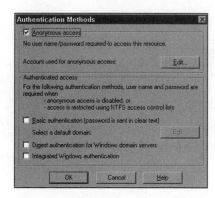

Figure 17-30: Setting IIS's Authentication Mode to prevent it from interfering with ASP.NET Forms Authentication

If you disabled Anonymous Access, IIS would try to authenticate users (using one of the standard HTTP authentication methods) before your ASP.NET code was ever loaded, in effect usurping your ASP.NET security model. With Forms Authentication, you don't want this to happen. When a user arrives at your site, you want to present him or her with your own custom Login page, where you can prompt for a user name, password, or anything else you want, like the mother's maiden name, the user's age, and so on.

Forms Authentication is completely customizable, but I don't have the space in this chapter to describe it in full detail. I'll cover the most common and simplest configurations. For additional information, see the ASP.NET online documentation.

Forms Authentication lets you take complete control over the login and authentication process. First, you create a Web Form that represents the login screen. You can lay the form out in any way and prompt the user for any information you like. When the user clicks the OK or Submit button, a postback event fires and the button's `Click` event handler is called on the server side. The handler can use any scheme you want to authenticate the user. If the user is not authenticated, you can return another Web Form with your own custom error message. If the user passes the authentication criteria, the user is allowed access to the secured Web resource.

Figure 17-31 shows the interaction diagram for a user attempting to access a Web Form of a Web application protected with Forms Authentication.

After successfully verifying the user's credentials in the login form postback handler, you issue an authentication ticket that is returned with the original Web Form requested by the user. The ticket is typically returned as a cookie to the user. The value of the cookie is also stored as a Web application Session variable, so the next time the user returns to the site during the same session, the cookie will be checked against the value stored in the `Session` variable. If the values don't match, the user is redirected again to the Login Form, otherwise the user is allowed to access the requested Web Form.

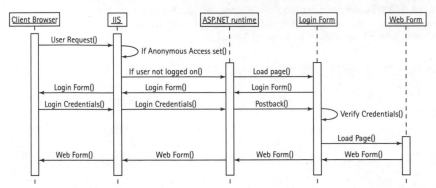

Figure 17-31: What happens when a user attempts to access a Web Form secured with Forms Authentication

A simple example

In this section, I'll show you how to create a simple Web application that uses Forms Authentication. Using the VS .NET New Project Wizard, I created a Web application called *MyWebApp_FormsAuthentication*. (I'll spare you the wizard details.) Using the Internet Services Manager, I disabled all authentication methods, to prevent any interference from IIS in authenticating users. The main form of the application displays a greeting message, as shown in Figure 17-32.

Figure 17-32: A simple page that is protected with Forms Authentication

You can put any content you want on the Web Form. I just put a couple of Label controls. Assume this main form is the home page of a Web site. The interesting part of the example is not what's on the form, but how Forms Authentication forces the user to log in using a custom Web Form. I created a login form called *MyLoginWebForm.aspx,* as shown in Figure 17-33.

To make ASP.NET redirect new users to the login form, I edited the web.config file as shown in Listing 17-4.

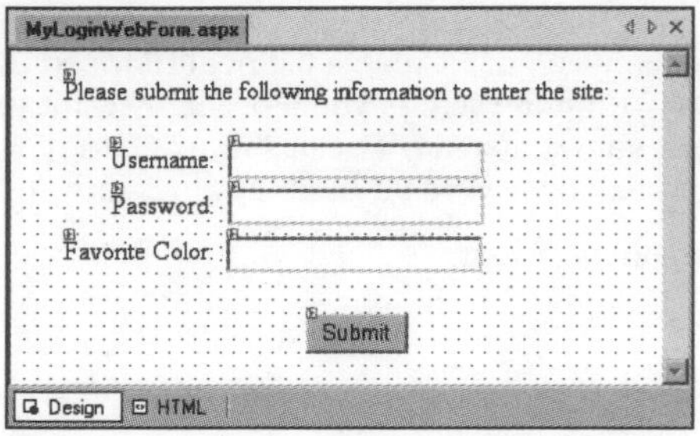

Figure 17-33: A customized login form

Listing 17-4: The web.config File Changes Made to Support Forms Authentication

```
<authentication mode="Forms">
  <forms name="MyAuthCookieName"
         loginUrl="MyLoginWebForm.aspx"
         protection="All" timeout="30">
    <credentials passwordFormat="Clear">
      <user name="Mary" password="mary" />
      <user name="John" password="john" />
    </credentials>
  </forms>
</authentication>

<authorization>
   <deny users="?" />
</authorization>
```

A few words about the web.config code: The `<authentication>` element tells the ASP.NET runtime to use Forms Authentication with the `mode` attribute set to `Forms`. The `<forms>` element sets up a number of Forms Authentication parameters. The `loginUrl` attribute contains the URI of the Web Form to use for prompting the user for login credentials. You'll probably want to redirect the user to a form that uses SSL, to avoid the user credentials from traveling over the wire in clear text. The login form doesn't necessarily have to be on the same server with the rest of your Web application. For example, you could have a `loginUrl` that looked like this:

```
https://www.myloginserver.mycompany.com
```

The `<form>` element's `protection` attribute defines how to protect the authentication cookie returned to the user from tampering. Possible values are:

✦ `None` — The cookie is sent in Base64 clear text.

✦ `Encryption` — The cookie is encrypted using DES or Triple-DES.

✦ `Validation` — The cookie is digitally signed to allow tamper-detection.

✦ `All` — Uses both Encryption and Validation. This is the default value.

The <credentials> element is where you specify the user names and passwords of allowed users. For simple Web applications, it might be convenient to keep a list of authorized users in the web.config file. Since passwords can also be put in the file, you'll probably want to avoid adding clear text passwords and use hash values instead. The passwordFormat attribute indicates what algorithm was used to hash passwords. Possible values are:

✦ Clear—No hashing used. Passwords are in clear text.

✦ MD5—Message Digest 5 algorithm used.

✦ SHA1—Secure Hash Algorithm-1 used.

At the time of this writing, there were no built-in .NET tools to produce hashed passwords. Fortunately, all hope isn't lost—you can use a couple of lines of code to produce hashed passwords with the method

```
FormsAuthentication.HashPasswordForStoringInConfigFile()
```

The following code would suffice:

```
using System.Web.Security;

string hashedPassword =
    FormsAuthentication.HashPasswordForStoringInConfigFile(
                        "MyPassword", "MD5");
```

The first parameter is the password to hash; the second parameter is the hashing algorithm to use. You can use the string "MD5" or "SHA1". The previous code produces the following hash string:

```
33BDF009F1CC358314D06D363FB5E8F2
```

The <authorization> defines which users to reject from the Web application. By using the following element, all anonymous users will be rejected and forced to go through your login mechanism to get in:

```
<deny users="?" />
```

Note   If you omit the <authorization> element with its child element <deny users="?" />, Forms Authentication is effectively disabled, because any anonymous users will be able to get in.

Getting back to my sample Web application, when new users fill out the login form and click the Submit button, a postback occurs and the button's Click handler is called. Listing 17-5 shows the handler and its related methods.

Listing 17-5: The Login Form's Event Handler that Authenticates Users

```
private void ButtonSubmit_Click(object sender,
                                System.EventArgs e)
{
  if (FormsAuthentication.Authenticate(TextBoxUsername.Text,
                            TextBoxPassword.Text) )
    AcceptUser();
  else
```

```
      RejectUser();
}

private void AcceptUser()
{
  // save the user's login settings
  Session ["Favorite Color"] = TextBoxFavoriteColor.Text;

  // tell the ASP.NET Framework to send back the main form
  // with an authentication ticket attached to it, in the
  // form of a cookie
  FormsAuthentication.RedirectFromLoginPage(
                         TextBoxUsername.Text,
                         false);
}

private void RejectUser()
{
  LabelTitle.Text = "Invalid User Credentials. Try again.";
}
```

You can prompt the user for all the data you want on the login form. In the `Click` handler, or a method called by the `Click` handler, you'll probably need to save the data somewhere. I stored the user's favorite color in a `Session` variable, but I could have used a database as well. The `FormsAuthentication` class has the static method `Authenticate()`, which is a helper method that checks the web.config file for the user's user name and password. If the method returns `true`, a match was found and my code calls the method `AcceptUser()`.

The key to a successful authentication is the call to `FormsAuthentication.RedirectFromLoginPage()`.This method generates an authentication ticket for the given user, and then returns to the user the Web Form originally requested. When the user gets this page, he or she will also get an authentication ticket as a cookie. Each time this user returns to your site, the ASP.NET Framework will automatically check the ticket to make sure it is valid. By default, tickets expire 30 minutes after a user requests a Web Form from your site.

That's all there is to it. It may seem like a lot of work, but it really isn't. All you have to do is add a small section of code to the web.config file, create a simple login Web Form, and handle its Submit button's `Click` event.

Keeping authentication information in a database

For very small systems, it might make sense to keep user names and passwords in the web.config file, but this solution won't fly for many Web applications. Most applications use a database to store user names and passwords, to keep them away from prying eyes. The Forms Authentication scheme enables you to store your authentication information in a database or any place you want.

To demonstrate how to authenticate users whose credentials are stored in a database, I created a simple SQL Server database called *MyDatabase* with a table called *MyUsers*. The table has two columns named *Username* and *Password*. I populated the table with a couple of entries, as shown in Figure 17-34.

Figure 17-34: Storing user names and passwords in a database table

To access the database from `MyLoginForm`, I used the VS .NET Add Connection Wizard on the Server Explorer to create a connection to MyDatabase. Figure 17-35 shows the new connection in the Server Explorer.

Figure 17-35: Creating a Connection component to access the table of user names and passwords

Next, I dragged an `SQLDataAdapter` component from the Toolbox onto `MyLoginWebForm`. The Data Adapter Configuration Wizard started, and I configured the adapter to check the MyUsers database for a given user name and password. Figure 17-36 shows the query statement used.

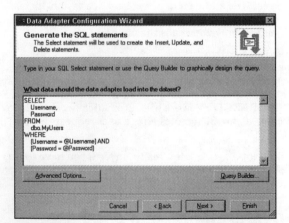

Figure 17-36: The SQL query used to look up user names and passwords in the MyUsers table

As you can see, the statement used two SQL parameters named `Username` and `Password`. The parameter names are identified by the @ character. After closing the wizard, `SqlDataAdapter` and `SqlConnection` components were added to `MyLoginWebForm`, as shown in Figure 17-37.

To look up user names and passwords in the MyUsers table, I created a short method called `Authenticate()` that mimics the behavior of `FormsAuthentication.Authenticate()`. Listing 17-6 shows the code.

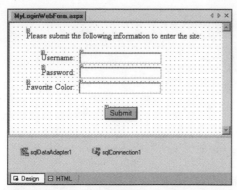

Figure 17-37: The login form after adding SqlConnection and SqlDataAdapter components

---

Listing 17-6: A Custom Authenticate Method that Looks Up Usernames and Passwords in a Database

```
private bool Authenticate(string theUsername, string thePassword)
{
  SqlParameter username = new SqlParameter("@Username",
                                   theUsername);
  SqlParameter password = new SqlParameter("@Password",
                                   thePassword);

  sqlDataAdapter1.SelectCommand.Parameters.Clear();
  sqlDataAdapter1.SelectCommand.Parameters.Add(username);
  sqlDataAdapter1.SelectCommand.Parameters.Add(password);

  sqlConnection1.Open();
  string s = (string) sqlDataAdapter1.SelectCommand.ExecuteScalar();
  sqlConnection1.Close();

  if (s != null)
    return true;
  else
    return false;
}
```

The method `SqlCommand.ExecuteScalar()` returns a single object representing the first field of the first item of the result set. If the user name and password are found in the table, then one row will be found and its first field will contain the user name. I just check to see if a string is present, without bothering to verify what the string is.

To use the new database version of the `Authenticate()` method, I changed one line of code in the Submit button `Click` event handler, as shown in Listing 17-7.

Listing 17-7: Using a Custom Authenticate() Method

```
private void ButtonSubmit_Click(object sender, System.EventArgs e)
{
  if (Authenticate(TextBoxUsername.Text, TextBoxPassword.Text) )
    AcceptUser();
  else
    RejectUser();
}
```

Nothing too complicated, as you can see. Like I said earlier, ASP.NET Forms Authentication has many options and configuration settings you can customize. Hopefully, I addressed the issues that matter to the great majority of readers. For those I couldn't satisfy, you'll just have to wait for my next book.

Passport Authentication

One of the frustrations users experience on the Web is the need to continually provide user names and passwords to sites. To eliminate or reduce the need to enter the same information over and over, a mechanism would need to be set up that maintained user information in a central location. When the user visited a site that required a login, his or her information could be stored in the central location. When navigating to another site, the first site could simply hand over a special ticket obtained from the central repository indicating the user had already logged in.

This is basically what Passport Authentication is all about: letting a user log in once and then navigate to any number of Passport-supported sites without having to log in again. The Passport technology has been around for some time now, and has a growing number of participating sites. Now it is available as a .NET Web Service, so it is much easier than before to use. For it to really become important though, the number of participants will have to hit critical mass. The details of Passport Authentication are beyond the scope of this book, but you can check out http://www.passport.com for more information.

Summary

In the new world of Internet computing, security has become a critical issue, because potentially anyone can access an unprotected Web site. No Web application should be deployed in a production environment without appropriate security measures to authenticate and authorize users. Hackers often penetrate a system just to prove they can do it, but the criminally inclined may have other plans once inside a system. Once a user has gained control of a Web server, he or she may have unlimited access to other resources on the server's network, potentially giving them access to highly confidential information.

It's interesting to note that computer security, like other types of security such as home security, is often considered of little importance until the day an intrusion is actually experienced. Don't wait for hackers to penetrate your system: Plan your Web security model carefully and be diligent about installing security patches as they become available for your Web server.

✦　　✦　　✦

Back-End Components

The ADO.NET Architecture

When you've spent half your political life dealing with humdrum issues like the environment . . . it's exciting to have a real crisis on your hands.

— Former U.K. Prime Minister M. Thatcher, referring to the Falkland Islands conflict

While Prime Ministers may enjoy having an occasional crisis on their hands, software engineers and systems administrators working with back-end systems are somewhat less enthusiastic about the idea of a crisis. In fact, learning how to avoid critical situations, or how to cope with them when they do occur, is a lifetime learning experience for many of us, and certainly a source of stress we would gladly do without.

This last part of the book deals with the components, tools, and techniques that deal with the back-end of a multitier system. Just to make sure we're all on the same page, let me describe what I mean by *back-end*.

What Is the Back-End?

The back-end of a multitier application is where the rubber meets the road. It's all about moving data, handling transactions, running multi-threaded code, and managing enterprise information. Speed, stability, and the capability to handle large volumes of traffic are often critical. Typical back-end servers run relational database-management systems, file servers, e-mail services, and caching services. Or they provide gateway access to information services running on a remote system. Two important measurements with many back-end systems are their availability and their speed. Let's take a look at how availability and speed are characterized:

✦ *Availability* is expressed as a number, indicating the fraction of time that the system is in operation over a given time span. For example, if you have to take a system down once a week for an hour to fix it or update it, the system will be available for all but 1 hour out of the 168 hours of the week. The availability of the system will be 167 / 168, or 0.994. Most people use percentages to express system availability, so the value would be 99.4 %. While that sounds like a pretty good number, it's actually fairly poor. Good systems are those that are unavailable for only a few hours or minutes out of a *year*. If a system were down for 1 hour a year, its availability would be 99.988 %. That's a very respectable number, and one that will take a lot of work to achieve. Nevertheless, there are a lot of systems out there that achieve it. Some even exceed it. Most of them are mainframes or high-end UNIX systems, but Microsoft is trying hard to get the Windows platform in that category. Windows 2000 was the first serious step in that direction.

✦ *Speed* is usually measured in operations per second, or *transactions per second (TPS)*. The speed of most back-end systems is constrained by the DBMS running on it. High-end systems often use multiple processors to improve performance. These machines may reach TPS values in the 100–1000 range. More expensive systems may rely on hardware to push speed higher, by using arrays of disks (RAID) or large amounts of RAM. Ultra-high speed systems may achieve TPS values of 10,000 or more by loading the entire database into memory and eliminating disk access completely. These systems use gigabytes or even terabytes of RAM, and have expensive hardware to maintain data redundancy. The systems periodically copy changed records to disk, to reduce the possibility of data loss in the event of a fault of any kind. Needless to say, these systems run with battery backup power supplies.

Depending on the traffic your application is designed to handle, back-end components can be spread among more than one server. For example, you might have a database server running Oracle or SQL Server on one machine. On a different machine, you might be running database Web Services that access the database and produce resultsets that are consumed by Web Forms on a separate Web Server machine. Such a system would look something like Figure 18-1.

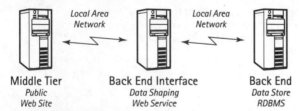

Figure 18-1: A system configured with two back-end levels

By moving the database-intensive components off the middle-tier to a separate machine, the public Web site machine (or machines) is able to service a much larger number of concurrent users.

For applications with lower expected traffic, such as intranet applications, you may not need all the horsepower of a multiback-end architecture. In many cases you can get by with a single machine running the private Web site, the back-end components, and the RDBMS together.

So, what is a back-end component? Is it a DMBS, a Web Server, or what? Strictly speaking, it is the service running on a back-end computer that reads and writes data. The data may be stored on the same computer, or it may be stored remotely. For example, if your back-end system is designed to get consumer credit reports, it might just be a gateway to a remote national service located who-knows-where. The back-end system would encapsulate all access to the national service, acting as a gateway to it. To other computers in the system, it would appear that your back-end system was the actual source of the credit information.

Now that I've described what the back-end is, let's explore the world of ADO.NET components. Database processing is a typical activity of back-end systems and ADO.NET is the backbone of all database operations in the .NET Framework.

ADO.NET Basics

ADO.NET is an evolutionary change from ADO, and a fairly big one, too. How is it different from ADO? Besides some changes in the programming model, a big difference is native support for XML. The ADO.NET architecture is designed from the ground up to support distributed architectures like the Web, passing data among distributed components with XML. Also, ADO.NET incorporates logic to handle disconnected recordsets containing arbitrary data types, so you can develop applications for portable devices that work even when the connection to the database is lost. While disconnected, users can work with the resultset. The ADO.NET components cache all the changes made. A connection is necessary only when you want to post changes made to the local data back to the database. The connection is used only briefly to post in a single pass all the inserts, updates, and deletions you made to the local data.

When data is moved internally among the various ADO.NET components and layers, it is often moved using XML packets. The total adoption of XML, in conjunction with the disconnected model, works eminently with client-server and multitier architectures, because it relieves the front-end from installing massive amounts of database client software and supports a thin client model. The use of XML and the disconnected model is also a boon for Web applications, because it fits the HTTP connection model very well.

In the following sections, I'll describe the basic ADO.NET components, showing how to use them. I created a sample program called *ADO.NET_Examples* that contains all the code shown. The complete code for this application is provided at the end of the chapter.

The DataSet

This component is the focal point of the entire ADO.NET architecture. A *DataSet* is the equivalent of an in-memory database, containing tables and relationships (such as Master-Detail relationships) among the tables. A DataSet loads records from an XML stream or file and makes them available to clients, who generally consume the data to present it on a user interface. A DataSet can also store all its tables and relationships in an xml file or to an XML stream. As you can see, DataSets are all about database schemas, records, and XML.

A very important thing to remember about DataSets is that they read and write XML data streams representing database records. Where these streams come from or where they go is completely irrelevant to a DataSet. Figure 18-2 shows a conceptual representation of a DataSet.

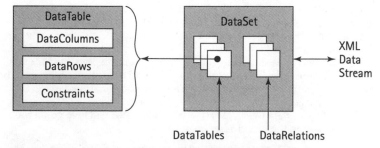

Figure 18-2: A conceptual representation of a DataSet

As you can see from the figure, `DataSets` are repositories of records. You can manipulate these records in various ways, using the DataRows collection. Once a `DataSet` is populated with records, no further database connection is needed to work with the records locally.

Besides supporting disconnected result sets, another really cool feature of `DataSet` is support for nonrectangular record sets. Traditional relational databases deal with tables using the familiar table construct. A table is a rectangular description of data, because the data is represented by a two-dimensional array of rows and columns, and all the rows have the same number of fields. There are many examples of nonrectangular collections of things that don't all have the same structure or layout. You don't have to look far to find them—the lines of text in this book, the hierarchy of folders displayed in Windows Explorer, or the nodes of an XML DOM are all examples.

The `DataSet` component has full support for XML, so you can feed it XML data on one side and then access the data with the disconnected record set metaphor on the other. Support for nonrectangular data enables a `DataSet` to store just about any kind of data you can think of, excluding binary or streaming data. `DataSets` are powerful components, but everything has a price and there are situations in which you may not want to use them. Since they offer the disconnected record-set feature, they obviously must cache entire record sets. If your record sets are big, that could be a problem, especially if you expect to have many `DataSet` instances at the same time, each with their own record set cache.

Not only do `DataSets` understand XML well, xml is in fact the *only* format they understand when populating themselves from a stream. The next logical question is: Where does the XML data stream come from or go to? The short answer is a *DataAdapter*.

The DataAdapter

`DataAdapter` components are responsible for maintaining and running the SQL commands necessary to move data back and forth between a `DataSet` and a data source (which is typically a database). A `DataAdapter` has four important properties that must be set up:

✦ `SelectCommand`

✦ `InsertCommand`

✦ `UpdateCommand`

✦ `DeleteCommand`

To populate a `DataSet`, you need to run a `DataAdapter`'s `SelectCommand` to fetch a result-set. The records in the resultset are passed as XML packets from the `DataAdapter` to the `DataSet`. The `DataSet` stores the records locally inside its own `DataTable` subcomponents. If you make any changes to the records managed by a `DataSet`, you need to post those changes to the database to make them permanent. Call `DataAdapter.Update()`, which gets all the changed records and runs the `InsertCommand`, `UpdateCommand`, and `DeleteCommand` statements to post the changes to the database. `DataAdapters` are responsible for establishing a connection to the data source, using the connection to read or write records, and then closing the connection. `DataAdapters` therefore work in close coordination with `Connection` components to open a communication channel with the data source, and with `Command` components to control the transfer of data over that channel. Figure 18-3 will give you a rough idea of where `DataAdapters` fit in the grand scheme of things.

There are two different versions of `DataAdapter`: *SqlDataAdapter* for SQL Server 7 and later databases, and *OleDbDataAdapter* for all other databases. You can associate a connection to a `DataAdapter` in two ways: implicitly and explicitly. In the former case, you call the `DataAdapter` constructor with the connection string, as shown in Listing 18-1.

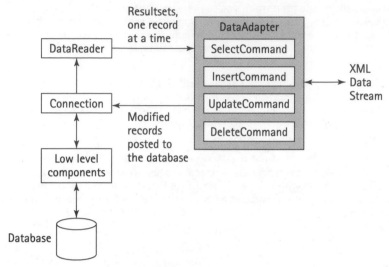

Figure 18-3: The role of a DataAdapter

Listing 18-1: Making a DataAdapter Instantiate Its Own Internal Connection Component

```
string conn = "...your connection string...";
string select = "Select au_id, au_lname, au_fname from authors";

// just pass a connection string to the DataAdapter
OleDbDataAdapter dataAdapter = new OleDbDataAdapter(select, conn);
```

The DataAdapter will then instantiate an internal Connection component, open it, use it, close it, and dispose of it at the right times. With the explicit way, you pass an existing Connection component to the DataAdapter as shown in Listing 18-2.

Listing 18-2: Passing an Existing Connection Component to a DataAdapter

```
// create a Connection component
string conn = "...your connection string...";
OleDbConnection connection = new OleDbConnection(conn);

// pass an existing Connection component to a DataAdapter
string select = "Select au_id, au_lname, au_fname from authors";
OleDbDataAdapter dataAdapter = new OleDbDataAdapter(select,
connection);
```

Do you need to close the connection when you're done with the `DataAdapter`? That depends: If you pass an open `Connection`, the `DataAdapter` uses it and leaves it open, so you'll need to close the `Connection` yourself. The assumption made by the `DataAdapter` is that if a connection is already open, you may want to continue to use it after the `DataAdapter` is finished.

If you pass a closed `Connection`, the `DataAdapter` will close it, use it, and then close it again. If you're not sure whether a `Connection` needs to be closed or not, call `Connection.Close()` just to be on the safe side: Database connections are one of the most valuable resources in your application, and failing to close unused connections will eventually cause serious database problems.

OK. So far, you know that `DataSets` hold database records in memory using `DataTables`. `DataSets` get these records from an XML data stream coming from a `DataAdapter`. `Data-Adapters` use `SelectCommand` with a `DataReader` to get this data from a data source. The `SelectCommand` component instantiates a `DataReader` to fetch the records from the resultset, one at a time.

The DataReader

Think of a *DataReader* as a forward-scrolling resultset cursor. Although it may not appear that `DataReaders` do very much, their main purpose is to insulate `DataAdapters` from the details of fetching records in a resultset.

A `DataReader` exposes only one way to fetch records: the `Read()` method. The `DataReader` component has no internal buffer of its own to store result sets, so client components are expected to call `Read()` to fetch the records one at a time. Once a record has been fetched, a `DataAdapter` can iterate over each field in the record and retrieve the field types and values.

Data passed between the `DataReader` and `DataAdapter` is not XML. The `DataAdapter` makes explicit method calls to the `DataReader` to fetch each field by type. For example, if the first field of the record is of type *integer,* the `DataAdapter` will call the method `DataReader.GetInt32(0)` to fetch the field's data. When the method `DataReader.Read()` returns `false`, it means the end of the resultset has been reached. Listing 18-3 shows how you might use a `DataReader` to programmatically get a resultset and iterate over it.

Listing 18-3: **Fetching Records One at a Time Using a DataReader**

```
void Fetch(System.Data.OleDb.OleDbConnection theConnection)
{
  string select = "Select au_lname, contract from authors";
  System.Data.OleDb.OleDbCommand command =
    new System.Data.OleDb.OleDbCommand(select, theConnection);
  theConnection.Open();
  System.Data.OleDb.OleDbDataReader dataReader;
  dataReader = command.ExecuteReader();
  while (dataReader.Read() )
  {
    String lastName = dataReader.GetString(0);
    bool contract   = dataReader.GetBoolean(1);
  }

  // closing the DataReader also closes its associated connection
```

```
    dataReader.Close();

    // you must explicitly close connections!

    connection.Close();
}
```

Note   A `DataReader` has no way of knowing how many records there are in a resultset. Each time you call its `Read()` method, it will fetch the next record and return `true`. If no more records are available, the method will return `false`. If you need to know in advance how many records there are, you'll need to run a separate `select count (*)` statement to find out.

Remember to always close a `DataReader` when you're done with it. You must also explicitly close any connections used. If you don't close the connection, the connection to the database will continue to remain open, and will not be reusable for other database operations.

The DataTable

All data in a `DataSet` is actually stored inside one or more `DataTables` managed by the `DataSet`. The number of tables created and managed by a `DataSet` depends entirely on the `select` statement used in the `DataAdapter` that populates the `DataSet`. For example, the following statement generates a result set for a single `DataTable`:

```
select * from authors
```

If you specify joins in the `select` statement, more than one table will be created in the `DataSet`. For example, the following statement generates two `DataTables`, one for `authors` and one for `title_author`:

```
select * from authors, title_author
where authors.au_id = title_author
```

A `DataRelation` will also be created to describe the join that relates the two `DataTables`.

To access one of the `DataTables`, you can use the `Tables` indexer property like this:

```
DataTable authorsTable = myDataSet.Tables[0];
```

To determine the number of `DataTables` set up in a `DataSet`, use the `Tables.Count` property like this:

```
int c = dataSet.Tables.Count;
```

The DataView

As mentioned earlier, `DataSets` contain the cached records returned by the `select` statement used in the associated `DataAdapter`. A `DataView` component enables you to further process the records in a `DataTable`, supporting filtering and searching. You can attach more than one `DataView` to the same `DataTable` and have each view filter out different records and apply different sorting criteria. Figure 18-4 shows the basic relationship between a `DataView`, a `DataTable`, and a consumer of data.

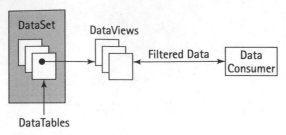

Figure 18-4: The relationship between DataSets, DataViews, and data consumers

The following sections describe the main filtering and sorting operations that can be performed with DataViews. Keep in mind that filtered or sorted records are stored locally inside each DataView, so the records in the associated DataTable are not altered or rearranged in any way.

Sorting records

It's easy to make a DataView sort the records contained in a DataTable. The sorting can be in either ascending or descending order, and can include multiple columns. Listing 18-4 shows how to sort the authors table in descending order on the au_lname column and ascending order on the au_fname column.

Listing 18-4: Using a DataView to Sort a resultset on Two Different Columns

```
String conn;  // ... assume this is the connection string
string select = "Select au_id, au_lname, au_fname from authors";
OleDbDataAdapter dataAdapter = new OleDbDataAdapter(select, conn);
DataSet dataSet = new DataSet();

dataAdapter.Fill(dataSet);
DataView dataView = new DataView(dataSet.Tables[0]);

dataView.Sort = @"au_lname DESC, au_fname ASC";

for (int i = 0; i < dataView.Count; i++)
{
  String lastName = dataView [i]["au_lname"].ToString();
  String firstName = dataView [i]["au_fname"].ToString();
}
```

Remember, sorting records with a DataView doesn't affect the records stored in the underlying DataTable.

Filtering records

You can also use a DataView to extract from a DataTable all those records that satisfy some filtering criterion. Class DataView has a property called RowFilter that can be assigned an expression that will then be used internally as the where clause in a select statement against the records in the DataTable. Listing 18-5 shows how to use RowFilter to effect row resultset filtering with a DataView component.

Listing 18-5: Using a DataView to Filter the Records in a DataTable

```
String conn;  // ... assume this is the connection string
string select = "Select au_id, au_lname, au_fname from authors";
OleDbDataAdapter dataAdapter = new OleDbDataAdapter(select, conn);
DataSet dataSet = new DataSet();
dataAdapter.Fill(dataSet);
DataView dataView = new DataView(dataSet.Tables[0]);

// select all the authors whose last names start with
// letters between 'A' and 'G'
dataView.RowFilter = @"au_lname >= 'A' and au_lname <= 'G'";

for (int i = 0; i < dataView.Count; i++)
{
  String lastName = dataView [i]["au_lname"].ToString();
}
```

Getting a list of the modified records

Another type of filtering that DataViews support is based on a row's type, as opposed to its data. When you insert, update, or delete rows in a DataView, the component tags these modified rows, so they can be retrieved separately if you need them. The ADO.NET Framework uses modified rows to post changes to the database, as described later. Listing 18-6 shows how to add a new record to a DataView and then iterate over the DataView to get a list of all the added records.

Listing 18-6: Using a DataView to Filter the Added Records

```
String conn;  // ... assume this is the connection string
string select = "Select au_id, au_lname, au_fname from authors";
OleDbDataAdapter dataAdapter = new OleDbDataAdapter(select, conn);
DataSet dataSet = new DataSet();
dataAdapter.Fill(dataSet);
DataView dataView = new DataView(dataSet.Tables[0]);


DataRowView addedRow = theDataView.AddNew();
addedRow ["au_lname"] = "<New last name>";



theDataView.RowStateFilter = DataViewRowState.Added;
```

Continued

Listing 18-6 *(continued)*

```
for (int i = 0; i < theDataView.Count; i++)
{
  String lastName = theDataView[i]["au_lname"].ToString();
}
```

To filter out updated or deleted rows, use these two filters:

✦ `DataViewRowState.ModifiedCurrent`

✦ `DataViewRowState.Deleted`

The `ModifiedCurrent` filter shows the new value of updated records. To see the old value of the records, use the property `DataViewRowState.ModifiedOriginal`. You can use multiple filters at once. For example, to get the number of added, updated, and deleted rows, you could do this:

```
dataView.RowStateFilter =  DataViewRowState.Added |
                           DataViewRowState.ModifiedCurrent |
                           DataViewRowState.Deleted;
```

You can also get the records that weren't changed using the following filter:

```
dataView.RowStateFilter = DataViewRowState.OriginalRows;
```

Note Remember that changes made to a `DataView` are not automatically posted to the database. In fact, they aren't even posted to the `DataTable` that the `DataView` is associated with. To write changes to the database, you need to explicitly post them, as described in the later section titled "Validating changes and resolving errors."

Locating records

Class `DataView` has a `Find()` method you can use to locate a record based on its primary key. Listing 18-7 shows how to use it to locate an author whose `au_id` value has a given value.

Listing 18-7: Locating a Record by Its Primary Key

```
String conn;  // ... assume this is the connection string
string select = "Select au_id, au_lname, au_fname from authors";
OleDbDataAdapter dataAdapter = new OleDbDataAdapter(select, conn);
DataSet dataSet = new DataSet();
dataAdapter.Fill(dataSet);
DataView dataView = new DataView(dataSet.Tables[0]);

dataView.Sort = "au_id";

int i = dataView.Find("672-71-3249");
if (i < 0)
  return;  // record not found
```

```
DataRowView locatedRow = dataView [i];

String lastName = locatedRow["au_lname"].ToString();
String firstName = locatedRow["au_fname"].ToString();
```

If the primary key of a table includes multiple columns, you need to pass the values of each key column as an array. Suppose the columns au_id, au_lname, and au_fname were all part of the primary key of the authors table. In this case, you would have to call the Find() method, as shown in Listing 18-8.

Listing 18-8: Calling DataView.Find() When a Table Has Multiple Columns in the Primary Key

```
Object[] keyValue = new Object[] {"672-71-3249",
                                  "Yokomoto",
                                  "Akiko"};
int i = theDataView.Find(keyValue);
```

Make sure the table you use Find() with has a primary key. If it does not, a Missing-PrimaryKeyException will be occur when Find() is invoked .

Other DataView features

Searching and sorting are probably the most well known features of DataViews, but there are a few other useful ones. For example, you can set up a DataView to refuse inserts, updates, or deletes on its records using the following properties:

 ✦ AllowNew

 ✦ AllowEdit

 ✦ AllowDelete

When a filtering criterion is changed and the records in a DataView are updated, the component fires a ListChanged event that you can use to synchronize other components that might be affected.

Data binding

User interface controls that display data contained in a database or a generic data source have a simple way of connecting with the data, using an infrastructure known as *data binding*. Data binding is not a new concept at all, but ADO.NET uses a different architecture from ADO to achieve it.

The most spectacular aspect added by ADO.NET is that Windows Forms and Web Forms use the same data-binding architecture and components. The ADO.NET components provide the necessary transport and packaging code to move resultsets between components and even computers. Figure 18-5 shows some of the UI controls and data sources that can be bound together.

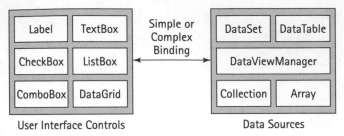

Figure 18-5: Typical user-interface controls and data sources involved in data binding

There are two types of data binding: simple and complex. The following sections describe both types.

Simple binding

Simple data binding applies to UI controls that can only display one value at a time, such a `Labels`, `TextBoxes`, and `CheckBoxes`. To create a simple binding between a control and a data source, create a `Binding` object and then add it to the control's `BindingContext` like this:

```
Binding binding = new Binding("Text", table, "au_lname");
textBoxName.DataBindings.Add(binding);
```

The first parameter in the `Binding` constructor is the name of the control's property you want to bind to the data source. The second parameter is the data source object to bind to. The third parameter is the name of the column in the data source to bind to.

If the control is already bound when you call `DataBindings.Add()`, an exception will be thrown. To avoid the exception, remove all bindings before adding the new one, as shown in Listing 18-9.

Listing 18-9: Using Simple Data Binding with a TextBox

```
Binding binding = new Binding("Text", datasource, "au_lname");

mytextBox.DataBindings.Clear(); // to remove old bindings
mytextBox.DataBindings.Add(binding);
```

You can use data binding on any property you want, such as the Text, Size, BackColor, or Visible properties. See Chapter 11, titled "Database Front Ends," for additional information on binding arbitrary properties.

Complex binding

Complex data binding applies to UI controls that can display lists of values. Don't get the idea that complex binding is complicated to program or set up. This type of binding is complex only because of the way it maps multiple rows and columns in a data source to a UI control. Complex data binding doesn't usually take more than one or two lines of code to establish. `ListBoxes`, `ComboBoxes`, and `DataGrids` all use complex binding. With complex binding, you simply set the UI control's `DataSource` property to the name of the data source object.

With single-column complex binding, used with ListBoxes and ComboBoxes, you also need to supply the name of the column to use by setting the DisplayMember property, as shown in Listing 18-10.

Listing 18-10: Complex Binding with a ComboBox

```
myComboBox.DataSource = datasource;
myComboBox.DisplayMember = "au_lname";
```

ListBoxes and ComboBoxes will display the entire column of data they are bound to. With ListBoxes, the current record will be highlighted in the list. With ComboBoxes, the current record will be the selected item.

With multicolumn complex binding, used with DataGrids, you don't need to supply column names, because all the columns in the data source will be displayed. The code to bind a DataGrid is shown in Listing 18-11.

Listing 18-11: Using Complex Binding with a DataGrid

```
dataGrid1.DataSource = datasource;
```

You can also set up a DataGrid to display only a subset of all the columns in a data source. As you can see, the code to bind controls to a data source is trivial. What I haven't shown yet is how the various types of data sources, like DataSets and DataTables, can be used.

Binding to various data source types

Probably the most common type of data source is a database field. Listing 18-12 shows how you would set up a DataSet, populate it with records from the authors table, and then bind the table's au_lname column to a TextBox.

Listing 18-12: Binding a TextBox to a Database Field

```
string conn = @"Provider=SQLOLEDB.1;Integrated Security=SSPI;" +
  @"Persist Security Info=False;User ID=Ted;Initial Catalog=pubs;" +
  @"Data Source=(local);Use Procedure for Prepare=1;" +
  @"Auto Translate=True;Packet Size=4096;" +
  @"Workstation ID=FRANCESCA;" +
  @"Use Encryption for Data=False;" +
  @"Tag with column collation when possible=False";

// setup the data source

string select = "Select * from authors";
OleDbDataAdapter dataAdapter = new OleDbDataAdapter(select, conn);
```

Continued

Listing 18-12 *(continued)*

```
DataSet dataSet = new DataSet();
dataAdapter.Fill(dataSet);
DataTable authors = dataSet.Tables[0];

// bind TextBox

binding = new Binding("Text", authors, "au_lname");
textBoxName.DataBindings.Clear(); // to remove old bindings
textBoxName.DataBindings.Add(binding);
```

The code in the listing is part of the ADO.NET_Examples program, shown at the end of the chapter. To see the effect of the code, run the program, select the DataBinding tab, and click the Bind To Database button. Figure 18-6 shows various user interface controls populated through both simple and complex binding from a database.

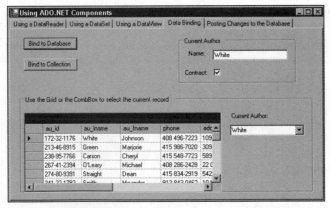

Figure 18-6: Populating user interface controls using simple and complex data binding

You don't necessarily need a database to support data binding. You can also use a collection as data source. The easiest collection is use is the DataRowCollection, managed by a DataTable. Each item in a DataRowCollection is a DataRow, and each DataRow can have any number of columns. The one restriction is that all DataRows have the same number and type of columns. Listing 18-13 shows how to use a DataTable to populate a DataRowCollection, which is then used as the data source for the UI controls shown in the previous figure.

Listing 18-13: Using a DataRowCollection as a Data Source in Data Binding

```
Binding binding;

String s = "";
```

```
bool b = false;

DataColumn columnLastName =
           new DataColumn("au_lname", s.GetType() );
DataColumn columnContract =
           new DataColumn("contract", b.GetType() );

DataTable table = new DataTable();

table.Columns.Add(columnLastName);
table.Columns.Add(columnContract);


DataRow row = table.NewRow();
row["au_lname"] = "Carson";
row["contract"] = true;
table.Rows.Add(row);

row = table.NewRow();
row["au_lname"] = "Hunter";
row["contract"] = false;
table.Rows.Add(row);

row = table.NewRow();
row["au_lname"] = "Johnson";
row["contract"] = true;
table.Rows.Add(row);

row = table.NewRow();
row["au_lname"] = "Smith";
row["contract"] = true;
table.Rows.Add(row);

// bind DataGrid
dataGrid1.DataSource = table;

// bind TextBox
binding = new Binding("Text", table, "au_lname");
textBoxName.DataBindings.Clear(); // to remove old bindings
textBoxName.DataBindings.Add(binding);

// bind CheckBox
binding = new Binding("Checked", table, "contract");
checkBoxContract.DataBindings.Clear(); // to remove old bindings
checkBoxContract.DataBindings.Add(binding);

// bind ComboBox
comboBoxCurrentAuthor.DataSource = table;
comboBoxCurrentAuthor.DisplayMember = "au_lname";
```

Running the code produces the results shown in Figure 18-7.

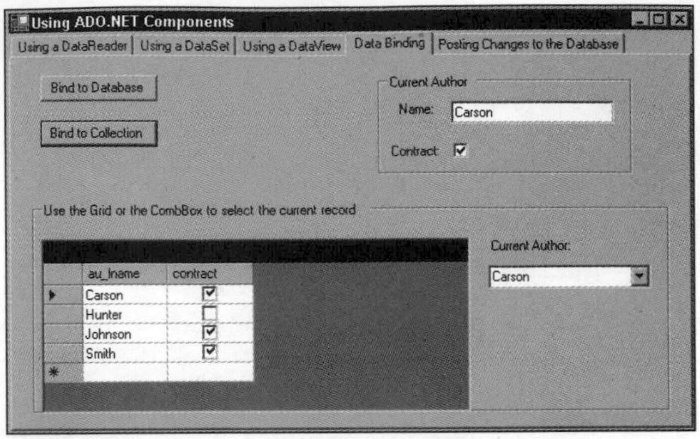

Figure 18-7: Using a collection as a data source in data binding

As stated earlier, you can use many different kinds of objects as data sources, such as collections, arrays, `DataSets`, `DataViews`, and `DataTables`. The process for filling the data source with records may be different for each type, but the way you bind a UI control to a data source is always the same.

Connecting to the Database

Back in Figure 18-3, I showed you a component called `Connection`. The role of this component is to encapsulate the details of managing a connection to the database. There are two versions of the component: one to handle connections to Microsoft SQL Server 7 and later, and one for all other kinds of databases. The first is called *SqlConnection,* and the latter is *OleDbConnection.* The main property of both components is `ConnectionString`. This string has a semicolon-separated list of properties that are passed to the low-level managed components that ultimately talk to the database-specific data provider. The most commonly used properties are these:

- ✦ `Provider`
- ✦ `DataSource`
- ✦ `Database`
- ✦ `UserId`

The name and number of attributes is strictly database-dependent. The password can also be passed in the connection string, but in most production software, the password is not supplied. It's not a good idea to embed passwords in the source code of production software. When the password is not supplied in the `ConnectionString`, the database will prompt the user for the password at runtime.

A `ConnectionString` for SQL Server might look like this:

```
string conn = @"Provider=SQLOLEDB.1;"+
              @"User ID=Ted;"+
              @"Initial Catalog=pubs;"+
              @" Data Source=(local);"+
              @"Packet Size=4096";
```

When connecting to the database, the `SqlConnection` and `OleDbConnection` components will talk with managed components that in turn may interact with unmanaged OLE DB providers. Figure 18-8 shows where the connection components come into the picture with respect to the other important ADO.NET components and the database.

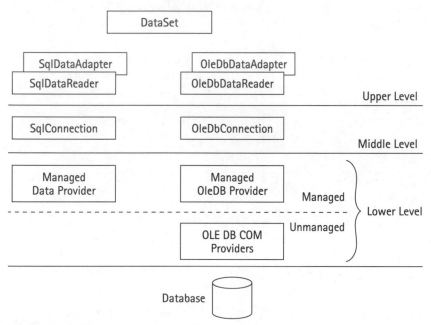

Figure 18-8: The database connection components in the ADO.NET architecture

Opening and closing connections

When you create database applications using the VS .NET wizards, all the database connection details are automatically taken care of for you, so you rarely deal with database connection objects directly. If you are writing your own code to open a connection and use it, then you need to make sure you close the connection when you're done. When the connection object is finalized and garbage-collected, the connection is *not* closed automatically. Listing 18-14 shows how to programmatically create, open, use, and close a connection.

Listing 18-14: **Opening and Closing a Connection Programmatically**

```
string conn = @"Provider=SQLOLEDB.1;Integrated Security=SSPI;" +
  @"Persist Security Info=False;User ID=Ted;Initial Catalog=pubs;" +
  @"Data Source=(local);Use Procedure for Prepare=1;" +
  @"Auto Translate=True;Packet Size=4096; " +
  @"Workstation ID=FRANCESCA;" +
  @"Use Encryption for Data=False;" +
```

Continued

Listing 18-14 *(continued)*

```
    @"Tag with column collation when possible=False";

OleDbConnection connection = new OleDbConnection();
connection.ConnectionString = conn;

// use the connection with a DataReader
string select = "Select au_lname from authors order by au_lname";
OleDbCommand command = new OleDbCommand(select, connection);

// open the connection
connection.Open();

// get a resultset using the connection
OleDbDataReader dataReader = command.ExecuteReader();

// iterate over the resultset...
while (dataReader.Read() )
{
   String lastName = dataReader.GetString(0);
}

// close the DataReader
dataReader.Close();

// close the connection
connection.Close();
```

As mentioned earlier, DataAdapters may or may not close the Connection they use. If you create your own Connection, open it, and then pass it to a DataAdapter constructor, the DataAdapter will leave the connection open. If you pass the DataAdapter constructor a closed connection, or just provide a connection string, a connection will be opened, used, and closed automatically where necessary. If you use a DataReader, remember to close it when you're done with it, but don't forget to also close the connection used.

When in doubt, always call a connection's Close() method. Calling Close() on a closed connection will not cause errors or other problems.

Connection pooling

Many types of applications are designed for large numbers of simultaneous users. Web applications often have many thousands of users at any given time. When an application like this uses a database, it is very important to manage who connects to the database, when, and for how long. Database connections are very precious and limited resources that need to be managed carefully.

If you use DataViews, DataSets, and DataAdapters to access data, then the ADO.NET Framework will automatically use database connections for the shortest amount of time possible. When retrieving a resultset, DataAdapters typically open a connection, run a SQL select statement on it, fetch the resultset, and immediately close the connection. When posting changes to the database, DataAdapters open a connection, run all inserts, updates, and deletes, and then immediately close the connection.

In order for these operations to be quick, ADO.NET needs to pool database connections. When you run a program and request data for the first time against a database, ADO.NET creates a connection component (either an SqlConnection or an OleDbConnection) and uses it to connect to the database. This connection operation can take anywhere from milliseconds to seconds, depending on the database used, its load, and other factors. You don't want to incur this connection time overhead every time you perform a database operation, so ADO.NET sets up and manages pools of database connections automatically.

You can disable connection pooling if you want. When you close an SqlConnection or OleDbConnection component, ADO.NET doesn't really close the low-level database connection. Instead, it takes the connection handle and puts it in a connection pool. The next time you open a connection to the same database, the connection handle is obtained from the pool and used. Since the connection is still open, it can be used instantly.

Each database you connect to will have its own pool. For example, if you have an application that uses connections to two databases called Pubs and Northwind, there will be two entirely separate connection pools for the connection handles. What's more, every connection string uses its own pool. If you create two connections to the same database that are different in any way, even if they access the same database and tables, the system will create separate connection pools for them. In order for two connections to share the same pool, their connection strings must match exactly, because the connection pool manager is extremely conservative when deciding if two connections can share a pool: Even the simple changing of the parameter order will cause a new connection pool to be created.

Maximizing performance

It's important to understand how and when a connection is returned to the connection pool. When a connection goes out of scope, whether in the open or closed state, it becomes available for garbage collection. When the garbage collector kicks in and comes across the connection, it calls the object's Finalize() method. If the connection is in the closed state, the finalizer calls the connection's Dispose() method. Dispose() moves the low-level connection handle into the connection pool, making it available for reuse. In high-performance systems, you need to make sure connection handles are returned to the pool as quickly as possible, so you should manually dispose of connections as soon as you're finished using them. Listing 18-15 shows you how to do this.

Listing 18-15: Disposing of a Connection to Force Its Immediate Return to the Connection Pool

```
OleDbConnection connection = new OleDbConnection();
// set connection string...

// open the connection
connection.Open();

// use the connection...

// close and return connection to pool
connection.Dispose();
```

Calling a connection's `Dispose()` method automatically closes the connection and then immediately returns the connection handle to the connection pool. It may be a good idea to wrap your database operations in a `try` block, and call `connection.Dispose()` in the final section, as shown in Listing 18-16.

Listing 18-16: Disposing of a Connection Even If Exceptions Occur

```
System.Data.OleDb.OleDbConnection connection = null;
try
{
  connection = new System.Data.OleDb.OleDbConnection();
  // set connection string...

  // open the connection
  connection.Open();

  // use the connection...
}
finally
{
  if (connection != null)
    connection.Dispose();
}
```

When the application is shut down, the ADO.NET Framework automatically shuts down the low-level database connections associated with the connection handles in the connection pools. Remember that dangling open connections are not returned to the connection pool and may represent a resource leak even after your application terminates. In some cases, you may have to restart the DBMS to recover the leaked connection handles.

Configuring the connection pool

Connection pooling is provided by managed SQL Server data providers and unmanaged OLE DB COM providers. To configure a connection pool, you pass attributes to a `Connection` object in the `ConnectionString`. Table 18-1 shows the pooling properties you can change with `SqlConnections`.

Table 18-1 Connection Pooling Attributes

Attribute	Description	Default
Connection Lifetime	Determines how many seconds an idle connection is kept in the pool before being disposed of. The value 0 makes an idle connection remain indefinitely in the pool.	0
Connection Reset	When `true`, this causes a connection to be reset when acquired from the pool.	true
Enlist	If `true`, the connections added to the pool use the same transaction context as the current thread.	true

Attribute	Description	Default
Max Pool Size	The maximum number of connections cached in the pool.	100
Min Pool Size	The minimum number of connections cached in the pool.	0
Pooling	When true, this enables connection pooling. Pooling can be set to true or false for each SqlConnection you create.	true

With OleDb connections, connection pooling is considered an OLE DB service made available by the OLE DB provider component. You can set connection pooling attributes using the OLE DB Services attribute in the connectionString like this:

```
String conn = @"Provider=SQLOLEDB;OLE DB Services=???; ...";
OleDbConnection connection = new OleDbConnection();
connection.ConnectionString = conn;
```

where the value assigned to the OLE DB Services attribute will determine what connection pooling options are enabled or disabled. Which attributes can be set is strictly provider-dependent. The Microsoft OLE DB providers for SQL Server and Oracle both support connection pooling by default.

Making Changes to the Database

Changing records in a DataSet, DataTable, or DataView is strictly an in-memory affair. The database is never touched. Once you have made all the changes you wanted, you must post them all to the database. The following sections show you how to change records and immediately post the changes to the database.

Adding records

To add a new record, the procedure is simple. You call the DataTable.NewRow() method, initialize the row fields and call the DataAdapter.Update() method to add the row to the database. Listing 18-17 shows the code.

Listing 18-17: **Inserting a New Row**

```
// assume you setup a DataAdapter with Select, Insert,
// Update and Delete statements. The easiest way to do
// this is with the DataAdapter wizard

OleDbDataAdapter oleDbDataAdapter1= new OleDbDataAdapter();

DataSet dataSet = new DataSet();
oleDbDataAdapter1.Fill(dataSet);

// create a new, empty row in the DataTable
DataRow newAuthor = dataSet.Tables [0].NewRow();
```

Continued

Listing 18-17 *(continued)*

```
// initialize all the required fields
newAuthor ["au_id"] ="999-99-9999" ;
newAuthor ["au_lname"] ="Last Name";
newAuthor ["au_fname"] ="First Name";

// add the row to the DataTable
dataSet.Tables [0].Rows.Add(newAuthor);

// post the new row to the database

oleDbDataAdapter1.Update(dataSet);

// commit all changes

dataSet.AcceptChanges();
```

The `DataTable.NewRow()` method returns an empty row with the same schema (column types) as the other rows in the `DataTable`. Then you initialize the fields, add the row to the `DataTable`, post the changes to the database, and commit the changes. You only call `DataAdapter.Update()` and `DataSet.AcceptChanges()` when you're done making changes. The changes may apply to any number of records, and include updates and deletes. Calls to `AcceptChanges` are fairly expensive for most databases, so try to call this method only once, after all your changes are made.

Updating records

Changing an existing record is also straightforward. First you need to locate the record to change. The code that changes the record needs to be bracketed by calls to `BeginEdit()` and `EndEdit()`. Listing 18-18 shows the complete details.

Listing 18-18: Updating an Existing Row

```
DataSet dataSet = new DataSet();
oleDbDataAdapter1.Fill(dataSet);

// find an item to update
DataTable authors = dataSet.Tables [0];
DataRow[] rows = authors.Select("au_id = '999-99-9999'");
if (rows.Length == 0) return;

// edit the item
DataRow rowToChange = rows[0];
rowToChange.BeginEdit();
rowToChange ["address"] = "New Address";
rowToChange.EndEdit();

// commit the changes to the database
```

```
oleDbDataAdapter1.Update(dataSet); // post changes to the database
dataSet.AcceptChanges();           // to commit all changes
```

Deleting records

Deleting records is also pretty easy. You specify which row or rows to delete, delete them from the DataTable, and then post the changes to the database. Listing 18-19 shows how you could delete a single row.

Listing 18-19: **Deleting a Single Row**

```
DataSet dataSet = new DataSet();
oleDbDataAdapter1.Fill(dataSet);

// find an item to update
DataTable authors = dataSet.Tables [0];

DataRow[] rows = authors.Select("au_id = '999-99-9999'");
if (rows.Length == 0) return;

// delete the item
DataRow rowToDelete = rows[0];
rowToDelete.Delete();

// commit the changes to the database
oleDbDataAdapter1.Update(dataSet); // post changes to the database
dataSet.AcceptChanges();           // to commit all changes
```

To delete multiple rows, you can use DataTable.Select() to retrieve a collection of rows to delete, and then delete each row as shown in Listing 18-20.

Listing 18-20: **Deleting Multiple Rows**

```
// delete all the authors whose names start with H
DataRow[] authors = authors.Select("au_lname like 'H%'");
foreach (DataRow author in authors)
  author.Delete();
oleDbDataAdapter1.Update(myDataSet); // post changes to the database
dataSet.AcceptChanges();             // to commit all changes
```

As stated earlier, the DataTable.Select() method takes a SQL filter expression and returns a DataRow collection with the rows that satisfy the expression.

To delete all the rows in a table, you can use DataTable.Clear() to remove all rows, and then update the database as usual, as shown in Listing 18-21.

Listing 18-21: Deleting All Rows in a Table

```
// delete all authors from the table
authors.Clear();
oleDbDataAdapter1.Update(dataSet); // post changes to the database
dataSet.AcceptChanges();          // to commit all changes
```

When you use `DataAdapter.Update(DataSet)` to post changes to the database, the target `DataSet` is automatically updated, so it should contain the same records as the database.

Another way to delete all the rows in a table is by using a direct SQL DELETE command, in conjunction with a `SQLCommand.ExecuteNonQuery()` call as shown in Listing 18-22. The advantage of this second approach is speed.

Listing 18-22: Another Way to Delete All Rows in a Table

```
SqlCommand myCommand = new SqlCommand("Delete from authors",
                                      sqlConnection1);
myCommand.Connection.Open();

// use a try block, so we can close the connection in
// the finally clause even if exceptions occur
try {
  myCommand.ExecuteNonQuery();
}
finally
{
  myCommand.Connection.Close();
}
```

Pay special attention to the fact that `ExecuteNonQuery()` is a method of class `SqlCommand`, not of `DataAdapter` or `DataSet`. The method executes SQL commands directly against the database, bypassing any `DataAdapters` or `DataSets` you may be using in your application.

 Note Performing an Insert, Update or Delete using `SqlCommand.ExecuteNonQuery()` leaves your `DataSet` components out-of-sync with the database. To resynchronize affected `DataSets` with the database, you'll want to call `DataAdapter.Fill(DataSet)` to repopulate the `DataSets`.

At this point, you should be able to accomplish the basic tasks of inserting, updating, and deleting records. Unfortunately, in the real world things don't always go as expected. Database operations don't always succeed, so you have to be prepared to deal with problems, which can hit you in the form of exceptions.

Dealing with DataSet problems

The most common type of problem is an exception caused by referencing a nonexistent table or column. In the previous examples, I accessed the `DataTable` component in a `DataSet` using an integer index. I knew for sure there was one table in the `DataSet.Tables` collection, so I didn't have any problems. But what if you used an incorrect index to retrieve a nonexistent table, by doing the following:

```
DataTable table = myDataSet.Tables [50];
```

You would get a `System.IndexOutOfRange` exception.

More often than not, instead of using numeric indexes to retrieve a table, you'll probably use table names like this:

```
DataTable table = myDataSet.Tables ["authors"];
```

If there is no table with the given name, the code won't throw an exception. Instead it will return a null object. Any attempts to access the object's methods or properties will obviously provoke a `System.NullReferenceException` with the following message:

```
Attempted to dereference a null object reference.
```

Specifying an incorrect column name in a `DataTable.Select()` filter will provoke a `System.Data.EvaluateException`, For example the code:

```
DataRow[] rows = authors.Select("au_idasdf = '999-99-9999'");
```

will throw an `EvaluateException` with the message

```
Cannot find column [au_idasdf].
```

Another source of problems is data-related. If you insert a new record into a table that conflicts with a record already in the table, as shown in Listing 18-23, a constraint violation exception may be thrown.

Listing 18-23: **Attempting to Insert Duplicate Records**

```
// create an author
DataRow author = myDataSet.Tables [0].NewRow();
author1 ["au_id"] ="999-99-9999" ;
author1 ["au_lname"] ="Last Name";
author1 ["au_fname"] ="First Name";
author1 ["phone"] ="555-1212";
author1 ["address"] ="Address";
author1 ["city"] ="City";
author1 ["state"] ="CA";
author1 ["zip"] ="55555";
author1 ["contract"] = 1;

// add the same row twice to the DataTable
myDataSet.Tables [0].Rows.Add(author);
myDataSet.Tables [0].Rows.Add(author);

adoDataSetCommand1.Update(myDataSet); // fl exception thrown here
myDataSet.AcceptChanges();
```

The code attempts to insert the same record twice. On the second attempt, this code will throw an ArgumentException with the following message:

```
This row already belongs to the table.
```

The moral of the story is that you should wrap code that deals with database operations in a try block. Be prepared to handle the exceptions I mentioned as well as others.

Validating changes and resolving errors

Errors caused by incorrect data are a major source of headaches in database applications. The following are just some of the things you need to check for:

✦ Nulls in non-nullable fields

✦ Duplicate records

✦ Attempts to delete nonexistent records

✦ Invalid or incorrectly formatted data

When you insert, update, or delete a row in a DataTable, a DataRowChangeEvent is fired both before and after the change is made. If you install an event handler for the RowChanging event, you can validate the data immediately, avoiding database errors later when the changes are posted to the database. You can also install a RowChanged handler to see what the records look like after being applied to the local DataTable. Listing 18-24 shows how to install the event handler for the authors table used in my sample program *ADO.NET_Examples*.

Listing 18-24: **Installing the Event Handler**

```
DataTable authors = dataSet.Tables [0];

authors.RowChanging +=
    new DataRowChangeEventHandler(MyRowChangingHandler);
```

Listing 18-25 shows a simple handler.

Listing 18-25: **An Event Handler to Validate Changes to a DataRow**

```
public void MyRowChangeHandler(Object sender,
                                DataRowChangeEventArgs e)
{
  DataRow rowToCheck = e.Row;

  switch (e.Action)
  {

    case DataRowAction.Add:
      // validate rowToCheck;
      break;
    case DataRowAction.Change: ;
      // validate rowToCheck;
```

```
            break;
         case DataRowAction.Delete: ;
            // verify if it is OK to delete rowToCheck
            break;

         default:
            break;
      }
   }
```

The event argument passed to the handler tells you which row was changed and how. If you determine that one or more fields in the row are invalid, you'll probably want to do one or more of the following things:

✦ Display an error message to the user.

✦ Apply a safe default for the incorrect data.

✦ Set the row's HasErrors property to true.

✦ Throw an exception.

To prevent the row from being changed, throw an exception. It doesn't matter what type of exception, any will do. The DataTable code that fired the DataRowChange event will catch the exception and refrain from changing the record. If you don't throw an exception and you can't fix the data for some reason, you can set the changed row's HasErrors property to true. Later, before posting the table changes to the database, you can check the DataTable.HasErrors property and attempt to fix the errors.

Listing 18-26 shows how you might check for errors, fix them, and post all the changes to the database.

Note The listing is fairly long, so I numbered the lines to simplify the discussion of the code.

Listing 18-26: Fixing Errors Flagged with the HasErrors Property

```
1  void CheckAndFixErrors(DataSet myDataSet)
2  {
3    if (!myDataSet.HasChanges() ) return;
4
5    // get a list of the New, Modified or Deleted rows
6
7    DataSet changedDataSet = myDataSet.GetChanges(DataRowState.Added);
8    // DataSet changedDataSet = myDataSet.GetChanges(DataRowState.Modified);
9    // DataSet changedDataSet = myDataSet.GetChanges(DataRowState.Deleted);
10
11   if (!changedDataSet.Tables [0].HasErrors) return;
12
13   // handle the errors
14   foreach (DataRow changedRow in changedDataSet.Tables [0].Rows)
15   {
16     if (!changedRow.HasErrors) continue;
```

Continued

Listing 18-26 *(continued)*

```
17
18      // get a list of the columns with bad data
19      DataColumn[] cols = changedRow.GetColumnsInError();
20
21      // tell the user which columns need to be fixed
22      if (cols != null)
23      {
24        Console.Write("The following columns have bad data:\n");
25        for (int i = 0; i < cols.Length; i++)
26          // show the name of the column
27          Console.WriteLine(cols[i].ColumnName + " ");
28      }
29
30      // get the original row
31      String originalLastName, currentLastName;
32
33      // no original value for New records
34      // if (changedRow ["au_lname", DataRowVersion.Original] != null)
35      // originalLastName =
36      //    changedRow ["au_lname", DataRowVersion.Original].ToString();
37
38      // get the current row, with the user's changes
39      if (changedRow ["au_lname", DataRowVersion.Current] != null)
40        currentLastName =
41          changedRow ["au_lname", DataRowVersion.Current].ToString();
42
43      // show the row to the user and ask for corrections
44      // ...
45
46      // clear all the HasError flags on the fields of the row,
47      // assuming the errors were fixes
48      changedRow.ClearErrors();
49    }
50
51    // merge the changed data back with the original data
52    myDataSet.Merge(changedDataSet);
53
54    oleDbDataAdapter1.Update(myDataSet);
55    myDataSet.AcceptChanges(); // to commit all changes
56}
```

Note   The `HasErrors` properties I refer to in the code will return `false` unless you set them to true somewhere in your code. The place you'll most likely do this is inside a `RowChangedEvent` handler, as discussed earlier. The ADO.NET code does *not* set `HasErrors` properties automatically: The properties were created to help you add your own error-handling code.

On line 3, the call to `DataSet.HasChanges()` checks to see if any rows were inserted, added, or deleted in any of the tables of the `DataSet`. Keep in mind that there can be more than one table, and the various tables can (and probably do) have different schemas.

If the code discovers that changes have occurred, the next step is to get a list of the changed rows. This is accomplished on line 7, 8, or 9 by calling `DataSet.GetChanges(DataRowState)`, indicating whether you're interested in getting the `New`, `Modified`, or `Deleted` rows. If you want all changes, including `New`, `Modified`, and `Deleted` rows, call `DataSet.GetChanges()` without any parameters. What the method returns is not a `RowsCollection`, but a full-fledged `DataSet`. You'll work with this subset of the original `DataSet` and merge it back with the original one later on line 52, but I don't want to get ahead of myself here.

On line 11, I check to see if the first table in the `DataSet` has errors. In a real program, you'll probably want to iterate over all the tables in the `DataSet` and call `DataTable.HasErrors` on each one. For my example, I'm only interested in the first table.

Once the code determines the table has errors, it iterates over all the rows and searches for rows that are flagged with errors (lines 14–16). When such a row is found, I call `changedRow.GetColumnsInError()` on line 19 to retrieve a list of the columns containing errors.

Lines 22–28 iterate over the collection of bad columns and print out the names of the columns.

Lines 30–41 show how to access the data for each field in a row. There are four different values that are managed for each field: the `Original` value, the `Current` value, the `Proposed` value, and the `Default` value.

Line 34 shows how to get the `Original` value of a field (the value that was read from the database). You might want to use this value to restore the changed data if you don't know how to fix the error. I commented out lines 34–36 because there is no `Original` value for newly added rows. Since my sample code is only looking at `New` rows (see line 7), there is no point in looking at `Original` values.

Line 39 gets the `Current` value for a field, which is the value entered by the user. I check to see if the field is null, because some fields may be null. If a field is left null, there won't be any object to access on lines 40–41.

Line 44 is where you would add code to fix the errors detected.

Line 48 clears all the `HasErrors` flags in the fields managed by the `DataRow`. This method saves you the effort of iterating over the fields in the `DataRow` and calling `SetColumnError(false)` for each field.

Line 52 is how you take the changes made to the `DataSet` subset (containing only the rows with flagged errors) and merge them back into the original `DataSet`. If you forget to merge the `DataSet` back, all your corrections will be lost. Note that you don't have to create a `DataSet` subset to work with. You could skip the call `GetChanges()` on lines 7–9 and iterate over the rows in `myDataSet`, and then use the `DataRow.HasErrors` flag to find rows that need fixing. After fixing all of the problems, you wouldn't need to call `Merge()`.

Lines 54–55 take the corrected `DataSet`, post all the changes to the database server, and commit the changes for good.

A Complete Example

Listing 18-27 shows the complete code for ADO.NET_Examples.

Listing 18-27: The Complete Code for ADO.NET_Examples, Showing How to Use DataSets, DataReaders, DataViews, and Data Binding

```csharp
using System;
using System.Data;
using System.Data.SqlClient;
using System.Data.OleDb;
using System.Drawing;
using System.Collections;
using System.ComponentModel;
using System.Windows.Forms;

namespace ADO.NET_Examples
{
  public class Form1 : System.Windows.Forms.Form
  {
    private System.Windows.Forms.TabControl tabControl1;
    // declare other UI controls...
    private System.ComponentModel.Container components = null;

    public Form1()
    {
      InitializeComponent();
    }

    protected override void Dispose( bool disposing )
    {
      // standard wizard-generated code...
    }

    private void InitializeComponent()
    {
      // wizard-generated code...
    }

    [STAThread]
    static void Main()
    {
      Application.Run(new Form1());
    }

    private void buttonUseDataReader_Click(object sender,
                                    System.EventArgs e)
    {
      string conn =
        @"Provider=SQLOLEDB.1;Integrated Security=SSPI;" +
        @"Persist Security Info=False;User ID=Ted; " +
        @"Initial Catalog=pubs;" +
        @"Data Source=(local);Use Procedure for Prepare=1;" +
        @"Auto Translate=True;Packet Size=4096; " +
        @"Workstation ID=FRANCESCA;" +
```

```
      @"Use Encryption for Data=False;" +
      @"Tag with column collation when possible=False";

    Cursor.Current = Cursors.WaitCursor;
    OleDbConnection connection = new OleDbConnection();
    connection.ConnectionString = conn;
    string select =
      "Select au_lname from authors order by au_lname";
    OleDbCommand command = new OleDbCommand(select, connection);
    connection.Open();
    OleDbDataReader dataReader = command.ExecuteReader();
    listBoxWithDataReader.Items.Clear();

    while (dataReader.Read() )
    {
      String lastName = dataReader.GetString(0);
      listBoxWithDataReader.Items.Add(lastName);
    }

    dataReader.Close();
    connection.Close();
    connection.Close();
    Cursor.Current = Cursors.Default;
}

private void buttonUseDataSet_Click(object sender,
                                    System.EventArgs e)
{
  string conn =
    @"Provider=SQLOLEDB.1;Integrated Security=SSPI;" +
    @"Persist Security Info=False;User ID=Ted; " +
    @"Initial Catalog=pubs;" +
    @"Data Source=(local);Use Procedure for Prepare=1;" +
    @"Auto Translate=True;Packet Size=4096; " +
    @"Workstation ID=FRANCESCA;" +
    @"Use Encryption for Data=False;" +
    @"Tag with column collation when possible=False";

  Cursor.Current = Cursors.WaitCursor;

  string select =
    "Select au_lname from authors order by au_lname";
  OleDbDataAdapter dataAdapter =
    new OleDbDataAdapter(select, conn);
  DataSet dataSet = new DataSet();
  dataAdapter.Fill(dataSet);

  listBoxWithDataSet.Items.Clear();
  DataRowCollection rows = dataSet.Tables[0].Rows;
  foreach (DataRow r in rows)
  {
    String lastName = r ["au_lname"].ToString();
```

Continued

Listing 18-27 *(continued)*

```csharp
      listBoxWithDataSet.Items.Add(lastName);
    }

    Cursor.Current = Cursors.Default;
}

private void buttonUseDataView_Click(object sender,
                                     System.EventArgs e)
{
    string conn =
      @"Provider=SQLOLEDB.1;Integrated Security=SSPI;" +
      @"Persist Security Info=False;User ID=Ted; " +
      @"Initial Catalog=pubs;" +
      @"Data Source=(local);Use Procedure for Prepare=1;" +
      @"Auto Translate=True;Packet Size=4096; " +
      @"Workstation ID=FRANCESCA;" +
      @"Use Encryption for Data=False;" +
      @"Tag with column collation when possible=False";

    Cursor.Current = Cursors.WaitCursor;

    string select =
      "Select au_id, au_lname, au_fname from authors";
    OleDbDataAdapter dataAdapter =
      new OleDbDataAdapter(select, conn);

    DataSet dataSet = new DataSet();
    dataAdapter.Fill(dataSet);
    DataView dataView = new DataView(dataSet.Tables[0]);

    listBoxWithDataView.Items.Clear();

    if (radioButtonAscendingOrder.Checked)
      showAscendingOrder(dataView);
    if (radioButtonDescendingOrder.Checked)
      showDescendingOrder(dataView);
    if (radioButtonNamesAtoG.Checked)
      showNamesAtoG(dataView);
    if (radioButtonAddedRows.Checked)
      showAddedRows(dataView);
    if (radioButtonEditedRows.Checked)
      showEditedRows(dataView);
    if (radioButtonDeletedRows.Checked)
      showDeletedRows(dataView);
    if (radioButtonLocateRecord.Checked)
      showLocateRecord(dataView);
    if (radioButtonEditRecord.Checked)
      showEditRecord(dataView);

    Cursor.Current = Cursors.Default;
}
```

```csharp
void showAscendingOrder(DataView theDataView)
{
  theDataView.Sort = @"au_lname ASC, au_fname ASC";

  for (int i = 0; i < theDataView.Count; i++)
  {
    String lastName = theDataView[i]["au_lname"].ToString();
    String firstName = theDataView[i]["au_fname"].ToString();
    listBoxWithDataView.Items.Add(lastName + ", " + firstName);
  }
}

void showDescendingOrder(DataView theDataView)
{
  theDataView.Sort = @"au_lname DESC, au_fname ASC";

  for (int i = 0; i < theDataView.Count; i++)
  {
    String lastName = theDataView[i]["au_lname"].ToString();
    String firstName = theDataView[i]["au_fname"].ToString();
    listBoxWithDataView.Items.Add(lastName + ", " + firstName);
  }
}

void showNamesAtoG(DataView theDataView)
{
  theDataView.RowFilter =
    @"au_lname >= 'A' and au_lname <= 'G'";

  for (int i = 0; i < theDataView.Count; i++)
  {
    String lastName = theDataView[i]["au_lname"].ToString();
    listBoxWithDataView.Items.Add(lastName);
  }
}

void showAddedRows(DataView theDataView)
{
  // add a row
  DataRowView addedRow = theDataView.AddNew();
  addedRow ["au_lname"] = "<New last name>";

  theDataView.RowStateFilter = DataViewRowState.Added;

  for (int i = 0; i < theDataView.Count; i++)
  {
    String lastName =theDataView[i]["au_lname"].ToString();
    listBoxWithDataView.Items.Add("Added record: " + lastName);
  }
}
```

Continued

Listing 18-27 *(continued)*

```
void showEditedRows(DataView theDataView)
  {
    // edit a row
    DataRowView editedRow = theDataView [6];
    editedRow ["au_fname"] = "<New first name>";
    theDataView.RowStateFilter = DataViewRowState.ModifiedCurrent;

    for (int i = 0; i < theDataView.Count; i++)
    {
      String lastName = theDataView[i]["au_lname"].ToString();
      String firstName = theDataView[i]["au_fname"].ToString();
      listBoxWithDataView.Items.Add(
          "Edited record: " + lastName + ", " + firstName);
    }
  }

  void showDeletedRows(DataView theDataView)
  {
    // delete a row
    theDataView.Delete(6);
    theDataView.RowStateFilter = DataViewRowState.Deleted;

    for (int i = 0; i < theDataView.Count; i++)
    {
      String lastName = theDataView[i]["au_lname"].ToString();
      String firstName = theDataView[i]["au_fname"].ToString();
      listBoxWithDataView.Items.Add(
          "Deleted record: " + lastName + ", " + firstName);
    }
  }

  void showLocateRecord(DataView theDataView)
  {
    // locate a key
    theDataView.Sort = "au_id";
    int i = theDataView.Find("672-71-3249");  // find Yokomoto
    if (i < 0)
      return;  // record not found

    DataRowView locatedRow = theDataView[i];

    String lastName = locatedRow["au_lname"].ToString();
    String firstName = locatedRow["au_fname"].ToString();
    listBoxWithDataView.Items.Add(
          "Located record: " + lastName + ", " + firstName);
  }

  void showEditRecord(DataView theDataView)
  {
    // edit a few rows
    DataRowView editedRow;
```

```csharp
    editedRow = theDataView [6];
    editedRow ["au_fname"] = "<New first name 1>";

    editedRow = theDataView [10];
    editedRow ["au_fname"] = "<New first name 2>";

    theDataView.RowStateFilter = DataViewRowState.ModifiedCurrent;

    for (int i = 0; i < theDataView.Count; i++)
    {
      String lastName = theDataView[i]["au_lname"].ToString();
      String firstName = theDataView[i]["au_fname"].ToString();
      listBoxWithDataView.Items.Add(
            "Edited records: " + lastName + ", " + firstName);
    }
}

private void buttonBindToDatabase_Click(object sender,
                                        System.EventArgs e)
{
  Binding binding;
  string conn =
    @"Provider=SQLOLEDB.1;Integrated Security=SSPI;" +
    @"Persist Security Info=False;User ID=Ted; " +
    @"Initial Catalog=pubs;" +
    @"Data Source=(local);Use Procedure for Prepare=1;" +
    @"Auto Translate=True;Packet Size=4096; " +
    @"Workstation ID=FRANCESCA;" +
    @"Use Encryption for Data=False;" +
    @"Tag with column collation when possible=False";

  Cursor.Current = Cursors.WaitCursor;

  string select = "Select * from authors";
  OleDbDataAdapter dataAdapter =
                   new OleDbDataAdapter(select, conn);
  DataSet dataSet = new DataSet();
  dataAdapter.Fill(dataSet);
  DataTable authors = dataSet.Tables[0];

  // bind DataGrid
  dataGrid1.DataSource = authors;

  // bind TextBox
  binding = new Binding("Text", authors, "au_lname");
  textBoxName.DataBindings.Clear(); // remove old bindings
  textBoxName.DataBindings.Add(binding);

  // bind CheckBox
  binding = new Binding("Checked", authors, "contract");
  checkBoxContract.DataBindings.Clear(); // remove old bindings
  checkBoxContract.DataBindings.Add(binding);
```

Continued

Listing 18-27 *(continued)*

```csharp
    // bind ComboBox
    comboBoxCurrentAuthor.DataSource = authors;
    comboBoxCurrentAuthor.DisplayMember = "au_lname";

    Cursor.Current = Cursors.Default;
}

private void buttonBindToCollection_Click(object sender,
                                          System.EventArgs e)
{
    Binding binding;

    String s = "";
    bool b = false;
    DataColumn columnLastName =
                new DataColumn("au_lname", s.GetType() );
    DataColumn columnContract =
                new DataColumn("contract", b.GetType() );
    DataTable table = new DataTable();
    table.Columns.Add(columnLastName);
    table.Columns.Add(columnContract);

    DataRow row = table.NewRow();
    row["au_lname"] = "Carson";
    row["contract"] = true;
    table.Rows.Add(row);

    row = table.NewRow();
    row["au_lname"] = "Hunter";
    row["contract"] = false;
    table.Rows.Add(row);

    row = table.NewRow();
    row["au_lname"] = "Johnson";
    row["contract"] = true;
    table.Rows.Add(row);

    row = table.NewRow();
    row["au_lname"] = "Smith";
    row["contract"] = true;
    table.Rows.Add(row);

    // bind DataGrid
    dataGrid1.DataSource = table;

    // bind TextBox
    binding = new Binding("Text", table, "au_lname");
    textBoxName.DataBindings.Clear(); // remove old bindings
    textBoxName.DataBindings.Add(binding);
```

```
    // bind CheckBox
    binding = new Binding("Checked", table, "contract");
    checkBoxContract.DataBindings.Clear(); // remove old bindings
    checkBoxContract.DataBindings.Add(binding);

    // bind ComboBox
    comboBoxCurrentAuthor.DataSource = table;
    comboBoxCurrentAuthor.DisplayMember = "au_lname";
}

private void buttonPostInserts_Click(object sender,
                                    System.EventArgs e)
{
    DataSet dataSet = new DataSet();
    oleDbDataAdapter1.Fill(dataSet);

    // create a new, empty row in the DataTable
    DataTable authors = dataSet.Tables [0];
    authors.RowChanging +=
       new DataRowChangeEventHandler(MyRowChangingHandler);

    DataRow newAuthor = authors.NewRow();

    // initialize all the required fields
    newAuthor ["au_id"] ="999-99-9999" ;
    newAuthor ["au_lname"] ="Last Name";
    newAuthor ["au_fname"] ="First Name";
    newAuthor ["phone"] ="555-1212";
    newAuthor ["address"] ="address";
    newAuthor ["contract"] = false;

    // add the row to the DataTable
    dataSet.Tables [0].Rows.Add(newAuthor);

    // post the new row to the database
    oleDbDataAdapter1.Update(dataSet);

    // commit all changes
    dataSet.AcceptChanges();
}

private void buttonPostUpdates_Click(object sender,
                                    System.EventArgs e)
{
    DataSet dataSet = new DataSet();
    oleDbDataAdapter1.Fill(dataSet);

    // find an item to update
    DataTable authors = dataSet.Tables [0];

    authors.RowChanging +=
       new DataRowChangeEventHandler(MyRowChangingHandler);
```

Continued

Listing 18-27 *(continued)*

```csharp
    DataRow[] rows = authors.Select("au_id = '999-99-9999'");
    if (rows.Length == 0)
    {
      MessageBox.Show(
          "Click on the 'Post Inserts' button first, to " +
          "create a record to change.");
      return;
    }

    // edit the item
    DataRow rowToChange = rows[0];
    rowToChange.BeginEdit();
    rowToChange ["address"] = "New Address";
    rowToChange.EndEdit();

    // commit the changes to the database
    oleDbDataAdapter1.Update(dataSet);
    dataSet.AcceptChanges();              // to commit all changes
}

private void buttonPostDeletes_Click(object sender,
                                     System.EventArgs e)
{
  DataSet dataSet = new DataSet();
  oleDbDataAdapter1.Fill(dataSet);

  // find an item to update
  DataTable authors = dataSet.Tables [0];
  authors.RowChanging +=
    new DataRowChangeEventHandler(MyRowChangingHandler);

  DataRow[] rows = authors.Select("au_id = '999-99-9999'");
  if (rows.Length == 0)
  {
    MessageBox.Show(
      "Click on the 'Post Inserts' button first, to " +
      "create a record to delete.");
    return;
  }

  // delete the item
  DataRow rowToDelete = rows[0];
  rowToDelete.Delete();

  // commit the changes to the database
  oleDbDataAdapter1.Update(dataSet);
  dataSet.AcceptChanges();              // to commit all changes
}

public void MyRowChangingHandler(Object sender,
```

```
                                    DataRowChangeEventArgs e)
{
  DataRow rowToCheck = e.Row;

  switch (e.Action)
  {
    case DataRowAction.Add:
      // validate rowToCheck;
      break;
    case DataRowAction.Change: ;
      // validate rowToCheck;
      break;
    case DataRowAction.Delete: ;
      // verify if it is OK to delete rowToCheck
      break;

    default:
      break;
  }
}

void CheckAndFixErrors(DataSet myDataSet)
{
  if (!myDataSet.HasChanges() ) return;

  // get a list of the New, Modified or Deleted rows

  DataSet changedDataSet =
          myDataSet.GetChanges(DataRowState.Added);
  // DataSet changedDataSet =
  //        myDataSet.GetChanges(DataRowState.Modified);
  // DataSet changedDataSet =
  //        myDataSet.GetChanges(DataRowState.Deleted);

  if (!changedDataSet.Tables [0].HasErrors) return;

  // handle the errors
  foreach (DataRow changedRow in changedDataSet.Tables [0].Rows)
  {
    if (!changedRow.HasErrors) continue;

    // get a list of the columns with bad data
    DataColumn[] cols = changedRow.GetColumnsInError();

    // tell the user which columns need to be fixed
    if (cols != null)
    {
      Console.Write("The following columns have bad data:\n");
      for (int i = 0; i < cols.Length; i++)
        // show the name of the column
        Console.WriteLine(cols[i].ColumnName + " ");
    }
```

Continued

Listing 18-27 *(continued)*

```
        // get the original row
        String originalLastName, currentLastName;

        // no original value for New records
        // if (changedRow ["au_lname", DataRowVersion.Original] !=
            null)
        // originalLastName =
        //     changedRow ["au_lname",
        //     DataRowVersion.Original].ToString();

        // get the current row, with the user's changes
        if (changedRow ["au_lname", DataRowVersion.Current] != null)
          currentLastName =
            changedRow ["au_lname",
            DataRowVersion.Current].ToString();

        // show the row to the user and ask for corrections
        // ...

        // clear all the HasError flags on the fields of the row,
        // assuming the errors were fixes
        changedRow.ClearErrors();
      }

      // merge the changed data back with the original data
      myDataSet.Merge(changedDataSet);

      oleDbDataAdapter1.Update(myDataSet);
      myDataSet.AcceptChanges(); // to commit all changes
    }
  }
}
```

Summary

As I've shown with all the examples in this chapter, the ADO.NET Framework has some very powerful components that can save you lots of programming time, if you understand how to use them. Coupled with the built-in support for XML and nonrectangular data, the ADO.NET Framework is a truly versatile architecture.

✦   ✦   ✦

Database Web Services

We are ready for an unforeseen event that may or may not occur at any time.

—Former U.S. Vice President Dan Quayle

Database operations need to be fast, but they also must be reliable, so they need to be approached using extremely defensive programming. Unlike Dan Quayle's world of politics and power, the realm of .NET database programming actually does make it possible to handle unforeseen events that may or may not occur at any time: Just use exception handling. Through judicious use of `try-catch` blocks, you can trap any type of exception, including unforeseen ones.

This chapter has a certain amount of overlap with the chapters on Web Services, Database front-end components, and ADO.NET. I decided to duplicate some of the information here, to save you the trouble of constantly jumping to other chapters to locate text, figures, and listings.

What Is a Database Web Service?

For those readers who may have skipped reading the section on middle-tier components and Web Services, a Web Service is a component that exposes methods you can call over an HTTP connection using a URI. The format of the data passed to and from the Web Service is XML. You can use a standard Web browser to test a Web Service, entering a URI that calls the service. Any data returned by the call will be XML. Web Services are always activated through IIS. When a request comes in identifying the URI of a Web Service, IIS gets a thread from its thread pool and runs the service on this thread.

What I call a *Database Web Service* is just a Web Service that exposes methods to access data stored in a database. Typically, a client calls a Web Service method to get a record set. The service issues a select statement against the database, gets the response, puts it into a `DataSet` and returns the `DataSet` in XML format to the client. The client reads the XML data, feeds it to a local `DataSet` and consumes the data as a resultset, as if the data was local. Figure 19-1 may help you understand this concept.

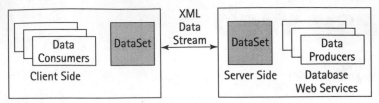

Figure 19-1: The general architecture of a distributed system using a Database Web Service

A good reason to use a Database Web Service is to simplify the front-end. By keeping all the DBMS-dependent code away from the client side, the front-end is much smaller, faster, and easier to deploy.

To show how all the parts fit together, there is no better way than an example. In the next few sections, I show how to develop a Web Service that acts as a Database Service. The service exposes methods for clients to call to get data and post changes back to the database. The program deals with the `authors` table, which comes with Microsoft SQL Server. The service has one method to retrieve a list of all the records in the `authors` table, and another method to post changes to the `authors` table.

If you just finished reading the previous chapter, you may recall that I already walked you through the steps of creating a Web Service that returns a database resultset. In the following sections, I'll place much more emphasis on how the database plumbing works, and less on how to create a generic Web Service.

Designing the Service

My Database Web Service uses standard VS .NET components to achieve its goals. As stated earlier, there are only two methods that need to be exposed to the client: one for retrieving the record set and another for posting changes back to the database. The class diagram in Figure 19-2 shows the basic architecture of the service.

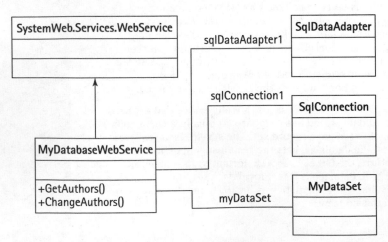

Figure 19-2: The class diagram of the service

The two methods, `GetAuthors()` and `ChangeAuthors()`, are Web Methods that will be available to clients. Both use standard ADO.NET DataSets to send record sets, encoded as XML documents, over the wire.

Two of the components on the right — `SqlDataAdapter` and `SqlConnection` — provide access to a SQL Server database and offer superior performance over the equivalent OleDb counterparts. To access other databases, such as Oracle or Sybase, you must use the OleDb classes `OleDbConnection` and `OleDbDataAdapter`. They're not as fast as the SQL components, because they rely on unmanaged OLE DB providers, which adds a bit of complexity to the path between you and the database.

Implementing the Service

Creating a Database Web Service with VS .NET is easy. I used the New Project Wizard and selected the template ASP.NET Web Service, as shown in Figure 19-3.

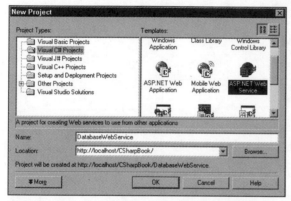

Figure 19-3: Creating the Web Service with the New Project Wizard

By default, the wizard places the project on the localhost. This is probably the best place to develop and test your Web Service, but requires your computer to have IIS running on it.

The wizard creates a default Web Service project with an empty Web Service class called `Service1`. To rename the class, the easiest way is to open the Class View window, drill down to the `Service1` class, and then go to the Properties windows and change the (`Name`) property. I changed the class name to `MyDatabaseWebService`.

Now that I have a skeleton Web Service to work with, the next step is to set up a connection to the database. I could do this in a number of ways. I'll use the Add Connection command in the Server Explorer window, as shown in Figure 19-4. If this window isn't already visible, use the View ➪ Server Explorer command on the main menu.

I've showed how to create database connections in other chapters of the book, but to save you the effort of going and looking up how to do it, I'll summarize the process here again. The Add Connection command opens the Data Link Properties window, as shown in Figure 19-5.

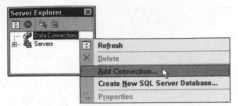

Figure 19-4: Using the Server Explorer to create a new database connection

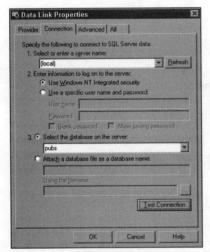

Figure 19-5: The Data Link Properties window for creating new database connections

Enter the name of the server where the DBMS is running, or use *(local)* if the database is on your computer. During development, it's a good idea to run everything locally if you can, or at least use a database on a server that is not accessed by production code. For the user name and password, I chose "Use Windows NT Integrated security," meaning the connection will be opened using the Security Account that I used to log in to Windows.

To finish filling in the Data Link Properties fields, I selected the pubs database, which is installed with SQL Server. Clicking the OK button concludes the creation of the new database connection.

Now I can use the new connection to set up a DataAdapter. Since my service will be accessing a SQL Server database, I can use either an OleDbDataAdapter or an SqlDataAdapter. The latter is optimized for SQL Server and doesn't use unmanaged data providers. All the code along the path between the SqlDataAdapter and SQL Server is managed code, so there are no process switches into unmanaged code to slow you down. Dropping an SqlDataAdapter component on the service starts the Data Adapter Configuration Wizard. I entered the selections shown in Figure 19-6.

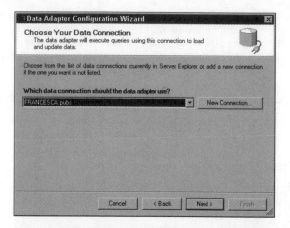

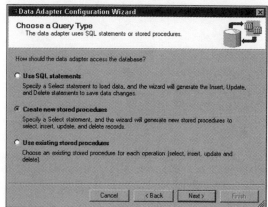

Figure 19-6: Selecting the database connection created earlier

Notice that I chose the "Create new stored procedures" option on the second screen. Components that run on the middle-tier and the back-end are normally for performance. Stored procedures are much faster than in-line SQL statements, so you should use them whenever possible. My stored procedure is really simple, consisting of the following query:

```
Select * from authors
```

Since most queries are more complicated, I clicked the Query Builder button to launch the Query Builder Wizard and show you how to use it. The wizard first prompts for the table or tables to use. I selected the authors table, as shown in Figure 19-7.

Figure 19-7: Selecting the tables to use in a query statement

Closing the dialog box put me back in the Query Builder Wizard. I selected all the columns for the query and then right-clicked in the top portion of the window and chose Run from the pop-up menu. This command populated the bottom list with records, to show a sample of the data returned by the query, as shown in Figure 19-8.

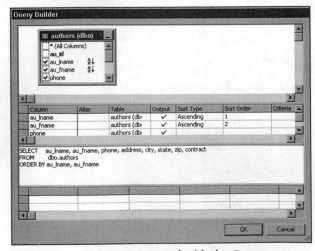

Figure 19-8: The query created with the Query Builder Wizard

Notice that I added two sorting criteria, on the au_lname and au_fname columns. Closing out the window with the OK button put me back in the Data Adapter Configuration Wizard with the new query statement, as shown in Figure 19-9.

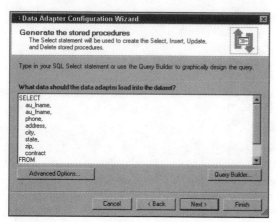

Figure 19-9: The initial part of the SQL statement generated by the Query Builder Wizard

Clicking the Next button displays the screen on which you can enter names for the four stored procedures the Data Adapter Configuration Wizard will add to the database, as shown in Figure 19-10.

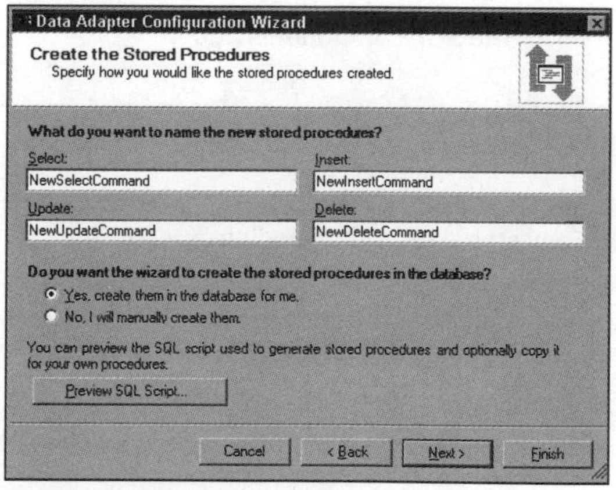

Figure 19-10: Configuring the names of the stored procedures to create

As you can see, the wizard proposes default names for the stored procedures. I'll leave the default names, and later show how to use SQL Server Enterprise Manager to rename them. Near the bottom of the window, notice the selected radio button labeled "Yes, create them in the database for me." With this setting, four stored procedures will be created and stored in the database automatically by running an SQL script. To see what the script looks like, I clicked the Preview SQL Script button and got the window shown in Figure 19-11.

Figure 19-11: The Preview SQL Script window, showing the script that will be used to add the four new stored procedures to the database

The dialog box doesn't let you make any changes, but you can save the script on the clipboard or in a file. Close the dialog box and click the Next button on the DataAdapter Configuration Wizard. The wizard will finish, adding a number of SQL components to the Service Designer, as shown in Figure 19-12.

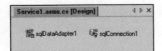

Figure 19-12: The SQL components added by the wizard

The wizard makes it just as easy to use stored procedures as SQL statements, completely obviating, in many cases, the need to do any stored procedure coding or learn stored procedure syntax.

You need one more component in the Web Service to make it functional: a `DataSet` configured to work with the `DataAdapter` created by the wizard. You may recall that a `DataSet` component acts as an in-memory mini database, storing records from queries. Most services or applications that use ADO.NET components require one or more `DataSets`. A `DataSet` must be configured with a schema that describes the layout of the records managed. Creating and configuring a `DataSet` is easy. In the Service Designer, right-click on the `DataAdapter` and select Generate DataSet from the pop-up menu, as shown in Figure 19-13.

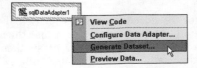

Figure 19-13: Generating a DataSet the easy way

The Generate DataSet Wizard prompts for the name to use for the DataSet. I chose *MyDataSet,* as shown in Figure 19-14.

Figure 19-14: Configuring the new DataSet

Make sure the checkbox labeled "Add this dataset to the designer" is not checked. The DataSet being created will be handled through code that I will add to the Web Service shortly, so I don't want it to be instantiated automatically and added to the Service Designer.

DataSets use schemas that are defined in files of type .xsd (for *XML schema definition*). When the wizard creates a DataSet, it also adds the schema file to the Solution Explorer. For the component named MyDataSet, the wizard created a schema file named *MyDataSet.xsd.* Figure 19-15 shows the .xsd file added to the Solution Explorer.

Figure 19-15: The Solution Explorer, showing the XML schema definition file for MyDataSet

Since one of the selections I used in the Data Adapter Configuration Wizard specified the use of stored procedures, I'll briefly describe where those procedures went and how to test them. In my previous example, I used a connection to the Pubs database on the server named Francesca. Using the Server Explorer, select the connection Francesca.Pubs, expand the node, and also expand the Stored Procedures node, as shown in Figure 19-16.

By default, the Data Adapter Configuration Wizard creates procedures with rather uninteresting names, like NewDeleteCommand. If you didn't rename the procedures back in Figure 19-10, you can use the SQL Server Enterprise Manager, as shown in Figure 19-17.

Figure 19-16: The four stored procedures created by the Data Adapter Configuration Wizard

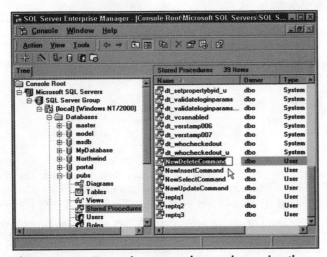

Figure 19-17: Renaming a stored procedure using the SQL Server Enterprise Manager

I renamed the procedures, replacing the word *command* with *author,* so NewDeleteCommand became NewDeleteAuthor, and so forth for the other three commands. Procedure names are completely arbitrary, but using a reasonable naming convention is a good thing. Six months from now, when your database has 200 stored procedures and you're looking for that special one that returns a list of authors in reverse order by last name and ascending order by telephone number, you'll appreciate the benefits of a good naming convention. Figure 19-18 shows the renamed stored procedures in the Server Explorer.

Figure 19-18: The renamed stored procedures in the Server Explorer

You can test the stored procedures immediately, if you want. For example, to run the `NewSelectAuthor` procedure, right-click on it in the Server Explorer and choose Run Stored Procedure from the pop-up menu, as shown in Figure 19-19.

Server Explorer
FRANCESCA.MyDatabase
FRANCESCA.pubs
Tables
Views
Stored Procedures
byroyalty (dbo)
NewDeleteAuthor (dbo)
NewInsertAuthor (dbo)
NewSelectAuthor (dbo)
NewUpdateAuthor (dbo)
Run Stored Procedure
Refresh
Copy
Properties

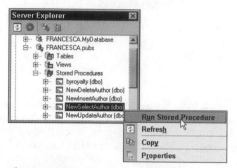

Figure 19-19: Running a stored procedure from the Server Explorer

The resultset appears in the VS .NET Output pane, as shown in Figure 19-20.

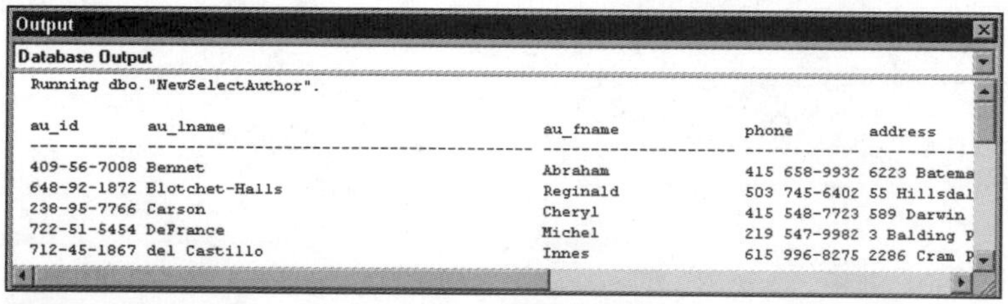

Output
Database Output
Running dbo."NewSelectAuthor".
au_id au_lname au_fname phone address
409-56-7008 Bennet Abraham 415 658-9932 6223 Batema
648-92-1872 Blotchet-Halls Reginald 503 745-6402 55 Hillsdal
238-95-7766 Carson Cheryl 415 548-7723 589 Darwin
722-51-5454 DeFrance Michel 219 547-9982 3 Balding P
712-45-1867 del Castillo Innes 615 996-8275 2286 Cram P

Figure 19-20: The resultset produced by the stored procedure

If you try to run the other three procedures, you'll be prompted for parameters. Figure 19-21 shows the dialog box that appears if you try to run the `NewInsertAuthor` stored procedure.

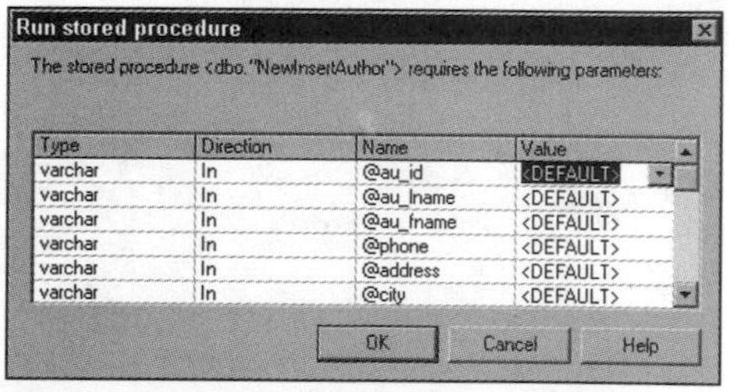

Run stored procedure
The stored procedure <dbo."NewInsertAuthor"> requires the following parameters:
Type Direction Name Value
varchar In @au_id <DEFAULT>
varchar In @au_lname <DEFAULT>
varchar In @au_fname <DEFAULT>
varchar In @phone <DEFAULT>
varchar In @address <DEFAULT>
varchar In @city <DEFAULT>
OK
Cancel
Help

Figure 19-21: How VS .NET prompts for parameters to run stored procedures with

Any procedure that takes parameters will produce a similar window. When running the procedure, the results will be shown in the Output pane, as before.

Exposing Web Methods to Clients

OK, so where am I in the discussion of Database Web Services? I used a couple of VS .NET wizards to create the database components needed by the Database Web Service to connect to a SQL Server database. I also have the necessary stored procedures to get and update the authors table. Now I need to create and expose the two Web Methods that clients will call. The first one is GetAuthors(), which returns a DataSet to the client with a list of all of the names in the authors table. The second method is ChangeAuthors(), which will take a DataSet parameter containing a list of all the changes made to the authors table. This method will post all changes to the database.

Before adding any code to the Web Service, switch from the Service Designer view to the Code view. To do this, click on the file Service1.asmx in the Solution Explorer and then click the View Code button on the Toolbar of the Solution Explorer. To declare a method as a Web Method (a method that can be invoked using a URI), you need to declare the method with the [WebMethod] attribute. The GetAuthors() method is simple—it only needs to create a DataSet, populate it, and return it, as shown in Listing 19-1.

Listing 19-1: **Creating the First Database Web Service Method**

```
[WebMethod]
public System.Data.DataSet GetAuthors()
{
  System.Data.DataSet dataSet = new MyDataSet();
  sqlDataAdapter1.Fill(dataSet);
  return dataSet;
}
```

Although the method is declared to return a DataSet, it doesn't actually return a binary representation of the DataSet over the wire back to the client. Since the method is a Web Method, the compiler generates code to take the returned DataSet object and convert it into an XML document. Basically the DataSet is serialized into an XML stream, which is returned to clients. Although the code for GetAuthors() looks completely harmless, it is a good idea to wrap it in a try block to prevent those pesky *unforeseen events that may or may not occur at any time* from sending exceptions over the wire back to the client. Defensive coding suggests changing the code into something like what's shown in Listing 19-2.

Listing 19-2: **Wrapping All Code in a Web Method in a try Block**

```
[WebMethod]
public System.Data.DataSet GetAuthors()
{
  try
  {
    System.Data.DataSet dataSet = new MyDataSet();
    sqlDataAdapter1.Fill(dataSet);
    return dataSet;
  }
  catch (Exception)
```

```
  {
    // handle the exception, or just kill it
    return null;
  }
}
```

Possible causes of exceptions include not being able to connect to the DBMS, not being able to open a connection to it, errors due to locked tables or records, and others. Just because you can't think of reasons that might cause a Web Method to fail doesn't mean it *can't* fail. For Web Services in general, and Database Web Services in particular, always try to avoid propagating exceptions from the server to the client. As you can see, my new version of the GetAuthors() method returns a null to the client if an exception occurs. The client code will need to check the returned value, to see if it is null or not.

The other method — ChangeAuthors() — is also pretty simple. It takes a DataSet parameter containing only the changes made on the client side, and applies those changes to the database. Listing 19-3 shows the code.

Listing 19-3: **Creating the Second Database Web Service Method**

```
[WebMethod]
public void ChangeAuthors(System.Data.DataSet changedDataSet)
{
  sqlDataAdapter1.Update(changedDataSet);
  changedDataSet.AcceptChanges();
}
```

To minimize network transmission overhead, the DataSet passed to ChangeAuthors(DataSet) should contain only the author records that were changed on the client side. Inserted, updated, and deleted records are all considered changes. The client can extract the changed rows from a client DataSet using the following code:

```
DataSet insertedRowsDataSet = myDataSet.GetChanges(DataRowState.Added);
DataSet modifiedRowsDataSet =
myDataSet.GetChanges(DataRowState.Modified);
DataSet deletedRowsDataSet  =
myDataSet.GetChanges(DataRowState.Deleted);
```

The client code will then need to call ChangedAuthors(DataSet) three times, to send the inserted, modified, and deleted record sets to the Web Service. If the service has a method capable of handling any kind of change, as in my example, then the client can get a list of all the changes like this:

```
DataSet changedDataSet =
        myDataSet.GetChanges(DataRowState.Added |
                             DataRowState.Modified |
                             DataRowState.Deleted);
```

Or even simpler, like this:

```
DataSet changedDataSet = myDataSet.GetChanges();
```

Once the client has a `DataSet` containing the changed records, it can call the Web Method `ChangeAuthors ()`, passing the `DataSet` to it.

Testing the Web Service

As indicated earlier in Chapter 16, there are three ways to test a Web Service: using the VS .NET Internal Web Browser, using a standalone test Windows Application, or with a Web application that uses Web Forms. I'll describe the first two methods in the following sections. For examples of testing with Web Forms, see Chapter 13.

Testing with the Internal Web Browser

Using the Internal Web Browser, you can easily test methods that take no parameters or methods that expect simple parameters like integers and strings. For example, to test `DatabaseWebService` with the browser, just right-click on the Service1.asmx folder in the Solution Explorer and select View in Browser from the pop-up menu, as shown in Figure 19-22.

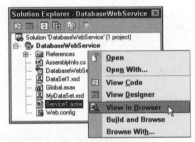

Figure 19-22: Using the VS .NET Internal Browser to test a Web Method

When you pass the URI of a .asmx file to a server running ASP.NET code, the ASP.NET runtime intercepts the request and generates an HTML page describing the Web Methods exposed (if any) by the .asmx file, as shown in Figure 19-23.

Figure 19-23: The HTML page displayed when viewing Service1.asmx in a browser

Most of the page contains boilerplate text. At the top, there is a list of the Web Methods discovered dynamically on the server. As described in detail in Chapter 16, titled "Services," the discovery process looks for .wsdl (for *Web Services Description Language*) files. These files contain a complete XML description of the Web Services, methods, and parameters available on a given server.

Clicking on the `GetAuthors` link brings up a new test page, with a test button on it, as shown in Figure 19-24.

Figure 19-24: The test page to invoke the Database Web Service from

Where does this page come from? Like the previous page, it comes from the ASP.NET runtime code running on the server machine. In case you're curious, the URI that generates this page is

```
http://localhost/DatabaseWebService/Service1.asmx?op=GetAuthors
```

When the ASP.NET runtime sees this type of URI, it builds an HTML test page for the given Web Method. Clicking the Invoke button on the page invokes the `GetAuthors()` Web Method, using the URI:

```
http://localhost/DatabaseWebService/Service1.asmx/GetAuthors?
```

The ASP.NET runtime then calls the `GetAuthors()` method and converts the response into an XML document, which is then returned to the client. The document is a serialized `DataSet`, containing a schema definition and a record set. Listing 19-4 shows the code for the XML document. This document can be deserialized on the client side to reconstruct a new `DataSet`. I removed all but two author records, to keep the code short.

Listing 19-4: **The XML Code Returned by the Database Web Service**

```xml
<?xml version="1.0" encoding="utf-8" ?>
<DataSet xmlns="http://tempuri.org/">
  <xsd:schema id="MyDataSet"
              targetNamespace=http://www.tempuri.org/MyDataSet.xsd
              xmlns=http://www.tempuri.org/MyDataSet.xsd
              xmlns:xsd="http://www.w3.org/2001/XMLSchema"
              xmlns:msdata="urn:schemas-microsoft-com:xml-msdata"
              attributeFormDefault="qualified"
elementFormDefault="qualified">
```

Continued

Listing 19-4 *(continued)*

```xml
<xsd:element name="MyDataSet" msdata:IsDataSet="true">
  <xsd:complexType>
    <xsd:choice maxOccurs="unbounded">
      <xsd:element name="authors">
        <xsd:complexType>
          <xsd:sequence>
            <xsd:element name="au_lname" type="xsd:string" />
            <xsd:element name="au_fname" type="xsd:string" />
            <xsd:element name="phone" type="xsd:string" />
            <xsd:element name="address" type="xsd:string"
                         minOccurs="0" />
            <xsd:element name="city" type="xsd:string"
                         minOccurs="0" />
            <xsd:element name="state" type="xsd:string"
                         minOccurs="0" />
            <xsd:element name="zip" type="xsd:string"
                         minOccurs="0" />
            <xsd:element name="contract" type="xsd:boolean" />
            <xsd:element name="au_id" type="xsd:string" />
          </xsd:sequence>
        </xsd:complexType>
      </xsd:element>
    </xsd:choice>
  </xsd:complexType>
  <xsd:unique name="Constraint1" msdata:PrimaryKey="true">
    <xsd:selector xpath=".//authors" />
    <xsd:field xpath="au_id" />
  </xsd:unique>
</xsd:element>
</xsd:schema>
<diffgr:diffgram
       xmlns:msdata="urn:schemas-microsoft-com:xml-msdata"
       xmlns:diffgr="urn:schemas-microsoft-com:xml-diffgram-v1">
  <MyDataSet xmlns="http://www.tempuri.org/MyDataSet.xsd">
    <authors diffgr:id="authors1" msdata:rowOrder="0">
      <au_lname>Bennet</au_lname>
      <au_fname>Abraham</au_fname>
      <phone>415 658-9932</phone>
      <address>6223 Bateman St.</address>
      <city>Berkeley</city>
      <state>CA</state>
      <zip>94705</zip>
      <contract>true</contract>
      <au_id>409-56-7008</au_id>
    </authors>
    <authors diffgr:id="authors23" msdata:rowOrder="22">
      <au_lname>Yokomoto</au_lname>
      <au_fname>Akiko</au_fname>
      <phone>415 935-4228</phone>
```

```
        <address>3 Silver Ct.</address>
        <city>Walnut Creek</city>
        <state>CA</state>
        <zip>94595</zip>
        <contract>true</contract>
        <au_id>672-71-3249</au_id>
      </authors>
    </MyDataSet>
  </diffgr:diffgram>
</DataSet>
```

To test the other Web Method, `ChangedAuthors()`, you need to set up a client program that populates a `DataSet` with changed rows and passes it to the method. I'll create such a program in the next section.

Testing with a Windows Application

When you create applications whose only purpose in life is to act as a test fixture, it's important to only add the minimum functionality needed to perform the required tests. In my case, I need the program to support the following features:

✦ Call the `DatabaseWebService` to get a record set of all the authors.

✦ Make changes to the record set.

✦ Call the `DatabaseWebService` to post the changes to the database.

I used the New Project Wizard to create a Windows Application called *TestFixture*. I saved the project in the TestFixture subfolder of DatabaseWebService, to keep the project closely associated with the component it tests, as shown in Figure 19-25.

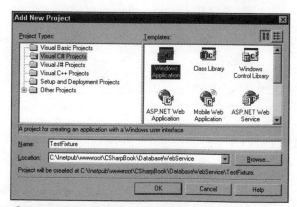

Figure 19-25: Creating a test fixture in a subfolder of the component to test

After adding the project to the solution that contains the Web Service, the Solution Explorer looked like Figure 19-26.

Figure 19-26: The Solution Explorer, after creating the test fixture

In order to call `DatabaseWebService` Web Methods from the test fixture, I added a Web Reference to the test fixture project. The reference makes it possible to make method calls to the Web Service using the same code you would use to invoke local methods. To add the reference, right-click on the TestFixture project in the Solution Explorer and select Project ➪ Add Web Reference from the pop-up menu. The Add Web Reference dialog box will open, as shown in Figure 19-27.

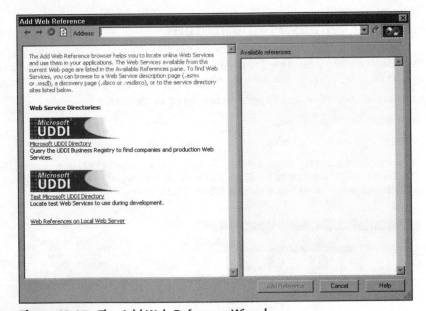

Figure 19-27: The Add Web Reference Wizard

In the Address bar at the top, enter the URL of the .asmx file for the service. For my example here, the URL is

```
http://localhost/DatabaseWebService/WebService1.asmx
```

If you don't know the path of the Web Service, you can locate it in two ways: by using UDDI (for *Universal Description, Discovery, and Integration*) or by clicking on the Web References on Local Web Server link at the lower left of the screen.

UDDI is an open standard developed by a consortium of companies and is available at `www.uddi.org`. UDDI supports the dynamic discovery of all Web Services published by a given company, or the discovery of all companies that support given types of business services.

Since I'm interested in testing only my local Web Service, I clicked on the Web References on Local Web Server link. The link references the URI `http://localhost/default.vsdisco`, which causes the ASP.NET runtime on the server to return an XML page describing all Web Services available on that server, as shown in Figure 19-28.

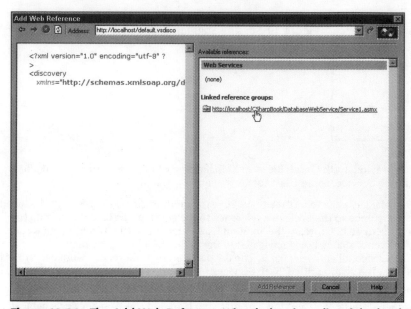

Figure 19-28: The Add Web Reference Wizard, showing a list of the local Web Services

Clicking on the hyperlink shown in the right pane allows you to see the XML contract file, in the form of a .wsdl (for *Web Services Description Language*) file, as shown in Figure 19-29.

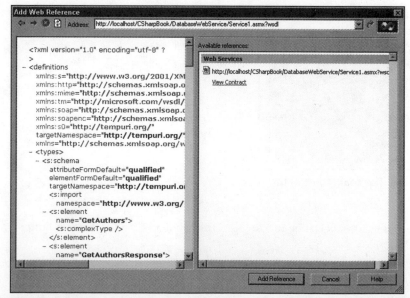

Figure 19-29: The .wsdl contract file displayed for my Web Service

To add a reference to my Web Service to the test fixture, I clicked the Add Reference button. A new Web References node called Service1.wsdl was added to the Solution Explorer, as shown in Figure 19-30.

Figure 19-30: The Solution Explorer, showing the newly added Service1.wsdl file

As described previously, the .wsdl file is an XML file describing the methods available through the Web Service, namely `GetAuthors()` and `ChangeAuthors()`.

Before I can make any calls to `DatabaseWebService` methods from the test fixture, I need to add another reference to the project: a reference to the service's DLL. Right-clicking the References node of TestFixture, in the Solution Explorer, I chose the Add Reference command. In the Add Reference dialog box, I navigated to the folder containing the file DatabaseWebService.dll and selected it. The details of adding references were described back in Chapter 16, in the section titled "Web Services."

Once the Web Service and DLL references are added to the TestFixture project, I can add code to interact with the Web Service. The first step is to add the Web Service's namespace to Form1.cs, which is the file where I'll put all the test code. All I need is the one line at the top of the file:

```
using DatabaseWebService;
```

On the form, I added two buttons and a `DataGrid`, as shown in Figure 19-31.

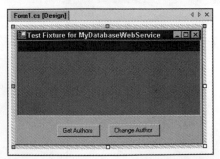

Figure 19-31: The main form of the test fixture

I added the code shown in Listing 19-5 to the `Click` handler of the Get Authors button.

Listing 19-5: The Code to Populate the DataGrid in the Test Fixture

```
private void buttonGetAuthors_Click(object sender, System.EventArgs e)
{
  Cursor.Current = Cursors.WaitCursor;

  MyDatabaseWebService myService = new MyDatabaseWebService();
  DataSet authorsDataSet = myService.GetAuthors();
  dataGrid1.DataSource = authorsDataSet;
  dataGrid1.DataMember = "authors";

  Cursor.Current = Cursors.Default;
}
```

The code is extremely simple. It uses a new operator to instantiate a `MyDatabaseWebService` component. Looking at these four lines of code by themselves, you can't tell whether the component being instantiated is local or remote. This is good, not only because it makes remote calls easy to write, but it also obviates the need for you to remember special rules or syntax to use with remote calls. Say good-bye to DCOM, RPC, and IDL.

The data returned from the call to `GetAuthors()` is an XML stream. This stream is used to create a `DataSet`, which is then bound to the `DataGrid` and used to populate it with authors. In my example, the `DataSet` component generating the XML stream in the Web Service is on the same computer as the client, but if I moved the Web Service to another computer, the client code wouldn't need to be changed at all. What would change is the Web Reference the test fixture uses. First, I would need to remove the local Web Reference I added earlier and then add a new one, specifying the new URI for the relocated Web Service.

Figure 19-32 shows what the test fixture looks like after clicking the Get Authors button.

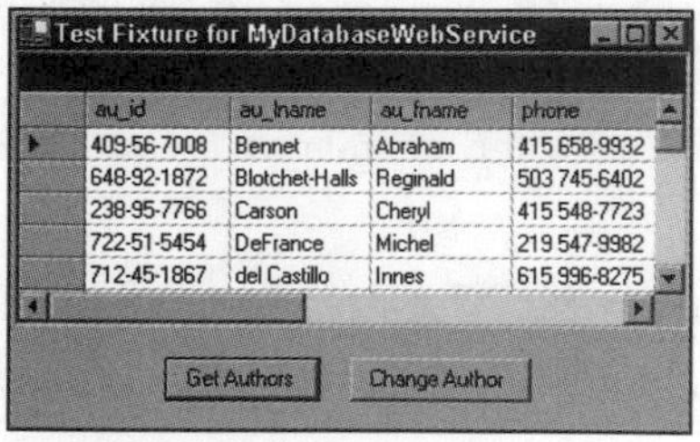

Figure 19-32: The DataGrid populated by clicking the Get Authors button

Piece of cake. To make changes to the `authors` table, I added the code shown in Listing 19-6 to the `Click` handler for the Change Author button.

Listing 19-6: Posting Changes to the Database Web Service

```
private void buttonChangeAuthors_Click(object sender, System.EventArgs
e)
{
  if (dataGrid1.DataSource == null)
    return;  // dataGrid never populated

  DataSet dataSet = dataGrid1.DataSource as DataSet;
  DataSet changes = dataSet.GetChanges();
  if (changes == null)
    return;  // no changes

  Cursor.Current = Cursors.WaitCursor;

  MyDatabaseWebService myService = new MyDatabaseWebService();
  myService.ChangeAuthors(changes);

  Cursor.Current = Cursors.Default;
}
```

The code is straightforward. If changes were made to the DataSet attached to the DataGrid, the code

```
DataSet changes = dataSet.GetChanges();
```

would return a DataSet containing only changed records — with all the added, edited, and deleted records. If a DataSet has no changes, DataSet.GetChanges() returns a null object. To post the changes to the Database Web Service, I created an instance of MyDatabaseWebService and called its ChangeAuthors() method. The DataSet passed to the method is automatically serialized into an XML document and sent to the Web Service. The Web Service receives the XML document, deserializes it, and reconstructs a new DataSet from it, containing only the changed records. This new DataSet is used over on the Web Service side to post the changes to the database using the code shown in Listing 19-7.

Listing 19-7: The Web Service Code that Posts Changes to the Database

```
[WebMethod]
public void ChangeAuthors(System.Data.DataSet changedDataSet)
{
  sqlDataAdapter1.Update(changedDataSet);
  // changedDataSet.AcceptChanges();  no need to call this
}
```

The posting is managed by the DataAdapter I created earlier, named sqlDataAdapter1. After posting the changes, notice how the code *doesn't* call DataSet.AcceptChanges().

This call is normally used after posting a DataSet's data, to clear all row flags indicating errors, or added, edited, and deleted rows. In the case of a Database Web Service, the DataSet is a temporary object that goes out of scope when the ChangeAuthors() method completes, so there is no need to clear any of its flags.

Handling Exceptions

As explained in Chapter 16, titled "Services," you need to be extremely careful about exceptions that may occur in a service. Since services don't have a user interface in most cases, exception messages may not be displayable. If an exception did occur, the server might try to display an invisible message box, waiting for someone to click the invisible OK or Cancel button. From the perspective of clients trying to use this service, it would appear that the service died.

Web Services are somewhat more tolerant of exceptions, because they have a built-in exception handler that sends a message over the wire back to the client, showing a description of the exception. For example, say a Web Service method has the code shown in Listing 19-8.

Listing 19-8: Throwing an Exception in a Web Method

```
[WebMethod]
public System.Data.DataSet GetAuthors()
{
    throw new Exception("The Database Web Service got hosed!");

    // other code...
}
```

When a client calls this method, the exception will show up on the client's machine with the message shown in Figure 19-33.

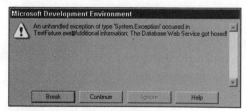

Figure 19-33: An exception propagated from a Web Service method back to the client machine

To avoid these ugly messages from getting back to the user, wrap all the code that may throw exceptions in a try block and handle the exceptions on the server side, when possible. For example, the ChangeAuthors() method would be better coded as shown in Listing 19-9.

Listing 19-9: Preventing Exceptions from Showing Up on the Client Side

```
[WebMethod]
public void ChangeAuthors(System.Data.DataSet changedDataSet)
{
  try
  {
    sqlDataAdapter1.Update(changedDataSet);
  }
  catch(Exception) {}  // squelch the exception completely
}
```

Rather than simply killing the exception, you should attempt corrective action, if possible. For example, if a parameter is missing, perhaps you could use a safe default value for it. Sometimes retrying the operation may lead to successful completion. Do whatever you can to handle server-side problems without involving the user.

The moral of the story is this: Services that send exceptions back to client machines are bad. Develop your services defensively. You may be convinced that a section of code can't possibly generate exceptions, but it's still a good idea to wrap everything in a `try` block. Just to handle those *unforeseen events* Dan Quayle talked about. There is only a negligible runtime penalty when adding `try` blocks to your code.

Transactions

When you have a group of database operations that are related, it's generally a good idea to execute them in the context of a database transaction. If all operations in the context succeed, the transaction can be committed, causing all the changes to be applied atomically. If one or more of the operations in the transaction fail, the transaction can be rolled back, canceling all the changes made in the transaction and restoring the database to the state it was in before the transaction was started. Listing 19-10 shows how to wrap a database operation inside a transaction.

Listing 19-10: Using Transactions with Database Operations

```
public void ChangeAuthors(DataSet changedDataSet)
{
  System.Data.SqlClient.SqlTransaction transaction = null;
  try
  {

    transaction = sqlConnection1.BeginTransaction();

    sqlInsertCommand1.Transaction = transaction;
    sqlUpdateCommand1.Transaction = transaction;
```

```
        sqlDeleteCommand1.Transaction = transaction;

        sqlDataAdapter1.Update(changedDataSet);

        transaction.Commit();
    }
    catch(Exception)
    {

        transaction.Rollback();
    }
}
```

As the code shows, you start a transaction by calling a `Connection`'s `BeginTransaction()` method. Each `Command` using that `Connection` (and that needs to be part of the transaction) must be passed a reference to the `Transaction` object. After calling the `DataAdapter`'s `Update()` method, you must commit all your changes by calling `Transaction.Commit()`. If an exception occurs during the `Update()` operation, the exception should be caught and the entire transaction rolled back.

Testing the Database Web Service

One of the most spectacular innovations in VS .NET and Web Services is in the debugging department. Now you can debug both the test fixture and the Web Service at the same time. If you set a breakpoint in the test fixture code, you can step right into a Web Method call as if the code was part of the test fixture. The switch from test fixture code to Web Service code is completely seamless. To see how cool this really is, I'll set a breakpoint in the test fixture code and show you the debugging windows when stepping through the code.

I set a breakpoint in the `Click` handler for the Get Authors button. After I clicked the button, the breakpoint was triggered, as shown in Figure 19-34.

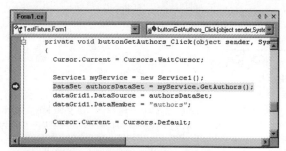

Figure 19-34: Setting a breakpoint just before calling a Web Service method

If you click the VS .NET debugger's Step Into button, the debugger steps across a process, and possibly even a machine boundary, into the Web Service code, as shown in Figure 19-35.

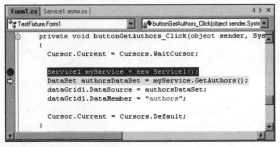

```
Form1.cs  Service1.asmx.cs                                    ◁ ▷ ×
❖ DatabaseWebService.Service1          ▼    ⊸◆ GetAuthors()              ▼
      [WebMethod]
      public System.Data.DataSet GetAuthors()
      {
        try
        {
          System.Data.DataSet dataSet = new MyDataSet();
          sqlDataAdapter1.Fill(dataSet);
          return dataSet;
        }
        catch (Exception)
        {
```

Figure 19-35: Seamlessly stepping from client code into a Web Service method

Take my word for it, there is a whole bunch of invisible .NET Framework code executed between the statement in the test fixture code and the first line of the Web Method code. The invisible code handles the details of SOAP packets, object serialization, and delivery of packets over the wire to the Web Server. The Web Server gets the SOAP message and hands it to the ASP.NET runtime. The runtime determines which Web Service and method the message is for and calls it. Like magic, the VS .NET debugger just switches to the Web Service code and places the execution point of the method's first line. For new programmers learning .NET programming, all this automatic activity is probably taken for granted. For programmers like me, used to all the headaches related to remote procedure calls, all I can say is *Hallelujah!*

If you single-step past the end of the method, the debugger switches back from the Web Service code to the client code, as shown in Figure 19-36.

```
Form1.cs  Service1.asmx.cs                                    ◁ ▷ ×
❖ TestFixture.Form1                    ▼    ≡◆ buttonGetAuthors_Click(object sender, Syste ▼
      private void buttonGetAuthors_Click(object sender, Sys
      {
        Cursor.Current = Cursors.WaitCursor;

        Service1 myService = new Service1();
        DataSet authorsDataSet = myService.GetAuthors();
        dataGrid1.DataSource = authorsDataSet;
        dataGrid1.DataMember = "authors";

        Cursor.Current = Cursors.Default;
      }
```

Figure 19-36: Seamlessly stepping from a Web Service method back into the client code

Simply spectacular. Debugging just doesn't get any better. There is one thing to keep in mind: To step into server-side code you need to have the appropriate permissions set up on the server, and also have remote debugging available on that machine. For more information on debugging, check Chapters 6 and 16.

Summary

In this chapter, I brought together a number of different topics, such as ADO.NET components, Web Services, debugging, and stored procedures. I did this to show how the various technologies work in the common scenario of database programming inside a Web Service. If you are interested in developing a Database Web Service, in many cases you can just read this single chapter, rather than reading bits and pieces of Chapters 6, 11, 16, and 18.

The ADO.NET Framework is superbly suited for use inside a Web Service. By using a Database Web Service, you can design thin clients that work reliably in both connected and disconnected modes. Because `DataSet` components intrinsically support serialization into XML documents, the details of moving resultsets across process and machine boundaries are automatically taken care of, enabling you to concentrate more on the business logic and less on the plumbing issues of your distributed systems.

✦   ✦   ✦

Multithreaded Components

He can compress the most words into the smallest idea of any man I know.

— Abraham Lincoln

Obviously, Mr. Lincoln wasn't talking about me, or the idea of multithreading. In any case, threads are no small idea. They provide developers with a fantastic means of making their programs more powerful. Before delving into the details of multithreaded components, let me say a few words about threads in the context of the .NET Framework.

What is a thread? Threads are the smallest slice of executable code you can define. When Windows starts up a program, it creates a process and a domain within that process, inside which the program's threads are run. In .NET nomenclature, the domain is called an *AppDomain*. More than one AppDomain can be created for a given process, although you'll generally have only one. Threads live inside this domain and can share variables and objects. Windows always creates a single startup thread for an application. From this thread, any number of additional threads can be started. Each of those threads can in turn start other threads, recursively to any depth.

Windows schedules threads to run in time slices, running short bursts of each thread in round-robin fashion. On single-processor machines, only one thread can run at a time. To end users, it appears that all the threads are running concurrently. If you run multithreaded code on a multiprocessor machine, Windows will run threads simultaneously on different processors, balancing the thread load. On multiprocessor machines, multiple threads really do run concurrently.

Multithreading is not a technique used only with back-end components, but I decided to discuss them in this last part of the book because the back end is about moving data. Back-end components are often measured by their TPS (number of *Transactions Per Second*) and by the number of concurrent users they can handle. The requirement to handle multiple users at the same time makes the use of multithreading almost a necessity. Middle-tier components are frequently run in a multithreaded mode, but when running under control of IIS or MTS, the threading details are taken care of for you.

Threading Concepts

If you have experience with multithreaded programming in the COM world, you know that COM threading was coordinated through the use of so-called *COM apartments*. Many programmers wonder what relationship exists between the old COM and the new .NET Framework models of threading. There are a number of recurring questions that pop up on discussion lists. Do .NET threads have dependencies on COM apartments? How many threads can run in an apartment? How do you synchronize multiple threads? These are some of the most frequently asked questions regarding threading in the .NET context. The short answers are:

✦ Threads don't require COM apartments, but can run in them.

✦ Any number of threads can run in an apartment.

✦ You synchronize threads using special objects, based on Win32 native objects.

To give you the long answer, I need to make a digression into COM and COM threading. If you could care less how threading works, and only want to read about how threading applies to component structure, skip the next section.

Apartment threading

The .NET *Common Language Runtime (CLR)* uses a threading model known as *Single Apartment Threading (STA)* to run your code. I know the term *apartment* sounds strange: it doesn't involve furniture or bedrooms, but the COM concept of apartment is fairly simple. An apartment is basically the execution context of one or more COM objects. More precisely, *apartments are the environments in which COM threads live and run.* Apartments were devised for COM as a means of dealing with the memory, concurrency, and reentrancy constraints of COM objects in a uniform manner. Before a COM object can be created, an apartment must be set up for it to execute in.

The CLR is really just a bunch of COM objects that are run in an STA. If you create a Windows Form application, it will be run in an STA, as shown in Figure 20-1.

Figure 20-1: A Windows Form application running inside a Single Threaded Apartment

If you create a different type of component, such as a class library or a custom controls library, no apartment is created and your code will run on the threads of calling applications. These threads may or may not be running in an apartment.

Whether your code runs in an STA or not, once your code is running, it can create as many threads as it wants. Part of the structure of the STA was devised to make code developed for Microsoft's old Dynamic Data Exchange (DDE) mechanism work. DDE was the component interaction method built into OLE 1. With DDE, components talked to each other by sending Windows messages. The messages were placed in the receiver's message queue, and subsequently processed by the receiver's message pump.

STAs are similar: There is a message queue on which incoming messages and method calls are placed. There is exactly one thread that runs the message pump to process the items in the message queue. The CLR runs inside the STA and handles the messages dispatched to it by the message pump, as shown in Figure 20-2.

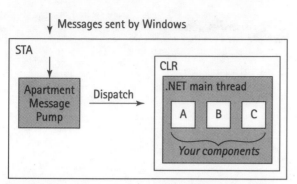

Figure 20-2: The .NET Framework STA your code runs in

By default, the components you create in your code are all run on the same thread: the main message pump thread. Since all your components are in the same apartment, as shown in the figure, they can call each other without having to marshal method calls across process or apartment boundaries. The components are also automatically thread-safe, because they all run on the same thread. Your components are protected by the STA from method calls originating in other apartments or processes.

There are a couple of essential points to keep in mind about apartments:

✦ An apartment can belong to only one process; in other words, processes *cannot* share apartments.

✦ A thread can belong to only one apartment; in other words, apartments *cannot* share threads.

If you feel an urge to better understand COM apartments, there are a couple of books you might want to check out, such as *Essential COM* [Box 1998] or *Inside COM* [Rogerson 1997].

.NET threads and synchronization

One of the rules stated earlier for STAs, namely that there can only be one thread in an STA, seems to preclude multithreaded programming in the .NET Framework. Relax—multithreaded programming is not only possible, but even easy. All you need to do is break the rules, or interpret them creatively. The requirement for an STA to contain only one thread is a COM edict, necessary so the COM apartment can synchronize calls into COM objects it contains. If the objects aren't COM objects, then the apartment doesn't know about them and you can create all the threads you want.

Creating threads is the easy part, regardless of whether your code is running in an apartment or not. Marshalling will be necessary when a .NET thread makes a call to code in an apartment it doesn't belong to. The calling thread may be in another apartment, or in no apartment at all. Synchronizing threads is also very important. If threads aren't synchronized properly, there may be problems such as race conditions, concurrency issues, and deadlocks in the code. Not always easy stuff to debug. The .NET Framework supports code synchronization at various levels. With COM components, this work was largely performed behind the scenes by the apartment infrastructure. Now you have to take over and manage all the details of synchronization.

But first, let's take a look at how to create and run a simple thread, as shown in Listing 20-1.

Listing 20-1: **Creating and Running a Thread**

```
using System.Threading;

public class WorkerClass
{
  public void DoThis() {}
}

public class ThreadClient
{
  public void RunTheWorkerClass()
  {
    WorkerClass myWorker = new WorkerClass();
    Thread myThread = new Thread(new ThreadStart(myWorker.DoThis));
    myThread.Start();
    while (!myThread.IsAlive)
      ;  // wait for thread to start
    myThread.Join();
  }
}
```

A word on semantics: When one thread creates another, the former is called the *parent* thread, and the latter is called the *child* or *worker* thread. When creating a child thread, the code you want to run on the new thread must be in a method with the following signature:

```
public void MethodName();
```

This method may be part of the class (such as `ThreadClient`) creating the worker thread, or a different class, as shown in the previous listing—it's up to you. To run this method, you need to create a new `Thread` object, and pass the method to it as a delegate. To start the thread, just call `Thread.Start()`. The call returns immediately, but if problems occur while the thread is started up, an exception will be raised. The thread terminates when the method returns. How does the thread owner know when the thread terminates? One way is to call the method `Thread.Join()`. The method will wait (possibly forever) for the thread to terminate. If you can't wait that long, you can also indicate a timeout value in the call, as shown in Listing 20-2.

Listing 20-2: **Checking to See If a Thread Timed Out Before Completing**

```
if (myThread.Join(20) )  // wait for no more than 20 ms
  Console.WriteLine("Thread ran normally");
else
  Console.WriteLine("Thread timed out");
```

`Thread.Join()` is a synchronization method that forces the running thread to stop until the other thread terminates (or times out).

Sending information back to the parent thread

Often the parent thread is interested in the outcome of the child thread. Did it work or not? Did errors occur, and if so, which ones? The child thread obviously needs a way to communicate information back to the parent thread. One simple way is to create a variable that is shared between parent and child. The parent could initialize it and run the child thread. The child could store a value in the shared variable, and the parent thread could check the value after the child terminates. This technique works fine if there is only one child thread, and as long as you're sure that two threads will not try to update the value at the same time. But what if you run multiple child threads concurrently? Read on.

Multiple threads executing the same code

To novice programmers, the idea of having multiple threads execute the same piece of code seems strange. Why would you want to do the same thing multiple times, and at the same time? There are good reasons. In practice it is a fairly common requirement. Consider what your Web browser does when you type in a URL: It creates a thread to download the HTML page requested. Then it parses the page and for each embedded object it finds (such as images), it creates a child thread to download it. If the page had five images on it, there would be five threads, all running the same code to download the images.

If threads share the same code, you need to coordinate them so they don't step on each other. What you need is *synchronization*. Synchronized code is code that is protected by some type of software lock, which ensures that only one thread executes the code at any given time. A common way to synchronize code in C# is with the `lock` statement, as shown in Listing 20-3.

Listing 20-3: **Using a lock Statement to Synchronize Code**

```
public class WorkerClass
{
  public void DoThis()
  {
    lock(this)
    {
      // only one thread allowed to enter at a time
    }
  }
}
```

If you run two child threads concurrently, the first will execute the `lock` statement. When the second thread tries to execute the `lock` statement, the system will find that a thread has already acquired the lock, so the second thread will be put to sleep. When the first thread exits the locked region, it frees the `lock` for the second thread. The system wakes the second thread up and runs it. See "Pausing and synchronizing a thread," later in this chapter, for other details on synchronizing threads.

When using a `Monitor` or other technique to synchronize sections of your child threads, you have to be very careful you don't cause deadlocks. Here is a simple example of deadlock: Thread 1 puts a lock on resource R1 and then waits for resource R2. Thread 2 has a lock on R2 and is waiting for R1. The two threads will wait forever. One way to eliminate deadlocks is to never put a lock on a resource if you plan to acquire another lockable resource while you hold the first lock. Or it may be possible to use one lock to access both resources. Avoiding deadlock requires forethought and careful design work.

Waiting for one of several events

When you have multiple child threads running together, you may need to monitor the status of each one, and perhaps take a different course of action based on which one terminates first. Using myChildThread.Join() won't work, because it will block until the child thread terminates. You could add a short timeout to the Join() call, say one millisecond, so if the child thread doesn't terminate within that time, the call to Join() would timeout and return. Then you could go on and check the next child thread. But there is a better way, based on the use of WaitHandle and Event objects.

Events have two states: non-signaled and signaled. The non-signaled state is used to denote an event that hasn't occurred yet. When the event occurs, you set the event state to signaled by calling the event's Set() method. Events can then be shared by parent and child threads and used to exchange information. Events come in two basic flavors: AutoResetEvent and ManualResetEvent. An auto-event resets itself automatically back to the non-signaled state when a thread that is waiting for this event is released. Manual events require you to call ManualResetEvent.Reset() to switch the state from signaled back to non-signaled.

The code in Listing 20-4 shows how to use both WaitHandles and Events. The parent thread starts up three child threads and then uses WaitHandle.WaitAny() to wait for any child thread to signal an event. In my example, child threads set events when the threads terminate.

Listing 20-4: Waiting for the First of Many Child Threads to Signal an Event

```
using System.Threading;

public class MyParentThread
{
  // initially non-signaled events
  AutoResetEvent event1 = new AutoResetEvent(false);
  AutoResetEvent event2 = new AutoResetEvent(false);
  AutoResetEvent event3 = new AutoResetEvent(false);

  public void Use3ChildThreads()
  {
    Thread t1 = new Thread(new ThreadStart(Thread1) );
    Thread t2 = new Thread(new ThreadStart(Thread2) );
    Thread t3 = new Thread(new ThreadStart(Thread3) );

    // setup a list of events to wait for
    AutoResetEvent[] EventsInProgress = new AutoResetEvent[3]
    {
      event1,
      event2,
      event3
    };

    // start all the child threads
```

```
   t1.Start();
   t2.Start();
   t3.Start();

   // wait for one of the events to be sigaled


   WaitHandle.WaitAny(EventsInProgress);

   // at least one thread has terminated
}

public void Thread1()
{
   // pretend to do something...
   Thread.Sleep(1000);

   // signal the fact that we're done
   event1.Set();
}

public void Thread2()
{
   // pretend to do something...
   Thread.Sleep(2000);

   // signal the fact that we're done
   event2.Set();
}

public void Thread3()
{
   // pretend to do something...
   Thread.Sleep(3000);

   // signal the fact that we're done
   event3.Set();
}
}
```

You can also use the method `WaitHandle.WaitAll()` to wait for all the events to be signaled. Both `WaitAny()` and `WaitAll()` can be passed a timeout value, to prevent them from blocking for too long. A thread can manage more than just one event. Although my example shows the child threads signaling events when they terminate, it is perfectly possible to have a thread continue running after signaling an event.

Threads and COM objects

If you plan on instantiating and running COM objects in a .NET thread, the thread needs to have an apartment. As stated earlier, there are two kinds of apartments: Single Threaded Apartments (STAs) and Multithreaded Apartments (MTAs). The `Thread` class has a property called `ApartmentState` that indicates the type of apartment set up for the thread. By default, the VS .NET Windows Application New Project Wizard sets the state to STA, using the code shown in Listing 20-5.

Listing 20-5: The STAThread Attribute Generated by the Windows Application Project Wizard

```
[STAThread]
static void Main()
{
  Application.Run(new Form1());
}
```

STA threading is set because Windows Forms are based on native Win32 Windows that require an STA. Apart from the main thread of the application, you can create additional threads with single-threaded apartments, multithreaded apartments, or even no apartment. The default is no apartment, because apartments are not needed when dealing with your own .NET classes unless they deal with COM objects.

Setting up an apartment for a thread is an expensive process, so do it only when necessary. Listing 20-6 shows how you would setup an STA for a thread and then instantiate and call a COM object.

Listing 20-6: Using a COM Object in a .NET Thread

```
using System.Threading;
using System.Reflection

public class MyThread
{
  Object myComServer;
  Type t;

  public void UseComObjectInsideThread()
  {

    Thread.CurrentThread.ApartmentState = ApartmentState.STA;


    t = Type.GetTypeFromProgID("MyCOMobject.TopLevelObject");
    if (t == null)
      throw new Exception("MyCOMobject not registered.");


    myComServer = Activator.CreateInstance(t);

    // assume the method to call takes 3 parameters
    Object [] args = new Object[3];
```

```
        args[0] = "Hello";        // Assume 1st parameter is a string
        args[1] = 1;              // Assume 2nd parameter is a number



        args[2] = Missing.Value;  // Use a default for the third
                                  //  parameter


    t.InvokeMember("DoThis", BindingFlags.InvokeMethod,
                null, myComServer, args);
    }
}
```

The code uses the static method `Type.GetTypeFromProgID()` to obtain a .NET-compatible type from data stored in the system registry. The static method `Activator.CreateInstance()` is then used to instantiate the COM object. To call methods of the COM object, you can use early or late binding. I used late binding in the example, invoking COM methods indirectly via `Type.InvokeMember()`. Notice the use of `Missing.Value` in the parameter array. This special value can be used to denote a default value.

Nonblocking calls

There are times when you need to call a method that will take a long time to complete. During this time, you don't want the program to just hang and wait for the method to finish. Perhaps the code has a user interface, and you want to let the user continue working while the lengthy operation completes. What you need is to make the call to the lengthy method return immediately, while the operation executes in the background. A threading model that will support this type of scenario is shown in Figure 20-3.

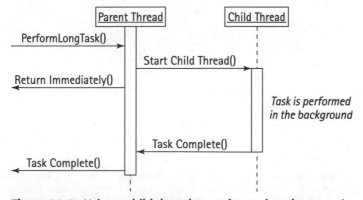

Figure 20-3: Using a child thread to perform a lengthy operation with a nonblocking method

To callers of the parent thread's `PerformLongTask()` method, the call is a nonblocking one, because it returns control immediately, before the task has been carried out. The `Task Complete` callback notification can be implemented with a delegate. Listing 20-7 shows how you might implement nonblocking calls:

Listing 20-7: Implementing Nonblocking Calls Using a Child Thread

```
using System.Threading;


public delegate void TerminationHandler();

public class MyClientComponent
{
  public void PerformLengthyOperation()
  {
    MyNonBlockingClass helper = new MyNonBlockingClass();
    helper.DoLongTask(new TerminationHandler(TaskIsComplete) );
  }

  void TaskIsComplete()
  {
    Console.WriteLine("Task is complete.");
  }
}

public class MyNonBlockingClass
{
  private TerminationHandler terminationHandler;

  public void DoLongTask(TerminationHandler whoToCallWhenDone)
  {
    terminationHandler = whoToCallWhenDone;
    Thread childThread = new Thread(new ThreadStart(DoTheWork) );
    childThread.Start();
  }

  void DoTheWork()
  {
    // pretend to do something...
    Thread.Sleep(2000);

    // tell the caller we're done
    terminationHandler();
  }
}
```

The nonblocking call scenario is so common (relatively speaking) that the .NET Framework has a built-in architecture to support it, known as the *Asynchronous Programming Model (APM)*. The model enables you to code lengthy methods as though they were called synchronously, doing away with the need to signal events. The calling code decides whether the worker method is executed asynchronously or not. Another nice thing about the built-in model is its support for remote calls: The lengthy operation method can be in a different process or even on a different machine from the client.

For more details on asynchronous method calls, see "Synchronous and asynchronous calls," later in this chapter.

Thread pools

Threads are fairly expensive resources to create. If you have a component that uses threads frequently for different tasks, it may be advantageous to create a pool of threads at startup time. The .NET Framework comes with a built-in ThreadPool class that is adequate for many different situations, but you may have requirements that force you to build your own thread pool, so I'll show you how in the next section.

Building your own thread pool

Why would you want to build your own thread pool class if there is a built-in class? One reason might be that you need access to the threads in the pool while they are running. Perhaps you need to coordinate actions between two or more of the threads in the pool. The built-in ThreadPool class doesn't give you direct access to the threads it manages, so you would need to build your own pool.

Let's take a look at how this could be done. You need the class to initially create a number of sleeping pools that users can run over and over again. When you need a thread, you get one from the pool, give it a method to execute, and run it. When the task completes, the idle thread is returned to the pool. Figure 20-4 shows the relationship between a component that uses threads and the thread pool.

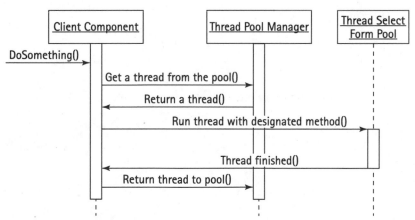

Figure 20-4: Using a thread pool to manage threads

One obstacle to reusing a thread is the fact that you can only pass the name of the method to run in the Thread() constructor. Once the thread is constructed, you can no longer change this method. Are we stuck with threads that can run only one method? Not really. You just have to be creative with what that one method is. I'll make this method a standard startup method that will use a delegate to call the real method to run. By using a delegate, the real method can be changed at any time, without violating the rule that a thread's startup method is immutable. Listing 20-8 shows a simple thread pool implementation.

Listing 20-8: The Implementation of a Simple Thread Pool

```csharp
using System.Threading;

class MyThreadPool
{
  ReusableThread[] threadPool;

  public MyThreadPool(int theSize)
  {
    threadPool = new ReusableThread [theSize];
    for (int i=0; i<theSize; i++)
    threadPool[i] = new ReusableThread();
  }

    public ReusableThread GetThread()
    {
      lock(this)
      {
        r = GetAvailableThread();
      }
      return r;
    }

    public ReusableThread GetAvailableThread()
    {
      foreach (ReusableThread rt in threadPool)
      {
        if (rt.isAvailable)
        {
          rt.isAvailable = false;
          return rt;
        }
      }
      return null;
    }

  public void PutThread(ReusableThread theThread)
  {
    lock(this)
    {
      theThread.isAvailable = true;
    }
  }
}

public delegate void StartupMethod();

class ReusableThread
{
  public bool isAvailable = true;
  private Thread thread;
```

```
      private StartupMethod startupMethod;

      public ReusableThread()
      {
        thread = new Thread(new ThreadStart(CommonStart) );
      }

      public void Join()
      {
        thread.Join();
      }

      public void Run(StartupMethod theStartupMethod)
      {
        startupMethod = theStartupMethod;
        thread.Start();
      }

      public void CommonStart()
      {
        if (startupMethod == null) return;
        startupMethod();
        startupMethod = null;
      }
    }
```

Notice the `lock` statement used in `MyThreadPool.GetThread()` and `PutThread()` to prevent concurrent accesses. Actually, `PutThread()` probably doesn't need the `lock` statement, because only one thread at a time should ever be releasing the same `ReusableThread` back to the pool. In any case, defensive programming may prevent unforeseen concurrency problems that could be hard to debug.

Look at the implementation of `MyThreadPool.GetThread()`. If no threads are available, the method simply returns `null`. An alternative approach is to wait for a short period to see if any threads become available before giving up.

You might wonder, on first glance, why I went to the effort of creating a `ReusableThread` class, rather than just using `Thread`. As stated earlier, the problem with class `Thread` is that it lets you set the startup method only once, in the constructor. For this reason, a common startup method is set for all threads, in class `ReusableThread`. This method then calls a delegate, which points to the startup method the client component wants to run. Listing 20-9 shows how a client object would use the thread pool to execute a method.

Listing 20-9: **An Example of a Client Using the Simple Thread Pool**

```
public class MyClient
{

  public void RunWithThread()
  {
```

Continued

Listing 20-9 *(continued)*

```
      MyThreadPool pool = new MyThreadPool(20);
      ReusableThread thread = pool.GetThread();
      if (thread == null) return;
      thread.Run(new StartupMethod(MyCode) );   // run the thread
      thread.Join(); // wait for thread to finish
      pool.PutThread(thread); // return thread to pool
   }

   public void MyCode()
   {
      // pretend to do some work...
      Thread.Sleep(2000);
   }
}
```

Using the built-in ThreadPool class

Because thread pooling is such a recurring requirement in high-performance components, a built-in `ThreadPool` class was added to the .NET Framework. The class works a bit differently from `MyThreadPool`. The idea is to let a calling application put in a request to execute some code with a thread from the thread pool. As soon as a thread becomes available, the code is executed. Figure 20-5 shows what the interaction diagram looks like when using the built-in `ThreadPool` object.

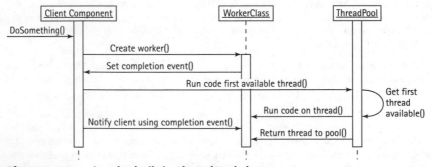

Figure 20-5: Using the built-in ThreadPool class

A `ThreadPool` runs in its own thread, to isolate your application from the timing details of managing the pool and scheduling new threads to run. You have no control over the number of threads that are created in a `ThreadPool`. The `ThreadPool` object itself decides how many threads to create, using a number of internal heuristics. To schedule a task to run, you call `ThreadPool.QueueUserWorkItem()` like this:

```
// passing no parameters
ThreadPool.QueueUserWorkItem(new WaitCallback(StartRequest) );

// ... or passing a state parameter
ThreadPool.QueueUserWorkItem(new WaitCallback(StartRequest), state);
```

The `state` parameter is stored internally in the `ThreadPool` and is an object with as many fields as you need to convey your state information. The `WaitCallback` parameter specifies the callback method you want to execute on a thread from the pool. When a thread is allocated for the callback, the `state` parameter (if available) is retrieved and passed to the callback. This way you can indirectly pass any information you want, such as context or state information, to the callback.

The callback method is simply a class method whose signature is:

```
void MethodName(Object state);
```

So you would need a class that looked something like Listing 20-10.

Listing 20-10: A Class Containing a Method that Could Be Passed to the ThreadPool Queuing Method

```
class MyClass
{
  public void MyCallback(Object state) {...}

  // other fields and methods
  //...
}
```

If no state information was passed to `ThreadPool.QueueUserWorkItem()`, the `state` parameter will be `null`. There are two common ways to use thread pools, based on whether the requester needs to know the outcome of a request or not.

Class `ThreadPool` never gives you a reference to the `Thread` object it chose to execute your code on, so you can't use methods like `Thread.Join()` to determine when the thread terminates. You need to use other techniques, such as signaled events, as shown in Listing 20-11.

Listing 20-11: Using the Built-In ThreadPool Class

```
public class ParametersToUse
{
  public int parameter1, parameter2, parameter3;

  public ParametersToUse(int p1, int p2, int p3)
  {
    parameter1 = p1;
    parameter2 = p2;
    parameter3 = p3;
  }
}

public class MyWorkerClass
{
```

Continued

Listing 20-11 *(continued)*

```
   private AutoResetEvent terminationEvent;

   public MyWorkerClass(AutoResetEvent theEvent)
   {
     terminationEvent = theEvent;
   }

   public void MyCode(Object theParameters)
   {
     // get the parameters to use

     ParametersToUse myParameters = (ParametersToUse) theParameters;

     // pretend to do something...
     Thread.Sleep(2000);

     // signal the fact that we're done
     terminationEvent.Set();
   }
}

public class MyThreadPoolClient
{
  public void UseTheThreadPool()
  {
    AutoResetEvent workerTermination = new AutoResetEvent(false);
    MyWorkerClass myWorker = new MyWorkerClass(workerTermination);

    ThreadPool.QueueUserWorkItem(new WaitCallback(myWorker.MyCode),
                          new ParametersToUse(1, 2, 3) );

    workerTermination.WaitOne(5000, true);
  }
}
```

The WorkerClass is where the code to run is placed. The callback method MyCode() is passed an object by the ThreadPool, containing any parameters needed. The parameters are contained in an ad hoc class, called ParametersToUse in the listing. For synchronization purposes, the WorkerClass is passed an AutoResetEvent object in the constructor. Class MyThreadPoolClient queues up thread requests by calling ThreadPool.QueueUserWorkItem(). When a thread becomes available in the pool, it is run automatically by the ThreadPool. When the task is completed in the method MyCode(), the AutoResetEvent object is set to the signaled state, so the client component in the parent thread can be notified.

The client component is a class called MyThreadPoolClient. The method UseThe ThreadPool() is where the thread pool is used. The last line in this method, with the call to the method AutoResetEvent.WaitOne(), makes the client wait for up to five seconds for the WorkerClass to terminate.

Thread Management

Having discussed the main concepts of threading, I'll now look at the details of thread management: starting, pausing, aborting, and synchronizing threads.

There are a couple of ways you are most likely to handle threads in a component. You'll either create a thread to carry out a task in the background, or you'll need to handle a whole slew of threads using a thread pool. I'll describe both of these methods in the next few sections.

Starting a thread

The first thing you can do to a thread is to create it and run it. In the .NET Framework, starting a thread is almost trivial. You create a Thread object and pass it a delegate, which is just reference to a method of a class. Listing 20-12 shows the code.

Listing 20-12: **Creating and Starting a Thread**

```
using System.Threading;

public class MyMultiThreadedApp
{
  public static void Main()
  {
    MyClass myClass       = new MyClass();
    Thread myThread = new Thread(new ThreadStart(myClass.EntryPoint) );
    myThread.Start();
  }
}

public class MyClass
{
  public void EntryPoint() {}
}
```

After creating a thread, you start it by calling Thread.Start(). This method returns immediately, often before the thread actually starts. Calling Thread.Start() results in the thread's entry point method being called. In the listing, the entry point was named MyClass.EntryPoint(). Entry point methods can't return a value, since the caller is the Thread class and wouldn't know what to do with a returned value.

If you need a way to check the results of running MyClass in a thread, create some fields in MyClass. The threaded code in EntryPoint() could set the field values. When the thread terminates — or even while the thread is running — class MyMultiThreadedApp could access the MyClass fields.

Checking the state of a thread

Since Thread.Start() returns immediately, you can't assume that the thread is running. It takes a certain amount of time for the operating system to start up a thread. To monitor the state of a thread, there are two main properties: `IsAlive` and `ThreadState`. The former tells you essentially whether the thread has started; the latter indicates the internal state of the thread, according to the Table 20-1.

Table 20-1: The States of a Thread

Thread State	When State Applies
Unstarted	Right after a thread was created, but before it is run.
Running	Once the thread starts running, following a Run or Resume command.
WaitSleepJoin	After a Wait, Sleep, or Join command.
StopRequested	After a Stop command, while a thread is attempting to stop.
Stopped	After a thread has come to a stop.
AbortRequested	After an Abort command, while a thread is attempting to abort.
Aborted	After a thread has aborted.
SuspendRequested	After a Suspend command, while a thread is attempting to pause.
Suspended	After a thread has paused.

If you wanted to start a thread and wait for it to actually start, you could use the code in Listing 20-13.

Listing 20-13: **Waiting for a Thread to Start Running**

```
Thread myThread = new Thread(new ThreadStart(myDelegate) );
myThread.Start();
while (myThread.ThreadState != System.Threading.ThreadState.Running)
  Thread.Sleep(10); // wait until the thread starts running
```

You need to be a bit careful with this code. It looks safe on the surface, but if for some reason the thread can't be started, the `while` loop will never end. What could cause a thread to not start? The most common reason is an exception during the thread startup. To prevent the code from getting stuck in the `while` loop, you could use a simple timer in the code, as shown in Listing 20-14.

Listing 20-14: **Adding a Timer to Prevent Hangs if a Thread Couldn't Be Started**

```
Thread myThread = new Thread(new ThreadStart(myDelegate) );
myThread.Start();

const int OneSecond = 1000;
```

```
int startTime = Environment.TickCount;

// wait up to 1 second for the thread to start
while (myThread.ThreadState != System.Threading.ThreadState.Running)
{
  Thread.Sleep(10);
  if ( Math.Abs(Environment.TickCount - startTime) > OneSecond)
    break;
}
```

`Environment.TickCount` is a 32-bit unsigned integer that is set to 0 (zero) when Windows starts and incremented every millisecond. It takes about 50 days for the value to wrap around to 0. The `Math.Abs()` method in the timer code is necessary in the case the `Environment.TickCount` overflows and wraps around to 0.

Pausing and synchronizing a thread

To novices, the idea of pausing a thread may seem like we're asking our software to do nothing for a while. Actually, the typical reason for pausing a thread is to make it wait until a certain event occurs, at which time the thread is woken up. There are several ways to pause a thread, as described in the next sections.

Using Sleep()

You can call `Thread.Sleep()`, telling it the amount of time to pause the thread. This method immediately pauses the thread. While the thread is paused, the other threads in the system will get more runtime.

Using Suspend()

You can also call `Thread.Suspend()`. If a thread suspends itself, the call to `Suspend()` blocks until another thread resumes it. When one thread suspends another thread, the call puts the latter thread in the `SuspendRequested` state and returns immediately. Some time later, the thread transitions to the `Suspended` state.

Using Join()

You can also pause a thread by telling it to wait for another thread to terminate, using the `Thread.Join()` method. You can also pass it a parameter to tell it how long to wait. The method returns `true` only if the other thread terminates within that timeframe.

Using lock statements

Threads can also be forced to pause to prevent concurrent access to a section of code. Probably the easiest way to prevent multiple threads from executing the same code concurrently is by using a C# `lock` statement. This statement takes the form:

```
lock(object or class to lock)
{
  block of code to lock
}
```

Locked code is protected with a `Monitor`. When one thread acquires the lock, other threads trying to acquire it will block, forming a queue of paused threads. When the first thread exits the locked section, the next thread waiting will unblock and acquire the lock. Listing 20-15 shows two examples of lock statements — one for an object and one for a class.

Listing 20-15: Using Locks with Instances and Classes

```
Class MyClass
{
  int x, y;
  static int a, b;

  void UseAnInstanceLock()
  {
    lock(this) // lock an instance
    {
      // code protected by lock
      x = x + y;
    }
  }

  static void UseAClassLock ()
  {
    lock(typeof(MyClass) ) // we're in static method:
                           // lock the whole class
    {
      // code protected by lock
      a = a + b;
    }
  }
}
```

Locking an object prevents concurrent access to instance variables and methods. Locking a class prevents concurrent access to static fields and methods.

Using the Synchronization attribute

As shown in the last section, an entire class can be synchronized using a lock. You can also use an attribute to synchronize classes. Listing 20-16 shows an example.

Listing 20-16: Synchronizing an Entire Class

```
using System.Threading;
using System.Runtime.Remoting;

[Synchronization()]
public class WorkerClass
{
  public void DoThis() {}
}
```

This `Synchronization` attribute causes an entire class to be synchronized, including every instance field and instance method. Note that static fields and static methods are not synchronized. Synchronizing a whole class is generally excessive, but it's easy to do. If performance is important, you'll probably want to study your code and synchronize only the areas that need to be, using locks or `Monitors`.

Using Monitors

Another way of making a thread pause is with a `Monitor` object. As with locks, the purpose of a `Monitor` is to guard a section of code from being executed simultaneously by more than one thread. `Monitors` are used like this:

```
Monitor.Enter(objectToLock);

// code that can't be accessed concurrently
// ...

Monitor.Exit(objectToLock);
```

When the `Monitor.Enter()` method is called, the thread will be paused if another thread has already entered the `Monitor` on the same object. The section of code guarded by a pair of `Monitor.Enter()` and `Monitor.Exit()` calls is called a synchronized block. When your code is in one of these blocks, it can call `Monitor.Wait()` and `Monitor.Pulse()`. Calls to `Wait()` make the `Monitor` unlock access the object it is called on, causing the thread to pause until another thread calls `Monitor.Pulse()` on the object. At this time, the `Monitor.Wait()` call returns and the thread resumes. There can be multiple threads paused on a `Monitor.Wait()` call on the same object. Each time someone calls `Monitor.Pulse()` on that object, the next thread on the waiting queue is resumed. To make all waiting threads resume (that called `Monitor.Wait()` on a given object), you can use `Monitor.PulseAll()`. Listing 20-17 how you might use `Monitors` in threaded code.

Listing 20-17: Using Monitors to Guard Sections of Code from Being Accessed Concurrently by Threads

```
Monitor.Enter(this);  // enter a synchronized block

try
{
  // do some processing...

  Monitor.Wait(anotherObject);  // wait for the object to
                                // do something, otherwise
                                // pulse the monitor
}

catch SynchronizationLockException e)
{
  // a Monitor.Pulse occurred before we called Monitor.Wait
}
catch (ThreadInterruptedException e)
```

Continued

Listing 20-17 *(continued)*

```
{
  // someone called Thread.Interrupt
}

// ... do more processing...

Monitor.Pulse(this); // tell other parts of this object we're done

Monitor.Exit(this); // exit the synchronized block
```

The call to Monitor.Wait() is wrapped in a try block to catch exceptions that could be caused by external events. A SynchronizationLockException exception will occur if you call synchronizing Monitor methods from unsynchronized code. For example, consider the code in Listing 20-18.

Listing 20-18: Code that Will Cause a SynchronizationLockException to Be Thrown

```
void BadMethod()
{
  // assume we haven't called Monitor.Enter(this) yet

  Monitor.Pulse(this); // this call will provoke a
SynchronizationLockException
}
```

Before calling the Monitor methods Wait(), Exit(), Pulse(), and PulseAll(), you must have first called Monitor.Enter(). The code in Listing 20-17 didn't really need to catch SynchronizationLockException exceptions, but I added a handler for them just to point out the existence of these exceptions. Another type of exception — ThreadInterrupted Exception — can also occur when a thread is blocked. The exception will occur if another thread calls Thread.Interrupt() on the blocked thread.

Getting back to the code in Listing 20-17, Monitor.Wait() will block until another thread calls Monitor.Pulse() or Monitor.PulseAll() with the designated object. You can also pass a timeout value to Monitor.Wait(), to prevent your code from waiting indefinitely.

Using thread events

Thread events are operating system objects that are used between threads to exchange signals. Here's how they work. Say you have a thread called A that needs to stop at some point and wait for another thread called B to do something. Events are the signaling mechanism. Thread A would issue a call to wait for a certain event signal. If the signal has already been given, the call will return immediately and thread A will carry on happily. If the signal hasn't been given yet, thread A will block until B sends the signal. The interaction diagram in Figure 20-6 gives an overview of the process.

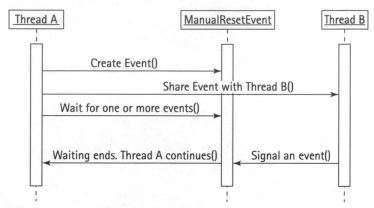

Figure 20-6: Synchronizing two threads with a ManualResetEvent object

The diagram refers to one of the thread event-signaling classes called ManualResetEvent. Listings 20-19 and 20-20 show what the code of threads A and B might look like.

Listing 20-19: **The Code for Thread A**

```
public class ThreadA
{
  ManualResetEvent waitForThreadB = new ManualResetEvent(false);
  ManualResetEvent[] events = new ManualResetEvent[1];
  ThreadB threadB;  // assume we have a reference to Thread B

  void RunAndWaitForSignal()
  {
    // share the event with Thread B
    threadB.SetEventToSignal(waitForThreadB);

    // do some processing...

    // wait for Thread B to signal it's done
    events [0] = waitForThreadB;
    ManualResetEvent.WaitAny(events);  // use WaitOne() if only 1 event

    // signal occurred: continue processing...
  }
}
```

Listing 20-20: The Code for Thread B

```
public class ThreadB
{
  ManualResetEvent eventToSignal;

  public void SetEventToSignal(ManualResetEvent theEvent)
  {
    eventToSignal = theEvent;
  }

  void RunAndWaitForSignal()
  {
    // do some processing...

    // signal that we finished
    if (eventToSignal != null)
      eventToSignal.Set();
  }
}
```

Thread A creates a `ManualResetEvent` and gives a reference to it to the other thread. A executes some code, and then waits for a signal from B. When thread B finishes its task, it sets the shared event to the signaled state and A carries on. Thread A blocks on the call:

```
ManualResetEvent.WaitAny(events);
```

The events array can be set up with any number of events to wait for. The first event in the list to become signaled will cause the calling thread to resume. If you need to wait until all events in the array get signaled, you can call the static method `WaitAll()`.

If you only need to wait for a single event to occur, you can dispense with the events array and just call the method `WaitOne()`, like this:

```
ManualResetEvent waitForThreadB = new ManualResetEvent(false);
waitForThreadB. WaitOne();
```

Up to this point, I have shown the use of class `ManualResetEvent`, but there is also another class called `AutoResetEvent`. The former changes state only if you call its `Set()` or `Reset()` methods. The latter will change the signaled state from `true` to `false` when a thread waiting for the signal is released.

If a thread waits for an event that never occurs, the blocked thread will never resume. To prevent this, all the `Wait` methods take some optional parameters to indicate how long you are willing to wait before the wait times out.

Using Interlocking

If you have multiple threads accessing a common variable, it's possible for threads to interfere with each other. Say two threads, A and B, try to execute the following statement at the same time:

```
x = x + 1;
```

where x is a shared variable. Both threads load the value of x, increment it, and save it. Depending on the exact timing with which A and B read and write x, the variable might be incremented once or twice. To prevent situations like this, you need to guard the statement against concurrent execution. You could use a Monitor or one of the other event classes described earlier, but the most efficient way is to use the Interlocked class, as shown in Listing 20-21.

Listing 20-21: Using an Interlock to Increment a Variable Shared Among Threads

```
// assume this code can run on multiple threads
public class MyClass
{
  int sharedVariable = 0;

  void UseSharedVariable()
  {
    // use an interlock to increment a shared variable
    int newValue = Interlocked.Increment(ref sharedVariable);

    // use newValue...
  }
}
```

The method Interlocked.Increment() guarantees that the operation will be performed *automatically,* meaning a thread will read, update, and write the variable without another thread interrupting it. There is also a method called Interlocked.Decrement(). If two threads attempt to execute an interlocked operation on the same variable at exactly the same time (a case that may occur if the operating system runs the threads on different CPUs), the interlocking mechanism will still work correctly.

Resuming a paused thread

If a thread is paused, there are a few ways to make it resume, based on how the thread was paused. If you paused it by calling Thread.Suspend(), you can resume it with the method Thread.Resume().

If the thread is in the WaitSleepJoin state, it can be resumed by calling Thread.Interrupt(). This method can be tricky. If you call it before a thread is in the WaitSleepJoin state, the call will set an internal flag in the thread. The next time the thread enters the WaitSleepJoin state, it will resume immediately. Keep in mind that calling Thread.Interrupt() for a blocked thread will cause the blocked statement to unblock by throwing a ThreadInterruptedException exception.

Stopping a thread

A thread will stop by itself when the entry point method passed to the thread constructor returns. You can also have one thread stop another. There are two typical ways to do this: the polite way and the rude way. The first uses a flag that is known to both threads. The controlling thread sets the flag when it wants the controlled thread to terminate. The controlled thread must periodically check this flag and terminate if the flag is found to be set.

Listing 20-22 shows how you might use a flag to support a controlled and orderly termination of a thread.

Listing 20-22: Using a Flag to Stop a Thread Gracefully

```
public class Worker
{
  public bool requestTermination;  // this flag is visible to
                                   // the controlling thread

  public void DoYourThing()
    {
        requestTermination = false;

        for (int i = 0; i < 10000; i++)
        {
          // Do some work here. We're lazy so
          // we'll just sleep for a while
          Thread.Sleep(2000);  // 2 seconds for each iteration

          // stop if we requested to do so
          if (requestTermination)
            return;
        }
    }
}

public class ControllingThread
{
  protected void RunAndStopAnotherThread()
  {
    Worker worker = new Worker();
    Thread myThread =
          new Thread(new ThreadStart(worker.DoYourThing) );
    myThread.Start();
    Thread.Sleep(3000);  // pretend we go off and do something...
    worker.requestTermination = true;  // ask the thread to stop

    // thread will stop within 2 seconds...
  }
}
```

The class Worker is the controlled thread. It has a field called requestTermination that is checked in the work loop. Class ControllingThread creates and runs Worker objects in a separate thread. The method RunAndStopAnotherThread() sleeps for a few seconds to simulate some work, and then sets the requestTermination flag. The controlled thread checks this flag every two seconds (the loop iteration time of DoYourThing) and shuts down as soon as it detects a request to stop.

Another way to stop a thread is by calling Thread.Abort(), which causes the controlled thread to throw a ThreadAbortException and terminate immediately. Use Thread.Abort()

carefully. If the controlled thread has acquired or locked resources, such as a file, a database connection, or a network connection, the resource will not be freed or unlocked when the thread is aborted.

Once a thread has been stopped, it can't be restarted or resumed. If you want to reuse threads over and over again, you'll need to use a `ThreadPool`.

Asynchronous processing

This technique processes requests without blocking them. When a request arrives, it is queued with the thread pool and the request call returns immediately. The caller regains control before the request is actually processed, and therefore doesn't know the outcome of the request operation. The interaction diagram in Figure 20-7 shows this type of arrangement.

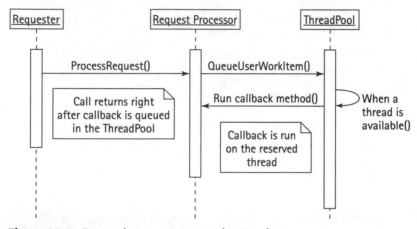

Figure 20-7: Processing requests asynchronously

Listing 20-23 shows how the relevant code might look.

Listing 20-23: Scheduling a Request Asynchronously

```
public void ProcessRequest()
{
  ThreadPool.QueueUserWorkItem(new WaitCallback(StartRequest);
}

void StartRequest(Object state)
{
  // execute the request...
}
```

As you can see, the method returns immediately after posting the `StartRequest()` callback to the thread pool. The caller doesn't get a returned value from the call, because `StartRequest()` hasn't run yet.

Synchronous processing

This technique blocks the requester's thread until the request has completed, as shown in the interaction diagram in Figure 20-8.

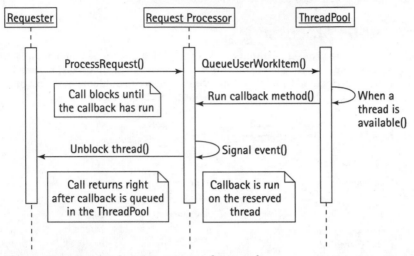

Figure 20-8: Processing requests synchronously

Listing 20-24 shows the relevant code.

Listing 20-24: **Scheduling a Request to Run on the Thread Pool**

```
public void ProcessRequest()
{
  // create a synchronization object
  AutoResetEvent waitForCompletion = new AutoResetEvent(false);

  // pass the synchronization object indirectly to the callback
  ThreadPool.QueueUserWorkItem(new WaitCallback(StartRequest),
                               waitForCompletion);

  // block until the callback executes
  waitForCompletion.WaitOne();  // calling thread will block bere
}

void StartRequest(Object state)
{
  // execute the request...

  // let the caller know we're done
  ((AutoResetEvent)state).Set();
}
```

The requesting thread sets up an `AutoResetEvent` object and passes it to the thread pool as the `state` parameter in the call to `ThreadPool.QueueUserWorkItem()`. When this method returns right after queuing the request, the thread blocks until the worker thread signals the `AutoResetEvent` event. To synchronize the requesting thread and the callback thread, I used an `AutoResetEvent` object, but other types of synchronization objects can be used as well.

Sharing resources across threads

Threads are often required to share information with other threads. A common requirement is for threads to share synchronization objects, like `ManualResetEvents`, `AutoResetEvents`, and `Monitors`. You may want to share your own objects across multiple threads. First you need to assign the object to a field. The .NET Framework makes it easy — trivial in fact — to control whether a field is shared among threads or not, according to the following rules:

✦ All nonstatic fields of classes are unique by thread.

✦ All static fields of a class are shared among all the threads using that class.

For example, consider the class in Listing 20-25.

Listing 20-25: A Class with Instance and Static Fields

```
class MyClass
{
  int a = 0;         // not shared across threads
  static int b = 0;  // shared across threads

  public void DoSomething()
  {
    a = a + 1;
    b = b + 1;
  }
}
```

Say you ran `MyClass.DoSomething()` in two separate threads as shown in Listing 20-26.

Listing 20-26: Running Two Instances of a Class in Separate Threads

```
MyClass myClass1 = new MyClass();
MyClass myClass2 = new MyClass();

Thread myThread1 =
      new Thread(new ThreadStart(myClass1.DoSomething) );
Thread myThread2 =
      new Thread(new ThreadStart(myClass2.DoSomething) );

MyThread1.Start();
MyThread2.Start();
```

The field a is not static, so it is unique by object. Each object instance will have its own copy. The field b is static, so both the objects on both threads will access the same field. What if you want to create a static field that is not shared across threads? No problem—just declare it with ThreadStatic attribute, as shown in Listing 20-27.

Listing 20-27: Using the ThreadStatic Attribute to Force a Static Field to be Thread-Unique

```
class MyClass
{
  int a = 0;

  [ThreadStatic]
   static int b = 0;   // this static field is NOT shared across threads

  public void DoSomething()
  {
    a = a + 1;
    b = b + 1;
  }
}
```

Now each thread will have its own copy of both a and b. There is another way to declare thread-unique data, using slots, but this technique is beyond the scope of this book.

Having now given you a quick look at the salient properties and issues of threads, it's time to have some fun and create a simple, but useful, multithreaded application.

Calling Windows form controls from other threads

If you create your own threads in a Windows application, there are some restrictions on how the Windows controls and forms can be accessed by those threads. Since Windows Forms run in an STA, they must only be accessed from code in the apartment's one and only thread.

Say you have a FileSearch application in which a worker thread is created to search a directory path for files, much like the Windows Explorer Search program. The list of files found is shown in a ListView control. The main thread runs the UI, while the worker thread searches for files. One way to add files found to the ListView is to have the worker thread update the UI directly, by calling ListView.Items.Add(). When calling UI objects from any thread that isn't the main one, you need to have the parameters marshaled into the UI's apartment. The easy way to handle the marshaling is to call the UI method indirectly using the method Control.Invoke().

An example will show all the details. To keep things simple, I'll create a simple program called *CallWinFromWorkerThread* that has some text labels and a button called Start. When the button is clicked, the current time is displayed in the top label. A worker thread is spawned to carry out some work. I'll just make the thread sleep for two seconds, after which it will update the bottom label on the UI with the current time. Figure 20-9 shows the UI after I clicked the Start button and made the worker thread run.

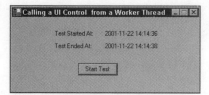

Figure 20-9: A simple program whose UI controls are updated by a worker thread

Listing 20-28 shows the code for the main form.

> ## Listing 20-28: **The Code for the Main Form of CallWinFormFromWorkerThread**

```
using System.Threading;

namespace CallWinFormFromWorkerThread
{
  public class Form1 : System.Windows.Forms.Form
  {
    // other declarations...
    Label labelTestStartedAt;
    Label labelTestEndedAt;
    Button buttonStart;
    // other declarations...

    public Form1() {...}
    protected override void Dispose(bool disposing) {...}
    private void InitializeComponent(){...}

    [STAThread]
    static void Main()
    {
      Application.Run(new Form1());
    }

    public delegate void UpdateEndTimeDelegate(DateTime theTime);

    private void buttonStart_Click(object sender,
                                   System.EventArgs e)
    {
      labelTestStartedAt.Text = DateTime.Now.ToString();

      UpdateEndTimeDelegate methodToCall =
                          new UpdateEndTimeDelegate(SetEndTime);

      WorkerThread workerThread = new WorkerThread(this, methodToCall);
```

Continued

Listing 20-28 *(continued)*

```
    Thread thread =
            new Thread(new ThreadStart(workerThread.Run) );
    thread.Start();
    }

    private void SetEndTime(DateTime theTime)
    {
        labelTestEndedAt.Text = theTime.ToString();
    }
  }
}
```

The method `buttonStart_Click()` is the interesting part. The method displays the current time on the top label of the UI. Then the code creates a delegate, passes it to the `WorkerThread` constructor, and starts up the thread. Figure 20-10 shows the class diagram.

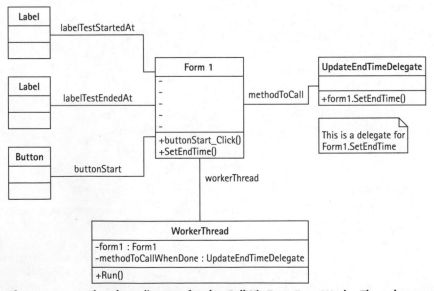

Figure 20-10: The class diagram for the CallWinFormFromWorkerThread program

The main form creates a delegate for the method `Form1.SetEndTime()`. Rather than allow the worker thread to access the `Label.Text` property directly, I created a method in Form1 called `SetEndTime()` that updates the `Label`. The delegate is then used by the `WorkerThread` to call `Form1.SetEndTime()`. The code for `WorkerThread` is shown in Listing 20-29.

Listing 20-29: The WorkerThread Code

```csharp
using System;
using System.Threading;

namespace CallWinFormFromWorkerThread
{
  public class WorkerThread
  {
    private Form1 form1;
    private Form1.UpdateEndTimeDelegate methodToCallWhenDone;

    public WorkerThread(
            Form1 theForm,
            Form1.UpdateEndTimeDelegate theMethodToCallWhenDone)
    {
      form1 = theForm;
      methodToCallWhenDone = theMethodToCallWhenDone;
    }

  public void Run()
  {
    Thread.Sleep(2000);  // stop for 2 seconds


    if (form1.InvokeRequired)
    {
      Object[] parameters = new Object[] {DateTime.Now};

      form1.Invoke(methodToCallWhenDone, parameters);
    }
    else
      methodToCallWhenDone(DateTime.Now);
    }
  }
}
```

The WorkerThread saves the delegate passed to the constructor. When the Run() method finishes sleeping, it calls the delegate. As stated earlier, when accessing methods and properties of UI controls, you need to use Control.Invoke() if the caller is in a different thread from the UI.

If you have code that updates the UI that could run both in the main thread or a worker thread, you can check at runtime to see if you need to use Control.Invoke() or not. Just check the property InvokeRequired of the UI element to access. You could also blindly use Control.Invoke() regardless of which thread your code is in, but this is not a good idea, because Invoke() is an expensive operation that you should avoid where possible.

In my example code in the previous listing, I already know the worker thread is not the same thread as the UI thread, so I didn't need to check InvokeRequired. I put the check there just to show you how to do it.

Synchronous and asynchronous calls

There are actually two types of `Invoke` methods in the base class `Control`: synchronous and asynchronous. The former is handled by the `Invoke()` method I just discussed. The latter is handled by the method `BeginInvoke()`.

Calls to `Invoke()` don't return until the delegate method returns. Calls to `BeginInvoke()` return immediately, giving back an `IAsyncResult` object that you can later use to check if the delegate has finished and get its return value back. Listing 20-30 shows an example.

Listing 20-30: **Calling a Delegate Asynchronously**

```
Object[] myParameters = new Object[] {DateTime.Now};
IAsyncResult ar = form1.BeginInvoke(methodToCallWhenDone,
                                    myParameters);

//go off and do something...

// check to see if methodToCallWhenDone has finished

if (ar.IsCompleted)
{
   // methodToCallWhenDone has completed
}
```

The `IAsyncResult` object returned by `BeginInvoke()` also contains a `WaitHandle` object that you can use, as shown in Listing 20-31.

Listing 20-31: **Using a WaitHandle to Limit the Amount of Time to Wait for an Asynchronous Call to Complete**

```
Object[] myParameters = new Object[] {DateTime.Now};
IAsyncResult ar = form1.BeginInvoke(methodToCallWhenDone,
                                    myParameters);

//go off and do something...

// wait up to 1 second for methodToCallWhenDone to finish
const int oneSecond = 1000;

ar.AsyncWaitHandle.WaitOne(oneSecond, false);

// see if the method finished within the allotted time

if (ar.IsCompleted)
  // the method finished
else
  // the method timed out
```

The `IAsyncResult` object returned by `BeginInvoke()` signals the `AsyncWaitHandle` automatically when the delegate method returns.

Getting a returned value

If you need the delegate method to return a value to the caller, you need to declare the delegate with a return type. Say you wanted to return a `String`. The delegate would be declared, as shown in Listing 20-32.

Listing 20-32: **Setting Up a Delegate Method to Return a String Value**

```
public delegate String UpdateEndTimeDelegate(DateTime theTime);
```

The method to call would then need to return a `String`, like this:

```
private String SetEndTime(DateTime theTime)
{
  labelTestEndedAt.Text = theTime.ToString();
  return "I'm done!";
}
```

The worker thread calling the delegate would then get a `String` as the returned value. For synchronous calls, the code would look something like Listing 20-33.

Listing 20-33: **Getting a Returned Value from a Synchronous Call**

```
Object[] parameters = new Object[] {DateTime.Now};
String s = (String) form1.Invoke(methodToCallWhenDone,
                                 parameters);
MessageBox.Show(s);
```

For asynchronous calls, the code would look like Listing 20-34.

Listing 20-34: **Getting a Returned Value from an Asynchronous Call**

```
Object[] myParameters = new Object[] {DateTime.Now};
IAsyncResult ar = form1.BeginInvoke(methodToCallWhenDone,
                                    myParameters);

//go off and do something...

// check to see if methodToCallWhenDone has finished
String s;
if (ar.IsCompleted)
{
  s = (String) form1.EndInvoke(ar);
  MessageBox.Show(s);
}
```

The .NET Framework's support for asynchronous methods is really spectacular, hiding all the gory details and letting you concentrate on getting your job done. Creating asynchronous method calls using `BeginInvoke()`, `EndInvoke()`, and `IAsyncResult` objects is part of a .NET programming model known as the *Asynchronous Programming Model*.

Regarding the UI methods or properties, just remember this: If you access the methods or properties from a thread other than the main UI thread, you need to use one of the `Invoke` methods to handle parameter marshaling. If you're not sure what thread the call is being made on, use `Control.InvokeRequired` to find out at runtime.

Creating a Multithreaded Component: StressTester

Components designed for the middle tier and the back end are often required to service large numbers of concurrent users. When developing such components, a recurring problem is how to test them realistically. You need a way to simulate the presence of many users accessing your components at the same time.

Enter the StressTester application. This is a small program I created that accomplishes a number of things:

✦ It is a complete multithreaded application.

✦ It uses a number of thread-related features.

✦ It performs a useful task.

✦ It is simple to understand and customize.

Commercial stress testers that test Web sites are available from a number of vendors, but they have price tags in the thousands or tens of thousands of dollars, and generally can't be tweaked to test components that run outside the context of a Web site. StressTester obviously can't compete with the commercial products in terms of bells and whistles, but when it comes down to just running multiple test threads simultaneously, it gets the job done eminently. Moreover, it is simple to customize, so you can use it to test any components you want—including front-end components, Web services, database services, and .NET Remoting components.

Designing the component

To stress test a component using thread loading, you need a way to start a large number of threads. Each thread can then be used to call the component under test. There are two basic ways you might want to use the threads to stress test a component: by having each thread create a new instance of the component, or by creating a single instance of the component and sharing it across the threads. StressTester uses the former approach, but can be changed to support the latter one by changing a single line of code. To share a single instance among the threads, the component under test needs to be thread-safe. The component doesn't necessarily have to be multithreaded, although thread stress testing is commonly used to test multithreaded components.

Besides being able to run multiple threads, StressTester must also maintain some statistical information, including the total number of method calls made to the component under test and the number of calls per second. On the UI of StressTester, I'll use the expression *Transactions Per Second* to denote the number of calls-per-second made to the component under test. Figure 20-11 shows how StressTester appears after running a test.

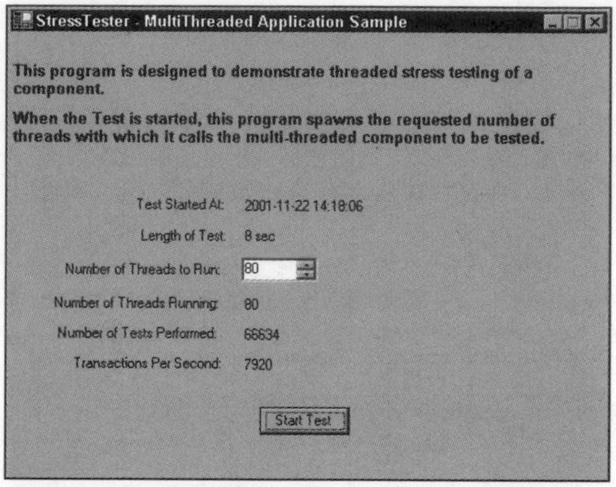

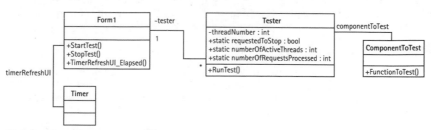

Figure 20-11: How the StressTester application appears after running a test

As you can see, StressTester lets you select the number of threads to run concurrently. I set the thread limit to 100, because I have a single processor computer. Threads are fairly expensive resources to run, and you'll find that your machine will have a certain threshold in the number of threads it can handle, before it starts getting bogged down by the thread-management overhead. Of course, if many of your threads are idle, you'll be able to create a large number of them. What counts more than anything else is how many threads are actually running. Blocked threads consume very little processor time.

Note that in this section I won't be developing a real component to test — just the StressTester fixture and a stub component. To keep things simple and not get caught up in too many details, StressTester just creates a new instance of a simple object for each thread it runs. In a real test scenario, each StressTester thread might reference the same instance of a multithreaded object. Figure 20-12 shows the class diagram for StressTester.

Figure 20-12: The class diagram for StressTester

The user interface component Form1 creates a number of threads on which it runs the method `Tester.RunTest()`. Form1 controls the threads using the static field `Tester.requestedToStop`. When a test is started, the field is set to `false`. `Tester.RunTest()` runs a continuous loop that checks the value of `requestedToStop` at each iteration. Because the field is static, it is shared across all the threads, giving me a simple way to stop all the `Tester` threads. For each iteration of `RunTest()`, `Tester` makes a call to `ComponentToTest.FunctionToTest()`.

A couple other static `Tester` fields are `numberOfActiveThreads` and `numberOf RequestsProcessed`. Both are used to keep track of total thread activity on the user interface.

Like I said earlier, the `ComponentToTest` class is just a stub for a multithreaded component to be tested. The class is not actually multithreaded, so `StressTester` instantiates a new copy of it for each thread it runs. The method `ComponentToTest.FunctionToTest()` doesn't do much—it just sleeps for awhile to simulate the time that a real component may require to process a request.

The `Timer` class is used to update the screen every tenth of a second. Each second, StressTester calculates the number of transactions executed and shows the value on the user interface.

Figure 20-13 shows the interaction diagram for StressTester.

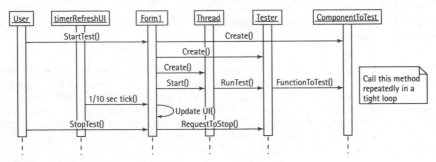

Figure 20-13: The interaction diagram for StressTester

The diagram shows the interactions for a single test thread. If the user specifies multiple test threads, then multiple instances of `Tester` and `ComponentToTest` are created and run on separate threads. When the user clicks the Stop Test button, the method `Form1.StopTest()` is called, which sets the static field `Tester.requestedToStop` to `false`, causing all `Tester.RunTest()` loops to exit and terminate the threads they were running on.

Implementing the component

Writing a multithreaded component can be challenging, because you have to try to visualize the threads running in parallel and anticipate how they might interact. Setting up the scaffolding and user interface for StressTester is easy. The interesting part of StressTester is not the UI, but the threading details.

First let's take a look at the simpler UI code. Using the VS .NET New Project Wizard, I created a standard C# application. On the main form, I added the controls for configuring and monitoring the progress of a test. Listing 20-35 shows the salient code for the user interface.

> **Listing 20-35: The Main User Interface Code for StressTester**

```
using System;
using System.Drawing;
using System.Collections;
```

```csharp
using System.ComponentModel;
using System.Windows.Forms;
using System.Data;
using System.Threading;

namespace StressTester
{
  public class Form1 : System.Windows.Forms.Form
  {
    bool isTestRunning = false;
    int numberOfTimeEvents = 0;      // to determine when 1
                                     // second goes by
    int totalRequestsProcessed = 0;  // to track Transactions
                                     // per Second

    private System.Windows.Forms.NumericUpDown numberOfThreadsToRun;
    private System.Windows.Forms.Button buttonStartStop;
    private System.Timers.Timer timerRefreshUI;

    // other UI elemtents...

    private System.ComponentModel.Container components = null;

    public Form1()
    {
      InitializeComponent();

      Thread.CurrentThread.Name = "Main Thread";
      timerRefreshUI.Enabled = false;
    }

    protected override void Dispose(bool disposing) {...}

    #region Windows Form Designer generated code
    private void InitializeComponent()
    {
      // create all the form components...
    }
    #endregion

    [STAThread]
    static void Main()
    {
      Application.Run(new Form1());
    }

    private void buttonStartStop_Click(object sender,
                                  System.EventArgs e)
    {
      if (!isTestRunning)
        StartTest();
      else
```

Continued

Listing 20-35 *(continued)*

```csharp
    StopTest();
}

void StartTest()
{
  isTestRunning          = true;
  timerRefreshUI.Enabled = true;

  buttonStartStop.Text    = "Stop Test";
  labelTestStartedAt.Text = DateTime.Now.ToString();

  Tester.numberOfActiveThreads     = 0;
  Tester.numberOfRequestsProcessed = 0;
  NumberOfTimeEvents = 0;
  TotalRequestsProcessed    = 0;

  labelNumberOfRequestsProcessed.Text = "0";
  labelNumberOfThreadsRunning.Text    = "0";
  labelTransactionsPerSecond.Text     = "0";
  labelLengthOfTest.Text              = "0 sec";

  decimal numberOfThreads = numberOfThreadsToRun.Value;

  for (int i = 1; i <= numberOfThreads; i++)
  {
    MyComponentToTest c = new MyComponentToTest();
    Tester tester = new Tester(c, i);
    Thread thread =
          new Thread(new ThreadStart(tester.RunTest) );
    thread.Name = "TestThread-" + i.ToString();
    thread.Start();
  }
}

void StopTest()
{
  isTestRunning = false;
  timerRefreshUI.Enabled = false;
  buttonStartStop.Text = "Start Test";
  Tester.requestedToStop = true;
}

bool HasOneSecondElapsed()
{
  return (numberOfTimeEvents % 10 == 0);
}

private void timerRefreshUI_Elapsed(object sender,
          System.Timers.ElapsedEventArgs e)
{
```

```
            labelNumberOfRequestsProcessed.Text =
                Tester.numberOfRequestsProcessed.ToString();
            labelNumberOfThreadsRunning.Text =
                Tester.numberOfActiveThreads.ToString();
            numberOfTimeEvents++;

            if (HasOneSecondElapsed() )
            {
              // update the running time
              labelLengthOfTest.Text =
                String.Format("{0} sec",
                              (numberOfTimeEvents / 10).ToString() );

              // update the TPS value
              int transactionsPerSecond =
                  Tester.numberOfRequestsProcessed -
                  totalRequestsProcessed;
              labelTransactionsPerSecond.Text =
                  transactionsPerSecond.ToString();
              totalRequestsProcessed = Tester.numberOfRequestsProcessed;
            }
          }
        }
      }
```

When the user clicks the Start Test button, StressTester creates and runs the requested number of threads with the code shown in Listing 20-36.

Listing 20-36: **How StressTester Starts the Test Threads**

```
void StartTest()
{
  //...

  for (int i = 1; i <= numberOfThreads; i++)
  {
    MyComponentToTest c = new MyComponentToTest();
    Tester tester = new Tester(c, i);
    Thread thread = new Thread(new ThreadStart(tester.RunTest) );
    thread.Name = "TestThread-" + i.ToString();
    thread.Start();
  }
}
```

Each thread instantiates a new copy of MyComponentToTest and passes it to the Tester component. If you want to create a single instance of MyComponentToTest and share it among the threads, the code needs to be changed slightly, bringing the MyComponentToTest instantiation out of the for loop as shown in Listing 20-37.

Listing 20-37: Using a Single Instance of MyComponentToTest with All Threads

```
// create a single instance of the component to test
MyComponentToTest c = new MyComponentToTest();

for (int i = 1; i <= numberOfThreads; i++)
{
  Tester tester = new Tester(c, i);
  Thread thread = new Thread(new ThreadStart(tester.RunTest) );
  thread.Name = "TestThread-" + i.ToString();
  thread.Start();
}
}
```

Notice the statement that assigns a name to each thread:

```
thread.Name = "TestThread-" + i.ToString();
```

Do you really care what name a thread has? Only if you plan to debug the code. The VS .NET integrated debugger has a Threads window that lists threads by name. The default name for a thread is <No Name>. To tell one thread from another, you need to give them individual names. I just named them with the number of the test thread. Later, in the debugging section, I'll show you how the thread name appears in the debugger.

Clicking the Stop Test button shuts down all the threads with the code shown in Listing 20-38.

Listing 20-38: How StressTester Stops the Test Threads

```
void StopTest()
{
  //...
  Tester.requestedToStop = true;
}
```

Listing 20-39 shows the code for the Tester and ComponentToTest components. I numbered the lines in order to point out a couple of interesting items in my discussion.

Listing 20-39: The Code for Tester and ComponentToTest

```
1   using System;
2   using System.Threading;
3
4   namespace StressTester
5   {
6     public class Tester
7     {
8       // unique for each thread
```

```
 9        private MyComponentToTest componentToTest
10        private int threadNumber;
11
12        // shared across threads
13        public static bool requestedToStop;
14        public static int numberOfActiveThreads = 0;
15        public static int numberOfRequestsProcessed = 0;
16
17        public Tester(MyComponentToTest theComponent,
18                      int theThreadNumber)
19        {
20          componentToTest = theComponent;
21          threadNumber = theThreadNumber;
22        }
23
24      public void RunTest()
25      {
26        requestedToStop = false;
27
28        Interlocked.Increment(ref numberOfActiveThreads);
29
30        Console.WriteLine("Starting thread {0}", threadNumber);
31
32        while (!requestedToStop)
33        {
34          componentToTest.FunctionToTest();
35          Interlocked.Increment(ref numberOfRequestsProcessed);
36        }
37
38        Console.WriteLine("Stopping thread {0}", threadNumber);
39      }
40    }
41
42    public class MyComponentToTest
43    {
44      public void FunctionToTest()
45      {
46        Thread.Sleep(10);  // simulate a small amount
47                           // of processing
48      }
49    }
50  }
```

Notice the Interlocked operations on the static fields numberOfActiveThreads and numberOfRequestsProcessed on lines 28 and 35. Since the test threads all share these static fields, it is important to prevent concurrent access to them.

Debugging the component

If you have multiple threads executing the same piece of code and put a breakpoint somewhere in the code, how do you know which thread triggered the breakpoint? The VS .NET integrated debugger has a Threads window that lists the running threads of your application.

The threads are listed by name. Running StressTester with three threads, and putting a breakpoint on line 33 in the previous listing will cause the breakpoint to trigger immediately. Figure 20-14 shows what the Threads window looks like when the program stops.

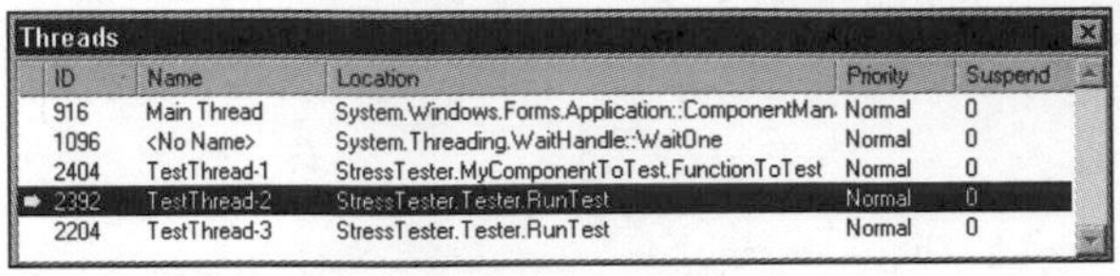

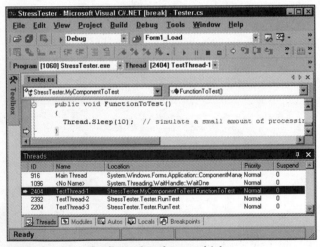

Figure 20-14: The Threads window, showing StressTester's threads

Looking at the window, you can immediately tell that TestThread-2 hit the breakpoint. The window also tells you which methods TestThreads 1 and 3 were in when TestThread-2 hit the breakpoint. If you double-click TestThread-2 in the Threads window, the debugger will display the source code the thread stopped on, which you already know is the line with the breakpoint.

It might be more interesting to see where TestThreads 1 and 3 were when the breakpoint was triggered. In the Threads window, just double-click the thread you're interested in. For example, double-clicking TestThread1 moves the arrow in the left margin to the TestThread1 line and shows the Code window in Figure 20-15.

Figure 20-15: The line of code on which TestThread-1 stopped

The line that TestThread-1 was about to execute when TestThread-2 hit the breakpoint is displayed with a yellow arrow and highlight. Clicking the threads listed in the Threads window makes it easy to see what each thread was doing when a breakpoint was triggered.

But there's more. Say you suspect a thread of causing a problem and want to stop it from running, to see how the rest of the system behaves without that thread. Just right-click the thread in the Threads window and select the Freeze command from the pop-up menu. Now the thread will be suspended by the debugger and displayed with a blue marker in the Threads window, as shown in Figure 20-16.

```
Threads                                                                    [X]
  ID      Name          Location                                    Priority  Suspend  ▲
  916    Main Thread    System.Windows.Forms.Application::ComponentMan. Normal   0
  1096   <No Name>      System.Threading.WaitHandle::WaitOne        Normal   0
II 2404  TestThread-1   StressTester.MyComponentToTest.FunctionToTest Normal  1
  2392   TestThread-2   StressTester.MyComponentToTest.FunctionToTest Normal  0
  2204   TestThread-3   StressTester.Tester.RunTest                 Normal   0       ▼
```

Figure 20-16: The Threads window, showing TestThread1 as frozen

The rightmost column in the Threads window shows a 1 (one) for the Suspend count of TestThread-1. Now when you click the debugger's Continue button, TestThread-1 will remain frozen at the statement it was on. All the other threads will run normally. To unfreeze a thread, right-click it in the Threads window and select Thaw from the pop-up menu.

Freezing a thread can be useful for checking concurrency issues. Say you have a section of code that you suspect has a concurrency problem. You could set a breakpoint in it, which would then be triggered by the first thread to execute the code. Now you could freeze all of the threads except for the one you suspect is causing the problem. When you click the Step Into or Step Over button, the suspect thread will run by itself. Now you can set breakpoints to see what happens when it hits the code you think is causing the problem. You might find, for example, that the code blocks unexpectedly on a synchronization object, causing a deadlock or other timing problem.

By being able to pause and resume threads at will, debugging multithreaded components is much easier than it ever has been. Just remember to name each of your threads, so you can tell them apart in the Threads window.

Summary

Multithreaded code is not difficult to write, but debugging can be difficult if threads aren't synchronized correctly. When you plan to develop multithreaded code, defensive coding and careful design are extremely important. Forgetting a simple lock statement or accidentally allowing concurrent access to a variable can cause a multithreaded program to behave erratically. To compound matters, stepping through the code with a debugger will often tell you little about where the problem is, because once you start single stepping through the code, the program no longer runs at normal speed and all timing-related problems seem to change.

In this chapter, I have described the most important and commonly used threading components and techniques. A golden rule with multithreaded programming is to keep thread code simple. Try to keep the synchronization logic and interaction between threads as straightforward as possible, to minimize the likelihood of introducing defects. Always plan to build and use a test fixture to verify the performance of your multithreaded code under stress. Never release a component to production unless it has been properly tested.

✦   ✦   ✦

Gateway Services

If you're going through hell, keep going.

—Winston Churchill

Unless you understand the performance and scalability issues that are essential with gateway services, you might feel like you're going through hell when the service is deployed and a barrage of customers hit it. By making good use of system resources and using the new features of the .NET Remoting Framework, you can avoid lots of problems from the start.

What Is a Gateway Service?

A *gateway service* is any service that runs on a back-end system designed to handle large numbers of concurrent requests. The requests are sometimes processed locally. More commonly, they are funneled to another remote system using a communication channel, such as a leased TCP/IP line, a VPN (Virtual Private Network) connection, or a secured connection over the Internet. This remote system is generally capable of servicing multiple requests concurrently. In this chapter, I'll call this latter system the *Service Provider*. Examples of Service Providers are Stock Quote Servers, Geographic Map Servers, and News Servers. Keep in mind that Service Providers often support numerous services, some of which may be handled by relaying requests to yet another Service Provider. Figure 21-1 shows the basic layout of a distributed system using a gateway service.

Gateway services are part of a more general class of components known as *remote services*. The remote services described previously were all based on the Web, where client requests would arrive as HTTP messages, and IIS would receive the messages and dispatch the appropriate Web Service component to handle it. All parameter-passing details were completely hidden and the task of running each request on its own thread was hidden by the Web Services infrastructure.

Not all remote services can or want to run as Web Services. One reason could be the desire to avoid deploying IIS on the back-end system to handle incoming requests. Also, Web Services implicitly use HTTP and XML, both of which have a nontrivial impact on performance when large amounts of data need to be transferred over the wire. Finally, the remote service may be required to support a specific network protocol, message encoding format, or security arrangement, to interact with legacy systems or to satisfy special customer requirements. For these types of situations, Web Services are not the answer. But all hope is not lost.

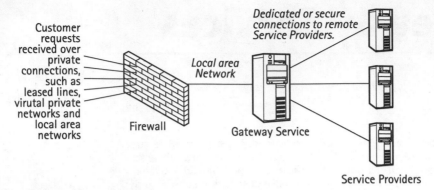

Figure 21-1: The basic architecture of a back-end system using a gateway service

The Remoting Framework

There is an extensive .NET component infrastructure known as the *Remoting Framework,* which provides everything necessary to allow your components to call remote components, regardless of whether they are in a different process, on a different machine, or even on a different network. As long as there is a network path that connects the components, the Remoting Framework will allow them to call each other. The Remoting Framework was designed to support seamless connectivity between components, abstracting away the connection details into a series of standard component types. *Channels* encapsulate the details of creating and maintaining a wire connection between the components. Components known as *formatters* take the parameters in method calls, and serialize them into an appropriate form for delivery over a connection. Parameters are marshaled automatically without the need for stuff like IDL or other unspeakable gunk.

The basic Remoting components

In a nutshell, the Remoting Framework is an elegant component-based infrastructure that supports remote method calls. The infrastructure uses a number of built-in components for transparently establishing communication channels, formatting messages, moving messages over a connection, ensuring messages are delivered, marshaling parameters, and a slew of other details. Figure 21-2 shows a high-level view of the Remoting Framework.

When a client accesses a remote object, a proxy is created on the client side. The creation and management of the proxy is completely automatic and hidden. The proxy forwards method calls to the remote object, creating the illusion that the object is local. Behind the scenes, the Remoting Framework might be converting the parameters to XML, packaging the call as a SOAP packet, sending the packet over an HTTP connection to other components, and managing the lifecycle of remote objects created to service the method call. In fact, this is exactly how calls to Web Services work. The main component in the Remoting Framework is the *channel.* This component uses a few pluggable components to get the job done. The pluggable components can be replaced with your own components if the available ones don't suit your needs. Figure 21-3 shows the three pluggable components that handle security, formatting, and wire protocol.

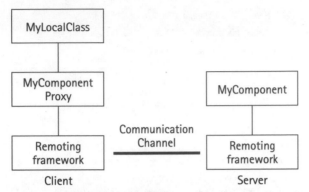

Figure 21-2: The basic role of the Remoting Framework in connecting remote components

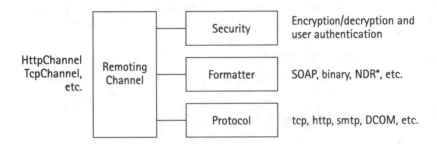

* NDR: Network Data Representation, used with DCOM

Figure 21-3: The pluggable components of a Remoting channel

A simple server-side object

Using the .NET Remoting Framework, you can create components that are *remotable*. Remotable components can be called from both local and remote processes. If the remotable component is in the same process as the calling component, the remotable component is local to the caller. If the remotable component is in a different process or on a different machine, the component is remote with respect to the caller. There are no code changes required to change local calls into remote ones. The only difference is in the way the called component is registered with the Remoting Framework. As far as the remotable class goes, it's just a regular class, as shown in Listing 21-1.

Listing 21-1: A Simple Remotable Object

```
using System;
using System.Runtime.Remoting;

namespace MyRemoteNamespace
{
```

Continued

Listing 21-1 *(continued)*

```
public class MyRemoteObject: MarshalByRefObject
{
  public String DoSomething(String theUserName)
  {
    return theUserName + ": Hello from a remote object";
  }
}
}
```

Other than importing the `System.Runtime.Remoting` namespace and using the `MarshalByRefObject` base class, there are no other Remoting-related items in it. Most of the objects created in this book were derived directly or indirectly from `MarshalByRefObject`. Class `MyRemoteObject` has a single method called `DoSomething()` that takes a `String` parameter and returns a `String`. Not much of a method, but sufficient for explaining the basics of Remoting. I'll be referring back to `MyRemoteObject` in the next sections.

Accessing remote objects from the client side

As stated earlier, the Remoting Framework makes it possible to create and manipulate remote objects with the same code you would use on a local object. Before instantiating a remote object in your client code, you need to give the Remoting Framework some information about where the object is, and how you want to connect to it. The code in Listing 21-2 will suffice on the client side.

Listing 21-2: A Simple Client Accessing a Remote Object

```
using System;
using System.Runtime.Remoting;
using MyRemoteNamespace;

namespace MyClientNamespace
{
  public class MyClient
  {
    void MyClientMethod()
    {
      // tell the Remoting Framework how to
      //access the remote object
      RemotingConfiguration.Configure("MyClient.exe.config");

      // create and access the object like a local one
      MyRemoteObject obj = new MyRemoteObject();
      String s = obj.DoSomething("Ted");
      Console.WriteLine(s);
    }
  }
}
```

The client instantiates the remote object using the regular new operator, and then accesses its methods and properties with the usual dot notation. How does the client know where the remote object is located and how to access it? There are a few different ways to solve this problem. In Listing 21-2, I called the method `RemotingConfiguration.Configure()`, and passed it a configuration file with the necessary information. (I'll describe configuration files in the next section.)

Although my examples all set up the Remoting Framework using configuration files, you can also do the setup programmatically. Since Remoting configuration files contain XML and reside on both the client and server machines, they can potentially expose the details of the connection between the client and server to end users. You might want to use a programmatic setup to hide the connection details. On the other hand, using a configuration file allows the configuration to be changed after deployment, by editing the XML file.

Hooking the client up with the server

At this point, you might be wondering where all the plumbing code is, to bridge the client code with the server code. The client needs to know where the remote code is running and how to connect to the server machine. The server side needs to be set up to listen for client requests somehow, so when the client calls, the server-side object responds.

Configuring the client side

The client Remoting configuration can be set up both programmatically and through a configuration file. As I mentioned earlier, the second method is more flexible, because it lets you change configuration settings without recompiling any code. For a component named MyClient.exe, the configuration file is named MyClient.exe.config. Listing 21-3 shows what information needs to be in the file MyClient.exe.config.

Listing 21-3: A Simple Application-Level Configuration File, Setting the Attributes of a Remote Object

```
configuration>
  <system.runtime.remoting>
    <application>

      <client url="http://YourServer.com/MyRemoteObject">
        <activated type="MyRemoteNamespace.MyRemoteObject,
                   MyRemoteNamespace"/>
      </client>

      <channels>
        <channel
          type="System.Runtime.Remoting.Channels.Http.HttpChannel,
               System.Runtime.Remoting"/>
      </channels>

    </application>
  </system.runtime.remoting>
</configuration>
```

The `<client>` node indicates *where* the remote object is located. The node has a `url` attribute that points to the host and directory that contains the remote object. You can also specify a port number in the URL. To use port 8000, you would specify it in the URL like this:

```
<client url="http:8000//YourServer.com/MyRemoteObject">
```

In my example, the remote object is a component called `MyRemoteObject`. The namespace for `MyRemoteServer` is `MyRemoteNamespace`.

The `<channel>` node indicates *how* to connect to the remote object. In my example, the channel is configured to use `HttpChannel`, which by default will use SOAP message formatting over an HTTP connection. There is another built-in channel you can use, called `TcpChannel`, which defaults to binary formatting with TCP sockets. At the time of this writing, Microsoft had published only these two channels, but others are expected to be in the final release. You can create your own channel, if the built-in ones don't meet your requirements. The procedure is beyond the scope of this book.

Configuring the server side

Configuring the server side is more complicated than the client side, because there's an additional component involved, known as the *Remote Service Host,* described in the next section. The host needs to be configured to listen for client requests, and the server-side object needs to be registered with the Remoting Framework, so incoming requests can be dispatched to it. Let's take a look at the Host component first.

The Remote Service Host

It may seem strange at first, but a .NET remote service component is actually not a service, in the operating system sense. It's not a component that you start and stop with the Windows Service Control Manager, like IIS is. A .NET remote service is just a component that is activated by the .NET Remoting infrastructure when a client request arrives. The remote service doesn't activate itself automatically.

The reason is simple: Since a remote service component isn't activated until a client request arrives, it is elementary that some other process must be involved, to listen for client requests and activate the remote service at the right time. As I mentioned, this process is the Remote Service Host. Remember that the host is not the remote service component itself. The host just sets up the .NET Remoting environment to listen for client requests on given channels. The host can either be a regular .exe application or a Windows service. Common Remote Service Hosts are IIS (which hosts Web Services) and COM+ Component Services. The latter provide support for asynchronous messaging and transactions. Figure 21-4 may help you better understand the basic relationship between the host, the Remoting Framework, and the server-side component.

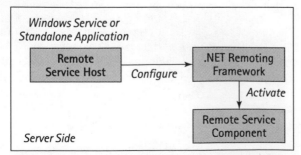

Figure 21-4: The relationship between the Remote Service Host and the rest of the system

As the figure shows, there really is no connection between the Remote Service Component and the host program. The host simply configures the Remoting Framework to listen for requests. The framework starts listening and dispatches requests to the Remote Service Component directly, without intervention from the host program.

From a design standpoint, the Remote Service Host is just a simple application or windows service. Listing 21-4 shows a fragment of the code for creating a host as a standalone application.

Listing 21-4: Configuring the Remoting Framework in the Remote Service Host Using a Configuration File

```
// various imports...

using System.Runtime.Remoting;

namespace RemoteServiceHost
{
  public class Form1 : System.Windows.Forms.Form
  {
    // various Form methods...

    [STAThread]
    static void Main()
    {
      RemotingConfiguration.Configure("RemoteServiceHost.exe.config");
      Application.Run(new Form1());
    }
  }
}
```

There is really only one line of code to talk about: the call to `RemotingConfiguration.Configure()`. This call passes a configuration filename to the Remoting Framework. The file contains detailed information about the communication channels to listen on and which objects to expose for remote invocation. When the host application program terminates, all of the channels and objects configured for it will be released and garbage collected. Listing 21-5 shows a simple configuration file.

Listing 21-5: A Configuration File Used in a Remote Service Host to Set Up the Remoting Framework

```
<configuration>
  <system.runtime.remoting>
    <application name="Server">

      <service>
        <wellknown mode="SingleCall"
                   type="MyRemoteNamespace.MyRemoteObject,
```

Continued

Listing 21-5 *(continued)*

```
                              MyRemoteNamespace"/>
        </service>

        <channels>
          <channel
              type="System.Runtime.Remoting.Channels.Http.HttpChannel,
                    System.Runtime.Remoting"
                    port="8000"/>
        </channels>

      </application>
    </system.runtime.remoting>
</configuration>
```

There are two interesting parts to the file: the `<wellknown>` node and the `<channel>` node. Let's look at both in detail, starting with the former:

```
<wellknown mode="SingleCall"
           type="MyRemoteNamespace.MyRemoteObject,
                 MyRemoteNamespace"/>
```

The `mode` attribute determines the server-side activation model we want for MyRemoteObject. Possible values are `"Singleton"` and `"Single Call"`. Don't worry about activation models, for the moment. I'll talk about them in future sections.

The `type` attribute shows the `Assembly.Classname` of the remote object to expose, followed by the remote object's namespace.

The `<channel>` node looks like this:

```
<channel type=" System.Runtime.Remoting.Channels.Http.HttpChannel,
                System.Runtime.Remoting"
         port="8000"/>
```

The `type` attribute specifies the communication channel on which to listen for client requests, followed by the namespace containing the channel component.

The `port` attribute specifies the port to listen on. The default port for HTTP channels is 80.

Remote object activation models

Not all .NET remote objects are used the same way. What if you wanted to create a remote object that maintained state information and acted just like a local object? The remote object would need to come into existence when the client created it, maintain any properties that were set, and disappear when the client was through with it. What if you didn't need the object to maintain state information across successive calls? Maybe you just need the object to expose a single method, such as `TransferFundsToAccount()`, which passes all relevant information to the object as method parameters? These and other scenarios are possible using the two object activation models supported by the Remoting Framework: *client-activated objects* and *server-activated objects,* as described in the next few sections.

Client-activated objects

When a client controls the lifetime of a remote object created on the server side of a Remoting connection, the remote object is called a *client-activated object (CAO)*. Assume the client uses the code shown in Listing 21-6.

Listing 21-6: Creating a CAO Remote Object with a New Operator

```
import MyServerNamespace;

// tell the Remoting Framework how to access the remote object
RemotingConfiguration.Configure("MyClient.exe.config");

// create a reference to a remote CAO
MyRemoteObject obj = new MyRemoteObject();
```

When the client executes the statement containing the new operator, the Remoting Framework makes a call from the client to the server. The client is set up with a local MyRemoteObject proxy object, which connects to a real MyRemoteObject object on the server side. The client can deal with the local proxy exactly as if it were the real object. Behind the scenes, the Remoting Framework manages the server-side object. The configuration file tells the Remoting Framework where the server-side component is, and how the remote object should be set up. There are two ways the server-side object can be set up: as a single instance that all clients share, or as a separate instance for each client. I'll discuss both cases in the next section.

In my example above, the configuration file might look be the one previously shown in Listing 21-5. To recap briefly, the sections of the file shown in Listing 21-7 are most important.

Listing 21-7: The Essential Part of the Configuration File

```
<service>
  <wellknown mode="SingleCall"
             type=" MyRemoteNamespace.MyRemoteObject,
                    MyRemoteNamespace"/>
</service>

<channels>
  <channel type=" System.Runtime.Remoting.Channels.Http.HttpChannel,
                  System.Runtime.Remoting"
           port="8000"/>
</channels>
```

The <wellknown> element indicates the namespace, assembly, and class name of the server object the client wants to create. In this case, I defined the component MyRemoteObject in the assembly MyRemoteNamespace. The component's namespace is the last parameter in the type attribute, or MyRemoteNamespace in my example.

The `mode` attribute indicates how to connect the client to the server computer. The example uses the built-in `HttpChannel` component, and selects the port `8080`.

Once created, the server-side object will hang around until the client no longer references it. Each time the client accesses a method, event, or property of `obj`, it will be referencing the same instance of `MyRemoteObject` on the server side. Because CAO objects are instantiated explicitly by calling the new operator with a constructor, the constructor can take parameters. As you'll see in the next section, Server-Activated Objects can only have a single, parameter-less, constructor.

Server-activated objects

In the previous section, I showed a client-side code fragment creating an instance of a remote object. The Remoting Framework on the server side responded by hooking up the client with an instance of `MyRemoteObject` on the server side. Because there are two kinds of `MyRemoteObject` objects involved — one on the client and one on the server — the server object is called a *Server-Activated Object (SAO)* to distinguish it from the proxy object created on the client side.

There are two types of SAOs: `Singleton` and `SingleCall`. You specify the type you want in the Remoting configuration file, in a `<wellknown>` element, as shown in Listing 21-8.

> **Listing 21-8: A Remoting Configuration File Specifying Both a Singleton and a SingleCall SAO**

```
<configuration>
  <system.runtime.remoting>
    <application name="Server">

      <service>
        <wellknown mode="Singleton"
                   type=" MyRemoteNamespace.MySingletonObject,
                   MyRemoteNamespace"/>

        <wellknown mode="SingleCall"
                   type=" MyRemoteNamespace.MySingleCallObject,
                   MyRemoteNamespace"/>
      </service>

      <channels>
        <channel
            type="System.Runtime.Remoting.Channels.Http.HttpChannel,
                  System.Runtime.Remoting"
                  port="8000"/>
      </channels>

    </application>
  </system.runtime.remoting>
</configuration>
```

This configuration file assumes the server computer has two Remoting components: one called `MySingletonObject` and the other called `MySingleCallObject`. The former is defined as a Singleton object, the latter as a SingleCall object.

With Singleton SAOs, only one instance of the server-side object is created. All client requests are dispatched to this single object, so it will need to be multithreaded to handle concurrent client requests. Since the server-side object is shared across client requests, it may contain state information that applies to all clients, such as a counter that tracks the number of client requests handled.

With `SingleCall` SAOs, the Remoting Framework on the server side instantiates a new object for each client request. Each request is processed with a separate thread. Since these SAOs come and go with every client request, the server-side object can't contain any state information. If the server component blocks while processing the client request, other clients are not affected, because every client request deals with a different server-side instance.

The difference between a CAO and an SAO

People just learning about the Remoting Framework tend to get confused with the CAO and SAO terminology, so I'll dedicate this short section to clearing up any lingering doubts.

Both CAOs and SAOs are server-side objects. When a client-side program uses the new operator to instantiate a local instance of a remote object, it's instantiating just a local proxy to the remote object. The remote object will either be a `Singleton` or a `SingleCall` object. If it is a `Singleton`, the first client-side instantiation will cause a server-side object to be created. While this server-side object is alive, other client instantiations will get hooked up to the same server-side instance.

If the server object is a `SingleCall` object, each client instantiation will cause the server to instantiate a new copy of the server-side object.

Just remember this: With a CAO, the client program determines *when* a server-side object is created and destroyed. Without a CAO, the server determines when the server-side object is destroyed.

If the client uses a URL to reference a server-side object, there is no CAO. The client might be a Web browser referencing the URL of the server-side component. The server will instantiate either a Singleton or SingleCall object, as before, but this time the server determines the lifetime of the server-side object. The process involves the use of *leases*. When a lease expires, the server-side object is destroyed automatically.

CAOs allow a client program to store state information in the remote object, just like it would if the object were local. If you don't use a CAO, you don't have a local proxy object, so you don't have control over which server-side instance you'll be connected to.

Creating a Gateway Service

To show how the various parts of the .NET Remoting Framework come together, I'll get to the meat of this chapter: *creating a simple gateway service*. Before designing the service, I need some requirements. Let's say the gateway will be used to perform a credit-check on a person. The end user will input data describing the person. I'll keep things simple and use a Social Security Number (SSN).

The service will send this information to a remote credit-checking Service Provider, which will return a message containing the SSN and a credit rating as an integer value between 0 and 9. A 9 represents a perfect credit history, and a 0 represents the kind of person that makes you want to count your fingers after shaking his or her hand.

Let's say the upper-management of your company has already decided to use a Service Provider company called *MyCredit.com*. This service has a fixed format for the messages it can handle, so the gateway service is constrained to interact with the Service Provider using a pre-established and fixed protocol. Let's assume the messages must contain ASCII data and be formatted as shown in Table 21-1. (All field sizes in the table are in bytes.)

Table 21-1: Messages Used by the Credit Reporting Service Provider

REQUESTS

Field Name	Size
SocialSecurityNumber	9

RESPONSES

Field Name	Size
Social Security Number	9
CreditRating	1

Another very important requirement is the amount of traffic the gateway service needs to support. Let's say your gateway service must handle 10 requests per second. How fast responses come back is determined by the Service Provider. Let's say MyCredit.com guarantees that each request will get a response in less than 10 seconds.

End users will connect to the gateway service through the company's Web site, which uses a Web Farm with three computers. End users will enter requests on a Web page form and submit the data to the Web site. The Web site will handle the request by calling the gateway service component.

Your mission, should you decide to accept it, is to create a .NET Remoting component that will take a credit-check request, send it to MyCredit.com, and return a numeric value to the caller, indicating the credit rating.

Establishing the system architecture

Before getting into the low-level details of the gateway service's design, first let's decide on how all the pieces will fit together. We have Web sites, Web Farms, gateways, Service Providers, and other systems. The gateway service must always be protected from unauthorized access by a firewall. For this example, let's assume your company has a LAN behind the firewall that operates at 100 Mbps. The gateway must sit on this LAN and use a dedicated leased line to connect to the Service Provider. What bandwidth do we need on the link to the Service Provider? We know that each request has roughly 10 bytes (from Table 21-1) and that we need to be able to send 10 requests per second. So we'll need a connection that can handle about $10 \times 10 = 100$ bytes per second. Counting 8 bits per byte, that's 0.8 Kbps. Accounting for TCP/IP packet overhead, I'll round it up to 10 Kbps, because the packet overhead is high compared to a payload of 10 bytes for each message. Let's say the cheapest connection you can get is a standard leased telephone line conditioned for 56 Kbps. Such a line offers more that adequate bandwidth. The block diagram of the system is shown in Figure 21-5.

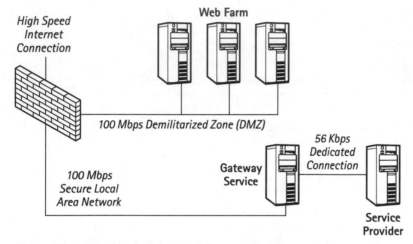

Figure 21-5: The block diagram of the system using a gateway service

The servers in the Web Farm sit on a demilitarized zone (DMZ) network that runs at 100 Mbps, so there is more than enough bandwidth to comfortably get 10 requests per second to the gateway service.

Note A DMZ is a network that is separated from both the Internet and your internal LAN by a firewall. The purpose of a DMZ is to enhance security. If a cracker hacks his way into a Web server, he or she might gain control over the DMZ network, but still will not be able to access your company's internal LAN. A DMZ network is where companies typically place servers that are publicly accessible from the Internet, such as mail servers and Web servers.

With the overall system architecture defined, we're ready to dive into the design process of the gateway service.

Designing the Gateway Service

In this section, I'll walk you through some of the design considerations that are important for a gateway service. In the process, I'll design a service called *MyGatewayService*. Client requests will originate from one of the systems in the Web Farm, outside the firewall. To keep the design simple, I'll set up `MyGatewayService` as a `Single-Call` Client-Activated Object. For each client request received, the .NET Remote Framework will spawn a separate `MyGatewayService` thread to process it. Although I won't be showing the ASP.NET code on the Web Farm computers that instantiate the client-side objects, the code would look like Listing 21-9.

Listing 21-9: A Fragment of the ASP.NET Code Used to Connect to MyGatewayService

```
import MyGatewayService;

RemotingConfiguration.Configure("MyWebApp.config");
MyGatewayService myService = new MyGatewayService();

// use the gateway
int creditRating =
    myService.GetCreditRating(socialSecurityNumber);
```

The file MyWebApp.config contains the instructions on how the Web application connects to `MyGatewayService`. The file will look like this:

```
<configuration>
  <system.runtime.remoting>
    <application name="MyWebApp">

      <service>
        <wellknown mode="SingleCall"
                   type="MyGatewayService.ServerSide,
                         MyGatewayService "/>
      </service>

      <channels>
        <channel
            type="System.Runtime.Remoting.Channels.Tcp.TcpChannel,
                  System.Runtime.Remoting"
            port="6000"/>
      </channels>

    </application>
  </system.runtime.remoting>
</configuration>
```

The file configures the connection to MyGatewayService to use TCP/IP on port 6000. For each client instantiation, a new thread is allocated on the server and a separate instance of the ServerSide object is executed in it. Each service thread will create a TCP socket, use it to connect to the Service Provider, send the message, and get the response back. While the Service Provider is busy working on the request, the calling thread on the gateway will block. If a response isn't received within a predefined interval, the blocked thread will timeout and return an error to the client. Remember, the client here is one of the Web Farm computers. If a response is returned before a timeout occurs, the blocked thread will be awakened and the response will be returned to the client. Figure 21-6 shows the high-level architecture of the gateway.

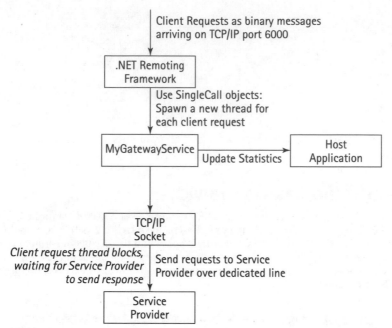

Client Requests as binary messages
arriving on TCP/IP port 6000

.NET Remoting
Framework

Use SingleCall objects:
Spawn a new thread for
each client request

MyGatewayService ⟶ Update Statistics ⟶ Host
Application

TCP/IP
Socket

Client request thread blocks,
waiting for Service Provider
to send response

Send requests to Service
Provider over dedicated line

Service
Provider

Figure 21-6: A high-level component view of the gateway service

Each CAO results in a new instance of MyGatewayService being instantiated on the server side. Each server-side instance uses its own TCP socket to talk to the remote Service Provider.

The Gateway Service doesn't do a lot of processing. The service just needs to convert client requests into the Service Provider message format, send the message, and then block the thread. Most of the time, a request thread is in the blocked state. When a response comes back, it is converted back to the format expected by the Web Farm computers and sent back. Figure 21-7 shows the class diagram for the server-side component of the gateway service.

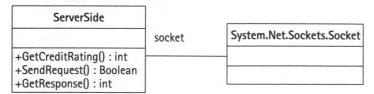

ServerSide	socket	System.Net.Sockets.Socket
+GetCreditRating() : int		
+SendRequest() : Boolean		
+GetResponse() : int		

Figure 21-7: The class diagram for MyRemotableServer

The class diagram for the ServerSide component of MyGatewayService tells you little about how it works. Let's take a look at the interaction diagram for ServerSide in the context of the whole gateway service, which is shown in Figure 21-8.

MyGatewayService is a collection of components drawn inside the Server Side box, on the right side of the interaction diagram. The service is actually implemented by a single class I called `ServerSide`. Let's see how this class needs to be implemented.

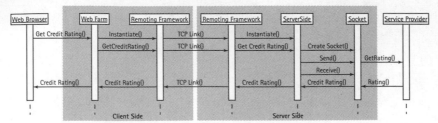

Figure 21-8: The interaction diagram for the various components involved in MyGatewayService

Implementing the Gateway Service

VS .NET doesn't have a project wizard to create .NET Remoting server-side components. The reason is that such components are nothing more than plain DLLs. To create a server-side component, you just use the Class Library Wizard. I'll spare you the details of running the wizard here, because it does nothing more than ask for the project name and create an empty project. Figure 21-9 shows the Solution Explorer after running the wizard and creating a project called *MyGatewayService*.

Figure 21-9: The project created by the Class Library wizard for MyGatewayService

By default, the wizard adds a file named Class1.cs to the project. I renamed this file to ServerSide.cs, as shown at the bottom of the figure. The implementation of class ServerSide in the file is shown in Listing 21-10.

Listing 21-10: **The Implementation of Class ServerSide**

```
1 using System;
2 using System.Net;
3 using System.Net.Sockets;
4 using System.Text;
5 using System.Threading;
6
7 namespace MyGatewayService
8 {
9 public class ServerSide
10 {
11   // statistics regarding traffic
12   static private int numberOfRequestsProcessed = 0;
13   static private DateTime lastRequestProcessedAt;
14   static private int requestsBeingHandled = 0;
15   static private int maxNumberOfSimultaneousRequests = 0;
```

```
16
17    // IP networking stuff
18    const int spPort = 8001;
19    IPAddress ipAddress;
20    IPEndPoint spAddress;
21    Socket socket;
22
23    public ServerSide()
24    {
25      ipAddress = IPAddress.Parse("127.0.0.1");  // address of
Service Provider
26      spAddress = new IPEndPoint(ipAddress, spPort);
27      socket = new Socket(AddressFamily.InterNetwork,
28                          SocketType.Stream, ProtocolType.Tcp );
29       socket.Connect(spAddress);
30    }
31
32    // update statistics shared by all instances of ServerSide
33    private void UpdateStatistics()
34    {
35      lock(this)
36      {
37        numberOfRequestsProcessed++;
38        lastRequestProcessedAt = DateTime.Now;
39      }
40    }
41
42    private void UpdateHighWatermark()
43    {
44      lock(this)
45      {
46        if (requestsBeingHandled > maxNumberOfSimultaneousRequests)
47          maxNumberOfSimultaneousRequests = requestsBeingHandled;
48      }
49    }
50
51    // given a Social Security Number, return the person's rating
52    public int GetCreditRating(String theSSN)
53    {
54      UpdateStatistics();
55      Interlocked.Increment(ref requestsBeingHandled);
56      UpdateHighWatermark();
57
58      int rating = HandleRequest(theSSN);
59
60      Interlocked.Decrement(ref requestsBeingHandled);
61      return rating;
62    }
63
64    // handle a request
65    private int HandleRequest(String theSSN)
```

Continued

Listing 21-10 *(continued)*

```
 66   {
 67     if (!SendRequest(socket, theSSN) ) return -1;
 68     int response = GetResponse(socket);
 69     return response;
 70   }
 71
 72   private bool SendRequest(Socket theSocket, String theSSN)
 73   {
 74     if (!theSocket.Connected) return false;
 75
 76     // truncate the SSN to 9 chars
 77     theSSN = theSSN.Substring(0, 9);
 78
 79     // convert string to array of octets
 80
 81     Encoding ASCII = Encoding.ASCII;
 82     Byte[] bytesToSend = ASCII.GetBytes(theSSN.ToCharArray());
 83
 84     // establish a connection with the service provider
 85
 86     int bytesSent = theSocket.Send(bytesToSend);
 87     return bytesSent == bytesToSend.Length ? true : false;
 88   }
 89
 90   private int GetResponse(Socket theSocket)
 91   {
 92     Byte[] response = new Byte[10];
 93     int charsReceived = 0;
 94     int startTime = Environment.TickCount;
 95     const int TenSeconds = 10000;   // in milliseconds
 96     while (charsReceived < response.Length)
 97     {
 98
 99       charsReceived = theSocket.Receive(response);
100       int elapsedTime = Environment.TickCount - startTime;
101       if (elapsedTime > TenSeconds) return -1;
102     }
103
104     // convert array of octets to integer
105     Encoding ASCII = Encoding.ASCII;
106     String rating = ASCII.GetString(response);
107     if (!Char.IsDigit(rating[9]) ) return -1;
108
109     return Convert.ToInt32(rating[9] - '0');
110   }
111
112   public int GetNumberOfRequestsProcessed()
113   {
114     return numberOfRequestsProcessed;
```

```
115    }
116
117    public DateTime GetLastRequestProcessedAt()
118    {
119       return lastRequestProcessedAt;
120    }
121
122    public int GetMaxNumberOfSimulataneousRequests()
123    {
124       return maxNumberOfSimultaneousRequests;
125    }
126 }
127 }
```

Notice the static fields on lines 12–15. They are used to maintain information shared by all instances of MyGatewayService, and will later be used to provide information about the service to the host program.

Lines 18–21 set up a variety of TCP variables for connecting to the remote Service Provider. The code in ServerSide assumes the connection is on port 8001. On line 25, the IP address of the Service Provider is set. I'll use a small program to emulate the Service Provider and run it on the same machine as MyGatewayService, hence the 127.0.0.1 local address. For those of you who are new to TCP programming, the special address 127.0.0.1 is the TCP/IP *loopback* address, and always refers to the machine the code is running on.

Notice on line 29 that the socket connection to the Service Provider is created in the class constructor. For each client connection, one socket is created and used to handle all traffic.

The remote entry point into the class is the method GetCreditRating(), which starts on line 52. This method calls UpdateStatistics() to update the traffic information to be displayed by the host program. Since all instances of MyGatewayService reference the same statistics variables, I used a lock() statement on line 35 to prevent concurrent access to the code that changes the static fields.

Class ServerSide also maintains a field known as a *watermark*. Watermarks are used to track maximum and minimum conditions in a program. In my case, the watermark tracks the highest number of concurrent accesses to MyGatewayService.

Client requests are sent to the Service Provider by the method SendRequest(), beginning on line 72. This method just sends the Social Security Number to the Service Provider. The credit rating is read back in the method GetResponse(), starting on line 90. Notice the while loop, starting on line 96. The loop waits until the entire expected response message is returned. If only part of it is received, the loop will wait up to 10 seconds and then time out. On lines 105–106 the response is converted from a character ('0'..'9') into an integer and returned to the caller. The remainder of the code handles access to the shared fields that describe traffic statistics.

Designing the service host application

As I mentioned earlier, a Remoting server-side object requires a host program to register the object with the Remoting Framework, set up the framework to listen for requests on TCP/IP port 6000, and dispatch incoming requests to the component named ServerSide.

I'll call the host program *MyGatewayServiceHost* and design it to have a main form showing some statistics about traffic handled by MyGatewayService. Each time a request arrives, the component ServerSide will store the date and time in a static field. Using a static field forces all client requests to share the same variable.

But how will all this work? When a client request arrives, if there are no instances of ServerSide, one is created. Then the instance processes the request and updates the static variables. If no requests arrive for a certain amount of time, the server object's lease could expire and the object could be garbage collected. If this happened, the values stored in the static fields would be lost.

I need a way to prevent the server-side object from going away while MyGatewayService is running. No sweat. I'll just create a Client-Activated Object (CAO) for ServerSide in the host program. The existence of the CAO will guarantee that the server-side object will continue to exist until the host program shuts down. The class diagram for the host program will look like Figure 21-10.

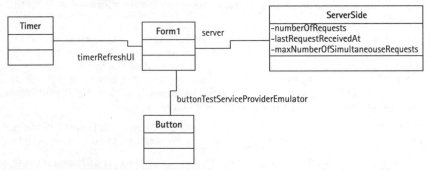

Figure 21-10: The class diagram for the host program on the server side

The host program uses a timer to periodically poll the ServerSide component for the statistics stored in the static fields. Figure 21-11 shows what the host program's user interface looks after a few requests have been handled.

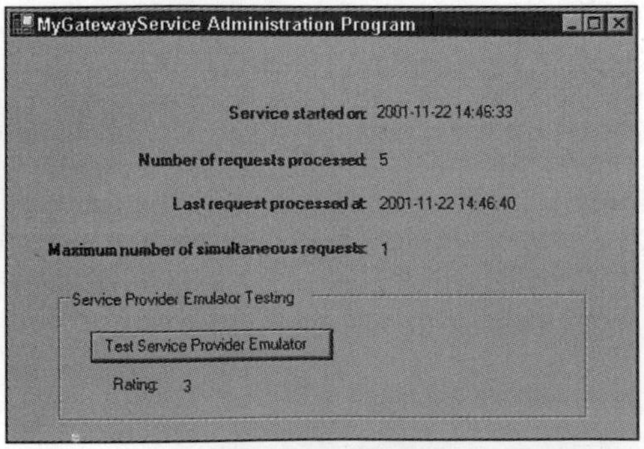

Figure 21-11: The user interface of the host program for MyGatewayService

As you can see, the host program is not used just to configure the Remoting Framework and set up the server side component. It also acts as the administration console for the gateway service.

The button at the bottom of the form, labeled *Test Service Provider Emulator,* is for testing MyGatewayService before connecting it to the real Service Provider. You don't want to be debugging your service component by sending requests to the Service Provider for two reasons. Besides the obvious reason that you may send invalid data until the code is debugged, the service will probably also charge you for each request. To avoid hitting the Service Provider while testing a gateway service, you'll need to develop a test fixture that emulates the Service Provider, discussed later.

Implementing the service host application

As stated earlier, a .NET Remoting Framework server-side component must be hosted, to register the service with the framework and designate the channels and protocols the service will handle. The host can be a Windows service, a console application, or a regular Windows application. I'll use the latter, because I want to use the host program to display a form with statistics about the running gateway service. I'll call the host program *MyGatewayServiceHost.exe.*

An important thing to remember is that a .NET Remoting Service is active only while the host is running. When the host shuts down, the service is unregistered and client requests will no longer be handled.

To create the host program, I used the VS .NET Windows Application wizard. (I'll spare you the details of running the wizard.) Figure 21-12 shows what the project looks like in the Solution Explorer.

Figure 21-12: The project files that are part of the MyGatewayServiceHost program

The figure contains a couple of items I added after running the wizard: a reference to MyGatewayService, and the configuration file MyGatewayServiceHost.exe.config. The former was added using the Add Reference dialog box. You display this dialog box by right-clicking the project node MyGatewayServiceHost in the Solution Explorer and selecting Add Reference from the list of commands. Select the Programs tab and select the project named MyGatewayService, as shown in Figure 21-13.

Once the reference is added, I add the following statement to the top of the code for Form1, because I'll be creating an instance of ServerSide in this class:

```
using MyGatewayService;
```

Before showing you the code for ServerSide, let me finish talking about the configuration file MyGatewayServiceHost.exe.config. The file is shown in Listing 21-11.

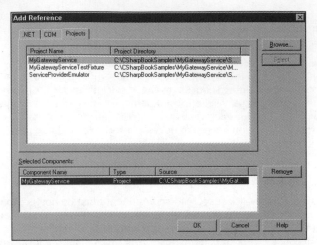

Figure 21-13: Adding a reference to MyGatewayService to the host program

---

Listing 21-11: **The Remote Configuration File Used by the Host Program**

```
<configuration>
  <system.runtime.remoting>
    <application name="MyGatewayServiceHost">
      <service>
        <wellknown mode="SingleCall"
                   type="MyGatewayService.ServerSide,
                         MyGatewayService" />
      </service>
      <channels>
        <channel
           type="System.Runtime.Remoting.Channels.Tcp.TcpChannel,
                 System.Runtime.Remoting" port="6000" />
      </channels>
    </application>
  </system.runtime.remoting>
</configuration>
```

As you can see, the configuration file sets up the Remoting Framework to listen for TCP requests on port 6000. The port number can be any value not already in use on your machine.

The configuration file is passed to the .NET Remoting Framework by the host program, whose code is shown in Listing 21-12.

Listing 21-12: The Code of the Host Program's Main Form

```
using System;
using System.Drawing;
using System.Collections;
using System.ComponentModel;
using System.Windows.Forms;
using System.Data;
using System.Runtime.Remoting;

using MyGatewayService;

namespace MyGatewayServiceHost
{
public class Form1 : System.Windows.Forms.Form
{
  // declare all the child controls
  private System.Windows.Forms.Label label1;

  // ...

  private ServerSide server = null;

  private System.ComponentModel.Container components = null;

  public Form1()
  {
    InitializeComponent();

    labelServiceStartedOn.Text = DateTime.Now.ToString();

    // create a Client Activate Object to keep an instance of
    // ServerSide running until this Host program shuts down
    server = new ServerSide();
  }

  protected override void Dispose( bool disposing )
  {
    // ... code generated by wizard
  }

  #region Windows Form Designer generated code
  private void InitializeComponent()
  {
    // ... code generated by wizard
  }
  #endregion

  [STAThread]
  static void Main()
```

Continued

Listing 21-12 *(continued)*

```
  {
    Application.Run(new Form1());
  }

  private void timerRefreshUI_Elapsed(
              object sender,
              System.Timers.ElapsedEventArgs e)
  {
    if (server == null) return;

    // read the latest statistics from the Server-Side remotable
    // component and update the User Interface
    int requestsProcessed = server.GetNumberOfRequestsProcessed();
    labelNumberOfRequestsProcessed.Text =
      requestsProcessed.ToString();
    if (requestsProcessed > 0)
    labelLastRequestProcessedAt.Text =
      server.GetLastRequestProcessedAt().ToString();
    labelMaximumNumberOfSimultaneousRequests.Text =
      server.GetMaxNumberOfSimulataneousRequests().ToString();
  }

  private void buttonTestServiceProviderEmulator_Click(
              object sender,
              System.EventArgs e)
  {
    int rating = server.GetCreditRating("123456789");
    labelRating.Text = rating.ToString();
  }
 }
 }
```

The constructor creates an instance of ServerSide, causing the server side to set up a CAO. The existence of this object guarantees that there will always be at least one instance of MyGatewayService running on the server. This is essential, because the traffic statistics of MyGatewayService are maintained in static fields in class ServerSide. If all instances of the class were garbage collected, the statistical information would be lost.

The method buttonTestServiceProviderEmulator() is used to test the connection to MyGatewayService. Although I labeled the button *Test Service Provider Emulator,* the button handler really tests MyGatewayService and any Service Provider that MyGatewayService uses. My code just uses a simple Service Provider emulator program, described later. Notice how simple buttonTestServiceProviderEmulator is. It just calls the method GetCreditRating() and displays the value returned. Looking solely at buttonTestServiceProviderEmulator, you can't tell whether the component server is local or remote. That's the beauty of the Remoting Framework. The architects of the framework worked hard to make it as painless as possible to write Remoting code.

Another nice feature of the Remoting Framework is debugging support. If you put a breakpoint on the line

```
int rating = server.GetCreditRating("123456789");
```

you can step into the method call, effectively stepping over the remote connection into the remote process. You can step through all the server-side code as if it were local.

All this debugging support is out-of-the-box. There are no tools or magic settings to configure to make it happen. If you have prior experience debugging DCOM or other remote procedure-calling methods, you'll appreciate the simplicity of the .NET Remoting Framework.

Designing the Service Provider emulator

As I mentioned earlier, to test a gateway service, you need to create a test fixture that takes the place of the Service Provider and emulates its basic behavior. The emulator required to test MyGatewayService is not too complicated: It needs to listen for TCP requests and return a response. To make it more realistic, I'll make it wait for a variable amount of time before responding. The wait will simulate the amount of time the Service Provider may take to return a response. I'll make the emulator wait for a period of time in the range (0..999) milliseconds. Figure 21-14 shows the user interface of the emulator, after processing four messages.

Figure 21-14: The user interface of the Service Provider emulator

The main form has a button to initiate the TCP socket listening process. When a request is received, it is timestamped and displayed in a ListBox. Only the last 10 requests are displayed. The UI also maintains a counter for the total number of requests received.

The design of the emulator is straightforward: The emulator is a standalone application that listens for TCP/IP traffic on a designated port, gets requests, and returns responses.

Although fairly simple, the emulator program is an interesting application in its own right, because it demonstrates TCP socket programming and the use of threads. I'll make the emulator listen on TCP port 8001, assuming this is the port the real Service Provider is using. Figure 21-15 shows the class diagram for the emulator.

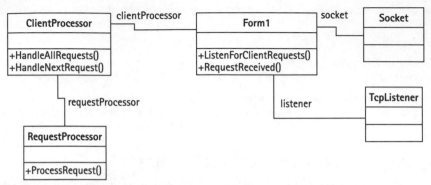

Figure 21-15: The class diagram of the Service Provider emulator

The class diagram tells you little about how the emulator works. To see how the parts work together, take a look at the interaction diagram shown in Figure 21-16.

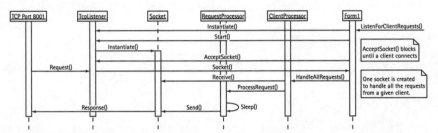

Figure 21-16: The interaction diagram of the Service Provider emulator

Even though the emulator is fairly simple, there is quite a bit going on in terms of interactions. Not all the components run in the same thread. When the emulator is processing a request, represented by the `Sleep()` method at the bottom of the interaction diagram, the application must continue to listen for other requests, making it necessary to use multiple threads in the emulator. The interaction diagram doesn't show the threading model of the system, so Figure 21-17 shows you the various threads.

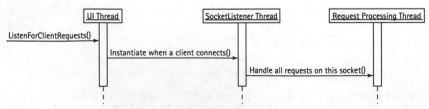

Figure 21-17: The threading model for the Service Provider emulator

The UI runs on the application's main thread. Since the processing of requests can entail blocking the request thread, you don't want the UI to get blocked as well. The UI should always be alive, so the user can click its buttons, resize the form, and close it at any time. When `TcpListener.AcceptSocket()` is called from the main form, the call blocks until a TCP connection is detected. While it is waiting for a connection, the method keeps the UI alive, so all the main form controls continue to work normally. When `AcceptSocket()` is called, it creates a new client connection. When `AcceptSocket()` returns, it passes back a new `Socket` object that will handle all the traffic on the new connection.

To keep all of the client connections independent from each other in terms of timing, the emulator application creates a second thread to handle each connection. And since I want the emulator to be able to handle concurrent requests on the same socket, the emulator creates a third thread to handle each request. While a request is being handled asynchronously on this third thread, the second thread is active listening for other requests from the same client. The first thread is also active listening for new client connections. It actually sounds more complicated than it is. The next section should clear up any confusion.

Implementing the Service Provider emulator

The UI is really simple. It consists of just a form with one button and a few text fields, as shown previously in Figure 21-14. The UI code is shown in Listing 21-13.

Listing 21-13: The Code for the UI Portion of the Service Provider Emulator

```
using System;
using System.Drawing;
using System.Collections;
using System.ComponentModel;
using System.Windows.Forms;
using System.Data;
using System.Threading;
using System.Net;
using System.Net.Sockets;
using System.Globalization;

namespace ServiceProviderEmulator
{
public class Form1 : System.Windows.Forms.Form
{
  private System.Windows.Forms.Label label1;
  private System.Windows.Forms.Label labelLastRequestReceivedAt;
  private System.Windows.Forms.Label label3;
  private System.Windows.Forms.Label labelNumberOfRequestsReceived;
  private System.Windows.Forms.Label label5;
  private System.Windows.Forms.Label labelEmulatorStartedAt;
  private System.Windows.Forms.Label label2;
  private System.Windows.Forms.ListBox
                            listBoxLastTenRequestsReceived;
  private System.Windows.Forms.Button buttonStartListening;

  int numberOfRequestsReceived = 0;
  TcpListener listener;

  private System.ComponentModel.Container components = null;
```

Continued

Listing 21-13 *(continued)*

```csharp
public Form1()
{
  InitializeComponent();

  labelNumberOfRequestsReceived.Text = "0";
  labelEmulatorStartedAt.Text = DateTime.Now.ToString();
}

protected override void Dispose( bool disposing )
{
  if (disposing)
  {
    if (components != null)
      components.Dispose();
  }
  base.Dispose( disposing );
}

protected void ListenForClientRequests()
{


  listener = new TcpListener(8001); // listen on port 8001
  listener.Start();

  while (true)
  {
    // block until a client connects
    Socket socket = listener.AcceptSocket();
    socket.Blocking = false;

    // dispatch a thread to handle all the client requests
    // on the connected socket
    ClientProcessor clientProcessor =
      new ClientProcessor(this, socket);
    Thread myThread = new Thread(
        new ThreadStart(clientProcessor.HandleAllRequests) );
    myThread.Start();
  }
}

public void RequestReceived(String theRequest)
{
  lock(this) // prevent concurrent access to this code
  {
    numberOfRequestsReceived++;
    String timestamp = DateTime.Now.ToString();
    labelLastRequestReceivedAt.Text = timestamp;
    labelNumberOfRequestsReceived.Text =
        numberOfRequestsReceived.ToString();
    listBoxLastTenRequestsReceived.Items.Insert(0,
```

```
                    timestamp + ": " + theRequest);
            if (listBoxLastTenRequestsReceived.Items.Count > 10)
                listBoxLastTenRequestsReceived.Items.RemoveAt(10);
        }
    }

    #region Windows Form Designer generated code
    private void InitializeComponent()
    {
        // initialize all the UI controls...
    }
    #endregion

    [STAThread]
    static void Main()
    {
        Application.Run(new Form1());
    }

    private void buttonStartListening_Click(object sender,
                                            System.EventArgs e)
    {
        buttonStartListening.Enabled = false;  // we can only start
                                               // listening once

        // listen for client requests on a separate thread, so
        // listening doesn't interfere with the UI events
        Thread thread = new Thread(
                new ThreadStart(ListenForClientRequests) );
        thread.Start();
    }

    private void Form1_Closed(object sender, System.EventArgs e)
    {
        // this code shouldn't be necessary in the release version of
        // the .NET Framework. The prerelease version I used for this
        // book failed to stop an active TcpListener when destroying the
        // object. As a result, the ServiceProviderEmulator program
        // would have a dangling thread running after the main
        // application
        // was shut down.

        listener.Stop();
    }
    }
}
```

Pay attention to the lock used in the method RequestReceived(). This method is called by the client socket handler when a client request is received. The purpose of RequestReceived() is to update the UI with various statistics. Since multiple request handling threads could call the method concurrently, it is important to guard the UI code with a lock, so only one thread has access to it at a time.

The last method in the listing (Form1_Closed) is a workaround for a problem in the prerelease version of the .NET Framework code I used for the sample programs. You should be able to safely delete the entire method without experiencing any problems with the release .NET Framework code.

When a client connection is detected, the method AcceptSocket() returns a socket for handling the connection. The code then creates a new thread for each connection and instantiates a new ClientProcessor object to handle the connection. The code for ClientProcessor is shown in Listing 21-14.

Listing 21-14: The Code for ClientProcessor

```
using System;
using System.Collections;
using System.Text;
using System.Threading;
using System.Net;
using System.Net.Sockets;
using System.Globalization;


namespace ServiceProviderEmulator
{
public class ClientProcessor
{
  Form1 parentForm;
  Socket socket;

  public ClientProcessor(Form1 theParentForm, Socket theSocket)
  {
    parentForm = theParentForm;
    socket = theSocket;
  }

  public void HandleAllRequests()
  {
    while (socket.Connected)
      HandleNextRequest();
  }

  public void HandleNextRequest()
  {
    const int OneMs = 1000;

    if (!socket.Poll(OneMs, SelectMode.SelectRead) ) return;

    // wait for the next request

    Byte[] request = new Byte[9];  // request is 9 chars long
    try {

      socket.Receive(request);
```

```
      }

    catch (SocketException) {
      return;
    }

    // dispatch a new thread to handle the request
    RequestProcessor requestProcessor =
            new RequestProcessor(parentForm, socket, request);
    Thread thread = new Thread(
            new ThreadStart(requestProcessor.ProcessRequest) );
    thread.Start();
  }
 }
 }
```

The method `HandleAllRequests()` waits in a loop and handles all the messages received over a given client connection. The method calls `HandleNextRequest()` to check for incoming messages. When a message arrives, a new thread is created to handle it using the class `RequestProcessor`. The code for this last class is shown in Listing 21-15.

Listing 21-15: The Code for Class RequestProcessor

```csharp
using System;
using System.Text;
using System.Threading;
using System.Net;
using System.Net.Sockets;
using System.Globalization;

namespace ServiceProviderEmulator
{
public class RequestProcessor
{
  Form1 parentForm;
  Socket socket;
  Byte[] request;

  public RequestProcessor(Form1 theParentForm,
                          Socket theSocket,
                          Byte[] theRequest)
  {
    parentForm = theParentForm;
    socket = theSocket;
    request = theRequest;
  }

  public void ProcessRequest()
  {
```

Continued

Listing 21-15 *(continued)*

```csharp
        // truncate SSN to 9 characters
        Encoding ASCII = Encoding.ASCII;
        String SSN = ASCII.GetString(request);
        SSN = SSN.Substring(0, 9);

        // update the statistics on the main form
        parentForm.RequestReceived(SSN);

        // randomly pick a rating to return

        Random random = new Random();

        int rating = random.Next(10);  // rating is 0..9

        // spend a random amount of time to simulate
        // processing time
        int processingTime = random.Next(1000);  // 0..999 ms
        Thread.Sleep(processingTime);

        // convert string to array of octets


        String response = SSN + rating.ToString();
        Byte[] bytesToSend = ASCII.GetBytes(response.ToCharArray());

        // send response back to client
        try
        {


           socket.Send(bytesToSend);
        }
        catch (SocketException) {}
        }
      }
    }
    }
```

The method `ProcessRequest()` is called each time a message arrives. The method calls `Form1.RequestReceived()` to update the user interface. The received message is truncated to nine characters, because the Social Security Number expected can only be that long. Next, the method chooses a random credit rating between 0 and 9. The method then puts the thread to sleep for a short amount of time to simulate the time it would take a real Service Provider to process the request. Finally, a response is returned to the client. Notice how the `Socket.Send()` call is wrapped in a `try` block. This is necessary to catch exceptions that occur when the client closes the socket connection.

Testing MyGatewayService

Since I won't be implementing the ASP.NET code that would typically run on a Web Farm computer and call MyGatewayService, I'll need to create a small test fixture program to test the service. Nothing fancy: just a plain Windows Application with one form. The form has a place to enter a Social Security Number, a button to call MyGatewayService, and a label for showing the returned credit rating. Figure 21-18 shows the form.

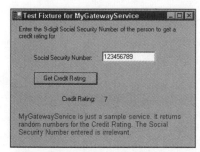

Figure 21-18: The main form of the test fixture for MyGatewayService

In order to reference the MyGatewayService remote components in the test fixture project, I'll need to add a reference to the service to the test fixture, using the procedure described back in the section "Implementing the service host application." Once the reference is added, the Solution Explorer for the test fixture project will have an item called *MyGatewayService* under the References node, as shown in Figure 21-19.

Figure 21-19: The Solution Explorer, showing the newly added reference to MyGatewayService

The code for the test fixture is simple. It's shown in Listing 21-16.

Listing 21-16: **The Code for the Main Form of the Test Fixture**

```
using System;
using System.Drawing;
using System.Collections;
```

Continued

Listing 21-16 *(continued)*

```
using System.ComponentModel;
using System.Windows.Forms;
using System.Data;
using System.Runtime.Remoting;

using MyGatewayService;

namespace MyGatewayServiceTestFixture
{
  public class Form1 : System.Windows.Forms.Form
  {
  // declare all the components...

  private System.ComponentModel.Container components = null;

  public Form1()
  {
    InitializeComponent();
  }

  protected override void Dispose( bool disposing )
  {
    // wizard-generated code...
  }

  #region Windows Form Designer generated code
  private void InitializeComponent()
  {
    // initialize all the components...
  }
  #endregion

  [STAThread]
  static void Main()
  {
    RemotingConfiguration.Configure(
        "MyGatewayServiceTestFixture.exe.config");
    Application.Run(new Form1());
  }

  private void buttonGetCreditRating_Click(object sender,
                                     System.EventArgs e)
  {

    ServerSide myService = new ServerSide();
    String ssn = textBoxSSN.Text;
    int creditRating = myService.GetCreditRating(ssn);
    labelCreditRating.Text = creditRating.ToString();
  }
 }
}
```

The code registers the Remoting configuration file in the `Main()` method. Alternatively, I could have registered the configuration file in the constructor code for Form1. The important thing is that the configuration file be registered only once; otherwise, you'll get a Remoting Framework exception. For the configuration file, I used a copy of the file used by the host program. I just changed the `<application>` node to use the string `"MyGatewayServiceTestFixture"`. Listing 21-17 shows the configuration file.

Listing 21-17: The Configuration File Used by the Test Fixture

```
<configuration>
  <system.runtime.remoting>
    <application name="MyGatewayServiceTestFixture">
      <service>
        <wellknown mode="SingleCall"
                   type="MyGatewayService.ServerSide,
                         MyGatewayService" />
      </service>
      <channels>
        <channel
            type="System.Runtime.Remoting.Channels.Tcp.TcpChannel,
                  System.Runtime.Remoting" port="6000" />
      </channels>
    </application>
  </system.runtime.remoting>
</configuration>
```

Putting it all together

OK. So far I have shown the implementation of four separate components: `MyGatewayService`, `MyGatewayServiceHost`, `ServiceProviderEmulator`, and `MyGatewayServiceTestFixture`. Figure 21-20 shows how the components fit together.

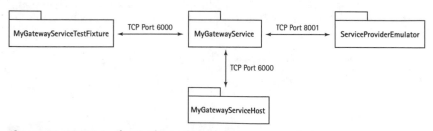

Figure 21-20: How the main components are connected

To see the whole gateway service in action, you need to start the components in a given order. First start the Service Provider Emulator. This will listen on port 8001 for client connections. Now start the host program. This will register MyGatewayService and immediately create an instance of MyGatewayService. The service will then open a TCP connection with the Service Provider Emulator on port 8001, and wait for client requests on port 6000.

Now you can click the host program's Test Service Provider Emulator button to verify connectivity to the emulator program. Once this works, you can start `MyGatewayServiceTestFixture`. When you click the test fixture's Get Credit Rating button, the events in the interaction diagram shown in Figure 21-21 will occur.

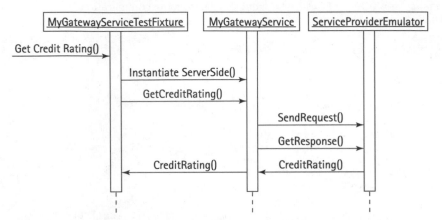

Figure 21-21: The interaction diagram showing the overall activity when testing MyGatewayService

The interaction diagram doesn't depict the host program, because the host program doesn't participate in client-request processing. The host program has only two purposes: to register MyGatewayService with the Remoting Framework, and to display a form showing statistics about the traffic handled by the MyGatewayService.

Dealing with remote exceptions

In the world of distributed components, there is a new layer of communication code that connects client components to servers. Method calls to remote components can fail if the Remoting Framework infrastructure can't make a connection to the server component. To make remote calls bulletproof, you should wrap them in a `try` block and catch exceptions thrown by the Remoting Framework. The code in Listing 21-18 shows how to do this.

Listing 21-18: Handling Exceptions that May Occur in a Call to a Remote Object

```
// instantiate a remote object...
MyRemoteObject obj = new MyRemoteObject();

// try accessing it
try
{
  obj.DoSomething();
}
catch (RemotingTimeoutException) {}  // Service not responding.
                                     // The server may have been
```

```
                                    // turned off or disconnected
                                    // from the network. The
                                    // URI used by the channel may
                                    // be incorrect

catch (RemotingException) {}        // Other remoting problems,
                                    //  such as message
                                    // serialization problems,
                                    // network transport problems,
                                    // etc.

catch (ServerException) {}          // A problem originating on a
                                    // server that doesn't use .NET
                                    // Remoting

catch (Exception) {}                // Whatever exceptions
                                    // DoSomething() can
                                    // be expected to throw, if the
                                    // service is running on a .NET
                                    // server.
```

The code I described in this chapter didn't have handlers for Remoting exceptions, to keep things simple. However, it is always a good idea to add handlers to your code. To get more information on the precise causes of each exception, check out the VS .NET online documentation for the classes shown in the various `catch` blocks shown in the previous listing.

Summary

Building gateway services is not too complicated. They make use of multithreaded components, so they can be a little tricky to debug. Moreover, they deal with TCP/IP networking issues and socket programming fairly extensively. To make debugging easier, follow the guidelines I have shown and split the work into small increments that can be handled by small components.

With gateway services, you need to watch for bottlenecks that may be caused by insufficient network bandwidth or processor horsepower. Although gateway services aren't as commonly used as other components described in this book, I chose to include them in a separate chapter to demonstrate the way Remoting components are used in the real world.

If you read every chapter of this book, my congratulations to you. It covered a tremendous amount of material, and showed you how to get the most out of .NET Framework from the perspective of the multitier application developer. Most of you will probably be interested in only one or two tiers, but as you go through your career as a developer or architect, your interests may change over time.

My hope is for this book to be a silent companion for the long run. No book can possibly describe every detail of the .NET Framework, but perhaps the tier approach that I've used will serve as a clear way to introduce you to some of the most exciting and useful features. If you learned anything from this book, remember the importance of keeping things simple, and maintaining a sound development process. Good luck!

✦   ✦   ✦

Bibliography

[Adams 1997] Adams, D. *The Hitchhiker's Guide to the Galaxy*. Ballantine, New York, NY. Reprinted in 1997. ISBN: 0-345-41891-3.

[Allen 1997] Allen, R. J. "A Formal Approach to Software Architecture." PhD Thesis, School of Computer Science, Carnegie Mellon University, Pittsburgh, PA. 1997. Document No. CMU-CS-97-144, page 52.

[Arnold 2000] Arnold, K, Gosling, J., Holmes, D. *The Java Programming Language*. 3rd Edition. Addison-Wesley, Reading, MA. 2000. ISBN: 0-201-70433-1.

[Bäumer 1998] Bäumer, D., Riehle, D. *Pattern Languages of Program Design 3*. Editors: Martin, R., Riehle, D., Buschmann, F. Addison-Wesley, Reading, MA. 1998. Chapter 3. ISBN 0-201-31011-2.

[Boehm 1981] Boehm, B. *Software Engineering Economics*. Prentice-Hall, New York. NY. 1981. ISBN: 0-138-22122-7.

[Boehm 1988] Boehm, B. "A Spiral Model of Software Development and Enhancement," *IEEE Computer*, Vol. 21 No. 5 (May 1988) Pages 61–72.

[Boehm 2000] Boehm, B. et al. *Software Cost Estimation with Cocomo II*. Prentice-Hall, New York. NY. 2000. ISBN: 0130266922.

[Boehm 2001] Boehm, B., Basili, V. "Software Defect Reduction Top 10 List," *Computer*, Vol. 34, No. 1 (Jan 2001). Pages 135–137. For IEEE Computer Society members, the paper is available online at http://dlib.computer.org/co/books/co2001/pdf/r1.zip.

[Booch 1994] Booch, G. *Object-Oriented Analysis and Design with Applications*. 2nd Edition. Addison-Wesley, Reading, MA. 1994. ISBN 0-805-35340-2.

[Booch 1998] Booch, G., Jacobson, I., Rumbaugh, J. *The Unified Modeling Language User Guide*. Addison-Wesley, Reading, MA. 1998. ISBN 0-201-57168-4.

[Bossomaier 1998] Bossomaier, T., Green, D. *Patterns in the Sand — Computers, Complexity and Everyday Life*. Perseus Books, Australia. 1998. ISBN 0-7382-0015-8.

[Box 1998] Box, D. *Essential COM*. Addison-Wesley. Reading, MA. 1998. Pages 199–205. ISBN: 0-201-63446-5

[Brooks 1986] Brooks, F. "No Silver Bullet — Essence and Accident in Software Engineering." *Proceedings of IFIP 10th World Computing Conference*. Ed. H. Krugler. 1986. Elsevier Science B.V. Amsterdam, The Netherlands. A reprint of the essay can also be found in the book *The Mythical Man-Month*, 20th anniversary edition, 1995, Addison-Wesley, ISBN 0-201-83595-9

[Brooks 1995] Brooks, F. *The Mythical Man-Month*. Addison-Wesley. Reading, MA. 1995. 20th year anniversary edition. ISBN 0-201-83595-9.

[Brown 1997] Brown, A.W., Short, K. *"On Components and Objects: The Foundations of Component Based Development," Proceedings of the 5th International Symposium on Assessment of Software Tools and Technologies.* 1997. IEEE Computer Society Press. ISBN 0-8186-7940-9.

[Brown 1998] Brown, A.W., Wallnau, K.C. "The Current State of CBSE," *IEEE Software*, No. 5 Vol. 15 (Sept/Oct 1998), pp37-46.

[Brown 2000] Brown, W. et al. *AntiPatterns in Project Management*. John Wiley & Sons. New York, NY. 2000. ISBN 0-471-36366-9.

[Buschmann 1995] Buschmann, F. *Pattern Languages of Program Design*. Editors: Coplien, J., Schmidt, D. Addison-Wesley, Reading, MA 1995. Chapter 9. ISBN 0-201-60734-4.

[Cheesman 2000] Cheesman, J., Daniels, J. *UML Components: A Simple Process for Specifying Component-Based Software*. Addison-Wesley, Reading, MA 2000. ISBN 0-201-70851-5.

[Conway 1968] Conway, M. E. "How Do Committees Invent?" *Datamation*, Vol. 14, No. 4 (April 1968), pp-28-31.

[Cusumano 1997] Cusumano, M. A., Selby, R. W. "How Microsoft Builds Software," *Communications of the ACM*, Vol. 40, No. 6 (June 1997).

[DOD 1988] U.S. Department of Defense. *Military Standard, Defense System Software Development. DOD-STD-2167A*. 1988.

[Eisenstadt 1997] Eisenstadt, M. "My Hairiest Bug War Stories," *Communications of the ACM*, Vol. 40, No. 4 (April 1997), pages 30-37.

[Enderton 1977] Enderton, H. B. *Elements of Set Theory*. Academic Press, San Diego, CA. 1997. ISBN 0-12-238440-7. Page 6.

[Faison 1998] Faison, T. "Interaction Patterns for Communicating Processes." PLoP98, *Pattern Languages of Programs Conference*. 1998. Monticello, IL. Available online at http://jerry.cs.uiuc.edu/~plop/plop98/final_submissions/P02.pdf.

[Gamma 1995] Gamma, E., Helm, R., Johnson, R., Vlissides, J. *Design Patterns – Elements of Reusable Object-Oriented Software*. Addison-Wesley, Reading, MA 1995. ISBN 0-201-63361-2.

[Gamma 1998] Gamma, E. *Pattern Languages of Program Design 3*. Editors: Martin, R., Riehle, D., Buschmann, F. Addison-Wesley, Reading, MA 1998. Chapter 6. ISBN 0-201-31011-2.

[Girardi 1993] Girardi, M. R., Ibrahim, B. "A Software Reuse System based on Natural Language Specifications." *Proceedings of the 5th International Conference on Computing and Information* (ICCI'93), Sudbury, Ontario, Canada. 1993. Pages 507-511.

[Hoare 1985] Hoare, C. A. R. *Communicating Sequential Processes*. Prentice Hall. New York, NY 1985. ISBN 0-13-153289-8.

[Humphrey 1989] Humphrey, W. *Managing the Software Process*. Addison-Wesley, Reading, MA. 1989. ISBN 0-201-18095-2.

[Humphrey 1995] Humphrey, W. *A Discipline for Software Engineering*. Addison-Wesley, Reading, MA. 1995. ISBN 0-201-54610-8.

[Jacobsen 1994] Jacobsen, I. *Object-Oriented Software Engineering: A Use Case Driven Approach*. Addison-Wesley, Reading, MA. 1994. ISBN 0-201-54435-0.

[Jones 1997] Jones, C. *What Are Function Points?* Online paper available at http://www.spr. com/library/0funcmet.htm. 1997.

[Keil 1998] Keil, M., Cule, P. E., Lyytinen, K., Schmidt, R. C. "A Framework for Identifying Software Project Risks," *Communications of the ACM*, Vol. 41, No. 11 (Nov 1998), pp. 77-79.

[Kougiouris 2001] Kougiouris, P. "Application Center 2000 Offers World-Class Scalability," *MSDN Magazine*, Vol. 16, No. 5 (May 2001), pages 84-91.

[Krieger 1998] Krieger, D., Adler R.M. "The Emergence of Distributed Component Platforms," *IEEE Computer*, Vol. 31 No. 3 (March 1998), pp 43-53.

[Littlewood 1993] Littlewood, B., Strigini, L. "Validation of Ultrahigh Dependability for Software-Based Systems," *Communications of the ACM*, Vol. 36, No. 11 (Nov. 1993).

[Mayr 1997] Mayr, E. *This is Biology – The science of the living world*. Belknap Press of Harvard University Press. Cambridge, MA. 1997. ISBN 0-674-88468-X.

[Meyer 1999] Meyer, B. "On to Components," *IEEE Computer*, Vol. 32 No. 1 (Jan 1999), pp. 139-140.

[NHSE 1998] National HPCC Software Exchange. *Repository in a Box – Repository Planning Guide*. Online document at http://www.nhse.org/RIB/plan.html.

[Nierstrasz 1995] Nierstrasz, O., Dami, L. *Component-Oriented Software Technology. Object-Oriented Software Composition,* Ed. Nierstrasz and Tsichritzis. 1995. Prentice Hall, pp 3-28. ISBN 0-1322-0674-9.

[Ohno 1988] Ohno, T., *Toyota Production System: Beyond Large-Scale Production*. Productivity Press, Portland, OR, 1988. ISBN 0-915-29914-3.

[Oestereich 1997] Oestereich, B. *Developing Software with UML, Object-Oriented Analysis and Design in Practice*. Addison Wesley. Reading, MA. 1997. ISBN 0-201-39826-5.

[Oestereich 1999], Oestereich, B. *Developing Software with UML*. Addison-Wesley. Reading, MA. 1999. Pages 53-71. ISBN 0-201-39826-5.

[Pais 1983] Pais, A. *Subtle Is the Lord: The Science and the Life of Albert Einstein*. Oxford University Press. Oxford, UK. 1983. ISBN: 0-195-20438-7.

[Pattison 1999] Pattison, T. "Advanced Basics — Working on a Web Farm," *Microsoft Internet Developer*, Vol. 4, No. 6 (June 1999), pages 61-66. Available online at http://www.microsoft. com/mind/defaulttop.asp?page=/mind/0699/basics/basics0699.htm&nav=/mind/ 0699/inthisissuecolumns0699.htm.

[Penix 1995] Penix, J., Baraona, P., Alexander, P. "Classification and Retrieval of Reusable Components Using Semantic Features." *Proceedings from KBSE '95, the 10th Knowledge-Based Software Engineering Conference*. Boston, MA. 1995. pp. 131-138.

[Pfleeger 1997] Pfleeger, S. K., Hatton, L. "Investigating the Influence of Formal Methods," *IEEE Computer*, Vol. 30, No. 2 (Feb 1997), page 41.

[Potter 1996] Potter, B., Sinclair, J., Till, D. *An Introduction to Formal Specification and Z*. 2nd Edition. Prentice Hall. New York, NY 1996. ISBN 0-13-242207-7.

[Prieto-Diaz 1991] Prieto-Diaz, R. "Implementing Faceted Classification for Software Reuse," *Communications of the ACM*, Vol. 34, No. 5, (May 1991). Pages 88-97.

[Pyarali 1998] Pyarali, I., Harrison, T., Schmidt, D. *Pattern Languages of Program Design 3*. Editors: Martin, R., Riehle, D., Buschmann, F. Addison-Wesley, Reading, MA 1998. Chapter 14. ISBN 0-201-31011-2.

[Rittri 1990] Rittri, M. "Retrieving Library Identificatiers via Equational Matching of Types." *Proceedings from the 10th International Conference on Automated Deduction.* Kaiserslauten, Germany. 1990. Pages 603-617.

[Robertson 2000] Robertson, S., Robertson, J. *Mastering the Requirements Process.* Addison-Wesley. Reading, MA. 2000. ISBN 0-201-36046-2.

[Rogerson 1997] Rogerson, D. *Inside COM.* Microsoft Press. Redmond, WA. 1997. Pages 312-319. ISBN: 1-57231-349-8.

[Ropponen 2000] Ropponen, J., Lyytinen, K. "Components of Software Development Risk: How to Address Them? A Project Manager Survey," *IEEE Transactions on Software Engineering*, Vol. 26, No. 2 (Feb 2000), pages 98-112. For IEEE Computer Society members, the paper is available online at `http://dlib.computer.org/ts/books/ts2000/pdf/e2.zip`.

[Royce 1970] Royce, W. W. "Managing the Development of Large Software Systems." *Proceedings of IEEE Wescon.* August 1970.

[Schmidt 1995] D. *Pattern Languages of Program Design.* Editors: Coplien, J., Schmidt, D. Addison-Wesley, Reading, MA 1995. Chapter 29. ISBN 0-201-60734-4.

[Sommerlad 1998] Sommerlad, P. *Pattern Languages of Program Design 3.* Editors: Martin, R., Riehle, D., Buschmann, F. Addison-Wesley, Reading, MA 1998. Chapter 2. ISBN 0-201-31011-2.

[Sotirovski 2001]. Sotirovski, D. "Heuristics for Iterative Software Development," *IEEE Software.* Vol. 18, No. 3 (May/June 2001), Pages 66-73.

[Szyperski 1999] Szyperski, C. *Component Software – Beyond Object-Oriented Programming.* Addison-WesleyReading, MA. 1999. ISBN 0-201-17888-5.

[Wang 1999] Wang, G., Ungar, L., Klawitter, D. "Component Assembly for OO Distributed Systems," *IEEE Computer.* Vol. 32, No. 7 (July 1999), pp. 71-78.

[Yourdon 1979] Yourdon, E., Constantine, L. *Structured Design: Fundamentals of a Discipline of Computer Program and Systems Design.* Prentice Hall. New York, NY. 1979. ISBN 0-138-54471-9.

[Yourdon 1999] Yourdon , E. *Death March: The Complete Software Developer's Guide to Surviving 'Mission Impossible' Projects.* Prentice Hall. New York. NY. 1999. ISBN: 0-130-14659-5.

[Zaremski 1997] Zaremski, A. M., Wing, J. M. "Specification Matching of Software Components," *ACM Transactions on Software Engineering and Methodology.* Vol. 6, No. 4 (Oct 1997). Pages 333-369.

◆   ◆   ◆

Index